CIM
TUTORIAL TEXT

Diploma

Strategic Marketing Management: Analysis and Decision

by Dr David Pearson (CIM Examiner)

First edition 1993
Fifth edition September 1997

ISBN 0 7517 4063 2 (previous edition 0 7517 4051 9)

British Library Cataloguing-in-Publication Data
A catalogue record for this book
is available from the British Library

Published by

BPP Publishing Limited
Aldine House, Aldine Place
London W12 8AW

All our rights reserved. No part of this publication may be reproduced, stored in a retrieval system or transmitted, in any form or by any means, electronic, mechanical, photocopying, recording or otherwise, without the prior written permission of BPP Publishing Limited and Dr David Pearson.

The author is grateful to Dr Paul Fifield for permission to use his case studies, to Northern Consultancy Associates for permission to use their case analyses and to CIM tutors and students for their contributions.

Printed by Ashford Colour Press, Gosport, Hants

©
Dr David Pearson and BPP Publishing Limited
1997

Contents

		Page
PREFACE		(v)

INTRODUCTION
How to use this Tutorial Text - syllabus overview   (vi)

PART A: BACKGROUND KNOWLEDGE RELEVANT TO ANALYSIS AND DECISION

1	Strategic marketing management: planning and control	3
2	Marketing communications strategy	74
3	International marketing strategy	120
4	Financial aspects of marketing	142
5	Significant current issues	172

PART B: THE CIM CASE STUDY EXAMINATION

| 6 | The CIM case study examination | 185 |

PART C: HOW TO ANALYSE THE CIM CASE STUDY

7	How to analyse a CIM case study: a general overview	197
8	The case study analysis methods recommended by the CIM senior examiner	201
9	Adopting the role and creating the plan	225

PART D: EXAMINATION TECHNIQUES: PLANNING YOUR EXAMINATION

| 10 | Examination techniques: planning your examination | 231 |

PART E: LEARNING FROM EXPERIENCE: ENSURING YOU PASS

| 11 | Introduction to past cases | 243 |

Gravesend Town Centre (June 1996 exam)

12	Gravesend Town Centre: case study documentation	245
13	Gravesend Town Centre: précis, marketing audit, SWOT	294
14	Gravesend Town Centre: analyses of appendices	318
15	Gravesend Town Centre: situational analysis, key issues, mission statement, broad aims, major problems	323
16	Gravesend Town Centre: outline marketing planning	334
17	Gravesend Town Centre: detailed marketing planning	353
18	Gravesend Town Centre: the examination paper, examiner's report and indicative marking guides	371
19	Consultants' analysis of Gravesend Town Centre	381

Mistral (December 96 exam)

20	Mistral: case study documentation	396
21	Mistral: précis, marketing audit, SWOT	426
22	Mistral: analyses of appendices	459
23	Mistral: situational analysis, key issues, mission statement, broad aims, major problems	466
24	Mistral: outline marketing planning	484
25	Mistral: detailed marketing planning	500
26	Mistral: the examination paper, examiner's report and indicative marking guides	509

Contents

Sentinel Aviation (June 1997 exam)

27	Sentinel Aviation: case study documentation	519
28	Sentinel Aviation: précis, marketing audit, SWOT	538
29	Sentinel Aviation: situational analysis, key issues, mission statement, broad aims, major problems	557
30	Sentinel Aviation: outline marketing planning	564
31	Sentinel Aviation: detailed marketing planning	597
32	Sentinel Aviation: the examination paper, examiner's report and indicative marking guides	627
33	Consultants' analysis of Sentinel Aviation	639

INDEX 659

ORDER FORMS

REVIEW FORM & FREE PRIZE DRAW

PREFACE

The exam

The Diploma awarded by the Chartered Institute of Marketing is a management qualification which puts a major emphasis on the practical understanding of marketing activities. At the same time, the Institute's examinations recognise that the marketing professional works in a fast changing organisational, economic and social environment.

Strategic Marketing Management: Analysis and Decision is one of the two compulsory CIM Diploma papers. It is compulsory as the marketing professional is expected to be a *manager*. Knowledge and skills in analysis and decision, together with an appreciation of the role of marketing in the corporate structure, are essential ingredients of managerial competence in this field.

This BPP Tutorial Text (September 1997 edition)

The secret of exam success is effective study material which is focused and relevant to the exam *you* will be sitting. This is the philosophy underpinning this Tutorial Text, which has been especially written for candidates sitting this case study examination. It is divided into five parts.

A   Background knowledge relevant to analysis and decision

B   The CIM case study examination

C   How to analyse the CIM case study (including the senior examiner's recommended 28-step method)

D   Examination techniques: planning your examination

E   Learning from experience: ensuring you pass. This includes detailed step-by-step analyses of three recent case studies (*Gravesend Town Centre (6/96)*, *Mistral (12/96)* and *Sentinel Aviation (6/97)*). You will view a variety of approaches to the material, which will help you set up a good file of data to take with you into the examination room. This approach helps you to take a reasoned, methodical approach to the case material which, by its nature, reflects the uncertainties of the commercial world.

The author

The author, *Dr David Pearson*, is a former Senior Examiner for Analysis and Decision, a former Senior Examiner for Marketing Planning and Control and the previous CIM Co-ordinator for all Diploma subjects. Dr Pearson has accumulated a total of 11 years experience in examining CIM Diploma subjects and continues to mark Analysis and Decision papers.

A final word

This Tutorial Text offers a professional solution to your needs in preparing for this challenging exam!

BPP Publishing
September 1997

For details of the other BPP titles relevant to your studies for this examination and for a full list of books in the BPP CIM range, please turn to the end of the text. If you send us your comments on this Tutorial Text, you will automatically be entered in our FREE PRIZE DRAW.

Introduction

HOW TO USE THIS TUTORIAL TEXT

1 *What is the CIM case study?*

There is no formal syllabus for the CIM's examination *Strategic Marketing Management: Analysis and Decision*. Instead the examination is based on a case study normally comprising 30 to 40 pages of narrative, charts and tables and issued to examinees by post about *four weeks in advance of the examination*.

The issue of the case study some four weeks in advance allows time for considerable analysis and discussion.

The case study is a *practical* test of the candidates' knowledge of marketing (gained in Certificate and Diploma, or equivalent, studies) and their ability to apply it. Normally candidates will also have some practical experience in marketing to bring to bear.

At the same time, some background knowledge is necessary. Those who are coming to the case study 'cold' will find the theoretical underpinning a useful complement to their practical experience. This is provided in Part A of this Tutorial Text. Some current issues in marketing of general relevance are also described here. The background material indicates the examiners' views as to what is relevant for the Analysis and Decision paper.

Whilst case study methods vary according to the institution and lecturer concerned, a particular model embodying a comprehensive 28-step approach is detailed in this Tutorial Text.

2 *Discussing the case study*

Students are strongly advised to conduct in-depth discussion with colleagues on the case study analysis and its issues. This is often accomplished at colleges by the forming of *syndicate groups* of four to six people and the holding of frequent *plenary sessions* where all candidates gather together. In this way, a syndicate member not only hears the view of his or her syndicate, but also those of other syndicates. In this way a much more balanced, integrated and secure approach can be developed. Students who forgo this sort of discussion are likely to fail, no matter how individually clever at analysis they might be.

Having said this, candidates should not copy out word for word *group answers*: these will be failed. Candidates must offer their own *individual* work on the day of the examination.

3 *The examination*

There are a number of different methods of dealing with case studies and students are exposed to some of these in Parts B and C of this Tutorial Text, so as to promote a reasonably wide appreciation of the subject. However, some method eventually needs to be chosen, and the one recommended has been thoroughly tried and tested, and has been found to achieve a high degree of success in the CIM examinations.

One of the key success factors in case study examination (apart from being thoroughly prepared) is to be well organised in the exam room itself, freeing the mind to think more calmly and clearly about the exam questions. Students are advised to study Part D on exam techniques very thoroughly.

4 *Practice*

Part E contains three recent case studies, examination questions and marking guides for self-assessment. You are strongly recommended to conduct a practice run on at least one of these previous case studies together with a mock exam and to get your answers assessed against the frameworks provided. This is the most effective way of preparing yourself for the problems you will eventually have to face in the examination room.

A note on pronouns

On occasions in this Study Text, 'he' is used for 'he or she', 'him' for 'him or her' and so forth. Whilst we try to avoid this practice it is sometimes necessary for reasons of style. No prejudice or stereotyping according to sex is intended or assumed.

SYLLABUS OVERVIEW

Aims and objectives

- To extend the practice of the student in the quantitative and qualitative analysis of marketing situations
- To develop powers of diagnosis and to create a firm basis in decision making

Learning outcomes

Students will be able to:

- apply their accumulated marketing knowledge and techniques to real world settings
- conduct detailed and comprehensive analysis of complex marketing situations
- assess critically marketing data of both a qualitative and quantitative nature
- comprehend and resolve a wide variety of marketing problems
- decide priorities and appropriate marketing objectives, strategies and tactics
- draw up a comprehensive and convincing marketing plan with accompanying costs and schedules
- suggest appropriate control mechanisms and contingency plans

Indicative content and weighting

Ideally, preparation for this module should be undertaken consecutively with Planning and Control allowing the various models and techniques introduced within Planning and Control to be practised on previous CIM case studies. Although there is no formal syllabus, the subject is intended to cover Analysis and Decision in equal weighting.

Whilst case study methods vary according to the institution and lecturer concerned, a particular model embodying a comprehensive 28-step approach is detailed in this Study Text.

Whilst the case study for this subject is intended to be a practical test of the candidate's ability to apply *all* his/her marketing knowledge (including the Certificate, Advanced Certificate and Diploma stages), the following aspects are particularly pertinent.

1 The marketing audit/situation analysis (30%)

2 Environmental analysis (PEST)

3 Competitor analysis (Porter's models)

3.1 Customer analysis (segmentation, positioning, buying behaviour)
3.2 Financial analysis - P&L and balance sheet, cash flow, ratio analysis
3.3 Review of the marketing planning process and marketing mix
3.4 The SWOT analysis

4 Company mission and corporation setting (5%)

5 Marketing organisation (5%)

5.1 Structure follows strategy
5.2 Marketing orientation
5.3 Internal marketing and TQM
5.4 Mergers and joint ventures

6 Marketing planning and control decisions (40%)

6.1 Marketing strategies (Ansoff, Boston, Porter etc)
6.2 The comprehensive marketing plan including the mix, budgets, action schedules and contingency planning

Introduction

7 Marketing research decisions (10%)

7.1 Types of marketing research
7.2 Information specifications and justifications
7.3 Methods of data collection
7.4 The marketing research plan
7.5 The marketing information system

8 Financial implications of the marketing plan (10%)

8.1 Costs, cash flow, working capital investment, risk, ROCE etc

Part A
Background knowledge relevant to analysis and decision

Chapter 1

STRATEGIC MARKETING MANAGEMENT: PLANNING AND CONTROL

This chapter covers the following topics.

1. Introduction to planning and control: overview
2. Strategic and marketing analysis (where are we now?)
3. Strategic direction and strategy formulation (where do we want to be?)
4. Strategic evaluation and choice (how might we get there and which way is best?)
5. Strategic implementation and control (how can we ensure arrival?)
6. Marketing research and the marketing information system (MkIS)

Introduction

The case study examination for *Strategic Marketing Management: Analysis and Decision* is intended to bring together and to test all your previous studies and knowledge of marketing. It would be impossible to cover all that here in just one part of one book. To do this, you would need to consult the CIM's full list of recommended publications. However, it is possible to review here a number of key subjects and to revise with you those elements which are most likely to be required for the case study examination. These key subjects are considered to be the following.

(a) The other diploma subjects of:

    (i) Strategic Marketing Management: Planning and Control (this chapter);
    (ii) Marketing Communications Strategy (Chapter 2);
    (iii) International Marketing Strategy (Chapter 3).

(b) Other relevant material including:

    (i) a discussion of financial information and its use (Chapter 4);
    (ii) a brief description of some significant current issues (Chapter 6).

This chapter will revise the syllabus for *Strategic Marketing Management: Planning and Control*, stage by stage. Rather than focusing on the detail required for the Planning and Control examination, it will however concentrate on those syllabus items *most relevant to case analysis and decision*. Theoretical detail is deliberately excluded in favour of practical application, for our purposes. (In other words, the material here will not be sufficient for you to pass that paper: buy the BPP Study Text for that subject if you are taking it.)

1 INTRODUCTION TO PLANNING AND CONTROL: OVERVIEW

1.1 Planning and control are essentially *management* functions. Planning and control are required at all levels of management. For our purposes we are concerned with the top level of marketing management, the level responsible for the critical strategic decisions.

1.2 However, marketing cannot be managed in a vacuum. Marketing directors and managers cannot take strategic decisions on their own without reference to the Managing Director and the Directors of other functions - ie corporate management as a team. True marketing orientation is found, after all, where everyone in the company from top to bottom accepts the marketing concept, and believes in customer sovereignty.

1.3 Nevertheless, marketing can be claimed with some justification to be the *key* activity in an organisation. As Drucker points out, a basic objective of any organisation is to survive. Organisations cannot normally survive without selling goods or providing services to people (customers) and this involves marketing.

1.4 A commercial organisation's long term survival usually rests on ensuring that revenue earned exceeds costs incurred and it is marketing managers' role to market profitably. The definition of *marketing* by the Chartered Institute of Marketing is: 'The *management* process which identifies, anticipates and satisfies customer requirements *profitably*'.

1.5 The marketing plan is only one of the functional plans which make up the total plan or corporate plan.

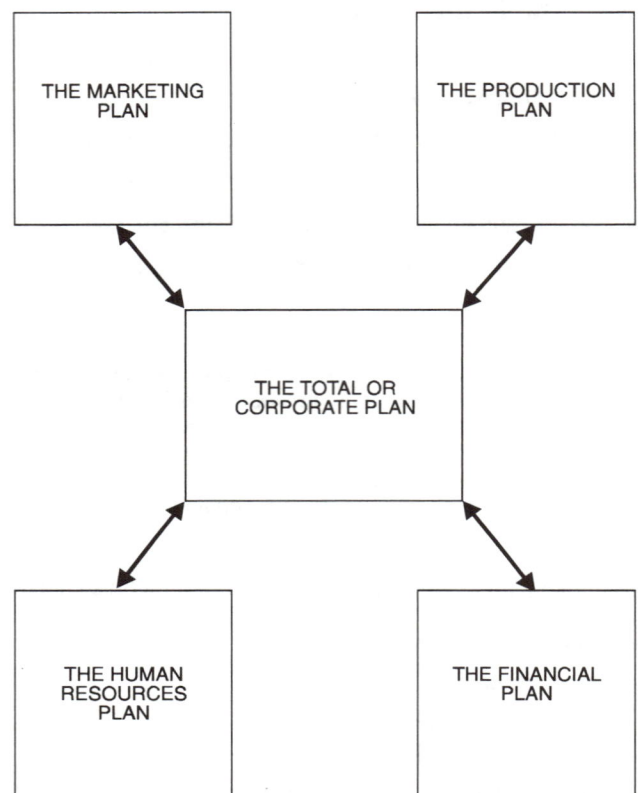

1.6 The marketing plan leads the other functional plans. Only after sales volumes have been forecast and agreed can the other functional plans be drawn up. Sales volumes determine the amount of goods that are to be produced in most industries (although in some industries, the costs of shutting down the production may be so huge so as to justify continued production).

1.7 The above figure reminds us of the importance of people. Again Drucker suggests that the art of management is 'getting things done through people'. It does, therefore, involve a process (getting things done) and people.

1.8 'Getting things done' is however an insufficient description of a manager's role. A manager has to 'do the right things' (strategy) and 'to do things right' (tactics) to be effective.

1.9 In order to do the right things, managers need to examine the organisation's current position, to understand how it got there, and to decide where they would *like* the organisation's future position to be.

Strategies and tactics

1.10 In deciding where the organisation *can* be in the future, rather than where they would like the organisation to be, managers have to assess the *feasibility* of the desired state of affairs, which in turn means examining options for achieving it and constraints on reaching it.

1.11 There will be many options or ways of getting to where the organisation wants to be, each of which will entail barriers and costs. Comparing these options and deciding which is best is clearly a key management role.

1.12 Having decided on the right things, managers have to 'do things right' and this involves technical planning, implementation and control.

1.13 We can therefore see that all management has a common basis. All plans drawn up by managers can be said to follow a broadly similar process.

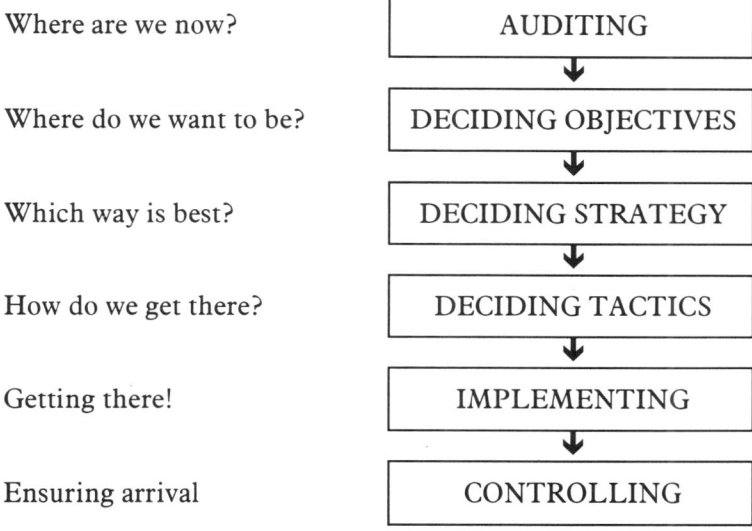

1.14 Marketing management can therefore be seen to have a great deal in common with other functional management.

1.15 Students often find it difficult to relate marketing objectives clearly to corporate objectives and even more difficult to distinguish clearly marketing objectives from corporate objectives. The latter is hardly surprising since corporate objectives are really marketing objectives. There can be no corporate plan which does not involve products/services and customers. The following diagram from Kotler clearly expresses the interactive two-way relationship between marketing plans and strategic business planning.

Part A: Background knowledge relevant to analysis and decision

1.16 A good way to achieve greater understanding of marketing in a corporate setting is to recognise that there is no real separation. *Corporate management* does not exist on its own. The only corporate manager is the Managing Director or Chief Executive and even then he or she will have come from a functional background.

1.17 The word corporate is derived from corpus, meaning the body. The body corporate is the body *whole*. The body consists of parts - the trunk, arms, legs, head etc. It does not exist on its own, it is the sum of the parts.

1.18 Corporate objectives can be said to be largely concerned with achieving growth (ie in size, in the number of activities, in profitability) consistent with limiting risk. The *stakeholders* in an organisation (ie all those, not only shareholders, who have an interest in what the organisation does) would not normally support high growth objectives which demanded the taking of very high risks. The prospect of an immediate growth of 300 times in the liquid capital of an organisation might sound attractive, but not if it was based on betting the organisation's liquid capital on a 300 to 1 outsider in the Grand National.

1.19 The pursuit of growth takes many forms - growth in number of employees, outlets, customers, profit, profitability etc. In a way growth itself, if achieved in a steady way, reduces risk. Not to grow and certainly to decline is seen within the organisation as a threat to an organisation's survival. Normally some profit (surplus of income over expenditure) is needed just to stand still, since assets can depreciate more than planned, employees will hope to improve their earnings and investors will want to see a return on their capital.

1.20 Corporate management in seeking to grow profitably and reduce risk will deploy the functional activities of the business to these ends. For example marketing activities can be deployed to increase (profitable) sales, the production function to reduce unit costs, the finance function to secure funding at lower rates and human resources to employ less people or recruit more productive/effective people. All these measures could help to increase profit and reduce risk. In this scenario, therefore, the functions are deployed *strategically* to meet corporate *objectives* since the functions are means to achieve the corporate ends.

1.21 Once you understand this, we can move on to see that, for a marketing director growth in profitable sales becomes the marketing objective. It derives from, and is consistent with but not separate from, the corporate objectives.

1.22 The *marketing strategy* is the way in which the marketing function organises its activities to achieve a profitable growth in sales. It could for example seek to do this by introducing new products/services (Ansoff's growth strategy of product development) or by seeking new customers (Ansoff's marketing development). At a marketing mix level, sales might be increased profitably by increasing/decreasing prices, by expanding the sales force, investing more money in advertising etc.

1.23 It is important to recognise that both strategy and tactics are means to ends, in other words, ways of achieving objectives. The difference between strategy and tactics is simply one of detail and depends on the level from which you are looking. To a marketing director, the cleanliness of a room will be a mere detail. To the office cleaner it will however be an objective and entail a plan. The cleaner will:

(a) audit (take stock, decide what state of cleanliness the room is currently in);
(b) decide objectives (what state the room needs to be in by a given time);
(c) decide broad strategies (vacuuming, tidying, dusting);
(d) decide tactics (where to start, what to use); and
(e) schedule the order of actions.

1.24 Once you realise that the difference between strategy and tactics is a movable line you should feel a great deal more comfortable when drawing up your marketing plans for the case study. You do not really need to be precise in your categorisation. The word 'tactics' does not really need to be employed at all. You could move from objectives to strategies (using the Ansoff growth matrix) to the marketing mix. In drawing up your plans for the marketing mix you should move from the general to the particular. For example a marketing communications manager will decide the balance between *pull and push* strategies, before getting down to the detail of which particular exhibitions to show the firm's wares in.

1.25 It is very important to get your thinking clear about this, otherwise your marketing plan and its relationship to the corporate plan will appear confused and your proposals will lose their credibility. To help you further in your thinking please examine and reflect upon the following table.

Eight ways to distinguish between Strategic and Tactical Decisions

1 *Importance:* Strategic decisions are significantly more important.

2 *Level at which conducted:* Strategic decisions usually taken by top management.

3 *Time Horizon:* Strategics = long term. Tactics = short term

4 *Regularity:* Strategy formulation is continuous whereas tactics are periodic.

5 *Nature of problem:* Strategic problems are unstructured and often unique, involving considerable risk and uncertainty. Tactical problems are more structured and repetitive with risks easier to assess.

6 *Information Needed:* Strategies require large amounts of external information much of which is subjective and futuristic. Tactics depend much more on internally generated accounting or marketing research information.

7 *Detail:* Strategy is broad. Tactics are narrow and specific.

8 *Ease of Evaluation:* Strategic decisions are more difficult to make and evaluate.

Source: adapted from 'Strategic Marketing' Weitz and Wensley (ex George Steiner and John Miner)

1.26 You should now have a clearer understanding of how the marketing planning process relates to the corporate planning process. It is therefore appropriate here to return to the other aspect of marketing management namely 'getting things done through people' (as mentioned in Paragraph 1.7).

Personnel issues

1.27 Writers such as Nigel *Piercy* have rightly pointed out that the marketing manager's plans are often frustrated by other people in the organisation. These 'blockers' can be people in the marketing department but are more likely to be people in other departments. The less an organisation is truly marketing orientated, the more likely it is that marketing plans are ineffective.

1.28 In the case study it is vital to look at your role and your relationships with other people in the organisation. You cannot do everything yourself and therefore have to rely on 'getting things done through other people'. Sometimes you may be cast in the role of a consultant, when you can only advise. Sometimes you will have only a *staff authority* (ie the authority to advise but not to direct) and need to *persuade*. At other times you may have *line responsibility* and be in a position to *command*.

1.29 Whatever your role in the case study, you will need to recognise the importance of *internal marketing* and *relationship marketing* in getting things done. You might also have to recommend ways of improving the marketing orientation of the organisation in the case. You will find some useful additional notes on these items in the final chapter of this book headed 'Significant Current Issues'.

1.30 This introduction to Marketing Planning and Control would not be complete without some mention of information inputs for decision outputs. Marketing makes a particularly important input to the corporate planning decisions in the following ways.

   (a) The *environmental audit* reviews the organisation's position in relation to changes in the external environment (sociological, legal, economic, political and technological) and provides information which directly affects the setting of corporate objectives.

   (b) The *competitor audit* provides competitor intelligence, competitor response models and so on which again influence corporate objectives, strategy and contingency planning.

   (c) The *customer audit* assesses the existing and potential customer bases to provide information as to whether to develop new markets.

   (d) *Product portfolio analysis* provides input for decisions as to whether to drop particular products and/or add new ones.

   (e) The *sales forecast* provides the basis for all other functional activities as well as marketing.

1.31 We have already seen how the corporate plan breaks down into the marketing plan and the other functional plans. Information inputs to the *corporate* planning decisions as suggested above perform a double duty in that they also provide the bases for deciding marketing objectives and strategies.

1.32 However marketing research is vital to *all stages* of the marketing plan. We need information in order to make sensible decisions on the marketing mix, for example product research, pricing research and advertising research. We also need information in order to implement and control the marketing plan and to assess the extent to which marketing objectives have been achieved.

1.33 *Marketing research* and an effective *marketing information system (MkIS)* are therefore essential components of the marketing planning process. You will find the outline of a marketing research plan in Chapter 7 (the methods recommended by the CIM senior examiner).

1.34 Further outline notes on marketing research and MkIS are given in Section 6 of this chapter.

1.35 Before moving on to the next section of this chapter it is felt appropriate to present a *concise* framework for the marketing plan which is our ultimate aim in the case study. Like all concise frameworks it suffers from omissions but many of our students have welcomed the following single page approach as a means of achieving an overview. You will find it on the next page.

2 STRATEGIC AND MARKETING ANALYSIS (WHERE ARE WE NOW?)

2.1 This is of course an area with a great deal of applicability to the case study *analysis* and decision. The amount of applicability of any one particular item within this section of the syllabus will obviously depend upon the specific case being analysed and the data it contains.

2.2 The actual case study on which you will be examined is unpredictable and the nature of the case study will change over time. It is thus in your best interests to revise thoroughly the marketing audit.

The marketing audit

2.3 *The marketing audit* is a thorough examination of all the external and internal factors affecting the marketing planning and control process. A useful way of portraying these factors is by reference to the various environments which surround the *customer*, the customer being the focus of our marketing plan.

Different environments impacting upon the satisfaction of customer needs (adapted from Buttle)

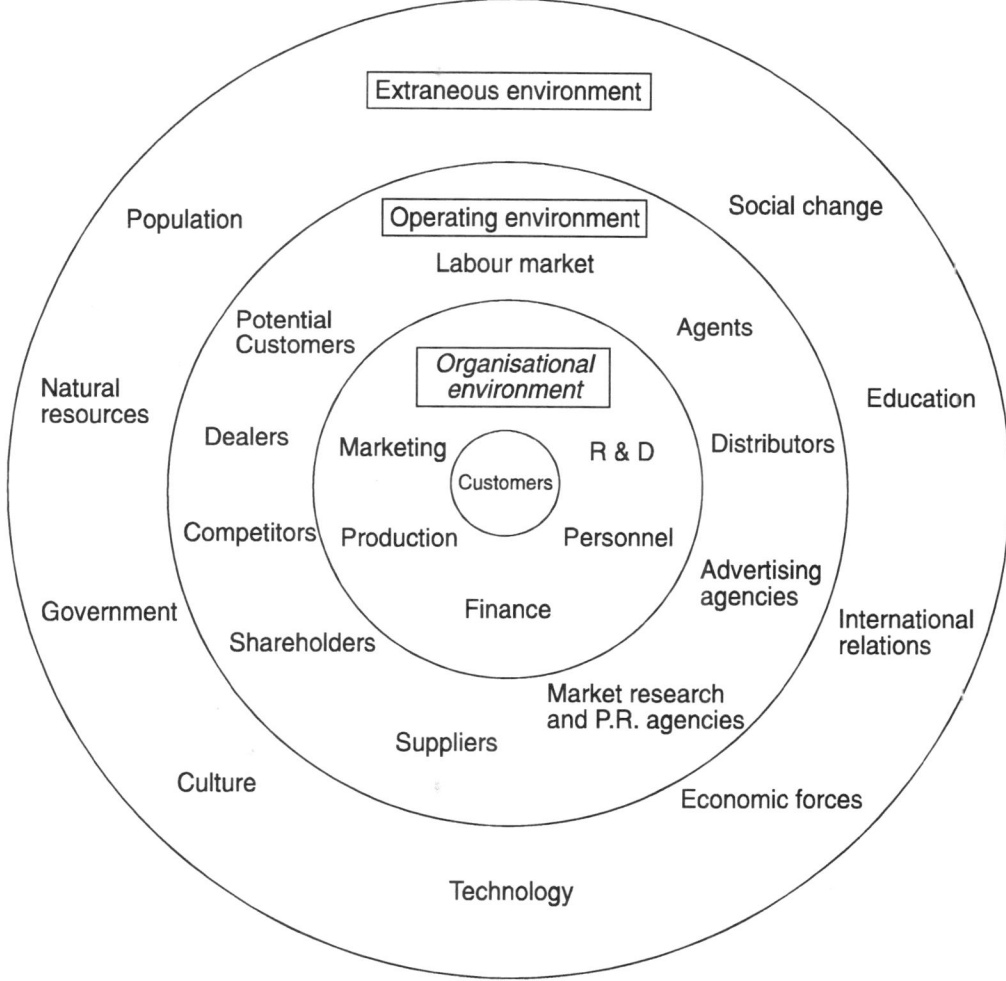

A CONCISE FRAMEWORK FOR A MARKETING PLAN

1. ANALYSIS OF CURRENT SITUATION (Using Marketing Research)

1.1 THE MARKET

Mkt size (units) | 96 | 97 | 98 | 99 | 00 | 01 | 02 | 03 | 04 | 05 | 06 |
Mkt share (units)

Mkt size (cash)
Mkt share (cash)
Mkt trends/forecasts
Company strengths/weaknesses and key features of marketing mixes
Brand strengths/weaknesses and key features of marketing mixes
Competitor strengths/weaknesses and key features of marketing mixes
Customer profiles, buying behaviours, needs
Company sales forecasts

1.2 DISTRIBUTION
Available channels
Sales by outlet
Competitors' distribution methods

1.3 ENVIRONMENTAL FACTORS

2. BUSINESS MISSION/OBJECTIVES

What business are we in?
What business would we like to be in 5-10 years hence?
Corporate objectives - profitability, growth, risk reduction.
Marketing objectives - market share, sales.

3. STRATEGIES - ANSOFF

	Existing Markets	New Markets
Existing Products	Market Penetration	Market Development
New Products	Product Development	Diversification

SEGMENTATION
- Bases
- Characteristics and measurement
- Strategy

4. TACTICS/OPERATION PLAN - MKG MIX PROPOSALS

4.1 PRODUCT DECISIONS
- Objectives
- Branding
- Packaging
- Pre/After sales service

4.2 PRICING DECISIONS
- Objectives
- Strategy - penetration v. skimming
- Discounts

4.3 DISTRIBUTION DECISIONS
- Objectives
- Channels
- Intensive/selective/exclusive distribution

4.4 PROMOTION DECISIONS
- Objectives - roles
- Salesforce size/organisation/motivation
- Sales promotion/PR, merchandising
- Advertising expenditure
- Media - target audiences
- Copy/creative platforms
- Agencies

5. BUDGETS

Sales forecasts, Sales budgets
Periods - 1-5 years
Costs - selling, marketing, advertising etc

1: Strategic marketing management: planning and control

2.4 The *external variables* are often referred to as the *uncontrollable variables* as opposed to the more controllable variables represented by the internal factors. It is in the external environment that opportunities and threats can be found which help to forge long-term strategy whereas the marketing mix decisions are internal, of a shorter term and are more tactical in nature.

2.5 Although the external variables are said to be uncontrollable, they can and must be anticipated and modelled. Having done this marketing planners can find ways to exploit opportunities and avoid threats. In this way the external variables become more controllable.

2.6 The more *comprehensive* the marketing audit, the clearer is the picture that emerges of the current situation and the better placed the company is to set *realistic* objectives for future achievement.

2.7 Ideally speaking the marketing audit should examine every item exhaustively. For example, an audit of advertising effectiveness should not only cover the detail of media, timing, copy platform, size, advertising research data, but also *changes* made over the past years and a similar examination of each *competitor's* advertising in the same period. Only in this way can a really thorough understanding be achieved the pay-off for which will be gained in better advertising plan decisions.

Internal checklist

2.8 (a) *Current position*

    (i) *Performance*

        (1) Total sales in value and in units.
        (2) Total gross profit, expenses and net profit.
        (3) Percentage of sales for sales expenses, advertising etc.
        (4) Percentage of sales in each segment.
        (5) Value and volume sales by area, month, model size etc.
        (6) Sales per thousand consumers, per factory, in segments.
        (7) Market share in total market and in segments.

    (ii) *Customers*

        (1) Number of actual and potential buyers by area.
        (2) Characteristics of consumer buyers, eg income, occupation, education, sex, size of family etc.
        (3) Characteristics of industrial buyers, eg primary, secondary, tertiary, manufacturing; type of industry; size etc.
        (4) Characteristics of users, if different from buyers.
        (5) Location of buyers, users.
        (6) When purchases made: time of day, week, month, year; frequency of purchase; size of average purchase or typical purchase.
        (7) How purchases are made: specification or competition; by sample, inspection, impulse, rotation, system; cash or credit.
        (8) Attitudes, motivation to purchase; influences on buying decision; decision making unit in organisation.
        (9) Product uses - primary and secondary.

(b) *Products*

    (i) *Firm's current product information*

        (1) Quality: materials, workmanship, design, method of manufacture, manufacturing cycle, inputs-outputs.
        (2) Technical characteristics, attributes that may be considered as selling points, buying points.

(3) Models, sizes, styles, ranges, colours etc.
(4) Essential or non-essential, convenience or speciality.
(5) Similarities with other company products.
(6) Relation of product features to user's needs, wants, desires.
(7) Development of branding and brand image.
(8) Degree of product differentiation, actual and possible.
(9) Packaging used, functional, promotional.
(10) Materials, sizes, shapes, construction, closure.

(ii) *Competitors*
(1) Competitive and competing products.
(2) Main competitors and leading brands.
(3) Comparison of design and performance differences with leading competitors.
(4) Comparison of offering of competitors, images, value etc.

(iii) *Future product development*
(1) Likely future product developments in company.
(2) Likely future, or possible future, developments in industry.
(3) Further product line or mix contraction, modification or expansion.

(c) *Distribution*

(i) *Current distribution position*
(1) Current company distribution structure.
(2) Channels and methods used in channels.
(3) Total number of outlets (consumer or industrial) by type.
(4) Total number of wholesalers or industrial middlemen, broken down into areas and by types.
(5) Percentage of outlets of each type handling product broken down into areas.
(6) Attitudes of outlets by area, type, size.
(7) Degree of cooperation, current and possible.
(8) Multi-brand policy, possible or current.
(9) Strengths and weaknesses in distribution system, functionally and geographically.
(10) Number and type of warehouses; location.
(11) Transportation and communications.
(12) Stock control; delivery periods; control of information.

(ii) *Competitors*
(1) Competitive distribution structure; strengths and weaknesses.
(2) Market coverage and penetration.
(3) Transportation methods used by competitors.
(4) Delivery of competitors.
(5) Specific competitive selling conditions.

(iii) *Future developments*
(1) Further likely and possible developments in industry as a whole or from one or more competitors.
(2) Probable changes in distribution system of company.
(3) Possibilities of any future fundamental changes in outlets.

1: Strategic marketing management: planning and control

- (d) *Promotional and personal selling*
  - (i) *Firm's position*
    - (1) Size and composition of sales force.
    - (2) Calls per day, week, month, year by salesperson.
    - (3) Conversion rate of orders to calls.
    - (4) Selling cost per value and volume of sales achieved.
    - (5) Selling cost per customer.
    - (6) Internal and external sales promotion.
    - (7) Recruiting, selection, training, control procedures.
    - (8) Methods of motivation of salesmen.
    - (9) Remuneration schemes.
    - (10) Advertising appropriation and media schedule, copy theme.
    - (11) Cost of trade, technical, professional, consumer media.
    - (12) Cost of advertising per unit, per value of unit, per customer.
    - (13) Advertising expenditure per thousand readers, viewers of main and all media used.
    - (14) Methods and costs of merchandising.
    - (15) Public and press relations; exhibitions.
  - (ii) *Competitors*
    - (1) Competitive selling activities and methods of selling and advertising; strengths and weaknesses.
    - (2) Review of competitors' promotion, sales contests, etc.
    - (3) Competitor's advertising themes, media used.
  - (iii) *Future developments* likely in selling, promotional and advertising activities.
- (e) *Pricing*
  - (i) *Firms' current pricing*
    - (1) Pricing strategy and general methods of price structuring in company.
    - (2) High or low policies, reasons why.
    - (3) Prevailing pricing policies in industry.
    - (4) Current wholesaler, retailer margins in consumer markets or middlemen margins in industrial markets.
    - (5) Discounts, functional, quantity, cash, reward, incentive.
    - (6) Pricing objectives, profit objectives, financial implications such as breakeven figures, cash budgeting.
  - (ii) *Competitors*
    - (1) Prices and price structures of competitors.
    - (2) Value analysis of own and competitors' products.
    - (3) Discounts, credit offered by competitors.
  - (iii) *Future developments*
    - (1) Future developments in costs likely to affect price structures.
    - (2) Possibilities of more/less costly raw materials or labour that would affect prices.
    - (3) Possible competitive price attacks.
- (f) *Service*
  - (i) *Firm's current service*
    - (1) Extent of pre-sales or customer service and after-sales or product service required by products.

Part A: Background knowledge relevant to analysis and decision

                    (2) Survey of customer needs.
                    (3) Installation, education in use, inspection, maintenance, repair, accessories provision.
                    (4) Guarantees, warranty period.
                    (5) Methods, procedures for carrying out service. Returned goods, complaints.
            (ii) *Competitors*
                    (1) Services supplied by competitive manufacturers and service organisations.
                    (2) Types of guarantee, warranty, credit provided.
            (iii) *Future possible developments* that might require a revised service policy.
    (g) Organisational points (eg design of marketing organisation, sales, production or marketing orientation)

External checklist

2.9 (a) Environmental audit: national and international
    (i) Social and cultural factors likely to impact upon the market, in the short and long term.
    (ii) Legal factors and codes of practice likely to affect the market in the short and long term.
    (iii) Economic factors likely to affect market demand in the short and long term.
    (iv) Political changes and military action likely to impact upon national and international markets.
    (v) Technological changes anticipated and likely to create new opportunities and threats.

(b) *Marketing objectives and strategies*
    (i) Short term plans and objectives for current year, in light of current political and economic situation.
    (ii) Construction of standards for measurement of progress towards achieving of objectives; management ratios that can be translated into control procedures.
    (iii) Breakdown of turnover into periods, areas, segments, outlets, salesmen etc.
    (iv) Which personnel required to undertaken what responsibilities, actions etc when.
    (v) Review of competitors' strengths and weaknesses, likely competitive reactions and possible company responses that could be made.
    (vi) Long term plans, objectives and strategies related to products, price, places of distribution, promotion, personnel selling and service.

2.10 We are now in a position to revise the various specific tools, frameworks and techniques relevant to particular sections of the checklist above.

The environmental audit

2.11 Nearly all the case studies are positioned in an environmental situation of considerable change which represents both an opportunity and a threat. Here are some examples.

(a) With *Regional Railways* (December 1992) the environmental change was largely politically inspired, and involved the impending privatisation of British Rail.

(b) With regard to the *Royal Mail* case study (June 1993) environmental changes included greater liberalisation orchestrated by an EC Green Paper, technological change (increasing electronification within the communications industry) and economic change.

1: Strategic marketing management: planning and control

(c) In *GT Student Aids Ltd* (December 1993), the educational market setting was subject to radical environmental changes (including sociological, legal, political, technological and economic factors).

(d) In *Purbeck Financial Services* (June 1994), the company was faced with a competitive threat (direct writers) made possible by advances in technology.

(e) In *Australian Tourist Commission* (December 1994), the Olympic Games in the Year 2000 represent a massive opportunity but also raises questions of sustainability and a number of environmental concerns.

(f) For *FirstrATE Europe* (June 1995), the setting is an industrial one and the main environmental threat/opportunity is that of technological change.

(g) In *Leffe* (December 1995) there are sociological and legal overtones.

(h) In the case of *Gravesend Town Centre* (June 1996) which is set in the public sector, almost the full raft of environment issues apply.

(i) In *Mistral*, demographic factors and changes in public sector procurement policies have an impact.

2.12 All these changes posed threats but also offered opportunities, the analysis of which greatly affected the choice and viability of marketing strategies.

2.13 In both deciding 'where we are now' and indeed 'where we want to be in the future' the environmental audit is therefore instrumental. The analytical framework commonly used for the environmental audit is given by the PEST acronym (political, economic, social, technological) but SLEPT as given below is perhaps more searching.

S = Socio-cultural
L = Legal
E = Economic
P = Political
T = Technological

2.14 Sometimes it is difficult to say whether a factor such as privatisation is political or legal. It is in fact politically led but legally (by Act of Parliament) implemented. However, the exact category an item falls under is less important than identifying it in the first place so do not waste time splitting hairs. Analytical tools and techniques do in any case need to be adapted where necessary rather than dismissed as unsuitable because of a little difficulty in applying them.

2.15 A review of recent *major* changes under the above framework, which are likely to affect marketing strategies in case studies is given below.

(a) *Socio-cultural trends*

(i) People in the UK are increasingly cohabiting before marriage or in place of marriage.

(ii) People in the UK are tending to have babies at a later age.

(iii) The UK population is living longer and ageing in profile.

(iv) Unemployment is high and likely to remain high in the UK and throughout Europe. Also there is a greater mobility of labour throughout the EC.

(v) More people are seeking higher education.

(vi) Ethnicity is changing in the UK and throughout Europe.

(vii) There is an increasing awareness of consumer rights.

(viii) The importance of corporate culture is reflected in mission statements, TQM, internal marketing and relationship marketing.

(b) *Legal factors* affecting marketing include the following.

(i) Trade Descriptions Act
(ii) Consumer Credit Act

(iii) Product liability legislation
(iv) Sale of Goods Act
(v) Law of Contract
(vi) Law of Agency
(vii) Data Protection Act (eg limits use of customer databases)
(viii) Changes in the presentation of company accounts
(ix) Restrictions on parking (for sales people, distributors etc).

The above list is illustrative only as there are continual changes in UK law which affect particular industries to a greater degree than others. Legal changes often cause changes to be made to the marketing mix eg price, packaging and distribution. To legal changes must be added an increasing proliferation of *EU regulations* and the non-legal but closely allied *Codes of Practice* (eg Banking Code of Practice) which constrain marketing decisions.

(c) *Economic factors*

(i) General economic depression in the western world.

(ii) UK/USA pulling out of recession faster than Germany, France and Eastern European countries.

(iii) A tendency towards protectionism in the larger economic groupings, although this is to some extent counteracted by the World Trade Organisation (1995).

(iv) The development of the single European market - in particular the lowering of trade barriers and the opening up to tender of public sector as well as private sector markets.

(v) The Department of Trade and Industry urges UK organisations to address the following nine key issues affecting future business strategy.

(1) Who in the organisation is to be made responsible for exploiting EU opportunities and negating threats?

(2) What other structural changes are necessary?

(3) In what particular ways has/will the single market affect the organisation?

(4) Will the organisation change from being a UK one servicing a UK market to being a European one with a European market?

(5) If we become European, how will this affect the scale of our business?

(6) How much more vulnerable will we be to new or greater competition?

(7) To what extent do we need to broaden our product range?

(8) To what extent do we need to strengthen our market position?

(9) To what extent should we (in order to broaden our product range and/or strengthen our market position and/or spread our financial risk) seek mergers, take-overs or joint ventures?

(vi) Generally low/slow growth in world markets but relatively high/fast growth in the 'Pacific Rim' and China.

(d) *Political factors*

(i) A move towards the right throughout Europe
(ii) A lack of strong political leadership throughout Europe and in the USA
(iii) A decrease in the relative power of trade unions
(iv) Increased opportunities for political lobbying
(v) The use of sanctions against 'offending' countries (eg in trade policy)
(vi) Political instability in eastern Europe.

(e) *Technological factors*

(i) Electronic data transfer (communications, EPOS, EFTPOS etc.)

(ii) Infrastructure including the Channel Tunnel

(iii) Computerisation, PC's, networking

(iv) Biotechnology

(v) Robotisation

(vi) New ways of designing production and procedures (eg TQM, Business process re-engineering).

2.16 Some examples of the impact of environmental forces on marketing mix decisions are given in the box below. We have selected two examples, legal and economic factors. To get you thinking about these issues yourself, you might like to do a similar task for socio-cultural, political and technological factors.

Factor	Mix element	
LEGAL	PRICE	Laws against agreements which lessen competition, change advertising descriptions, illustrations, ban slush funds etc.
	PROMOTION	Laws on labelling, packaging, publicity, sales promotion, lotteries, selling door to door etc.
	PRODUCT	Laws on safety, function, 'fitness for use'
	DISTRIBUTION	Laws on monopoly, foreign markets, restricted sales (eg drugs through certain outlets) opening days/times parking etc.
ECONOMIC	PRICE	Intensity of competition, credit restrictions, consumers willingness to spend.
	PROMOTION	Features emphasised eg cost savings.
	PRODUCT	Recession increases competition and pressure to reduce costs, and add features
	DISTRIBUTION	In recession there is more direct marketing and foreign markets are sought after.

SWOT analysis

2.17 *SWOT analysis* is one of the most useful tools in deciding 'where are we now?' in terms of Strengths, Weaknesses, Opportunities and Threats. Strengths and weaknesses are those of the organisation (ie internal and are controllable). Opportunities and Threats emanate from outside the organisation (ie external variables).

(a) Organisations should of course exploit opportunities for which their strengths are particularly suitable, correct weaknesses and avoid threats.

(b) In many ways, therefore, the organisation's strengths and weaknesses are a blueprint for the short-term operational or tactical plan whilst opportunities and threats influence the nature of longer-term strategic planning.

(c) It does however need to be emphasised that the SWOT analysis is a subjective technique. Whether an item is categorised as a strength or a weakness depends both upon the circumstances and the analyst's point of view. Taking a consensus of the organisation's staff (or a case study syndicate) helps to remove some of the subjectivity and clarify the individual's thinking.

(d) In the case study *Leffe* one of the key issues is that of gaining critical mass for the brand in the UK market. How best to achieve this entails a choice from a number of evaluated options. An opportunity exists to achieve market growth in the premium lager market but others might see Leffe as better positioned outside this already fragmented and highly competitive market. Weaknesses exist in the poor penetration of the brand so far and the lack of promotional funds.

(e) A format for the SWOT analysis is given in Chapter 8 (the examiner's recommended methods of analysing the CIM case study).

(f) When analysing strengths, weaknesses, opportunities and threats, a greater degree of sophistication may be achieved by scoring each item as being *major, medium* or *minor* and then whether that item is of *high, medium* or *low importance*.

Part A: Background knowledge relevant to analysis and decision

A *major strength* can be of relatively *low importance* in terms of the opportunities and threats facing the firm. A strength of high importance needs to be capitalised upon and play a key part in strategy formulation. For example, a major strength in the domestic market may be unimportant if there is a strategic imperative to expand into overseas markets.

2.18 *SWOT and issues analysis*. The findings of the SWOT analysis help to define the basic issues underlying the case study situation. In the case of Leffe some of these might be as follows.

(a) Should all promotional expenditure continue to be below-the-line?
(b) How should Leffe be positioned in its chosen markets?
(c) What should be the best distribution outlets for this brand.

2.19 *Ratio analysis*

(a) Ratio analysis can play a major role both in deciding where the company is now and in quantitatively defining where the company would ideally like to be in the future. This analysis can also be applied to competitors.

(b) Most case studies contain Profit and Loss Accounts and Balance Sheets which lend themselves to this form of analysis. Other case studies might actually present some ratios to you. To help you to familiarise yourself with this form of analysis, a section giving more detail has been included in Chapter 4.

2.20 *Productivity analysis* is a type of ratio analysis given here by way of example.

(a) Probably the simplest way of defining the productivity of marketing is:

$$\frac{\text{Marketing outputs}}{\text{Marketing inputs}}$$

(b) This can then be applied to individual marketing activities, eg:

(i) $$\frac{\text{Increase in numbers aware of products}}{\text{Cost of advertising}}$$

(ii) $$\frac{\text{Units shipped through distribution channel X}}{\text{Cost of distribution channel X}}$$

(iii) $$\frac{\text{Number of redemptions}}{\text{Cost of sales promotion}}$$

(c) As can be seen, productivity analysis and ratio analysis are closely related. However, care needs to be taken between efficiency and effectiveness. For example, sales *efficiency* might be increased in terms of numbers of orders taken by the sales force but if they are very small orders or mainly orders for a product with a relatively low contribution then *effectiveness* in terms of profitability may be reduced.

(d) The case study data will often encourage you to seek to improve the organisation's effectiveness in terms of sales.

3 STRATEGIC DIRECTION AND STRATEGY FORMULATION (WHERE DO WE WANT TO BE?)

Auditing the present and forecasting the future

3.1 It is only when we have a clear picture of where we are now (and how we've come to arrive here) that we can decide realistically where we want to be in the future. This relationship between auditing and forecasting can be seen in the following figure.

1: Strategic marketing management: planning and control

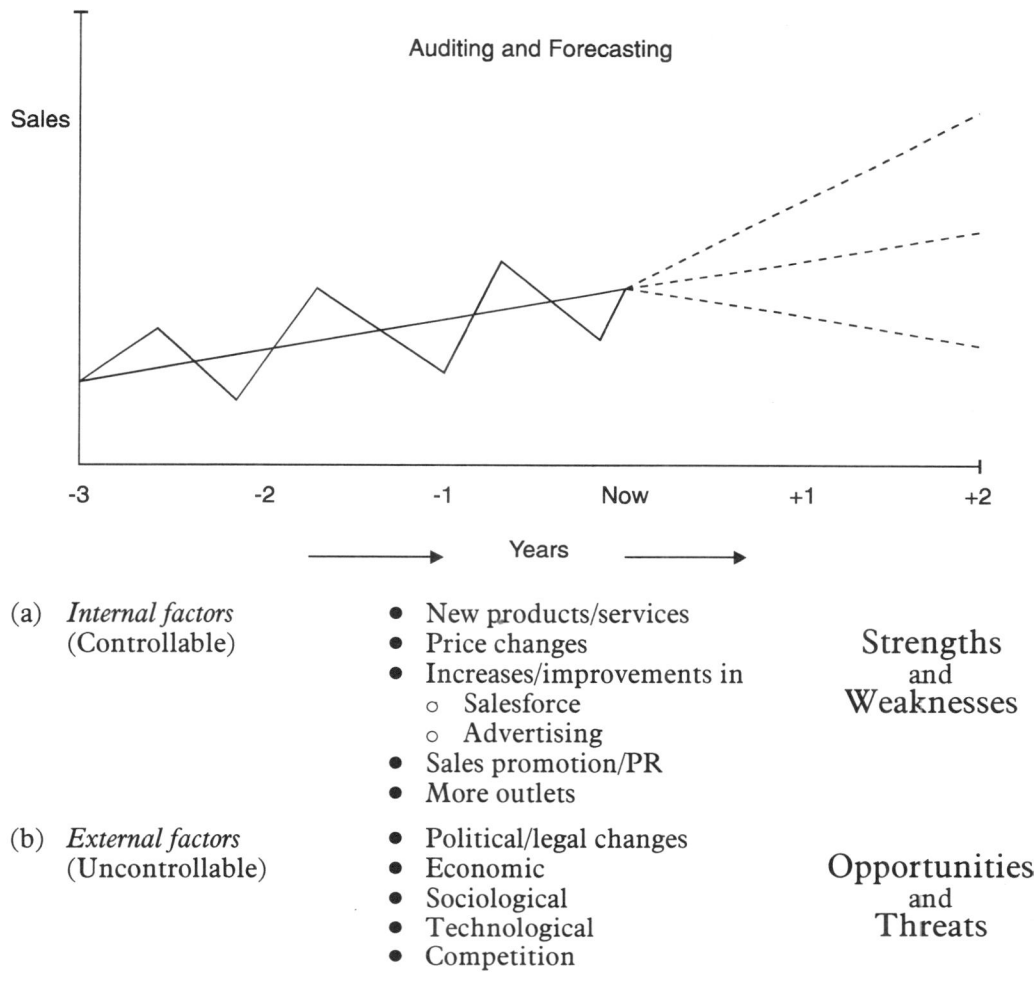

3.2 Referring to the above figure we can see how sales can be plotted for previous years and use statistical techniques or simply 'the line of best fit' to establish the base trend. This straight line trend can then be extended or extrapolated to indicate where (all things being equal) we are likely to be in the period which lies ahead.

3.3 However, all things are not equal. Some people might argue that the *more recent* past is a more reliable indicator of the future than the more distant past and so weight the last year accordingly. Furthermore one or more of the external environmental factors may be on the verge of radical change, for example Europe going into recession or (in the case of *Gravesend Town Centre*) the siting of the Channel Tunnel rail link. Finally your company might be planning to increase the size of the sales force, introduce a major new product, reduce prices or take other actions that will significantly affect future sales.

3.4 Now is perhaps a good time to revise *forecasting*. In your exam case study you are likely to be presented with a set of accounts for previous years which will include sales and costs of sales. You can therefore use these to extrapolate into the future as indicated above. Your environmental analysis will suggest upward or downward variations on this extrapolation and your marketing plans will do likewise. You can also take actions to reduce or increase the costs of sales and therefore forecast future profit. If for example you were planning to introduce a major new product next year, this could add significantly to costs but not impact significantly on sales until say the year after.

Sales forecasting

3.5 Sales forecasting can be defined as an estimate of the anticipated volume of sales which the business expects to make over a given period of time. Its purpose is to reduce to a minimum the risks and uncertainties involved in making decisions affecting the future. The sales forecast is central to decisions on all aspects of business.

(a) Production schedules
(b) Human resources
(c) Purchasing requirements
(d) Financial requirements
(e) Price determination
(f) R & D priorities
(g) Promotional effort

3.6 Firms should consider the following.

(a) The international situation (and its likely effects on both exports and government policy at home)

(b) The national situation (expanding or stagnant).

(c) The industrial situation (which may show contrary trends to the above, eg electronics likely to expand even in a stagnant economy).

(d) The company situation (better or worse than competitors).

(e) The product situation (growing and declining products).

(f) In addition to this market information a firm will also consider its own:

(i) current orders;
(ii) stock levels;
(iii) production capacity.

3.7 The time period for the forecast can be short - medium or long term.

(a) *Short term* is the most common, usually one year or less depending on purchasing patterns for the production capacity to current order and stock levels.

(b) *Medium term* is from one to three years ahead. This will guide decisions on budgets, salesmen's quotas etc, and will require information on market trends.

(c) *Long term* is up to 10 years ahead. This guides decisions on capital expenditure, research and development programmes, new product development. Information on growth trends, changes in taste, movements in population etc is required.

(d) In addition we can add *long term objective forecasts:* will we be in business with our present products in ten or twenty years time? This will require information on all major trends - technological, social ethical and economic. It will aid decisions on diversification, capital expenditure etc.

3.8 Factors influencing the forecast fall into two main groups.

(a) Those *outside* the company's control (including SLEPT and competitive factors). Information can come from published data and commissioned field research.

(b) Those *within* the company's control (including, for example, product range, distribution, advertising, selling and pricing). Information will come from internal documentation.

3.9 Forecasting techniques fall into two main groups, subjective techniques and objective techniques.

3.10 Subjective techniques of forecasting include the following.

(a) *Sales force opinion*. This is a composite company forecast based on individual salesmen's estimates of sales in their respective termination.

(i) *Advantages*

(1) Close acquaintance with customers.
(2) Helps salespeople's morale.
(3) Allows a detailed forecast to be made - by salesperson/customer/product or product group.

(ii) *Disadvantages*

(1) Few salespeople are objective.
(2) They may have a narrow view of life - eg may be unaware of broader economic and technical trends.
(3) The salesperson is paid to sell - not to forecast.

(iii) Its *main use* is in situations where the company has few customers, there is close liaison between customers and the salesperson and orders are large and rare.

(b) *Executive opinion* is a forecast made by obtaining the opinions of those inside the company (Board or senior managers) and also some outsiders (eg banks, brokers etc).

(i) *Advantages*

(1) It is cheap and quick.
(2) A range of views is represented.

(ii) Disadvantages

(1) It is more likely to be based on opinion than fact.
(2) It is only useful for aggregate forecasts (as there will be no analysis by product or customer).

(c) *Surveys of buyers' intentions*. Forecasting is essentially anticipating what *buyers* will do in a given set of conditions, so why not ask them what they will be buying, how much, when and from whom?

(i) *Advantages*

(1) Information comes straight from the horse's mouth.
(2) Information is detailed.

(ii) *Disadvantages*

(1) You may not always know who your customers are (eg what about new customers?). In a consumer market you cannot contact *all* buyers.
(2) Will your customer tell you what you want to know? Buyers may not be willing or able to provide the correct information eg defence buyers. Buyers may deliberately mislead.
(3) There may be difficulties in discerning who makes the buying decisions.

3.11 Objective techniques of forecasting generally involve some form of statistical analysis. Here are two examples.

(a) *Time series analysis* is a method of forecasting the future on the basis of what is happening now and what happened in the past. Data are analysed in an attempt to discover any pattern that may help to predict future sales.

(i) Extending graphical curves into the future is complicated by short and long term fluctuations in the curve. A number of techniques exist to 'smooth out' these fluctuations including:

(1) least squares
(2) moving averages and
(3) exponential smoothing

(ii) Statistical trends show only *what* has happened not *why* it happened. Extrapolating from past sales implies that past situations will be exactly repeated in the future - an unlikely occurrence.

(iii) Historical data is required - but is not available in new firms or for new products.

(iv) Statistical trends have limited value for short term forecasts.

(b) Correlation analysis is a measure of relationship between two or more variables, one dependent on the other. For example a cloudy sky is the independent variable, rain is the dependent variable (as without clouds there will be no rain, but you can have clouds without rain).

- (i) It is often possible for a firm to isolate an independent variable on which its future sales will depend. For example if national income goes up 1%, then car sales will go up 2½%. Thus, forecasts for national income can be used to predict car sales.
- (ii) Problems are as follows.
  - (1) Ensuring that the relationship is real and rational and not merely *coincidental*.
  - (2) The independent variable itself may be difficult to forecast.
  - (3) The relationship might change.

Technological forecasting

3.12 For organisations in recent CIM case studies such as FirstrATE, Leffe and Gravesend Town Centre, technological advances can present major opportunities and threats which you need to take into account when developing your future marketing strategy. For example increasing technological flexibility within the market is obliging FirstrATE to become more innovative; the opening of the Channel Tunnel and its rail links will impact on Gravesend's accessibility to tourists; and the introduction of widgets has certainly affected the canned ale market in the case of Leffe. The ability to predict future technological change may therefore be a critical success factor. There are a number of ways in which this might be accomplished.

- (a) Panels of experts or 'think tanks' can be asked to build future scenarios and assign probabilities.
- (b) The Delphi technique uses individual experts to make initial predictions which are then circulated to other individual experts in the group. Individuals are then asked whether they wish to modify their predictions in light of the other experts' opinions. This process is repeated until modifications become marginal.
- (c) Competitor intelligence can range from the planting of 'moles' or electronic surveillance devices to simply asking the sales force to keep their ears and eyes open.
- (d) Checking Patents Office registrations.
- (e) Attending exhibitions in developed countries.
- (f) Subscribing to published industry forecasts
- (g) Enlisting specialist agencies or consultants. There are a number of institutions with established reputations (eg the Henley Centre for Forecasting) and indeed individuals whose services can be sought.

Corporate planning

3.13 The *corporate plan* describes a plan for the *total future activity* including resource allocation of a business, usually for a period of about five years. More detailed plans are developed to cover annual operations. It might be based on a *long term sales forecast*. We will not go into detail here, but merely say that marketing issues affect the plan, and that marketing activities are determined by it. Marketing's first concern is to take part in the planning process by contributing an assessment of what the marketing opportunities are likely to be. Once the corporate objectives have been agreed, the plans for carrying them out will include tasks for the marketing side of the business. These are embraced in the marketing plan. The corporate plan clarifies tasks of the marketing department.

- (a) What is our current situation?
- (b) Where are we heading if no action is taken?
- (c) Objective - where should we be heading?
- (d) Strategy is about the broad ways of achieving objectives.

Marketing budgets: the purpose of budgets

3.14 It is likely that you will have to draw up financial data to support your marketing proposals. The resources available to you are determined by the corporate plan, but now is perhaps a good time to sharpen up your knowledge of the budgetary implications of where you want to be at the completion of your *marketing* plan. Budgets are compiled for three main reasons.

   (a) To assist and express planning.

   (b) To control expenditure.

   (c) To calculate the cost of products at standard cost and enable priced catalogues etc to be produced and distributed.

3.15 Business forecasting is an important element of budgetary control as it forms the basis of the revenue forecast on which the various expenditure budgets depend. A budget may be regarded as the expression of an objective but having prepared a plan it is equally important to watch performance. Differences between actual results and the budget are termed *variances* and may indicate the need for corrective action so as to assure the realisation of the forward plan.

3.16 One of the main dangers in the practical use of budgetary control is to regard the budgets as fixed and immutable. The budget is a planned course for the future and that course must be altered as necessary to deal with developments that may arise on the journey. The budget idea then combines the features of *forecasting*, of *setting objectives* and of *control* over activities.

3.17 Budgets also aim to secure co-ordination of effort in all the various departments towards the common end. One of the best ways to achieving this is to form a Budget Committee, comprising all the departmental heads responsible for carrying out the various budget activities, under the chairmanship of the Financial Director or the MD. (See Paragraph 3.34 below.)

3.18 Some definitions relevant to marketing are given below.

   (a) 'Budgetary control is an exact and rigorous analysis of the past and the probable and desired future experience; with a view to substituting considered intention for opportunism in Management'...*International Management Institute*.

   (b) 'A comparison of forecast cost and income objectives, with actual results achieved at sufficiently short intervals to allow remedial action to be taken'...*College of Marketing*.

3.19 Production, sales and finance functions are often in conflict.

   (a) Often the production function wants a minimum of variety in the goods with long runs, whilst the sales department prefers to cater for every whim of the market with the widest possible range and even with specials produced quickly to individual customers' requirements.

   (b) Both sales and production functions may favour large stocks but the finance function might argue for a low stock investment with the maximum return on capital.

3.20 Budgetary control aims at co-ordinating these conflicting requirements in such a way that the best possible overall result is achieved. It is fundamentally concerned with the analysis of probable results of alternative courses of action. The result of these considerations is expressed in a budget which can serve in effect as a planned path for the business to follow. If the path is followed the result will be the optimum. Departures from the path are signals for corrective action or a sign of change of circumstances calling for a review of plans. The real value of budgeting in business is not in the figures that go down on paper but in the planning process that they illustrate.

Part A: Background knowledge relevant to analysis and decision

3.21 Budgetary control shorn of its trimmings is a pattern for thinking which removes the unexpected from day to day control of operations and facilitates the process of making decisions in terms of the general good of the business as a whole.

3.22 *Marketing budgets* have some unique characteristics.

(a) Non marketing budgets tend to be a mathematical calculation based on the expected sales volume (eg the purchasing budget). The sales budget contains elements of uncertainty and dynamism.

(b) The conventional one year period used as the budget period for other departmental activities and reflected in the annual accounts of the enterprise is not necessarily applicable to the marketing budgets. A totally marketing orientated company making use of the brand management principle might need to draw up separate budgets for each product. New products might have budgeted losses for the first three years and their costs will be offset against budgeted profits from *established* products in the annual budget. The marketing budgets for each product could have a variable time base, covering a period from the time of launching through the break-even point and finishing at the anticipated time in the product's life-cycle when the profit return no longer justified production.

3.23 The principal budgets linked with marketing will of course depend on the marketing mix. However, they will be subsumed in the Sales Budget, when this is compared to the other budgets for production, finance, administration, personnel.

Budgets and cost

3.24 Sales budgets help identify the maximum costs that can be contained within the *revenue* of the business. An enterprise can only produce at a given time up to the limit of its existing capacity and it must therefore be able to cover all its cost and make a profit out of the revenue which this output can realise. When output is restricted to a maximum number of units and price is determined by market conditions, the key variable in this situation is the total cost of supplying and selling the product, which must be contained within the *fixed revenue*. The cost structure in this case could be represented by the following diagram

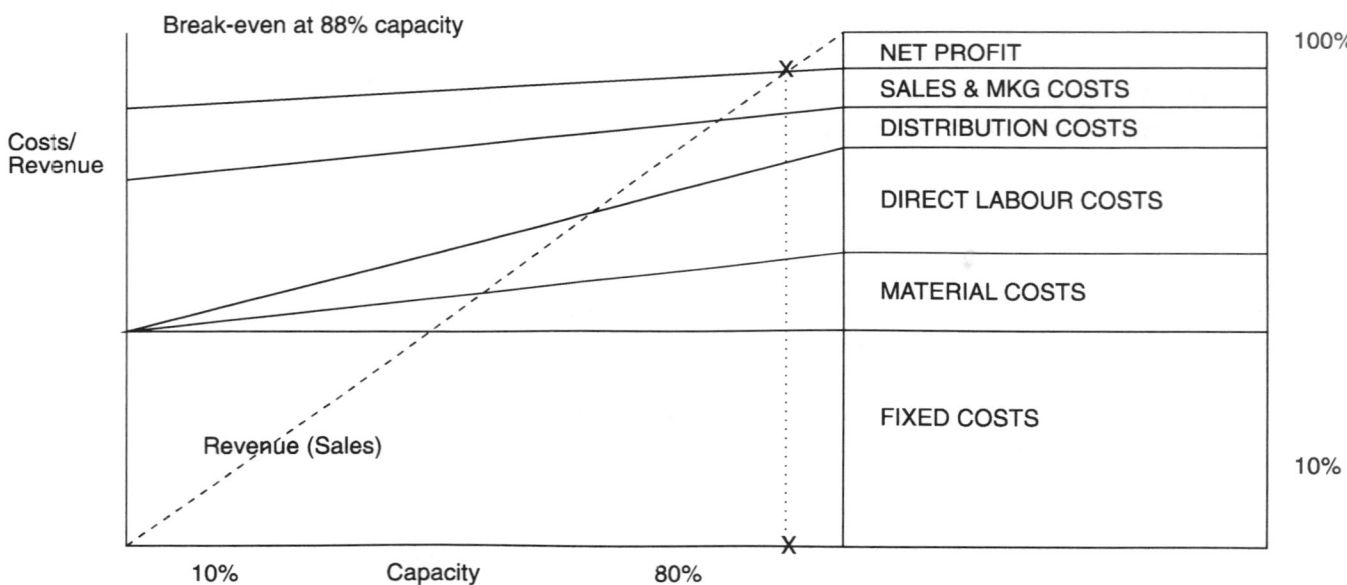

3.25 Distribution, like selling, helps ensure the realisation of revenue. The more efficient the distribution of a product, the greater the market which can be profitably reached at a given price. As soon as manufacturers set up their own distribution networks, the budgets for this will be similar to those for production budgets; physical input and output can be estimated with reasonable exactness; a vehicle or depot together with a

1: Strategic marketing management: planning and control

certain labour complement can be expected to handle a specific quantity of goods, and the financial implications of holding stocks are known.

3.26 After sales service aimed at maximising goodwill must be regarded as a selling cost, even where this is extended through the distribution network. Where customers give top priority to after sales service, the provision of this facility is pre-requisite to credible sales promotion.

3.27 Analysing marketing costs is sometimes a matter of judgement.

(a) It is easy to analyse costs on a functional basis. For example, the total cost of the advertising department can be easily identified and allocated to the sales and marketing department.

(b) It is also relatively easy to identify some of the variable costs of selling (eg sales commission).

(c) However, it is very hard to do a more sophisticated cost allocation to market segments, product brands, customers etc. (For example, when a salesman is visiting a town to sell a range of goods, it is extremely hard to estimate accurately the cost of individual calls in that town and the cost of selling particular products.)

3.28 (a) The main difficulty is caused by fixed costs. *Fixed costs* do not, in the short run, vary with the volume of production. In a marketing context, fixed costs would be incurred whether you sold one product or one hundred. For example, you may be contracted to pay rent on your warehouse for years ahead. The rent will have to be paid, irrespective of any change in sales level. Fixed costs include warehousing depots, and even advertising, in the short run. (The advertising expenditure is incurred before the products are sold, when those sales are uncertain).

(b) Variable costs vary with the volume produced. The amount of dough a baker uses depends precisely on the number of loaves he or she decides to bake. Even so, it is still hard to allocate variable costs sometimes (eg what is the 'cost' of an individual sales call?)

3.29 A useful way of dealing with these problems is of *contribution analysis*. For example in a bakery a different proportion of variable costs to price received might be incurred as seen in the following figure.

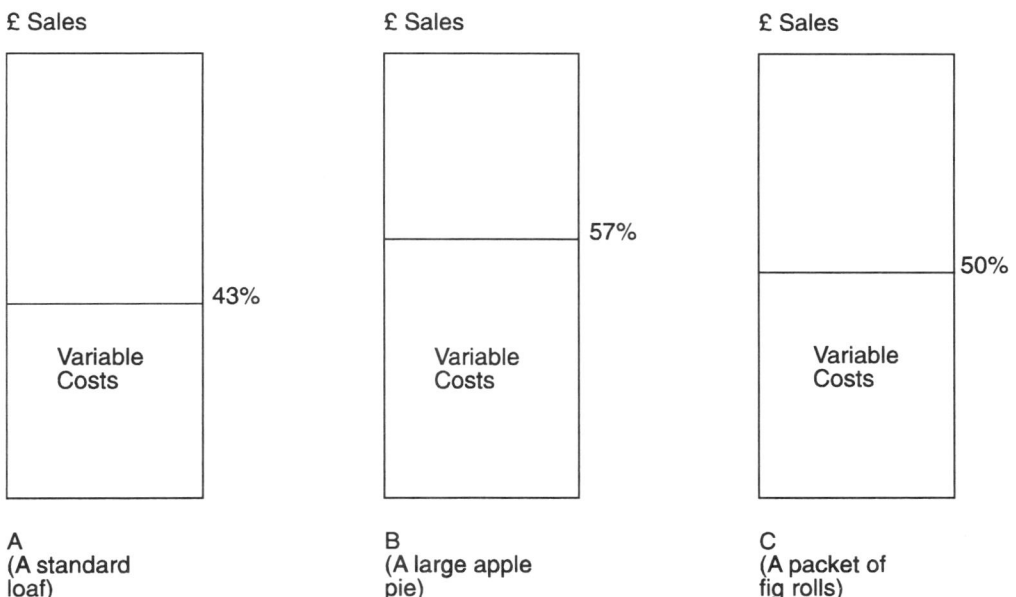

Put another way, Product A makes a contribution of 57% to all other costs and profit. Product B's contribution is 43% and Product C's contribution is 50%.

3.30 The variable costs shown above (those which vary directly and in the short term with the amount of goods produced or sold) are largely those of labour and materials, which can be directly attributed to these products.

Cost ratios

3.31 Ratios can be set between any two sets of functional costs eg advertising to distribution but more importantly they can be set between any functional costs and sales revenue or profit. Any ratio can be selected which is considered likely to improve control of costs (eg advertising to sales, transport to sales, salespeople's expenses to revenues etc).

3.32 Ratios are means of identifying and controlling trends in inputs and outputs. Comparisons can be made:

(a) between the standard ratio and that actually achieved;
(b) between one region and another;
(c) between one period of time and another;
(d) between various means of promotion and sales;
(e) and between the ratios for specific segments such as goods, customers, brands etc.

3.33 Ratios are no more sacrosanct than the budget of which they form a part. The dynamics of marketing make acceptance of changes in the ratios inevitable and a changed ratio will suggest the need for an enquiry into the reasons and into methods of rectifying the situation insofar as possible.

3.34 In order to abandon unprofitable sales, use can be made of the concept of avoidable and unavoidable costs. If removal of a product, order or outlet relieves the enterprise of costs in excess of the profits gained from it, then profits will be increased.

(a) The problem is that of identifying those costs which can and cannot be avoided by the elimination of a product, order or outlet. If one product in a range is removed, brand advertising, sales force, depot and transport costs are not likely to be materially affected. If many products are removed then some inroads into these costs will be made.

(b) The expenditure, escapable and inescapable involved in handling products suspected of being unprofitable, may be more profitably used on the rest of the range, on other calls or on new products. The time spent by a representative on an unprofitable call involves not only the loss on the current call but also the loss of *potential* profit on an alternative call (ie opportunity cost).

(c) Nevertheless, a range of products may only be attractive because of its *overall* content. To remove products from this range may reduce its attractiveness and thereby diminish profits. (This is especially true where customers are motivated by convenience of purchase and do not want any duplication of buying activity). Similarly the extra cost of handling apparently unprofitable orders or outlets may be more than offset by economies of scale in manufacturing operations made possible by the total orders.

The budget process

3.35 The principal budgets linked with marketing are of course the sales budget, based on the sales estimate or forecast, the selling expense budgets, the distribution budget and the research and development budget. (They are analysed in detail later on.)

3.36 The *budget period* is the time period to which the budget relates. Except for capital expenditure budgets, the budget period is commonly the accounting year (sub-divided into 12 or 13 control periods).

(a) Sometimes a main budget will be prepared for a twelve months period, with a three month budget in detail.

(b) A *rolling budget* is continually updated and so at defined periods, the budget is changed and the next twelve months is on view. A rolling budget is therefore a 12-month budget prepared several times a year.

(c) Note that certain items do not easily slot into a twelve month time period (see Paragraph 3.22).

3.37 To co-ordinate the budget a budget committee is often set up (with the managing director perhaps as chairman). The preparation and administration of budgets is usually its responsibility. The staff work of the budget committee is delegated to a budget officer who is usually an accountant. Every part of the organisation should be represented on the committee, ie there should be a representative from sales, production, marketing etc. The functions of the budget committee include the following.

(a) Co-ordination of the preparation of budgets, which includes the issue of the budget manual.

(b) Issuing of timetables for the preparation of functional budgets.

(c) Allocation of responsibilities for the preparation of functional budgets.

(d) Provision of information to assist in the preparation of budgets.

(e) Communication of final budgets to the appropriate managers.

(f) Comparison of actual results with budget and the investigation of variances.

(g) Continuous assessment of the budgeting and planning process, in order to improve it.

(h) Issuing of timetables for the preparation of functional budgets.

(i) Allocation of responsibilities for the preparation of functional budgets.

(j) Provision of information to assist in the preparation of budgets.

(k) Communication of final budgets to the appropriate managers.

(l) Comparison of actual results with budget and the investigation of variances.

3.38 The principal budget factor must then be identified.

(a) The principal budget factor is usually sales demand: a company is usually restricted from making and selling more of its products because there would be no sales demand for the increased output at a price which would be acceptable/profitable to the company.

(b) The principal budget factor may also be machine capacity, distribution and selling resources, the availability of key raw materials or the availability of cash. Once this factor is defined then the rest of the budget can be prepared. For example, if sales are the principal budget factor then the production manager can only prepare his budget after the sales budget is complete. In other words, the sales department may predict vast quantities of sales, but there may be no production capacity to satisfy them. The volume of activity will thus depend on the production capacity, not demand, in this case.

3.39 If production is a limiting factor, then, rather than face unmet demand and the frustration of consumers, the marketing strategy might be adjusted, for example, by raising the price or altering the marketing mix in some other way.

3.40 The functional budgets would then be prepared.

(a) The production budget, in units produced, is based on the budgets for units sold adjusted for the levels of opening and closing stocks, and manufacturing lead times. From this would be derived budgets for raw materials.

(b) The marketing department, as well as being responsible for determining sales revenue, is also a cost centre. Budgets for selling expenses, advertising and so forth will have to be prepared.

Naturally, the budgets for expenditure will have to be scrutinised.

3.41 A *master budget* is then prepared in which all the functional budgets are integrated.

3.42 An important aspect of budgeting is the balance sheet side. In other words, an estimate is needed of the resources required to fund production, and timing of major items of expenditure or revenue. For example the firm might have to commit a great deal of money 'up front' for production facilities, but only receive the revenue later. The firm might have to borrow money. A *cash budget* shows the inflow and outflow of money. This is vitally important, as a failure to plan the cash properly can encourage a too swift expansion and possible collapse.

The sales budget

3.43 The practical success of any budget system depends to a large extent upon the accuracy with which future sales can be forecast since the sales estimate is the foundation for the purchasing and production budgets, the guide to plant-extension requirements and as the prime source of cash receipts, the basis of any plan for financing the business. If the sales forecast is a guess (eg previous years sales plus 10%) rather than a logical researched estimate, the practical value of the budget system may be entirely lost.

3.44 As we have seen, there is no standard method of estimating future sales as different businesses demand different methods. However, in every case the estimate must be based fundamentally on a study of past experience, modified by anticipated trade conditions and proposed future plans. The relative emphasis on these three elements will vary considerably from one company to another.

(a) The structure of past/sales may provide a pattern that can be projected into the future with some degree of reliability.

(b) The essence of the forecast may lie on the general economic background, anticipated during the forecast period.

(c) In a third case the key influence may be sales promotion activity with the sales forecast virtually a plan rather than a forecast. The only logical approach to the problem is through an understanding of the factors which affect sales results.

3.45 Once finalised, the sales estimate will show the likely sales quantities for the budget period, as totals. It will have been adjusted according to the following factors.

(a) Profit and earning capacity of the various lines.
(b) Production and purchasing capacity of the business.
(c) Selling and administration expenses involved.
(d) Financial requirements.

3.46 It is the function of the sales budget to split down these total quantities into quantities for the control periods - usually monthly or quarterly or both and to convert the quantities into value and revenue. Thus the sales budget splits naturally into two sections - the *sales quantity budget* and the *sales revenue budget*. In industrial marketing, particularly where long and variable delivery delays are concerned, it is useful to split the sales revenue budget into the following.

(a) Value of orders received budget
(b) Value of orders delivered budget, so as better to ascertain the true position.

3.47 The actual sales revenue received will of course depend upon the credit period allowed, actual promptness of payment experienced and the amount of bad debts. This is usually the responsibility of the financial departments. For sales budget purposes, the sales revenue budget may be regarded as the *planned value of sales*.

3.48 In order to convert quantities into values it is of course necessary to fix selling prices. Selling prices are ultimately determined by market conditions and the balance between supply and demand. Note that simply deriving sales price as a percentage increase on cost may not work and may be suboptimal.

(a) In the case of a manufacturer basing his prices on prime cost and overheads and a fixed profit margin, when the shop was working at a normal (say 90%) capacity, overheads might be 12.5%; when at full capacity, 10%; and when at 50% capacity, 20%.

(b) In other words when business was good and orders such that the plant was working at full capacity, a reduction in price based on the given formula would merely result in increased orders which could not be met.

(c) On the other hand, when business was slack, increased prices would limit his chances of keeping his share of the reduced volume of business.

3.49 If then, a manufacturer is unwise to base prices on the *cost of production*, by what method should prices be determined? Several firms have found the answer by *price-volume* studies for each product. Price-Volume studies are attempts to forecast the elasticity of demand, so as to determine the probable volume of sales against various price levels and thus to arrive at the optimum price for each product, bearing in mind competitors' prices, to yield the largest net profit.

In this example, the cost of making a unit is £8.00

Proposed selling price £	Expected sales Units	Value of sales £	Cost of goods sold £	Surplus over cost £
12.50	1,100	13,750	8,800	4,950
12.00	1,200	14,400	9,600	4,800
11.50	1,400	16,100	11,200	4,900
11.00	1,700	18,700	13,600	5,100
10.50	2,000	21,000	16,000	5,000
10.00	2,200	22,000	17,600	4,400

3.50 In the example above it has been assumed that the cost remains at £8 per unit whether output is 1,100 or 2,200 per year. In practice economies would probably result from higher quantities. For example, if you buy materials in bulk you might obtain a discount. This is relevant to differential costing used in special order-industries where contracts have to be tendered for. The principle is that:

(a) there is a cost above which a manufacturer would begin to lose money by accepting an additional order;

(b) the average cost per unit decreases as the volume of output increases, up to a certain level, which enables a manufacturer to charge a lower price on this extra output.

3.51 To justify the use of differential costs on a particular job the situation must be that:

(a) prices on the remainder of the company's output are unaffected;

(b) the job must represent a definite addition to output that could not be obtained in any other way.

3.52 Suppose a company has established a normal selling price of £6,000 per unit and the sales estimate for the budget period suggests an output of 60 units which represents a production capacity of 80%. (Total capacity is therefore $60/0.8 = 75$ units.) It may so happen that the company could secure orders for a further 10 units providing the price was considerably reduced. By consulting the following table of differential costs, the minimum price would be £1,900.

Part A: Background knowledge relevant to analysis and decision

Item	Cost of 60 units £	Cost of 70 units £
Materials	83,000	91,000
Labour	78,000	85,000
Supplies	30,000	31,000
Variable o/h	56,000	59,000
Fixed o/h	65,000	65,000
Total cost	312,000	331,000
Unit cost	£5,200	£4,730
Cost per extra 10 units (£331,000 – £312,000)		£19,000*
Differential cost per extra unit		£1,900

The company would profit by selling an extra 10 units at any price in excess of £1,900 per unit *providing it maintains its previous price against the normal output quantity of 60 units*. It might be possible to charge different prices in different, perhaps secluded, market segments. It is the existence of such conditions as these which results in the adoption of *dumping policies* overseas by manufacturers with a protected home market.

3.53 In the above example the extra 10 units would bring the output up to 93% of production capacity and enable shop workers to earn higher wages. An alternative policy might be to hire out the additional labour and machine capacity to non-competing manufacturers whose demand exceeds their capacity.

Sales budget: summary

3.54 The preparation of the sales budget involves the following.

(a) A preliminary sales estimate based on:

(i) a study of normal business growth;

(ii) a forecast of general business conditions;

(iii) a measure of the relationship between the company and (ii);

(iv) a knowledge of potential markets for each product;

(v) the practical judgement of salesmen, sales management and general management staff;

(vi) a realisation of the effect on sales of basic changes in company policy.

(b) The adjustment of the above preliminary sales estimate in light of:

(i) the seasonal nature of the business;
(ii) from the viewpoint of optimum selling prices;
(iii) the overall production or purchasing capacity;
(iv) the viewpoint of securing even manufacturing loads;
(v) overall selling expenses and net profits;
(vi) the financial capacity of the business.

(c) The adjusted anticipated sales by value and quantity contained in the sales budget should then be classified by commodities, departments, customers, salesmen, countries, terms of sale, methods of sale, methods of delivery and urgency of delivery (rush or normal).

The expense budgets related to marketing

3.55 As a summary checklist, if you are preparing schedules of selling expenses you should concentrate on the following.

(a) *The selling expenses budget*

(i) Salaries and commission
(ii) Materials, literature, samples
(iii) Travelling (car cost, petrol, insurance) and entertaining
(iv) Staff recruitment and selection and training

- (v) Telephones and telegrams, postage
- (vi) After sales service
- (vii) Royalties/patents
- (viii) Office rent and rates, lighting, heating etc.
- (ix) Office equipment
- (x) Credit costs, bad debts etc

(b) *Advertising budget*

- (i) Trade journal - space
- (ii) Prestige media - space
- (iii) PR space (costs of releases, entertainment etc)
- (iv) Blocks and artwork
- (v) Advertising agents commission or
- (vi) Staff salaries, office costs, etc
- (vii) Posters
- (viii) Cinema
- (ix) TV
- (x) Signs

(c) *The sales promotion budget*

- (i) Exhibitions: space, equipment, staff, transport, hotels, bar etc
- (ii) Literature: leaflets, catalogues
- (iii) Samples/working models
- (iv) Point of sale display, window or showroom displays
- (v) Special offers
- (vi) Direct mail shots - enclosure, postage, design costs.

(d) *Research and development budget*

- (i) Market research - design and development and analysis costs
- (ii) Packaging and product research - departmental costs, materials, equipment.
- (iii) Pure research - departmental costs materials, equipment
- (iv) Sales analysis and research
- (v) Economic surveys
- (vi) Product planning
- (vii) Patents

(e) *The distribution budget*

- (i) Warehouse/deposits - rent, rates, lighting, heating
- (ii) Transport - capital costs
- (iii) Fuel - running costs
- (iv) Warehouse/depot and transport staff wages
- (v) Packing (as opposed to packaging).

Indicative marketing costs

3.56 You will probably be required to indicate the approximate costs of your marketing proposals in your case study examination. Hopefully as a practising marketer you will either be aware of current cost levels or will be able to find out fairly easily. You will not be expected to present *precisely* accurate costs but rather to have an awareness of their scales. To help you with this, and bearing in mind costs can vary widely between London and the provinces, we are providing some indications as follows. *Note that this data is only approximate, and is for case study purposes only.*

3.57 Of the terrestrial TV channels, three take advertising (ITV, Channel 4 and Channel 5). ITV operates on a regional basis with approximately 15 commercial channels in total, but GMTV provides breakfast broadcasting. There is an ever increasing number of satellite TV channels, some (eg Sky Sports) catering to specialist audiences. Moreover, over the next few years, *digital terrestrial television* will massively increase the number of channels available.

	ITV	Channel 4
Cost of 30 second advertising break at peak times	£85,000	£56,000
Off peak cost (minimum)	£24,000	£12,000

Part A: Background knowledge relevant to analysis and decision

3.58 *Newspapers.* The cost per full page of some national newspapers and magazines is given below. Circulations refers to the numbers of copies sold per day. Readership, perhaps more subjective, is based on research into the number of people who read each copy. Penetration refers to the proportion of the population reading the paper.

(a) *Daily papers*

Title	Circulation (millions)	Readership (millions)	Penetration Men %	Penetration Women %	Page cost black/white £
Sun	4.1	10.2	29	24	32,000
Daily Mirror	2.5	6.7	23	17	26,000
Daily Express	1.3	3.4	10	9	18,000
Daily Mail	1.8	4.5	11	10	20,000
Guardian*	0.4	1.3	4	2	15,000
Times*	0.6	1.5	3	3	17,000
Independent*	0.3	0.9	3	2	114,000

(b) *Sunday papers*

Title	Circulation (millions)	Readership (millions)	Penetration Men %	Penetration Women %	Page cost black/white £
News of the World	4.8	12.3	29	28	36,000
Sunday Mirror	2.6	8.0	23	20	29,000
Sunday Times*	1.3	3.7	9	7	47,000
Observer*	0.5	1.5	6	4	24,000
Mail on Sunday	1.9	5.8	12	11	28,000

(c) *Some Sunday colour supplements*

	Page cost (black and white) £	Page cost (colour) £
Sunday Times*	11,000	16,000
Sunday Mirror	–	25,000
Observer*	7,000	10,000

*Up market, quality press

(d) *There is a very wide choice of women's magazines.*

(i) Weekly

Title	Circulation (million)	Readership (million)	Housewives (million)	Page cost colour £	Page cost black/white £
Woman's Own	0.8	4.0	3.4	22,000	16,000
Woman	0.8	3.0	2.7	18,000	13,000
Woman's Weekly	0.8	2.4	2.0	12,000	9,000

(ii) Monthly

Title	Circulation (million)	Readership (million)	Housewives (million)	Page cost colour £	Page cost black&white £
Options	0.2	0.5	0.4	5,000	3,500
Woman and Home	0.4	1.9	1.8	8,000	5,000
Ideal Home	0.2	2.0	1.5	8,100	5,500
Essential	0.4	1.3	1.1	7,700	4,900

3.59 *Radio.* There are over 45 independent stations. Until recently, these have only been local (eg Capital Radio) but national commercial radio (eg Classic FM) now exists. The cost of a 30 second peak spot might be £4,000, but varies considerably.

3.60 *Cinema* attracts a mainly young adult audience (under 25). A four week campaign might reach 20% of under the 25 age group. The average 'network' cost of a 30 second spot would be £31,000 in such a campaign.

3.61 *Posters.* The average cost of a 48 sheet poster site for one month is £265. A national campaign would require 1,500 - 2,000 of such sites.

3.62 The production cost of an average 30 second TV commercial is £84,000.

Useful analytical techniques and models in deciding 'where do we want to be?'

3.63 There are a variety of analyses, techniques, concepts and models which can help us in deciding our future *marketing* objectives and strategies. These include the following.

(a) The mission statement
(b) Market structure analysis
(c) Buying behaviour analysis
(d) Segmentation analysis
(e) Product life cycle (PLC) analysis
(f) Ansoff's growth matrix
(g) The Boston matrix
(h) Gap analysis
(i) PIMS data base
(j) Critical success factors

3.64 It is most important that you recognise the universality of most of these approaches. In the same way that Marketing Research helps marketing planning in all its stages, these models/analyses can be applied throughout.

(a) The plotting of product sales to look for evidence of the product life cycle (growth or decline) not only tells us where we are now but also predicts where we are likely to be in the future (up or down) and prompts action where necessary. This is of course also a control mechanism.

(b) Similar remarks could be made with regard to segmental analysis which will show us where we are now (sales by segment) where we would like to be (new segments) and act as a control device (did we get there?)

We are simply dealing with these other approaches now because of convenience and because deciding where we want to be could be said to be the most critical marketing strategy decision of all. In the following notes, we will provide you with the essential details of the above approaches in the order in which they are given.

Mission statement

3.65 The mission statement is an important part of strategy. It has an important role in providing a *consensus* between different viewpoints and a *focus* for business activity. The mission statement is likely to have a degree of *generality* so that it can integrate various stakeholders over a long period of time. Stakeholders could be defined as 'any group or individual who can affect or is affected by the achievement of an organisation's purpose'

Market place stakeholders	*External stakeholders*	*Internal stakeholders*
Customers Competitors Suppliers	Government Political groups Financial community Trade associations Activist groups	Owners Decision makers Unions and employers

(a) The use of *open* objectives is appropriate for areas that are difficult to quantify or express in measurable terms, eg 'to be a leader in technology'. Open objectives can avoid overformalisation, opposition, rigidity to change and alerting competitors. Although generalised, they can still provide a focus to the activity of the business.

(b) The mission is shaped by five key elements.

(i) The organisation's history
(ii) The current preferences of owners and managers (stakeholders)
(iii) Environmental considerations

Part A: Background knowledge relevant to analysis and decision

    (iv) Resources
    (v) The organisation's distinctive competences

  (c) Examples of some mission statements are given below. These are all quite brief. Often mission statements are much longer.

    (i) *What business are we in?*

     Firm   *Product view*   *Market view*

Revlon	We make cosmetics	We sell hope
Xerox	We make copying equipment	We help improve office productivity

    (ii) RCA. 'To be technological leader again in its core business of electronics and communications.'

    (iii) Apple. 'Apple (computers) is not in the game or toy business but in the computer business. What Apple does best is to take a high cost ideal and turn it into a low cost, high quality solution.'

    (iv) 'To make a lot of money' is not a mission statement but Toyota's 'Global 10' mission, for example, 'to have 10 per cent of the world auto market by 1990' did give form to its business activity.

Market structure analysis

3.66 Every market will differ in its characteristics so that it is difficult to be specific about structure. However, the following general analytical framework can be applied to most markets.

  (a) What are the market parameters? In other words, what are its boundaries? The UK domestic market's parameters are the borders of the UK.

  (b) How big is the market within these parameters?

  (c) Is this market growing, stable or declining?

  (d) How does the market segment?

  (e) To what extent is each segment growing, stable or declining?

  (f) Who are the key players in the market or segments? (Manufacturers, distributors, others)

  (g) What are the key success factors in this market or segment?

  (h) What are the buying behaviour characteristics of this market or segment?

  (i) Who are the major market/segment competitors and what are their distinctive competencies.

  (j) What future environmental factors are likely to affect this market/segment?

  (k) How easy or difficult is market and/or segment to enter or exist?

Buying behaviour analysis

3.67 Buyer behaviour is a topic which connects the consumer's needs wishes and desires - normally studied by the psychologist - with the economic and commercial objectives of a firm. The model below indicates the main issues in buyer behaviour. One of the consequences of a purchase might be to encourage an additional purchase (especially true in service industries). Post-purchase feelings are therefore important.

1: Strategic marketing management: planning and control

STEPS IN THE BUYING PROCESS

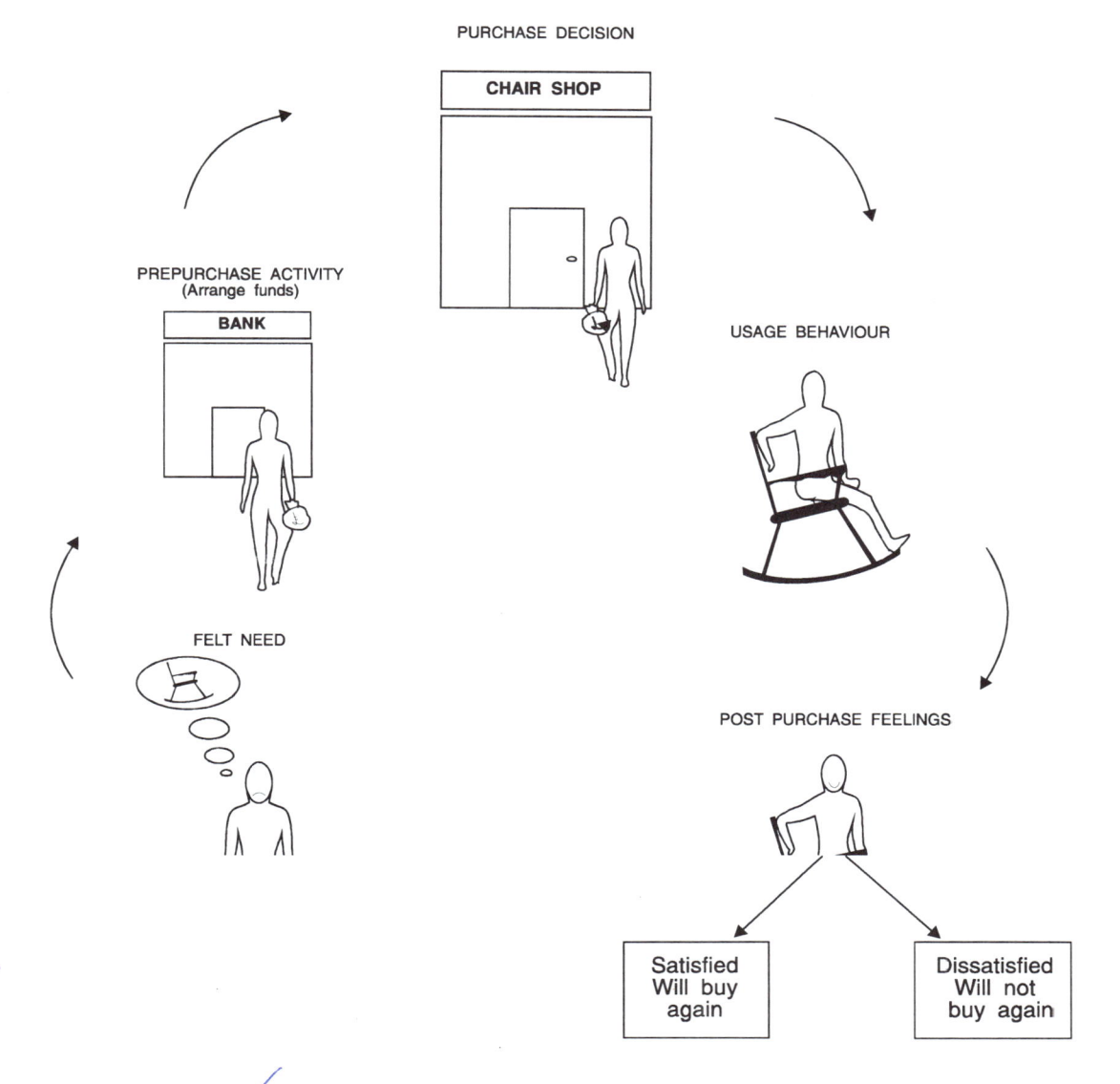

Buying decisions

3.68 The *decision making unit* is responsible for an organisation's purchases. It involves five roles, which may be played by different people. Several individuals may occupy the same role and one individual may occupy more than one role.

(a) *Users.* This group includes all those in the organisation who use or are going to use the product being purchased. It will include people at all levels in the organisation - thus the decision to purchase a particular type of powered hand-tool may well be influenced by the shop floor workers who tried out the samples.

(b) *Buyers.* In most organisations, there is a *purchasing or buying department*. Certain members of this department will have formal responsibility and authority for signing contracts for purchases on behalf of the organisation. These are, in this context, the purchasing agents together with any other persons with such authority.

(c) *Influencers.* This is usually a large ill-defined group as it includes all those who influence the decision process directly or indirectly by providing information and setting the criteria for evaluating alternative buying actions.

(d) *Deciders.* This is the group with authority to choose amongst alternative buying actions. A buyer is not always a decider and vice versa. Thus when purchasing a very complex product of an advanced technological nature, a group of engineers and scientists may pick or decide upon a particular supplier. Their decisions might then be passed to a purchasing agent to be implemented purely in the sense of drawing up the necessary formal documents to complete the legal aspects of the transaction.

(e) *Gate keepers.* Any decision-making unit will need, from time to time, to collect some information. Those supplying the information may influence the group's decision by withholding certain information available or by controlling access from personnel in the selling organisation to personnel in the buying organisation. This is not dishonesty or bias, but simply emphasises the fact that time does not usually make it possible to provide all relevant information and selections have to be made or a synopsis provided.

3.69 The principles of the industrial DMU can be applied in consumer goods marketing. Children can influence parents in their food purchasing decisions. For some types of household goods the decision is generally taken by the male and, for other types, by the female.

Diffusion of innovation ✓

3.70 The diffusion of innovation curve is another buyer behaviour model. Take the example of the compact disk player. When first introduced, it was a speciality item. Now, certainly for classical music, it has become standard.

Diffusion of innovation curve: statistical patterns in buyer behaviour

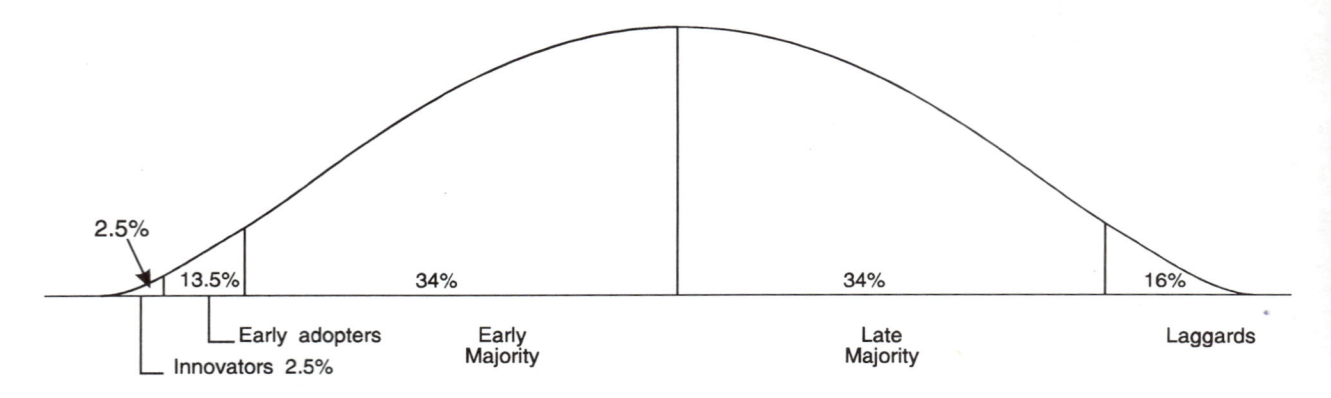

```
         2.5%
              13.5%       34%              34%              16%
              Early adopters   Early         Late           Laggards
         Innovators 2.5%       Majority      Majority
```

(a) This model can equally be applied to industrial as well as consumer marketing. Some companies (Rolls Royce, aero engines) may be seen and wish to be seen as technological leaders in their field and are, therefore, much more likely to be early adopters of innovations than other industrial companies who may have elected to follow rather than lead in this respect.

(b) In choosing where we want to be we may wish to specialise in meeting the needs of particular customers (the leaders in innovation as perhaps expressed in our mission statement).

(c) At a later stage (in the marketing mix) we will need to take account of how the buying system works, who makes the purchasing decisions and who influences these decisions.

Segmentation analysis ✓

3.71 Segmentation classifies the market so that there are fewer people in a market segment than in the whole market. They have more in common with each other than with others in the wider market. Some writers have said that segmentation and positioning within a segment are at the very heart of modern marketing.

(a) *Segmentation variables useful in deciding why people buy*

   (i) *Psychographic (the type of person)*

      (1) Life styles
      (2) Attitudes
      (3) Self concept
      (4) Culture

   (ii) *Benefits sought (from the product)*

      (1) Economy
      (2) Convenience
      (3) Prestige
      (4) Services

(b) *Segmentation variables useful in targeting marketing effort*

   (i) *Demographics*

      (1) Age, sex, education, religion
      (2) Social class, occupation
      (3) Residence, life cycle (eg with children)

   (ii) *Geographic*

      (1) Urban, suburban, rural
      (2) Climate

(c) *Other types of segmentation include usage behaviour*. In other words, what people do with the product. (Do you consider a watch simply as a time piece or as a fashion accessory? This is how SWATCH watches have been marketed.)

(d) Some segmentation variables for industrial markets include the following

   (i) Industrial demographics; industry, company size, geographical location.

   (ii) Usage: light, medium or heavy.

   (iii) Purchasing criteria: companies seeking lower prices or higher quality, better service etc

   (iv) Conditions of purchase: stringent or light?

   (v) Company personality: risk taking, loyal, bureaucratic, power seeking etc.

   (vi) Ordering characteristics: frequency, size of order, urgency of order etc.

The product life cycle (PLC)

3.72 This product life cycle concept suggests that most products and services, will, over time, exhibit stages of growth, maturity, and decline as follows.

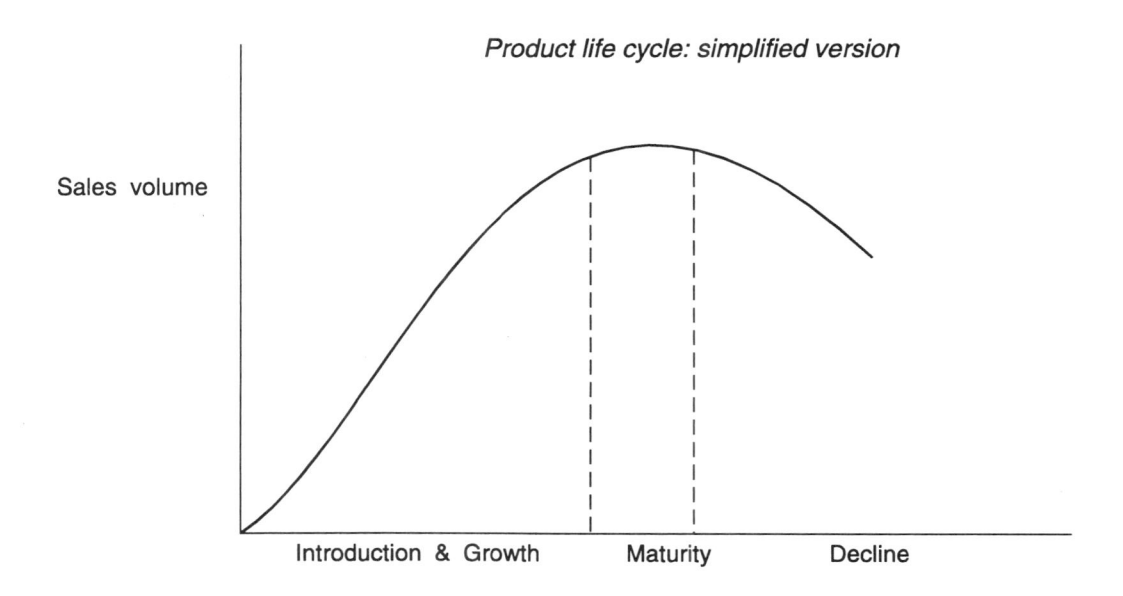

Product life cycle: simplified version

[Graph: Sales volume (y-axis) vs time, with stages labelled "Introduction & Growth", "Maturity", "Decline"]

Notes   **Part A: Background knowledge relevant to analysis and decision**

(a) The concept is useful inasmuch as it draws attention to the need for marketing action to lengthen a product's life, regenerate or replace it. Whilst some critics argue that the PLC has been responsible for far too many premature product withdrawals and others argue that coal, bread etc. have been in demand for thousands of years, there is little doubt that a great many individual products do exhibit PLC tendencies unless modified. Thus, smokeless fuels replaced standard coal in the home and now most homes have central heating. Likewise less bread is eaten in terms of ounces per capita and new varieties (eg slimming breads) have now appeared to challenge the standard British loaf. Hovis is now packaged and available in a sliced variety, more in tune with modern needs.

(b) In practice, some products and services can be re-cycled as in the case of sixties' music and mini-skirts. However, it would be difficult to accept the possibility of a future boom in horse-drawn carriages in place of the motor car as a viable means of modern transportation!

3.73 The utility of the PLC in indicating the need for action is perhaps best demonstrated in the following diagram where it can be seen that unless something is done urgently, the likelihood is that total turnover and profit will radically decline. This is because Product A is in decline whilst Products B and C have reached maturity and are about to enter into decline.

(a)

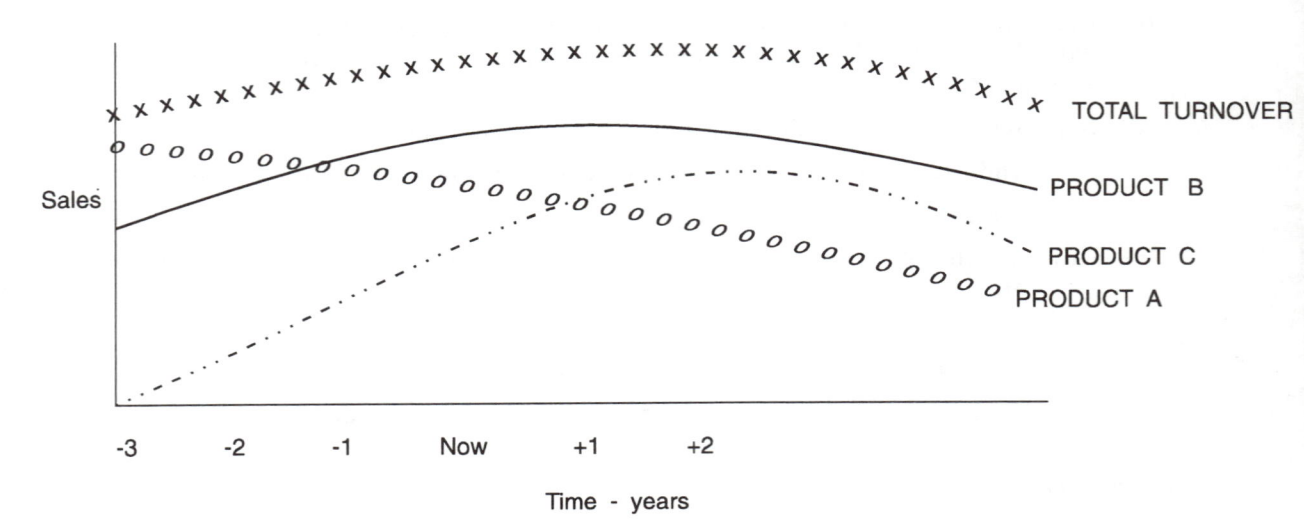

[Graph showing Sales vs Time (years) from -3 to +2, with curves labelled TOTAL TURNOVER, PRODUCT B, PRODUCT C, and PRODUCT A]

3.74 We can now move to a more sophisticated treatment of the PLC, one that adds the pre-launch and the deletion stages to the picture and paints in the aspects of cash flow and profitability.

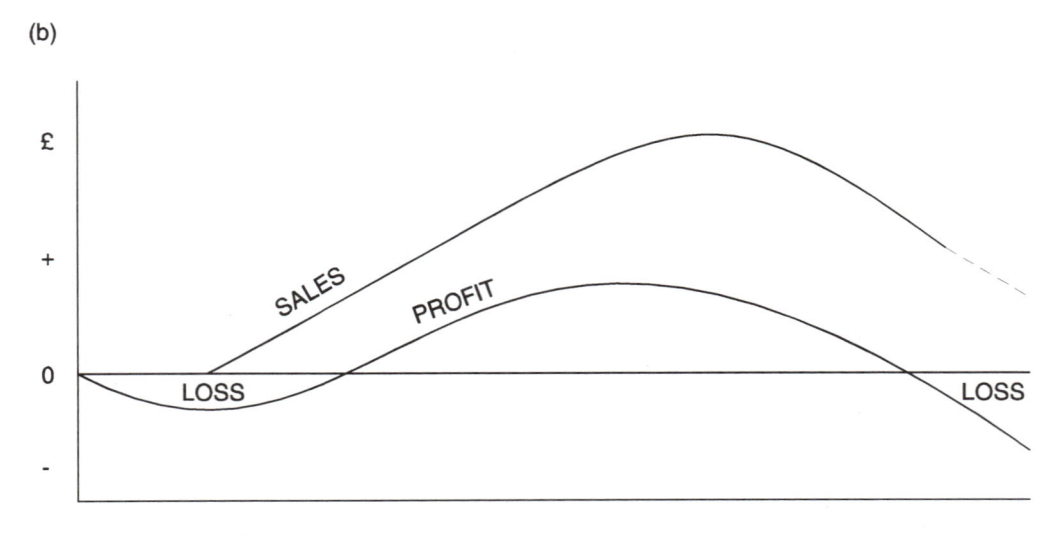

(b)

[Graph showing £ (+/0/-) over stages, with SALES and PROFIT curves, LOSS regions at both ends]

Research - Launch - Growth - Consolidation - Saturation - Decay - Deletion
Gestation - Birth - Youth - Maturity - Middle age - Old age - Death

1: Strategic marketing management: planning and control

(a) At the pre-birth stage, costs are involved in conducting research and product development so that a negative cash flow occurs. This situation tends to worsen on launch, in that heavy promotion and distribution are added whilst relatively few sales are made. However, during the growth stage, marketing planners expect to generate positive cash flow and go into profit, a position which should last until a point in the decline stage where sales drop below break-even and deletion becomes desirable unless regeneration is possible

(b) It should be noted in the above diagram that the profit curve is shown to peak before the sales curve. This is often the case when competitors enter what can be seen to be a growing and potentially lucrative market and prices are, therefore, forced down further than can be compensated for by lower costs due to increased sales volume.

(c) Marketing planners can deploy elements of the marketing mix to varying degrees over the PLC so as to enjoy maximum cost benefit relationships. The PLC can also be used as a strategic tool to identify, for example, the need for replacement products and/or product modification, as illustrated in the diagram below.

Marketing mix relative to product life cycle

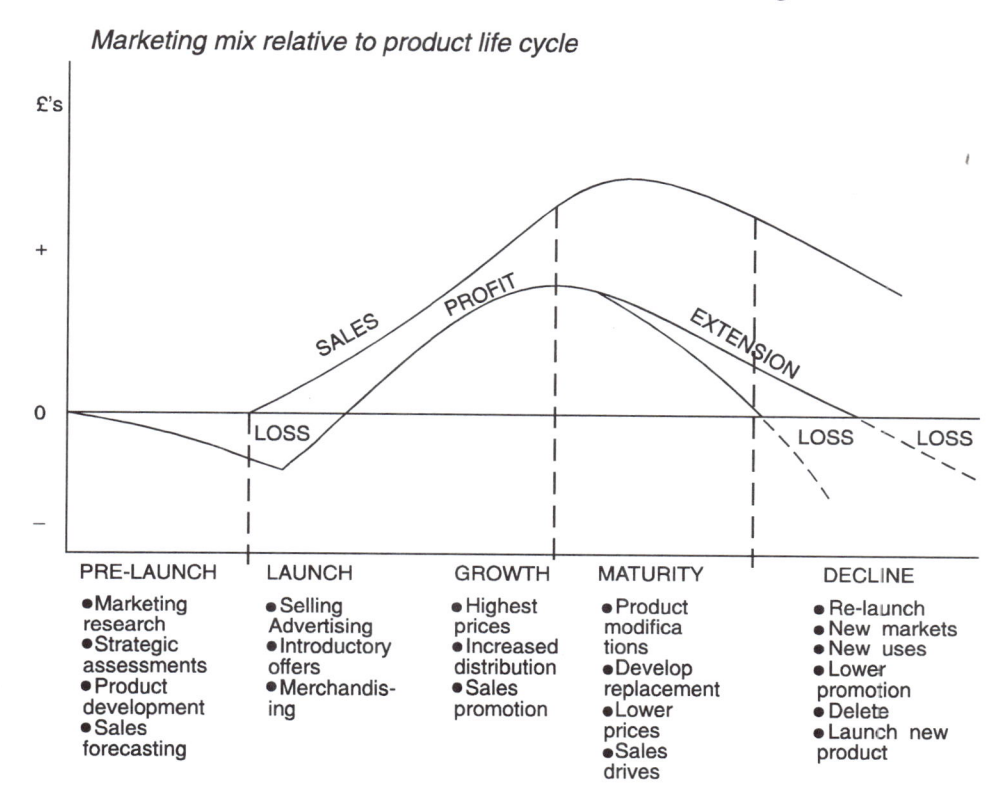

	PRE-LAUNCH	LAUNCH	GROWTH	MATURITY	DECLINE
	• Marketing research	• Selling Advertising	• Highest prices	• Product modifications	• Re-launch
	• Strategic assessments	• Introductory offers	• Increased distribution	• Develop replacement	• New markets
	• Product development	• Merchandising	• Sales promotion	• Lower prices	• New uses
	• Sales forecasting			• Sales drives	• Lower promotion
					• Delete
					• Launch new product

3.75 *New product development, sales forecasting, market research.* Identification of the position of existing products on the life cycle by the simple process of plotting sales will indicate a possible need to re-develop existing product or develop new ones. It also assists in sales forecasting and highlights the potential need for marketing research, particularly at the decay stage of an existing product and/or the generation stage of a new product.

3.76 *Advertising, sales promotion, selling.* The communications job will be particularly demanding at the selling stage of a new products and will continue at somewhat lower levels during the stages of growth and maturity. Lower prices, special offers, development of the existing product, improvement of the service element etc. are resorted to in an attempt to counter decline which, if continued, will lead to efforts to find new outlets, new uses and new markets. If decline continues, promotional support is often removed in order to postpone the point at which the product's sales fall to break-even and efforts to develop a new replacement product are increased.

3.77 *Distribution and pricing.* The planning of increases in the number of outlets in harmony with production (and transport) capacity is particularly important during the growth stage. New outlets, particularly in less sophisticated markets abroad, may be sought during the decline stage. Price levels may be high during the period of high demand in order to recover development costs but may be forced down before sales peak, with the onset of competition.

3.78 *Arresting decline.* Where new products to replace those in decline are not available in time, marketing planners can attempt to arrest decline by finding new users, perhaps in developing markets overseas. New uses may be developed for existing products or they can be modified in some way or perhaps re-packaged. Thus, the Ford Escort's PLC has been extended by a continuous process of product modification. The addition of diesel engined versions may lead to new users, ie those interested more in economy than acceleration. The development of estate or hatchback versions may lead to new uses, eg as a freight carrier.

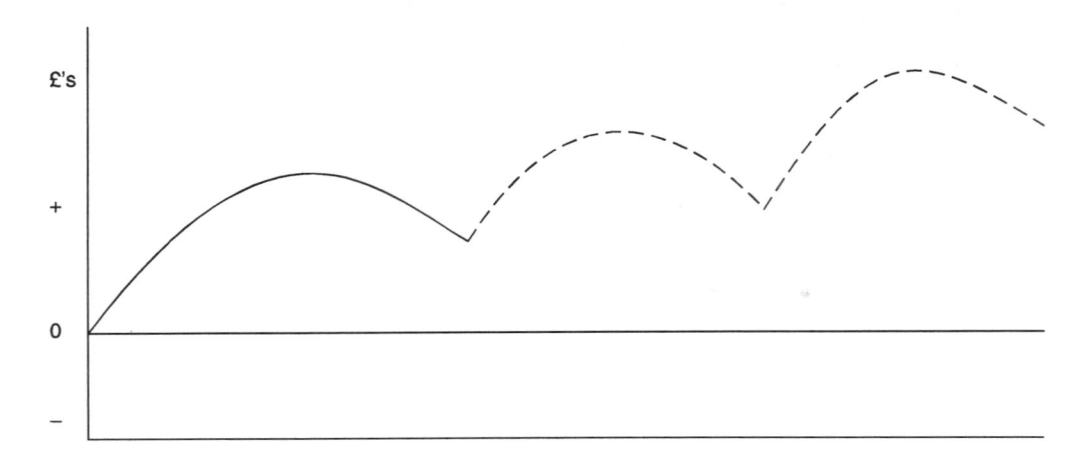

3.79 A further strategic aspect of the PLC is that of considering the relative buying behaviour patterns. Studies by Midgeley and Wills, 1974 indicated that relationships between types of buyers and PLC exists in fashion markets, which can be exploited in terms of more accurate targeting of the marketing mix over time. Thus, at the launch stage, buyers are likely to be the more adventurous, innovative, leader types. Promotional messages, media chosen, pricing and distribution outlets can be targeted accordingly.

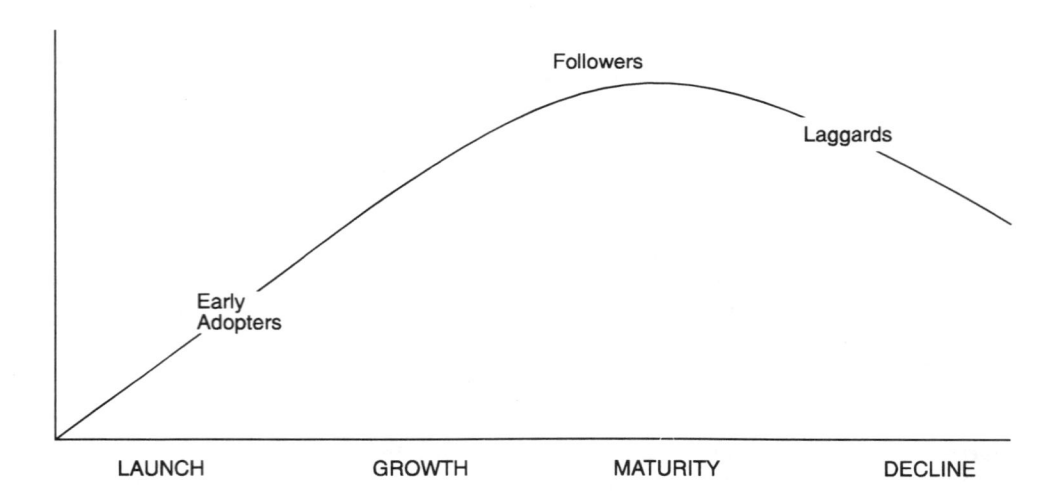

(a) At the growth stage, the marketing strategy can move towards mass media and mass distribution outlets with alterations in messages appealing to the followers of the trend setters and opinion leaders (early adopters).

(b) At the decline stage, promotion and distribution strategy can aim at the laggards, ie those buyers who react more slowly than the norm to fashion trends. It is suggested that most buyers of goods exhibit a spectrum of buying behaviour similar to that identified by Midgeley and Wills. For example, industrial equipment innovators may target particular companies, known for being at the leading edge of technology, by inviting them to preview demonstrations, offering trials and special terms. Press releases could also be targeted at the more innovative trade media. Case histories of successful trials with leading companies are then used to persuade the less adventurous companies to buy.

Ansoff's growth matrix ✓

3.80 The Ansoff matrix is used to analyse the appropriate product - market strategies, by the type of product and market.

		Product	
		Existing	New
Market	Existing	Market penetration	Product development
	New	Market development	Diversification

3.81 Here are some examples of the type of strategies that might be used.

	Existing products	New products
Existing markets	**Market penetration strategy** 1. More purchasing and usage from existing customers 2. Gain customers from competitors 3. Convert non-users into users (where both are in same market segment).	**Product development strategy** 1. Product modification via new features 2. Different quality levels 3. 'New' product
New markets	**Market development strategy** 1. New market segments 2. New distribution channels 3. New geographic areas eg exports	**Diversification strategy** 1. Joint ventures 2. Mergers 3. Acquisition/take-over

The Boston matrix

3.82 You may find the Boston Consulting Group's analysis of products into stars, cash cows, dogs and question marks quite a useful one. Bear in mind, though that this is simply a *model* and a tool, involving subjective judgements and prone to change over time.

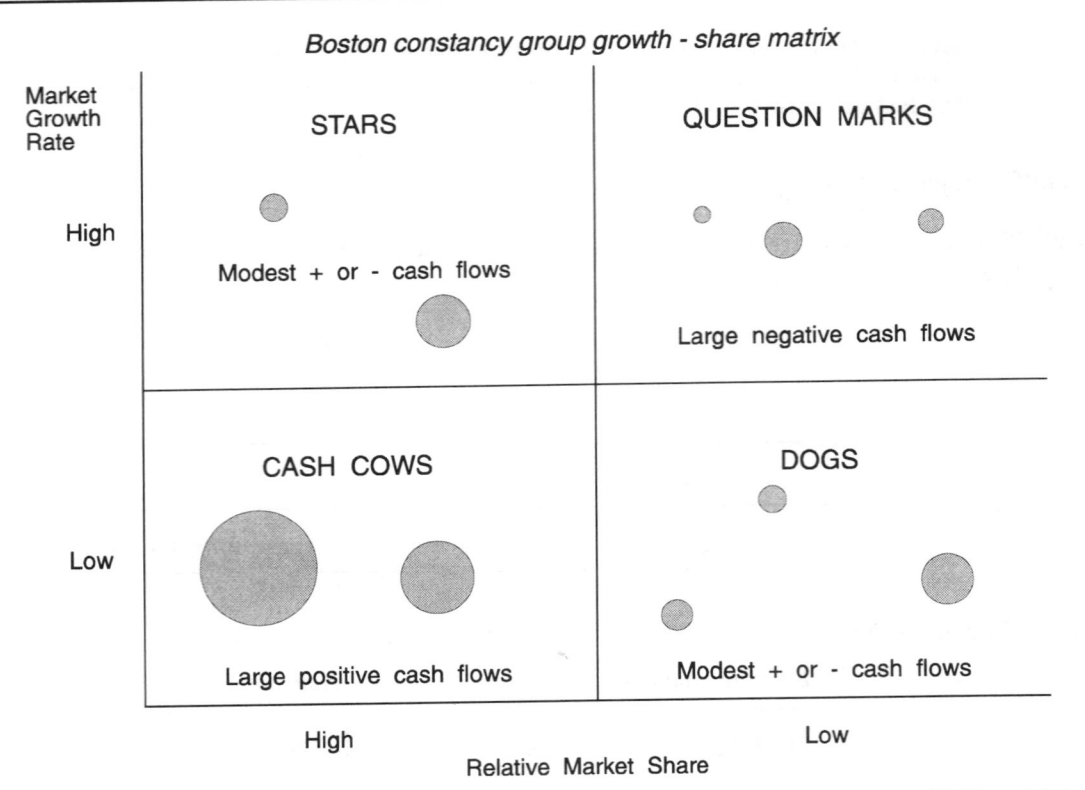

Notes   Part A: Background knowledge relevant to analysis and decision

Boston constancy group growth - share matrix

```
             High Relative Market Share  Low
Market
Growth    STARS              QUESTION MARKS
Rate
High      Modest + or -      Large negative
          cash flows         cash flows

Low       CASH COWS          DOGS
          Large positive     Modest + or -
          cash flows         cash flows
```

(a) The above model can also be applied to a strategic business unit (SBU) within a group or conglomerate particularly where the SBU is a single product manufacturer.

(b) The idea is to work towards a balanced portfolio. The Boston matrix is related to the product life cycle analysis in that question marks are often those products in the launch stage, stars are in the growth stage, cash cows are in the mature stage and dogs are in the decline stage.

(c) In the FirstrATE case study the Delta product could be said to be a question mark whilst Omega perhaps is a cash cow in danger of becoming a dog.

Gap analysis

3.83 By comparing the objectives with the current forecast, it is possible to measure the gap which is the discrepancy between what the firm wants and what it is likely to achieve. A task of corporate planning is to identify gaps and propose strategies whereby the gaps may be closed. In the diagram below, let us assume that re-examination of the current forecast shows that one of major products will not achieve sales targets (perhaps due to technological developments in market, increased competition etc).

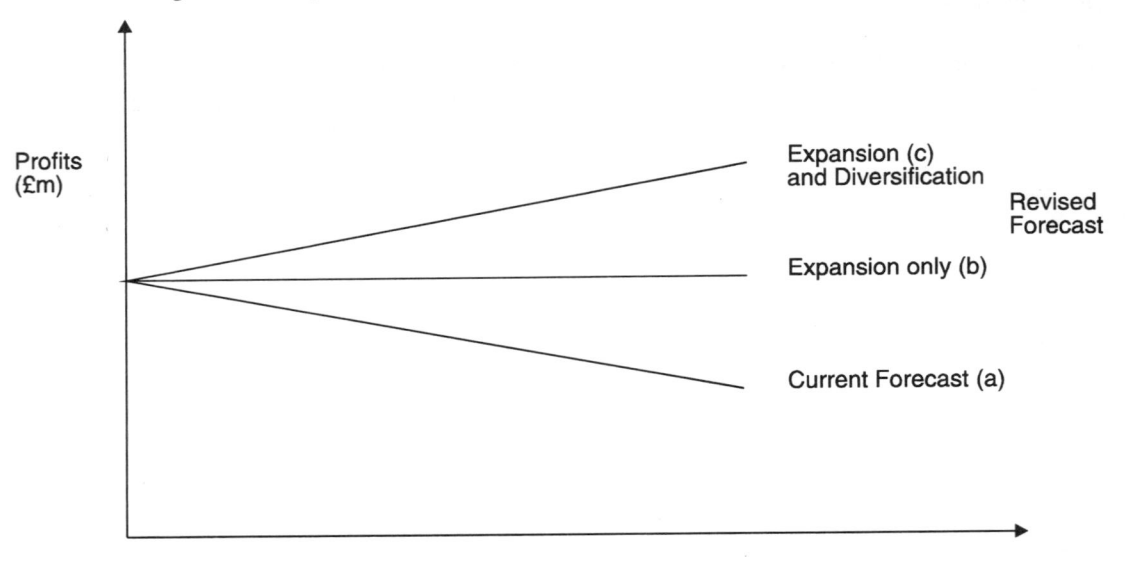

```
Profits
(£m)
                    Expansion (c)
                    and Diversification
                                         Revised
                                         Forecast
                    Expansion only (b)

                    Current Forecast (a)

                         Time
```

(a) The current forecast indicates that profits will decline in future

(b) Expansion in existing markets, by improving existing products, may maintain level of profits in future

(c) By expanding within existing markets and/or improving existing products and *diversifying* into new markets with new products, a higher level of profit may be obtained.

The PIMS database

3.84 PIMS (Profit Impact of Market Strategy) research is important to the decision of 'where we want to be' in that it uses an analysis of more than 2,800 businesses to show:

(a) that product innovation and quality are significant factors in achieving a dominant market share;

(b) that dominant market share is a key factor in achieving high levels of profitability.

If, as in most case studies the objective is to achieve profitable growth, PIMS can be quoted and leadership/innovation strategies proposed as ways of getting there.

Critical success factors

3.85 In the case of FirstrATE, flexibility seemed to be a critical success factor in a rapidly changing technological environment. Fortunately FirstrATE had an advantage in flexibility and this could therefore be developed into a distinctive competitive advantage.

4 STRATEGIC EVALUATION AND CHOICE (HOW MIGHT WE GET THERE AND WHICH WAY IS BEST?)

4.1 The decision on which strategy is best is the most difficult and risky decision that marketing managers have to take. In the case study many students find themselves unable to take it. They want to go on analysing until the decision becomes crystal clear and fail-safe. Forced into it by the question, they will opt for all four Ansoff growth strategies rather than decide which one is best. In real life of course we *have* to take marketing decisions on imperfect and insufficient information and analysis if we wish to take advantage of 'a window of opportunity' which opens for a limited amount of time. Limited resources means that we cannot pursue all available strategies and if we tried to do this, failure would be almost certain.

(a) In deciding which of the growth strategies on the Ansoff matrix is best, consideration has to be given to the risk factor associated with each strategy.

	Existing product	*New product*
Existing market	1	4
New market	2	16

The numbers in the matrix indicate notional levels of risk. Note, however, that market penetration (existing products and markets), while easy, may be risky in the long term if a new competitor is about to leap in, or if a new technology can render yours obsolete overnight, or if the market you are in is saturated. New products are always risky (research has shown that 8 out of 10 grocery products 'fail'). However, in some situations it can be *more* risky to go into new markets than to launch new products into a market that you know and understand well.

(b) Trade offs inevitably occur between levels of risk and levels of return. When considering entering new markets or new market segments for example (Ansoff's market development strategy) the following trade-offs are likely.

Part A: Background knowledge relevant to analysis and decision

	Low exit barrier	High exit barrier
Low entry barrier	Low stable returns	Low risk returns
High entry barrier	High stable returns	High risky returns

4.2 There is a variety of matrix analyses which can be used. You can invent your own according to your particular product - market situation or better still, the one in the case study. However, here are some established matrices which have a degree of universality as well as a history of success.

(a) *The directional policy matrix (George Day)*

The directional policy matrix (George Day)

Market attractiveness: High / Medium / Low
Degree of competition: Strong / Medium / Weak

High / Strong — PROTECT POSITION
- invest to grow at maximum digestible rate
- concentrate effort on maintaining strength

High / Medium — INVEST TO BUILD
- challenge for leadership
- build selectively on strengths
- reinforce vulnerable areas

High / Weak — BUILDS SELECTIVELY
- specialize around limited strengths
- seeks ways to overcome weaknesses
- withdraw if indications

Medium / Strong — BUILD SELECTIVELY
- invest heavily in most attractive segments
- build up ability to counter competition
- emphasize profitability by raising productivity

Medium / Medium — SELECTIVITY/MANAGE FOR EARNINGS
- protect existing program
- concentrate investments in segments where profitability is good and risk is relatively low

Medium / Weak — LIMITED EXPANSION OR HARVEST
- look for ways to expand without high risk otherwise, minimize investment and rationalize operations

Low / Strong — PROTECT AND REFOCUS
- manage for current earnings
- concentrate on attractive segments
- defend strengths

Low / Medium — MANAGE FOR EARNINGS
- protect position in most profitable segments
- upgrade product line
- minimize investment

Low / Weak — DIVEST
- sell at time that will maximize cash value
- cut fixed costs and avoid investment meanwhile

1: Strategic marketing management: planning and control

(b) *Arthur D Little matrix*

		Stage of industry maturity			
		Embryonic	Growth	Mature	Ageing
Competitive position	Dominant	Grow fast. Build barriers. Act offensively.	Grow fast. Aim for cost leadership. Defend position. Act offensively.	Defend position. Increase the importance of cost. Act offensively.	Defend position. Focus. Consider withdrawal.
	Strong	Grow fast. Differentiate.	Lower cost. Differentiate. Attack small firms.	Lower costs. Differentiate. Focus.	Harvest.
	Favourable	Grow fast. Differentiate.	Focus. Differentiate. Defend.	Focus. Differentiate. Hit smaller firms.	Harvest.
	Tenable	Grow with the industry. Focus.	Hold-on or withdraw. Niche. Aim for growth.	Hold-on or withdraw. Niche.	Withdraw.
	Weak	Search for a niche. Attempt to catch others.	Niche or withdraw.	Withdraw.	Withdraw.

(c) *Porter's five factor map of segment attractiveness*

Porter's five factor map of segment attractiveness

Customer groups: M_1, M_2, M_3
Products: P_1, P_2, P_3

- Potential entrants (Threat of mobility)
- Suppliers (Suppliers power)
- Industry competitors (Segment rivalry)
- Buyers (Buyer power)
- Substitute products (Threat of substitutes)

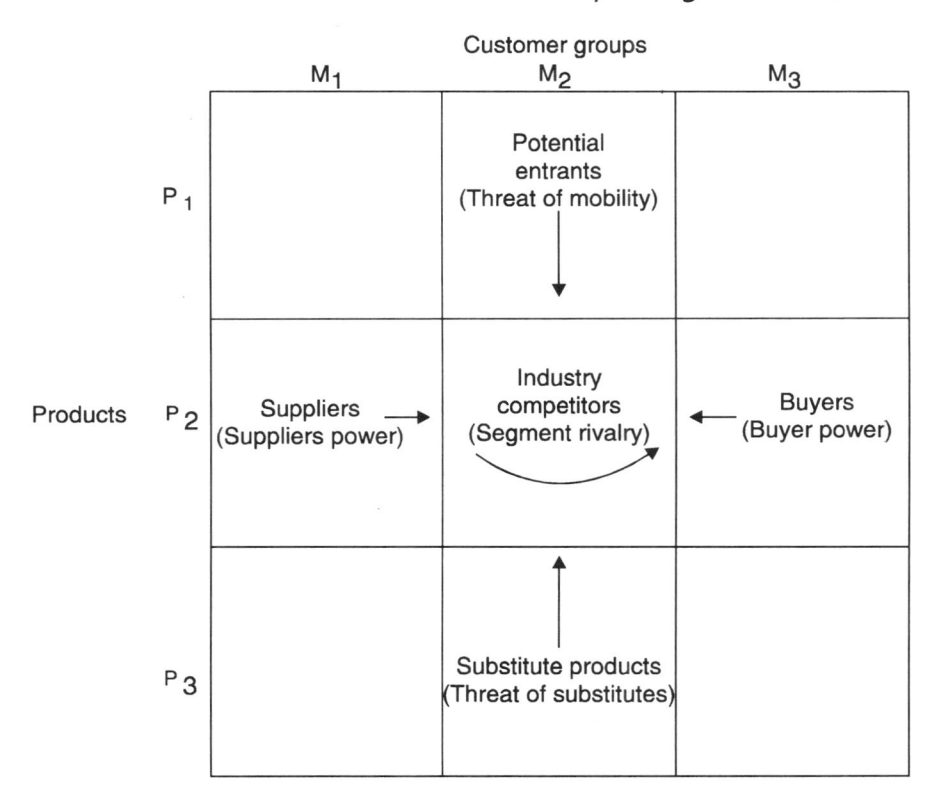

Part A: Background knowledge relevant to analysis and decision

4.3 There are a number of other approaches to the formulation of strategy which can be relevant to the case study. Michael Porter suggests three generic competitive strategies which are described below.

(a) *Overall cost leadership strategy*

The business works hard to achieve the *lowest costs of production and distribution* so the firm must be good at engineering, purchasing, manufacturing and physical distribution. Less skill perhaps is needed in marketing as the firm which pursues this strategy will *always* be able to compete on price, and will stay profitable for longer. But remember only *one* firm in a product market can follow this strategy. Texas Instruments is a leading practitioner of this strategy.

(b) *Differentiation strategy*

Here the business concentrates on achieving superior performance in some important customer benefit area valued by the market as a whole. It can strive to be the service leader, the quality leader, the style leader, the technology leader etc but it is hardly possible to be all of these things. The firm cultivates those strengths that will give a differential performance advantage along some benefit line. Thus, the firm seeking quality leadership must make or buy the best components, put them together expertly, inspect them carefully and so on. This has been Canon's strategy in the copy machine field.

(c) *Focus strategy*

Here the business focuses on one or more narrow market segments rather than going after the whole market. The firm gets to know the needs of these segments and pursues either cost leadership or some form of differentiation within the target segment. Thus, Armstrong Rubber has specialised in making superior tyres for farm equipment vehicles and recreational vehicles, and it keeps looking for new niches to serve.

4.4 A further approach to the formulation of strategy which is both corporate and marketing lies in deciding where to position the company in the market place along the leader-follower spectrum. A firm can choose between a market leader strategy and a market follower strategy.

(a) *Market leader strategy*. This has the following requirements.

    (i) Research-intensive effort
    (ii) Major development resources
    (iii) Technical personnel (eg scientists)
    (iv) Close relationship between marketing and technical staff
    (v) Flexible organisation structure
    (vi) Innovative product

This is risky and expensive, especially as innovators do not always reap the rewards of their hard work.

(b) *'Follow the leader' strategy*. In this case, the leader is copied quickly. The advantages are that the firm can offer customer benefits over those offered by the leader. Success requires a true marketing orientation: the firm has to pursue customers more fiercely. This strategy is most successful in large volume markets. The requirements are as follows.

    (i) Streamlined organisation
    (ii) Rapid response time in product development
    (iii) High quality development engineers

(c) *'Me too' strategy* is another follower strategy. Companies follow this because they have to, just to keep up with competition. By this time, the technology will have become more widely available. The requirements are as follows.

    (i) Minimal research and development
    (ii) Strong manufacturing function
    (iii) The ability to copy designs quickly
    (iv) Product modification to reduce production costs
    (v) Competitive strategy based on price and delivery

Competitor response models

4.5 A great deal can be accomplished in understanding competitors by relatively simple numerical analysis, and financial and market review. No business exists in a vacuum and marketing strategists need to assess competitors and their reactions to a firm's plans. Here is a checklist of questions about your competitors you should find answers to.

   (a) How many?
   (b) Size?
   (c) Growing or declining?
   (d) Market shares and/or rank orders
   (e) Likely objectives and strategies
   (f) Changes in management personnel
   (g) Past reactions to:
       (i) price changes
       (ii) promotional campaigns
       (iii) new product launches
       (iv) distribution drives
   (h) Analysis of marketing mix strengths and weaknesses
   (i) Leaders or followers?
   (j) National or international
   (k) Analysis of published accounts.

4.6 Adding to the above data obtained from competitor intelligence (observation, asking customers, planting moles etc) and from maintaining comprehensive records of competitors' past behaviour and you can begin to develop competitor response models. These attempt to predict for example, what competitor A will do if you launch a radical new product (do nothing, retaliate by non-product means, copy you, develop superior product etc), or what competitor B will do if you raise your prices (nothing, immediately copy, increase theirs less, increase theirs more, wait a bit and then copy etc). Such modelling can be an invaluable aid to strategic choice.

Experimentation and test marketing

4.7 Writers like RMS Wilson have continuously encouraged marketers to conduct more experimentation when making the decision which way is best. This is particularly appropriate when applied to the marketing mix. We can experiment with different price levels and study price-volume-profit relationships. We can try out a new sales promotion in a small geographical area, we can ask selected customers to test new products etc. In these ways marketers can avoid the possibly disastrous consequences of a failed strategy. A failure of a new product launch on a national scale is measured not only by unrecovered costs but also in the loss of credibility which can jeopardise future initiatives.

You will learn more about concept testing and test marketing in Section 6 of this chapter which can be put to good use in your case study examination. In the case study 'Brewsters' the company had developed three new drinks concepts but needed to conduct concept testing in order to make the best choice.

The marketing mix

4.8 The assumption has to be made that you already know something about the marketing mix and so the following pages are in the form of outline notes only.

4.9 In terms of marketing, strategy is achieved by deploying the elements of the marketing mix. This essentially entails developing products and services to meet target segments' needs (established by marketing research), communicating their benefits to target audiences and ensuring they are available in the right place, at the right price and at the right time. At its simplest, the marketing mix can, therefore, be defined (after McCarthy) as the 4 P's, namely:

> P1 = PRODUCT (or service)
> P2 = PRICE
> P3 = PROMOTION (communications)
> P4 = PLACE (Distribution)

4.10 Each of these four elements subsumes other elements which might be termed sub-elements or submixes. The exact nature or make-up of these submixes is determined both by the product or service itself and by the marketer's choice. For example, branding may not be a consideration for industrial raw materials, whereas a consumer goods marketer might decide to seek a differential competitive advantage through distinctive packaging, unique product design and style of advertising, as in the case of TIC-TAC Mints.

4.11 With these points in mind, we can identify submixes as follows.

(a) *Product submix*

   (i) Pre-sales service
   (ii) Product range
   (iii) Packaging
   (iv) Patenting
   (v) Design
   (vi) Positioning
   (vii) Warranties
   (viii) Demonstration/trial
   (ix) Standardisation
   (x) Modification
   (xi) Rationalisation
   (xii) Innovation
   (xiii) After-sales services
   (xiv) Evaluation

(b) *Pricing submix*

   (i) Costings
   (ii) Demand
   (iii) Profitability
   (iv) Competitive pricing
   (v) Promotional pricing
   (vi) Product-mix pricing
   (vii) Discounts
   (viii) Price Increases
   (xi) Evaluation

(c) The *promotional submix* consists of four submixes, which are themselves further analysed.

Advertising	Sales promotion	Public relations	Selling
Objectives Budget Messages Media Scheduling Evaluation	Literature Incentives (consumer, dealer, sales force) Exhibitions Direct mail Merchandising Trade presentations Point of sale display materials In-house visits Evaluation	Corporate identity Internal communications Publicity Media receptions Evaluation	Sales force size Structure of sales force Remuneration Training Motivation Evaluation

(d) *Distribution submix*
   (i) Channels
   (ii) Stocking levels
   (iii) Ordering systems
   (iv) Speed of response
   (v) Dealer relationships evaluation
   (vi) Depots
   (vii) Channel costing and evaluation

4.12 These submixes at least form the framework for marketing operations planning and control, although the amount of detail can be debated.

4.13 We should also note that the elements of the marketing mix/submixes are, in practice, interdependent and interactive. They need to combine harmoniously to form an integrated and tailored whole, so as to be attractive to the target market or segment.

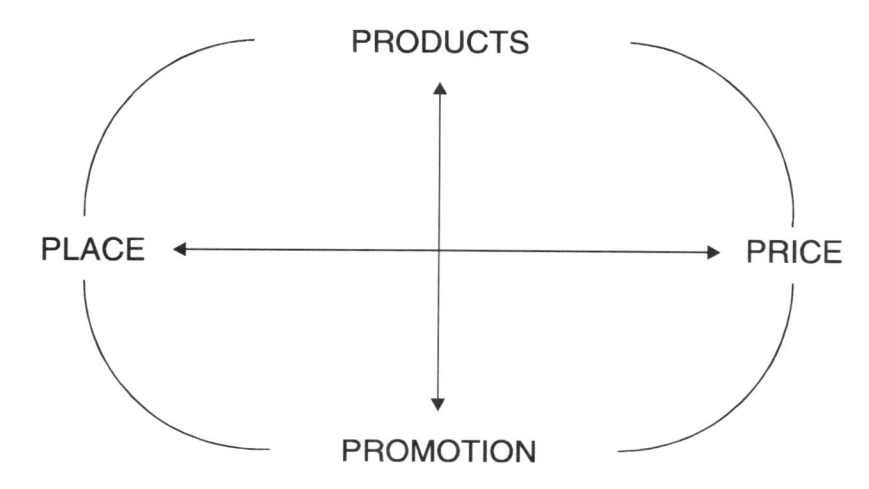

Interrelationships of the marketing mix

(a) *Price* is to some extent dependent on *product* in the sense that any price below variable costs (labour plus materials) would fail to generate any contribution. The nature of the product might also determine its method and/or channel of distribution(place). An industrial product would not normally be advertised in consumer media (promotion). Heavy promotional expenditures and high quality packaging costs might need to be recovered in the price charged, depending upon the extra volume generated.

(b) As an example of interaction, the sales force will refer to advertising support in their personal presentations. Point-of-sale display material will embody the advertising theme and the advertisements themselves might well refer to company benefits in the form of sales force and merchandising support. Price communicates a degree of value and, therefore, could be considered to be part of the communications mix as well as an element in itself. Packaging in a self-service environment becomes 'the silent salesman' to the consumer.

Products and services

4.14 Most authors attempt to differentiate between products and service (Foxall, for example, differentiates on grounds of tangibility and durability). Lovelock in his book on service marketing, quotes who states: 'Services are relatively intangible, produced and consumed simultaneously, and often less standardised than goods. These unique characteristics of services present special challenges and strategic marketing opportunities to the services marketer.'

(a) Three fundamental characteristics of services are as follows.

   (i) intangibility;
   (ii) a service is an activity rather than a thing;
   (iii) production and consumption are to some extent simultaneous activities.

(b) Service marketing involves three additional 'P's:

    (i) people;
    (ii) process;
    (iii) physical evidence. (See paras 4.18 - 4.10 below.)

4.15 However, most products purchased entail some element of service, if only that of availability, delivery or credit, which facilitate the sale and most services have tangible elements eg dry cleaners provide coat hangers and bags. Cowell concludes that there are four categories:

(a) a pure tangible good;
(b) a tangible good with accompanying services;
(c) a service with accompanying goods;
(d) a pure service.

4.16 When marketing goods or services, we should remember the maxim that people do not buy goods or services, they buy what products and services will do for them that they want doing, ie *they buy benefits*. In this context, it can be useful to view the product (for service) as an input-output device, so as to gain a clearer insight of how to communicate product features in the form of user benefits.

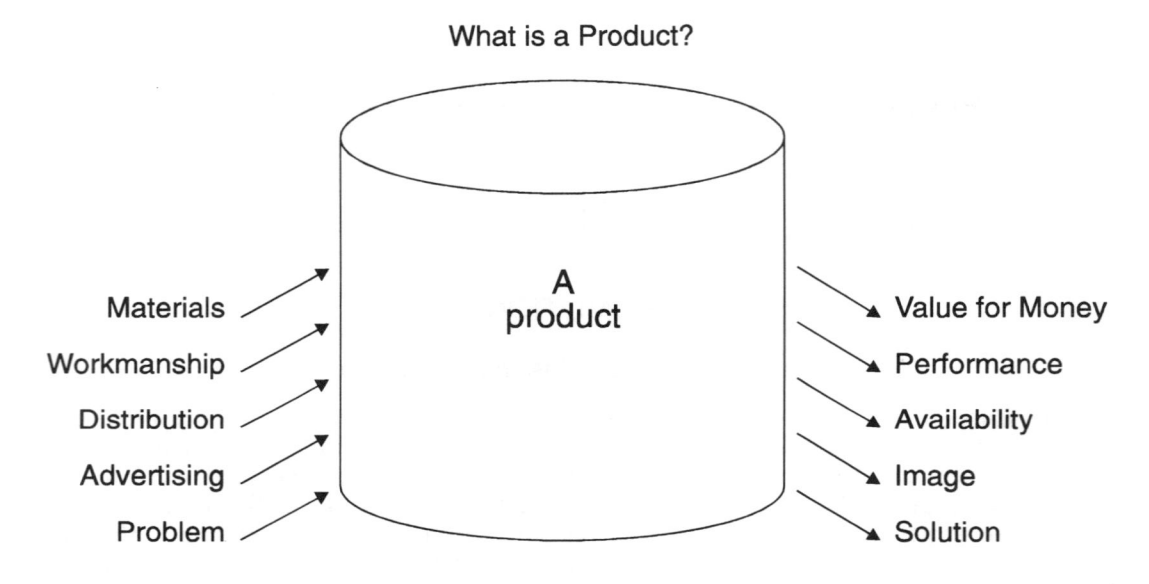

What is a Product?

Inputs: Materials, Workmanship, Distribution, Advertising, Problem → A product → Outputs: Value for Money, Performance, Availability, Image, Solution

The product as an input-output device

4.17 Extending the above idea, we can now say a product is everything a purchaser gets in exchange for his money, including the following possible 'extras'. It is also useful to acknowledge here that different people seek different benefits, giving rise to market segmentation. In general, people seek new and/or better benefits, such as image enhancement, greater reliability and more convenience, giving rise to new market segments and the concept of product life cycle.

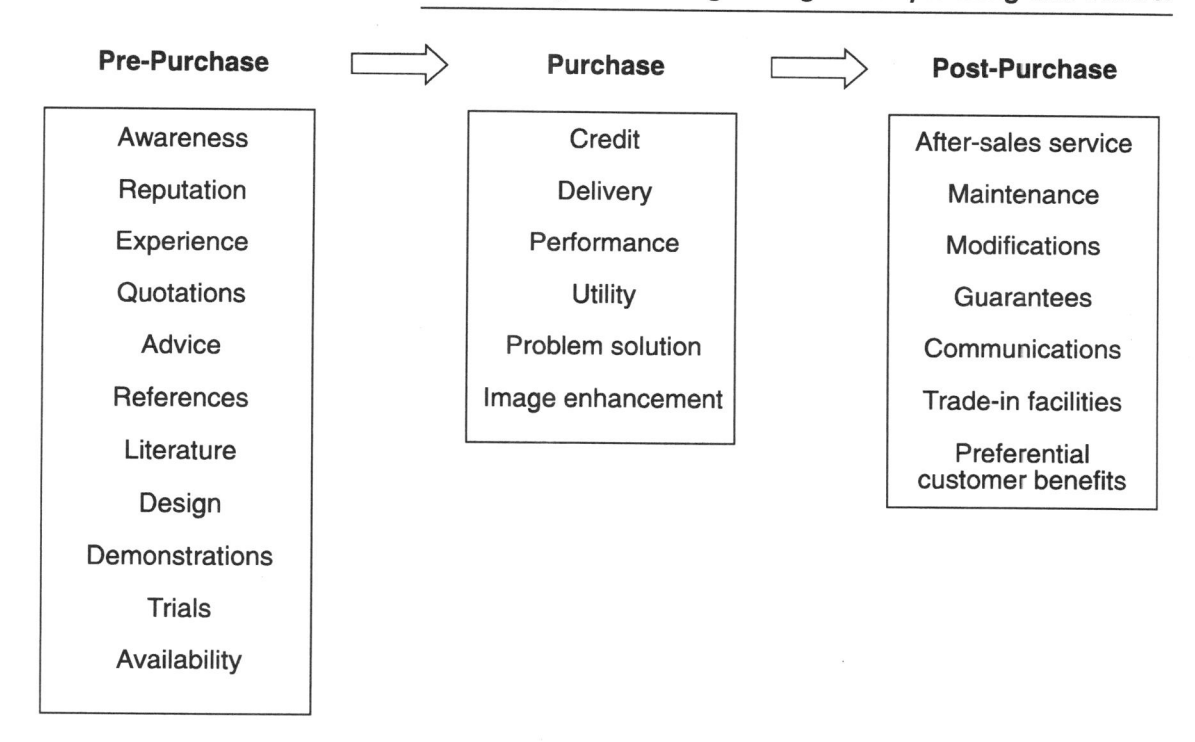

Pre-Purchase	Purchase	Post-Purchase
Awareness	Credit	After-sales service
Reputation	Delivery	Maintenance
Experience	Performance	Modifications
Quotations	Utility	Guarantees
Advice	Problem solution	Communications
References	Image enhancement	Trade-in facilities
Literature		Preferential customer benefits
Design		
Demonstrations		
Trials		
Availability		

Product inputs-outputs related to the buying cycle

4.18 *People*

(a) *Employees.* The importance of employees as an element in the marketing mix is particularly evident in service industries. After all, if you have had poor service in a shop or restaurant, you may not be willing to go there again. An American retailing firm estimated that there was an identifiable relationship between lower staff turnover and repeat purchases. Managing front-line workers (eg cabin-crew on aircraft) who are the lowest in the organisational hierarchy but whose behaviour has most effect on customers, is an important task for senior management. It involves corporate culture, job design and motivational issues.

  (i) Appearance
  (ii) Attitude
  (iii) Commitment
  (iv) Behaviour
  (v) Professionalism
  (vi) Skills
  (vii) Numbers
  (viii) Discretion

(b) *Customers.* At first sight, having customers here might seem strange. Customers are, after all, the destination of the efforts of the marketing professional. However, customer, values and attitudes are important.

  (i) Behaviour
  (ii) Appearance
  (iii) Numbers
  (iv) Customer/customer contact

4.19 *Process.* Processes involve the ways in which the marketer's task is achieved. Efficient processes can become a marketing advantage in their own right. For example, if an airline develops a sophisticated ticketing system, it can encourage customers to take connecting flights offered by allied airlines. Efficient processing of purchase orders received from customers can decrease the time it takes to satisfy them. Efficient procedures in the long term save money.

(a) Procedures
(b) Policies
(c) Mechanisation
(d) Queuing
(e) Information
(f) Capacity levels
(g) Speed/timing
(h) Accessibility

4.20 *Physical evidence*. Again, this is particularly important in service industries, for example where the ambience of a restaurant is important. Logos and uniforms help create a sense of corporate identity.

(a) *Environment*
    (i) Furnishings
    (ii) Colours
    (iii) Layout
    (iv) Noise levels
    (v) Smells
    (vi) Ambience

(b) *Facilities*
    (i) Vans/vehicles/aeroplanes
    (ii) Equipment/tools
    (iii) Uniforms
    (iv) Paperwork

(c) *Tangible evidence*
    (i) Labels
    (ii) Tickets
    (iii) Logos
    (iv) Packaging

New product development

4.21 The process of new product generation entails three basic stages

(a) Generating ideas
(b) Screening
(c) Developing the launch strategy

Generating ideas

4.22 Ideas for new products and/or services can come from employees, customers, suppliers, intermediaries, competitors and the general public.

4.23 In recognising the need for a continuous stream of new product ideas, many companies formalise their approach. For example, they may install suggestion boxes at various points within the company and offer rewards for ideas brought to fruition. *Quality circles* are used to seek ideas for improvements from production staff in organised discussion groups. Some of these ideas will give rise to product modification. Other companies scour *complaints files* periodically for product/service improvement ideas.

4.24 *Value analysis* usually involves obtaining a range of competitive products, adding your own and subjecting this combination to a rigorous and detailed critique. For example, the following questions might be asked about a range of electric fan heaters. (This list is not exhaustive.)

(a) Why do we need 3 fan speeds?
(b) What price reduction could we make if only 2 fan speeds were offered?
(c) Would this modification result in better value?
(d) Why use stainless steel screws?

(e) Would mild steel screws be almost as good?
(f) What price reduction would this make?
(g) Would this represent better value?
(h) Why use 20 gauge casting which vibrates without reinforcement?
(i) Would 18 gauge casting be vibration free without reinforcement?
(j) What would be the relative cost of 18 gauge?
(k) Would using 18 gauge represent better value?

4.25 Some organisations use *brainstorming* techniques. Individuals are gathered together in groups and are asked to contribute ideas without forethought, embarrassment or inhibition. Original guidelines suggested by Osborn were as follows.

(a) Nothing should be held back, however wild.
(b) The greater the number of ideas generated, the higher the probability of a good one.
(c) Ideas should be combined, and interesting ones improved, during the session.

4.26 The *sales force* can be a good source for new ideas, being closer than anyone else in the organisation of customers and competitors. However, formal *market research* can be applied to discover both new needs and existing attitudes towards your own and competitive products, on a number of attributes, in the form of gap analysis.

4.27 Scaling techniques can be applied to discover the perfect mix of a product's attributes and how far existing products fall short of ideal product improvement. For example, research could give us an idea of what customers regard as the ideal or perfect loaf. Its attributes can include taste, freshness, nutritional value, non-staling characteristics etc. Existing types of bread are then tested to see how far they fall short of the ideal. If we could then develop a loaf which comprised a better fit, this would fill a gap in the market.

4.28 Technological forecasting is another way of generating new product ideas, along with the building of 'what if?' scenarios. The process involves an examination of current technological and current research progress (see Paragraph 3.12). The next step is to see what products might be developed. There is currently research into superconductivity: this will make energy distribution cheaper. A number of possible applications might exist. There is speculation on what will happen if the gap in the ozone layer widens - what new products/services might be needed?

4.29 How far a new product is in fact *new*, rather than a modification of an existing product, is less important than whether potential customers *see* it as a new product. (Thus, mushy peas in a can were portrayed and accepted as a new product, despite having been available loose or in cardboard containers in chip shops in the UK for decades).

Screening

4.30 New product ideas need to be screened against a set of criteria in order to prevent expensive failures, but guarding against the premature dismissal of ideas which could turn out to be winners. Here is a general purpose or generic screening model.

Part A: Background knowledge relevant to analysis and decision

General purpose screening model for new product ideas

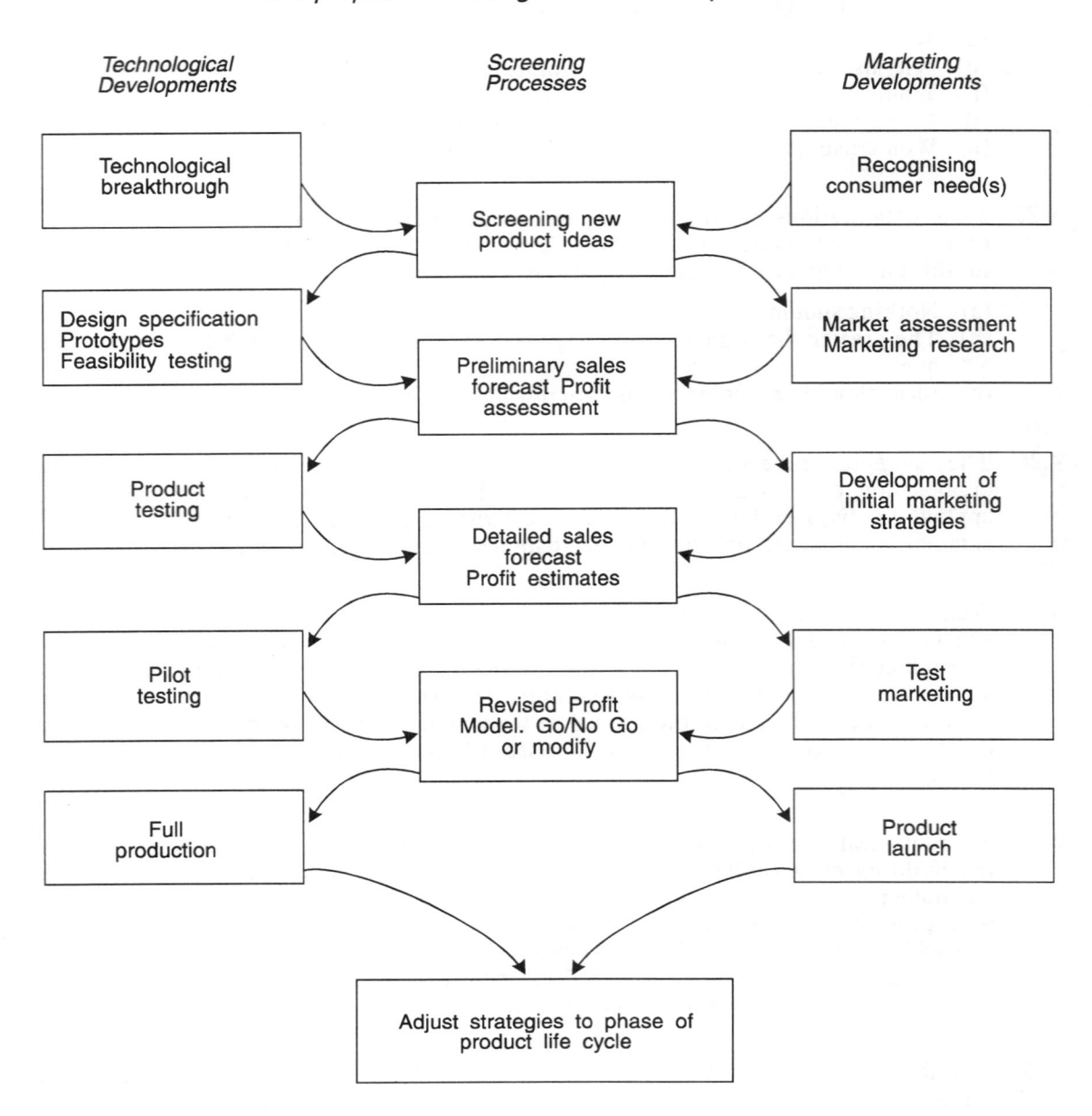

```
Technological              Screening              Marketing
Developments               Processes              Developments

[Technological                                    [Recognising
 breakthrough]      →  [Screening new    ←         consumer need(s)]
                        product ideas]
                              ↓
[Design specification                             [Market assessment
 Prototypes         →  [Preliminary sales ←        Marketing research]
 Feasibility testing]   forecast Profit
                        assessment]
                              ↓
[Product                                          [Development of
 testing]           →  [Detailed sales   ←         initial marketing
                        forecast                   strategies]
                        Profit estimates]
                              ↓
[Pilot                                            [Test
 testing]           →  [Revised Profit   ←         marketing]
                        Model. Go/No Go
                        or modify]
                              ↓
[Full                                             [Product
 production]        →                     ←        launch]
                              ↓
                       [Adjust strategies to phase of
                        product life cycle]
```

Promotion

4.31   This element is covered in detail in Chapter 2 on Marketing Communications Strategy.

5   STRATEGIC IMPLEMENTATION AND CONTROL (HOW CAN WE ENSURE ARRIVAL?)

Implementation

5.1   Getting things done entails delegating responsibility and granting the necessary authority. In case study exams you may well be asked for action plans and, if so, you are expected to specify not only who is responsible, but also the sequence and timing of the actions. This could be expressed in columnar form as follows.

	Actions in sequence	Person responsible	Timing	Estimated cost (£'000)
1	Conduct full marketing audit	MkIS manager	January 98	10
2	Summarise situation from this audit	Marketing manager	February 98	1
3	Agree sales forecast for 98-99	Marketing manager, sales manager	February 98	-
4	Finalise marketing plans	Marketing team	March 98	3

Control

5.2 The implementation schedule acts as a control document. Checks can be made that the action has been carried out by the agreed deadlines and within the agreed cost. More often than not, outline schedules like the example given above, will be backed by more detailed documents which can then contain the control procedures. In addition to budgetary control which has been covered earlier in this chapter (and also in Chapter 4) are the human controls and the contingency plan. The range of potential control techniques are as follows.

(a) Budgetary control
(b) Ratio analysis
(c) Cost-volume-profit analysis
(d) Net present value analysis
(e) Distribution cost analysis
(f) Quality controls
(g) Marketing audits
(h) Marketing research
(i) Marketing experimentation and test marketing
(j) Management science (eg operational research, systems analysis and design)
(k) Meetings and discussions
(l) Contingency planning

Most of the above have already been covered or will be covered in subsequent chapters.

5.3 *Management science* is an area of increasing importance. It can relate to systems, in particular control systems, in which control action is built into the very operation of a system (like a thermostat).

(a) It would for example include systems which automatically signal when an event occurred outside the tolerances laid down. (In a stock control system this could be whenever stock exceeds maximum or falls below planned levels.)

(b) Flowcharts, programming, networks, critical path analysis all come under the aegis of management science.

(c) In retailing, systems such as EPOS (Electronic Point of Sale) can be programmed to automatically debit stock and re-order as goods sold are registered by the tills.

5.4 Most companies hold regular (weekly, monthly and quarterly) meetings at which performance is discussed and any remedial action necessary is agreed and documented. Special meetings can be called when for example a competitor action seriously threatens existing plans.

5.5 Events can be predicted, assigned degrees of probability of occurrence and for events most likely to happen *contingency plans* drawn up in advance detailing the actions to be taken. Again, the control action is premeditated.

5.6 It is possible to use ratio analysis in a control system.

$$\frac{\text{Selling expenses}}{\text{Sales revenue}} \qquad \frac{\text{Advertising expenditure}}{\text{Sales revenue}} \qquad \frac{\text{Below the line expenditure}}{\text{Sales revenue}}$$

$$\frac{\text{Promotional expenditure}}{\text{Net profit before tax}} \qquad \frac{\text{Net profit before tax}}{\text{Sales revenue}} \qquad \frac{\text{Total marketing expenditure}}{\text{Sales revenue}}$$

5.7 A ratio can be historically assessed and new ratios agreed which can then act as control mechanisms

Total market expenditure	1995	1996	1997	1998	1999	2000	2001
% of sales revenue =	5	5.5	6.0	6.5	7.0	7.5	7.5

In the above case, a company bent on gaining dominant share might have to be prepared to increase advertising expenditure, as a proportion of sales revenue as well as expecting sales volumes to rise, so that marketing expenditure would in practice get a double boost. The drawback of this particular form of control lies in the difficulty of forecasting future revenues. A mechanism for partially coping with fluctuating revenues is to agree tolerances. For example in 1999 we would accept a ratio in between 6.8 and 7.2%.

6 MARKETING RESEARCH AND THE MARKETING INFORMATION SYSTEM (MkIS)

6.1 Marketing research and marketing information systems (MkIS) are favourite areas for testing in the case study and so it is often necessary for you to draw up a marketing research plan as part of your examination preparation. A format for the marketing research plan will be found in Chapter 8 paragraph 5.13 of this Tutorial Text.

6.2 However, a thorough underpinning in marketing research (and the MkIS) is pre-requisite to the drawing up of a marketing research plan and the aim of the following pages is to provide this for you in a succinct manner.

6.3 *Marketing research* can be defined as follows, either:

(a) research into all aspects of marketing (markets, sales, advertising, products, price, distribution); or

(b) the systematic gathering, recording and analysing of data relating to the marketing of goods and services.

Market research is research into markets (sizes, segments, trends, manufacturer and distributor shares etc) whereas marketing research is research into all elements of the marketing mix (price, product/service, promotion etc) *and* markets.

6.4 The basic rationale for marketing research is the widening communications gap between an organisation and its customers in a modern economy and the need to provide a more informed basis for strategic decisions than mere hunches. There are other reasons, too.

(a) Increasing competition necessitates a detailed knowledge of competitors' activities.
(b) Rapid changes in technology must be noted
(c) Growing affluence creates changes in tastes and purchasing habits
(d) Marketing costs (largely labour costs) are increasing faster than production costs.

6.5 What does a firm need to know? An *information specification* is suggested here.

(a) *Markets*. Who are our customers? What are they like? How are buying decisions made? This information is vital to every marketing decision

(b) *Share of the market* What are total sales of our product? our sales? competitors' sales?

(c) *Products*. What do customers think of our product? What do they do with it? Are our products in a 'growth' or 'decline' stage of their life cycle? Should we extend our range?

Types of marketing research

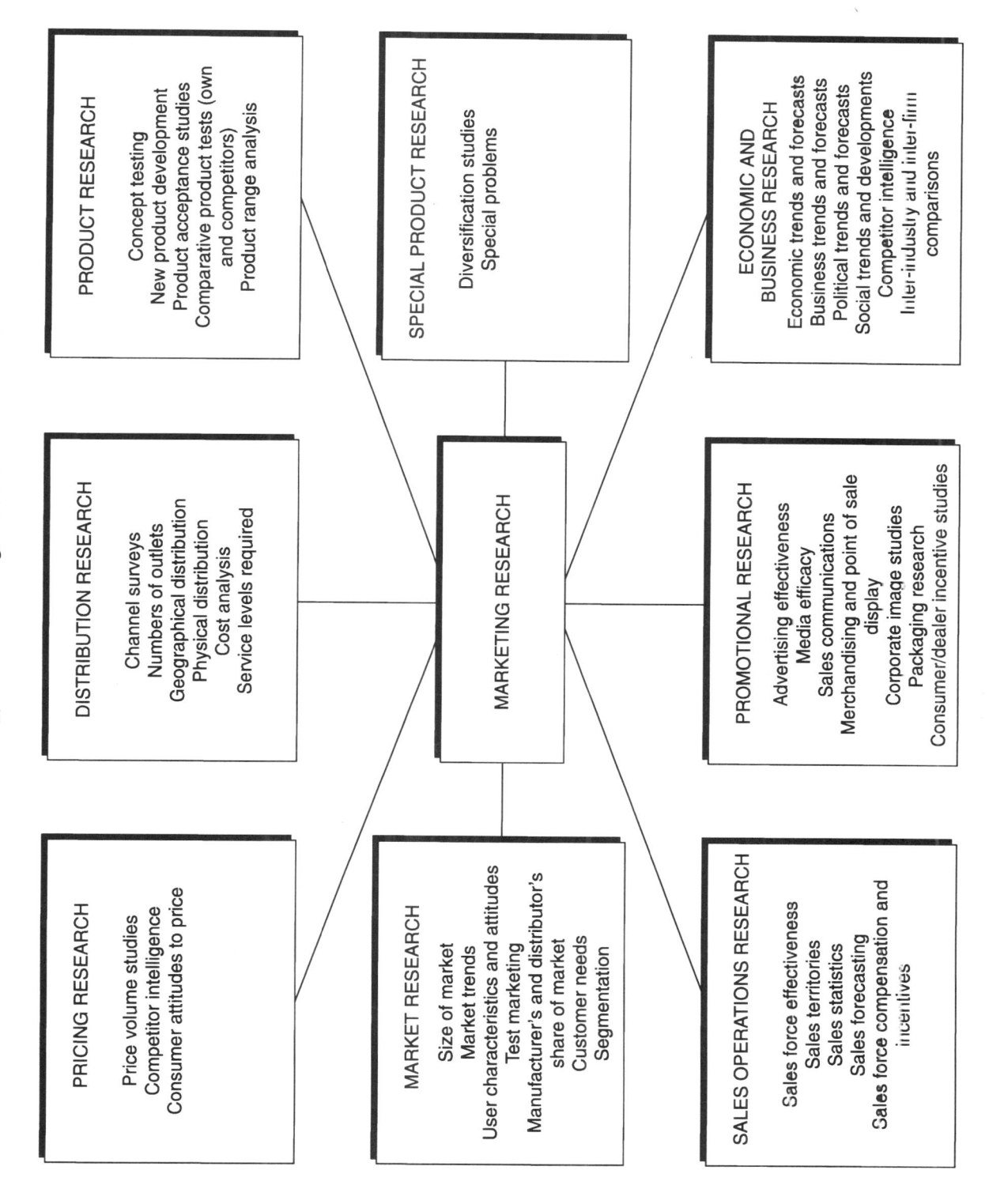

PRODUCT RESEARCH
- Concept testing
- New product development
- Product acceptance studies
- Comparative product tests (own and competitors)
- Product range analysis

SPECIAL PRODUCT RESEARCH
- Diversification studies
- Special problems

ECONOMIC AND BUSINESS RESEARCH
- Economic trends and forecasts
- Business trends and forecasts
- Political trends and forecasts
- Social trends and developments
- Competitor intelligence
- Inter-industry and inter-firm comparisons

DISTRIBUTION RESEARCH
- Channel surveys
- Numbers of outlets
- Geographical distribution
- Physical distribution
- Cost analysis
- Service levels required

MARKETING RESEARCH

PROMOTIONAL RESEARCH
- Advertising effectiveness
- Media efficacy
- Sales communications
- Merchandising and point of sale display
- Corporate image studies
- Packaging research
- Consumer/dealer incentive studies

PRICING RESEARCH
- Price volume studies
- Competitor intelligence
- Consumer attitudes to price

MARKET RESEARCH
- Size of market
- Market trends
- User characteristics and attitudes
- Test marketing
- Manufacturer's and distributor's share of market
- Customer needs
- Segmentation

SALES OPERATIONS RESEARCH
- Sales force effectiveness
- Sales territories
- Sales statistics
- Sales forecasting
- Sales force compensation and incentives

(d) *Price.* How do we compare: high, average, low? Is the market price sensitive?

(e) *Distribution.* Should we distribute directly, indirectly or both? What discounts are required?

(f) *Sales force.* Do we have enough/too many salesmen? Are their territories equal to their potential? Are they contacting the right people? Should we pay commission?

(g) *Advertising.* Do we use the right media? Do we communicate the right message? Is it effective?

(h) *Customer attitudes.* What do they think of our product? firm? service? delivery?

(i) *Competitors' activities.* All aspects

(j) *Environmental* factors impacting on marketing planning (SLEPT factors)

Building on the above, the marketing applications to which marketing research can contribute, can be categorised as given in the table on the previous page.

6.6 In seeking data for decision taking purposes marketing managers should follow a logical series of steps, starting with internal sources and ending with the conducting of ad-hoc surveys only as a last step when proceeding sources have failed. This process can be best expressed as a flow diagram.

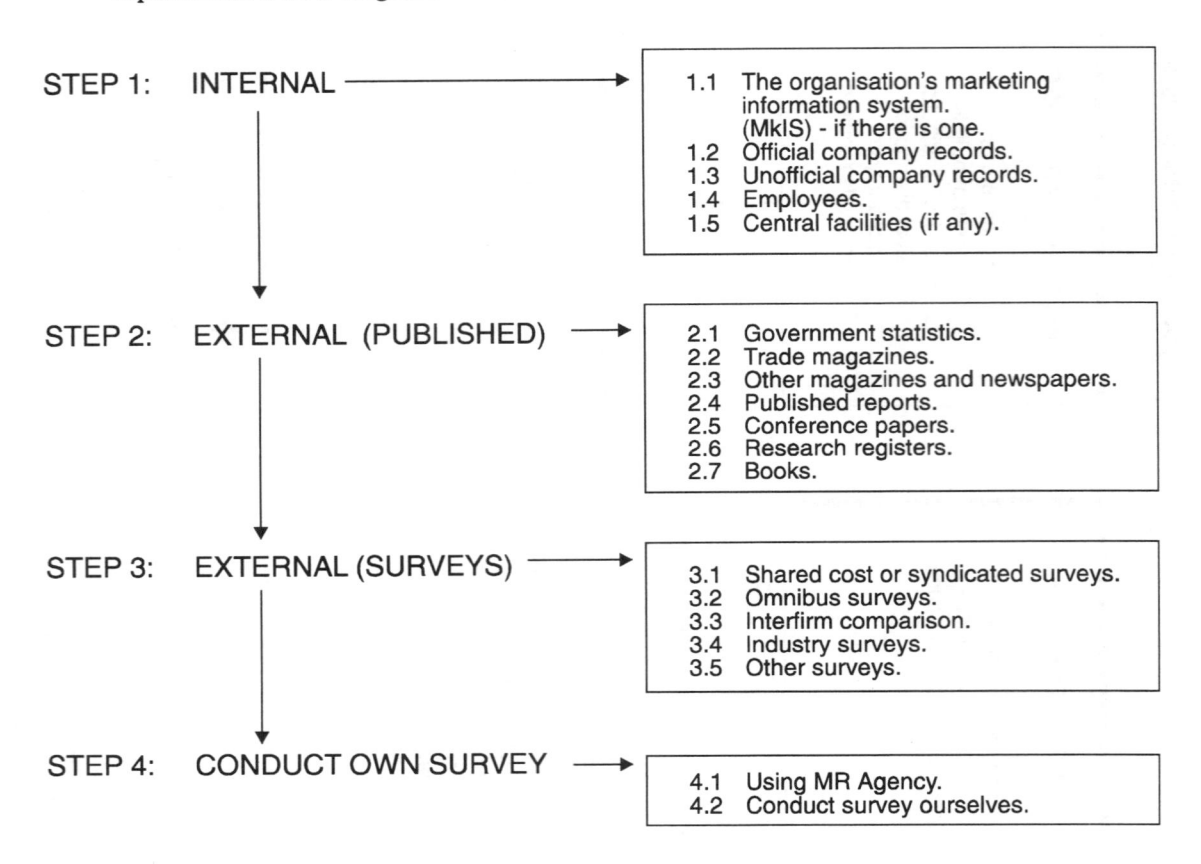

STEP 1: INTERNAL
- 1.1 The organisation's marketing information system. (MkIS) - if there is one.
- 1.2 Official company records.
- 1.3 Unofficial company records.
- 1.4 Employees.
- 1.5 Central facilities (if any).

STEP 2: EXTERNAL (PUBLISHED)
- 2.1 Government statistics.
- 2.2 Trade magazines.
- 2.3 Other magazines and newspapers.
- 2.4 Published reports.
- 2.5 Conference papers.
- 2.6 Research registers.
- 2.7 Books.

STEP 3: EXTERNAL (SURVEYS)
- 3.1 Shared cost or syndicated surveys.
- 3.2 Omnibus surveys.
- 3.3 Interfirm comparison.
- 3.4 Industry surveys.
- 3.5 Other surveys.

STEP 4: CONDUCT OWN SURVEY
- 4.1 Using MR Agency.
- 4.2 Conduct survey ourselves.

6.7 To fully cover all data sources in detail would take several volumes and be beyond the scope of this book. However the following guide to locations of data should be helpful not only for answering exam questions but also for career purposes.

Sources of marketing research data

6.8 (a) *Government statistics*

Central Government has an army of statisticians producing data in the national interest and like everyone else, wanting the results of their labour to be put to use. ('Consumption is the sole end and purpose of all production'. Adam Smith *The Wealth of Nations*, 1776.) The *Office of National Statistics* can be reached by contacting, at first instance. The ONS Library (1 Drummond Gate, Pimlico,

London SW1 2QQ, phone 0171 533 6262, fax 0171 533 6261, E-mail info@ons.gov.uk) who will provide a free booklet giving a brief guide to sources. Alternatively phone the ONS sales desk on 0171 533 5678). The following more specific statistics are often available in your town/city public library.

- (i) Monthly Digest of Statistics
- (ii) Annual Abstract of Statistics
- (iii) Population Trends, Economic Trends, Social Trends, Regional Trends
- (iv) Family Expenditure Survey and the General Household Survey
- (v) Distribution Monitors (shops and stores) and Transport Statistics
- (vi) Production Monitors
- (vii) Special Monitors eg Travel and Tourism

(b) *Business directories.* Examples include, although there are many others:

- (i) Kompass Register (Kompass)
- (ii) Who owns Whom (Dunn and Bradstreet)
- (iii) Key British Enterprises (Dunn and Bradstreet)

(c) Some *digests and pocket books*

- (i) Lifestyle Pocket Book (annual by the Advertising Association)
- (ii) Retail Pocket Book (annual by Nielson)
- (iii) A to Z of UK Marketing Data (Euromonitor)
- (iv) UK in Figures (annual, free from CSO)

(d) *International data*

- (i) Overseas Trade Statistics (CSO) General Statistical Bulletin (EC)
- (ii) Consumer Europe (bi-annual, Euromonitor)
- (iii) International Directory of Published Market Research
- (iv) Statistics and Market Intelligence Library (DTI London)

(e) *Some important periodicals (often available in the public libraries)*

- (i) Economist (general)
- (ii) Campaign (advertising)
- (iii) Marketing Week
- (iv) Mintel (consumer market reports)
- (v) Retail Business (consumer market reports)
- (vi) BRAD (all newspapers and magazines published in UK)

(f) *Some special data bases*

- (i) ACORN (consumption indices by class of neighbourhood)
- (ii) PRESTEL (British Telecom)
- (iii) TEXTLINE (abstracts articles from c.80 newspapers)
- (iv) Marketing Surveys Index (CIM)
- (v) MRS Yearbook (Market Research Agencies and their specialisms)

(g) *Some retail audits and consumer panels*

- (i) Nielsen Retail Audits
- (ii) AGB Home Audit
- (iii) Television Consumer Audit (TVA)
- (iv) Attwood Consumer Panel
- (v) BMRB Target Group Index (TGI)

(h) *Shared cost/syndicated research and omnibus surveys.* If the expense of conducting their own surveys is too great, companies and organisations can obtain general surveys they can buy into on a shared cost basis. Some of these are given above (eg the Nielsen Retail Audit). A particular form of shared cost research is the omnibus survey a variety of which are advertised in the Market Research Society Newsletters and range from general weekly surveys done by telephone (eg phonebus) to special sector surveys (eg Omnicar - motoring, Carrick James - children and youth, small businesses etc).

(i) The advantage is that for a few hundred as opposed to a few thousand, pounds a company can ask a few questions of a reasonably representative sample and have a report sent within 2 or 3 weeks.

Notes   **Part A: Background knowledge relevant to analysis and decision**

(j) Companies can also link up with others in an industry through their federations so as to conduct shared cost marketing research surveys.

6.9 *External assistance.* Few firms can carry out all the research they may find necessary. Employing outside agencies is often the answer and need not be too expensive.

(a) *Government bodies.* The DTI will often advise on these matters and is particularly helpful on export marketing research. Practical and financial assistance will be given in some instances.

(b) *Marketing research agencies and consultants.* Their numbers are increasing in response to demand for their services. The two professional associations in this sphere, the Market Research Society and the Industrial Marketing Research Association both issue lists of agencies and will often recommend a suitable agency.

(c) *Other bodies.* An increasing number of universities have business schools where advice and help can be obtained, often at small or no cost.

Field surveys

6.10 *Field surveys.* Few companies should undertake their own field surveys without expert help in survey design, sampling, questionnaire design and questionnaire administering. As the old saying goes 'rubbish in equals rubbish out'. It would be counter-productive if critical and expensive decisions were made on the basis of faulty research. However, companies should at least be aware of the basics of fieldwork in order to brief agencies adequately.

6.11 Field surveys generally speaking involve posing a number of questions to a *respondent*, who answers them. Respondents can be contacted in several ways. These are now briefly described.

(a) *Personal interview.* This is the most common method. Skilled interviewers attempt to obtain information from selected individuals. Formal questionnaires are usually used.

  (i) *Advantages*

   (1) It yields a high percentage of acceptable returns.
   (2) There is a low refusal rate.
   (3) The sample can be an almost perfect cross-section of the population.
   (4) Interviewers can clear up contradictory statements at once.
   (5) Answers are likely to be spontaneous.
   (6) Much information can be obtained (ie a questionnaire can be longer than any other method).

  (ii) *Disadvantages*

   (1) High cost per interview - travel, wages, etc.
   (2) Interviewer bias can occur: the interviewer may influence the answers.
   (3) Inaccuracies in recording can occur.
   (4) The number of interviews per day is restricted.

(b) *Telephone interview.* This is, of course, restricted to samples of people with telephones. Contact is made by telephone and the people are then questioned.

  (i) *Advantages*

   (1) Speed.
   (2) Interviewers are easily supervised.
   (3) The cost per interview is low.
   (4) The sample can be widely spread over the country - no travel expenses.
   (5) It is better for surveys of higher social classes.
   (6) People who might otherwise be inaccessible can be contacted.

1: Strategic marketing management: planning and control

(7) Advantage over mail (postal) survey in that the respondent hears only one question at a time. Therefore, there is no bias due to *subsequent* questions.

(ii) *Disadvantages*

(1) Telephone subscribers are not always representative of the general population.

(2) Only a short questionnaire can be used.

(3) Observation is not possible, so no information can be obtained in this way.

(4) It is difficult to predict suitable times to telephone the respondents.

(5) Recalls are necessary when a number is engaged.

(6) It is possible that a secretary may prevent you getting to the person you want.

(7) The quality of the interviewer must be very high indeed.

(c) *Postal or mail survey method.* Respondents are contacted by post. Questionnaires to be completed and returned are sent to randomly selected individuals. Follow-up letters may have to be sent to those who have not replied. Sometimes a small gift is enclosed as an incentive to complete the questionnaire. The questionnaire needs to be short and easy to follow. The questionnaires may be enclosed in newspapers, periodicals or attached to some consumer product.

(i) *Advantages*

(1) A widely spread sample can be reached without increased costs.

(2) It can be much cheaper than field survey method.

(3) No interviewer training is required.

(4) Interviewer bias is avoided.

(5) Certain groups which cannot be reached easily by other methods can be reached by post.

(6) The respondent can fill in the form at his or her own convenience.

(7) Information regarding several members of a household can be obtained at one go.

(8) Information which the respondent has to verify can also be obtained

(ii) *Disadvantages*

(1) Respondents select themselves and are therefore not fully representative of the population.

(2) The refusal rate tends to be very high - higher than any other method of inquiry. Returns will usually fall between 10 and 50 per cent. Moreover, those that do respond are unusual in displaying an interest. The chief problem is that of non-response. The size of this depends on several things:
- the population under survey;
- the subject of the survey;
- the effectiveness of the covering letter; and
- the sponsorship (ie who is wanting the information).

(3) Respondents may not understand the questions and no interviewer is there to explain them.

(4) The questionnaire has to be simple and short which limits the obtainable information.

(5) Up to date address lists are difficult to obtain and maintain.

(6) Returns can dribble in slowly and this stage of the survey can take considerable time.

(7) Personal questions may alienate the respondent and may have to be omitted.

(8) The answers may be influenced by the opinions of other people - there is no way this can be checked. Therefore, they are not appropriate for testing a person's knowledge on a topic.

(9) The wording has to be perfect.

(10) There is no chance to add observational data (eg type of house, the person's appearance, etc).

(iii) Some methods of increasing response rates include the following.

(1) Include a stamped addressed envelope.

(2) Pay great attention to the covering letter.

(3) Use code numbers so you can tell who has not responded. This will need explanation probably in the covering letter. While this may put a few respondents off it is likely that the gains will outweigh the losses.

(4) Follow up to non-respondents ie sending another copy and writing 'You probably did not receive...' One government survey obtained 38% response rate at the first attempt, an extra 32% on the first reminder, and an extra 7% in a second reminder, lifting the total response rate to 77%.

(5) Use of incentives - free sample or payment (as in the Family Expenditure Survey).

(d) *Group interview method.* A small, carefully selected group of people is invited to discuss whatever topic is under review. A questionnaire can be used, the discussion can be taped or an observer can take notes.

(i) *Advantages*

(1) Useful for research concerned with motives and opinions where factors such as social status and acceptance are involved.

(2) Reasonably cheap - one observer can handle up to ten people at a time.

(3) The spontaneous discussion may provide information not obtainable by other means.

(ii) *Disadvantages*

(1) Doubtful if such a group can be regarded as really representative of the population.

(2) The information obtained is not usually suitable for statistical analysis.

(3) It is possible that the more vocal members may have some undue influence on the group opinion.

(4) The observer must be a psychologist or similarly trained person. His job is not to intrude, only to keep the discussion to the point.

(e) *Panel method.* A group of people are selected, and their services are retained over a period of time to obtain a series of answers.

(i) Types of panel include the following.

(1) Consumer purchasing panel.
(2) Consumer product testing panel.
(3) Retail audit panel.
(4) Radio audience panel.
(5) Television audience panel.

(ii) Recruitment of panels is by personal interview of a cross section of the population. Those chosen are given diaries in which they are asked to enter, for example, all their purchases of the commodities being surveyed. Diaries are returned at regular intervals (often weekly). Alternatively the panel can be interviewed periodically. This has been successfully used for radio, television and opinion research.

(iii) *Advantages*

(1) Because the people involved stay the same over a period of time it is useful for researching into trends eg changing TV viewing habits.

1: Strategic marketing management: planning and control

(2) Data gathered over a period of time can be accumulated and factors underlying changes in trends analysed.

(3) Case histories of respondents can be used to provide relevant background material to responses.

(4) The panel, once established, may be used for enquiries on other subjects.

(iv) *Disadvantages*

(1) The membership of the panel is not fixed (death, removal, etc).

(2) Refusal to join the panel may destroy its representativeness. Often the less literate section of the population refuses to join.

(3) The fact that the members belong to the panel may affect their reactions over a period of time. They may become *less* typical.

(4) Recruitment is expensive (a long time before it yields returns).

(5) Much interviewing is necessary to replace lost panel members.

(6) Panel members may have to be visited regularly to check on their activity and reliability. This is costly.

(7) Panel members usually have to be rewarded.

(f) *Observational methods.* An observer simply records what he sees.

(i) Types of observational method include the following.

(1) *Stock audits* can be made at regular intervals in order to establish sales trends for certain products.

(2) *Passenger counts* are useful if poster advertising is being considered. Counts could involve pedestrians, motorists and passengers on public transport.

(3) *Behaviour observation.* Movements and behaviour of store customers are monitored to check store display and layout.

(4) *Participant observation.* The observer remains with subject for a period of time to see what the subject really does.

(ii) *Advantages*

(1) Respondent mistakes deriving from faulty memory are eliminated.
(2) Interviewer bias is slight and may not occur at all.

(iii) *Disadvantages*

(1) People are not always reliable observers, although sometimes mechanical recording devices can be used.

(2) Only a limited amount of information can be obtained.

(3) The cost may be high.

Briefing a market research agency

6.12 In your marketing research plan you will need to decide whether to appoint an agency and if so how to go about this, and the selection criteria you will use. It is advisable to draw up a shortlist of agencies based on size, location, expertise, recommendation etc and approach, say, three of them for proposals and a quotation. The following notes will help you to draw up a brief.

6.13 *What the market research agency can expect from you*

(a) A research agency cannot be expected to provide satisfactory and comprehensive research proposals in the absence of any of the below; it is therefore in your interests to supply them.

(i) A statement of the research problems, preferably in the form of a written brief.

(ii) A setting of the problem in its general background and context. In some cases, users may be able to define their overall problem within its generalised context but not have the experience to define it in *research* terms.

(iii) An opportunity to meet and discuss the problem and its background

(iv) An indication of the decisions that are likely to be influenced by the research results and the uses to which the results are to be put (eg whether publication is envisaged).

(v) A broad indication of the budget available for the research project.

(b) There are three other things an agency can reasonably expect, though of themselves they will not necessarily affect the quality of research proposals.

(i) That you should only approach agencies on a formal basis when there is reasonable probability that the project under consideration will actually be commissioned.

(ii) If it is the type of project which you feel should be subject to tender, then you should restrict the agencies you approach to a reasonable number (say two to four), and inform them that they are competing. If you should submit a project to tender in this way, the agencies can reasonably expect an opportunity to meet you to discuss your reaction to the approach suggested in their research proposals before you make your final choice of agency. Agencies will often spend a considerable amount of time in the preparation of research proposals. It is desirable that this practice should continue but this will only be the case if agencies perceive their investment has some chance of paying off.

6.14 *What you can expect from the agency: general.* This first checklist details the criteria which can be used to assess the agency's general level of competence and will help in the decision as to whether, in principle, a particular agency will suit your requirements.

(a) Evidence of the background and quality of its research executives.

(b) Details of any specialists (psychologists, statisticians) employed full-time or on a consultant basis.

(c) Evidence of the company's experience that may be relevant to your particular situation; work on similar kinds of problems; work within the same market; experience of using relevant research techniques.

(d) Details of the field operation; selection and training of interviewers; levels of supervision; check on quality and accuracy.

(e) Details of editing, coding, and purchasing operations; quality and training of staff; supervision; checks on quality and accuracy.

(f) Details of analysis and tabulation, computers and machinery used, restrictions on numbers and types of tabulations.

(g) Details of normal standard of reporting; the style and content of reports.

(h) Details of accounting and legal aspects; normal billing procedures.

6.15 *What you can expect from the agency: specific*

This second check-list sets out the *specific points* you can expect an agency to include in its proposals for a particular project.

(a) It should be obvious from their statement of the research objectives and of the scope of the inquiry, that the agency understands your problem.

(b) Detailed descriptions of the research design including:

(i) a statement of the scope and nature of any preliminary desk research, qualitative work, or pilot studies;

(ii) for any quantitative study, a statement of the data collection technique (how the information is to be obtained) population to be sampled (who is to be interviewed). the size of the sample (how many are to be interviewed), the method of sample selection (how the individuals are to be selected).

(c) A statement of the cost of the project and a clear indication of the assumptions on which it is based and what is included eg assumptions made about length of interview, assumptions made about degree of executive involvement, whether personal briefing of interviewers is included, the number of copies of the report envisaged, the approximate number of tabulations envisaged; whether there will be a written interpretation of the tabulations, whether visual presentations of results is included.

(d) A reasonably detailed timetable for the project and a reasonably firm reporting date.

(e) The name(s) of the executive(s) responsible for the project.

6.16 *A marketing research programme* would contain the following.

(a) *Research brief.* This should define clearly the marketing problems to be investigated (eg the need for machines of a specific capacity, specific formulations of chemicals, likely demand for spares). It may be necessary to make some exploratory enquiries in certain areas of the organisation (eg selling arrangements, publicity methods, pricing structures in order to gain valuable background knowledge). The briefing must be thorough and honest on the part of the client, and the researcher must be prepared to probe, comment on unrealistic proposals, point out constraints. They should agree on the level of accuracy and the required submission date.

(b) *Work plan.* This should specify a simple model of the problem, specify the data to be collected and the methodology. It should give the timing of various operations. It should be shown how the work plan meets the objective of the research.

(c) *Collection of data* is the longest stage, and it is necessary to check the relative efficiency of alternative methods of data collection.

(d) *Analysis and evaluation of data.* Analysis pre-supposes sound data. Data have to be refined by means of tabulations analysis and interpretation. The analysis should ascertain significant relationships between variables. Systems of data storage and retrieval may be incorporated at this stage, with provision for updating and extending the data base as required.

6.17 *Presentation of findings.* Most findings have to be presented to two main groups, general management, and research specialists. Often, therefore, there have to be two reports - a fully documented technical report and a short, detailed account of major findings, conclusions and recommendations, abstracted from the first. The Market Research Society suggests the following minimum acceptable contents of a report should include the following.

Market research report

(a) Purpose of the survey
(b) For whom and by whom the survey was undertaken.
(c) General description of the universe covered
(d) Size and nature of the sample, including a description of any weighting methods used.
(e) The time when the field work was carried out.
(f) The method of interviewing employed.
(g) Adequate description of field staff and any control methods used.
(h) A copy of the questionnaire
(i) The factual findings
(j) Bases of percentages
(k) Geographical distribution of interviews.

6.18 A formal layout of an MR report is given below.

> 1 *Introduction*
> - Title of the report
> - Name of sponsor
> - Title of research organisation
> - Date of publication.
>
> 2 *Table of contents*
>
> 3 *Preface.* (Stating terms of reference and acknowledgement.)
>
> 4 *Statement of purpose.* (Elaboration of the terms of reference contained in the preface. It would outline the general nature of the problem and be investigated and specific hypotheses on which the research was based.)
>
> 5 *Methodology.* (Outline the stages through which the project passed, a statement of the definitions adopted, research techniques employed, sources of data used, details of sample size and composition, description of the methods of analysis employed, any explanatory observations.)
>
> 6 *Findings.* (Abstract of relevant data.)
>
> 7 *Conclusion.* (Used on findings.)
>
> 8 *Recommendations.* (Based on conclusions).
>
> 9 *Appendices.* (Detailed accounts of sample design and its theoretical reliability; copy of the questionnaire and instructions to interviewers; detailed statistical tables; bibliography and glossary of terms; details of any tests of reliability; theoretical proofs.)

(a) In a report intended for the management, conclusions and recommendations follow immediately after the statement of purpose or terms of reference, and methodology could be consigned to the appendixes.

(b) There will usually be a single page statement of the basic purpose and findings entitled Management or Executive Summary.

6.19 *Type of research.* Care needs to be taken to distinguish types of research (product research, advertising research, distribution research) and methods (desk research, field research, telephone research, observational research etc)

Retail audits and consumer panels

6.20 *Retail audits.* A retail audit is a form of market research which provides information for manufacturers about the sales, distribution and stocks of their products and of competing brands.

(a) It accounts for a substantial proportion of total expenditure on market research in this country, being sponsored mainly by manufacturers of food and pharmaceutical products.

(b) The need for a retail audit is apparent. Without it the manufacturer has little knowledge of how goods are reaching the final consumer. It is true that a manufacturer will know how much it is selling from the factory but, except for the rare case of direct selling to consumers, it will have very scanty knowledge of the movement of his product from the wholesaler to the retailer and on to the actual purchaser. Thus if ex-factory sales rise it will not be certain whether this is due to an increase in consumer demand or whether it is the result of wholesalers or retailers increasing their stocks. Moreover, a manufacturer's own sales figures tell nothing about how competitors are faring. A manufacturer might, for example, know that its own sales are up 5 per cent on last year. This gives no grounds for complacency if its main competitors' sales are up 20 per cent. Retail audits enable a company to watch its own and its competitors' sales trends and market shares and to modify its marketing strategy accordingly.

6.21 *Special panels for test marketing.* Retail audit panels provide a means for testing a new product in a restricted area before large-scale production and distribution are embarked upon. The product tested might be a completely new one or might only be new to a manufacturer wishing to get into a particular market.

(a) The basic operation in test auditing is to provide sales and market share information for three consecutive periods: before the product is launched, the launch period itself and after the launch.

(b) The object of this type of testing is to avoid making mistakes on a large scale, by confining the initial marketing operation to one area. The area chosen is usually an ITV region, preferably an area small enough to be reasonably inexpensive to test and at the same time sufficiently representative to the country as a whole to make test results valid.

(c) The test operation proceeds as follows.

(i) Before the product is launched audit data are collected to establish the existing market pattern. After the new brand has been launched the immediate impact is observed from the audit figures. Initial sales figures can, of course, be misleading: the auditing operation is therefore continued until the market has settled down to its new equilibrium level. The manufacturer, having noted the reception of his product in the test area can decide whether to extend the marketing area or whether any strengthening of the product or of the marketing method is necessary. Modifications to the product or to its presentation can be made and their effects measured. When the product is finally approved and the best marketing strategy has been decided, it is ready for launching over a wider area, maybe on a national scale. This may be up to two years after the initial launch in the test area, reflecting the care and detailed planning necessary when introducing a new product.

(ii) A test marketing area affords the first opportunity for a manufacturer to observe the reactions of consumers to his product under actual market conditions. Such reactions differ from those to other forms of product testing (eg free samples, in that the product is actually purchased over the counter by the consumer).

(iii) A test marketing operation also enables the manufacturer to assess the trade's reaction to the new product, in particular to such matters as margins, packaging, display material and advertising.

(iv) The test operation consists basically of a 'before, during and after' measurement, principally of market share. The 'before and after' periods should be 'as long as possible' but the actual length is determined as usual by the time and money available. Nevertheless, it is essential that the 'after' period should be sufficiently long to enable the *initial* impact to subside. What is really required is a knowledge of what proportion of the sales are repeat purchases. This question can be answered more precisely by consumer research than retail audit data, and both forms of research are sometimes used. Repeat purchase information can be implied from retail audit data if enough time after the initial launch is allowed for market conditions to settle at their new levels.

(v) Test marketing has been described up to now in terms of testing in a television area. This is how most test marketing is done, partly because of the variety of conditions to be found in such a large area and partly because the television companies are beginning to provide a test marketing service for advertisers, often in conjunction with one of the retail audit organisations. Product testing can, however, be confined to a single town or to a sample of a few towns.

(vi) The use of a test panel is not confined to the testing of a new product. The effect of changing the packaging, advertising or marketing policy for an established product may also be measured with the same idea of avoiding mistakes on a large scale with consequent waste of money or, worse, damage to the brand image.

6.22 *Limitations of retail audit*. The technique provides information which is of fundamental importance to manufacturers and which cannot satisfactorily be obtained by any other means. However, the research is based on sampling techniques which depart from random methods, sometimes to a considerable extent. Yet using extremely small samples (usually of the order of 1% of the population being sampled) it provides information on which marketing and production decisions can be based. Care is needed in the interpretation of results from retail audit. The limitations of the data and the danger of unwarranted generalisations must be fully appreciated. The main dangers are as follows.

(a) Generalising from the sample to a population wider than that from which the sample was drawn (eg assuming that results from stores who do co-operate apply to those who do not).

(b) Attempting to base large-scale marketing strategies on tests made in only one or two towns.

(c) Basing decisions on test figures before the effect of the *initial* launch or advertising impact has died down. (People might try out the product once.)

(d) Competitors might intervene to distort the data obtained.

Retail audit is now a firmly established and respectable form of research with most manufacturers of food, cosmetics, pharmaceutical, and other consumer goods. The money spent checking how a brand is selling against competitors' brands is small compared with the money spent on advertising the brand.

6.23 *Consumer panels*. Whilst retail audits provide a great deal of valuable data on sales, they do not tell you *who* buys from particular outlets. Bearing in mind that markets are essentially people (ie and their wants and needs) you should want to know more about your actual customers than the retail audit can tell you. This gap is addressed by a representative sample of consumers in the form of a panel or series of panels. These consumers maintain detailed records of what they buy and why they change brand loyalties or store loyalties.

6.24 Information obtainable from consumer panels is as follows.

(a) Who buys?
 (i) Socio-economic class.
 (ii) Age group

(b) How good is your distribution?
 (i) By area
 (ii) Town or country?
 (iii) How strong is your distribution through every type of outlet?

(c) How frequently do people purchase your product?
(d) Do people buy your product more than just once?
(e) Use of 'size of household' analysis.
(f) Where is your greatest appeal (eg to households with children)?
(g) Does seasonal change affect your sales unduly?
(h) What makes a customer switch brands?

6.25 Advertising/communications research is covered in Chapter 2 on Marketing Communications Strategy.

The marketing information system (MkIS)

6.26 Many marketing decisions are taken on a continuous basis (eg decisions are taken on various aspects of the marketing mix - sales, advertising, sales promotion at least annually). A continuous plan of information is also required for control purposes. A marketing information system (MkIS), normally part of the Management Information System (MIS), meets these needs. A diagram can be found on the following page.

6.27 The MkIS will contain the following subsystems.

(a) *Internal reports (and accounts) systems* provides the following.

(i) Results data.
(ii) Provides measures of current activity performance.
(iii) Sales, costs, stock information.
(iv) Possible areas for improvement include the timeliness, availability and distribution of reports.

(b) *Marketing intelligence system*

(i) *Happenings data* (eg what competitors are doing).
(ii) It provides information on developments in the environment.
(iii) It involves scanning and the dissemination of a wide range of intelligence.
(iv) Possible areas of improvement include:

(1) increased use of salesmen as intelligence agents;
(2) additional intelligence sources;
(3) purchasing data from special marketing intelligence services;
(4) processing of intelligence by improving the system for evaluation, abstraction, dissemination, storage and retrieval

(c) *Marketing research system contains* specific studies of marketing problems, opportunities and effectiveness.

(d) *Analytical marketing system (Management science)*. This uses models to explain, predict and improve marketing processes. Models may be descriptive, decisional, verbal, graphical or mathematical.

All subsystems should be interactive.

6.28 Data collected needs to be processed in some way to produce coherent information.

(a) Considerations for a good storage and retrieval system include the following.

(i) Manual or computerised, or some compromise?
(ii) The extent of hard copy back up.
(iii) Cross referencing of data.
(iv) Data protection legislation considerations.

(b) Irrelevant data must be eliminated.

(c) Information should be:

(i) relevant;
(ii) concise;
(iii) of an appropriate level of accuracy or detail (eg level of aggregation);
(iv) cost-effective;
(v) directed to the right person;
(vi) such as to inspire confidence in the user;
(vii) timely (current, or relevant to the time it is required).

(d) Dissemination of information considerations include:

(i) distribution list;
(ii) use of newsletters for standardised regular information;
(iii) how much value is added by system?

6.29 An MkIS has implications for costs and for the organisation's practices.

(a) Training of existing and new staff.

(b) Staff with specialist skills might be recruited. Job descriptions and specifications might need to change.

(c) Organisational considerations include:

(i) reallocation of duties
(ii) the degree to which the system should be centralised

(d) Costs incurred include:
  (i) specialist staff
  (ii) retraining
  (iii) equipment
  (iv) system running costs

(e) Time is needed before the system will display any benefits

6.30 The design of any MkIS should:

(a) recognise user limitations in defining and then fully using information;
(b) ensure users understand the systems and are in position to evaluate and control it;
(c) review the system regularly and improve feedback;
(d) clarify the true meaning and highlight the limitations of information provided;
(e) be flexible;
(f) recognise that a system is only as effective as designers and users make it.

6.31 It is important to remember, though, that:

(a) managers may not know what information they need and want;

(b) even if provided with the information, managers do not always make good use of it;

(c) more communication often means better performance;

(d) the managers do not have to understand how an information system works, but they should get some idea of the benefits it can give them to encourage them to use it.

1: Strategic marketing management: planning and control

The marketing information system

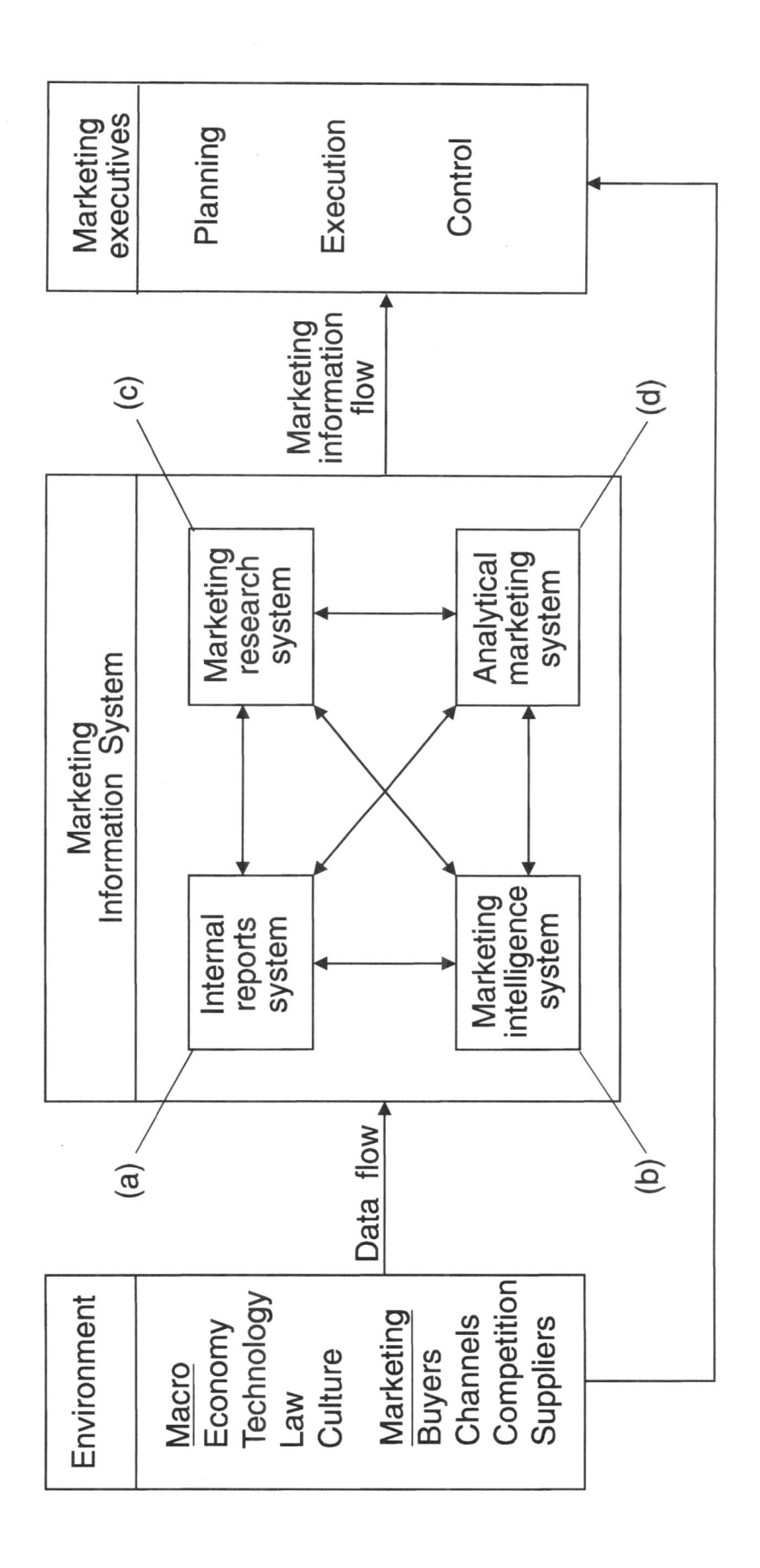

```
                    Marketing Information System
┌─────────────┐   ┌──────────────────────────────────────┐   ┌──────────────┐
│ Environment │   │   ┌──────────┐      ┌──────────┐     │   │  Marketing   │
│             │   │   │Marketing │◄────►│Analytical│     │   │  executives  │
│ Macro       │   │(c)│ research │      │marketing │(d)  │   │              │
│  Economy    │   │   │  system  │      │  system  │     │   │  Planning    │
│  Technology │   │   └──────────┘      └──────────┘     │──►│              │
│  Law        │──►│       ▲ ▲  ╲         ╱  ▲ ▲          │   │  Execution   │
│  Culture    │   │       │  ╲  ╲       ╱  ╱  │          │   │              │
│ Marketing   │   │       │   ╲  ╲     ╱  ╱   │          │   │  Control     │
│  Buyers     │   │       ▼    ╲  ╲   ╱  ╱    ▼          │   │              │
│  Channels   │   │   ┌──────────┐      ┌──────────┐     │   └──────────────┘
│  Competition│   │(a)│ Internal │◄────►│Marketing │(b)  │          ▲
│  Suppliers  │   │   │ reports  │      │intelligence│   │          │
│             │   │   │  system  │      │  system  │    │          │
└─────────────┘   │   └──────────┘      └──────────┘     │          │
      │           └──────────────────────────────────────┘          │
      │                      ▲          Marketing                   │
      │              Data flow          information flow            │
      └─────────────────────────────────────────────────────────────┘
```

6.32 The benefits possible with a sophisticated MkIS are outlined below.

Typical applications	Benefits	Examples
Control systems		
1. Control of marketing costs	1. More timely computerised reports	1. Undesirable cost trends are spotted quickly so that corrective action may be taken sooner
2. Diagnosis of poor sales performance	2. Flexible on-line retrieval of data	2. Executives can ask supplementary questions of the computer to help pinpoint reasons for a sales decline
3. Management of fashion goods	3. Automatic spotting of problems and opportunities	3. Fast-moving fashion items are reported daily for re-order and slow moving items are reported for price reduction
4. Flexible promotion strategy	4. Cheaper, more detailed and more frequent reports	4. On-going evaluation of a promotional campaign permits reallocation of funds to areas behind target
Planning systems		
1. Forecasting	1. Automatic translation of terms and classifications between departments	1. Survey-based forecasts of demand for industrial goods can be automatically translated into parts requirements and production schedules
2. Promotional planning and corporate long-range planning	2. Systematic testing of alternative promotional plans	2. Simulation models, both developed and operated with the help of data bank information can be used for promotional planning
3. Credit management	3. Programmed executive decision rules can operate on data bank information	3. Credit decisions are automatically made as each order is processed
4. Purchasing	4. Detailed sales reporting permits automation of management decisions	4. Computer automatically repurchases standard items on the basis of sales data with programmed decision rule
Research systems		
1. Advertising strategy	1. Additional manipulation of data is possible when stored on computer in an unaggregated file	1. Sales analysis is possible by new market segment breakdowns
2. Pricing strategy	2. Improved storage and retrieval capability allows new types of data to be collected and used	2. Systematic recording of information about past R&D contract bidding situation allows improved bidding strategies
3. Evaluation of advertising expenditures	3. Well-designed data banks permit integration and comparison of different sets of data	3. Advertising expenditures are compared to shipments by country to provide information about advertising effectiveness

Chapter roundup

- This chapter has endeavoured to cover those areas of the Strategic Marketing Management: Planning and Control syllabus relevant to the Analysis and Decision examination. Consequently it has dealt with the practical aspects of the issues you will face, rather than a theoretical examination of them.

- The marketing plan is one of many functional plans, but at strategic level it has a great impact on the organisation's corporate plan. After all, deciding the business the organisation is in (the products and services it provides to its chosen markets) is a corporate as well as a marketing issue. Growth in sales volumes and value is the overall marketing objective. Marketing planning requires:
    - an analysis of the current situation (a marketing audit);
    - an awareness of the business's mission (what business are we in now? what business would we like to be in in 5-10 years time?);
    - objectives, ensuring that corporate objectives are translated into marketing terms;
    - strategies (eg Ansoff, segmentation) for achieving those objectives;
    - tactics (marketing mix proposals: product, price, place, promotion and the three extra Ps for service marketing, people, processes and physical evidence).

- Marketing research and the marketing information system provide essential underpinning to the planning and control of marketing strategies.

Test your knowledge

1. Draw a diagram of the planning process. (see para 1.13)
2. What is the difference between strategy and tactics, in marketing? (1.22, 1.23)
3. Who or what is the focus of a marketing plan? (2.3)
4. What is SWOT? (2.17)
5. What subjective techniques of sales forecasting might you use? (3.10)
6. Why are budgets compiled? (3.14, 3.16)
7. What is the importance of the sales budget? (3.24)
8. Describe the expense budgets related to marketing (3.55)
9. What strategies are suggested by the Ansoff matrix? (3.80, 3.81)
10. What are critical success factors? (3.85)
11. What are three generic strategies for obtaining competitive advantage? (4.3)
12. Describe competitor response models. (4.5)
13. Distinguish between products and services (4.14, 4.15).
14. What is value analysis? (4.24)
15. What would be contained in an information specification for a firm? (6.5)
16. List some sources of marketing research data. (6.8)
17. At the back of this Tutorial Text you will find a review form which asks you for your comments on this Tutorial Text. How does this rate as MR in your opinion? (6.11) (Can you improve it?)
18. What are the drawbacks of a MkIS? (6.31)

Chapter 2

MARKETING COMMUNICATIONS STRATEGY

This chapter covers the following topics.

1. Marketing communications strategy at corporate level
2. Communications planning
3. Promotion and the promotional mix
4. Legal and other constraints
5. Campaign planning
6. Selecting and briefing agencies
7. Media and media research
8. Branding
9. Communications research
10. Internal communications and the organisation

Introduction

This chapter emphasises the practical aspects of marketing communications relevant to the case study. This material will *not* be sufficient to get you through the Marketing Communications Strategy exam: buy the BPP Study Text (written by the senior examiner for that subject) if you are taking it.

1 MARKETING COMMUNICATIONS STRATEGY AT CORPORATE LEVEL

1.1 Marketing communications are only a part of the total communications output of any company or organisation. Total communications breaks down into:

(a) external communications (to people outside the organisation);
(b) internal communications (to people within it).

Corporate identity

1.2 Any organisation cannot help having a *corporate identity*. The physical aspects of an organisation, eg premises, literature, staff duties, vehicles etc convey impressions or images. A corporate identity relating to the firm is sometimes promoted as distinct from the firm's products. The penalty for not having a good corporate identity is perhaps best expressed by the following statements.

> I don't know who you are
> I don't know your company
> I don't know your company's products
> I don't know what your company stands for
> I don't know your company's customers
> I don't know your company's record
> I don't know your company's reputation
> Now what was it you wanted to sell me?

2: Marketing communications strategy

1.3 The salesperson representing, say, Rolls Royce, a company with a recognisable image would be unlikely to have to face the above communication barriers. There are, however, many other reasons for developing appropriate corporate identities, including the following.

(a) The increasing importance of public relations (eg establishing the right relationships with governments, opinion influencing pressure groups, local communities in the vicinity of offices, factories, distribution centres).

(b) The need to attract and retain investment.

(c) The need to attract labour of the right kind in the right numbers (depending on the level of employment etc).

(d) The growing realisation of the importance of good relationships with suppliers and institutions involved in forward distribution processes: wholesalers, agents, distributors.

(e) The need to foster a feeling of belonging within an organisation-this is particularly in evidence in large, widely spread groups and/or merged or re-structured units.

(f) The realisation of the cumulative impact of multiple repetition.

1.4 You may find the following distinctions (Olms 1989) help to avoid confusion.

(a) *Corporate personality* 'is the soul, the persona, the spirit, the culture of the organisation manifested in some way. A corporate personality is not necessarily something tangible that you can see, feel or touch - although it may be'.

(b) *Corporate identity* 'is the tangible manifestation of a corporate personality......It is the identity that projects and reflects the reality of the corporate personality'.

(c) *Corporate image* 'is what people actually perceive of a corporate personality or corporate identity'.

We should all be aware that the image actually received is not always that intended by the message sender - hence the need for pre-testing. For example a bank sends messages saying that it is friendly and caring but potential customers might find these messages patronising and insincere.

1.5 *Corporate public relations*. Many companies which recognise the importance of having a good corporate identity manage their external/internal communications by the use of a Corporate PR function or department. The Institute of Public Relations defines public relations (PR) as 'the deliberate, planned and sustained effort to establish and maintain mutual understanding between an organisation and its publics'. There are eight basic publics for PR.

(a) The community at large - people living near the premises or affected by them.

(b) Employees and their unions

(c) Customers - past, present and future

(d) Suppliers - of materials and non-financial services

(e) The money market - shareholders, banks, insurers, potential investors.

(f) Distributors - agents, wholesalers, retailers etc

(g) Potential employees

(h) Opinion leaders - all those whose opinions could help or harm the organisation including media editors.

1.6 Care needs to be taken therefore to distinguish between corporate PR and marketing or product/service PR. You will find that some authors prefer to use the term 'publicity' to describe the sub-function of PR which seeks to gain favourable editorial publicity in the media about a firm's products and services. More about this comes later in Section 3 on the promotional mix.

1.7 Occasionally, firms use *corporate advertising* (eg Hanson Trust a little while ago) to build public awareness of their size and activities. Conglomerates do this for a variety of reasons(eg to purvey an image of ecological friendliness to communicate with shareholders, and influence public opinion).

2 COMMUNICATIONS PLANNING

Integration of marketing communications

2.1. It is essential that *marketing* communications are integrated with *corporate* communications and that all elements of the marketing communications (promotional) mix are also harmonised. All a firm's communications need to say the same thing to avoid confusing and alienating the firm's customers, potential customers, and publics.

2.2 A model of the process is given below.

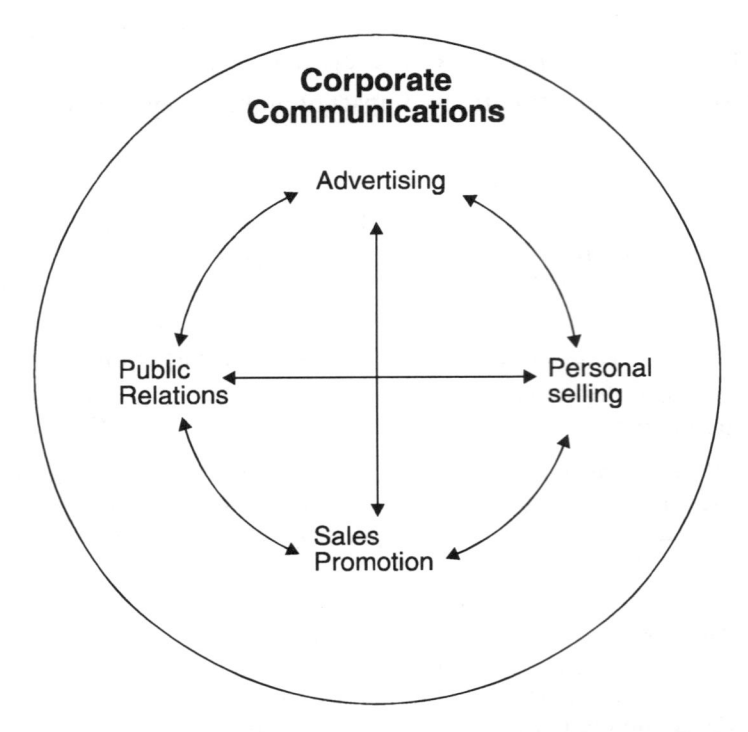

[Diagram: Corporate Communications encircling Advertising, Personal selling, Sales Promotion, Public Relations]

Communications planning formats follow the same general framework of any planning activity with the additional considerations that we need:

(a) to define clearly the target audiences with which we wish to communicate;

(b) to decide the messages we wish to send and the most appropriate media to carry these messages to the target audiences;

(c) to pre-test (to ensure the messages will have the desired effect);

(d) and to post-track (to ensure the messages have reached the target audiences at the right time, the measure of recall and conviction etc).

Corporate vs marketing communications objectives

2.3 Again we need to distinguish between corporate communications objectives and marketing communications objectives. Examples might be as follows.

(a) *Some potential corporate communications objectives*

(i) To assure the general public that the organisation's policies are environmentally friendly

(ii) To resist take-over by a bidder

(iii) To gain governmental assistance

(iv) To announce changes in the Board of Directors

(v) To promote awareness of the corporate mission

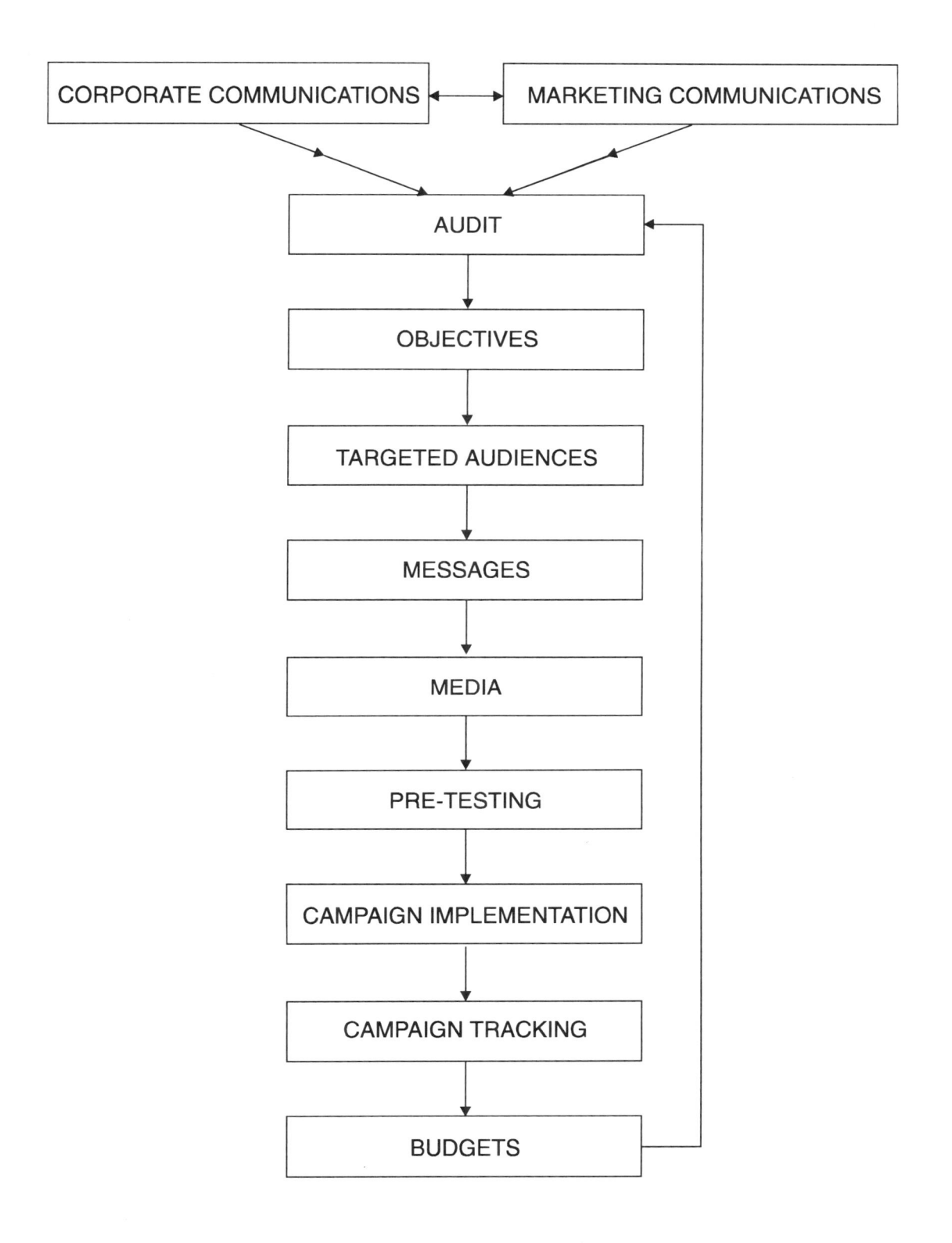

2: Marketing communications strategy

```
CORPORATE COMMUNICATIONS ⟷ MARKETING COMMUNICATIONS
              ↓           ↓
            AUDIT ←──────────────┐
              ↓                  │
          OBJECTIVES             │
              ↓                  │
       TARGETED AUDIENCES        │
              ↓                  │
           MESSAGES              │
              ↓                  │
            MEDIA                │
              ↓                  │
         PRE-TESTING             │
              ↓                  │
      CAMPAIGN IMPLEMENTATION    │
              ↓                  │
        CAMPAIGN TRACKING        │
              ↓                  │
           BUDGETS ──────────────┘
```

(b) Potential marketing communications objectives

   (i) *Consumer communications*
      (1) To inform about a new product
      (2) To correct misconceptions about a product
      (3) To increase frequency of use
      (4) To remind people about a product
      (5) To present special offers
      (6) To educate consumers in how to use a product
      (7) To build an image for the product/company
      (8) To build up consumer loyalty

   (ii) *Trade communications*
      (1) To provide information
      (2) To inform about promotional programmes
      (3) To present special trade offers
      (4) To avoid stockpiling
      (5) To educate the trade on product usage
      (5) To build patronage motives

(c) Some communications are quantitative (eg numbers of enquiries) and qualitative (eg aimed at changing attitudes).

3 PROMOTION AND THE PROMOTIONAL MIX

3.1 The words promotion and communications tend to be used synonymously but some authors prefer to use the terms *promotion* and *promotional mix* to distinguish marketing communications from corporate communications. The rest of this chapter is concerned with marketing communications.

3.2 Some benefits of promotion are as follows.

(a) Personal contact is expensive. Appropriate promotion takes the place of personal contact, and has a lower cost, for example by mailshots.

(b) Promotion helps prepare the ground for personal sales.

(c) Customers are forgetful. Promotion can remind customers or potential customers of the firm's products and services.

(d) Sales visits consume time. Promotion can convey some information in advance, making calls more productive.

(e) Promotion can promote the wide range of a firm's activities.

(f) The morale of staff can be boosted if the firm has a good image.

(g) Promotion can communicate to customers who are otherwise hard to contact.

(h) Promotion can help identify potential new customers, through enquiries received for follow-up.

3.3 Consider also the following example of a buying behaviour model for a retail setting and the effect of promotion (advertising, personal selling, PR/publicity and sales promotion) on the model's outcomes. 'Dupont' is a manufacturer of branded consumer goods distributed through retail outlets.

The Dupont consumer buying behaviour model

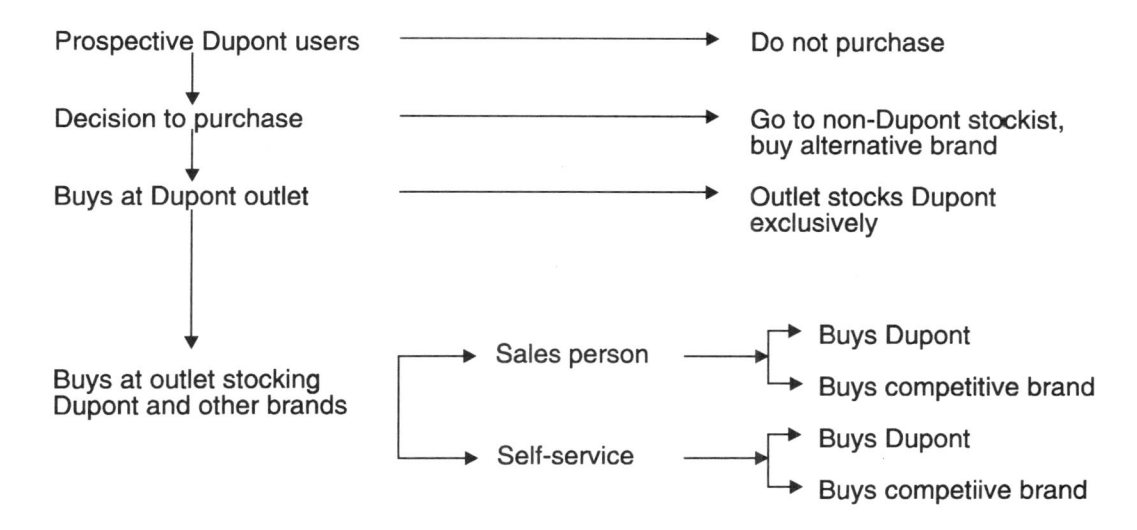

```
Prospective Dupont users  ─────────────▶  Do not purchase
        │
        ▼
Decision to purchase      ─────────────▶  Go to non-Dupont stockist,
        │                                  buy alternative brand
        ▼
Buys at Dupont outlet     ─────────────▶  Outlet stocks Dupont
        │                                  exclusively
        ▼
Buys at outlet stocking   ───▶ Sales person ───▶ Buys Dupont
Dupont and other brands                          Buys competitive brand
                          ───▶ Self-service ───▶ Buys Dupont
                                                 Buys competiive brand
```

The potentially beneficial effects of promotion on the above model for Dupont are as follows.

(a) It increases the number of prospective Dupont users.

(b) It increases the number of outlets stocking Dupont or the number of people using existing Dupont outlets.

(c) It influences more customers to specify Dupont despite what the salesperson may suggest.

(d) It increases the number of salespeople suggesting Dupont.

(e) It increases the number of self-service customers selecting Dupont.

A problem, of course, is that other people are 'promoting' as well.

3.4 Each of the four elements of the promotional mix has its own submix which requires planning and decisions, as illustrated in the following chart.

Part A: Background knowledge relevant to analysis and decision

ADVERTISING SUBMIX

The role of advertising
Target audiences
Creative approach
Deciding on the message
Deciding on the media
Selection of an agency
Deciding the advertising spend

SALES PROMOTION SUBMIX

The role of sales promotion
Target audiences
Creative approach
Deciding on the media
Selection of an agency
Deciding the advertising spend
Evaluating effectiveness

THE PROMOTIONAL SUBMIX

ADVERTISING
SALES PROMOTION
PUBLIC RELATIONS
PERSONAL SELLING

PERSONAL SELLING SUBMIX

The role of the Sales force
Determining buyer behaviour
Selling methods/strategies
Sales force support
Sales force size and structure
Recruitment and selection
Training
Direction and motivation
Remuneration
Evaluation and control

PUBLIC RELATIONS SUBMIX

The role of P.R.
Corporate identity and image
Publics
Internal marketing
Media relations
Agencies
Sponsorship
Exhibitions / PR events
Publicity

3.5 The elements of the promotional mix, like the elements of the marketing mix need to be harmonised for maximum productivity.

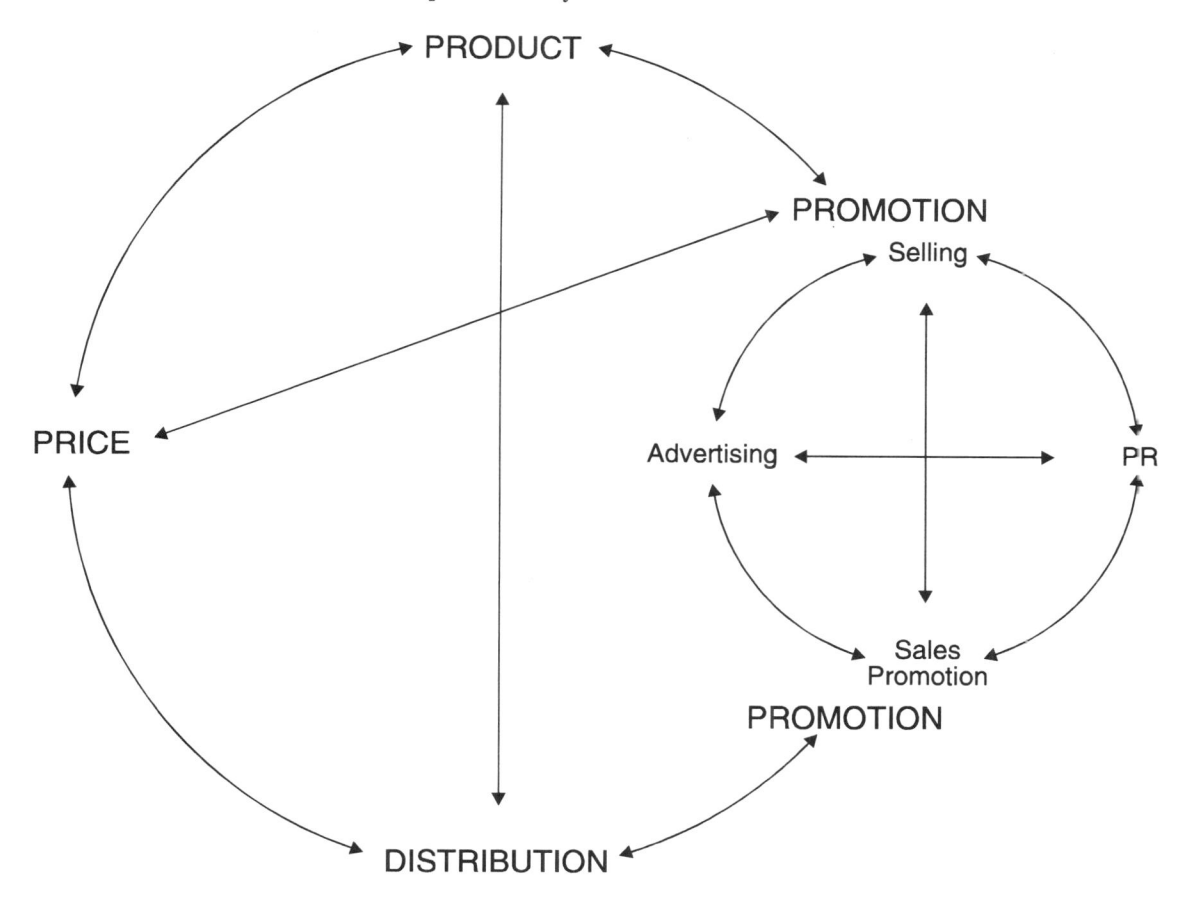

```
                    PRODUCT
                   ↗       ↖
                  /           ↘
                 /            PROMOTION
                /              ↗ Selling ↖
               /              /    ↑      \
         PRICE ←             /     |       \
              ↖            Advertising ←→ PR
                ↘            \     |      /
                  ↘           \    ↓     /
                    ↘          ↘ Sales  ↙
                      ↘         Promotion
                        ↘     PROMOTION
                          ↘  ↙
                       DISTRIBUTION
```

Deciding the right promotional mix

3.6 In trying to increase market share (a marketing objective) using a promotional strategy (rather than a price decrease or new product introduction) we do of course need to decide the right promotional mix. Increases in sales can be brought about by:

(a) more advertising; or
(b) more customer incentives; or
(c) better PR; or by
(d) enlarging the sales force; or
(e) as is usually the case by a mix of all four measures.

The decision then becomes how much more advertising, how many more salespeople etc.

3.7 In taking these decisions we ideally want to know the relative efficacy of each action. This can possibly be determined by experimentation and/or observation of competitor actions, or indeed similar actions in different markets. Unfortunately for marketing managers, favourable reactions to previous promotional initiatives are not always repeated. This is because markets change, competitors act differently etc. However, you should find the following general advantages and disadvantages of major promotion methods (as proposed by Peter and Olson) helpful in making your decisions.

Advertising	
Advantages	*Disadvantages*
Can reach many consumers simultaneously Relatively less cost per exposure Excellent for creating brand images High degree of flexibility and variety of media to choose from; can accomplish many different types of promotion objectives	Many consumers reached are not potential buyers (waste of promotion expenditure) High visibility makes advertising a major target of marketing critics Advertisement exposure time is usually brief Advertisements are often quickly and easily screened out by customers

Personal selling	
Advantages	*Disadvantages*
Can be the most persuasive promotion tool; salespeople can directly influence purchase behaviours Allows two-way communication Often necessary for technically complex products Allows direct one-on-one targeting of promotional effort	High cost per contact Sales training and motivation can be expensive and difficult Personal selling often has a poor image, making salesforce recruitment difficult Poorly done sales presentations can hurt sales as well as company, product and brand images

Sales promotion	
Advantages	*Disadvantages*
Excellent approach for short-term price reductions for stimulating demand A large variety of sales promotion tools to choose from Can be effective for changing a variety of consumer behaviours. Can be easily tied in with other promotion tools	May influence primarily brand-loyal customers to stock up at lower price but attract few new customers May have only short-term impact Overuse of price-related sales promotion tools may hurt brand image and profits Effective sales promotions are easily copied by competitors

Publicity	
Advantages	*Disadvantages*
As 'free advertising', publicity can be positive and stimulate demand at no cost May be perceived by consumers as more credible, because it is not paid for by the seller Consumers may pay more attention to these messages, because they are not quickly screened out as are many advertisements	Company cannot completely control the content of publicity messages Publicity is not always available Limited repetition of publicity messages; seldom a long-term promotion tool for brands Publicity can be negative and hurt sales as well as company product, and brand images

Pull and *push* promotional strategies in retail marketing

3.8 The following two diagrams illustrate these push and pull strategies.

(a) The push strategy is one where the producer concentrates on selling in to the channel in the hope that its goods will sell out.

(b) By contrast the pull strategy is where the producer advertises heavily and directly to consumers to create demand so that consumers ask for its goods which the channel is then induced to stock. In fast moving consumer goods most producers employ both policies to gain maximum effect.

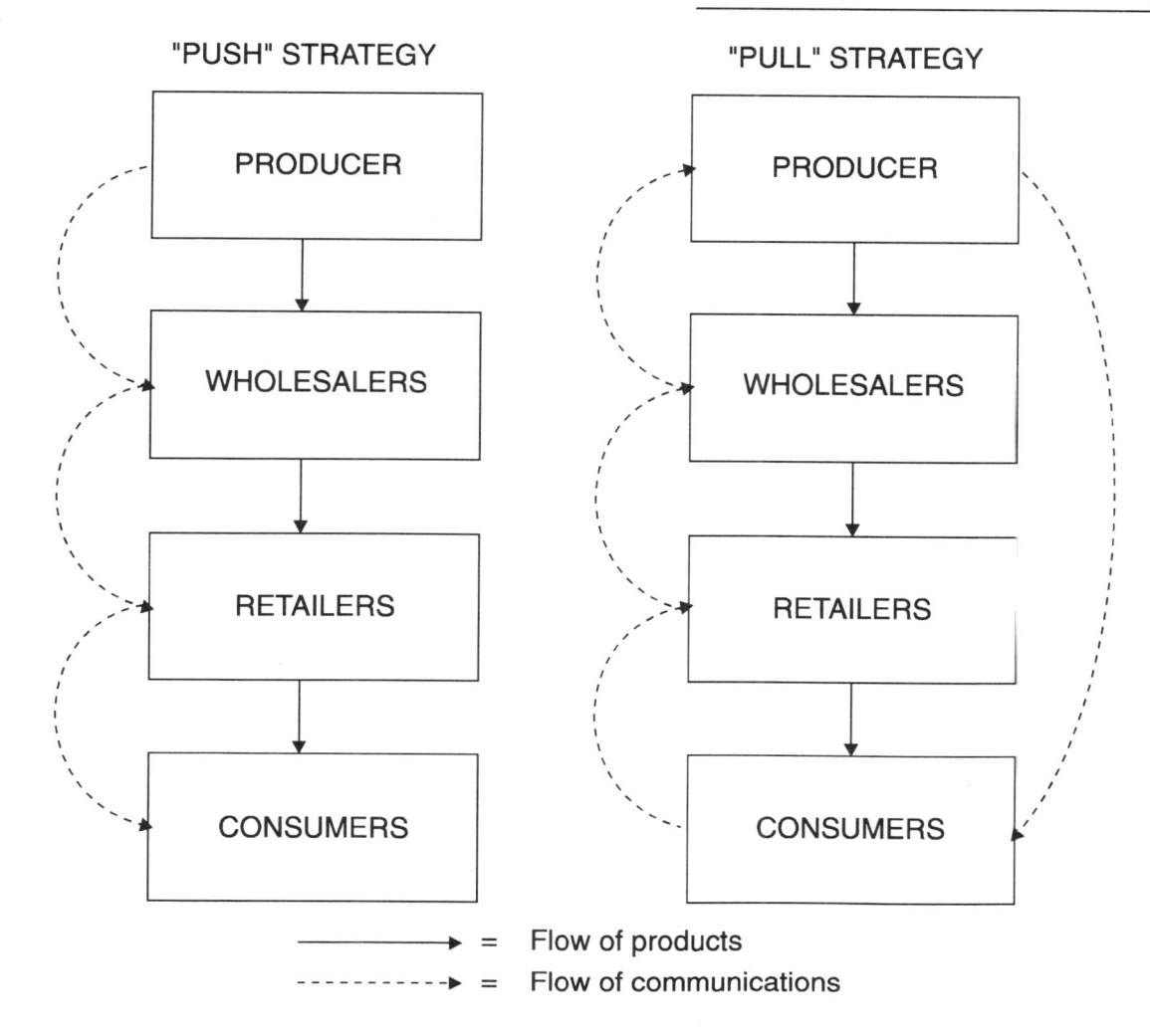

"PUSH" STRATEGY

PRODUCER → WHOLESALERS → RETAILERS → CONSUMERS

"PULL" STRATEGY

PRODUCER → WHOLESALERS → RETAILERS → CONSUMERS

⟶ = Flow of products
------⟶ = Flow of communications

Push versus pull strategies

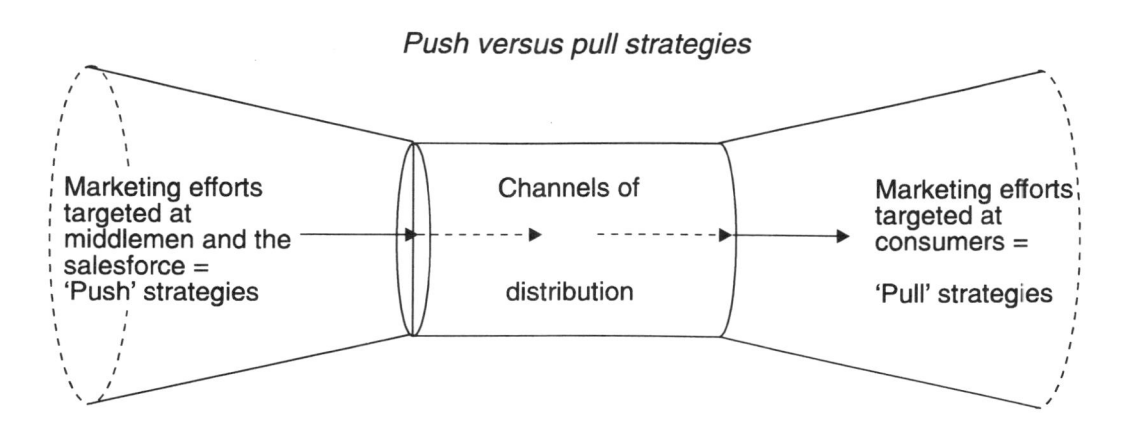

Marketing efforts targeted at middlemen and the salesforce = 'Push' strategies

Channels of distribution

Marketing efforts targeted at consumers = 'Pull' strategies

3.9 The use of a push strategy usually requires a sizeable amount of personal selling and sales promotion, whereas the pull policy demands mass media advertising to a larger degree. It is assumed that you will have some prior knowledge of each of the elements of the promotional mix so that outlines rather than full notes are provided below. These are presented in the following order:

(a) Selling
(b) Advertising
(c) Sales promotion
(d) PR/publicity

Notes **Part A: Background knowledge relevant to analysis and decision**

Selling decisions

3.10 The most *expensive* and the most *effective* form of promotion is personal selling

(a) The cost of selling includes:

(i) Salary
(ii) Meals
(iii) Accommodation
(iv) Car
(v) Commission
(vi) Supervision
(vii) Administration
(viii) Training

(b) The cost of actual selling time is greater than this because few salespeople spend more than 20% of their time actually selling. On average a salesperson's time can be broken down as follows.

	%
Travelling	40
Meals	10
Waiting	17
General chat	17
Selling	16

(c) Some alternative forms of selling include:

(i) Commando sales forces conducting 'raids' on particular areas
(ii) Telephone selling
(iii) Agents

(d) The effectiveness of personal selling is high because the salesperson can:

(i) Vary the approach to suit different customers
(ii) Answer questions and counter objections
(iii) Accept an order on the spot

3.11 The main *sales decisions* are as follows.

(a) Steps in determining the *size of the sales force*.

(i) Group customers by turnover

(ii) Determine the number of calls required per customer

(iii) Total work load = Number of customers × number of calls required per customer per annum.

(iv) Determine number of calls a salesperson can make each year.

(v) The number of salespeople required =

$$\frac{\text{Total number of calls per annum}}{\text{Average number of calls per sales person per annum}}.$$

(b) *Structure of the sales force*

(i) *By geographical area.* The basis can be either:

(1) equal potential sales per area (which gives unequal workloads, as one area may be much larger than another, or contain more customers, requiring more travelling); or

(2) equal workload (which gives unequal potential sales, the corollary of (i) above)

The practical compromise is a mixture of the two.

(ii) *By product* where there are technical problems.

(iii) *By customer* where customer needs differ.

(c) The sales force can be remunerated on the following basis
   (i) Commission only
   (ii) Salary only
   (iii) Salary and commission
   (iv) Salary and bonuses
   (v) Salary and commission and bonuses

   Commission is based on each individual sale. Bonuses might be based on the achievement of certain sales targets, and might even be paid on a group basis.

Advertising decisions

3.12 The main advertising decisions are as follows assuming that target audiences have been identified and responses sought have been clarified. (Further notes are given in Section 5 of this chapter.)

   (a) What are the objectives of advertising? The advertising objectives must be specific and well defined if advertising is to be successful and properly targeted.
      (i) To increase or move consumer through any of the following stages
      (ii) Awareness/knowledge/liking/preference/conviction/purchase
      (iii) Image building
      (iv) Convey message
      (v) Educate
      (vi) Increase sales volume
      (vii) Increase awareness
      (viii) Create loyalty
      (ix) Increase willingness to buy
      (x) As reminder

   (b) There are a number of possible methods of setting the advertising budget.
      (i) *Marginal analysis.* This tries to link variances in sales with changes in volumes of advertising, but in practice this is difficult to quantify.
      (ii) *Advertising expenditure as a percentage of sales revenue.* This is widely used, being a fixed percentage of forecast sales thus is affordable. is no scientific reason for using a particular % figure. This approach *implies* that advertising is being based on sales, rather than sales being generated by advertising. The amount will fluctuate each year depending on sales revenue - sales revenue falls, perhaps you should increase advertising, not decrease it.
      (iii) *Competitive parity.* In this case budget matches or exceeds competitors'. It is useful to know what competitors spend, but this information is not always obtainable. Any way, how do you know that competitors have got it right, or that the 'conventional wisdom' is, in fact, wisdom.
      (iv) *Affordable approach.* Firms allocate what they feel they can afford. However, the amount available will fluctuate, and the approach assumes advertising has no effect on its position. The implication is that advertising is low priority - has the entire promotional strategy been properly thought through?
      (v) *Budgets based on objectives*, ie the tasks to be achieved (precise quantification of advertising goals, choice of media, etc, and estimation of associated costs forces management to recognise what is needed and its cost).

   (c) *Message decisions* include the following.
      (i) Content (rational, emotional, moral?)
      (ii) Structure (draw conclusion? 1 or 2 sided argument?)
      (iii) Format (quantity of copy, coloured, size, pictorial?)

   (d) *Media decisions* include the following.
      (i) Reach (how many people exposed to advert?).
      (ii) Frequency (of exposure).
      (iii) Impact (of exposure).
      (iv) Selecting the *media type* you need to consider the following.

(1) *Audience research findings*
- Circulation and readership of newspapers
- Duplication of audience
- Number who would see advert
- Ability to reach target
- Does half or full page make it more noticeable

(2) *Prestige, mood, expertise of each media vehicle*

(3) *Merits of each media type.* For example TV is suitable for movement, for demonstration, sound and visual impact, and is flexible (regional/national). The disadvantages of TV advertisements are the expense of production, the necessity of repetition to achieve awareness and the fact that they are unsuitable for long explanations

(4) The media type's ability to deliver *reach, frequency and impact*

(v) Choice of specific media vehicle requires attention to the following.

(1) Circulation
(2) Costs for different advertisement sizes
(3) Colour options
(4) Advertisement positions
(5) Cost per thousand
(6) Credibility
(7) Prestige
(8) Reproduction quality
(9) Lead times
(10) Audience quality

(vi) Media scheduling

(1) Period of campaign?

(2) Timing of adverts?
- Concentrated? (ie for brand launches, seasonal products)
- Continuous? (very expensive)? Intermittent? (widely used, gives concentrated impact periodically)?

(3) Buying efficiency?
- Advertising agency used for everything
- Advertising agency used for creative work
- Own advertising agency or department
- Specialised media broking services
- Limited services creative agencies

(4) Should media timespace be purchased centrally?

(5) How often should the company change advertising agency?

(6) What benefits are there to be gained by changing? Being tied to one agency can be restrictive.

Sales promotion decisions

3.13 *Objectives of sales promotion*

(a) The objective of all promotions is to increase sales, either in the short or long-term. The *specific* objective will condition the strategy (ie persuade as many potential shoppers as possible to try it out).

(i) A new retail product must have the widest trial, so the appropriate methods would be coupons, free samples, in-store trial, banded offers, etc.

(ii) A new product requires a longer campaign than an established product.

(iii) An established product requires a more selective approach in order to concentrate on low user segments with a shorter campaign designed to increase brand loyalty.

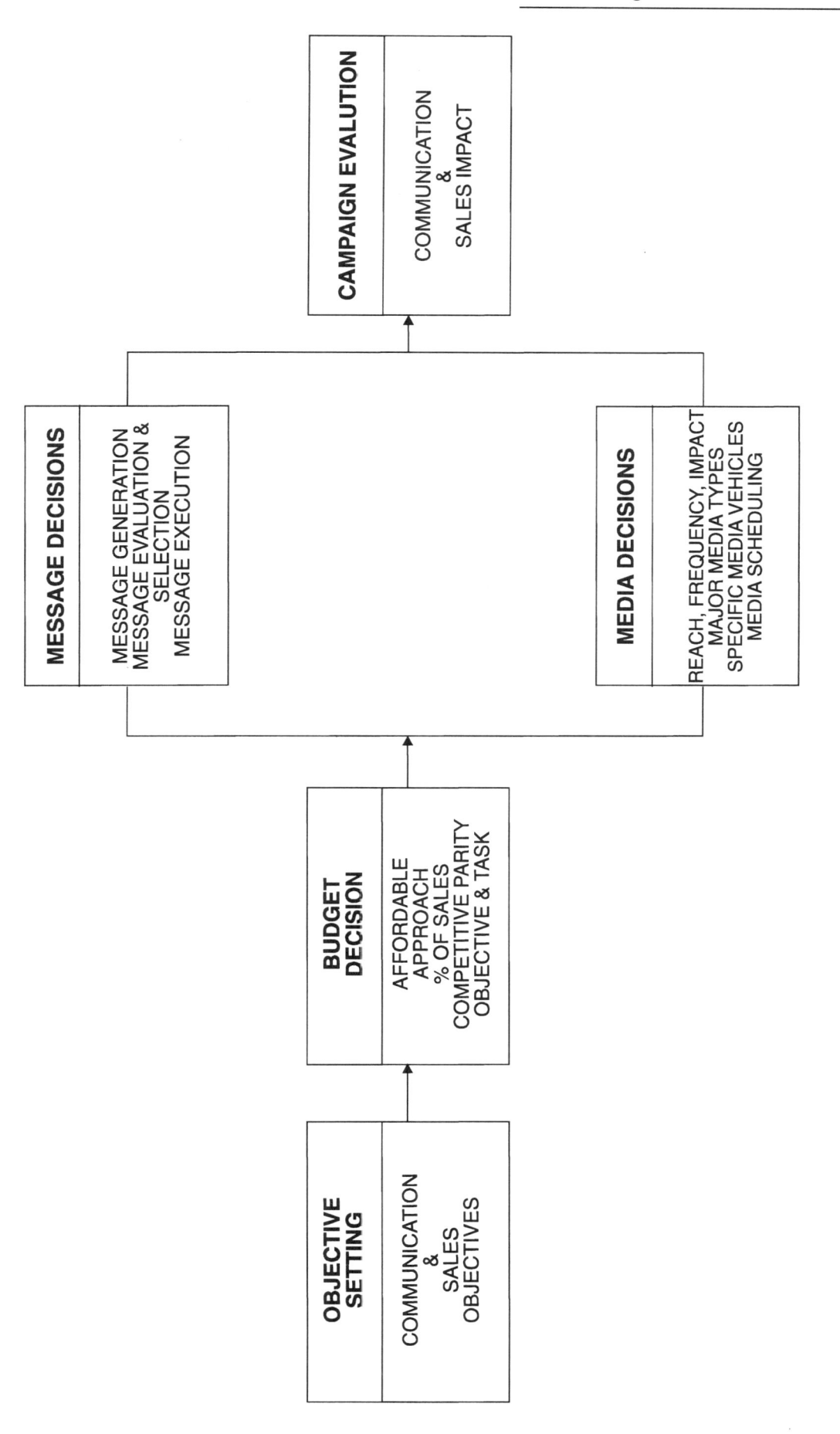

MAJOR DECISIONS IN ADVERTISING MANAGEMENT

OBJECTIVE SETTING
- COMMUNICATION & SALES OBJECTIVES

↓

BUDGET DECISION
- AFFORDABLE APPROACH
- % OF SALES
- COMPETITIVE PARITY
- OBJECTIVE & TASK

↓

MESSAGE DECISIONS
- MESSAGE GENERATION
- MESSAGE EVALUATION & SELECTION
- MESSAGE EXECUTION

MEDIA DECISIONS
- REACH, FREQUENCY, IMPACT
- MAJOR MEDIA TYPES
- SPECIFIC MEDIA VEHICLES
- MEDIA SCHEDULING

↓

CAMPAIGN EVALUATION
- COMMUNICATION & SALES IMPACT

(iv) In a highly competitive market (detergents, cereals etc), campaigns can be designed to increase short term sales, knowing that buyers will revert to a former brand or take advantage of a competitive promotion.

(b) Sales promotion is *tactical*, designed to achieve a short term and limited objective, and is normally concentrated at the point of sale. It usually takes place in close association with the dealers who stock the product. Some sales promotion activities (personality promotions for example) do take place in the street or on a door to door basis, but even then, there is usually a strong tie-in with local dealers.

(c) The distinction between advertising and sales promotion roughly equates to the distinction between 'above the line' and 'below the line'.

3.14 *Some typical sales promotion tasks*

(a) *Encouraging dealers to stock.* Dealers need persuasion to take on a new line, they must be convinced that it will be profitable for them, which means that they must be convinced that customers will buy it in reasonable volume. Sales promotion activities can be used to persuade and provide direct cash incentive (eg cash discounts or deals).

(b) *Encouraging customers to sample.* With food products, for example, it is often crucial that customers try the new product. A special price offer, 'two for one' or an exciting display may tempt them sufficiently to make the test. A new brand of tea might be sold with a free packet of biscuits for example.

(c) *Combating competition.* A competitive situation, such as someone else introducing a new product, may call for an intensive short-term promotion of an existing product to ensure that not too many present customers are wooed away, and that, if possible some new ones are gained.

(d) *Improving distribution.* An existing product may have a 'patchy' distribution and sales promotion techniques can be used to fill in the gaps and gain extra dealers in a poorly represented area.

(e) A well established product may suffer from over familiarity. Since most people are well aware of it, it can become boring. Sales promotions liven it up again and revive interest in it.

3.15 Some examples of sales promotions in current use are as follows.

(a) *Free samples* give the greatest chance of inducing trial. They are the most expensive method, and can only be used for brands with substantial annual sales.

(b) *Off-price labels.* This method is acceptable to consumers and retailers. There is no administration and they can feature the special offer in their advertising.

(c) *Banded offers* come in two forms.
  (i) Existing well known brand 'carries' a free sample of another non-competing product (eg soap and toothpaste).
  (ii) Two for the price of one.

(d) *Premium offers*
  (i) Free gift in the pack (plastic animals in breakfast cereals), attached to it (plastic rose, tea towel), given out at the checkout (china bowls, wastepaper bins, etc) the pack itself (instant coffee in storage jars, to encourage the collecting habit and extend the trial).
  (iii) Free, secondary premium. Free gift for proof of purchase.
  (iv) Self-liquidating premiums. The consumer sends money and proof of purchase, and secures merchandise, often a leading brand name, at a discount.

(e) *Competitions*

(f) Personality promotions (usually with fancy dress). A prize is offered if the housekeeper has the product in the home when the personality calls (Egg-chick, Ajax superman).

3.16 When should you run a promotion? Promotion works best when part of an advertising, product development, or trade incentives strategy, and also when integrated into the overall strategy.

   (a) Firstly, you need information. What is the target market for the product? Why do customers use the product and how? How frequently is it bought and where? What products are its main competitors?

   (b) Do you run a promotion?

   (i) Determine the priority of the problems facing the product.
   (ii) Determine the money available to solve the problems.
   (iii) Test and cost all possible solutions.
   (iv) Estimate effectiveness of each solution.

   (c) Which promotion do you choose?

   (i) Does the promotion offer an incentive to the people in target audience from *their* point of view?
   (ii) What is the likely impact of the promotion on the product's image?
   (iii) Which consumer problems can the promotion solve (eg measuring cup, applicators, etc)?

3.17 *Trade promotions*. The trade has to be persuaded to stock the goods and promote them to their customers. 'Dealer loading' may have repercussions on the manufacturer, although there are other situations where the dealer may need to carry higher stocks (eg preparation for a new product launch). You need to make provision for display material. Examples of trade promotions are as follows.

   (a) Co-operative advertising schemes (the producer and retailer act together).
   (b) Contests for the retailer's sales staff.
   (c) Special discounts to retail staff
   (d) Special quantity trade terms.

3.18 *Sales force promotions* include incentives to sales staff, eg gifts, holidays, prizes etc.

3.19 *Industrial promotions* include discounts, introductory offers, give aways, diaries, calendars, pens. In addition, firms can supply annual golf or racing parties for customers, yachts, holiday villas to entertain customer's staff, sponsorship of sporting events. There are certain limits, eg relating to business ethics and practices, which must be observed in certain countries.

3.20 *Trade exhibitions* include the Motor show, Ideal Home Exhibition, Packaging Exhibition, Plastics Exhibition. An exhibition is a specialist temporary market place. There is also growing use of individual company exhibitions, seminars and demonstrations, where the audience can be selected more closely at a lower cost.

   (a) Reasons for exhibiting are as follows.

   (i) The launch of a new product which cannot be demonstrated physically by sales personnel, but can be shown at an exhibition and reported by the press, TV etc.
   (ii) New markets can be developed rapidly, customers contacted and an image speedily created.
   (iii) Exhibitions help maintain or gain goodwill of sponsoring trade or professional organisations.
   (iv) They are sometimes the only way to make initial contact with professional personnel buying on behalf of foreign governments.

Part A: Background knowledge relevant to analysis and decision

(b) To ensure the cost effectiveness of your stand at the exhibition:
   (i) invite important customers to the stand;
   (ii) make sure the stand accords with the corporate image (size, positioning and lighting);
   (iii) avoid over or under manning;
   (iv) provide less costly literature for 'free loaders' rather than serious customers;
   (v) provide an eye catching stand design, and exhibit to appeal to target groups (eg working models etc);
   (vi) secure information from people who are interested to enable follow up;
   (vii) pay attention to press relations, with suitable releases and visual material.

(c) You should discern in advance
   (i) what kind of people will attend?
   (ii) whether they are a position to buy?
   (iii) what results are expected (actual sales, additional publicity, etc)?
   (iv) follow-up action.

3.21 *Direct mail* may be broadly defined as a method of sending unsolicited advertising or promotional material through the post to customers or potential customers at specific named addresses.

(a) *Advantages*
   (i) It enables direct contact to be made with specific individuals in the target market group.
   (ii) It is highly selective and avoids 'waste' circulation.
   (iii) It is not competing at the same time with other advertising messages.
   (iv) It is very flexible and can be phased and designed in terms of geographical areas, types of prospects, frequency.
   (v) Results are readily measurable.
   (vi) It is relatively cheap and quick.

(b) Response and cost effectiveness. Response rates depend on:
   (i) the user's ability to maintain accurate, up to date lists of potential respondents by appropriate categories;
   (ii) mailing packages of appropriate quality, attraction and format interest to appeal to the respondent;
   (iii) easiness of replying (eg business reply cards or envelopes included);
   (iv) speedy arrangement of personal and/or other forms of follow-up.

3.22 *Point of sale promotions*. The buyer's final decision is made at the point of sale. Showcases, windows, posters, special display material can all be used to persuade people to shop at one location in preference to another.

3.23 *Packaging:*
(a) should stand out clearly on the shelf;
(b) should be clearly identifiable, with strong brand name;
(c) should lend itself to displays.

3.24 Evaluating the success of sales promotion requires that you determine the following.
(a) The number of 'promoted' units taken up.
(b) The number of new users who repeat purchase.
(c) The profit per promoted unit, and profit per unpromoted unit
(d) Attitude towards brand among actual and potential users.

(e) Ascribable profit from new and former users who have taken up the promotion.

(f) Ascribable sales and profits against promotion costs.

(g) Distribution and display increases, increases in buying, sales, trade (and consumer) goodwill.

3.25 We have discussed the notions of *push* and *pull* promotional strategies in an earlier section. When we examine the role of sales promotion in relation to these two notions in more detail we can observe that its various techniques can be used in both contexts as shown in the figure below.

```
PUSH                                                    PULL

Distributor                                             Consumer
incentives    ─┐                                 ┌───   incentives
              ─┤                                 │
POS display   ─┤        THE CHANNEL              ├───   Instore
materials     ─┤                                 │      merchandising
              ─┤                                 │
Sales force   ─┘                                 └───   Packaging
incentives
```

3.26 When deciding whether or not to stock a new product a distributor can often be swayed by the amount of and quality of consumer sales promotion support. This is because the distributor's main fear is that of the product not selling and consumer incentives will help to ensure that products stocked are sold. In this way consumer incentives can help a sales force to sell in to the distribution channel. However, many manufacturers will also offer distributors some special incentives to stock and display a new product or to specially feature an existing product such as base bonuses, special trial offers, special display fittings etc. Sales promotion is thus an important contributor to the selling-in (to retailers) process as well as to that of selling-out (to customers).

Public relations and publicity decisions

3.27 Here are two definitions of public relations.

(a) PR practice is the deliberate, planned and sustained effort to establish and maintain mutual understanding between an organisation and its publics.

(b) PR consists of all forms of planned communications inward and outward, between an organisation and its publics for the purpose of achieving specific objectives concerning mutual understanding.

3.28 *Publicity* involves capitalising on specific events or opportunities relating to the organisation or its products/services, so that these are communicated to its defined publics, in line with the corporate or marketing communications objectives. As a result:

(a) PR is invariably a long term activity;
(b) publicity is more frequently short term.

3.29 PR and publicity depend on communications, both internal and external.

(a) Few organisations can avoid publicity whether may want to or not.

(b) PR is *not* free advertising.

(c) PR is not even free. (Somebody has to pay for lunch!)

(d) Every organisation has PR.

(e) PR involves communication with many groups and audiences, not just consumers or potential consumers.

(f) PR is not propaganda - it does not set out to indoctrinate.

(g) PR is a two-way process.

3.30 Good relations with relevant publics are essential for the well-being of the organisation whether (commercial, non-commercial, government, social, non profit making etc). PR publics are as follows.

(a) The consumers
(b) Employees
(c) Government
(d) Suppliers
(e) Distributors
(f) Financial community
(g) Opinion leaders
(h) The local or national community

3.31 Communication vehicles used in PR and publicity include the following.

(a) Personal communication (eg with journalists)
(b) Printed communication:

(i) direct mail;
(ii) literature (the press magazines visual communications - photographs);
(iii) videos/films, television, exhibitions, company logo/house style, airships, radio.

3.32 Effective public relations/publicity requires the setting of objectives which should *ultimately* reflect the corporate and/or marketing objectives.

(a) PR, being more subtle, may incorporate corporate objectives which are different from product objectives.
(b) PR is frequently wider based than just Marketing (product marketing).
(c) Its objectives are therefore often long term.
(d) Its effectiveness is difficult to quantify and measure.

But nevertheless, objectives as guidelines and direction pointers are important so that there exists a consistency in communication with the relevant publics.

4 LEGAL AND OTHER CONSTRAINTS

Non-legal constraints on promotion

4.1 Non-legal constraints on promotional decisions are of two kinds.

(a) Consumerism - watchdogs, protest bodies, consumer media programmes and features.
(b) Codes of practice - infringement of which can lead to recriminations by the industry.

4.2 It is increasingly difficult today for large companies operating in consumer markets to escape from bad media publicity in the event of transgressions, whether intended or not, against what is deemed to be the consumer interests. Consumers who feel that they, or indeed society at large, are being badly served will find a variety of newspaper columns, television or radio programmes willing to air their grievances to a wider audience.

4.3 Many organisations have adopted and published codes of practice (eg the CIM and most other professional institutes). These codes bind their members/staff to good practices upon penalty of expulsion or other sanctions. Cynics have said that organisations generally only adopted codes of practice as an attempt to ward off a further escalation in legal constraints.

4.4 In any event marketing managers not only need to observe the law, but also need to take note of consumerist pressures and codes of practice when making promotional decisions. A recent example is that of Hoover's offer of free airline tickets to America for purchases of their goods. This proved so popular that the company was unable to cope with demand and much unfavourable publicity has resulted over a long period of time. Marketing managers have to be wary of potential consumerist backlashes when, for example, designing attractive packaging for their company's goods. If the packaging is seen to be over-extravagant, wasteful or adding to the litter problem then bad publicity will almost certainly result. Manufacturers might achieve more sales by simplifying packaging, making this more bio-degradable and promoting this as being more environmentally friendly than competitors'.

Legal constraints on promotion

4.5 You will find in the pages which follow some details of the major laws affecting promotional decisions at the time of writing. Please bear in mind that new laws and changes in regulations are likely to occur which you need to take into account when making promotional decisions in the scenario of the case study. Also needed is an awareness that different legal constraints apply in different countries.

(a) *Trade Descriptions Acts, 1968 and 1972*

   (i) These acts detail three offences, false or misleading trade descriptions, false or misleading indications of price and false or misleading statements as to services, accommodation or facilities.

   (ii) The object of each Act is to protect consumers from misleading claims from retailers. For example, it is an offence to state. 'Reduced to 95p from £1.50' when the goods are seconds, specially purchased for the sale. Before reducing goods, the higher price must have been charged for at least 28 days continuously, unless the retailer displays a notice to the effect that these are genuine reductions although they have not been displayed at the higher price for 28 days during the last 6 months.

   (iii) It is also an offence to apply a 'false trade description' to goods. The Act defines a trade description under 10 headings.

   (1) Quantity, size, gauge.
   (2) Method of manufacture, production, processing.
   (3) Composition.
   (4) Fitness for the purpose, strength, performance.
   (5) Special characteristics.
   (6) Tests and results of tests.
   (7) Approval given by any person or body.
   (8) Place of manufacture: Date of manufacture.
   (9) Persons by whom manufactured.
   (10) Other history, including previous ownership or use.

   (iv) Breach of the Act can result in fines of up to £400 or two years imprisonment.

   (v) The National Consumer Council analysed 11,000 complaints in first 6 months of 1989. 55% concerned claims and description labels and packaging. 0.5% concerned claims made in advertisements. 44.5% concerned other types of claims and descriptions.

(b) *Supply of Goods (Implied Terms) Act 1973*. This act guarantees the consumer's rights and prevents vendors from entering clauses in contracts waiving the buyer's Common Law rights (unfair contract terms).

(c) *Fair Trading Act 1973*. This Act set up the Office of Fair Trading. Basically the OFT can look into almost any aspect of trading and if they feel it is unfair can put proposals to Parliament.

(d) There are other Acts that relate to the advertising of *specific* merchandise.

4.6 TV and radio advertising are subject to legal control under the terms of the Broadcasting Acts of 1981 and 1990. The ITC (Independent Television Commission) regulates the amount and content and has a Code of Advertising Standards and Practice. Other advertising media are governed by the British Code of Advertising Practice which is almost identical to the ITC code. The Code is run by the Advertising Standards Authority and is self regulatory.

Part A: Background knowledge relevant to analysis and decision

   (a) *Television* advertising:
      (i) is regulated by ITC;
      (ii) is subject to statutory control;
      (iii) is limited to maximum of seven minutes in any 'clock' hour, and an average of 6 minutes per hour;
      (iv) should amount to no more than 10% of broadcast time (25% in the USA).

   (b) *Radio* advertising:
      (i) is regulated by its own regulatory body;
      (ii) is subject to statutory control;
      (iii) is limited to a maximum of 9 minutes/per hour;
      (iv) must be no more than 15% of broadcast time.

   (c) *Press*
      (i) Currently, there is no formal control except by the publisher, although legislation is looming.
      (ii) In practice, the ratio of advertising to editorial is around 50% (tabloids) and 50% (glossy magazine).
      (iii) 'Freesheets' usually contain 90-100% advertising.

   (d) *Posters*
      (i) These are controlled by town and country planning regulations (1969).
      (ii) Poster advertising has decreased dramatically since 1900.
      (iii) Many other countries make more use of poster advertising.
      (iv) It can brighten up otherwise dull areas.

   (e) *Cinema*
      (i) No formal control exists.
      (ii) In practice an average of 12 minutes of advertising is shown in a two-and-a-half hour programme.

4.7 A survey on public attitudes on quantity of advertising (consumer regulation), based on 1,300 UK TV viewers took place in 1983, and the results were reported in *Which?* November 1983

   (a) Attitudes to amount of advertising on *existing* channels.
      (i)   Current levels about right   53%
      (ii) There should be less   35%
      (iii) There should be none   11%

   (b) Attitudes to amount of advertising on *future* ITV channels
      (i)   There should be less   41%
      (ii) There should be the same   41%
      (iii) There should be none   8%
      (iv) No opinion   10%

Control of advertising content

4.8 Two types of statutory regulation of advertising content exist.
   (a) Direct legislation, as we have seen.
   (b) Indirect statutory control.

4.9 Indirect statutory control includes the following.
   (a) The Independent Television Authority (ITA) set up when commercial broadcasting was first permitted; established an advisory code of practice in 1955. Its successor, the Independent Broadcasting Authority (IBA), also produced standards of practice.

2: Marketing communications strategy

(b) The Broadcasting Act (1990) makes it a statutory duty of the *Independent Television Commission* (ITC) to draw up and enforce a code covering television advertising. The Act states that: 'the general principle which will govern all broadcast advertising is that it should be legal, decent, honest and truthful'. Advertisements may not be included in the following.

  (i) Religious ceremonies or programmes
  (ii) Programmes designed for schools
  (iii) Formal royal ceremonies/occasions and appearances of Queen or Royal family
  (iv) Some half hour adult education programmes
  (v) Some current affairs programmes and documentaries

(c) Viewers sometimes find advertisements offensive, misleading or dishonest despite the controls (eg various campaigns in which women have been portrayed in stereotyped ways).

4.10 The ITC has also issued a code of advertising standards and practice. The ITC code is modelled closely on the former IBA and Cable Authority Codes which it replaces. It has many points in common with the self regulatory code for the non broadcast media (the British Code of Advertising Practice). The ITC code applies to all television services regulated by the ITC. In the main these are: ITV, GMTV, Channel 4, Channel 5, UK direct broadcast satellite (DBS) services. Separate provisions apply to Oracle Teletext. The enforcement of any self regulatory code is a problem. In this case it is the media owners who have agreed not to accept any advertising from an advertiser who has refused to abide by an ASA decision. The weakness of the scheme has not been in *enforcing* the code, but the willingness of media owners to print advertisements which contravene the Code, rather than upset advertisers. This tends to make the code a 'longstop' rather than a preventative measure.

4.11 Self regulation of advertising and sales promotion. The Advertising Standards Authority (ASA) has responsibility for supervising the advertising industry's system of self-regulation. It is recognised by the Office of Fair Trading and the government as a fundamental part of consumer protection. One of the Authority's specific tasks is to investigate complaints from the public that advertisements are in breach of the British Code of Advertising Practice (BCAP). The ASA is a wholly independent body which operates quite separately from the industry's Code of Advertising Practice Committee. The ASA was set up in 1962, and is a watchdog which oversees all advertisements *except* those on radio or TV. Complaints about radio and television advertising made to the ASA are passed on to the IBA.

4.12 The ASA is a voluntary body. Unlike the IBA it does not have the force of an act of Parliament behind it. In theory, non-broadcast media owners, agencies and advertisers follow the ASA's advice.

(a) The ASA's main functions are to see that the British Code of Advertising Practice is adhered to, and to deal with complaints from the general public. The ASA does, however, check all advertisements for cigarettes before publication, and in practice most advertisements for alcoholic drinks are also pre-vetted. Otherwise, it is clearly impractical for the ASA to vet every press advertisement, every poster and every advertising film before it was used.

(b) Between 7,000 and 8,000 complaints are received each year from the public. If, after an investigation, the complaint is upheld, the Authority seeks an assurance from the advertiser that the offence will not be repeated. Advertisers who do not agree to amend their advertisements in line with the ASA's recommendations are reported to media owners.

(c) The Authority issues a monthly case report which described the complaints received and the action taken. The January 1986 Case Report gave the results of 109 investigations into breaches of the British Code of Advertising Practice which had been completed. The complaints were upheld in 70 cases, and partly upheld in a further three. Many complainers were readers who had been attracted by price offers in advertisements which involved hidden extra costs, or to have suffered increases since the advert.

Part A: Background knowledge relevant to analysis and decision

4.13 The British Code of Sales Promotion Practice (BCSPP, 1982) is published by ASA's Code of Advertising Practices Committee. It aims to regulate marketing techniques, usually used on a temporary basis, to make goods and services more attractive to the consumer by providing some kind of additional benefit in cost or in kind.

(a) It covers:

   (i) all types of premium offer
   (ii) reduced price and free offers
   (iii) distribution of vouchers
   (iv) coupons and samples
   (v) personality promotions
   (vi) charity linked promotions
   (vii) all types of prize promotions
   (viii) sales and trade incentive promotions
   (ix) editorial promotions offers
   (x) aspects of sponsorship.

(b) It *defines* a promotional product as: 'a product which the consumer receives or may receive as a result of participation in a sales promotion'.

(c) The ASA implements the code, but primary responsibility for ensuring the code is implemented rests with the promoter (but in the case of a mailing of a cigarette promotion to a 17 year old girl, the complaint was not upheld, as she had previously completed a coupon declaring she was over 18 years old).

4.14 The British Direct Mail Association (BDMA) introduced a Code of Practice in 1982. It covers:

(a) direct mail
(b) direct response mail order advertising
(c) other direct response advertising
(d) telephone selling

Members of the BDMA are bound by the BCAP and the BCSPP. The *Direct Marketing Association* was formed in 1992 and issued a code in 1993.

Comparative advertising

4.15 Attitudes are very hard - and therefore expensive - to change. Thus, much advertising is highly competitive, with two objectives; to reinforce the attitudes of existing customers and to change the attitudes (or convert) competitors' customers. One of the most powerful but controversial tools available to advertisers in this respect is comparative advertising, known to the trade as knocking copy.

4.16 The control of knocking-copy and selective comparisons has always been a matter for controversy. Some advertising people have demanded the right to make comparisons in favour of a product advertised. Yet it would then be unfair to isolate one feature of a product and illustrate it in a discrediting way, giving the impression that the exceptional incident is the norm.

4.17 The view of the ASA is that 'knocking-copy' can only bring advertising into bad repute. Secondly, 'knocking-copy' is the refuge of the incompetent or lazy copywriter, who finds it only too easy to knock. Some critics consider that advertisements which make direct comparisons with competitive products or services are undesirable and should not be permitted.

4.18 The BCAP is very explicit on the subject:

'Advertisements containing comparisons ... including those where a competitor is named, are permissible in the interests of vigorous competition and public information,' provided that they comply with five specific clauses of the code. These may be summed up as saying that the comparisons must not be deliberately misleading, that it must be clear what is being compared with what, that the points of comparison must not be so selected as to confer an unrealistic margin of advantage, that price comparisons must use comparable and comprehensible units of measurement and that advertisers should not gratuitously attack one another.

4.19 The ITC Code of Advertising Standards and Practice offers the same guidelines, though in less detail. The five year battle of words between the leading UK manufacturers of hover and cylinder lawnmowers reached the point at which the hover mower manufacturers petitioned Parliament to restrain their competitors, on the grounds that the competitive comparisons were 'unfair', despite the fact that the ASA and ITC were both satisfied that their codes were no longer being breached in any way.

5 CAMPAIGN PLANNING

A campaign planning framework

5.1 From time to time companies will experience a need for a special promotional campaign. This might be to launch an entirely new product or service or to re-launch/re-position an existing product. Such campaigns would normally call for a new creative strategy, the forerunner to which would be a new creative brief. For such an important exercise, it would be highly likely that an advertising agency and/or a creative specialist would be heavily involved at an early stage. The framework for such a special campaign might therefore be as illustrated in the diagram on the following page.

5.2 Additional issues in campaign planning are as follows.

(a) Determine the *objective of the campaign*. This is a task for management and not for the advertising specialist who may, however, cause management objectives to be modified if it is felt they cannot be achieved because of copy, media, budget or other limitations. However, the advertising specialist should be involved in deciding the objectives of marketing communications.

(b) *The message (copy and design)*.

(i) Advertisements consist of verbal symbols, illustrations, colour, movement, sound etc. It is the task of the creative personnel in advertising to achieve the mix most likely to accomplish the purpose of the communication taking into account literal and emotional aspects.

(ii) Copy will be influenced by the choice of media as well as the target audiences. In general the most effective copy is that which concentrates on a limited selling appeal, and frequent repetition of a single appeal is a feature of many very successful campaigns. Certainly many campaigns are spoiled by the attempt to cover too many selling points in one advertisement.

(iii) Campaigns may, of course, be planned to cover a number of single objectives over a given time, in line with a multiple communications strategy.

(iv) Advertising can be pre-tested to determine whether the intended message is being communicated, and comparisons of the effectiveness of communication of a number of advertisements can also be made. Samples of prospective viewers or readers are exposed to advertisements, and certain reactions are measured. Sometimes, tests are carried out on specially constituted panels. The tests may be conducted on the basis of aided or unaided recall of advertisements to which the panel or sample member has been exposed. It should be noted that these tests relate to the effectiveness of the communication as such and do not give a measure of sales results.

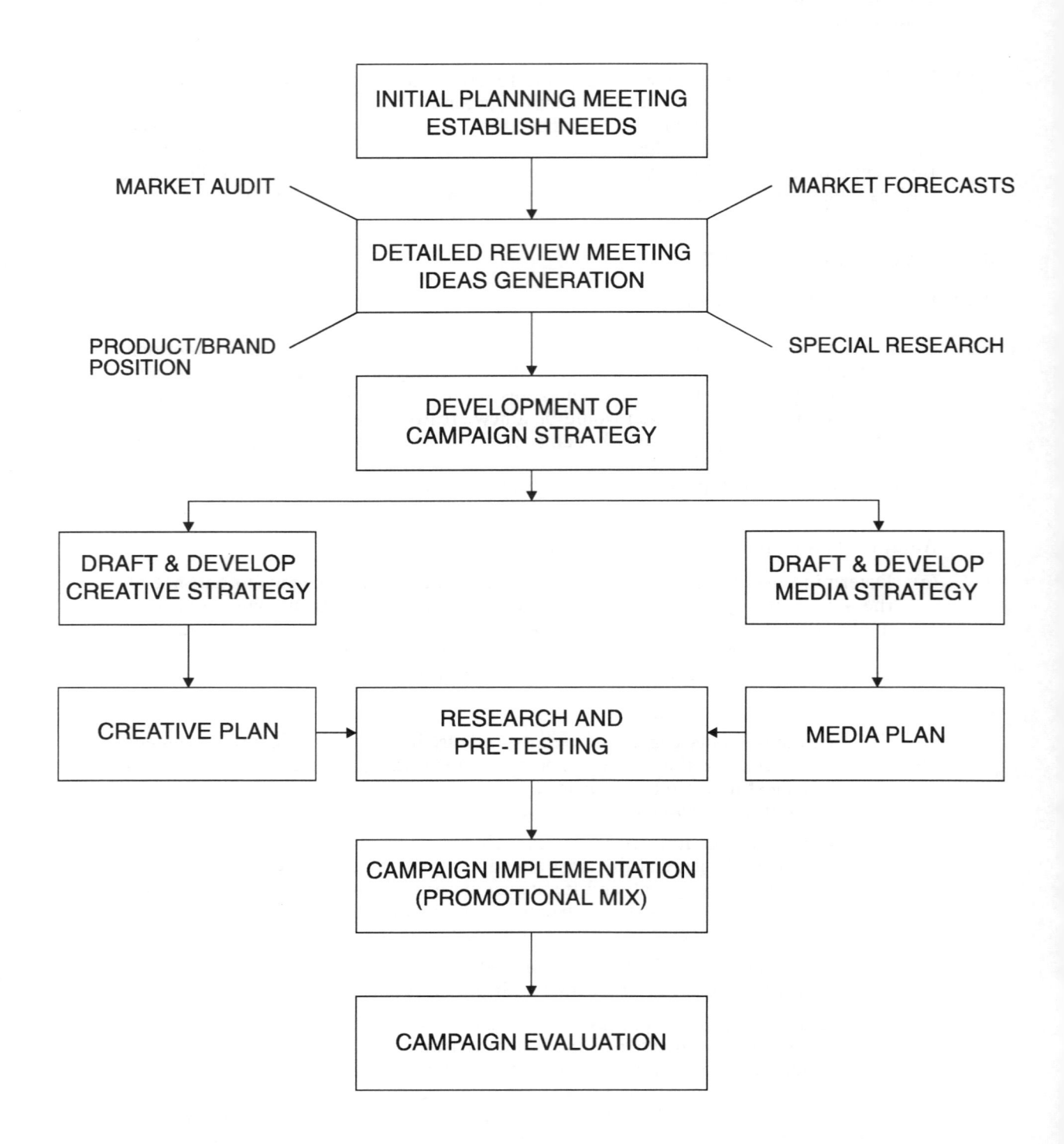

Notes   **Part A: Background knowledge relevant to analysis and decision**

```
                    ┌─────────────────────────┐
                    │ INITIAL PLANNING MEETING │
                    │    ESTABLISH NEEDS      │
                    └─────────────────────────┘
                                │
                                ▼
   MARKET AUDIT ──── ┌─────────────────────────┐ ──── MARKET FORECASTS
                    │  DETAILED REVIEW MEETING │
                    │     IDEAS GENERATION    │
                    └─────────────────────────┘
   PRODUCT/BRAND ───         │                   ──── SPECIAL RESEARCH
   POSITION                  ▼
                    ┌─────────────────────────┐
                    │     DEVELOPMENT OF      │
                    │    CAMPAIGN STRATEGY    │
                    └─────────────────────────┘
                       │                 │
            ┌──────────┘                 └──────────┐
            ▼                                       ▼
   ┌──────────────────┐                    ┌──────────────────┐
   │ DRAFT & DEVELOP  │                    │ DRAFT & DEVELOP  │
   │ CREATIVE STRATEGY│                    │  MEDIA STRATEGY  │
   └──────────────────┘                    └──────────────────┘
            │                                       │
            ▼                                       ▼
   ┌──────────────┐      ┌──────────────┐      ┌──────────────┐
   │ CREATIVE PLAN│─────▶│ RESEARCH AND │◀─────│  MEDIA PLAN  │
   │              │      │ PRE-TESTING  │      │              │
   └──────────────┘      └──────────────┘      └──────────────┘
                                │
                                ▼
                    ┌─────────────────────────┐
                    │ CAMPAIGN IMPLEMENTATION │
                    │    (PROMOTIONAL MIX)    │
                    └─────────────────────────┘
                                │
                                ▼
                    ┌─────────────────────────┐
                    │   CAMPAIGN EVALUATION   │
                    └─────────────────────────┘
```

(c) Select and schedule appropriate media. Problems of media selection include the following.

   (i) The extent of coverage required to reach potential buyers and its effective cost.

   (ii) The comparative communication effectiveness of various media (eg the compatibility of the advertising or editorial material with media audiences - an advertisement designed for the popular press might be totally unsuitable in a specialised journal).

   (iii) Is there a medium or specific newspaper or TV channel to reach your target audience?

   (iv) Location. Many national media have facilities to enable regional advertising. TV and Radio are obvious. Sunday colour press, TV and Radio Times and many national dailies have regional editions. Is your target market evenly spread?

   (v) Penetration. A free newspaper may have a larger circulation than the local 'paid for' paper. However, if you are a local advertiser the smaller circulation publication may be better, as it is probably read more thoroughly. Penetration is the proportion of the 'readers' who are registering the message.

   (vi) Timing. It is important that the advertisement appears at a time when the consumer is most responsive. Obviously, for a new product this is crucial, but it is also important for established products. Sunday newspapers are advertised on TV on Saturday night.

   (vii) Use by competitors. For example, if six dog food brands are already heavily using TV, would you be better off using a combination of radio, outdoor and press?

   (viii) Cost. The media planner must make best use of the budget. Firstly, a small budget will preclude media with high production costs (such as TV or cinema).

   (ix) The administrative, organisational and operating requirements of the media (eg frequency of publication and length of lead time required for placing advertisements).

   (x) Consideration of the ways in which competitors allocate expenditure to various media.

   (xi) The determination of advertising frequency - 'opportunities to see'.

   (xii) The size, positioning and/or timing of advertisements.

(d) Co-ordinate advertising with the total promotional plan. Amongst co-ordination problems would be those of assigning tasks and expenditure to promotions, personal selling efforts, handling and follow-up of enquiries, and public relations.

(e) Determine and control the advertising budget. The size of the budget will, in practice, determine very largely the selection of media, but ideally budgets should be determined by companies after due consideration of the cost of achieving communication objectives.

(f) Media planning. It is all too easy to say, 'that was a good advertisement' without asking, where did it appear, how often, who saw it, when and how often.

Advertising strategy

5.3 *Objectives*. The setting of advertising objectives, the strategy to achieve them, and the measurement of their effectiveness is stressed in the concept of DAGMAR. This concept was first described by Russell H Colley as 'Defining Advertising Goals for Measured Advertising Results'.

5.4 *Testing advertisements*. Everybody believes they can tell a good advertisement from a bad one. If the advertisement is shown to five or six people, the chances are there will be a divergence of opinion. Alternatively they may all like it, but not be able to tell you the name of the product the next day.

(a) When judging advertisements they must be judged against their stated objectives and they should be only tested on the target audience. There are a few characteristics that all good ads have in common.

   (i) Does it stop me and make me look?
   (ii) Is some element of it unusual or original?
   (iii) Is it a pleasing design?
   (iv) Is it relevant to the product?
   (v) Is it easy to understand?

(b) However, there are two questions we need to answer when testing an advertisement that are far more difficult to answer.

   (i) Does it fit the strategy?
   (ii) Will it work?

The answers to these questions can be arrived at before or after the advertisement has been run and this is called pre-testing and post-testing.

5.5 Pre-testing techniques normally involve showing the advertisement to members of your target group and soliciting their response. All the methods of doing this have the drawback that it is difficult to recreate the conditions under which they would really see the advertisement (ie passing a poster in a car, thumbing through a magazine, in the middle of a TV programme).

(a) The method normally employed is a discussion group, where a highly trained interviewer asks a number of groups questions that are not leading or rhetorical.

(b) For advertisements the proposed ad can be placed in a folder with alternative or competitors' advertisements and respondents questioned when they have been studied.

(c) Any pre-testing for TV advertisements is more problematical as it involves producing the advertisement before it can be tested and human nature is such that there is a reluctance to abandon an advertisement that tests badly. However, for a big campaign it is worth pre-testing. This is sometimes carried out using low cost story boards, animatics or a low budget video approach.

Defining advertising objectives

5.6 It is important to be able to distinguish between *marketing objectives* and advertising objectives. To increase sales or to increase market share are not advertising objectives but objectives, of the total marketing plan. Advertising objectives are much more specific to the communications process. Example of advertising objectives are given below. In practice, you would aim to quantify these objectives.

(a) To maintain the loyalty of existing buyers and encourage their greater usage.
(b) To encourage non-users to sample.
(c) To inform users, especially lapsed users, that the product has been improved.
(d) Develop the belief that it is better than other products for whatever reason.

5.7 Is must also be possible to measure the effectiveness of the campaign against these specific objectives. This can only be done by research before and after the campaign. It is fairly straight forward using 'ad hoc' research to establish attitudes and usage levels amongst users and non-users, within our target market.

Designing advertisements

5.8 The strategy involves two aspects.

(a) Who do we want to communicate with? We will normally want to communicate with our target market. This should be already established as it is *fundamental* to the whole marketing plan.

(b) What are the desired reactions to the advertisement.

5.9 Let us take the example of Black and Decker Power Drills aiming at the market segment of new home owners who do not own a power drill.

(a) Consumer reactions might range through the following.

  (i) 'Black & Decker is a name I've heard of and know is widely available.'
  (ii) 'I've also heard Bosch make drills, are German and make parts for cars so they might be better.'
  (iii) 'Power drills are expensive, I could make do with a hand drill.'
  (iv) 'I will probably need lots of extras such as drill bits, power leads, etc.'
  (v) 'Would I use a power drill enough to make it worth buying?'

(b) The strategy could be to reinforce the positive aspects, to change the negative aspects and to suggest new, previously unconsidered motives.

  (i) *Reinforce*
    (1) Black and Decker has been established 80 years
    (2) It has a wider dealer network (than Bosch)
    (3) The guarantees are good
    (4) Black and Decker are the most popular in the UK

  (ii) *Change*
    (1) Black and Decker only make power tools, so are specialist (knock Bosch)
    (2) Cable is included and can be used for hedge cutters, strimmers.
    (3) Drill bits are included
    (4) The power drill can also be used to power sanders, saws, screwdrivers
    (5) Prices start at £19.95

  (iii) *New*
    (1) A drill makes an ideal wedding/christmas/birthday present
    (2) The new model is more powerful

  (iv) *Emotional/psychological factors are also often added*
    (1) Power-tools are 'macho'.
    (2) They satisfy a 'need' to make an impressive home, impress family and neighbours.
    (3) They look professional and knowledgeable.
    (4) Tool advertisements often use 'the choice of the professional' partly to appeal to the ego but also to reduce perceived risk.
    (5) In addition to this, the advertising can give something extra, normally described as 'from the advertising'. In the case quoted, it could be a shot of some impressive shelves (bearing a lot of weight) or some other completed DIY job.

5.10 *Post-testing*. Accepting that the role of advertising is to sell, the obvious post testing method is to measure sales. However, as advertising is only one small part of the promotional and marketing mix, it is normally wrong to credit any change in sales purely to advertising except in very unusual circumstances, where a control is available and every other factor remains constant. This is the philosophy behind *area tests* where the advertisement is run in one area and the sales compared with the rest of the country. This has various drawbacks.

(a) The area chosen may respond to the message differently to the rest of the country.
(b) Obtaining information from individual branches of multiple retailers, who buy centrally, is difficult.
(c) The overlap of TV transmission areas.
(d) The time taken up in receiving results.

5.11 Press advertising has the advantage of enabling the inclusion of a direct response element, such as a coupon.

5.12 If it is difficult to test a single advertisement, it is even more difficult to test a complete campaign or prove that 'advertising works', and most text books completely ignore these topics. As previously stated, research should be used to measure changes in attitudes to the product and such research is probably the only way that we can realistically assess the value of a campaign.

Media buying

5.13 As previously explained, the media space is normally booked by the advertising agency, and it is one of the agency's main jobs to buy well. Personnel in some agencies believe they are so creatively brilliant that their advertisement can be sufficiently effective whenever or wherever they appear. There is a basic conflict between media buyer and seller in that within all media there are spots or positions less popular than others. To some extent this is accounted for by the rate card but even so, it is difficult to fill unpopular spots with advertisements. Consequently, a deal is normally struck that includes good, bad and indifferent spots at an advantageous price.

5.14 The task of converting your media plan into firm orders placed with media-owners is more than simply an administrative task, and here the difference between *media planning* and *media buying* becomes all important. For example, your approved media schedule might show a series of television commercials to be transmitted in various time segments on certain dates. When the plan was drawn up, however, it was impossible to know the programmes that would be transmitted or the viewing figures that would be achieved many months ahead. So a great deal of skill is called for in negotiating the best possible spots at times when your commercial will be seen by the largest number of people in your target market group. Similar detailed negotiations will be necessary with the owners of other media.

5.15 The up-to-the-minute buying function contrasts sharply with the earlier planning stage, which produced only an outline plan to be implemented in the light of subsequent information. Media buying calls for a highly competitive cut and thrust approach which many find more exciting than the abstract planning stage which, in contrast, seems a rather boring mechanical exercise. Some practitioners argue that the personal qualities called for in planners and buyers are so very different that few individuals can do both jobs properly. The vital importance of the buying side is illustrated by the growth of the media independents, by the separation within many agency media departments of the planning and buying functions, and by the fact that advertisers have been known to move their accounts from one agency to another simply because of its better buying performance. In such cases, media considerations clearly have just as high a priority as the creative side of advertising.

Schedule improvement

5.16 Few advertising campaigns ever appear exactly as originally planned, and you should keep your schedule under constant scrutiny and make whatever improvements are possible. A marginal improvement of, say, 10 percent in coverage is equivalent to a 10 percent increase in your appropriation, so you should keep your schedule under review and adjust it in the light of subsequent information.

5.17 With television advertising, schedule improvement is just as important as the original plan. Changes are less frequent with press or other media but the case for schedule improvement is just as valid. The publication of new readership data, the issue of a new rate card or the launch of a new publication, for example, should lead you to re-examine your current media plans.

6 SELECTING AND BRIEFING AGENCIES

6.1 Few companies can entirely satisfy their customers without calling upon other organisations to provide specialist services. Serving customers is a matter of getting the product, promotion, price and place right. In the case of promotion there are three major types of agency as illustrated in the model below. Note that there are four major participants in the communications system.

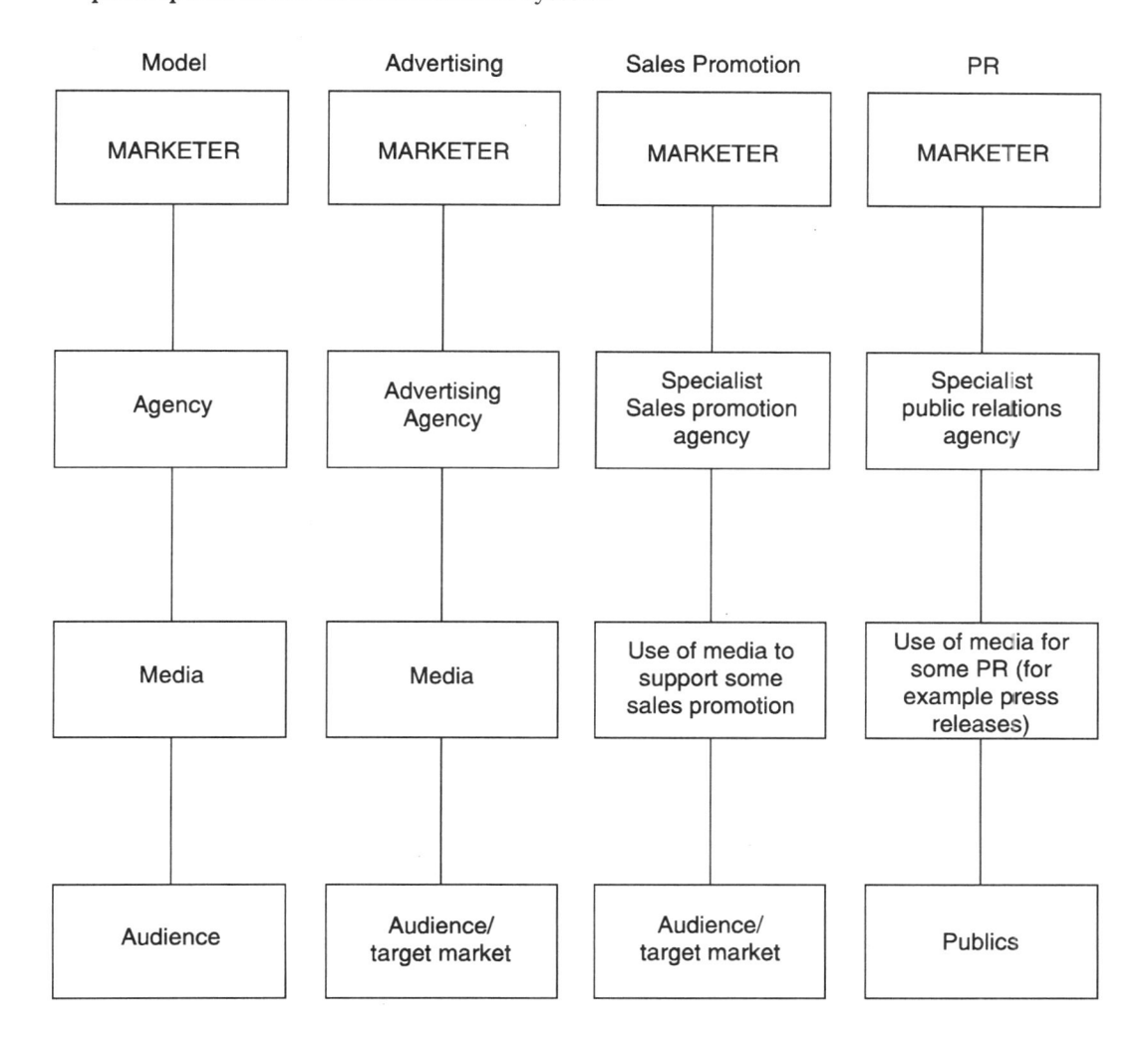

Model	Advertising	Sales Promotion	PR
MARKETER	MARKETER	MARKETER	MARKETER
Agency	Advertising Agency	Specialist Sales promotion agency	Specialist public relations agency
Media	Media	Use of media to support some sales promotion	Use of media for some PR (for example press releases)
Audience	Audience/ target market	Audience/ target market	Publics

The client

6.2 The advertiser is the party who wishes to advertise a product or a service. Advertising agencies refer to them as clients. Advertising is unusual in that it usually involves other organisations (agencies, media) whereas most marketing functions are carried out internally. Some companies do not use an agency and produce their own advertisements and buy their own media, but this is unusual. More common is an arrangement where the advertiser has a marketing or advertising department and uses an agency. An organisation's advertising manager will normally have the following roles:

(a) He or she will represent the sales promotion and advertising function, just as the sales manager will represent personal selling.

(b) He or she will lay down the advertising objectives for the organisation and appeal for the necessary appropriation.

(c) He or she will plan a strategy to make use of the available resources

(d) He or she will brief the advertising agency and control its activities in the interest of the organisation.

In many companies Product Managers and Brand Managers carry out many or all of the above roles.

The advertising agency

6.3 The main role of the agency is the preparation of advertisements for their clients and the purchase of advertising space. In this section we shall consider:

Part A: Background knowledge relevant to analysis and decision

(a) the services offered by agencies;
(b) how agencies are structured;
(c) selecting an agency;
(d) briefing an agency;
(e) remuneration of the agency.
(f) working with the agency;
(g) alternatives to the agency

The services offered

6.4 Agencies originally worked for the *media owners* to sell space to advertisers. They soon began to help the advertisers prepare their advertisements and today they specialise in preparing advertisements and placing them in appropriate media.

(a) At its most elaborate, the agency offers a full marketing resource and is able to provide assistance in business planning together with supporting show-material, sales literature, sales conferences, etc.

(b) On the other hand there are agencies which specialise in one market (eg often an industrial market). Whatever the size of the agency, they often use sub-contractors to produce artwork and print.

How agencies are structured

6.5 The main parts of most modern agencies are as follows.

(a) *Account management.* The agency functions by allocating an *account executive* to the client (the account). The account executive heads up a team (the account group) made up of specific members of the creative department, a planner and media specialists. Normally the whole team meets the client and get to know client needs and operations. The *account executive* is responsible to the client to ensure that the client is satisfied. The account executive is present at all meetings.

(b) The *account planner's* job is to assemble information about the product and the market, production of the advertising strategy which guides the creative team. The account planner will organise any research into the advertisement and its results. Planners have appeared for two reasons.

   (i) The account executive does not have time

   (ii) Planners redress the balance away from the creative side to channel the artistic resource in the right direction. This is becoming very important in times when clients are looking for accountability/measurability for the money spent on advertising.

(c) The *creative team* are the ideas people who actually think up the advertisement. The team normally consists of an artist or art director and a copy writer. A traditional stereotype is that they are nonconformist in terms of normal office practice.

(d) *Media.* The *media planner* gets involved from the beginning to decide which media are most appropriate. This enables the creative team to tailor their efforts according to the media. When the creative work is complete, the media planner will draw up the schedule and, when agreed, will go out and buy 'the space'.

(e) The *progress or traffic department* does not usually have a representative on the account team, but oils the wheels, making sure jobs go to and from the right places, on time. This is co-ordination.

(f) Similarly the *accounts* or billing department is not on the team, but is vitally important in keeping the client happy. Charging the client is complicated and advertising is expensive, consequently there is scope for friction. From an agency viewpoint the accounts department is important in minimising cash-flow difficulties.

Selecting an agency

6.6 The Institute of Practitioners in Advertising has over 300 member agencies and represents a wide choice for the advertiser. Apart from new advertisers, existing accounts are often on the move. *Campaign* magazine, which you should dig into from time to time, is often full of news of accounts (and personnel!) moving between agencies. Because of all this activity, it is important for the agency to be able to court and win new accounts, and for the client to be able to assess agencies.

6.7 *Recognition* of an agency by the trade associations that represent the *media owners* confers the automatic right to receive media *commission*. Media commission is not paid to unrecognised agencies or advertisers who deal directly with the media. Most agencies seek to be recognised.

Criteria for recognition include:

(a) existence in the business (a barrier to entry for new agencies needing media commission to become established);

(b) professional competence (poorly produced advertisements reflect badly on the media);

(c) solvency (the most important criterion as the agency is responsible for the client's debts if the client pays late or goes bust).

6.8 Incorporation of an agency is a status awarded by the Institute of Practitioners in Advertising (IPA) as professional associates, so that an incorporated agency can call itself 'Incorporated Practitioner in Advertising'. Criteria for the award of incorporated status include that the agency:

(a) must be completely independent of media owners;
(b) must agree to abide by the IPA code of conduct;
(c) must agree to abide by the British Code of Advertising Practice (BCAP).

6.9 IPA member agencies (ie incorporated agencies) account for around 40% of the 900 or more advertising agencies in the UK. These 40% of agencies account for a 90% of the total billings of advertising agencies. The larger and more successful agencies are IPA members. Some agencies do not have incorporated status because they choose not to adhere to the second criterion which involves strict rules on competition (ie IPA code).

6.10 The selection of an agency is very subjective and unscientific, but it does pay to approach the problem by first drawing up a shortlist of agencies using the following general criteria.

(a) *Size*. The size of the account should be in proportion to the size of the agency. Small agencies cannot always handle big accounts, and big agencies might not put all their weight behind a small account.

(b) *Track record*. Agencies grow and fail. Try to find a growing one as it will attract the best staff. If an agency has a record of gaining or holding on to other good accounts it is a good sign.

(c) *Compatibility*. Can you get on with the people, do they 'speak your language'?

(d) *Creativity*. All agencies claim to be creative. Look at their past work (are the staff who did the good work still there?). Make sure that the creativity is not so esoteric that it fails to sell.

(e) *Relevant experience*. Assume you are selling cheese. An agency does not need to have handled a cheese account to handle yours, but it may be a help to have handled other food accounts. The agency will know good photographers of food and may be able to get good deals from the media as they have used them before. You may wish to move to an agency which has just lost your *competitor's* account, particularly if the competitor is the market leader. The agency will know your market and your competitors' weaknesses. Agencies rarely take on *conflicting accounts* from competing clients.

6.11 You can start to talk to agencies at this stage to reduce the list still further as you need a final list of no more than four. Discount those who do not appear keen. You will get approaches from other agencies, try to put them off but consider those who are persistent or ingenious. If you need to reduce further, give them all the opportunity of a one hour presentation.

(a) The classic way of choosing an agency is to give three or four the same brief and ask them to present against it, giving them a number of weeks.

(b) There are draw-backs to such a system. It is rather artificial as the timescale is short. The decision tends to be made too much on the creativity of the advertising copy whereas the advertising *plan* is just as important.

(c) From the agency's viewpoint, they can spend £000's on preparing a pitch and get less than nothing as they are giving away their creative ideas. Some of the very biggest refuse to join in.

6.12 When the final decision has been made, a standard letter of terms is drawn up by the agency covering the following.

(a) The range of services to be provided.
(b) The basis of payment.
(c) Length of credit.
(d) Copyrights, confidentiality, etc.
(e) Conditions of termination.

Briefing the agency

6.13 Guinness's brief to the agencies involved in pitching for their account was 100 pages and probably the most expensive ever produced. Other clients produce two sheets of A4 culminating in the objective 'to increase sales'.

(a) The brief should comprise two parts, information on the company and the advertising objective. The information should include historical sales, financial and marketing information and research into attitudes to the product or brand and its current advertising.

(b) However, a company with limited marketing resources may replace the advertising objectives by a statement of its problems and ask for a complete promotional plan.

(c) There are obvious dangers in too little information but the dangers of the client trying to direct the creative approach are real and equally dangerous.

(d) A 'typical' brief could include some or all of the following.

Brief	
1	Marketing plan - include time scale for advertising guidelines
2	Communication objectives (be precise)
3	Campaign budget - penalties for overspend etc
4	Product profile - in consumer terms
5	Company profile
6	Market analysis - segmentation of market
7	Production schedules - can we cope with created demand?
8	Distribution policy
9	Pricing policy
10	Evaluation criteria (effectiveness of agency and efficiency of the advertising campaign)

Remuneration of the agency

6.14 The amount of advertising undertaken is usually determined by the size of the advertiser's budget. It is important, therefore, to understand how it is paid for. As already stated the agency originally worked for the media owner and this is still where the agency gets most of its revenue. Nearly all media owners give the agency 15% of the cost of the space as a commission. The media outlet bills the agency net of commission and the agency then bills the client for the full amount. This means that the commission is in fact 17.65% on the *cost*. For every £100 the client pays, the agency pays the *media* £85, ie

$$\frac{£15}{£85} \times 100 = 17.65\%$$

6.15 *Calculating media commission.* Assume the rate-card cost of time/space for an item is £10,000, and a standard rate of commission of 15%, which the agency receives if it is recognised. Commission discount on £10,000 is £1,500. The agency bills the client for £10,000. The media owner bills the agency for £10,000 *less* £1,500 commission, ie £8,500. The agency therefore makes £1,500 on the deal.

6.16 The agency also receives a mark-up on work supervised by the agency but bought from external suppliers. Let us assume that a market research survey cost £8,500. However the agency will charge to the client a fee of:

$$\frac{100\%}{85\%} \times £8,500 = £10,000.$$

The agency therefore makes £1,500 on the deal, which is equivalent to a 15% commission discount on £10,000 worth of media buying.

6.17 Whilst the commission system is almost universal, it tends to be replaced for very large or small accounts. If a campaign is very small the 15% will not cover the agency costs. In such a situation the agreement may be that the client pays for all the cost of preparing the advertisement or a flat fee. Alternatively a figure of, say £500, could be set and the client makes up any shortfall that the agency does not earn from commission. The fee system is rarely used however, and the commission system is as already stated above, almost universal.

6.18 As long as the commission system is the norm, agencies *cannot* compete with each other on price (of buying time/space) only on creative flair, management quality, customer service etc *unless* the agencies are willing to pass on to the client some of their commission. This is commission rebating. Agencies do not actually hand anything back they simply invoice the client for the media bill at rate card costs *less* the level of the rebate. Thus the agency may end up with only 10% to 12% media commission. Big spending clients can exert pressure on agencies to do this, due to the size of their accounts and therefore, the value of their commission. It is not known how widespread this practice is, but as an example in 1984 Allan Brady and Marsh resigned the £3.5 million B & Q account after being asked to rebate on an account they considered to be only marginally profitably anyway. (Media independents routinely rebate commission but this is different because they only provide the media *part* of the advertising agency service.) Conversely, a very expensive campaign (eg in millions) will earn the agency very large sums. Clients may resent the fact that they do not benefit from the discounts being given on their advertising. The client, in this case, is likely to negotiate a deal with the agency. Alternatively the client can pay the agency on the time spent on the campaign, and pay the media at cost.

Working with the agency

6.19 The agency exists to provide a service that the client needs, and consequently agency and client should work as partners, even if they are not equal. Bearing in mind the hard work involved in selecting a new agency, it is worthwhile making an effort to co-operate. An agency will work better once it is acquainted with the client and the client's marketing staff, and market. Consequently a series of regular reviews is becoming more common. These cover areas such as gaps in performance, the relationship, strategy and campaigns.

Part A: Background knowledge relevant to analysis and decision

Alternatives to the agency

6.20 Alternatives have become more popular. The use of a full-service advertising agency is still the norm, however, particularly in the USA, and creative consultants and media buying shops are at your service. We can distinguish four main types of alternatives to using a full-service agency.

(a) 'Do-it-yourself' or in-house advertising
(b) Use a creative shop (Hot House or Hot Shop)
(c) Use a media independent
(d) Go 'a la carte'

6.21 Whether you do it yourself, or use specialist services, it is down to you to co-ordinate the exercise and this requires skill and a considerable amount of time. The final result of using specialist services or indeed doing the job personally may be a lower paying out cost but will the advertising be as effective'?

6.22 The *media owner* is the independent broadcasting contractor, newspaper or magazine publisher, bill posting contractor, radio company, etc. Media owners normally have a department responsible for attracting advertisers (or agencies), and arranging for the appearance of the advertisements. The head of this department is the advertising manager. It is worth remembering that the media is itself a product and has to be marketed to readers/viewers and to advertisers as its revenue is derived from both.

6.23 We have seen that there are three parties to the relationship shown earlier. We focused on the agency-client relationship, but we must also consider what each party should be doing to nurture the *tri-partite* relationship, including the media owner, the agency and the advertiser.

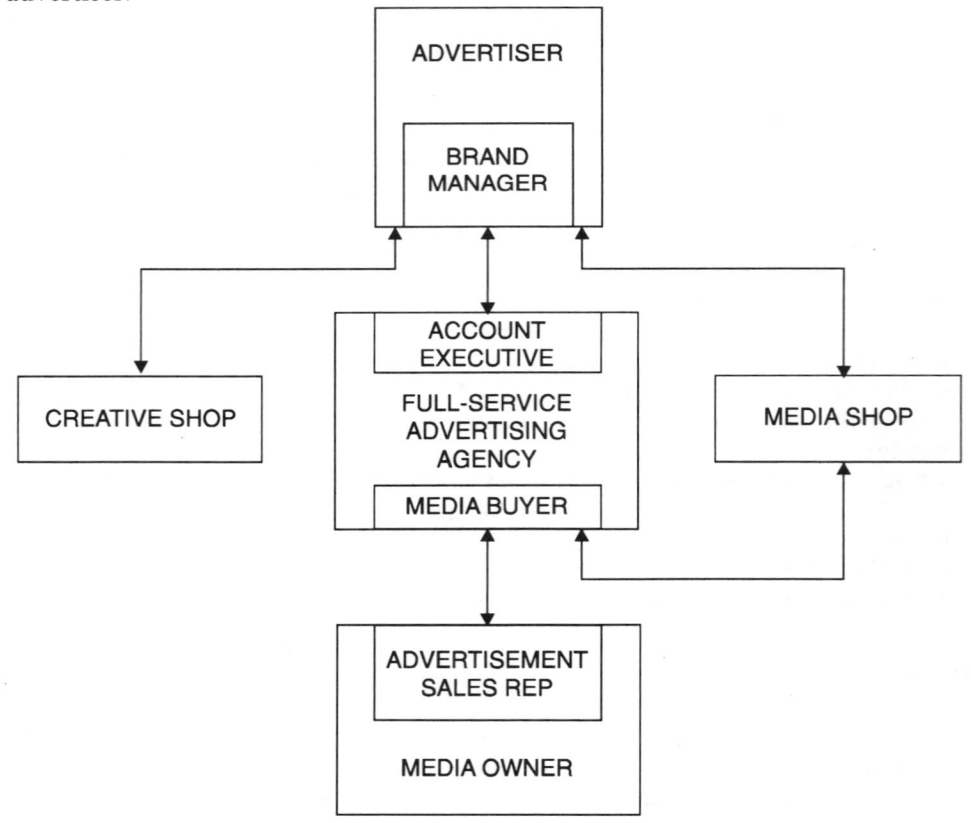

```
                    ┌─────────────┐
                    │  ADVERTISER │
                    ├─────────────┤
                    │    BRAND    │
                    │   MANAGER   │
                    └─────────────┘
        ┌──────────────────┼──────────────────┐
        │           ┌─────────────┐           │
        │           │   ACCOUNT   │           │
        │           │  EXECUTIVE  │           │
        ▼           ├─────────────┤           ▼
  ┌──────────┐     │ FULL-SERVICE│      ┌──────────┐
  │ CREATIVE │     │ ADVERTISING │      │  MEDIA   │
  │   SHOP   │     │   AGENCY    │      │   SHOP   │
  └──────────┘     ├─────────────┤      └──────────┘
                    │ MEDIA BUYER │           ▲
                    └─────────────┘           │
                           ▲                  │
                           │                  │
                    ┌─────────────┐           │
                    │ADVERTISEMENT│           │
                    │  SALES REP  │───────────┘
                    ├─────────────┤
                    │ MEDIA OWNER │
                    └─────────────┘
```

6.24 The media owner should:

(a) pay attention to the long-term quality of the media product;
(b) try to develop media that hit specific target markets;
(c) work closely with client and agency, keeping both informed about the medium;
(d) notify agencies in advance of future editorial comment;

(e) ensure an appropriate balance between editorial and advertising;
(f) invest in research or relevance to improving the media and its effectiveness;
(g) not misrepresent the reach of the medium;
(h) recognise the importance of flexibility, offering as many varied positions as possible;
(i) not sell time/space to a higher bidder once a firm contact has been signed;
(j) conduct extensive follow-ups on business already won;
(k) keep agencies informed of meetings with the clients;
(l) not quote different prices to agency and client;
(m) not offer deals cutting out the agency and, therefore its commission earnings;
(n) should not increase rates without adequate notice;
(o) should not omit advertisements without prior notice.

6.25 The advertiser should:

(a) have a good product (advertising is at its most effective when offering the consumer a benefit eg lower price, new version etc);
(b) make messages known to an appropriate audience using the correct media;
(c) be the expert on the brand and the market;
(d) be completely clear as to the objectives of the advertising;
(e) learn and understand media characteristics;
(f) initiate planning well in advance of campaign date to allow professional media operations, copy dates to be met and early booking discounts to be gained;
(g) contribute to the agency's and media owner's knowledge of the market;
(h) give a clear, easily understood briefing with complete background information;
(i) involve the agency in the total marketing strategy;
(j) fix the budget, target audience and media objectives in advance;
(k) reward the agency and recognise it has to be allowed to make a profit;
(l) be ruthless in removing business if performance is substandard;
(m) give the media schedule time to do its job.

6.26 The agency should:

(a) encourage three-way contact (advertiser-media owner-agency);
(b) have close personal ties with the media, to secure time and space, when these are scarce;
(c) involve the media reps in producing media and market information;
(d) make full use of media facilities/run/research etc;
(e) understand overall marketing plans for brands;
(f) keep clients informed of changes in media, expanding clients' media knowledge;
(g) remember it is the clients' money (they have the final say);
(h) not treat the client like an idiot or dictate to the client;
(i) periodically review media schedules to ensure the reasons for choice still hold good;
(j) ensure the method of remuneration allows the agency to give unbiased recommendations;
(k) not object to the client demanding changes provided adequate reason is given;
(l) explain precisely to the client how media schedules are arrived at;
(m) do not ignore clients' views on media matters;
(n) remember that in most cases the client will understand the needs of customers best of all.

Part A: Background knowledge relevant to analysis and decision

Role of the media independents

6.27 As mentioned earlier, some agencies, rather than expand by diversifying their departments, prefer to *concentrate* their abilities. Rather than provide the full service of advertisement creation, media planning and buying, and production work, they restrict their expertise to one of these areas. These independent companies now form such an important part of the current advertising scene that they merit separate attention.

6.28 What was originally thought to be a temporary phenomenon has turned out to be substantial and permanent feature of the advertising industry. These organisations are no longer described, as they were originally, as media-brokers or buying shops. The term 'media independent' is not fully adequate, but does describe these companies which specialise in an aspect of the media side of advertising, yet are independent of the traditional agency structure, and of any specialist creative or production company

6.29 In order to understand why these specialist media planning and buying companies have prospered, we must examine both the service they provide and the clients who use it.

(a) What service is provided? Media independents are specialised and have grown because they are cost-effective streamlined organisations which employ skilled media talent.

(b) Why should any organisation call on the services of a media independent? There is no single answer. A number of advertisers found that conventional full-service agencies did not meet their particular needs or budgets The economic climate forced some companies to look for alternative systems and, as media costs continued to rise, many advertisers turned with new interest to ways of stretching their budgets The media independents offered them a system that side-stepped the fixed 15% commission rate and employed some of the best time-buyers in the business. Clients with expert marketing departments could formulate their own products, select a skilled team of creative people to prepare the advertisements and appoint a separate team of experts to plan and book the schedule.

6.30 As marketing departments grow more skilful, so they are better able - and are often more inclined - to commission specific tasks, and they now have a far wider range of smaller specialist teams, to perform these selected tasks Some companies use several creative companies to develop different campaigns for different products, and one media independent to place the advertisements. As clients become more sophisticated, and the media independents (and complimentary creative services) prosper, some extremists have suggested that full-service agencies will have to hive off their media departments and run them like independents (some already have) or perhaps break down their range of services into four or five specialist departments operating like a conglomerate of independents - a self-service advertising cafeteria from which clients can select the dishes they want.

6.31 One view - held by many independents - is that this trend will mean the end of many traditional agencies, particularly those of a medium size which cannot afford to match the talents available within independents. With a full-service agency, the client might find some services extremely good but others, particularly media, weak. The independents are not cheap, but claim to give better value for money. There is no reason for advertisers to use a full-service agency to plan and buy their media requirements, unless the agency is prepared to waive the fixed 15% commission rate in favour of a payment system better than that offered by the independents and, even if this were granted, the independents would still do a better job

6.32 The opposing school of thought - found, of course, in the agencies - is that there will always be a need for the superior resources and fertile interconnections of the full-service agency. Companies without internal resources of experienced advertising and marketing staff need all the help they can get in straightening out their advertising strategies and marketing planning. Whilst a media independent can perform its allocated task very efficiently, its effectiveness depends on what it is asked to do, and the independent may not have the agency's wide knowledge of marketing and of the client's market in particular. Advertisers with a wide variety of communication needs, and different levels of campaign running simultaneously for a range of different products, need a full-service agency to co-ordinate for them. Independents are often divorced from the creative strategy, so are less efficient then their agency counterparts in making choices which acknowledge creative demands, and the penalty of not using a full-service agency must be measured by the loss in effectiveness of the total advertising investment.

6.33 The client profile for the media independents now covers the whole gamut of opportunities - advertisers, agencies, creative consultancies and design groups, and even media-owners and management consultancies

6.34 Many small agencies and some medium-sized now place some or all of their media planning or buying in the hands of the media specialists, but it is not only the small firms who do this: quite a few medium-sized agencies enlist outside media assistance, particularly where TV buying is concerned. Media independents are also getting business from new agencies without media dependents. These companies are providing the top creative and account-handling experience that complement the media independents' own services to clients. Added to this, the rise of separate media-buying companies has also opened up the field for the creative consultants. whose work has multiplied over the years.

6.35 The media independents are now in a period of evolution rather than revolution and the 'either/or' syndrome no longer applies so rigidly - advertisers and agencies recognise that the independents have a lot to offer can save time and money and cut down administration costs.

Services provided

6.36 It is interesting to note the wide variety of services now offered. Some independents work in an advisory capacity but do not plan or buy campaigns, while others specialise in international business. Furthermore, the ways in which the media independents are integrating have become increasingly flexible, they co-operate not only with creative consultancies and the new-type agencies but also work freely with advertiser/agency partnerships direct. Some advertisers now use media independents working alongside their existing agencies, rather than seeing them as competitors. the growth of new media opportunities (eg cable and satellite channels), along with the proliferation of selective press media has meant increased demand on the independents' talents.

6.37 There is no longer any need to argue for the respectability of what were called buying shops - it is now firmly established that most media independents are run by professionals. This professionalism was recognised more formally by the formation in 1981 of the Association of Media Independents. In order to establish the calibre of companies seeking membership, the Association checks that applicants meet various criteria as laid clown in its memorandum and articles.

   (a) The applicant company must be in the business of media buying, with billings and a client list which show that its capacity extends across major media and that its practice is not unduly restricted. The company must also have received recognition by the various media trade bodies.

   (b) The applicant firms are of high professional standing: they must give a written understanding to provide any first-hand client with copies of invoices from media-owners, showing prices at which space or time was bought on their behalf. The applicant firm must also give a formal undertaking to abide by the Code of Advertising Practice.

   (c) They should be of sound financial standing and, to this end, must provide the last set of accounts as submitted to one of the recognition bodies.

   (d) The applicant company should be independent of any advertiser, agency or media-owner and to establish this independence the applicant company must submit to the Association details of its company share holdings and corporate structure.

Part A: Background knowledge relevant to analysis and decision

7 MEDIA AND MEDIA RESEARCH

Main media types

7.1 There are five main media types available in the UK.

(a) Television (TV)
(b) Press (newspapers and magazines)
(c) Radio
(d) Outdoor (mainly posters)
(e) Cinema

You will need to consider the reach frequency and impact of the above media when planning a campaign. These aspects will influence your decision as to the best media mix for any given campaign. See the table on the next page.

	TV	Press	Radio	Outdoor (posters)	Cinema
Strengths	Creative opportunities; Sound and real movement; Mass economic coverage; Regional (but with national image); Time control; Intrusive	Very selective therefore cost efficient; Detailed message possible; No time limit; Personal communication; Production costs not excessive	Cheap; Flexible; Good creative opportunities; Precise timing; High trade interest	Continuous presence; Highly visible; Regionally selective; High coverage; High trade awareness	Selective coverage of your audience; Captive audience; Sound movement + Big sound; Regionally flexible; Trade involvement
Weaknesses	Time limit on message; No reference back; Rarely selective; Expensive for both advertising time and production costs	Not intrusive; Little control over timing; Long lead times - especially colour; Regional media have no national image	Sound only; Limited geographical cover; Limited penetration (variable); Limited research	Creative limitations; Best sites committed long term; High demand - limited availability; High capital outlay; High production cost; Little reliable research	Low coverage of total population; High production costs

7.2 Media are constantly changing. For example electronic media are being increasingly used. Particular instances are outdoor programmable electronic signs (eg a theatre advertising future plays or shows) and indoor videos advertising to queues inside major city post offices. It is important for your Diploma examination and indeed your marketing career that you keep up to date with the latest developments.

7.3 Some references to media research have been made in earlier pages and it is not proposed to go into a great more detail here since it is unlikely that you will be asked a detailed question on this in your case study exam. However you should be aware that media research takes two major forms.

(a) Client or agency research on the media.
(b) Media owners' research on the media's audiences.

2: Marketing communications strategy

7.4 Clearly you would as a client want to know the general advantages and disadvantages of the various media as given on the previous pages. However, you would also want to know:

(a) media costs;
(b) media audiences;
(c) media reach - geographical, percentages of target audience;
(d) media images;
(e) media effectiveness.

7.5 Reputable media conduct their audience research on viewers, listeners, readers, passers-by and so on in the knowledge that clients/agencies will be interested not only in the numbers reached but also in the type of persons reached (eg, sex, age, social class, lifestyle etc).

7.6 You may find a knowledge of the following other data sources for media research helpful. Most research is controlled by committees within the governing bodies of advertising, as it is in the industry's interest to be able to provide accurate information and have a co-ordinated scheme providing accurate information and comparable statistics. (These bodies are called *Joint Industry Committees or JIC's*).

(a) *Audit Bureau of Circulations (ABC)* is a limited company, independent of media owners, advertising agencies and advertisers but which has members representing each. Founded in 1931, it certifies net (per issue) sales figures for newspapers and magazines. These figures are averaged over the six month periods from the end of June and December each year. *Sales* is defined as a copy bought by an individual and not received in any other way ie it excludes bulk purchases for organisations and free copies. The certified figure-is described as the 'ABC circulation' of the publication. These figures are found in BRAD (see (c) below).

(b) *Broadcaster's Audience Research Board (BARB)*. Its remit is to commission and supervise TV audience research in the UK. Before BARB was established in 1981, JICTAR (The ITV JIC) and the BBC had independently measured the total TV audience, but their figures rarely tallied due to differences in measurement techniques. BARB is based on a survey of 24,000 households to determine the demographics of the TV area, and who can receive which channels. From the 24,000, 4,500 households are chosen which are representative of the TV area and the nation. Each of these has a set meter that records when the TV was on, the channel the programmes watched. Each member of the family over 4 years old also keeps a record of what they watched. The research can therefore tell us how many people watched a programme in total, which members of the family and their socio-economic group.

(c) *British Rate and Data (BRAD)* is a monthly index of current advertising rates and mechanical data for almost every separate media vehicle available to UK advertisers. Press vehicles also normally include ABC or VFD circulation figures or a publisher's statement of claimed circulation. BRAD is the media buyer's indispensable reference book. (Its American counterpart is Standard Rate and Data.)

(d) JICNARS is the *Joint Industry Committee for National Readership Surveys*. It was set up in 1968 to co-ordinate and commission research into *readership* of UK newspapers and magazines. Readership is the number of people who read (or scan through) the publication. Certain publications are passed onto other readers (Vogue, Cosmopolitan), some end up in waiting rooms (National Geographical, Readers Digest, Country Life) significantly increasing the potential of each advertisement. There is a variation amongst national dailies and the tabloids being read during breaks at work while the more serious titles are taken home to read in the evening. A continuous programme of 35,000 personal interviews is carried out each year, asking about readership of around 230 publications. Readership figures are calculated from frequency/last read scores. Respondents are shown the mastheads of publications and asked when they last read or looked at it. If the answer was yesterday/today for a daily publication, within the previous 7 days for a weekly, or within the last 4 weeks for a monthly, that respondent is classified as an average issue reader for that title. The percentage of average issue readers in the samples is the statistic from which a total average issue readership figure is estimated. Their aggregate demographic make-up defines the title's *readership profile*.

(e) JICPAR is the *Joint Industry Committee for Poster Audience Research*. In addition there is OSCAR (Outdoor Site Classification and Audience Research).

    (i) OSCAR calculates the 'opportunities to see (OTS) rates for every member's sites (95% of all sites) using a mathematical model and a census of sites.

    (ii) Gross audience - estimated number of people passing each site.

    (iii) OTS are less than the gross audience to allow for factors such as:

        (1) illumination
        (2) height and reflection
        (3) permanent obstructions
        (4) other poster panels
        (5) visibility distance
        (6) angle of panel to sightline

(f) Radio research tells us if the set was switched on during a particular period, and the demographics of the audience. Radio research is less involved partly because it only accounts for 2.3% of advertising expenditure and cannot afford the £1m that BARB costs. The information is collected via a diary scheme giving audience details for 1/2 hour periods, together with demographic details and socio-economic groups. RAJAR (Radio Joint Audience Research) now conducts audience research for both the BBC and independent local radio.

8 BRANDING

8.1 Branding has provided exam questions in recent cases. Firstly, some definitions.

(a) *Brand:* 'a name, term, sign, symbol, or design (or a combination of them) which is intended to signify the goods or services of one seller or group of sellers and to differentiate them from those of competitors'. (Kotler)

(b) *Brand name:* is that part of a brand which can be vocalised or uttered.

(c) *Brand mark:* that part of a brand which can be recognised but cannot be uttered (symbols, design, or distinctive colouring or lettering).

(d) *Trademark*: a brand or part of a brand that is given legal protection because it is capable of exclusive appropriation.

(e) *Copyright:* the exclusive legal right to reproduce, publish, and sell the matter and form of literary, musical, or artistic work.

8.2 From the buyer's viewpoint, a brand tells the buyer something about the product's quality. Brand names contribute to shopping efficiency. Brand names help attract consumers' attention to new products.

8.3 From the seller's viewpoint, brand names help the seller to handle orders and track down problems. Brand names and trademarks give legal protection when there are unique product features, which would otherwise be easy to copy. (Illegal brand copying is a big problem in international marketing.) Branding gives the seller the opportunity to attract a loyal set of customers whose regular purchase give more sales stability and long-run profit. Brands are usually supported by good product quality and promotion. Brand recognition, brand preference, and ultimately brand insistence represent the aims of many companies in FMCG (fast moving consumer goods) markets.

8.4 From the viewpoint of society as a whole, branding has advantages and disadvantages.

(a) Branding leads to higher and more consistent product quality. A brand essentially makes a promise to customers about delivering certain satisfactions. The seller cannot easily tamper with the brand's quality or be careless.

(b) Branding increases the rate of innovation in society. Without branding, producers would not have an incentive to look for new features that could be protecting a product against imitating competitors. Branding gives producers an incentive to seek distinctive product features, and this results in much more product variety and choice for consumers.

(c) Branding increases shopper efficiency, since it provides much information about the product and where to buy it. It enables cost benefits of self selection in large retailing outlets. These benefits can result in higher profits for manufacturers and retailers and/or lower prices for consumers.

(d) Branding leads to higher prices, false and unnecessary differentiation of goods. Branding increases the status consciousness of people who buy certain brands to impress.

Naming

8.5 The essentials of a good brand name are as follows.

(a) Is it distinctive? Does it have individuality? It is different from others in the field?

(b) Does it lend itself easily to display and use in advertising? Short names can be printed larger than long ones.

(c) Is it easy to say? Audi should be pronounced Owdy, but people outside Europe tend to call it Ordy.

(d) It is easy to remember? (eg OXO, Coco-Cola, Rentokil, Yamaha, Heineken). Sometimes new names are adopted, to indicate a change in management, or to overcome the bad associations of the old ones. Think of the motor company of Hillman that became Rootes, then Chrysler, then Talbot, then Peugeot. Morris became BMC, then British Leyland and now Rover.

8.6 The marketing and PR implications of a name are therefore very important. The Japanese car names Cherry and Laurel sound odd in the West where car names usually suggest power or prestige. The *Economist Pocket Marketing* says: 'When Chrysler introduced a new car into the Mexican Market called the Nova it forgot that in Mexico *no va* means "it does not go"'.

Company names

8.7 Choice of a corporate name is important because it will become an identity (including a legal identity) to which will become attached a good or bad reputation forming a corporate image. It will have a character or personality.

(a) Some are based on the founder's name - Ford, Cadbury, Guinness, Lipton and Singer. Others are more general, but perhaps have imposing nature - Premier, National, British, Perfect or Marvellous.

(b) Others based on the product Coca-Cola, or mention the service (eg First Bank of Nigeria)

Some firms use initials (eg FIAT, BMW for Bayerische Motoren Werke or form words based on the initials of the company.

(c) Long and difficult names such as Tokyo Shibaura Electrical Company become short, like Toshiba. The Royal Dutch Airlines has a long name in the Dutch language, but the airline has readily been recognised as KLM for over 50 years.

(d) The names of long established organisations may have been chosen haphazardly, or for personal reasons, long before marketing considerations demanded more careful choice of names. Today, one is less able to choose any name because it may already exist. In most countries business names may have to be registered under company law.

Notes Part A: Background knowledge relevant to analysis and decision

Brand names

8.8 Brand names are the specially devised names used to distinguish products. They may also be company names, like, Heinz, Guinness, or Sanyo, but they can be quite different names of which DAZ, OMO, Ultrabrite, Lux, Marlboro, Sprite, Elephant, or Lion are examples. Such names are usually registered as trade marks by designing the name in a distinctive way.

(a) Unregistered names are usually called trade names.

(b) Granada TV failed to prevent the Ford Motor Company using the name Granada. At the moment there are two Budweiser beers on sale in Europe: the American one and one produced in Czechoslovakia (called Budweiser Budvar).

(c) The 'halo' effect operates when a new product benefits from the already established good name of the manufacturer.

9 COMMUNICATIONS RESEARCH

9.1 Advertising research as described above is but one aspect of communications research. As a marketing manager you will be concerned with the following aspects of your decision making.

(a) *Economy* - the need to minimise the cost of inputs.

(b) *Efficiency* - the process of maximising the productivity of inputs.

(c) *Effectiveness* - the extent to which the output generated meets the objectives set for the organisation.

9.2 You will therefore be continuously assessing the effectiveness as well as the relative costs of each element of the promotional mix using research methods.

(a) *Sales research*
   (i) What are the selling costs for different customers?
   (ii) How can we improve sales presentations so as to obtain more orders?
   (iii) Should we have fewer personal visits and more telephone calls?
   (iv) Is personal selling more effective than direct marketing?

(b) *Sales promotion research*
   (i) What extra sales resulted from the extra costs for these promotions?
   (ii) What level of retention of extra sales was there post-promotion?
   (iii) What proportion of the budget should go on consumer incentives as opposed to dealer incentives or salesforce incentives?

(c) *PR/publicity research*
   (i) How effective is PR relative to other forms of promotion?
   (ii) How can changes in image and attitudes be measured..
   (iii) How much notice do potential customers take of editorials?

10 INTERNAL COMMUNICATIONS AND THE ORGANISATION

Internal communications and internal marketing

10.1 With the advent of Total Quality Management and its increasing adoption more and more companies have come to realise that without the wholehearted co-operation of all employees (whether in direct contact with the customer or not) any extra marketing effort can be wasted. As previously mentioned you will find additional material on internal marketing in Chapter 5. However you might find the following internal marketing framework helpful bearing in mind that questions on internal marketing have been posed in recent cases.

10.2 Communications within the organisation fall into two types.

(a) *Vertical communication* is mainly formal, and it reflects the organisation hierarchy - in other words it is communication from boss to subordinate and from subordinate to boss.

   (i) Organisations are geared to relay orders/instructions regarding specific tasks
   (ii) Length of *chain of command* (the number of people the order goes through eg managing director, marketing director, product group manager, brand manager, secretary etc).
   (iii) Distortion is a risk especially if communication is verbal.
   (iv) There is a need for the provision of upward communication (feedback).
   (v) Difficulties can arise if the decision-making area is divorced from areas where the decisions are implemented.
   (vi) Authoritarian attitudes can cause resentment amongst subordinates.
   (vii) Problems related to co-operation.

(b) *Horizontal communication* is between departments and individuals of the same level. It is often informal.
   (i) There is a need to communicate at equal levels.
   (ii) It relies on good relations between departments and co-operation to achieve success.
   (iii) There are problems related to demarcation of responsibilities.
   (iv) Distortion of information can be caused by specialist jargon.

Effective internal communication

10.3 Communication may break down inside an organisation for one or more of the following reasons.

(a) Gaps in transmission, eg between office and field salesforce.
(b) Bureaucratic structures with formalisation of communication.
(c) The manufacturing and marketing of a large number of different products
(d) The size of the organisation (eg Unilever) may add to its communication problems because of the volume of information to be transmitted.
(e) Inflexibility of structures.
(f) Isolation of departments (eg legal department within a company).
(g) Reluctance of subordinates to report upwards that some things are not going according to plan.
(h) Misinterpretation of messages (is a *cost reduction programme* the same as redundancy or reorganisation, or what?)
(i) Shortcomings in communications skills:
   (i) low standards of written communication
   (ii) poor speaking, listening
   (iii) ambiguity
   (iv) verbosity, etc.

10.4 An organisation must identify the internal groups with whom it is or ought to be communicating and decide what messages should be sent along which channels to reach them.

10.5 Internal marketing, discussed in more detail in Chapter 5, is a means by which organisations can address these issues.

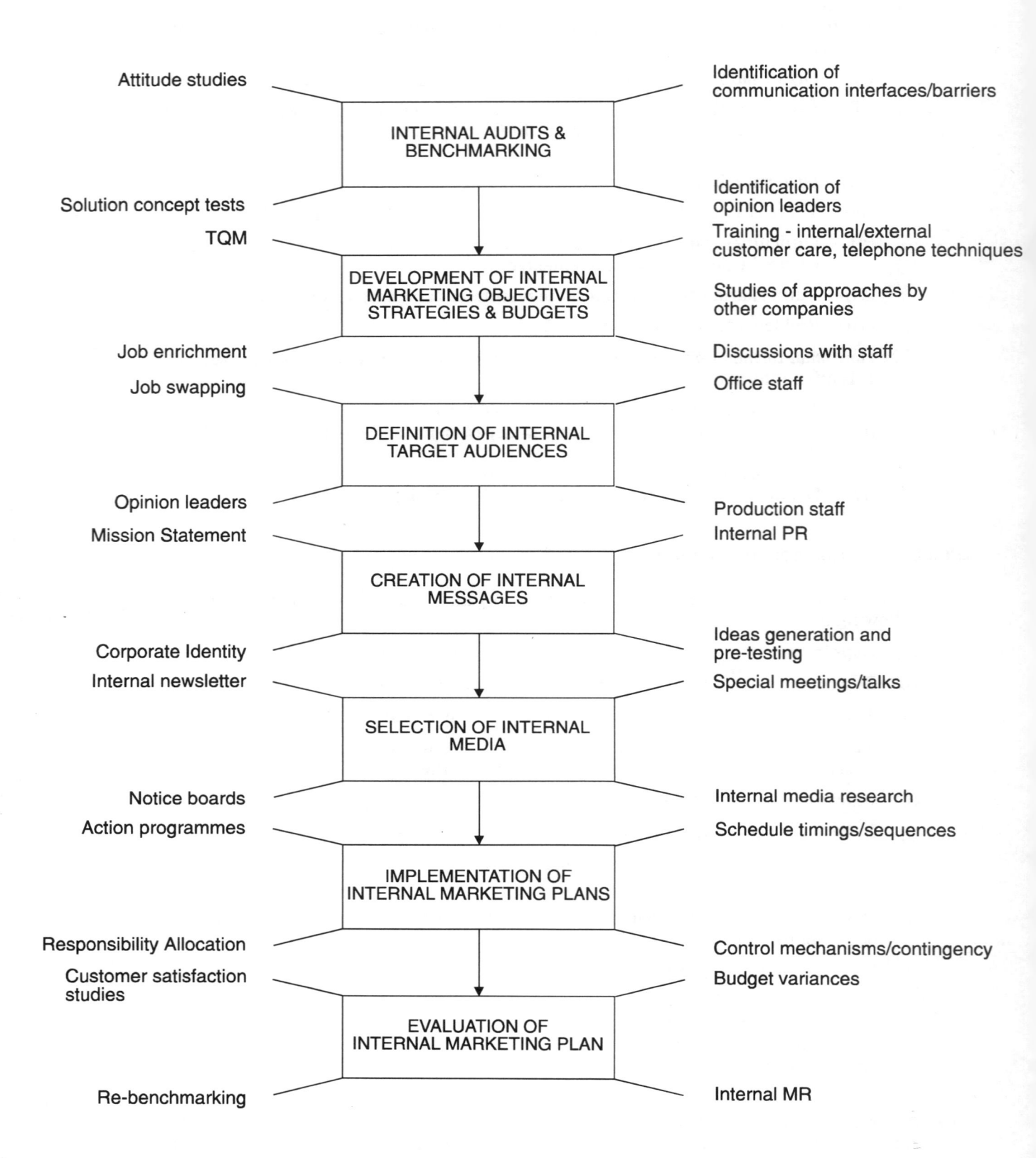

Part A: Background knowledge relevant to analysis and decision

Left items	Process	Right items
Attitude studies	**INTERNAL AUDITS & BENCHMARKING**	Identification of communication interfaces/barriers
Solution concept tests		Identification of opinion leaders
TQM		Training - internal/external customer care, telephone techniques
	DEVELOPMENT OF INTERNAL MARKETING OBJECTIVES STRATEGIES & BUDGETS	Studies of approaches by other companies
Job enrichment		Discussions with staff
Job swapping		Office staff
	DEFINITION OF INTERNAL TARGET AUDIENCES	
Opinion leaders		Production staff
Mission Statement		Internal PR
	CREATION OF INTERNAL MESSAGES	
Corporate Identity		Ideas generation and pre-testing
Internal newsletter		Special meetings/talks
	SELECTION OF INTERNAL MEDIA	
Notice boards		Internal media research
Action programmes		Schedule timings/sequences
	IMPLEMENTATION OF INTERNAL MARKETING PLANS	
Responsibility Allocation		Control mechanisms/contingency
Customer satisfaction studies		Budget variances
	EVALUATION OF INTERNAL MARKETING PLAN	
Re-benchmarking		Internal MR

Chapter roundup

- Promotion is an aspect of an organisation's total communications with its environment. Promotion deals with distinct products and services. Corporate communications promotes the organisation.

- Promotion is necessary because personal contact is expensive and impractical for many products and services.

- The promotional mix includes:
    - advertising;
    - sales promotion;
    - personal selling;
    - public relations (PR).

- The choice of mix depends on the promotion objectives, the competition, the type of product/service and budget. Industrial goods (eg power stations, turbines) are likely to require a heavy degree of personal selling.

- For most campaigns, the services of an advertising agency are required, even though there are also media independents who provide a part of the service. Advertising agencies are generally divided between account management and creative tasks.

- Messages must reflect communication objectives and be tailored to the specific needs of each public.

Test your knowledge

1. Distinguish between corporate personality, corporate identity and corporate image (see para 1.4)
2. List some marketing communications objectives. (2.3(b)).
3. What are the benefits of promotion, in the context of buyer behaviour? (3.3)
4. Distinguish between pull and push strategies. (3.8)
5. What decisions have to be taken in an advertising campaign? (3.12)
6. What is a 'false trade description'? (4.5(a)(iii))
7. Draw a framework for campaign planning. (5.1)
8. How would you select an advertising agency? (6.6 - 6.12)
9. What are the pros and cons of TV, press, radio, poster and cinema advertising? (7.1 diagram)
10. What is a brand? (8.1(a))

Chapter 3

INTERNATIONAL MARKETING STRATEGY

This chapter covers the following topics.

1. International marketing (IM) and the CIM case study examination
2. The rationale for international marketing
3. Barriers, problems and risks involved in marketing internationally
4. Cultural differences affecting marketing
5. Other environmental factors affecting marketing strategies
6. International market entry options and evaluation
7. International marketing research
8. Planning and organisational aspects of international marketing

Introduction

This chapter does not purport to be a *comprehensive* treatment of International Marketing. In other words, if you are sitting the separate Diploma examination in *International Marketing Strategy* you should buy the BPP Study Text on that subject. This chapter draws heavily on material provided for CIM courses by Dr Paul Fifield and Keith Lewis.

1 INTERNATIONAL MARKETING (IM) AND THE CIM CASE STUDY EXAMINATION

1.1 Most, if not all, of the companies featured in recent CIM case studies have had international interests. Although these interests have been mainly in Europe, there have also been opportunities to market in the wider world. Examples include the following.

(a) The *Australian Tourist Commission* (ATC) case was placed in a setting of international tourism and growth of international competition. International buying behaviours with regard to travel were also part of the ATC case study setting.

(b) In the case of *FirstrATE Europe*, part of your responsibilities as European Marketing Manager is to 'ensure all necessary contacts are made with ATE Group personnel in Princetown, such that the "marketing pipeline" between the USA and Europe grows stronger and becomes more effective in both directions'.

1.2 You need to bear in mind that the major part of international marketing is *marketing*, the basics of which have been covered in Chapters 1 and 2.

1.3 All we need to do in this chapter, therefore, is to examine how planning and control and the marketing mix might differ when marketing abroad. We can also confine ourselves to those aspects of international marketing likely to be needed for CIM case study examinations.

2 THE RATIONALE FOR INTERNATIONAL MARKETING

2.1 Some countries are not self-sufficient in food, in raw materials or both. They therefore need to import in order that their populations can survive, grow and prosper.

2.2 The UK is not self sufficient either in food or in all its needs for raw materials. It has traditionally imported a large proportion of its food and some of its raw materials, converting the latter into manufactured goods which have then been exported in order to pay for the imports. The UK is also a major international investor, earning dividends on overseas investments. The UK is also a major provider of services.

2.3 The difference between payments for imports of goods and services and the revenue received for exports of goods and services is sometimes known as the Balance of Payments (current account) and is an important factor in determining the economy of a country. Adverse balances have to be financed by borrowing from overseas investors (even the International Monetary Fund) but in the long term these debts will have to be repaid.

2.4 Some countries have more raw materials or can produce more food than they need and will naturally be tempted to export so as to raise their standard of living.

Comparative advantage

2.5 Ricardo, a 19th century economist, demonstrated that because certain industries enjoyed advantages in certain countries, it would be of mutual advantage for *countries* to trade in those goods where their *comparative* advantage, compared to other countries, was most favourable.

2.6 Ricardo's doctrine of comparative cost (1817) can be illustrated below in this simple example. Compare England and Portugal.

(a)

	England (Cost)		Portugal (Cost)	
One gallon of wine	120	hours work	80	hours of work
One yard of cloth	100	hours work	90	hours of work
Total hours work	220		170	

(b) Portugal has an *absolute* advantage in both wine and cloth. Portugal also has a comparative advantage in wine: it is better at producing wine than cloth. England is better at producing cloth than wine. *Despite* the fact that Portugal is more efficient than England in producing cloth, it should still produce wine, and England should specialise in cloth. Why?

(i) Assume that one yard of English cloth is traded for one gallon of Portuguese wine. In other words, for 80 hours work producing a gallon of wine, the Portuguese can import one yard of cloth. Therefore, for the cost of 160 hours of work (one gallon of wine for domestic consumption, and one for export) it can have its gallon of wine (home made) and its yard of cloth (imported), a saving of ten hours work. England fares even better. For the cost of 200 hours work (one yard of cloth for domestic use and one for export) it can have its gallon of wine (imported) and its yard of cloth, a saving of 20 hours of work.

(ii) In other words, it *still* benefits Portugal to produce wine and import cloth, even though it is more efficient at making cloth than England.

(c) Portugal has *absolute* advantage in both wine and cloth but a *comparatively* greater advantage in wine.

2.7 Reasons why industries may benefit from a comparative advantage include the following.

(a) Raw materials industries benefit from the existence of raw material, if it is efficiently produced and constitutes a large part of final product costs for user industries.

(b) Transport, if the effect of transport costs are high in comparison to the value of the product.

(c) Wages and employment structure leads to high labour productivity, but cheap labour can be a source of comparative advantage (in the short term).

(d) Economies of scale. If a market is large enough to permit the establishment of economically sized plants where scale economies are important, this can give an industry an advantage.

(e) Acquired skills: the existence of experience and know how based on historical specialisation can provide advantages.

2.8 The example of fairly simple goods like wine and cloth was chosen because trade in high-tech goods or specialised services is much more complex. This has been demonstrated by Michael Porter in his *Competitive Advantage of Nations*. Cost is only one factor, not perhaps the most important. Porter proposes that the competitive advantage of a country's firms, that is their ability to pursue successfully strategies of cost leadership, differentiation or focus, derives from a country's:

(a) factor conditions (human resources, physical resources, knowledge, capital, infrastructure, divided into basic factors such as cheap labour or raw materials which are unsustainable as a source of long term competitive advantage and *advanced factors* such as proprietary technology);

(b) demand conditions (which determine how firms interpret buyer behaviour: sophisticated domestic consumers are a good discipline for global success);

(c) related and supporting industries (eg suppliers, industries using similar technologies);

(d) competitive rivalry.

2.9 When you are considering international markets, then you need to consider the extent to which your distinctive competences are enhanced by those conditions identified above.

2.10 The main reasons for *companies* marketing internationally may be summarised as follows.

(a) Product nearing the end of its life cycle on the home market.
(b) Excess production capacity and/or surplus production.
(c) Competition in overseas markets may be less intense.
(d) To gain economies of scale.
(e) For prestige purposes and/or patriotic concerns.
(f) To gain political favour and/or government subsidies.
(g) To lessen risk (ie wide customer/market base).
(h) Comparative advantage.
(i) Saturated home market.
(j) Organisational ambitions/desires - shareholder pressure
(k) Perhaps most important of all - the potential for extra profits.
(l) Survival.
(m) To compete against overseas firms which are entering the domestic market.

3 BARRIERS, PROBLEMS AND RISKS INVOLVED IN MARKETING INTERNATIONALLY

3.1 Two types of barriers exist in international trade.

(a) Tariff barriers
(b) Non tariff barriers

3.2 *Tariff barriers* are visible and straightforward. They simply consist of a surcharge on all goods described in detail by the special tariff concerned. This can be applied as a percentage of the *value* of the goods or on volume (ie the quantity). There can be different levels of tariffs for different volumes. Both tariff and non-tariff barriers are used by governments to protect home industries but also as a means of discouraging imports so as to obtain a more favourable balance of payments. The EU has a standard 4% tariff for most non-EU imports.

3.3 *Non-tariff barriers* are many, varied and usually less visible than tariff barriers (which attract reprisals from other countries). They may be summarised as follows.

(a) *Technical barriers* can be

(i) *deliberate,* such as noise level restrictions on aero engines or exhaust emission levels in the USA; or

(ii) *incidental,* such as electrical supply (different voltages, incompatible equipment etc).

(b) *Administrative barriers*

(i) *Deliberate barriers* include bureaucratic 'red tape' delays (such as against Japanese imports to France).

(ii) *Incidental barriers* include over zealous officials.

(c) *Cultural barriers* are dealt with in more detail in Section 4 of this chapter.

(d) *Quotas* are restrictions on the amount of particular types of goods allowed into the country. These may be for limited periods only.

(e) *Prohibitions* are the result of deliberate government policy banning the import of certain goods (eg made from the skins of endangered species).

(f) *Monetary controls* on payments/currency leaving the country, although fluctuating exchange rates can also make exporting difficult.

(g) *Government pressure* ('Buy British' campaigns policies etc).

(h) Other *legal barriers* are described in Paragraph 3.4 below.

3.4 Legal constraints affecting international markets include the following.

(a) *Markets*
   (i) Export controls
   (ii) Import controls
   (iii) International law
   (iv) Treaties (eg GATT/WTO)
   (v) Patents/trademarks
   (vi) Regional economic groupings (eg the EU)

(b) *Marketing mix.* Specific country laws govern products/services, pricing, promotion and distribution (too many and varied to cover here).

(c) *Organisation*
   (i) Ownership and capital structure
   (ii) Permits for:
      (1) location of plant
      (2) employment of labour
      (3) types of product or process
      (4) monopoly, trusts etc.

(d) *Financial*
   (i) Minimum wages
   (ii) Expatriation of profits
   (iii) Methods of payment

(e) *Legal administration*
   (i) Contracts

Part A: Background knowledge relevant to analysis and decision

      (ii)   Which law prevails, importing country, exporting country, third country
      (iii)   Which courts settle disputes.

3.5   Although perhaps a little over-detailed for our needs and subject to updating, Beatrice Bondy's (1983) study of protectionism in the 1980s is very revealing. We give below her detailed categorisation of non tariff barriers. Note that there is a movement towards free trade, with the GATT agreement of November 1993 and the founding of the World Trade Organisation 1995. At best non-tariff barriers are being converted into tariff barriers.

Non tariff trade barriers in detail

Formal trade restrictions	Administrative trade restrictions
A *Non tariff import restrictions (Price related measures)*	D *State participation in trade*
Surcharges at border	Subsidies and other government support
	Government trade, government monopolies,
Port and statistical taxes	and granting of concessions or licences
Non discriminatory excise	Laws and ordinances discouraging imports
Taxes and registration charges	Problems relating to general government policy
Discriminatory excise taxes	
Government insurance requirements	Government procurement
Non discriminatory turnover taxes	Tax relief, granting of credit and guarantees
Discriminatory turnover taxes	Boycott
Import deposit	
Variable levies	E *Technical norms, standards and consumer protection regulations*
Consular fees	
Stamp taxes	
Various special taxes and surcharges	Health and safety regulations
	Pharmaceutical control regulations
B *Quantitative restrictions and similar specific trade limitations (Quantity-related measures)*	Product design regulations
	Industrial standards
	Size and weight regulations
	Packing and labelling regulations
Licensing regulations	Package marking regulations
Ceilings and quotas	Regulations pertaining to use
Embargoes	Regulations for the protection of intellectual property
Export restrictions and prohibitions	
Foreign exchange and other monetary or financial controls	Trademark regulations
Government price setting and surveillance	F *Customs processing and other administrative regulations*
Purchase and performance requirements	
	Antidumping policy
Restrictive business conditions	Customs calculations bases
Discriminatory bilateral arrangements	Formalities required by consular officials
Discriminatory regulations regarding countries of origin	Certification regulations
International cartels	Administrative obstacles
Orderly marketing agreements	Merchandise classification
Various related regulations	Regulations regarding sample shipments return shipments, and re-exports
C *Discriminatory freight rates*	Countervailing duties and taxes
	Appeal law
	Emergency law

3.6 There are of course risks involved in international marketing but depending on the country concerned these may not necessarily be any greater than trading in the home country.

3.7 Many organisations exist to encourage you and give you tangible help when exporting. You could start with the Overseas Trade Services, the Institute of Export and the banks. The following is based on an extract from a brochure detailing Barclays' services offered to all businesses. Such services help you:

   (a) find new outlets and sources of overseas trade, enabling you to develop your sales markets and identify sources of supply by providing you with impartial information about prospective overseas trading partners;

   (b) gain efficient access to a vast international market place (by providing you with information about international markets on a scale inaccessible to most companies);

   (c) determine your costs in advance as such services are offered on a fixed cost basis, so that you know exactly how much you will have to pay at the outset;

   (d) advertise your products or services (eg on a *worldwide trade opportunity database* which provides 24-hour exposure to a vast international marketplace);

   (e) find potential trading partners, by scanning the trade opportunity database;.

   (f) obtain export finance, foreign currency accounts, documentary credits, foreign exchange hedging contracts and options.

4 CULTURAL DIFFERENCES AFFECTING MARKETING

4.1 There are approximately 200 different countries each of which contains many different cultures, each with a myriad of beliefs, norms and taboos. It is helpful for us to have a framework used on CIM courses showing the major categories as follows.

Part A: Background knowledge relevant to analysis and decision

A cultural framework

```
        LANGUAGE              RELIGION           VALUES AND
        Spoken language       Sacred objects     ATTITUDES
        Written language      Philosophical      towards:
        Official language     systems             * time
        Linguistic pluralism  Beliefs & norms     * achievement
        Language              Prayer              * work
        Hierarchy             Taboos              * health
        International         Holidays            * change
        languages             Rituals             * scientific
        Mass media                                  method
                                                  * risk taking

        AESTHETICS                                EDUCATION
        Beauty                                    Formal education
        Good taste                                Vocational training
        Design                → CULTURES ←        Primary education
        Colour                                    Secondary
        Music                                     education
        Architecture                              Higher education
        Brand names                               Literacy level
                                                  Human resources
                                                  Planning

        LAW & POLITICS        TECHNOLOGY         SOCIAL
        Home country law      AND MATERNAL       ORGANISATIONS
        Foreign law           CULTURE            Kinship
        International law     Transportation     Social institutions
        Regulation            Energy systems     Authority structures
        Political risk        Tools & objects    Interest groups
        Ideologies            Communications     Social mobility
        National interest     Urbanisation       Social stratification
                              Science            Status systems
                              Invention
```

4.2 It is of course impossible for us to cover the above without reference to specific countries, specific sub-cultures, specific religions etc. However just taking the example of religion, this can affect market entry (religious conflict) marketing organisation (days of prayer) goods (type of clothes worn, types of food eaten) promotion (images shown), methods of doing business (eg Islamic banks) and so forth.

5 OTHER ENVIRONMENTAL FACTORS AFFECTING MARKETING STRATEGIES

5.1 We have already touched upon some of the cultural and legal factors affecting marketing decisions. We can now look in more detail at some of the *political, technological* and *economic* factors as follows:

5.2 *Political factors* include the following.

(a) *Role of government* in the economy

    (i)   Participator and/or regulator
    (ii) Trade, prices, wages, budget process

(b) *Ideologies*

    (i)   Capitalism
    (ii) Socialism
    (iii) Nationalism

(c) Political stability assists long term planning

3: International marketing strategy

(d) *International relations*
  (i) Between home and host governments
  (ii) Between different host governments

(e) *Major trends*
  (i) Central planning - democracy?
  (ii) Environmental pressures: the 'Green' dimension
  (iii) Fundamentalism

5.3 Technological factors include the following.

(a) Basic technology levels (Including infrastructural support, electrical power, skills available etc).

(b) Industrialisation (Importance of agriculture, manufacturing base, industrial growth or decline, level of automation etc).

(c) Investment (political supports, sphere of influence, international dependency etc).

5.4 *Economic factors* relating to an overseas market are as follows.

(a) *Market size*
  (i) Population size and growth
  (ii) Population density and concentration
  (iii) Population age and distribution
  (iv) Disposable income and distribution
  (v) GNP

(b) *Nature of the economy*
  (i) National resources
  (ii) Topography
  (iii) Climate
  (iv) Economic activity
  (v) Infrastructure
  (vi) Energy and communications
  (vii) Urbanisation
  (viii) Inflation
  (ix) Role of government

(c) Financial factors (eg currency controls)

5.5 It is also possible to identify the marketing characteristics relating to the country's stage of economic development, although this model will not hold for all markets.

(a) *Self sufficiency*. The country is largely a farming economy. The marketing characteristics are:
  (i) the use of barter;
  (ii) the exchange of basic necessities;
  (iii) the limit of exchange to the immediate area (ie local markets).

(b) *Emergence*. Economic wealth has increased. The marketing characteristics are:
  (i) expanded local markets;
  (ii) supply surplus of basic goods;
  (iii) developing trade specialists and intermediaries;
  (iv) product orientation;
  (v) money-based economy;
  (vi) moderate consumption;
  (vii) developing middle class.

(c) *Industrialisation*. The country builds factories for mass production. More people live in towns, and fewer on the land. The marketing characteristics are:
  (i) trade in national and international markets;
  (ii) product differentiation;
  (iii) market segmentation;

Part A: Background knowledge relevant to analysis and decision

(iv) consumer orientation;
(v) modern technology;
(vi) rising levels of consumption;
(vii) rapid growth of middle class.

(d) *Mass consumption and post industrialisation?* The marketing characteristics are:

(i) economic affluence;
(ii) credit based economy;
(iii) mass application of technology;
(iv) pervasive middle class;
(v) growing concern for quality of life, environment and conservation.

5.6 Geographic factors include the following.

(a) *Infrastructure/topography.* (Distribution planning, logistics, damage in transit considerations, handling/packaging methods etc.)

(b) *Distance.* (Delivery dates, product life deterioration, management control etc.)

(c) *Climate.* (It affects product quality/life, colour, fading, infestation etc.)

5.7 Let us illustrate the above with a brief anecdote. An engineering company supplied industrial heating and cooling equipment, and produced to specification a large number of very big water coolers using air as the cooling medium (like very large car radiators equipped with fans). Their purpose was to re-cool river water that had been used to cool the generators for a power station in a semi tropical climate (like a car radiator which cools the water which cools the engine). The product specification had not allowed for the amount of large winged insects propagated in that climate. These were sucked in by the fans and rapidly clogged up the radiator surface. This caused the equipment to stall and brought the power station to a halt within a few hours of start-up.

5.8 All the above factors affect international marketing strategies in the choice of suitable markets/market segments and the marketing mix.

The international marketing mix

5.9 The question then arises as to what extent marketing mixes need to be modified to cope with overseas market conditions. Distribution strategies are obviously affected. Different packaging methods and materials may be required and the channels of distribution in overseas countries are unlikely to replicate those in the UK.

5.10 Because of the greater distances entailed in trading in international markets compared with home market operations, transportation costs will no doubt be higher. Such extra costs may however be offset by lower production costs gained by greater economies of scale. Ways in which some of the SLEPT factors might affect *international pricing strategies* are listed below.

(a) *Social*

(i) Customer's perception of product and its quality.
(ii) Customer's preference for purchasing eg haggling.
(iii) Customer's perception of country of origin.
(vi) Social/cultural elements with influence price.
(v) Reference groups, lifestyles, beliefs etc.

(b) *Legal requirements* over:

(i) pricing and redistribution decisions;
(ii) margins in distribution network;
(iii) prices to be printed on packaging;
(iv) price promotions.

(c) *Economic*

(i) Number of competitors.

(ii) Role of price competition in marketing mix.
(iii) Potential response to price competition.
(iv) Pricing strategies pursued.
(v) General economic changes and their implication for price.

(d) *Political*

(i) Presence/absence of resale price maintenance
(ii) Level of sales or value added taxes
(iii) Role of trade associations in pricing decisions.
(iv) 'Consumer Association' lookalikes and their influence on consumer price perceptions

(e) *Technological*

(i) Recent developments in distribution technology.
(ii) Recent development in communications.

5.11 *Promotional strategies* will also be affected to some degree by the prevailing environment and market conditions in different countries as suggested below, in relation to advertising.

(a) *Environment* (eg culture; literacy levels; readership details; response to symbolism; general attitude to advertising; details of buyer, decider; influencer patterns; market segments; demography.)

(b) *Competition* (eg identification of competitive advertising practices and their expenditure and ratio to sales over a period. Research into strengths and weaknesses of competitors' advertising policies.)

(c) *Institutions* (eg total advertising expenditure in country; media available and growth in expenditure patterns; technical facilities. Media details: circulations, readership and segments, media costs, frequency; code of advertising.)

(d) *Legal system* (eg trade description legislation, special rules pertaining to various products (eg cigarettes, drugs, fertilisers), law limiting expenditure.)

(e) *Economics* (eg levels of consumption, disposable incomes, ownership of radios and TVs, readership of newspapers and magazines, socio-economic class structure, degree of social mobility.)

(f) *Language* (eg translation and 'back translation' of copy etc.)

(g) *Technology* (eg availability of satellite/cable communications etc and levels/organisation of research methodologies' microcomputer applications.)

5.12 *Distribution strategies* are affected by:

(a) physical infrastructure (extent, condition);
(b) existing distribution channels (eg large supermarket chains, small retailers);
(c) warehousing;
(d) competitors' dominance over distribution

5.13 This leaves us with the extent to which the product will need to be modified to suit overseas markets. The answer depends upon the type of product and the nature of the market. If we accept the marketing concept we will conduct research to establish needs before making the decision. Having said this the example of Coca Cola is often quoted as an example of successful global *standardisation*.

6 INTERNATIONAL MARKET ENTRY OPTIONS AND EVALUATION

6.1 Modes of entry to overseas markets may be summarised as follows:

(a) indirect exporting;
(b) direct exporting;
(c) overseas production.

Part A: Background knowledge relevant to analysis and decision

6.2 Indirect exporting without overseas involvement is usually by one of the routes below. The firm itself does not get involved in the process of exporting.

(a) *By default*. Goods sold to other home market manufacturers may find their way into overseas markets and ultimate users may then come to you for spares/replacements. (Eg you make electric motors which carry your nameplate and are bought by many engineering companies marketing say compressors, generators, pumps etc overseas).

(b) *UK buying offices*. These may be the subsidiaries of overseas businesses set up in the UK to buy UK goods. They buy from you in the normal way and arrange their own shipments overseas.

(c) *Export houses*. A variation on (b) but not foreign owned. These are often long-established companies set up to exploit demand for British goods. They provide the export services for British manufacturers who did not want the bother of exporting themselves.

(d) *Trade missions*. Overseas trade missions periodically visit the UK to buy goods direct, for example in the fashion industry.

(e) *Piggy backing*. You ask another manufacturer already trading overseas to sell your products along with his own.

6.3 Some advantages of indirect exporting are as follows.

(a) No language problems or literature translations.
(b) Transactions according to British law.
(c) Revenues paid through your bank in the normal way.
(d) Subject to your conditions of sale.
(e) No complex export documentation needed.
(f) No risks of non-payment due to foreign government interventions.
(g) No need to arrange shipment overseas.
(h) Ideal for start-up situations.

In summary, there is no hassle but the big disadvantage is that you may miss out on greater opportunities for profit.

6.4 *Direct exporting* is where the producer exports goods directly to the market. There are various degrees of involvement, as outlined below, but to summarise these are:

(a) overseas agents;
(b) overseas distributors;
(c) overseas sales office.

6.5 Overseas agents do *not* take title to goods (exceptions exist). They are restricted territorially and only sell (obtain orders - transmit to UK). The manufacturer delivers. An agent is paid commission and acts in role of substitute sales force. Agents are best suited to 'simple' standardised products, but are not suitable where high marketing involvement is necessary.

(a) *Advantages*

(i) Little cost involved
(ii) Risk factor low
(iii) Payment by result
(iv) Quick, easy to start
(v) Market and 'contacts' knowledge, language ability

(b) *Disadvantages*

(i) Variable quality
(ii) Lack of control
(iii) Conflicts of interest
(iv) Legal complexities (exit strategies)
(v) Communications
(vi) Motivation
(vii) EC interest in agency agreements (greater complexity)

6.6 *Distributors*, unlike agents, take title to goods buy and sell usually at their price, and absorb risks. They are restricted territorially. They are more involved than agents in the success of the product, and as well as increasing commitment, are likely to give more marketing assistance. Key factors in managing distributors are as follows.

   (a) Create loyalty
   (b) Create involvement and sense of teamwork
   (c) Ensure adequate payment, training/development programmes
   (d) Determine standards of performance
   (e) Evaluation of their performance
   (f) Efficient communications

6.7 Setting up an *overseas sales office* perhaps in the form of a subsidiary company offers potential cost savings, gives greater control, and perhaps offers faster feedback. The head office's marketing strategy can be transferred easily.

   (a) Drawbacks include:
      (i) higher capital costs
      (ii) back up support needed is higher
      (iii) training
      (iv) commitment (long term)
      (v) continuity (in personnel)
      (vi) organisational and administrative involvement
      (vii) time/speed of entry

   (b) Choosing a sales office. The choice depends on:
      (i) corporate objectives
      (ii) the nature of market
      (iii) speed of entry
      (iv) the level of marketing
      (v) the scale of effort
      (vi) the desired level of control
      (vii) risk
      (viii) the degree of the company's experience in international marketing.

Overseas production for overseas sales

6.8 Finally goods which would have been exported from the home country to the foreign market can be made in the foreign market.

6.9 *Licensing* confers a right to the licensee to utilise a company's specific patent or trademark for a defined period of time.

   (a) Benefits to the licenser are as follows.
      (i) No capital outlay, as the licensee provides capital for the operation.
      (ii) Trade restrictions are overcome.
      (iii) Little political risk.
      (iv) It is a quick and easy way of producing within the overseas market.
      (v) The licensee has access to local market knowledge.
      (vi) Considerable cost savings can be generated (eg saving on freight).

   (b) Disadvantages to the licenser are:
      (i) heavy dependence on licensee;
      (ii) limited returns (usually 2% to 5%);
      (iii) a lack of control of licensee (eg in product quality);
      (iv) a lack of control of marketing;
      (v) the licensee may learn enough to become a long-term competitor at the end of the licensing agreement

   (c) Managing the licensing agreement requires the following.
      (i) Careful selection of licensee if possible
      (ii) Careful drafting of agreement (in home language)
      (iii) Control of key components/formulation should be retained by licenser

(iv) Limit the geographic area covered
(v) Register trade marks/patents in licenser's name
(vi) An agreement attractive enough to retain the licensee.

6.10 *Franchising* is a special form of licensing. The franchiser provides a total marketing programme including the brand name, logo, product and method of operation. It usually involves selling a service and is thus open to small investors with only working capital. It allows small, independent, entrepreneurial individuals to enjoy the benefits of belonging to a large organisation whilst retaining owner-manager status. Franchising is fast growing, but not without its problems, which largely centre around standards/service levels, etc and reflect cultural expectations. Examples have included MacDonalds, Kentucky Fried Chicken, Hertz, Manpower, and Holiday Inns.

6.11 *Contract manufacturing* is where products are produced by an independent local company on a contractual basis. The manufacturer's responsibility is limited to production, and, in effect, the international company is 'renting' production capacity. It is different from licensing in legal terms.

(a) Its advantages are that it:

(i) avoids import barriers;
(ii) reduces risk;
(iii) can claim to be 'local'.

(b) It is suitable for low market volume combined with high tariff situations, and is usually employed where production technology is widely available and where *marketing* effort is crucial to success.

6.12 Assembly involves locating only a part of the manufacturing process overseas, typically the final stages of production. For example, some firms send components or parts from the home country for assembly into finished goods. It can takes advantages of low wage costs in the country of assembly, and lower transport costs. It can help overcome government restrictions, (quotas, tariffs, etc), but many governments are beginning to insist on a set percentage of local content.

6.13 An overseas joint venture is a foreign operation in which the international company has enough equity to have a voice in management but not enough to dominate or control. It is fast growing, increasingly important strategic business activity (eg GEC). It is insisted upon by many countries, whose governments wish to benefit from technology transfer.

(a) *Advantages*

(i) Faster development of product, if this process is shared.
(ii) Shared costs/risk.
(iii) Control over production and marketing.
(iv) Market feedback.
(v) The venturer gets more experience in international marketing.

(b) *Disadvantages*

(i) The need for greater capital investment.
(ii) More management involvement.
(iii) Cultural conflicts between the partners.
(iv) Disengagement problems.

6.14 Firms can buy or build factories overseas from scratch. Some also develop their own distribution networks, operating effectively, as domestic firms (a process which Kenichi Ohmae calls *insiderisation*).

(a) *Advantages*

(i) Complete control
(ii) Total commitment
(iii) No 'partner' conflicts
(iv) Profit

(b) *Disadvantages*

 (i) May be costly in time and money
 (ii) Political risk - expropriation
 (iii) Socio/economic risk (eg different management styles)

Which mode of entry?

6.15 Aside from the considerations above, strategic factors affecting mode of entry are given below.

 (a) Factors *specific* to the firm include:

  (i) goals;
  (ii) size;
  (iii) product line and nature of product;
  (iv) competition.

 (b) *General factors,* which are relatively independent of firm, include the following.

  (i) Number of markets
   (1) Different methods give different coverage.
   (2) Wholly owned foreign subsidiary may not be permitted.
   (3) Licensing may not be possible (no qualified licensees).

  (ii) Penetration within markets
   (1) Quality of coverage required
   (2) Some markets are more open than others.

  (iii) Market feedback
   (1) It is important that the method chosen provides feedback
   (2) Direct methods provide better possibilities for feedback
   (3) Management of the distribution channel ensures feedback

  (iv) Administrative requirements, including documentation, red tape, management and time can affect a mode's attractiveness.

  (v) Personnel requirements
   (1) These become more complicated with greater involvement.
   (2) Managing overseas staff requires skill.
   (3) International personnel need to be recruited.

  (vi) Exposure to foreign problems
   (1) New kinds of legislation
   (2) Regulation, taxes, labour problems

  (vii) Flexibility. The type of involvement might change in the long run

  (viii) Risk function of the method of involvement in addition to market itself. This is because risk is not just commercial, it is political, too

6.16 On a broader level still, Paliwoda gives us the following criteria.

 (a) Speed of market entry desired
 (b) Direct and indirect costs of entry
 (c) Degree of flexibility required
 (d) Risk factors involved
 (e) Investment payback period
 (f) Long-term profit objectives

6.17 When evaluating entry options in the CIM case study exam you need to recognise the question's *time constraints* and work from the *broad to the particular* in order to select the more viable options.

Notes   Part A: Background knowledge relevant to analysis and decision

7 INTERNATIONAL MARKETING RESEARCH

7.1 When making your proposals in the CIM case study exam, you need to take into account that the stage of economic development of your overseas market may not allow the same degree of sophistication as we might be used to in the UK. For example, telephone research may not be viable if only a small proportion of the population have one. Random sampling using street names and house numbers will be impossible if streets are not named (eg Tokyo) and numbers do not exist. Databases such as Acorn cannot be assumed to be universally available.

7.2 Special problems of international marketing research include the following.

(a) *Comparability*
   (i) Aggregation of data makes comparison difficult.
   (ii) Decision making is made locally, so there may be unique local marketing requirements.
   (iii) Comparing of results of decisions.

(b) *Sampling*
   (i) Validity of techniques varies from country to country.
   (ii) Poor transportation in some countries can affect the viability of the sampling
   (iii) Different languages or dialects in the same country reflect cultural or sub-cultural differences
   (iv) Different family structures may mean that the person taking the decisions are not the same as in the host structure (ie there is different household buyer behaviour)

(c) *Data collection methods*
   (i) Telephone and mail difficulties in developing countries
   (ii) Cultural problems
   (iii) Suspicion of interviewers (especially in countries with authoritarian regimes)

(d) *Response error*
   (i) Not-at-home problem/call backs
   (ii) Co-operation levels

(e) *Field force*
   (i) Training differences
   (ii) Composition. In some countries, female interviewers may not be acceptable.

(f) *Data*
   (i) Lack of historical data
   (ii) Few and poorly aggregated statistics may make it hard

7.3 Information sources used by UK companies (%) are as follows.

	%
Feedback from export sales staff	61
Trade associations and chambers of commerce	54
General knowledge	44
Press reports	32
Export departments of banks	29
Local press and journals	20
Test marketing	5
Financial institutions	14
No information base	15

7.4 Most frequently used *government services* in the UK are as follows.

Rank order	Service
1	Specific export opportunities
2	Help with overseas visits
3	Tariffs
4	Finding overseas agent
5	Calls for tender
	Economic reports
6	Status reports
	Market reports
	Export regulations

7.5 *Export facilitating agencies* provide a range of service and expertise which can provide a research, entry and promotional basis for the commercial and industrial sectors seeking to expand their sales operations into export markets. Here are some examples.

(a) British Export Houses' Association.

(b) British Importers' Confederation.

(c) International Export Association (incorporating the Export Merchants' Association).

(d) Accepting Houses Committee.

(e) Institute of Shipping and Forwarding Agents.

(f) Road Haulage Association.

(g) Chambers of Shipping.

(h) British Federation of Commodity Associations.

(i) Manufacturers' Association of Great Britain and Ireland.

(j) Conference Lines (scheduled shipping services to exporters).

7.6 *Evaluating market opportunities*. Market *opportunities* can be evaluated using the SLEPT factors with particular emphasis in the Social, Political, Economic and Legal dimensions.

(a) *Social*

(i) Major historical developments

(ii) Population and its composition (age, race, religion, occupation, residence, education)

(iii) Mobility (between jobs, places, social classes)

(iv) Communications (transport and media)

(v) General way of life and traditions

(b) *Political*

(i) Major political trends
(ii) Governmental structure and organisation
(iii) Prevailing political philosophy
(iv) Principal government activities
(v) Annual budgets (eg chief sources of revenue, chief expenditure)
(vi) Policies towards labour, business, agriculture, foreign trade

(c) *Economic*

(i) Gross national product, but also the *total* and main *components* of personal consumption (eg percentage spent on clothes), government expenditure, foreign trade balance, private investment

(ii) Agricultural production
(iii) Industrial production
(iv) Services
(v) Construction
(vi) Currency and exchange rates
(vii) Banking system and financial institutions
(viii) Labour force and wage rates
(ix) Incomes and standard of living
(x) Natural resources

(d) *Legal*

(i) Main laws affecting business (eg forms of organisation, capital and ownership, permits regarding location, employment, trademarks, patents).
(ii) Tariffs
(iii) Taxes
(iv) Currency and foreign exchange control
(v) import/export regulations
(vi) Antitrust regulations
(vii) Labour laws

7.7 Some data sources for international marketing research

(a) Information relating to the changes in the social, political, economic and legal dimensions can be found from the following.

(i) *The Europa Yearbook* is a two volume compendium providing reviews of every country. It is published annually.
(ii) *EIU World Outlook* annual publication by the Economist Intelligence Unit (an offshoot of 'The *Economist*') gives summary details of the economic and political trends in 165 countries.
(iii) *Clearing banks*. Many of the major banks of the world produce periodic reviews of the performance of each of the countries of the world.
(iv) *Department of trade and industry*. The *Hints to Exporters* series provides synopses of each of the countries of the world, and a wealth of other material.

7.8 Information relating to the activities of commercial organisations can be found in the following, amongst others.

(a) *Kompass publications*. Details of companies who subscribe to Kompass covering products and services offered, are supplied with an indication of export/import activities. A wide range of countries are covered but the Americas and Africa are not covered in as much detail (by country) as Europe, Australasia and parts of south-east Asia.
(b) *Thomas Register (TOM-CAT)* is the 'Kompass' equivalent in the USA.
(c) *Trade Association Publications* often provide details of like associations in other countries.

7.9 Statistics

(a) *Industrial Statistics Yearbook* is published by United Nations (UN) and details the manufacturing activities of each country. Data is usually two to six years old at time of publication depending on the country concerned.
(b) *International Trade Statistics Yearbook* (UN) contains details of the trade between countries by product (volume and value). Data is usually two years old when published.

(c) *Statistics of Foreign Trade* is published by the Organisation for Economic Co-operation and Development (OECD), and is similar to the UN publication but not as detailed. Statistics are usually one year old when published.

(d) *Eurostat* is published by the EC, and is a comprehensive set of statistics covering the activities of each country of the EC and their trading relationships with the world.

7.10 In addition, information can be supplied by the following.

(a) Government
(b) International institutions (OECD, IMF, WTO, EU)
(c) The World Bank
(d) Trade associations
(e) Professional bodies
(f) Chambers of commerce
(g) Market research agencies
(h) Consultants
(i) Service industries
(j) ESOMAR (European Society for Opinion and Market Research).

8 PLANNING AND ORGANISATIONAL ASPECTS OF INTERNATIONAL MARKETING

International marketing planning and control

8.1 International marketing and control is similar in essence to marketing planning as detailed in Chapter 1 with the difference of detail as indicated below.

Notes | **Part A: Background knowledge relevant to analysis and decision**

The international marketing planning process

```
┌─────────────────────┐          ┌─────────────────────┐
│ Information: Foreign│          │   Organisation's    │
│  Market potential,  │          │     objectives      │
│ Environmental Audit │          │                     │
│         etc         │          │                     │
└──────────┬──────────┘          └──────────┬──────────┘
           │                                │
           └───────────────┬────────────────┘
                           ▼
              ┌────────────────────────────┐
              │ Decision to "go international" │
              └──────────────┬─────────────┘
                             ▼
              ┌────────────────────────────┐
        ┌────▶│ Strategy, level of involvement │
        │     └──────────────┬─────────────┘
        │                    ▼
        │     ┌────────────────────────────┐
        │     │    Selection of markets    │
        │     └──────────────┬─────────────┘
        │                    ▼
        │     ┌────────────────────────────┐
        │     │ Methods of foreign market entry │
        │     └──────────────┬─────────────┘
```

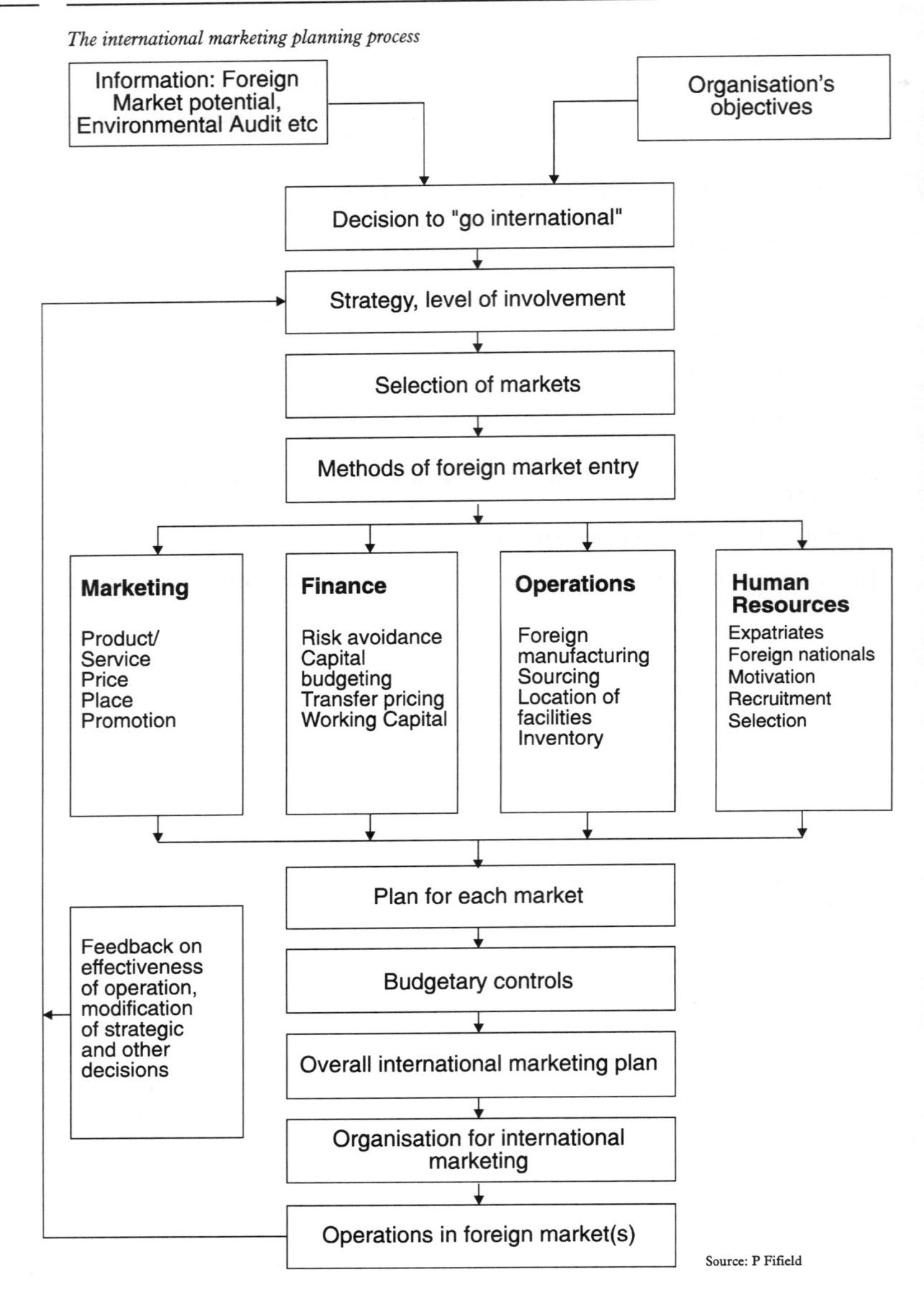

Marketing	**Finance**	**Operations**	**Human Resources**
Product/ Service	Risk avoidance	Foreign manufacturing	Expatriates
Price	Capital budgeting	Sourcing	Foreign nationals
Place	Transfer pricing	Location of facilities	Motivation
Promotion	Working Capital	Inventory	Recruitment
			Selection

```
                             ▼
              ┌────────────────────────────┐
              │    Plan for each market    │
              └──────────────┬─────────────┘
                             ▼
┌─────────────┐   ┌────────────────────────────┐
│ Feedback on │   │    Budgetary controls      │
│effectiveness│   └──────────────┬─────────────┘
│of operation,│                  ▼
│modification │   ┌────────────────────────────┐
│of strategic │   │ Overall international marketing plan │
│and other    │   └──────────────┬─────────────┘
│decisions    │                  ▼
└─────────────┘   ┌────────────────────────────┐
                  │ Organisation for international marketing │
                  └──────────────┬─────────────┘
                                 ▼
                  ┌────────────────────────────┐
                  │ Operations in foreign market(s) │
                  └────────────────────────────┘
```

Source: P Fifield.

Transfer pricing

8.2 A word about transfer pricing is perhaps appropriate here, although this decision would normally be addressed at corporate level. Transfer pricing is the term used to describe differences in prices as goods are transferred from division to division both within a country and across national boundaries.

(a) For example, the manufacture of a component might take place within country A, offering comparative advantage in labour and/or materials. These semi-manufactured goods are then transferred at price A to country B where manufacture is completed and the goods are transferred at price B to another division in country B for packaging, stocking and eventual sale to a number of other countries at different prices.

(b) Tensions arise within the company over pricing where divisions operate as separate strategic business units (SBUs). The reason is that if each SBU is supposed to make a profit, they will charge the highest price.

(c) Perhaps more importantly, political tensions arise (governments, consumer bodies, trade unions) when multinationals use transfer pricing to avoid tax. Transferring at a low price from a high-tax country allows a subsidiary in a low-tax country to make a larger profit and is in the interests of the multinational but not necessarily the high-tax country government or population.

Controlling international marketing

8.3 Distances and differences in language and culture affect communications effectiveness and thereby mechanisms for planning and control. Other factors previously discussed such as fluctuations in exchange rates and political stability can also adversely affect control systems for international markets. Some potential ways of overcoming these difficulties are given below.

(a) Methods of integrating international marketing

  (i) Standard planning system
  (ii) Standard reporting system
  (iii) International meetings/committees
  (iv) International task forces (trouble shooters)
  (v) International marketing publications
  (vi) Common marketing support systems
  (vii) Rotation of personnel

(b) This can be summarised as follows.

  (i) Centralisation of strategic decision-making (planning)
  (ii) A strong corporate culture (loyalty etc)
  (iii) Systems transfer
  (iv) Personnel transfer

The organisational implications of international marketing

8.4 Variables influencing organisational structure include the following.

(a) *Size* of business - overall volume and foreign volume.
(b) *Number* of markets in which operating
(c) Degree of *involvement* in foreign markets
(d) The company's *goals* for international business
(e) The company's international *experience*
(f) The *nature* of products - complexity etc
(g) The nature of marketing *task*
(h) Political factors, external *and* internal.

8.5 Some companies have an international division. In other words, all aspects of overseas activities are collected in *one* division.

(a) *Advantages*

    (i) Centralisation of all specialist skills/expertise
    (ii) International business can be focused upon
    (iii) Resources can be properly allocated
    (iv) Objective analysis of potential markets is provided

(b) *Disadvantages*

    (i) Separation of the two divisions may not mean equality between them
    (ii) Sub-optimisation may result from dilution of corporate resources
    (iii) Friction between international and domestic divisions

8.6 Structuring the organisation by area means that activities, especially marketing activities, are broken down by region.

(a) *Advantages*

    (i) Easy communications.
    (ii) Expertise can be grouped.
    (iii) Area problems can be identified and rectified at the right level.
    (iv) They reflect existing economic groups (eg EU).

(b) *Disadvantages*

    (i) Duplication leads to management inefficiency.
    (ii) Friction between areas and HQ.
    (iii) Limited communication between areas.
    (iv) Gaps emerge between countries in one area (increasing friction).

8.7 Centralisation and decentralisation of operations determine the relative power of corporate head office and local subsidiaries, ensuring a division of labour.

(a) *Corporate HQ* is in charge of international marketing at corporate level. It:

    (i) sets objectives/policies for world markets;
    (ii) plays a major role in planning;
    (iii) is a source of ideas and a back-up resource (trouble shooting);
    (iv) co-ordinates and integrates national programmes.

(b) The *local subsidiary* has its own roles. It:

    (i) implements the plan within broad guidelines;
    (ii) conducts market research;
    (iii) has a 'voice' in product policy and pricing;
    (iv) selects and administers distribution channels;
    (v) manages the sales operation;
    (vi) directs the promotional programme;
    (vii) ideally has dual reporting to local and HQ management.

Human resource implications of international marketing

8.8 We need to consider the effects of going international on our standard recruitment and training policies. Should we:

(a) recruit from expatriates in the foreign country?
(b) use foreign nationals? or
(c) use our own personnel recruited and trained in the home country?

8.9 Obviously circumstances alter cases but most companies have found that using a foreign sales force is on balance more effective than sending home country personnel with the accompanying language and cultural difficulties involved.

8.10 Many overseas countries have regulations concerning the proportion of indigenous/foreign employees for different levels - management, office staff, factory staff which are allowed for foreign companies.

8.11 You may also experience differences in foreign countries concerning the types of training available, laws on hire and fire, salary levels etc.

8.12 Whereas delegation of responsibility may be encouraged in one culture, only the top executives may be allowed to make decisions in another culture (as analysed by Hofstede). Similarly criteria for promotion can vary considerably from culture to culture. Any human resources plan has to be sensitive to these issues.

Chapter roundup

- International marketing is not a unique type of marketing in its own right, but does have specific problems of its own related to the different circumstance of each county and its culture (eg political stability, different levels of development, buyer behaviour).

- Other factors include international financial issues such as exchange rates, and trade liberalisation agreements.

- IM is often more risky than domestic marketing because of the variety of environmental influences involved, and there are additional organisational considerations to be taken into account. Help for exporters is available however.

Test your knowledge

1. What is the rationale for a *country* to trade? (see paras 2.2, 2.6)
2. Why do *companies* engage in IM? (2.10)
3. Describe some non-tariff barriers. (3.3, 3.5)
4. What are the distinct marketing characteristics of a country at different levels of development? (5.5)
5. Describe licensing. (6.9)
6. Draw a planning model for IM. (8.1)

Chapter 4

FINANCIAL ASPECTS OF MARKETING

> **This chapter covers the following topics.**
> 1 Financial aspects of the CIM case study
> 2 The balance sheet
> 3 The profit and loss account
> 4 The cash flow statement
> 5 Financial analysis: external ratio analysis
> 6 Financial analysis: internal ratio analysis
> 7 Value added statements
> 8 Inflation
> 9 Short-term decision making
> 10 Long-term decision making
> 11 Cash flow forecasting
> 12 Sources of finance
> 13 Feasibility and risk
>
> **Introduction**
> The CIM has in the past been criticised for turning out 'financially illiterate' diploma holders. It is now official CIM policy to ensure that marketing managers who become members are able to play their full part in corporate decisions. To do this, they need to know the financial status not only of their own organisation but also those of their leading competitors.

1 FINANCIAL ASPECTS OF THE CIM CASE STUDY

1.1 In this chapter we are examining only those aspects of finance which you are expected to apply to the case study. Almost all case studies have financial accounts which you are expected to analyse and understand. You also need to be able to assess the value of data (including financial data). Not all the data is accurate. This is something you will have to decide for yourself.

1.2 In addition to financial ratio analysis (and of course marketing costs ratio analysis) you are expected to have a basic knowledge of approaches to cost. This is necessary to understand pricing decisions.

1.3 The definition of marketing by the CIM ends with the word 'profitably'. You must therefore be aware of the financial implications of your marketing proposals and the importance of being able to demonstrate a return on investment at least equal to that of competing proposals.

1.4 With the above points in mind please read the following sections 2 to 13 assiduously. It is important not only for your CIM case study exam but also for your career and your own professional standing to have an adequate grasp of these financial aspects.

2 THE BALANCE SHEET

2.1 The balance sheet/position statement is a 'snapshot' of the financial picture/position of the business at a single moment in time (eg 12 o'clock midnight on 31 December). It shows us the total 'value' of the assets that the business owns and how these are represented by the liabilities that the business owes. In this respect the accounts may be looked at as *balancing assets with liabilities.*

2.2 *Assets* are items which have a *value to the company* at the balance sheet date. They may be long term/fixed assets, such as buildings, equipment and motor vehicles, or short term/current assets, such as stocks, debtors (money owed by your customers) and cash.

2.3 *Liabilities* are the *responsibilities* that the business has to pay suppliers for goods received (creditors), to repay loans and to account to the shareholders/investors for the money they originally put into the business, and the profit that has been earned to date but not paid out in dividends. *Share capital* is the money initially invested, *reserves* are the *profit retained. Equity* describes the total of capital and reserves.

2.4 *Presentation.* Accountants now use a combined vertical format which allows certain additional information (eg net current assets or working capital) to be readily shown. The general convention is to list assets down the page in descending order of permanence, ie land and buildings first, cash last. This is then followed, but in the opposite way, by liabilities.

2.5 *Historical costs.* The value of a company's assets shown in its accounts reflects the cost to the company *when the assets were purchased,* less of course any depreciation that has been charged so far. There is much debate on whether these historical costs are relevant to the users of accounting documents. (For example, a building may have an historical cost less depreciation of £50,000, but have a market value of £200,000.) Modification to historical costs is sometimes allowed.

2.6 *Tangible and intangible assets*

   (a) Tangible assets are those with a physical identity such as buildings, furniture and fittings, vehicles etc. They can be counted and verified each year.

   (b) Investments are financial investments in stocks and shares (occasionally in subsidiary companies).

   (c) Intangible assets are not physical assets.

      (i) Development costs of a new product should only be treated as an asset in special circumstances.

      (ii) Concessions, patents, licenses, trademarks (*not* brands) should only be treated as assets if acquired for valuable consideration.

      (iii) Brands, however, do not count as trademarks. They are 'goodwill' which is a 'combination of factors which is expected to produce enhanced earnings'. Treating brands as *assets* (like a company's head office building) is a very contentious topic, and it is possible that the practice will be so hedged around with restrictions that it will be effectively outlawed.

2.7 Consider though the position of a marketing department that wants to spend £10m establishing a new brand. They will rightly argue that the brand once established will last say five years and the cost should therefore be capitalised and written off over five years. The counter argument is that it should be written off in the first year as no one can say how long it will last or in fact whether it will achieve the desired results in the market place. Also, the value of a brand may suddenly fall: the price of Marlboro cigarettes was reduced in the US, to compete with low price competition, even though the owners of the brand had invested large sums of money in it. Thus the ability of a brand to command a premium price may be restricted.

2.8 Items contained in the balance sheet include the following: this is *not a standard layout*.

Item	*What the item represents*
1 Fixed Assets	1 Cost of long-term assets
2 Depreciation	2 Amounts charged to profit up to now to reflect the use of an asset over its life
3 Tangible assets	3 (1) - (2)
4 Current assets	4 Assets that can easily be converted into cash
• Stocks	• Raw materials, work in progress and finished goods
• Debtors	• Amounts owed to firm by customers.
• Cash	• Money in bank or actual cash
5 Current liabilities (under 1 year)	5 Amounts owned by firm (payable during year)
• Creditors	• Amounts owed to suppliers
• Overdrafts	• Owed to bank
• Taxation owing	• Owed to Inland Revenue
• Dividends owing	• Owed to shareholders
6 Net current assets (liabilities)	6 Current assets less current liabilities
7 Net Assets	7 Total assets (fixed assets plus net current assets)
8 Loans (over 1 year)	8 Borrowing, repayable in medium/long term
9 Share Capital	9 Money invested by owners
10 Reserves	10 Profits made, not distributed
11 Equity	11 Total owners' stake

2.9 For companies domiciled in the UK the rules governing balance sheets (and profit and loss accounts, and cash flow statements) are laid down by Act of Parliament (in the Companies Acts) and in Financial Reporting Standards (formerly Statements of Standard Accounting Practice) which can also have a legal effect. Note that the rules only apply to *external reporting*: a firm can arrange its internal management accounting information in any way it likes. CIM case studies may include companies domiciled overseas and therefore subject to other laws.

2.10 A typical balance sheet is given below.

WAY AHEAD INTERNATIONAL PLC
BALANCE SHEET

	19X9		*19X8*	
	£000	£000	£000	£000
Fixed assets				
Tangible assets		20,840		20,527
Investments		4,908		4,688
		25,748		25,215
Current assets				
Stocks	995		954	
Debtors	1,743		1,375	
Cash at bank and in hand	10,823		7,959	
	13,561		10,288	
Creditors				
Amounts falling due within one year	6,439		4,478	
Net current assets		7,122		5,810
Total assets less current liabilities		32,870		31,025
Creditors: Amounts falling due after more than one year		200		1,371
		32,670		29,654
Provisions for liabilities and charges		521		539
Net assets		32,149		29,115

	19X9		19X8	
	£000	£000	£000	£000
Capital and reserves				
Called-up share capital		1,675		1,675
Revaluation reserve		11,104		11,104
Other reserves		10,230		10,230
Profit and loss account		9,140		6,106
Shareholders' funds		32,149		29,115

Signed on behalf of the Board
Directors

3 THE PROFIT AND LOSS ACCOUNT

3.1 If the balance sheet is a snapshot at a *point* of time then the profit and loss account (or income statement) is a history, as it were, of, what has been happening to the business over a *period of time,* usually a year, a quarter, or a month. By deducting the total of all expenses from the income (revenue earned) a profit or loss for that time period will be left. In practice this is not quite as straightforward as it sounds.

3.2 The *accruals or matching principle*. Revenue and expenses must be matched to the time period to which they relate. The total sales will be the summation of all the invoiced or firm sales in the period. Expenses though consist of the items of expenditure which have been *enjoyed* by the firm *in the same time period*. This can be very *different* to the amounts that have been *paid for*.

(a) Some charges which must be taken into account may not even have been invoiced by the supplier until after the year end. For example the electricity consumed in December might not be billed until February. The accountant therefore has to estimate and provide for or *accrue* these charges, which is why they are called accruals. Similarly, you might buy and use goods from suppliers at the end of year 1, but not pay them until year 2 (which is why they appear as creditors on the balance sheet).

(b) Similarly some charges such as business rates are paid in advance from April to March. The accountant will therefore deduct a proportion of the total bill before calculating the profit. This is called a *prepayment*.

3.3 *Stock*. A company which manufactures or trades will hold stocks of goods for resale. At the end of the year when the cost of the goods sold is calculated, it is logical that a deduction is made in recognition of the stock that has *not* been sold, but has been made or received. This stock will then become a cost to the business in the *following* year. The calculation is performed as follows.

	£	£
Sales for year		10,000
Opening Stock (1 January 19X0)	900	
Purchases, other production costs etc	7,050	
Total cost	7,950	
Closing stock 31 December 19X0)	(800)	
Cost of goods sold		7,150
Gross profit		2,850

3.4 *Depreciation.* The costs of fixed assets/items which are purchased for use in the business over a long period ie over a year, need to be charged as expenses over the period of time in which those assets are *useful* to the business. The simplest way of doing this is to estimate how many years of life the asset will have and then divide the cost by the number of years.

(a) For example, a computer costs £5,000. Its estimated life before it wears out, becomes scrapped, or whatever, is five years. In each of the five years, £1,000 (£5,000 divided by five years) will be charged as depreciation to the profit and loss account. (The value of the asset in the balance sheet will be reduced by that amount.)

(b) There are a number of other methods of calculating the charge per year. Motor cars for example depreciate faster in the early years of their life and so non-linear methods are used which frontload the charges per year, such as the reducing balance or the sum of the digits method. In other words, most of the depreciation is charged early on.

3.5 Cash based expenses are often straightforward items such as fuel for salesmen's cars which require no adjustments.

3.6 *Profit.* To the economist profit is a straightforward concept, the reward of capital, land, and labour. The accounting concept is slightly different, as accountants analyse profit in several ways.

(a) *Gross profit* is the difference between the sales value and the cost of the goods which have been sold. In Paragraph 3.3 it was £2,850 or 28.5% of sales value (£10,000) *gross margin on sales*. This figure of £2,850 also represents the *mark-up on cost* of:

$$\frac{£2,850}{£7,150} = 39.9\%$$

(b) *Net profit* is the gross profit after deducting all other expenses and is usually shown before deducting the interest payable to the banks and other capital lenders (Net Profit Before Interest and Tax NPBIT) and then after interest but before the deduction of corporation tax. (NPBT).

(c) *Retained profit* is the profit that is left after deduction of the dividend payable to the company's shareholders. It is the money 'ploughed back' into the business.

	£	£
Turnover		10,000
Cost of sales (eg production wages, raw materials etc)		7,150
Gross Profit		2,850
Distribution costs	1,000	
Administrative expenses (eg personnel department)	475	
		1,475
Net profit on ordinary activities before interest and taxation		1,375
Interest payable and similar charges		300
Net profit on ordinary activities before taxation		1,075
Tax on profit on ordinary activities		250
Profit or loss for the financial year		825
Dividends paid or proposed		175
Retained profit		650

SSAP 25 Segmental reporting

3.7 Certain large companies are required, under Statement of Standard Accounting Practice 25 (SSAP 25), to analyse their profit and loss account in more detail, giving turnover and profit figures by:

(a) class of business (defined as 'a distinguishable component of an entity that provides a separate product or service or a separate group of related products or services', which sounds very much like a strategic business unit);

(b) geographical market ('a geographical area comprising an individual country or a group of counties in which an entity operates or to which it supplies products or services').

3.8 Turnover (ie sales) must be analysed by origin and destination and any sales between segments must be identified. Financial reports therefore give additional information about competitors' businesses, both how much they sell and, as importantly, how profitable they are in a particular segment.

4 THE CASH FLOW STATEMENT

4.1 The balance sheet shows us the financial value of the company at a single point in time, the profit and loss account tells the story of the increase or decrease in the company's net assets during a given period in time.

   (a) We have seen however, that profit is derived after charges in which no *cash* leaves the company, for example *depreciation* and accrued expenses.

   (b) Conversely, money is spent on assets, both fixed and current, but such spending does not *immediately* have an effect on the profit and loss account. The amount of money in the bank account or held as cash is therefore *independent* of the profit and loss account. Generally speaking, money, or cash as it is referred to, is not *directly* related to profit in the short or medium terms.

   (c) Moreover the *timing of payments* has an effect. The tax charge for Year 1 would appear in Year 1's profit and loss account even though it might not be paid from the firm's bank account until Year 2.

4.2 A profitable company can go bankrupt because it has insufficient cash in the business to meet its daily commitments. (For example, owning a £1,000-worth antique will be of no use to you if you are standing at a bus stop in the rain with no *cash* to pay the bus driver for your fare.) The effect of temporary cash difficulties is accelerated because once the word goes round a trade that someone is struggling, suppliers stop supplying goods until outstanding balances are cleared. If the company then decides to sell some of its assets then the prices that can be achieved are always much lower once buyers sense that it is a forced sale.

4.3 The importance of managing cash in the business cannot be over stressed, particularly in relation to marketing activities where strategies and tactics can have a significant impact on cash flow.

4.4 Money is brought into a business either through raising capital from shareholders and lenders or by generating and realising profit through trading activities. This money is then spent on either fixed assets (to keep) or current assets (needed in trading). In the course of trading, assets may be sold and loans repaid. Cash is therefore said to *flow* in the course of trading. There are two ways of viewing this flow.

   (a) As a forecast (eg to ensure that overdraft limits are not breached) this is concerned mainly with cash.

   (b) In terms of analysing where the money is coming from and going to by each category of the items shown in the balance sheet. Is the company for example raising loans to spend on fixed assets (long term funding) or spending its trading profits in ever expanding trade debtors? We call this analysis *funds flow* as it helps to explain how the business is being funded, as in the following example.

4.5 The recommended format for reporting these matters has changed. The old and current styles are briefly described below.

Old style funds flow statements - until March 31 1992

4.6 In some of your case analyses, you might be given financial data going back *several years*. Until March 1992, funds flow statements were disclosed as below. Note that from March 31 1992 a new format has been *required* for published accounts: there is no choice.

Part A: Background knowledge relevant to analysis and decision

Example: statement of source and application of funds

4.7 For the 52 weeks ended 31st December 19X9

	19X9 (52 weeks) £'000	19X9 (52 weeks) £'000	19X8 (52 weeks) £'000	19X8 (52 weeks) £'000
Source of funds				
Profit before taxation		5,358		4,404
Depreciation (added back as not a cash item)		632		588
Total generated from operations		5,990		4,992
Funds from other sources				
Sales of investments	553		1,733	
Sales of fixed assets	1,038		216	
Decrease in loans to customers and others	-		116	
		1,591		2,065
		7,581		7,057
Application of funds				
Dividends paid	1,292		1,128	
Tax paid	1,495		1,517	
Purchase of fixed assets	1,006		1,232	
Purchase of investments	558		1,737	
Increase in loans to customers and others	102		-	
		4,453		5,614
		3,128		1,443

	19X9 (52 weeks) £'000	19X9 (52 weeks) £'000	19X8 (52 weeks) £'000	19X8 (52 weeks) £'000
Increase/decrease in working capital				
Stocks	41		(85)	
Debtors	368		(33)	
Creditors	(145)		(3)	
		264		(121)
Movement in net liquid funds		2,864		1,564
		3,128		1,443

Cash flow statements

4.8 Candidates should be aware that the layout of the traditional funds flow statement has been altered by Financial Reporting Standard 1 (FRS 1). A revised format for presentation of information has been adopted from March 31st 1992. The intention of the new method is to relate cash movements more directly to their long term and short term impact on the business. Greater breakdown of the sources (receiving and earning) and applications (spending and repaying) are given to show more logically the cash consequences of the following activities.

(a) Trading and operating activities. These include the effect of working capital movements (eg stock, debtors. creditors, cash) as these items are directly related to operations.

(b) Servicing the existing finance requirements of the business (eg interest on loans and dividends to shareholders).

(c) The payment of taxation.

(d) Financing the business. This includes raising new capital and finance or repaying existing loans or share capital.

4.9 The revised layout taken from the standard is shown as follows. Some notes explaining how the figures are derived are also provided. (Cash flow as used here should not be confused with future cash flow planning, as described in Section 11 of this chapter.)

XYZ LIMITED
CASH FLOW STATEMENT FOR THE YEAR ENDED 31 MARCH 19X2

	£'000	£'000
Net cash inflow from operating activities		6,889
Returns on investments and servicing of finance		
Interest received	3,011	
Interest paid	(12)	
Dividends paid	(2,417)	
Net cash inflow from returns on Investments and servicing of finance		582
Taxation		
Corporation tax paid (including advance corporation tax)	2,922	
Tax paid		(2,922)
Investing activities		
Payments to acquire intangible fixed assets	(71)	
Payments to acquire tangible fixed assets	(1,496)	
Receipts from sales of tangible fixed assets	42	
Net cash outflow from investing activities		(1,525)
Net cash inflow before financing		3,024
Financing		
Issue of ordinary share capital	211	
Repurchase of debenture loan	(149)	
Expenses paid in connection with share issues	(5)	
Net cash inflow from financing		57
Increase in cash and cash equivalents		3,081

Notes to the cash flow statement

1   Reconciliation of operating profit to net cash inflow from operating activities

	£'000
Operating profit	6,022
Depreciation charges (added back, as no *cash* has left the business this year).	893
Loss on sale of tangible fixed assets (a 'book' loss)	6
Increase in stocks (since 1st April 19X1)	(194)
Increase in debtors (since 1st April 19X1)	(72)
Increase in creditors (since 1st April 19X1)	234
Net cash inflow from operating activities	6,889

2   Analysis of changes in cash and cash equivalents during the year

	£'000
Balance at 1 April 19X1	21,373
Net cash inflow	3,081
Balance at 31 March 19X2	24,454

3   Analysis of the balances of cash and cash equivalents as shown in the balance sheet

	19X2	*19X1*
Cash at bank and in hand	529	681
Short-term investments	23,936	20,700
Bank overdrafts	(11)	(8)
	24,454	21,373

Part A: Background knowledge relevant to analysis and decision

4   Analysis of changes in financing during the year

	Share Capital	Debenture Loan
Balance at 1 April 19X1	27,411	156
Cash inflow/(outflow) from financing	211	(149)
Profit on repurchase of debenture loan for less than its book value		(7)
Balance at 31 March 19X2	27,622	–

5   FINANCIAL ANALYSIS: EXTERNAL RATIO ANALYSIS

5.1   The three financial statements reviewed so far all give *absolute financial values*, which will answer the following questions.

(a) Has a profit or loss been made?
(b) Has it generated or consumed cash?

The historical values may not relate to the market value of the business or its ability to generate cash *in future*.

5.2   To understand more about the company from those statements we need to answer the following questions.

(a)   Is the company being run efficiently:
   (i)   in comparison with other firms in the same trade?
   (ii) in comparison with previous years?

(b)   Would you supply goods on credit to that company? Is the company able to continue trading and is it paying its creditors?

(c)   Would you recommend investing money in the business:
   (i)   in comparison with the return from say the building societies?
   (ii) in comparison with other companies with different profits and different share prices?

5.3   To answer these questions we need to use *ratio analysis*. It should be stressed that there are a number of variations of ratio formulae, but whatever format used must be applied *consistently* and to related account headings. For example comparing gross profit to the current liabilities is in itself meaningless but comparing net profit with the total capital employed is useful.

Example

5.4   For the purpose of illustration, study the figures below in relation to the questions posed in 5.2.

	X plc £'000	Y plc £'000
Gross profit	30	60
Net profit before tax and interest	20	40
Turnover (sales)	200	500
Capital employed	100	150
Bank loans (included in capital employed)	80	50
Share capital	20	100
Previous years' net profit	18	37
Interest Rate 10%		
Inflation rate 10%		

(a)   *Question:*   which management team is most effective?

(b)   *Question:*   which would you invest in?

4: Financial aspects of marketing   Notes

(c) *Question:* if you were beamed down from Mars into both companies could you tell which was which by observing their marketing strategies in relation to these figures?

Analysis

5.5 Y plc would appear to be much larger than X plc. Turnover is 2.5 times that of Y and net profit is double that of Y. This is as far as the absolute values can take us. By calculating a few simple ratios we can get a much better insight.

(a) *Gross profit percentage*

	X plc	*Y plc*
$\dfrac{\text{Gross profit}}{\text{Turnover}}$	$\dfrac{£30,000}{£200,000} = 15\%$	$\dfrac{£60,000}{£500,000} = 12\%$

X plc is more efficient than Y plc in realising gross margins from its sales. From this level of gross profit we might assume that they are involved in a trade such as food retailing which has similar gross margins. If both companies were buying and selling the same goods at the same prices we might assume that the 3% deficiency of Y is the result of shoplifting, poor stock rotation (selling out of date goods cheap), staff theft, damaged goods (through poor handling) etc.

(b) *Net profit percentage*

	X plc	*Y plc*
$\dfrac{\text{Net profit}}{\text{Turnover}}$	$\dfrac{£20,000}{£200,000} = 10\%$	$\dfrac{£40,000}{£500,000} = 8\%$

Again this is consistent with food retailing. The gap between them has now closed to a difference of 2%. Let us see why.

(c)

	X plc	*Y plc*
$\dfrac{\text{Operating / admin costs}}{\text{Turnover}}$	$\dfrac{£10,000}{£200,000} = 5\%$	$\dfrac{£20,000}{£500,000} = 4\%$

We can deduce these costs as the difference between gross profit and net profit (£10,000 and £20,000 respectively). We can now say that Y plc has lower overheads per £1 of goods sold than X plc. This saving on items such as administration, staff costs, lighting etc may contribute to the lower level of *control* and *efficiency* highlighted in (a).

(d) *Return on capital employed*

(i)

	X plc	*Y plc*
$\dfrac{\text{Net profit}}{\text{Capital employed}}$	$\dfrac{£20,000}{£100,000} = 20\%$	$\dfrac{£40,000}{£150,000} = 27\%$

This shows that Y plc is getting a better return on the money that has been invested in the business than X plc, because while Y plc net profit is double that of X plc it has only 50% more capital (£150,000 against £100,000). Y plc is making more efficient use of its funds.

(ii) If we now look at the two companies from the viewpoint of a shareholder, we notice that X has a higher proportion of bank loans than Y, 80% capital employed against 33%. If we take these loans out of the capital employed because they carry a 'fixed' interest charge (as opposed to receiving a share of the profits) then we can see that from a shareholder's viewpoint it is far more beneficial to invest in X in comparison with Y.

In calculating the ratios above we have to adjust for the interest charge that the banks will make. The full calculation is as follows.

	X plc	*Y plc*
$\dfrac{\text{Net profit (after interest)}}{\text{Share capital}} =$	$\dfrac{£20,000 - (£80,000 \times 10\%)}{£20,000}$	
	$\dfrac{£40,000 - (£50,000 \times 10\%)}{£100,000}$	

Part A: Background knowledge relevant to analysis and decision

$$= \frac{£12,000}{£20,000} \qquad \frac{£35,000}{£100,000}$$

$$= 60\% \qquad 35\%$$

(e) This effect is the result of *gearing* which is calculated as follows:

$$\frac{\text{Fixed interest loans}}{\text{Total capital employed}} = \frac{£80,000}{£100,000} \qquad \frac{£50,000}{£150,000}$$

High gearing is not always advantageous! No matter how low your profits are, you still have to pay the interest.

(f) We can see that both X and Y have attractions for the investor. If we assume for the sake of illustration that if we were to invest £1 in either company and that the relative merits had been fully reflected in the share price of the two companies which one should now be chosen?

	X plc	Y plc
$\frac{\text{Increase in profit}}{\text{Last year's profit}} =$	$\frac{£20,000 - £18,000}{£18,000} = 11.1\%$	$\frac{£40,000 - £37,000}{£37,000} = 8.1\%$

Company X would appear to be expanding faster than Y and so this would be the preferred investment. With the inflation rate at 10% the real growth of X at 1.1% looks very modest but Y is not even keeping pace with inflation and so is looking stagnant.

(g)

	X plc	Y plc
$\frac{\text{Turnover}}{\text{Net assets = capital employed}}$	$\frac{£200,000}{£100,000}$	$\frac{£500,000}{£150,000}$
	2 times	3.33 times

Here is another insight into the two companies. Y plc is achieving a far greater turnover from its assets. (Net assets are equivalent to the capital employed.) This ratio is probably the most revealing in terms of helping us to understand their different marketing strategies. If these do in fact represent supermarkets it should be possible to identify which one was which from this ratio.

(i) Supermarket Y is probably devoted to a high sales per square foot policy with minimum warehousing but the cramped conditions lead to stock 'drift' and damage.

(ii) Supermarket X, by contrast probably has an uncluttered layout with ample well laid out warehousing. This is speculation of course, but it should be seen that while ratio analysis will not lead to a single definitive assessment of a company it is however a powerful analytical tool which will generate questions and serve as a cross check on the other features of a business.

The management of working capital

5.6 Consider the following additional information at the year end and try to relate it to companies X plc and Y plc.

	X plc £000	Y plc £'000
Closing stock	10	22
Debtors	-	-
Creditors	30	80

Ratios can be calculated as follows.

(a) *Stock turnover*

	X plc	Y plc
$\frac{\text{Closing stock}}{\text{Cost of sales}^*} \times 365 =$	$\frac{£10,000}{£200,000 - £30,000} \times 365$	$\frac{£22,000}{£500,000 - £60,000} \times 365$
	= 21.5 days	= 14.9 days

★ Sales-Gross Profit

Where the stock turnover is low it is easier to think in terms of a number of times per year. A factor of 2.2 times is easier to relate to than 166 *days*. The calculation is simply done the other way round ie $\frac{\text{Cost of sales}}{\text{Stock}}$. This shows the rate at which stock is used.

The turnover rates of 21.5 days (X plc) and 14.9 days (Y plc) helps to explain how Y plc is getting a better asset turnover rate and also underpins the view that we are probably looking at two supermarkets. (Sainsbury's 1990 stock turnover was 18 days.)

(b) Creditor turnover

	X plc 64 Days	Y plc 54 Days
$\frac{\text{Creditors} \times 365 \text{ days}}{\text{Cost of sales}}$	$\frac{£30,000 \times £365}{£200,000 - £30,000}$	$\frac{£80,000 \times £365}{£500,000 - £60,000}$

Here X plc is, taking 10 days longer credit from its suppliers than Y plc.

(c) Debtor turnover is not relevant here. As there are no debtors, both businesses are trading exclusively on a cash basis. The calculation would normally be:

$\frac{\text{Debtors}}{\text{Sales}} \times 365$. It shows how long your customers are taking to pay you.

(On the other hand, they could have received money from debtors just before the balance sheet date - but this is unlikely given the other information.)

Liquidity ratios

5.7 The importance of cash to the financial survival of a company was highlighted above. The balance sheet will show what the immediate liabilities are at a certain point in time. The test here is to see if the value of the current (or non permanent) assets of the business will cover the current liabilities. In doing this we take a pessimistic but not implausible view that all the creditors may require payment in full on demand. Note, that in the event that one creditor cannot be paid then the word will quickly get around the other suppliers who will promptly stop supplying goods, effectively preventing the company from trading its way out of a problem.

There are two ratios used.

(a) The current ratio is $\frac{\text{Current assets}}{\text{Current liabilities}}$

Analysts will regard a benchmark of 2:1 as 'healthy'. This recognises that in the event of a sudden liquidation of current assets only a half of the value of those assets might be turned into cash fast enough to satisfy the creditors.

(b) The acid test or quick ratio is:

$\frac{\text{Current assets - stock}}{\text{Current liabilities}}$

This ratio reflects the difficulty of realising/converting stocks of raw materials, work in progress and finished goods, to pay liabilities. These items are now excluded from current assets to leave near cash or quick assets. These should ideally be £1 of quick assets for every £1 of current liabilities ie a 1: 1 ratio. (Remember that liabilities that do not have to be paid before 12 months such as bank loans, as opposed to overdrafts, are classed as long term and not current liabilities.)

5.8 '*Wealth*' *warning*. Ratios must not be viewed as rigid indicators. Their calculation, application and interpretation will vary from analyst to analyst and from company to company. It is possible for example for companies to influence or 'window dress' their results for ratio analysis. Consider for example the following.

Current assets	£200,000
Current liabilities	£300,000

The ratio of 0.66: 1 would not be considered favourably. However if on the last day of the year a £500,000 overdraft is drawn down and say shares are purchased for short term investment the figures are now:

Current assets	£700,000
Current liabilities	£800,000

0.88: 1 appears much more respectable!

Financial ratios

5.9 This final section of ratio analysis examines two aspects of the company's funding picture.

5.10 *Price earnings ratio*. The return to shareholders measured in terms of the profit or earnings per ordinary share compared with the market price of the share, so that the percentage return on purchasing one share can be compared with other similar companies and the risk free market return (eg the return that would be earned from investing money in government stocks ie gilts).

This is the $\dfrac{\text{Market price per share}}{\text{Earnings per share}}$

Earnings per share is, subject to sundry adjustments $= \dfrac{\text{Net profit}}{\text{Number of shares in issue}}$

A high PE ratio can indicate shareholders' expectations of growth, low risk etc. A low PE ratio suggest that, despite the high return, investors are not confident in the company.

5.11 Effects of *gearing*. The gearing ratio which looks at the sensitivity of the company's finances to changes in:

(a) the rate of interest levied by lenders on the money the company has borrowed;

(b) the way in which gearing affects profit attributable to shareholders in different trading conditions.

5.12 The gearing ratio is:

$\dfrac{\text{Long term interest bearing loans}}{\text{Total capital employed}^\star}\ \%$

★ TCE = Long term interest bearing loans + shareholders' funds.

The inclusion of *overdrafts* in the calculation is debatable because overdrafts are usually a short term function of working capital requirements and fluctuate daily. However many companies tend to run a significant and permanent overdraft as part of their overall funding. (Overdrafts are more flexible and sometimes cheaper than fixed interest loans, but they are repayable on demand.)

5.13 The significance of this sensitivity analysis is best demonstrated by means of an example.

Top Gear Plc has the following capital profile.

	£'000	£'000
Commercial mortgage	4,000	
Loan from merchant bank	5,000	
Total loans		9,000
Shareholders funds		
Share capital	500	
Reserves	500	
Total		1,000
Total capital		10,000

This gives a gearing ratio of 90%.

5.14 The profit before interest for 19X1 is £1m and analysts are looking forward to assess the prospects of the company in the following year. Two factors are being considered.

(a) Trade prospects will fluctuate between +10% and -10% of 19X1 levels.
(b) Interest rates will fluctuate between +1% and –1% around the 19X1 rate of 10%.

To demonstrate the impact these factors will have on the shareholders' fortunes calculate the interest payments and shareholders' profit in 19X2.

Scenario	Total profit £'000	Interest payments £'000	Profit to shareholders £'000
1 19X1 results	1,000	900	100
2 Trade prospects + 10%	1,100	900	200
3 Trade prospects -10%	900	900	NIL
4 Interest rates + 1%	1,000	990	10
5 Interest rates- 1%	1,000	810	190

The reality will depend on many other economic and political factors, particularly the underlying asset value of the company (sometimes called the break-up value).

5.15 The volatility induced by the gearing effect is plain to see and it often accounts for the large movements in share prices that affect some companies. The effects can be mitigated by borrowing at fixed interest rates and diversifying across different market segments and in different economies.

6 FINANCIAL ANALYSIS: INTERNAL RATIO ANALYSIS

6.1 Any segment of the business may be viewed as an accounting centre as follows.

(a) *Cost centre.* Costs are gathered together by function (eg export marketing), by activity (eg work on customer XYZ Ltd), or by location (eg Paris office).

(b) *Responsibility centre.* Costs are shown for a complete function, headed by an executive *directly responsible* for that function's expenditure (eg the marketing department).

(c) *Profit centre.* This is a part of the business which is accountable for both costs and revenues thereby producing a profit (eg the Intercity division of British Rail).

(d) *Investment centre.* This is a profit centre where the Return on Capital Employed is measured by comparing profit with the funds invested in that particular centre.

6.2 *Segmental productivity analysis.* In internal analysis, costs are usually compared with other comparable sections of the business to gain an insight into the way in which the section is being managed. For example the Scottish division may spend more money on salespeople's travelling expenses than the Southern division as a percentage of sales achieved. This may be due to any of the following.

(a) Inefficiency in route planning, and poor effectiveness of representatives in making sales.

(b) Differences in customer profiles, customer locations or the territory's geography.

(c) Alternatively it may be due to a *trade off* in *another item* in the *total expenditure* of the section. For example Southern salespeople may be allowed to stay in hotels more often than the Scottish salespeople. Their vehicles' travelling expenses will be lower but their accommodation costs will be higher. A *total cost* approach will be necessary before any management decisions are made.

6.3 The important thing is to devise appropriate ratios for the business. For a firm of road hauliers cost per tonne carried per mile identifies a crucial area for examination. For a hotel, useful ratios include the percentage of rooms occupied per night, the cost per room per day etc.

Part A: Background knowledge relevant to analysis and decision

7 VALUE ADDED STATEMENTS

7.1 A value added statement is an analysis of the profit and loss account to show the wealth created by the company as opposed to bought in goods and services. It puts profit into proper perspective and regards the whole enterprise as a collective effort by investors, management and employees. Here is an example.

STATEMENT OF VALUE ADDED
XYZ MANUFACTURING COMPANY LTD

	£'000	£'000
Turnover		103,900
Bought in materials and services		67,600
Value added		36,300
Applied in the following way:		
To pay employees		
Wages pension and fringe benefits		25,900
To pay provider of capital:		
Interest on loans	800	
Dividends to shareholders	900	
		1,700
To pay government:		
Corporation tax		3,900
To provide for maintenance and expansion of assets		
Depreciation	2,000	
Retained profits	2,800	
		4,800
Value added		36,300

7.2 The uses of value added statements are as follows.

(a) They provide additional information about a company's performance.
(b) They show increases in the firm's resources.
(c) They highlight the proportion of value added paid to employees.
(d) They show the contribution paid to government.
(e) They help implement profit schemes and encourage employee participation.

7.3 Their drawbacks are that they:

(a) are not widely used;
(b) are based on historical financial reports with accepted shortcomings;
(c) are used sometimes to deflect attention away from poor financial performance.
(d) are used as a 'political' statement.

7.4 Value added statements, moreover, are not compulsory, unlike the profit and loss account, the balance sheet and the cash flow statement.

8 INFLATION

8.1 Inflation, or the deterioration of monetary value, is a persistent economic phenomenon. The accountancy profession have attempted for a number of years to develop mechanisms to account for its effect on company finances but with little success. The effect of inflation is in essence quite simple. Companies lose money while ostensibly performing more successfully each year.

8.2 Consider the following example. A plc buys a piece of equipment, let's say a crane, to hire out to others. For the purposes of illustration we will assume that in hiring out the crane no expenses are incurred and no margin is levied. It cost £100,000, and it has an expected life of five years to run. Let us say that to replace it at the end of five years would cost £160,000. Inflation is 10% per annum. Also assume that shareholders leave all their money in the business.

The inflation on cranes is not quite 10% unlike the rate of general inflation of which there are a number of measures (RPI, manufacturers headline, underlying etc). The company's turnover revenue is affected by the general rate of inflation.

8.3 Let us now look at what the company will show in its accounts. Depreciation will be provided at £20,000 per annum and the turnover will increase in line with inflation at 10% per annum.

	Turnover from rental £'000	Depreciation on crane £'000	Profit £'000
Year 1	20,000	20,000	NIL
Year 2 (£20,000 + 10% of turnover)	22,000	20,000	2,000
Year 3 (£22,000 + 10% of turnover)	24,200	20,000	4,200
Year 4 (£24,200 + 10% of turnover)	26,600	20,000	6,600
Year 5 (£26,000 + 10% of turnover)	29,300	20,000	9,300
	122,100	100,000	22,100

Each year the company will report a record level of turnover and record profits, but has it made any 'money'? Well, the tax man will think so, charging tax on the £22,100. The shareholders will have a company with more money in the bank than it started with, but can the company continue trading? In other words can it buy another crane? The answer is no, unless it asks the shareholders for £37,900 (£160,000 - £122,100) and whatever the tax man has taken. At this stage it is clear that this is not a sound basis on which to carry on business. The company will argue that it was able to earn money on the original £100,000 and will do so again on the next £160,000. The problem comes when the company cannot raise further sums to keep up with inflation: it then continues with ageing plant and is uncompetitive until it goes broke. The same effect can be seen on working capital items such as stocks and debtors. Each year more cash is required just to `stand still'.

8.4 A more realistic approach might be to provide one fifth of the £160,000 *replacement cost* each year as follows.

	Turnover from rental £	Provision for replacement £	Profit/ (Loss) £
Year 1	20,000	32,000	(12,000)
Year 2	22,000	32,000	(10,000)
Year 3	24,200	32,000	(7,300)
Year 4	26,600	32,000	(5,400)
Year 5	29,300	32,000	(2,700)
	122,100	160,000	(37,900)

It would be a brave chairman that presented those results to his shareholders. In any event the rate of inflation may not be constant and the replacement cost could not realistically be predicted. (Try explaining to the customer that you are charging £32,000 pa for a crane they know only cost £100,000!)

8.5 If the provision for replacement is reassessed each year on the basis of *known inflation* then the effect is even more pronounced as there is a cumulative catching up effect.

	Turnover from rental £	Provision for replacement £	Calculations
Year 1	20,000	22,000	(£100 × 110%) × $^1/_5$
Year 2	20,000	26,400	(£100 × 110% × 110% × $^2/_5$) − £22,000
Year 3	24,200	31,500	etc
Year 4	26,600	37,200	
Year 5	29,300	42,900	
	122,100	160,000	

This effect of increasing provision is necessary because each year less provision is provided compared to the £32,000 which we know with hindsight *should* be provided.

Part A: Background knowledge relevant to analysis and decision

8.6 These tables and calculations are only shown to demonstrate how inflation causes businesses to go *bankrupt* while *appearing* reasonably healthy. The marketer should bear this in mind when setting prices and analysing business performance. Some companies such as oil retailers do put up prices as soon as replacement costs are known so that their cash flow is preserved but many other companies do not have the power to do this.

9 SHORT-TERM DECISION MAKING

9.1 Marketers make their decisions around the 4 P's: what to sell (product), where to sell (place) how to sell (promotion), and what to charge (price). If any degree of manufacturing or conversion is needed in the product, management has to decide how many should be made.

9.2 There are two ways of looking at this dilemma. In the long term we need to consider what production facilities are required (do we need one factory or two factories, how many production lines etc). In the short term such decisions are not relevant as we cannot just add another factory for say six months or close the existing one down for a few weeks. Such facilities and the associated costs are said to be *fixed*.

9.3 How much to charge? In theory this is easy. The right answer, from an economic and marketing view is how much will the market bear? In practice though much product pricing is done by working out what the product costs to produce and then adding a percentage on top for profits. The importance of costs is that too low a price will mean that products lose money. On the other hand, a low market price could be a stimulus to greater production or marketing efficiencies. The product may be a one off (eg there does not exist a market price for decorating a particular house). Alternatively it may be a part of a range and price positioning may be determined in relation to *comparative* costs.

The term given to this is *cost plus pricing*. The cost of the product is the full cost of producing it, ie the cost of materials, labour and a share of the overheads. For example, consider the following cost statement.

FACTORY XYZ LTD
YEAR ENDED 31 DECEMBER 19X1

	Total cost		Budgeted cost per unit at 20,000 production
	£	£	£
Materials		50,000	2.50
Direct labour		20,000	1.00
		70,000	3.50
Factory rent	10,000		
Factory rates	5,000		
Factory supervisor wages	5,000		
Administration and selling expenses	7,000		
Miscellaneous expenses	3,000		
Total overheads		30,000 ÷ 20,000 =	1.50
Total cost		100,000	5.00

If 20,000 units had been produced then the full cost per unit would be £5.00. The overheads of £30,000 would be *absorbed* onto each unit of production at £1.50 per unit. A 30% markup on cost (£5) would give a selling price of £6.50, and a profit of £1.50.

9.4 In the example above the costs have been divided into two categories:

 (a) materials together with direct labour (*direct costs*);
 (b) overheads (*indirect costs*).

Indirect costs cannot obviously be ascribed to any particular unit.

9.5 Suppose we now produce another 1,000 units, how much will it cost to make the additional 1,000? We would expect to use more materials, and more labour.

(a) If it costs £2.50 in materials to make each unit at present (£50,000 ÷ 20,000 units) then materials should cost £2,500 to make the *additional* units. In this case materials are said to be a *variable* cost. The same assumption could probably be made for the labour element.

(b) The factory rent will *not* increase if extra units are produced. That is said to be a *fixed cost* The same *may* be true for all the other overheads in which case the cost per unit of producing the additional 1000 units is as follows.

		£ unit	£
Materials	1000 units × 2.50 =	2.50	2,500
Labour	1000 units × 1.00 =	1.00	1,000
Total cost		3.50	3,500
Selling price (£1,000 × 6.50)		6.50	6,500
Contribution		3.00	3,000

It can now be seen that the profit from producing and selling the *additional* 1000 units is more profitable per unit than the first 20,000 units. This is because there are no extra overheads per unit other than the material and the labour.

9.6 Let us look at this in another way. Let us examine the cost of producing 20,000 units and the cost of producing 21,000 units and the profits that can be obtained.

	20,000 units £		21,000 units £	
Materials £2.50 per unit		50,000		52,500
Direct labour £1.00 per unit		20,000		21,000
		70,000		73,500
Factory rent	10,000		10,000	
rates	5,000		5,000	
Supervisor wages	5,000		5,000	
Administration and selling	7,000		7,000	
Miscellaneous	3,000		3,000	
		30,000		30,000
		100,000		103,500
Sales revenue 20,000 × £6.50		130,000		136,500 21,000 × £6.50
Profit		30,000		33,000
Profit per unit		£1.50p		£1.57p

Because some of the costs are fixed, irrespective of the level of production, producing and selling more increases profit.

Cost behaviour

9.7 In practice however the behaviour of costs between fixed and variable elements is not so straightforward. Some cost elements have a fixed and a variable element. The cost of electricity has a *fixed element,* (the standing charge and the cost of lighting the factory) irrespective of how many units are produced. It also has a *variable* element, depending on how many hours the production machines are running. Such a cost element is said to be *semi fixed* or *semi variable* depending on the proportion of fixed to variable cost involved.

9.8 There are also *stepped fixed costs* where the total cost increases in steps after certain levels of production have been exceeded. For example after 21,000 units the XYZ Factory may have to operate a night shift, the supervisory wages may double but other costs stay the same.

Part A: Background knowledge relevant to analysis and decision

Cost behaviour

TOTAL COST

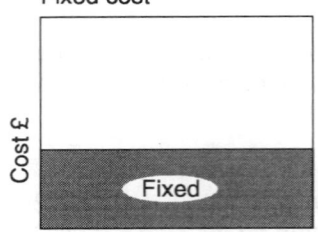

Fixed cost — Cost £ vs Activity level: no. of units (horizontal line, Fixed)

Variable cost — Cost £ vs Activity level: no. of units (upward sloping line from origin, Variable)

Total cost — Total cost £ vs Activity level: no. of units (Variable above Fixed)

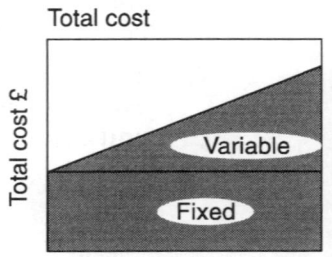

Stepped fixed cost — Total cost £ vs Activity level: no. of units (step function, Fixed)

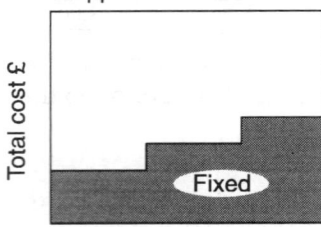

Semi-variable or semi fixed cost — Total cost £ vs Activity level: no. of units (Fixed then Variable)

Total cost £ vs Activity level: no. of units (Variable then Fixed)

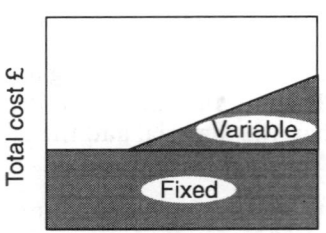

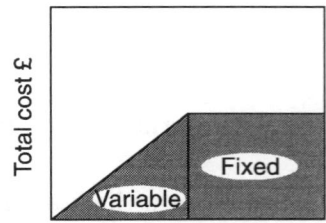

COST PER UNIT

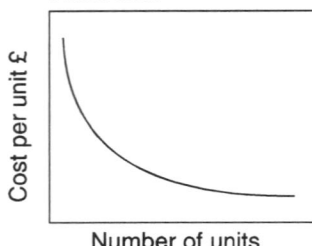

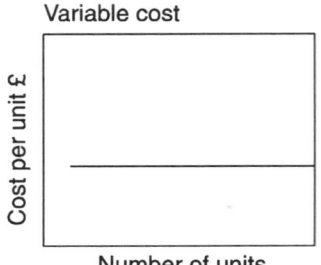

Fixed cost — Cost per unit £ vs Number of units (declining curve)

Variable cost — Cost per unit £ vs Number of units (horizontal line)

Total cost — Cost per unit £ vs Number of units (declining curve)

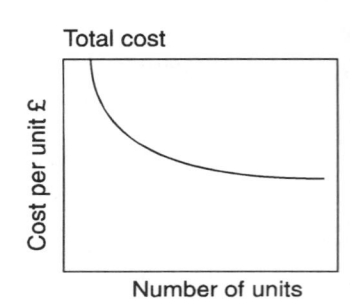

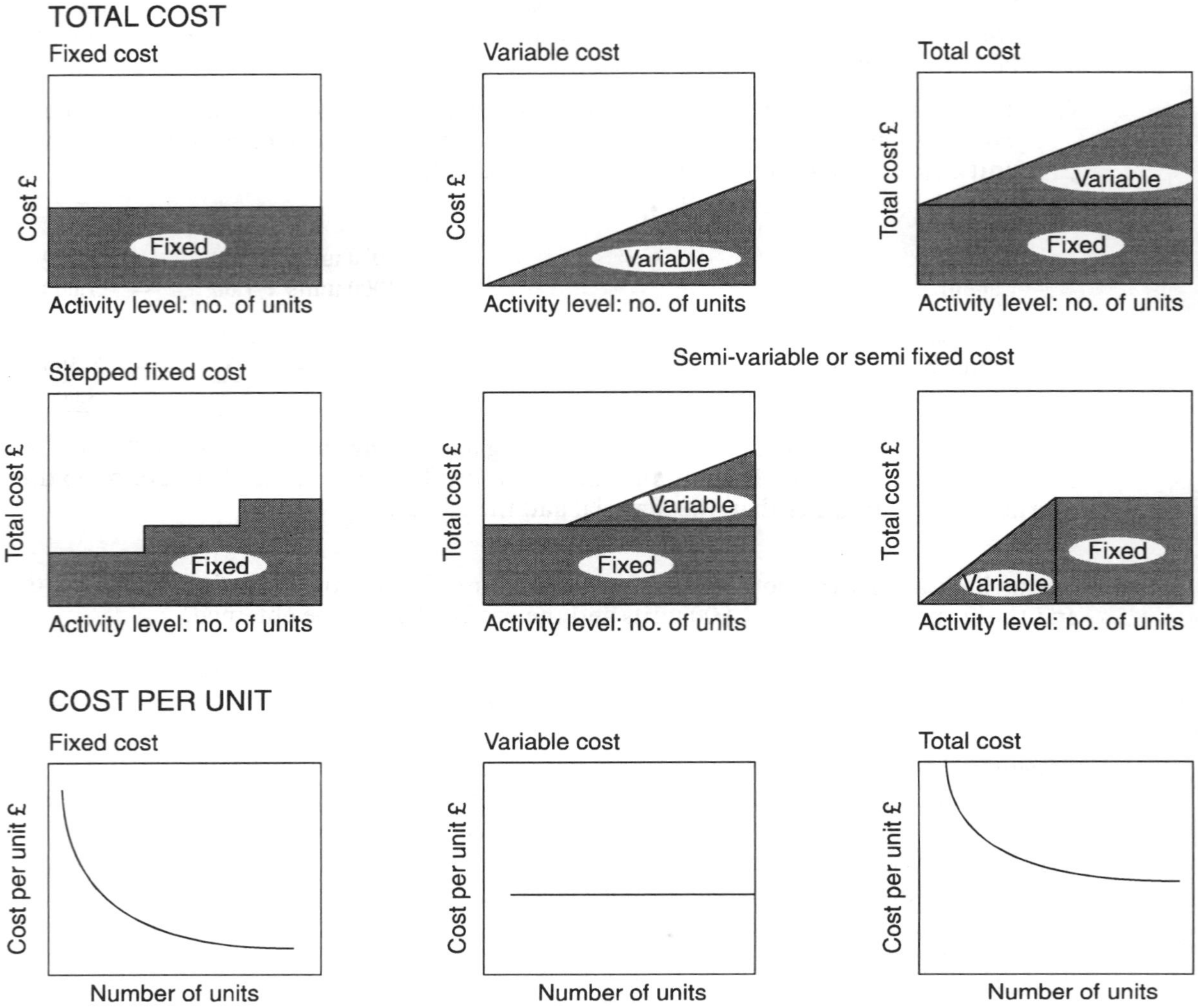

9.9 *Marginal cost.* The *marginal cost* of production is the *additional cost (variable cost)* of producing one additional unit of production or service. For this purpose the cost behaviour of each cost element must be analysed into fixed and variable components. The fixed costs are then viewed as a charge *relating to time* and *not related to the volume* of production. The factory rent of £10,000 is payable whether or not 20,000 units or zero units are made.

9.10 *Contribution.* The total fixed costs of £30,000 cannot be totally ignored or else the company will go out of business. For decision making purposes however they are *irrelevant* in the short term. The only decisions to make are *how much to charge* and *how many* should be produced based on recovering the fixed overheads. The difference between the selling price and the *variable* cost, £3.00 (£6.50 - £3.50) is referred to as the *contribution per unit*. We say that for each unit sold a contribution of £3.00 is made towards the fixed costs of £30,000. When the £30,000 has been recovered each unit sold will *contribute £3.00 towards profit*. The key questions now are these.

(a) How many units need to be sold to cover fixed costs. This is said to be the *break-even point* (BEP) calculated as follows:

$$\frac{\text{Fixed costs}}{\text{Contribution per unit}} = \frac{£30,000}{£3.00} = 10,000 \text{ units}$$

(b) The profit at the planned production levels of 20,000 units and 21,000 units calculated as follows, as we have seen, can also be calculated as:

	20,000 units £	21,000 units £
Contribution (ie revenue of £6.50 less variable costs of £3.50)	60,000	63,000
Fixed costs	30,000	30,000
Profit	30,000	33,000

The power of the marginal cost/contribution approach is that different permutations of fixed costs, variable costs, selling prices and sales volumes can be assimilated very quickly.

9.11 The *margin of safety* represents the difference between *planned sales volume* and the *break even point*. In the example above, sales could fall from 20,000 units to 10,000 units before a loss would occur. (ie 50% margin of safety). The contribution earned by 10,000 units is £30,000, exactly matching the fixed costs. The plan is for 20,000 units.

9.12 *Cost attribution*. In Paragraph 9.3 we calculated a total/full product cost of £5.00. We identified material and labour costs separately from the overheads. Materials and labour are *direct costs* of production and the overheads are indirect costs. This distinction is important in costing because it is seldom that only one product is involved. We need to identify the costs that are *directly associated* with a particular product. All other costs are *indirect*.

9.13 If two or more products are involved it is necessary to *attribute* the cost of the indirect/overhead expenses to each product. This is done in stages.

(a) Allocation of *identifiable* elements of expense to cost centres or to the products (eg the cost of foremen supervising workers making one particular product).

(b) Apportionment of *unidentifiable* elements to cost centres or products on some equitable basis (the rates would be divided between the production, sales and administration functions on the basis of the floor area occupied).

(c) Absorb the total overheads onto the cost per unit on some sensible basis. Sometimes, in single product firms, it is simply allocated on the number of units. For example, for 20,000 production we could identify overheads as follows.

	£	£ per unit
Factory rent	10,000	0.50
Factory rates	5,000	0.25
Factory supervision, wages	5,000	0.25
Administration and selling	7,000	0.35
Miscellaneous	3,000	0.15
Total overheads (per 9.3)	30,000 ÷ 20,000 units	1.50

Here we absorb them by expected units of production.

An example is the absorption of overheads on the basis of *direct labour hours*. In other words an estimate of the total labour hours is made. The overhead is divided by the estimate, and the overhead cost is allocated on that basis. If a product takes two hours to make, then it is allocated more overhead expense than product B which takes one hour to make. In some industries the labour content is very low so the *machine processing time* may be used instead.

9.14 *Absorption costing*. After all costs have been *absorbed* onto the product we then have the *full cost* which we calculated for XYZ Ltd in 9.3.

Marginal cost versus full cost

9.15 *Absorption versus marginal costing*. We have looked at two very different ways of preparing product costs. Both ways have advantages and disadvantages. The choice of approach will be particularly important in closing *stock valuations* and hence affect the calculation of profit. *Marginal* costing effectively writes off all fixed costs each year but absorption costing values some of the *fixed costs as a cost of stock* therefore *carrying these costs forward* into the next period. Financial accounting Statement of Standard Accounting Practice (SSAP) No. 9 recommends that the absorption principle should be used.

9.16 (a) *Marginal cost approach*

   (i) Fixed costs are period costs. In other words they are not carried forward in a stock valuation.

   (ii) Profit planning is best done using contribution per unit, and breakeven analysis.

   (iii) Decision making should focus on *relevant* costs. In the short term, fixed costs are irrelevant to a decision as you have to incur them whatever you do.

   (iv) The problems of cost allocation, apportionment and absorption are avoided. Time is saved, and subjectivity is reduced. There are many criticisms of absorption costing, too technical to go into here, but it is argued that it often gives misleading information.

   (v) Control of fixed costs is better. Fixed costs are incurred on a time basis, and should be controlled on that basis rather than hidden in stock.

 (b) *Absorption cost approach*

   (i) Production causes cost, therefore all costs should be reflected in unit costs.

   (ii) Products incur costs and use production facilities differently. A costing system should reflect this on an equitable basis.

   (iii) SSAP 9 acquires a full cost approach for disclosure of stock valuation in the year end financial statements.

   (iv) It is necessary for setting prices in some cases (eg new products, one off products with no market price, certain cost plus contracts).

9.17 Other decision making issues for which some of these techniques are useful, as well as breakeven analysis, include:

 (a) whether to accept or reject new orders;
 (b) changing the product mix;
 (c) making the best use of limited resources;
 (d) dropping product/range/line;
 (e) alter prices/production costs;
 (f) changing cost structure (eg incentive schemes);
 (g) automation/mechanisation;
 (h) whether to make something in-house or buy in from outside.

The classification of costs for decision making

9.18 We have so far looked at costs as being variable or fixed, direct or indirect. In terms of decision making there are a number of other classifications which can be used. Remember decision making is concerned with *future events* stemming from the *present decision point*. It is a very different concept to the recording of accountancy data to *deduce last year's profit*.

 (a) *Controllable costs.* Costs which can be *controlled* by a particular person are identified as such so that performance can be monitored and decisions made by the appropriate personnel. For example territory sales managers are *responsible* for the costs of *their* sales force. The manager can exert control over, say, travelling expenses but the advertising costs in that territory are dictated by the marketing director. Although the cost of advertising is charged to the sales manager's budget the manager *cannot control* that section of cost.

4: Financial aspects of marketing Notes

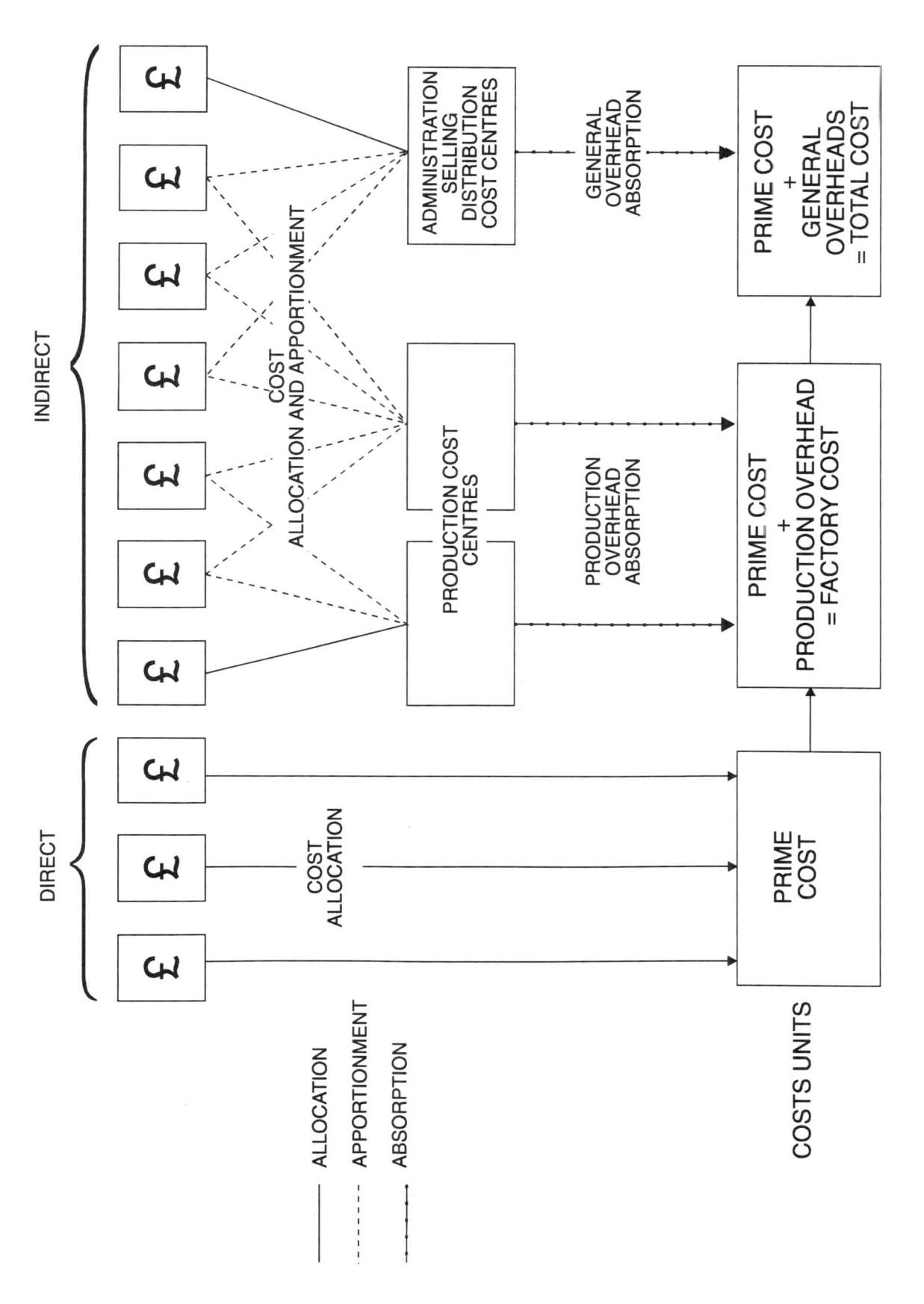

THE BUILD-UP OF TOTAL COST

Part A: Background knowledge relevant to analysis and decision

(b) *Avoidable costs.* Future costs may be split into those costs which are *avoidable* and those which are *unavoidable*. For example the decision to reduce the number/cost of employees will result in cost being *avoided* but reducing production levels will not in the short term avoid paying the rental on the factory's 21 year lease. Such a cost is *unavoidable*.

(c) *Sunk costs.* A cost which as already been incurred is said to be a *sunk* cost. That cost, as far as decision making is concerned, is no longer relevant. The fact that a football player cost £2 million last year is *not relevant* if now, through bad form, he is only worth £100,000. The decision to retain or sell him should be made *only* on the level of any offer that may be made for him.

(d) *Opportunity costs*

An *opportunity* cost is a *hypothetical* cost which represents the revenue that would be *received* if an *alternative* course of action was pursued.

(i) Let us take a simple example. You currently earn £8,000 pa. You have recently thought about setting up your own business, and you reckon you could earn £10,000 pa. The *opportunity cost* of your decision to go it alone is the £8,000 you could have earned by staying put.

(ii) Another example: a consignment of grey wool which was purchased last year and never used may be assumed to have no value in the financial accounts. It is now proposed to knit it up to make prison blankets. But if the yarn in its present form could be sold to a market trader or redyed then the money that could be received is effectively a *cost* of knitting the prison blankets. The cost is thus the benefit which will be forgone by knitting.

(e) *Incremental costs.* An incremental cost is the increased cost that will result from the decision being taken.

(f) *Differential cost.* A differential cost is the difference between the cost levels of two courses of action. The total costs of alternative A should be compared with the total costs of alternative B.

10 LONG-TERM DECISION MAKING

10.1 In the previous section we assumed that in the short term little effective control could be exerted over the level of *fixed costs*. If we extend the *time horizon*, then these fixed costs become unfixed and under management control. For example a firm may decide to reduce or increase a firm's capacity by acquiring alternative premises. Management need to estimate all the *differential* costs and revenues/benefits associated with such a change and evaluate the move as a distinct project. Should a move be made or not?

10.2 The same approach is also necessary to evaluate new projects where the *payback* timescale is over two years. In considering a long term project its costs can be split into two categories.

(a) *Capital* amounts where the expenditure will take place early in the project life and the benefits will last for several years.

(b) *Revenue* expenditure which will occur each year and will generally be linked directly to sales revenue or cost savings.

It is usual in examination questions to net income and revenue expenditure together to give a net cash inflow or outflow per annum.

Project viability: discounted cash flow

10.3 The financial viability of a long term project should consider three aspects.

(a) The *return on capital employed*. (Profit over capital employed ie the accounting measure.)

(b) The *risk* on investment. Exposure to uncertainty/risk increases as a function of time. Some investments are inherently riskier than others.

4: Financial aspects of marketing   Notes

(c) The *discounted return* on investment. Seen as the cash inflows of the project *less* the cash outflows taking into account the cost of borrowing or tying up money in the initial investment.

10.4 *The time value of money.* The view is to put it crudely, that cash now is better than money in future. £1,000 now is worth more than £1,000 in ten years time, because you can earn interest on it in that time, as well as taking inflation into account.

(a) Consider the cost of investing £100,000 in a project for 4 years before any return was achieved. How much would need to be received to break even if the interest rate is 10%?

	£
Initial capital	100,000
Interest for year 1 (£100,000 × 10%)	+10,000
Balance at end of year 1	110,000
Interest for year 2 (£110,000 × 10%)	+11,000
Balance at end of year 2	121,000
Interest for year 3 (£121,000 × 10%)	+12,100
Balance at end of year 3	133,100
Interest for year 4 (£133,100 × 10%)	+13,310
Balance at end of year 4	146,410

So, a return of *at least* £146,410 would be needed at the end of year four to break even. A short way of achieving the same result is by use of simple mathematics.

$$£100,000 (1 + 10\%)^4 = £100,000 (1.1)^4$$

(b) Rather than add interest to our capital now by applying an interest rate, we can divide future sums by a discount rate to set their value now. To demonstrate this let us compare two scenarios, one in which we expect £146,000 at the end of four years and one in which we expect £147,000. How do we 'work back' to their equivalent now? Just as we multiplied our sum *now* by an interest rate to get a future value, we can *divide* the future values by a discount rate. In other words, assuming the rate of 10%:

$$£100,000 \times 1.1^4 = £146,410$$

$$\frac{£146,410}{1.1^4} = £100,000 \text{ present value.}$$

(Try it on your calculator. You can also get *discount tables*). In other words £146,410 in four years time is equivalent to £100,000 now.

Let us take one or two figures.

$$\frac{£146,000}{1.1^4} \text{ (in four years time) has a present value of } = £99,720$$

$$\frac{£147,000}{1.1^4} \text{ (in four years time) has a present value of } = £100,403$$

(c) This can be used to assess the value of the project.

	£
Present value of £146,000 in year 4	99,720
Outlay	100,000
Net present value	(280)
Present value of £147,000 in year 4	100,403
Outlay	100,000
Net present value	403

If the profit were to give us £146,000 in four years time, we would be better off investing the £100,000 at 10% for the period in a bank account. The net present value is *negative*. If, on the other hand, we were to receive £147,000 in four years time, we would be better off investing in the project than leaving the money in the bank.

Part A: Background knowledge relevant to analysis and decision

(d) Tables showing DCF factors for a range of interest rates over periods up to 50 years are available and these will be supplied in any examination. The value of $\frac{1}{1.1^4}$ would be given as 0.683 so $\frac{£146,410}{1.1^4} = £146,410 \times 0.683$ (approx).

(e) By discounting, a point is reached whereby at an interest rate of 10% there is no difference between having the benefit of £100,000 now (which we could invest to earn 10% interest per annum) or alternatively receiving a sum (which we have worked out as £146,410) in 4 years time.

(f) In the example above, however, it would be a foolhardy person who accepted a return of exactly £146,410 in four years time because there is no guarantee that such a return will materialise. In four years anything could happen and 10% is not a particularly exciting return. In other words there is no account taken of the *exposure to risk*.

10.5 The approach of adding interest to the original capital cost to compare with future cash inflows, tends to be rather clumsy and impractical in practice, particularly when two projects of different *lives* are being compared. In real life, management will estimate the initial investment costs together with the estimated net cash inflows year by year and then evaluate the profitability after allowing for interest. Future cash flows (in or out) are therefore *discounted* by the compound interest rate to the first day of the project, as we have seen.

10.6 There are two techniques of DCF.

(a) Net present value is the *present value of surplus cash* flows over a number of years after deduction of initial outlay. A positive value should be accepted as in 10.4(c).

(b) The internal rate of return (IRR) compares the DCF interest rate achieved on a project with the required rate. The rate in the project is found by trial and error.

10.7 *Cumulative NPV tables*. To avoid calculating factors as individual factors powers we simply use cumulative discount tables. In simple calculations the single tables are quite sufficient but for amounts received constantly for a number of years the cumulative tables should be used. for example if we wanted a discount factor for 10% cumulatively for three years.

(a) The factor of 2.487 used above would be made up as follows:

From single year tables	0.909	$\left(\frac{1}{1.1}\right)$
	0.826	$\left(\frac{1}{1.1^2}\right)$
	0.752	$\left(\frac{1}{1.1^3}\right)$
From cumulative discount tables	2.487	

(b) For an investment of £1,000 giving £600 pa for three years we have the following.

	Present Value £
= £600 × 2.487 =	1,492
Less Investment	1,000
Net Present Value	492

(c) Working this out individually gives us:

Outlay	Cash/£ (1,000)			Present value £ (1,000)
Year 1	600	$\times \dfrac{1}{1.1}$	=	545
Year 2	600	$\times \dfrac{1}{1.1^2}$	=	496
Year 3	600	$\times \dfrac{1}{1.1^3}$	=	451
			Net present value	492

11 CASH FLOW FORECASTING

11.1 The managers of a firm need to monitor the factors which affect cash flows of the business. In this control activity, a formal annual cash flow statement will not give sufficient information regarding the timing of changes to cash resources. For example, a cash flow statement published in the financial accounts may show that the firm has a healthy bank balance at the beginning and end of the financial period. But the cash flow statement does not show whether the firm went into overdraft in the middle of that period.

11.2 However, for internal management information cash flow forecasts are designed to address the liquidity problem in more detail. They will attempt to show specific receipts and payments of cash during the month (or week or even day) in which the cash actually flows.

11.3 The managers of a business may regret or celebrate the cash position of the firm which has already occurred. But they can do little about that position. Their main concern will be future liquidity. Thus a cash flow statement tends to be a prediction (or budget or forecast) of what is likely to happen. Used in this way the cash flow forecast allows managers to foresee liquidity problems before they arise, and possibly take action to overcome them.

11.4 Balance sheets, income statements, and cash flow statements may be prepared either in retrospect (after the event) or in prospect (looking ahead). Analysts and other external users of accounts will normally have to rely on past data. But managers within the firm can (and normally will) make more use of forward looking accounting statements.

11.5 We now consider a 'forward looking' cash flow statement. Such a statement is normally referred to as a cash budget. The information relates to Cyclops (an imaginary firm) which makes and sells bicycles to retailers. This is a seasonal business and cash flow is critical around Christmas. Large quantities of bicycles have been produced and sold to the shops, but the cash for these sales will not be received until the New Year. Cyclops' cash budget for the period November-January is show below:

Notes   Part A: Background knowledge relevant to analysis and decision

Cyclops: - cash budget

		November £'000	December £'000	January £'000
Receipts from customers				
1	Paying in month of delivery (taking discount)	10	8	4
2	Paying two months after delivery	20	30	60
		30	38	64
Payments				
1	Materials	20	15	11
2	Labour Costs	20	15	11
3	Cash Expenses	5	5	5
4	Fixed Assets	10	-	10
5	Interest payments	-	3	-
		55	38	37
Surplus/(deficit) for the month		(25)	-	27
Cash balance - beginning of month		10	(15)	(15)
Cash balance/(overdraft) end of month		(15)	(15)	(12)

11.6 Many of Cyclops' customers take two months credit and this causes the firm problems of liquidity because payments for materials and labour are paid out before the cash is returned. Cyclops needs to talk with a sympathetic bank manager perhaps to set up temporary overdraft facilities during the Christmas period.

11.7 Remember that the figures in a cash budget are only predictions and must therefore be subject to various degrees of uncertainty. The cash budget is a view of the firm as a system of cash flows. An examination of the cash flow cycle of any firm can be very revealing. Business is not static and there will be continual movements between assets and liabilities. It is probably easier to see the cash flow cycle in diagrammatic form.

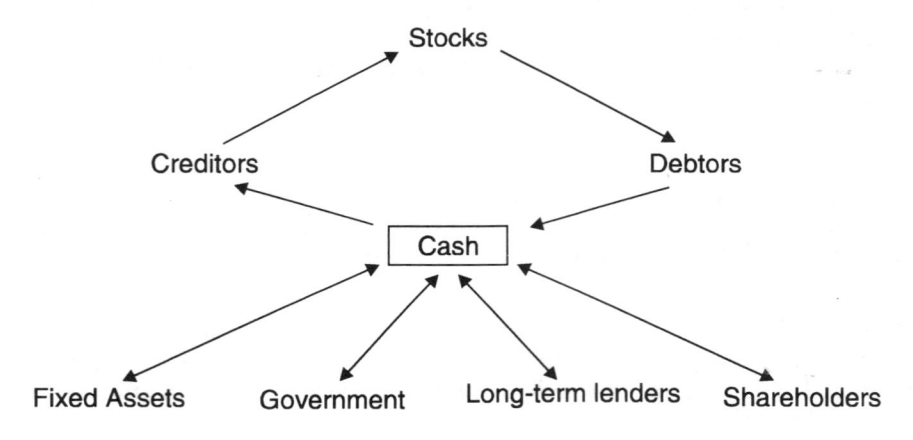

```
                    Stocks
                   ↗      ↘
            Creditors     Debtors
                ↖  ↕      ↙
                   Cash
                ↗  ↑  ↑  ↖
        Fixed Assets  Government  Long-term lenders  Shareholders
```

Eg	Items in stock	62 days
	Less credit period allowed from supplies	30 days
		32 days
	Plus credit period allowed to customers	55 day
	Total cash cycle time	87 days

The length of time between paying cash out to creditors and receiving cash in from debtors will be a critical aspect of a firm's liquidity. A manufacturing firm may have a cycle which takes several months to complete, whereas a retailer often receives cash for a sale before paying for the goods! The nature of the business will, therefore, largely determine the need for cash resources to carry the firm through its cash flow cycle.

12 SOURCES OF FINANCE

12.1 Although as a marketing manager you will not be involved in managing money (other than from sales, of course!), there are occasions when you will need to take account of how you are going to raise money, if your marketing strategy involves expense, and if the company is in a difficult position.

12.2 *Short term sources of finance*

(a) Delay payments to creditors
(b) Bank overdraft
(c) Factoring of sales (getting a bank to collect the debts)
(d) Export credit guarantee
(e) Profit (retained in the business)
(f) Sell investments

12.3 *Medium term*

(a) Bank overdraft
(b) Bank loan
(c) Leasing
(d) Hire purchase
(e) Government (and EC) loans and grants

12.4 *Long term*

(a) Merchant bank loans
(b) Bond home/overseas
(c) Debentures/mortgages
(d) Shares issues
(e) Retained profit

12.5 Sources of finance will, of course, vary for companies domiciled overseas. Credit can be restricted by a country's government or indeed directly and indirectly by the International Monetary Fund and World Bank. International companies and multinationals are better placed by virtue of their organisation to take advantage of low-cost sources of finance worldwide.

13 FEASIBILITY AND RISK

The financial implications of your marketing plan

13.1 In order to get your marketing plan implemented in real life, you will need to persuade your superiors and peers of its financial viability as well as its marketing feasibility. In the past this has been a weakness in the marketing plans of a high proportion of the CIM case study examinees, some of whom give the impression that they should have carte blanche to spend large sums of money without any regard to a return on these investments.

13.2 In Chapter 8 (Paragraph 5.21) there is a *financial implications checklist*. Please study this carefully. Many students interpret a request for the financial implications in an exam paper as a question on *costs*. Obviously cost is one of the financial implications of your marketing plan but it is *only* one. (Others might be revenues, return of investment, sources of investment finance, exchange rates etc.)

13.3 Consider your plan to increase sales. This will inevitably place strains on the organisation's working capital as you will no doubt be spending more money on raw materials, work in progress, stocks and wages. The increase in working capital needed will require funding and if this is external it will incur interest. If you need to buy new machinery this might be a capital investment: a return on capital employed will be required to justify the purchase. Having purchased the machinery it will be subject to depreciation. The planned increase in sales may have implications for debtors and the creditors (as a result of the increased production) debtors situation which in turn may affect your cash flow.

Risk

13.4 Now what about *risk*? Just supposing your planned increase in sales did not materialise. How would it affect the above issues? Do you need a contingency plan? Would you 'buy' your own marketing plan or is it too risky? Have you done your homework? Are your figures sound? Should you acquire new machinery on a lease and buy-back basis? Are projected increases in sales based upon properly conducted test marketing? What assurances can you give your superiors and peers on this element of risk?

13.5 If you were the finance director and you could obtain an 8% return on investment in securities after one year with very little risk, why should you support your marketing director's costly proposals to venture into new international markets with no prospect of breaking even in the first year? The finance director might suggest a risk premium. In other words, your marketing plan should not only match the return available from investing it, but should perhaps exceed it by a set percentage.

13.6 These and other questions need to be addressed at CIM Diploma level. You need to be able to demonstrate your acumen and grasp of these financial aspects if you are to succeed in your professional marketing career.

Feasibility studies

13.7 Very little appears to have been written specifically on this aspect in the marketing literature. The following guidelines should therefore be found useful in the event of a future question on this matter. The guidelines are based on a specimen answer to a specific question on feasibility in a previous CIM case study.

The form and content of a feasibility (viability) study

> 1   *Corporate audit*
>   - Objectives, five year plan,
>   - Key criteria for project appraisal/evaluation
>
> 2   *The scenario or project*
>
> 3   *Assumptions*
>
> 4   *Feasibility research*
>
>   (a) *Experimental/technical research*
>   Design studies, performance specification, timings, costs.
>
>   (b) *Market research*.
>   Demand analysis, competition, buying motives, pricing etc.
>
>   (c) *Commercial potential*. (to include analysis of the feasibility research in terms of timing, cost, human resource needs). Outline income and expenditure analysis.
>
>   (i)   DCF projections over 5 years, prices, break-even analysis
>   (ii)   Venture capital required
>   (iii) Cost of capital at current interest rate
>   (iv)   Working capital
>   (v)   Short-term loans/overdraft requirements
>   (vi)   Cash flow projections - funding periods
>   (vii) Contingencies
>   (viii) Payback periods and net gains

Chapter roundup

- An awareness of the financial implications of your marketing plans is becoming increasingly necessary for the examination.

- The balance sheet displays what a business possesses (assets) and what it owes (liabilities). The profit and loss account describes how a business has performed over time. A cash flow statement describes how the business has been financed.

- Ratio analysis is a way of using financial information to glean facts about an organisation's performance (eg gross margin). It should be used with care, as financial data is easily manipulated.

- Pricing decisions are often related to costs. Variable costs change with the volume of production. Fixed costs do not. Contribution (sales revenue less variable cost) is sometimes a better guide to decisions than information based on absorption costing.

- Any profit needs to be assessed for risk, especially new ventures or markets.

Test your knowledge

1. Distinguish between tangible and intangible assets. (see para 2.6)
2. What is the matching principle? (3.2)
3. What rule should be adopted for ratio analysis? (5.3)
4. What is the current ratio? (5.7)
5. Distinguish between fixed and variable costs (9.7)
6. What is marginal cost? (9.9)
7. Define net present value. (10.6)
8. List some short term sources of finance. (12.2)

Chapter 5

SIGNIFICANT CURRENT ISSUES

> **This chapter covers the following topics.**
> 1. Marketing myopia
> 2. Relationship marketing
> 3. Total marketing: total quality and the marketing concept
> 4. Improving marketing orientation
> 5. Internal marketing
> 6. Brand management: culture, values and change
> 7. Industrial (business to business) marketing
>
> **Introduction**
>
> This chapter contains notes on current issues which you should bear in mind in case study work.

1 MARKETING MYOPIA

1.1 The syndrome identified famously as 'Marketing Myopia' by Theodore Levitt in 1960 still exists today in many companies and organisations. Even today some customers seem blind to customers' needs and wants or couldn't care less. We still come across hotels and bars which are apparently run for the benefit of the management and staff rather than customers. Television sets are tuned to the programmes which the staff want to see and left on regardless of whether customers want to watch. Young bar staff play the music they want to hear at maximum volume irrespective of the fact that the clientele are trying to make conversation. Companies priding themselves on technological advance still become entranced with their products to the point when they cease to enquire what the customers really want. These companies push their products before customers and hard-sell benefits which most people may not relate to.

1.2 An innovation concept recently hyped up in the media comprises of a completely robotised hospital trolley which can deliver tea, newspapers etc to hospital beds without human assistance. Great for the hospital management, perhaps, but one wonders whether patients have been consulted.

1.3 Too many candidates fail CIM case study examinations because they do not understand that marketing is first and foremost about *customer pull* as opposed to *product push*. The most significant change in marketing thinking today is (or should be) from chasing a sale to creating and keeping a customer. The movement is towards relationship marketing and achieving a true, lasting marketing orientation: *read on!*

2 RELATIONSHIP MARKETING

2.1 The essence of relationship marketing is stated by Martin Christoper, Adrian Payne and David Ballantyne in their book of this title (Butterworth-Heinemann 1991) to be as follows.

   (a) Focus on customer retention.

(b) Orientation on customer benefits.
(c) Long time scale.
(d) High customer commitment.
(e) High customer contact.
(f) Quality is the concern of all.

2.2 It is claimed that gaining a new customer can cost four times as much as to keep an existing one, so that a focus on customer retention makes a great deal of sense.

2.3 The longer term approach can also be said to be eminently suited to the 1990s in many ways. Studies of successful Japanese companies are likely to reveal an underlying long term strategy in that:

(a) they will accept losses in the short term in order to gain a dominant market share and lasting profitability in the longer term;

(b) they form long-term contractual relationships with all their staff rather than the 'hire and fire' approach taken by many British companies;

(c) they build long-term partnerships with their suppliers in the interests of the customers rather than the 'cheapest price on the day' approach adopted by many British managements;

(d) once a Japanese company wins a customer it works hard to build the relationship rather than easing up;

(e) a long term approach is also taken with regard to location and the development of good relationships with the community.

2.4 Relationship marketing's emphasis on high customer commitment is in keeping with the TQM approach being taken by many British companies in the 1990s. There is increasing recognition that internal customers and indirect customer contacts play crucial roles in the quality of external customer service. Put quite simply if someone in the despatch department drops a case rather too heavily on the pallet, a subsequent customer complaint of damaged goods is likely to result. Failure of the works office to respond quickly to a sales office telephone enquiry on progress of a job means a customer is let down and an expensively built-up relationship is tarnished.

3 TOTAL MARKETING: TOTAL QUALITY AND THE MARKETING CONCEPT

3.1 The following is a summary of an article by Barry J Witcher of Durham University Business School published in the Quarterly Review of Marketing (Winter 1990).

3.2 Witcher's main contention is that marketing, as currently understood by management and the marketing profession, is generally too narrow a concept. In fact, it can be argued that the marketing concept has a great deal in common with total quality management (TQM).

3.3 Going back to Kotler, marketing is about identifying customer needs and targeting organisation resources at them in the most appropriate way. Segmentation is an important technique for ascertaining customer needs, although only 47% of UK companies, according to a report published in 1987, can identify their main types of customer.

3.4 Witcher feels that companies still follow rival philosophies to the marketing concept.

(a) Production orientation involves a focus on costs, quality and reliability, 'a pre-deterministic rather than a flexible and responsive approach to customer needs'.

(b) Product orientation involves a concentration of product features rather than customer benefits, leading to a misunderstanding as to the significance of product changes on the competitive offer.

(c) A selling orientation results in an emphasis on promotion and 'a hit-and-run attitude towards the customer which gives a distinctly short-term emphasis to a company's operations'.

3.5 Witcher argues that the marketing concept goes much deeper than ideas about 'segmentation' and 'targeting'. He holds that three conditions must be met for a true marketing orientation.

(a) All aspects of a company's organisation and functioning must be directed to customers. This deals with issues of the marketing environment, keeping in touch with customers etc.

(b) The company must coordinate its efforts and activities with those of its customers. This deals with targeting, segmentation and competitive advantage.

(c) There should be a total marketing environment for the whole company. The marketing philosophy must be embraced by the whole company (eg including the accounts department).

Internal marketing

3.6 In most UK companies, marketing is a separate activity, devoted to outsiders. For the marketing philosophy to be adopted, it must overcome the pattern of communication within the company.

3.7 Some examples by which this can be achieved are:

(a) internal communication (eg mission statements);

(b) linking business functions (eg production and marketing personnel should be trained together;

(c) relationships between marketing and staff.

3.8 Witcher quotes the example of BT's TQM programme.

(a) A mission statement was drawn up for the company, expressing what was required from the company by its users, in terms of 'customer service, product quality, involvement of suppliers and attainment of a positive market position.'

(b) Cross-functional training and workshops tried to build bridges between different parts of the company.

(c) Full discussion of TQM was encouraged.

Total quality management (TQM)

3.9 'The purpose was to implement planning and management through the use of team working, and by so doing create an understanding which leads to a greater spread of responsibilities, and pro-activity... TQM tries to make the process continuous.'

Relationship marketing

3.10 TQM matches with the concept of relationship marketing. Relationship marketing is concerned with 'more than just a short term event in a market place'. Rather, 'relationships take time to establish, and all long term phenomena which involve complete series of exchanges (however defined). In short, relationship marketing is orientated towards 'strong, lasting relationship with individual accounts.'

3.11 A simple example can be provided in the service sector. A restaurant management will want satisfied customers to return, as repeat custom will be a more important factor in the restaurant's success than new customers.

Business to business marketing

3.12 Marketing to other businesses has a different set of problems than marketing to consumers. Arguably, if TQM is encouraging customers to have a more restricted number of suppliers, then business-to-business marketing, on a relationship basis, will become more important.

Marketing and TQM

3.13 Marketing is perhaps 'too basic to be noticed' and, as it is not considered in the abstract, the marketing department often has little connection with TQM programs.

   (a) If 'quality' is fitness for use, then this should be part of internal marketing. Quality is not simply a matter of improving production processes.

   (b) If 'total quality management' is to be introduced, so perhaps must 'total marketing' in order that the firm's productive capacity can be tailored to customer needs. This would mean everybody in the firm knowing, or at least considering, 'the demands of customers.'

3.14 Witcher suggests that UK companies are culturally ill-suited to this approach.

   (a) The history of adversarial relations with suppliers does not encourage a 'partnership' approach, as noted in Paragraph 3.12 above.

   (b) UK firms' activities are compartmentalised, so that there are significant divisions within the company.

3.15 'The insularity of UK-based companies has probably prevented the full application of marketing in its modern sense. This is a British marketing failure. For the future, British companies should look to their corporate cultures, and change them. The marketing concept, like the total quality concept, applies totally and to everything. Both these things must be brought together through training and company identity schemes as a common programme to influence culture. Management have to understand that the marketing idea is not a functional activity but a way of business life. In the Japanese way of stating things, it is an important part of 'continuous improvement. This is not generally understood at the moment, which is why companies do not seem to be implementing modern marketing ideas. The marketing profession must understand it first.'

4 IMPROVING MARKETING ORIENTATION

4.1 Richard Wilson and Noel Fook of Nottingham Business School argue, in *Marketing Business* (June 1990) that the adoption by organisations of the marketing orientation improves their effectiveness in marketing specifically, and then in the effectiveness of the organisation throughout its activities.

4.2 The authors feel that marketing is a process by which 'an enterprise seeks to maintain a continuous match between its products and services'. A more precise definition is that the 'marketing orientation is the process by which an enterprise's target customers' needs and wants are effectively and efficiently satisfied within the resource limitation and long-term survival requirements of that enterprise'.

4.3 However, how far does the marketing orientation actually exist in UK companies? If so, how can you recognise it? The authors suggest that the existence of an effective marketing orientation can be identified by the following characteristics.

   (a) A 'good understanding of the needs, wants and behaviour patterns of targeted customers'.

   (b) The organisation should be concerned with profitable sales rather than just turnover.

(c) The chief executive should be a marketing strategist.

(d) The mission should be market driven.

(e) Marketing should be 'seen as being more important than other functions and orientations'.

(f) The marketing orientation should be recognised as superior.

(g) All managers should use marketing inputs in decision making.

(h) The cost-efficiency of the marketing function should be analysed.

(i) The marketing function should be involved in new product development.

(j) Marketing professionals should be employed for marketing functions.

(k) Marketing is the responsibility of everyone in the organisation.

(l) Decisions with marketing implications are made in a well-coordinated way and executed in an integrated manner.

4.4 Wilson and Fook go on to connect these issues with the 7 S framework (shared values, style, structure, skills and staffing, systems, strategy) outlined by Kinsey.

4.5 Developing a marketing orientation 'is a long term process and needs to be thought of as a form of investment. To a large extent this investment is in changing the organisation's culture, so that common values relating to the need to highlight service to customers, a concern for quality in all activities and so forth, are shared throughout the organisation. This is not an appropriate target for a quick fix.'

4.6 Wilson and Fook suggest the following stages to increase the marketing orientation of an organisation.

(a) Secure the support of senior management with the prestige and authority to push it through and overcome scepticism.

(b) There should be a specified mission relating to the development of the marketing orientation.

(c) A task force should be set up:

(i) to identify the current orientation;

(ii) to carry out an analysis of deficiencies between the current orientation and the desired marketing orientation;

(iii) to advise on change and implementation.

4.7 Progress must be monitored to ensure that the firm does not snap back into its old ways.

5 INTERNAL MARKETING

5.1 Kevin Thomson writing in *Marketing Business* (September 1991) stated that 'looking at the employee as a valued customer is the focus of the new discipline of internal marketing'.

5.2 'If total customer satisfaction is the responsibility of marketing, then it is no longer good enough for marketing people to simply look at the external customer's requirements. Quality can only come from inside the organisation, so marketing must start to turn its attention this way.'

5.3 Internal marketing is not just the responsibility of training staff (employed by the personnel department) but of marketing personnel because the author suggests that only marketing personnel possess all of the following.

(a) Knowledge of the organisation's overall strategy.

(b) Understanding of the needs of external customers.

(c) Marketing techniques and tools.
(d) Ability to use techniques and tools on internal customers.
(e) Budgets.

5.4 Internal marketing is a means to 'reach and teach' the internal customer. Internal products and services include education, information, strategy and planning.

5.5 Internal marketing also can be integrated with a company's external marketing practice. Service businesses in particular, which depend on customers being made to feel welcomed, depend on those personnel dealing directly with the customers. Internal marketers can affect these employees, or indeed, any other aspect of the organisation/customer relationship (eg quality).

5.6 Internal marketing combines:

(a) marketing;
(b) human resources;
(c) training;
(d) behavioural science.

5.7 It operates at three levels.

(a) It can be integrated at overall policy-making level as one of the objectives of the company.
(b) It is a strategic tool in the planning of organisational change.
(c) It is part of a way of implementing organisational change, or supporting an external marketing effort.

5.8 Internal marketing sees internal communications, and so forth (eg company magazines, services to employees) as products to be 'sold' to customers.

5.9 Internal marketing it is hoped, will provide the right framework for quality management. Internal marketing - identifying and meeting customer needs - can be seen as giving focus to quality control.

6 BRAND MANAGEMENT: CULTURE, VALUES AND CHANGE

6.1 Neil Pickup and John Smith argue, in *Marketing Business* (April 1990) that 'more organisations which have been successful in establishing a brand have directed their attention both inside and outside the organisation; not merely to the external environment within which the business operates, but also to the culture influencing and governing delivery of the package to the customer'.

6.2 Marketing has traditionally had an external focus. However, communicating these external issues to other members of the organisation, has been relegated to standard internal communications 'as the sole means to initiate what may well be major cultural change'.

6.3 Especially in service businesses, creating a corporate brand by which the business is known, and delivering it successfully, often requires changes in corporate culture. The major issues involve:

(a) corporate culture;
(b) procedures and processes;
(c) organisational design.

6.4 If a business's culture is in conflict with customer expectations, then corporate branding is a liability, as it might make claims which cannot be satisfied.

Notes **Part A: Background knowledge relevant to analysis and decision**

6.5 The authors hold that internal research is necessary, before any attempt is made to set up a corporate brand. Furthermore:

(a) both management and staff need to understand why the organisation exists and the role of the brand;

(b) both management and staff should 'own' the culture;

(c) there should be an 'objective and pragmatic analysis of the culture(s) and values operating within the business';

(d) there should be a 'change management' strategy.

6.6 The process of organisational change can be analysed in three phases.

(a) Phase 1. This is the 'pre-managerial' phase of a business. It thrives on entrepreneurial flair.

(b) Phase 2. However, this flair needs to be supported by good management if the business is to succeed. Management structures tend to become rigid in this phase.

(c) Phase 3. Businesses evolve from formal rigidities to Phase 3 and are held together not so much by procedures as by values.

6.7 In *phase 1*, the corporate brand image might be founded on the entrepreneur (eg 'Virgin' is Richard Branson). In *phase 2*, a corporate brand might be increased, as it were, from outside and imposed by formal procedures. However, as the brand is not connected with the underlying corporate culture, its claims, compared with the service actually provided, may founder. In *phase 3*, the corporate brand will reflect the corporate culture, and will be shared by managers and staff.

6.8 Managing the introduction is a major task as it requires a thorough review of all the behaviour patterns. 'Shared values and agreed standards must become inherent in all management activity, whether routine dealings with external and internal customers or non-routine activities such as management development programs'.

6.9 Corporate branding though required changes in behaviour so that the brand's ideals can be matched.

7 INDUSTRIAL (BUSINESS TO BUSINESS) MARKETING

7.1 A study of the series of CIM case studies will reveal that from time to time, cases will appear which involve companies engaged in business to business marketing eg FirstrATE. Such cases can catch students unawares especially if they have focused their studies entirely on consumer goods marketing.

7.2 It is important to distinguish between industrial and consumer goods in terms of buying behaviour. Such differences affect marketing strategy, the marketing mix and marketing research.

(a) What is *industrial marketing?* A definition from Aubrey Wilson is: 'All those activities concerned with purchases and sales of goods/services in industrial markets and between organisational buyers/sellers.'

(b) What are *industrial goods?* A definition from Professor Baker is: 'Goods which are destined for use in producing other goods or rendering services, as contrasted with goods destined to be sold to ultimate consumers', eg office furniture, fork lift trucks, weaving looms, aero-engines.

7.3 It has been estimated that the total of interfirm sales of industrial goods amounts to about two and a half times the *value* of total sales of consumer goods. This comes about because, for example, Company A will buy copper and make it into copper wire sell it to Company B who will wind it onto a motor which they will then sell to Company C who will use it in, say, a washing machine for final sale to a consumer. In other words, for each consumer sale there will probably have been several transactions within the industrial markets with the same basic product or raw materials (eg copper) changing hands and, perhaps, form in the process.

7.4 *Derived demand.* An important distinguishing factor in industrial markets is that demand for the majority of industrial products is derived, often indirectly, from the final demand for consumer products. Thus the industrialist is faced with the need for providing increased plant, equipment etc for anticipated increases in consumer demand or for curtailing expenditures in anticipation of decreased levels of consumer expenditure. He is also faced with the impact or sales changes at consumer level reflected back through the channel of distribution. These changes are magnified by changes in inventory levels and inventory policy and can even be distorted by time lag - ie with sales moving one way and manufactures' order moving in the opposite direction.

7.5 Industrial market buying behaviour typically differs from consumer markets in the following ways.

   (a) *Concentration of buyers.* The number of potential buyers for industrial goods tends to be rather smaller than for consumer goods.

   (b) *Scale of purchasing.* The scale of industrial purchasing tends to be considerably greater than consumer purchasing in absolute terms (not always true, however, in relation to disposable assets).

   (c) *Complexity of products.* Industrial products tend t be more complex technically thus requiring expertise on part of buyer and salesman.

   (d) *Buying motives.* Industrial purchasers must satisfy company objectives of profitability etc. This taken together with the points above tend to lead to more rational buying motives than in the consumer market. This does not preclude emotion from industrial buying nor logic from consumer buying.

   (e) *Group buying.* Again, stemming from the scale and complexity of purchases and the need for satisfaction of company objectives. Industrial buying tends to be a group process with some formalised evaluation and decision procedures.

   (f) *Negotiation.* Whereas in the consumer market the element of negotiation (or bartering) has almost disappeared it is still an important factor in the industrial market.

The decision making unit (DMU)

7.6 Expanding now on (e) above, there are several different roles in the DMU which industrial marketers need to take into account when planning marketing operations. The two key points are that the buyer may not be the decision taker and even if he is, you can still use other people within the buying organisation to influence the decision your way. The several distinct roles in the DMU which have been identified are users, influencers, buyers, deciders and gatekeepers. Several individuals may occupy the same role and one individual can occupy two or more roles. Let us now expand on these roles.

   (a) *Users* exert influence either individually or collectively. The influence can be a positive one, by suggesting the need for purchased materials and by defining standards of product quality, or a negative one, by refusing to work with the material of certain suppliers for certain reasons.

   (b) *Influencers* are organisational members who directly or indirectly influence buying or usage criteria. They exert influence either by defining criteria which constrain the choices or provide information with which to evaluate buying actions.

   In manufacturing organisations, technical personnel are significant influencers over the purchasing decision. Research and development personnel, design engineers, production engineers and manufacturing personnel may all be significant influences, and may emphasise different factors in the buying decision.

   (c) *Buyers* are organisational members with formal authority for selecting the supplier and arranging terms of purchase. Buyers may be the purchasing manager, purchasing agent or buyer or a vice-president manufacturing, an office manager may also have buying authority.

The choice available to the buyer may be significantly limited by the formal and informal influence of the others.

The influence of the Buyer is especially apparent in determining the set of feasible suppliers and selecting suppliers. The Buyer's influence depends on the nature of the buying task, ranging from the simple, routine, clerical operation, through the need to negotiate prices and conditions of sale, to the most complex, where a simultaneous definition of specification and alternative is necessary.

(d) *Deciders*. Organisational members with formal or informal power to determine 'final' selection of supplies. In practice it is not always easy to determine when the decision is actually made and by whom. A purchasing agent may be the person with formal authority to sign a buying contract, he may not be the true decider.

Many purchasing agent's job descriptions place an upper limit on the financial commitments they can make, reserving larger decisions for other members of the organisation.

(e) *Gatekeepers*. Group members who control the flow of information into the group. The purchasing agent or Buyer may often have this function, but salesmen employed by the buying organisation can also be sources of inflation, and similarly technical personnel may perform the role on an informal basis.

Gatekeepers exert influence at the stage of identifying buying alternatives, and hence they significantly determine the outcome of the purchase decision.

7.7 Reflecting on the above, it can be seen why industrial marketing communications strategies depend heavily on personal selling and below-the-line, rather than advertising (fewer buyers, more complex products, rational decision taking, price/terms negotiation etc). Exhibitions and technical literature feature strongly in industrial marketing budgets whilst advertising is usually limited to relatively infrequent appearances in trade magazines.

7.8 Industrial marketing research methodology also varies from that used in consumer markets. Again, respondents are much fewer and more accessible (all on the telephone and usually in the offices or in the factory). The industrial salesforce know their Buyers personally. Information can be obtained face to face either formally of informally relatively easily and cheaply. New product development is usually a participative process between seller and buyer.

Other significant current issues

7.9 It is suggested that candidates read more widely so as to be better able to spot other contemporary issues which they can then use in their answers.

Chapter roundup

- These articles suggest some general principles.
    - The marketing approach needs to be involved with all facets of an organisation's relationship with customers, including quality.
    - For service businesses, or in service activities of non-service businesses, the success of external marketing may depend on the spread of marketing values within the organisation.

Test your knowledge

1 What is the essence of relationship marketing? (see para 2.1)
2 What three conditions must be satisfied for there to be true marketing orientation? (3.5)
3 Why should marketing departments be involved in TQM programmes? (3.13)
4 What is internal marketing? (6.1)
5 What sort of research should be conducted before a corporate brand is set up? (6.5)
6 What are the salient characteristics of industrial buyer behaviour? (7.5)

Part B
The CIM case study examination

Chapter 6

THE CIM CASE STUDY EXAMINATION

This chapter covers the following topics.

1. The case study examination: rationale and role
2. What you can expect in the examination
3. Examination rules
4. Candidates' notes
5. Candidates' brief
6. The CIM Examiner's guidance notes

Introduction

The case study method of learning and teaching has played a major part in management education, training and development over the past twenty years. The Harvard Business School in the USA helped both to pioneer and to stimulate the development of the case study method on its senior management courses and quickly gained an international reputation in this field.

It has been demonstrated increasingly that:

(a) case studies make an extremely important contribution to the study, knowledge and understanding of management;

(b) case studies are being used more and more often as an examination technique by professional bodies, and in particular by the Chartered Institute of Marketing (CIM).

It is fitting that the final examination of the CIM Diploma, which once conferred, is in effect a licence to practise, should use this most searching test of management ability.

1 THE CASE STUDY EXAMINATION: RATIONALE AND ROLE

1.1 An understanding of the role of case studies is pre-requisite to being able to learn from them and how to handle them.

(a) A case study portrays, as far as possible, a real world situation and aims through its use to develop a greater ability to analyse, conclude and make decisions.

(b) Case studies are also used the encourage the application of theoretical concepts and techniques in a selective and evaluative way to solve practical problems.

(c) Case studies are often explored on a group basis, as opposed to individuals solitarily reviewing data, so as to develop broader perspectives.

1.2 In business and management education and training, the situation described by a case study is usually one faced by an organisation and would typically include some facts and figures on:

(a) the organisation's past development;
(b) its current situation;
(c) financial, marketing, and personnel aspects;
(d) competitors.

1.3 A case study can vary from a single page (often termed a mini-case or caselet) to fifty or more pages and appendices.

1.4 Cases also vary in the extent to which they are based on real life situations. Some are based entirely on a real world situation (sometimes distinguished by the term case history).

1.5 On the other hand, a case study might be one that is fabricated by the writer so as better to test particular aspects. Often case writers deliberately distort data so as to preserve confidentiality and will intentionally introduce anomalies, jumble logical sequences and omit data so as to make the case more challenging.

1.6 There is no one perfect solution to a case. Solutions not only depend upon an individual's interpretation of the data (which can in turn be influenced by the nature of the analytical techniques employed) but also upon the role and relationships of the people involved in the case.

1.7 For the foregoing reasons, students can find, on their first introduction to the case method, that case studies are intimidating, irritating and frustrating. However, given the right approach and the benefits of some experience the following advantages from the use of case studies are claimed.

1.8 According to Edge and Coleman (*The Guide to Case Analysis and Reporting*) students can benefit from increased skills in:

(a) clear thinking through complex situations;

(b) the ability to devise credible, consistent and creative plans;

(c) the application of analytical techniques;

(d) the recognition of the relative significance of information;

(e) the determination of informational needs;

(f) oral communication in groups;

(g) the writing of clear, forceful and convincing reports;

(h) choice of career paths;

(i) recognising the importance of personal values in organisational decision taking processes and self analysis.

1.9 With regard to the last item Wilson highlights individual behavioural differences pointing out that 'the more stakeholders there are, the greater is the scope for differing interpretations and assumptions'. (A stakeholder is a person, group or organisation with an interest in another organisation's performance.) He draws out the following four key propositions.

(a) People have different ways of relating to other people in the world.
(b) People have different ways of gathering and using information.
(c) People have different ways of using information and making decisions.
(d) People attach different priorities to gathering and using information.

1.10 The implications of these propositions are that:

(a) value judgements and other affective issues are essential in defining problems;

(b) the roles people play need to be made explicit, as do assumptions about the people in these roles, and this is part of the learning process. After all management is often held to be about 'getting things done through people'.

Making the most of case studies

1.11 Edge and Coleman place the emphasis on student responsibilities in case learning. Much greater effort and cooperation are needed from students in learning from cases as opposed to lectures.

1.12 A more positive attitude can be encouraged by students working as a team on a real management situation and by role adoption.

1.13 Students need to familiarise themselves with the case in advance of discussion. They should both participate in, and help to manage, the discussion.

1.14 A sense of humour helps groups to relax, to develop a team spirit and to enjoy discussion and feedback.

1.15 When a complex and lengthy case study and analysis takes place over a period of several weeks or sessions, regular attendance is essential. Otherwise a student might become a burden on the group, or be seen as a malingerer.

1.16 Students must respect the contributions made by and feelings of other group members, but at the same time they should be prepared to give and take constructive criticism.

1.17 Some sympathy for the case study leader's role and problems in the overall management of the project will also help.

1.18 Students need to appreciate the likelihood of initial dissatisfaction with the case, the necessity for learning, and the value of keeping an open mind. At the start, confusion and frustration will be caused by the following factors.
   (a) There is no one best answer.
   (b) Information can be ambiguous and/or irrelevant.
   (c) Vital information is missing.
   (d) The key issues may not be given or identified.
   (e) The case study leader does not direct.
   (f) The case study leader does not provide solutions.

   A constructive attitude should help allay these problems.

1.19 Attention to the two matters below should help students get the most out of their case study group.
   (a) The position of chairing syndicate groups and acting as spokesperson in plenary sessions should be rotated so that all concerned develop leadership and communication skills.
   (b) The adoption of stakeholder roles (eg one member to act as the finance manager, another as managing director, another as spokesperson for employees' interests) by group members helps to develop greater understanding of the human relations aspects of decision making.

How to handle case studies: an overview

1.20 All writers and most case study instructors recommend a step by step approach to case study analysis. Easton *(Learning from Case Studies)* summarises these as follows.

Notes   *Part B: The CIM case study examination*

Step 1	Understanding the situation
Step 2	Diagnosing problem areas
Step 3	Generating alternative solutions
Step 4	Predicting outcomes
Step 5	Evaluating alternatives
Step 6	Communicating the results

However the detailed methods of carrying out these steps can vary according to the nature of the case, its length and how far in advance (if at all) the case is issued.

1.21 Also, time constraints and other reasons may cause the case instructor to concentrate on particular steps. For example, the London Business School use a particular caselet purely for the purposes of generating as many alternative solutions as possible. This helps to encourage groups of mature business people to look beyond the first immediate solution that springs to mind.

1.22 Students being exposed to case studies as part of coursework will normally be issued with detailed guidelines on how to tackle each of the above steps or referred to recommended reading by the course instructor. For the purposes of this Workbook we are concentrating on how to handle case studies being used for examination purposes.

1.23 In the pages which follow, distinctions are drawn between:

(a) the recommended treatments for the unseen caselets (or mini-cases) which are used as part of the format for several Chartered Institute of Marketing examinations; and

(b) the major case study which is issued four weeks in advance and is the sole method of examination for the Institute's Diploma subject *Strategic Marketing Management: Analysis and Decision*.

2 WHAT YOU CAN EXPECT IN THE EXAMINATION

2.1 It is standard practice for the CIM to supply the examination case study in the form of an A5 booklet, printed on both sides of the page. There is not much room therefore for making notes in the booklet and you may prefer to expand each page on to A4 single sides for this purpose.

2.2 Typically, the CIM diploma case will be 30 to 40 pages long. It will consist of 5 to 10 pages of text followed by a number of appendices.

2.3 The information contained in the case study is likely to include some or all of the following matters.

(a) Background and historical data on the company featured.
(b) Corporate and group organisation.
(c) Marketing and sales organisation.
(d) Strengths, weaknesses, opportunities, threats (indicative only).
(e) Market size, segments, competitors, trends.
(f) Environmental factors.
(g) Marketing mix (product, price, promotion, distribution).
(h) Marketing research.
(i) Consolidated accounts (profit and loss, balance sheet).

2.4 As is usual in most management case studies, the CIM case will:

(a) include some information which is not particularly useful; and
(b) exclude some data which you might feel essential.

This is to test your powers of discrimination and also to suggest a blueprint for a marketing research plan and or improvements to the marketing information system.

2.5 You are also likely to find some anomalies and contradictions which will oblige you to make assumptions.

2.6 On the inside front cover of the case you will find *Important Notes* for candidates, followed by a page *Candidate's Brief* (see Chapter 8 for details), which you must, of course read thoroughly and have in mind when interpreting the subsequent data in the case itself.

2.7 The examiner reserves the right to issue *additional information* on the case with the examination paper on the day itself. This is to ensure thinking takes place in the examination room and to discourage excessive use of pre-prepared answers. In the most recent examinations, additional information *has* been provided in the examination paper and a proportion of the total marks has been allocated for its use when answering the questions set. Up to 20% of the marks might be allocated for this purpose as at 12/94 (15% in 6/94).

Questions in the examination

2.8 Typically, you may expect three or four questions of unequal marks requiring you to undertake some calculation of how much time to allocate to each question - see Chapter 10 on examination techniques. There is normally no choice and you are required to answer all questions.

2.9 It is normal for these three or four questions to be split between;
   (a) issues of strategy formulation;
   (b) issues of strategy implementation.

Trends in the examination paper

2.10 The current examiner has made it clear that he wishes (on behalf of the CIM) to encourage the adoption of longer-term strategic planning by marketing management. It is also current policy to try to ensure that future marketing managers are financially literate by asking candidates to state the financial implications of their proposals.

2.11 Finally, the examiner will normally expect candidates to think through the organisational implications posited by the case and to be aware of the contribution that an improved marketing orientation and internal marketing can make to corporate wellbeing.

3 EXAMINATION RULES

3.1 This subject is examined as a three hour 'open book' case study examination. This means you may take as much pre-prepared material, reference books etc into the examination room as you wish, provided this does not interfere with the space and comfort of other candidates. The use of electronic calculators not requiring mains electricity is also permitted providing of course that this does not distract other candidates.

3.2 If you have any doubts on this matter it would be as well to check with the CIM. However, you would be well advised to limit your equipment to that normally required for any examination plus a well-indexed ring binder of pre-prepared analysis (see Chapter 10 on examination techniques). All CIM examinations are held under the jurisdiction of a professional invigilator whose decisions on any point of order must be accepted as final.

Notes   **Part B: The CIM case study examination**

3.3 You must of course only start when the invigilator gives permission and you must stop writing immediately you are asked to do so.

3.4 All candidates will be provided with an examination slip which permits entry into the examination room. You will have been allocated an examination number which you must write on the examination script, together with the examination centre and the number of questions attempted, in the order in which they appear in the script. Your name must not appear on the script.

3.5 Additional pages must be securely fastened to the script booklet.

3.6 Answers must only be submitted on CIM script and/or paper such as graph paper supplied by the invigilator. You cannot submit pre-prepared pages and any material suspected of this will be treated as invalid.

4   CANDIDATES' NOTES

4.1 The Candidates' Notes are amended from time to time but stay broadly the same. The following example was used in the June 1997 case.

Diploma in Marketing: Marketing Analysis and Decision

Important notes

The examiners will be marking your scripts on the basis of questions put to you in the examination room. Questions *may not* carry equal marks and candidates are advised to pay particular attention to the mark allocation on the examination paper. Candidates are advised to budget their time accordingly.

Your role is outlined in the candidates' brief. In the position outlined you may be required to recommend clear courses of action.

You *will not* be awarded marks merely for analysis. This should have been undertaken before the examination day in preparation for meeting the specific tasks which will be specified in the examination paper.

Candidates are *instructed not to conduct research or analysis outside* the material provided within the case study. The introduction of extraneous material in examination answers will gain no marks and serves only to waste valuable time. Although cases are based upon real world situations, facts have been deliberately altered or omitted to preserve anonymity. No useful purpose will therefore be served by contacting companies in this industry and candidates are strictly instructed *not to do so,* as it would simply cause unnecessary confusion.

As in real life anomalies will be found in this case situation. Please simply state your assumptions where necessary when answering questions. The CIM is not in a position to answer queries on case data whether in writing or on the telephone. Candidates are tested on their overall grasp of the case and its key issues, not on minor details. There are no catch questions or hidden agendas.

Additional information will be introduced in the examination paper itself which candidates must take into account when answering the questions set. Up to 20 per cent of the marks will be allocated for this purpose.

Acquaint yourself thoroughly with the Case Study and be prepared to follow closely the instructions given to you on the examination day. *To answer examination questions effectively, candidates must adopt report format.*

The copying of pre-prepared 'group' answers written by consultants/tutors is strictly forbidden and will be penalised. The questions will demand thinking out in the examination itself and individually composed answers are required in order to pass.

---

5   CANDIDATES' BRIEF

5.1 The Candidates' Brief will of course be specific to the particular case and states your role and reporting relationships. It will normally include pointers to the areas for examination questions and is, to a degree, an indication of the stance you should take on the material. The following example has been taken from the June 1995 case.

> *Candidates' Brief*
>
> You are Thijs Van der Vliet, Marketing Manager of FirstrATE Europe. You report directly to Gareth Hall, Director of Sales and a member of the management team of FirstrATE Europe.
>
> FirstrATE Europe is a division of FirstrATE Inc, based in Princetown, New Jersey, USA. You have recently been appointed to your current position and are based in Frankfurt where you work in FirstrATE's Technology Support Centres. Your appointment formed part of FirstrATE's switch in focus from being a product-led organisation to becoming a customer-led organisation. This radical change in emphasis was borne out of sheer necessity since FirstrATE Europe had been reporting increasing losses in recent years. There were due partly to the increasingly competitive conditions in the maturing *automatic test equipment* (ATE) market and partly to the background of economic recession in many of the markets in which FirstrATE operates.
>
> Since you have joined FirstrATE, you have focused on tactical marketing and in particular you have organised a series of promotions which have been successful. In the past, marketing has been a weakness of FirstrATE and you have encountered considerable resistance to your ideas, frequently finding that you have no support from the country sales managers and on occasions you have encountered downright hostility. You continue to feel that you are operating in a vacuum. Gareth Hall, who is one of the architects of the new structure and a great proponent of the organisation being customer-led, has asked you to prepare a presentation on strategic marketing for the board meeting in June 1995.
>
> This is the first time that FirstrATE Europe has prepared strategic marketing plans, having previously relied upon the US parent to provide the product portfolio and dictate the transfer pricing. In the past, the products were distributed through a conventional hierarchical organisation structure with subsidiaries in the main countries in Europe, each with their own financial controls, sales force, promotional activities, technical support team and logistics. Over the past 18 months this has all changed. The Technology Support Centre in Germany provides technical support, training and marketing for all the countries in Europe while the financial controls and human resources are centred in the UK in the Thame office. The new structure is much more flexible, freeing the organisation to provide a 'flow of services to the customer' and allowed a head-count reduction of some 20%.
>
> This case material is based upon actual organisations and existing market conditions. However, the information provided and the real data has been significantly changed to preserve commercial confidentiality. Candidates are strictly instructed not to contact companies in the industry, and are advised that some additional information will be provided at the time of the examination.

6   THE CIM EXAMINER'S GUIDANCE NOTES

6.1   These are normally updated annually but remain substantially the same over a period of about three years. They contain important information on how to prepare for the examination and should be read carefully. The Guidance Notes are issued to providers of tuition for this subject for passing on to students at the tutor's discretion.

6.2   Tutors are told the following.

(a) Notional taught hours	45
(b) Method of assessment	3 hour written examination
(c) Number of questions	all questions to be attempted (3 or 4)
(d) Pass mark:	50%

Preferred sequence of studies

6.3   The culmination of the Certificate, Advanced Certificate, and Diploma course is the case study. The examination has the purpose of ensuring that those who hold the Diploma qualification have not only achieved a certain level of marketing knowledge, but also have the competence to use that knowledge in addressing simulated marketing management problems.

6.4   Any aspect of the entire Certificate and Diploma syllabuses may be applicable and if you have been exempted from parts of the course you should ensure you familiarise yourself with the detailed course requirements.

6.5 This paper should be taken at the end of your course of study.

Case study rationale

6.6 The guidance notes state the rationale of the case study as follows.

> **Aims and objectives**
>
> 'To extend the practice of candidates in the quantitative and qualitative analysis of marketing situations, both to develop their powers of diagnosis and to create a firm basis in decision making'
>
> By the end of their study students will be able:
>
> (a) to identify, define and rank the problem(s) contained in marketing case studies;
>
> (b) to formulate working hypotheses regarding the solution(s) to problems identified in marketing case studies;
>
> (c) to assemble, order, analyse and interpret both qualitative and quantitative data relating to a marketing case, using appropriate analytical procedures and models;
>
> (d) to describe and substantiate all working assumptions made regarding the case problem(s) working hypothesis and data;
>
> (e) to generate and evaluate the expected outcomes of alternative solutions to case problem(s);
>
> (g) to prepare and present appropriate marketing case reports.

Senior examiner's comments

6.7 The CIM Diploma is recognised increasingly widely as a licence to practise. It is in no-one's interests for it to be awarded lightly, as those who have striven hard to attain it will surely agree. The value of the Diploma depends directly upon the quality of the people holding it; in turn the respect earned from peers, superiors and clients depends on the value of the Diploma.

6.8 *Strategic Marketing Management: Analysis and Decision* is quite rightly the severest test in the CIM examinations. The examination is based upon a real-life major case and requires the application of theories, principles and techniques learned in the study of other subjects. It is not an examination to be passed by regurgitating knowledge.

6.9 Candidates must demonstrate beyond reasonable doubt that they are capable not only of in-depth analysis before the exam, but also are able to take decisions and write clear, concise and convincing marketing plans. These marketing plans need to show an understanding of the corporate and financial implications.

Question design and scope

6.10 Questions applied in case studies do not have any standardised format. They may vary in number. They may throw up a surprise situation. They will be action orientated. One inevitable and recurring theme will be the *strategic marketing* of products and services. It is likely that additional information will be provided in the examination paper which has to be taken into account when answering the questions set. The examiners are aware of the time constraint of three hours and the questions are designed to enable a candidate to cover them adequately if not well, within that period. Candidates should remember that they are expected to have knowledge equivalent to the syllabuses of the other three Diploma subjects. The whole course (Certificate, Advanced Certificate, and Diploma) is a legitimate source of questions.

Examination approach

6.11 Candidates are required to do what the examiners ask, to answer the question as put and in accordance with any mark allocation which is stated on the paper. This means the management of the time within the examination situation is crucial. In every case, candidates have a human role to play within the structure of either the case, the examination paper, or both, to which they are expected to be able to relate. Usually, this means that they have to respond and restructure their thinking within the examination itself; this is precisely what the examiners are seeking.

Preparation

6.12 There are two basic parts to this paper embodied in its title, Analysis and Decision. There can be no better description of these two parts than the questions put to his students by one lecturer as follows.

 (a) What is wrong?
 (b) What are you going to do to put it right?

Within the context of management, marketing or otherwise, the second question is the critical one, but cannot be answered without the problem identification implicit in the first.

6.13 There will be anomalies in the case, as in real life. Assumptions will therefore need to be made and clearly stated. (The CIM cannot enter into discussion on these aspects, either verbally or in writing.)

6.14 Problem identification will certainly require the application of statistical and financial analytical techniques, and of organisational and behavioural understanding and marketing knowledge. The examiners must know what the problems are, what alternative solutions to them have been considered and which alternative has been chosen by the candidate, in other words:

 (a) what is to be done?
 (b) in what time period?
 (c) by whom?
 (d) with what financial and human resource implications?
 (e) and with what projected outcome?

6.15 There is no such thing as a right answer to these questions. Above all, sensible recommendations are required, supported by reasoned argument. *Lists of problems and regurgitated materials from the case itself do candidates no credit.*

6.16 The evidence is overwhelming that a great many students try to seek refuge in analysis and come to their examination desks hoping that inspiration will suddenly flow to the tips of their ball-point pens! The case study is issued prior to the examination data to enable students to conduct their analysis *before* responding to the situation posed in the examination hall. *A restatement of this analysis is insufficient to pass the examination.* You have to make decisions, and clearly articulate them on the exam day.

Decisions

6.17 There is an apt Chinese proverb which says 'He who deliberates fully before taking a step will spend his entire life on one leg'. The question of taking decisions is a conceptual leap for many students. They need help. In the absence of full information, they have to make assumptions, use their judgement and be prepared to back it up on paper.

6.18 One of the difficulties, which the examiners fully understand, is the lack of knowledge about any particular industry used in the case. Marketing decisions however, are applicable in any environment based on sound principles relevant to the situation. The examiners will not tolerate academic essays: we need to be assured of practical management ability and this means that candidates should adopt *management report style* and format. The report should, of course, be structured according to the exam paper and use the terminology/headings suggested by the questions.

Further research

6.19 The examiners can state categorically that there is *no need* for any candidate to seek additional information outside the case study. There are three reasons for this.

(a) The examiners incorporate within the case itself enough information for the candidate to work on. It is a self-contained exercise.

(b) Some data within the case studies needs to be disguised to preserve confidentiality. Trying to search out the company concerned can thus not only be a waste of time but also lead to confusion.

(c) Access to additional research data is limited, particularly for overseas students.

6.20 Nevertheless, candidates may be expected to be able to state within the examination what additional research information they would seek, for what reason, in what time period, at what approximate cost and by what method. There is every justification for encouraging student research during the course of an academic year in order to have the experience and be able to apply it to the examination case. No students will earn additional marks for external research data introduced in the examination.

6.21 *Creativity and innovation*

The lack of imagination by the majority of candidates in this examination is a major weakness. Marketing is creative; it is one of the means by which companies distinguish themselves or their products from competition. Only on rare occasions are the examiners confronted by some illuminating or different approach and marks then have a tendency to soar!

6.22 *What tutors can, and should, do*

For the purposes of this section, the examiners must assume that students have, at the beginning of the year, the knowledge and skills required by the syllabus. What follows can also only be recommendations; there is no one way to teach case studies, just as there is no one answer.

Chapter roundup

- This chapter has presented you with a sense of the context regarding the case study exam.

- Firstly, you are given information in advance, not all of which will be relevant. You should not research outside information.

- In dealing with the information, group discussion is important.

- You are required to take reasoned decisions within the case's context, not to provide an ideal solution as one is not available. Do your analysis in *advance*. Take decisions in the exam.

- The questions asked in the case can cover topics contained in the *entire* CIM syllabus, from the Certificate, the Advanced Certificate and the Diploma.

Part C
How to analyse the CIM case study

Chapter 7

HOW TO ANALYSE A CIM CASE STUDY: A GENERAL OVERVIEW

> **This chapter covers the following topics.**
> 1. Case study methodology in general
> 2. Mini-cases
> 3. Longer case studies
>
> **Introduction**
>
> A case study element has featured in your CIM exams already. This chapter identifies the main differences between minicases in other CIM papers and the cases in the Analysis and Decision exam.

1 CASE STUDY METHODOLOGY IN GENERAL

1.1 A number of writers have endeavoured to summarise and express the vast amount of experience gained over many years by a host of institutions using the case study approach to teaching and learning. These institutions include universities, business schools and colleges.

1.2 The following few pages are devoted to introducing you to some of the best practice and custom expressed by these writers. This will enable you to develop a broad appreciation of the ways in which most institutions approach case study teaching.

1.3 Chapter 8 will then explain the specific methods recommended by CIM Senior Examiners for the purposes of the Diploma in Marketing case study examination. These specific methods do, of course, have their roots in the general custom and practice covered in this section.

1.4 Methods tend to vary in general according to the following factors.

   (a) The length of the case.
   (b) The content of the case.
   (c) The culture of the teaching institution.
   (d) The abilities of the students.
   (e) The personality of the case tutor.
   (f) The amount of time available.

2 MINI-CASES

2.1 Candidates used to handling short cases must take care not to assume that the methodology can be successfully applied to the longer case study. Clearly, the shorter the case study, the less is its content and the smaller is the amount of the analysis that can be conducted upon it. Another related criterion is the amount of numerical as opposed to textual data. This affects the nature of the analytical techniques that can be applied.

Part C: How to analyse the CIM case study

2.2 For those students sitting other CIM exam papers which feature unseen minicases, a former senior examiner gives this advice

2.3 'It needs to be stated unequivocally that the type of extremely short case (popularly called the mini-case) set in the examinations for Diploma subjects *other* than 'Analysis and Decision' cannot be treated in exactly the same way as the extremely long case set for the subject of marketing analysis and decision. If it could, there would be little point in going to all the trouble of writing an in-depth case study.

2.4 'Far too many students adopt a maxi-case approach, using a detailed marketing audit outline which is largely inappropriate to a case consisting only of two or three paragraphs. Others use the SWOT analysis and simply re-write the case under the four headings of strengths, weaknesses, opportunities and threats.

'Some students even go so far as to totally ignore the specific questions set and present a standard maxi case analysis outline including environmental reviews through to contingency plans.

2.5 'The CIM "mini-case" is not really a case at all, it is merely an outline of a given situation, a *scenario*. Its purpose is to test whether examinees can apply their knowledge of marketing theory and techniques to the company or organisation and the operating environment described in the scenario. For example, answers advocating retail audits as part of the marketing information system for a small industrial goods manufacturer, demonstrate a lack of practical awareness. Such answers confirm that the examinee has learned a given MkIS outline by rote and simply regurgitated this in complete disregard of the scenario. Such an approach would be disastrous in the real world and examinees adopting this approach cannot be passed, ie gain the confidence of the Institute as professional marketing practitioners. The correct approach to the scenario is a mental review of the area covered by the question and the selection by the examinee of those particular parts of knowledge and techniques which apply to the case. This implies a rejection of those parts of the student's knowledge which clearly do not apply to the scenario.

2.6 'All scenarios are based upon real world companies and situations which are written with a full knowledge of how that organisation actually operates in its planning environment. Often, the organisation described in the scenario will not be a giant fast-moving consumer good manufacturing and marketing company, since this would facilitate mindless regurgitation of textbook outlines and be counter to the intention of this section of the examination.

2.7 'More often, the scenarios will involve innovative small or medium sized firms which comprise the vast majority of UK companies and which lack the resources often assumed by the textbook approach. These firms do, however, have to market within these constraints and are just as much concerned in marketing communications, marketing planning and control and indeed (proportionately) in international marketing, particularly the EU.

2.8 'However, as marketing applications develop and expand and as changes take root, the Institute through its examiners will wish to test students' knowledge awareness of these changes and their implication with regard to marketing practice. For example, in the public sector increasing attention is being paid to the marketing of leisure services and the concept of "asset marketing", where the "product" is to a greater extent fixed and therefore the option of product as a variable in the marketing mix is somewhat more constrained. Internal marketing has been recognised as essential to the effective operation of TQM.

2.9 'Tutors and students are referred to Examiners' Reports which repeatedly complain of inappropriateness of answer detail which demonstrates a real lack of practical marketing grasp and confirms that a learned by rote textbook regurgitation is being used. Examples would include:

(a) the recommendation of national TV advertising for a small industrial company with a local market;

(b) the overnight installation of a marketing department comprising managing director, marketing manager, advertising manager, distribution manager, sales manager, etc into what has been described as a very small company;

(c) the inclusion of packaging, branded-packs, on-pack offers etc in the marketing mix recommendations for a service.

2.10 'It has been borne in mind that the award of the Diploma is in a very real sense the granting of a licence to practice marketing and certainly an endorsement of the candidate's practical as well as theoretical grasps of marketing. In these circumstances, such treatments of the mini-case, as described above, cannot be passed and *give rise to some concern that perhaps the teaching/learning approach to mini-cases has not been sufficiently differentiated from that recommended for the Analysis and Decision Paper.*'

3 LONGER CASE STUDIES

3.1 With the above comments in mind, it is suggested that the following approaches should be treated as being more appropriate to the longer case study.

3.2 Cravens and Lamb (1986) recommend a six step approach to case analysis along the following lines.

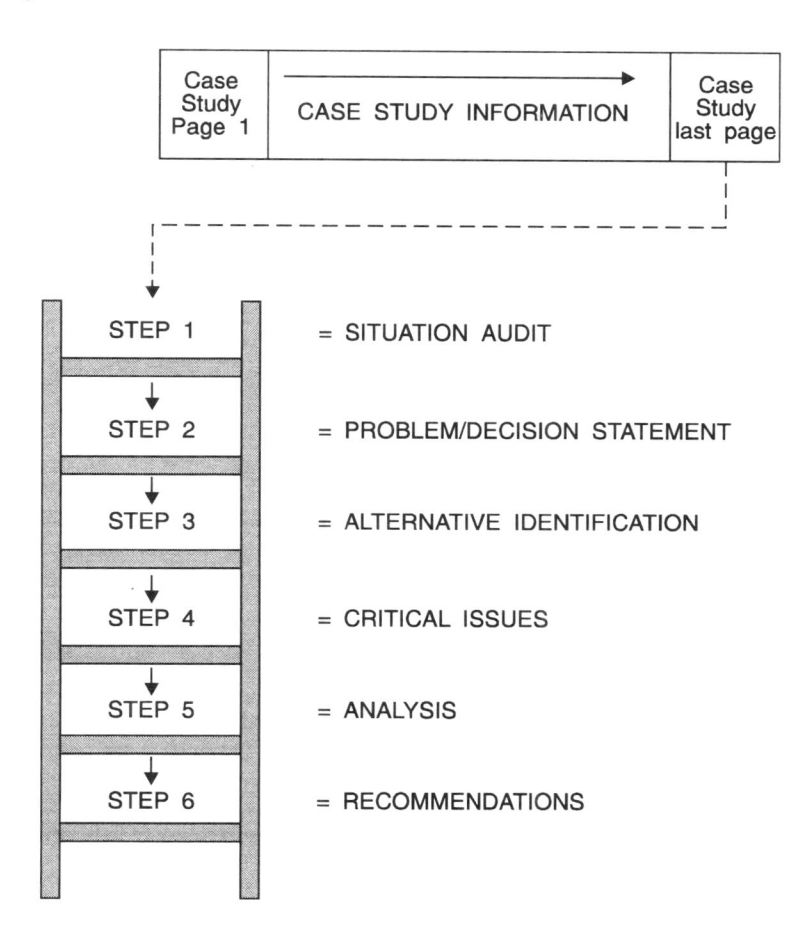

```
STEP 1 = SITUATION AUDIT
STEP 2 = PROBLEM/DECISION STATEMENT
STEP 3 = ALTERNATIVE IDENTIFICATION
STEP 4 = CRITICAL ISSUES
STEP 5 = ANALYSIS
STEP 6 = RECOMMENDATIONS
```

3.3 Whilst not disputing the appropriateness of any of the above steps, this model is insufficiently comprehensive for CIM major case study preparation. It suggests analysis as step 5 whereas analysis has to take place much earlier in the process. Also CIM examination candidates would need to take step 6 (recommendations) a great deal further, for example into costings, budgets, schedules and their financial/human resource implications.

Part C: How to analyse the CIM case study

3.4 Edge and Coleman's framework for case analysis also has six steps which are, however, somewhat different in their detail from those recommended by Cravens and Lamb.

1. Comprehend case situation
⬇
2. Diagnose problem areas
⬇
3. State problem
⬇
4. Generate alternatives
⬇
5. Evaluate and select
⬇
6. Defend implementation

3.5 The Edge and Coleman model adds to that of Cravens and Lamb, particularly in its first and last steps. Defending implementation is another way of saying 'justify your recommendations' which is certainly a necessity for the CIM Diploma case preparation.

3.6 Mention has already been made in Chapter 6 paragraph 1.20, of the Easton (*Learning from case studies* 1982) approach which is similar to the two outlined above but suggests a seventh step, namely that of communicating the results (of the analysis).

3.7 Easton refers to two basic methods of 'teaching' case studies in the classroom.

(a) One is the traditional Harvard method of open class discussion.

(b) The other basic method is that of asking individuals or groups (syndicates) to make formal presentations during each stage or step of the case study analysis, which then may be followed by questions and/or general discussion.

3.8 In the class discussion the case instructor may question individuals rigorously or may simply direct the groups attention to particular areas, issues or anomalies in the case. The case instructor may specify which analytical tools and techniques should be applied.

3.9 The less directive case leader will tend to chair the discussion and control the *process* rather than its *content*, guiding and advising rather than dictating solutions.

3.10 In the case of the CIM Diploma where the case study is given out at least four weeks before the examination, there is time for a structured approach aimed at developing both group and individual solutions, in the form of a complete and professional marketing plan. This is the approach which we shall be recommending in the next chapter.

Chapter roundup

- This chapter has introduced you to the contrasts between mini-cases you will encounter elsewhere and the longer case study sat in this paper.

- You have also been introduced to some of the underlying methodologies of approaching a case study.

Chapter 8

THE CASE STUDY ANALYSIS METHODS RECOMMENDED BY THE CIM SENIOR EXAMINER

This chapter covers the following topics.

1. The 28-step approach
2. Steps 1 to 5: confronting the case study
3. Steps 6 to 10: analysing the case study
4. Steps 11 to 16: identifying issues and developing strategies
5. Steps 17 to 23: developing your plans
6. Steps 24 to 26: control and contingencies
7. Steps 27 to 28: the examination

Introduction

It has been the traditional practice for CIM Senior Examiners for the subject *Strategic Marketing Management: Analysis and Decision* to write their own case studies dedicated to the particular standards and teaching/learning objectives set by the CIM and its academic Boards. These case studies are individually tailored to the testing of particular areas of marketing management abilities.

Over the years a considerable expertise has been built up through extensive dialogue with Course Tutors; by teaching and directing actual case study courses; through student appraisals and not least by the need for case study writers to submit marking schemes, examiner's reports and specimen answers.

This expertise is synthesised in the following recommendations.

---

1 THE 28-STEP APPROACH

Objectives

1.1 The *objectives of the case study* are as follows.

  (a) A thorough understanding of the situation and of the key issues should be gained through a rigorous analysis of the information provided in the specific examination case being tackled.

  (b) A complete and credible marketing plan should be produced which is appropriate to the specific case study, and which addresses the key issues and is underpinned by the prior analysis.

Rationale

1.2 Whilst it would be unlikely for the examiners to ask for the presentation of this complete marketing plan in the examination paper (owing to time constraints), the questions are inevitably going to invoke *parts* of this plan.

Notes *Part C: How to analyse the CIM case study*

1.3 Rather than gamble on which parts of the plan are likely to be tested in the exam *and therefore run the risk of failure*, it is better to be prepared for all eventualities. Whilst other subjects can be revised relatively easily in the event of failure, each case study is unique. To resit the case examination essentially means *starting again from scratch*.

Basic approach to a case study

1.4 A *group* approach to analysis and decision is recommended. It is extremely unlikely that a person working alone (however clever) will be able to develop the wider perspectives necessary to a thorough understanding of the case. Additionally, the challenges provided by the group to an individual's recommendations constitute an excellent forum for developing appropriate justification. This process also helps to moderate excesses and provide a balanced, reasoned report.

1.5 The *ideal* approach is that whereby a study group is formed consisting of a group of say 24 people who then work in four syndicates each of six people in a programmed way through each of the steps recommended below.

1.6 At the end of each syndicate session, the syndicates should report formally back to the plenary group of 24, through a rotating syndicate spokesperson. Each syndicate's presentation should be open to questions, challenges and constructive criticism from the other syndicates and be followed by general discussion. All sessions should ideally be programmed and guided by an objective case instructor of the less directive nature (see Chapter 7, paragraphs 3.7 to 3.9).

1.7 Continuity, commitment, discipline and organisation within the syndicates is essential to producing the quality of marketing planning required.

1.8 Failing this ideal, candidates working alone are, *as a minimum* urged to discuss aspects of the case with as many colleagues as they can muster and to continually challenge their own assumptions, conclusions and solutions. Analyses of the case are available at modest prices from a number of sources normally advertised in *Marketing Success* published by the CIM. These analyses do at least provide other perspectives, usually generated by a small group of marketing consultants.

8: The case study analysis methods recommended by the CIM senior examiner

Summary of the 28 steps recommended when tackling the CIM case

1.9   You can use this as a checklist to monitor your progress.

Step 1	Read the case.
Step 2	After an interval, re-read the case.
Step 3	Reflect on the instructions and candidate's brief.
Step 4	Think yourself into the role and the situation
Step 5	Re-read the case and write a précis. Discuss with colleagues.
Step 6	Conduct a marketing audit. Discuss with colleagues.
Step 7	Do a SWOT analysis. Discuss with colleagues.
Step 8	Conduct analyses/cross analyses of appendices. Discuss with colleagues.
Step 9	Reconsider your précis, marketing audit and SWOT analysis.
Step 10	Conduct a situational analysis. Discuss with colleagues.
Step 11	Decide key issues. Discuss with colleagues.
Step 12	Develop a mission statement. Discuss with colleagues.
Step 13	Decide broad aims. Discuss with colleagues.
Step 14	Identify and analyse major problems. Develop and analyse alternative solutions. Discuss with colleagues.
Step 15	Develop quantified and timescaled objectives. Discuss with colleagues.
Step 16	Consider alternative strategies and select those most appropriate. Discuss with colleagues.
Step 17	Draw up detailed tactical plans covering the marketing mix. Discuss with colleagues.
Step 18	Draw up a marketing research plan and MkIS (Marketing information system).
Step 19	Consider organisational issues and make recommendation for changes towards complete marketing orientation as felt necessary. Discuss with colleagues.
Step 20	Consider the organisation's culture and make recommendations for internal marketing programmes as felt necessary. Discuss with colleagues.
Step 21	Consider the financial and human resource implications of your plans/recommendations. Discuss with colleagues.
Step 22	Assess costs and draw up indicative budgets. Discuss with colleagues.
Step 23	Draw up schedules showing the timing/sequence of your plans/recommendations. Discuss with colleagues.
Step 24	Specify review procedures and control mechanisms. Discuss with colleagues.
Step 25	Outline contingency plans. Discuss with colleagues.
Step 26	Review your complete marketing plan.
Step 27	Draw up your examination plan.
Step 28	Practise writing in true report style.

1.10   This, then, is the 28 step approach to a thorough preparation for the CIM examination. It can be seen that this specific approach is necessarily more comprehensive than the more general approaches recommended by other authors. It encompasses many different steps of *analysis* and *decision* which are the basic ingredients of this subject and of marketing management in general. Nevertheless the above steps are only in summary form and need expansion into more practical detail in the remainder of this chapter.

Notes Part C: How to analyse the CIM case study

2 STEPS 1 TO 5: CONFRONTING THE CASE STUDY

Step 1. Read the case

2.1 The first thing to remember is not to panic when the actual case study falls through your letterbox. To panic is not good marketing management practice. Keep calm, remember you have at least four weeks (normally) to prepare and that thanks to this text, you have an excellent game plan. Resist the temptation to drop everything, miss your breakfast, frantically pore over the case and immediately start analysing all the tables.

2.2 Choose a time when your brain is receptive. Set aside no more than *one hour* for this purpose. Find somewhere quiet where you will not be disturbed.

2.3 Read the case through very quickly twice then put it away, ideally until the next day, when you've slept upon it and your sub-conscious mind will have sifted it through for you and made more sense of it.

> 2.4 Resist the temptation to read the case slowly and thoroughly because if you do, you are highly likely to become obsessed with the detail and never see the wood for the trees.

2.5 Speed reading tests show that quicker reading not only saves time but also actually *improves* retention of the content (up to a point of marginal returns). Reading very quickly twice, rather than very slowly once, is therefore more effective. Go on, try it. Force yourself.

Step 2. After an interval, re-read the case

2.6 This time read the case through *once* very quickly - as you did yesterday, then once again more slowly. Allow yourself a maximum of *two hours*.

Step 3. Reflect on the instructions and candidates' brief

2.7 All CIM case studies contain a page of instructions under the heading of *Important Notes* and a further page headed *Candidates' Brief* prior to the text of the actual case itself. Both pages give important clues, need to be read carefully and given close consideration.

(a) The *Important Notes* will tell you that no useful purpose will be served by conducting research or analysis outside the material in the case. So do not waste your valuable time by doing this. They also tell you that you will not be awarded marks for mere analysis. Analysis is expected to have been undertaken between receiving the case and the four week period before the examination. It is to be used in the examination solely for the purpose of underpinning your decisions. The notes will emphasise that you must adopt report format, hence the need for practice as recommended in Step 28 of our approach. Finally the notes will warn you that pre-prepared 'group' or syndicated answers written out blindly without reference to the actual questions set, will be failed. You really do have to think in the examination itself, *select* data from your analysis, manipulate it and add to it, in order to pass.

(b) The page headed *Candidates' Brief* is equally important since it will not only tell you which role to adopt but remind you of the need to justify the financial and human resources demanded by your proposals, against competing projects. The candidates' brief will often also indicate at least one of the key issues which act as pointers towards possible examination questions.

Step 4. Think yourself into the role and the situation

2.8 You will note later in the Examiner's Reports that candidates lose marks for failing to adopt the role designated in the Candidates' Brief, for example, writing 'What Irma should do...' when they are supposed to be Irma.

2.9 Sometimes candidates are placed in the role of a *consultant*. In this case, it would be unsuitable to adopt the tell style and more appropriate to position yourself in an advisory capacity. The more you can adopt your role and think yourself into the situation described in the case, the better will be your grasp, and the more realistic will be your recommendations.

2.10 *Without* re-reading the case, start thinking about it and make strong efforts to adopt the company/organisation as your own. What are the major problems? What business are you in? What is the present position? Where would you like to take the company over the next few years?

2.11 *Avoid detail*. You are in the position of an artist trying to decide the nature of your next painting. You decide upon a rural scene, approximate size and *broad* content: sky, water, trees, a hill. This is sufficient for a visualisation, a rough sketch. The details of cloud types, tree varieties, number of leaves etc can come later. *This overview is most important.* The ability to see the most *important* things in the case situation is crucial. You need to see the ball clearly *now* in order to keep your eye firmly upon it in subsequent and more detailed stages.

2.12 You will find the précis called for in the next step is a useful technique towards confirming your overall initial grip on the situation.

Step 5. Re-read the case and write a précis. Discuss with colleagues

2.13 The pre-précis reading of the case should be a quick one, merely serving as a reminder to you of its contents and to confirm initial impressions of the more important facts.

2.14 You are now asked to précis the 30-40 pages of the case in *not more than two A4 sides*. This is a really good way of forcing yourself to decide what is truly basic to the case and what is relatively less important.

2.15 One case study tutor has remarked that some of his course members, when put to the task of doing a précis, produce one considerably longer than the original text. Let us therefore remind ourselves of what a précis is.

'A concise summary of the essential facts or statements of a book article or other text'. (Dictionary)

2.16 *Stick to the facts*. It is important to avoid putting your own opinions, assumptions or interpretations into your précis. Many people find it difficult to avoid suggesting solutions to problems in their précis, a sign that they will find it difficult to stick to the question in their examination. This is not the purpose of the précis.

2.17 How to do the précis? Well, one way is to do it in easy stages. Go through each page and pencil lightly at the side I for important, VI for very important. Try not to treat each page the same. Some pages may have no important information on them and others a great deal.

2.18 You may find you have pencilled about a third. If so you can boil it down still further until you really have condensed it down to two pages or can do so when using your *own* words, rather than those given in the text. Now you can either maintain the order in which the case is printed or you can re-order. You might want to add structure, such as which parts of your précis come under the headings of objectives (or problems or opportunities or indeed the marketing mix), if you think this will help to give you a better grip on the essential facts.

2.19 Now, and only now, *discuss* your précis and what you feel to be most relevant important issues, with your colleagues. Remember there is no one wholly correct answer. It is quite normal to find that someone with an *accounting background* will think the *financial data* to be more important than someone from the social sciences. You should find that while there are a number of different perspectives, all should share some common ground and that your own knowledge of the case study has been significantly improved.

3 STEPS 6 TO 10: ANALYSING THE CASE STUDY

Step 6. Conduct a marketing audit. Discuss with colleagues

3.1 What is a marketing audit? Here is Kotler's definition.

'A marketing audit is a comprehensive, systematic, independent and periodic examination of a company's - or business unit's - marketing environment, objectives, strategies and activities, with a view to determining problem areas and opportunities and recommending a plan of action to improve the company's performance'.

3.2 It is, therefore, a pre-requisite to the setting of objectives. If you think about it, the clearer the view of where we are now and how we arrived at this position, the more likely we are to set realistic objectives. The further our actual position is from that imagined, the more unrealistic will be the targets set.

3.3 The marketing audit should, therefore be rigorous. It is well worth a considerable investment in time and resources. Wherever possible, comparisons should be drawn with competitors. For example, in discussing advertising you might ask the following questions.

(a) How much did we spend on advertising last year?

(b) How much did our competitors spend?

(c) How effective is our advertising compared with competitors?

(d) How do our advertisements compare in terms of media used, size of advertisements, the use of colour, copy platforms etc?

3.4 The full marketing audit has two parts, the internal (or micro) audit and the external (or macro) audit, a summary of which follows.

(a) *Marketing environmental audit*. Political, legal, economic, sociological and technological factors. Markets, competitors, distributors, suppliers, publics.

(b) *Marketing strategy audit*. Mission, objectives, strategies.

(c) *Marketing organisation audit*. Formal structure, functional efficiency, interface efficiency.

(d) *Marketing systems audit*. MIS, planning systems, control systems. Marketing research inputs.

(e) *Marketing productivity audit*. Profitability analysis, cost-effectiveness, analysis.

(f) *Marketing function audits*. Products/services, price, distribution, selling, advertising, sales promotion and public relations. If services add people, process and physical evidence (see paragraphs 5.6, 5.7, 5.8 in this chapter).

3.5 In the context of the CIM case study we have to adapt models, frameworks, tools and techniques to suit our own purposes. It would, for example, be folly not to examine the financial position of the company in the case bearing in mind we are likely to be required to give the financial implications of our proposals. With this in mind it is suggested that you add audits of other functions as follows.

8: The case study analysis methods recommended by the CIM senior examiner

(a) *Financial audit*. Revenue/profit trends, financial ratio trends, financial accounts.
(b) *Production audit*. Production facilities, constraints, developments.
(c) *Personnel audit*. Organisation, training, human resources.

3.6 When auditing the case study, it would also be sensible to use a *marketing planning framework* bearing in mind what we are trying to accomplish is a comprehensive marketing plan. We could ask questions such as 'What do we know about the corporate mission? Do we have one? Is it good, bad or indifferent?' etc. A simple schematic approach for this is suggested below.

Auditing the marketing plan - schematic approach	
Planning	*Auditing*
Corporate mission	Correct? Understood?
Corporate objectives	Feasible? Being achieved?
Corporate strategies	Appropriate? Have environmental factors changes? What are competitors doing?
Marketing objectives	Feasible? Being achieved?
Marketing strategies	Appropriate? Working? Competitors? (Direct, indirect)
Marketing mix plans	Harmonised? Tailored for each segment? Positioning OK? Check price, place, product/ service and promotion. Internal audits, customer audits
Marketing research plan	Is the right data provided at the right time in the right format?
Budgets/performance measures	Appropriate? Being achieved?
Organisation, integration, co-ordination	Working harmoniously? Is the organisation effective?
Overall	How do we compare with last year and the years before? How do we compare with competitors?

3.7 It is recognised that a full marketing audit using the checklist in Chapter 1 (section 2 of that chapter), is difficult to apply on the relatively scant information given in the typical case study. However, you could use this checklist to identify *the information you have not got* but would ideally require and which therefore might constitute part of the information specification for your marketing research plan or marketing information system.

3.8 After completing this audit and discussing it with your colleagues, your understanding of the case should have again improved. However, a great more analysis is needed before we can start our decision making process.

Step 7. Do a SWOT analysis. Discuss with colleagues

3.9 The following sheet (purposely designed for use on CIM case studies) illustrates the approach used to identify from the comprehensive marketing audit those areas of Strengths and Weaknesses, Opportunities and Threats. You should have come across SWOT earlier.

3.10 It is a popular analytical tool because it is quick and easy to use and it can form the blueprint for the marketing plan. Companies can attempt to exploit strengths and correct weaknesses so as to form the basis of a short-term tactical plan. Strengths and weaknesses emanate from within the company and are, therefore, classed as internal, controllable variables.

Notes *Part C: How to analyse the CIM case study*

SWOT ANALYSIS SHEET

STRENGTHS	Ref	Function	WEAKNESSES	Ref	Function
1			1		
2			2		
3			3		
4			4		
5			5		
6			6		
7			7		
8			8		
9			9		
10			10		
11			11		
12			12		
13			13		
14			14		
15			15		
16			16		
17			17		
18			18		
19			19		
20			20		

OPPORTUNITIES	Ref	Function	THREATS	Ref	Function
1			1		
2			2		
3			3		
4			4		
5			5		
6			6		
7			7		
8			8		
9			9		
10			10		
11			11		
12			12		
13			13		
14			14		
15			15		
16			16		
17			17		
18			18		
19			19		
20			20		

BPP Publishing

8: The case study analysis methods recommended by the CIM senior examiner

3.11 Opportunities and threats come from outside the company. These variables being external are, to a greater extent, uncontrollable (eg we cannot directly control competitors). Operating in ways to seize and develop opportunities, and so stave off or negate threats, can form the basis of longer term strategic plans.

3.12 The SWOT analysis has its limitations.

(a) It is essentially subjective.

(b) One person can see an attribute as a strength, whilst another might see it as a weakness.

(c) Under particular circumstances, a strength can become a weakness and vice versa.

(d) People have difficulty in deciding whether something is a strength or an opportunity and whether something is a weakness or a threat.

(e) It can produce almost endless lists with variations on themes and so can result in too much detail to be effective.

3.13 Ways in which the SWOT analysis can be made more effective are as follows.

(a) Keep strictly to the internal versus external criteria when deciding between strengths and opportunities, weaknesses and threats.

(b) Categorise all items by function, for example a particular strength as being a marketing strength, or a financial strength and so forth.

(c) Rank each strength in relative importance on a scale of major to minor.

(d) Draw up a list to show in descending order of ranks which items are most important.

(e) Take it as read that there are always opportunities to correct weaknesses and exploit strengths.

(f) Use the broad frameworks of other techniques to develop the SWOT analysis. Here are two examples.

(i) Ansoff: we have a broad opportunity to develop new products/services for existing markets (which new products and for which existing markets?).

(ii) SLEPT (Social, legal, economic, political and technological) factors representing opportunities or threats - which particular legal factors? - do these emanate from the national legislation, or Europe or other international sources?

(g) Do not equivocate. Decide, for the purposes of what follows, how an item should be categorised.

(h) Keep the SWOT analysis under continuous review.

(i) Use the ref. column to indicate the page number in the text of the case (p1) and/or appendix number (A10) from which you have extracted each item. This not only underpins your analysis more objectively, but saves time during the discussion periods, and other occasions when disputes may arise.

Step 8. Conduct analyses/cross analyses of appendices. Discuss with colleagues

3.14 CIM case study appendices normally considerably enrich the information afforded by the text. However, many of the appendices may be in the form of tables and the data contained therein may need analysis and interpretation in order to extract information for decision-taking purposes. Remember, information which cannot be used for taking decisions is by definition useless as far as we are concerned.

3.15 The analysis of numerical and financial data poses two pitfalls.

(a) Many people (usually the more numerate ones) get carried away by figures and will argue endlessly whether the extra cost of switching from hard toilet paper to soft is £2.27 per week or £2.35 per week, depending on whether or not we can negotiate a retrospective volume discount. Quite honestly, such debates waste the valuable time of a group and so the format suggested below is designed deliberately to simplify the data.

(b) What do the figures *mean*? Without meaning, figures are useless. We must also recognise that some tables may be deliberate red herrings and add very little to our understanding. Be aware that *figures can be interpreted differently*. For example, a series (representing annual turnover net of inflation as an index, 1988 = 100) reading 100, 99.8, 99.5, 99.4 may be interpreted by the more statistically minded person as a declining trend. However, looked at from a marketing management viewpoint the series could, on the contrary, be said to represent a highly stable market.

3.16 Does the appendix corroborate data in the text, in other words, does it strengthen or contradict something in the text? If so, which is right? You are, in the latter case, entitled to make your own assumptions but if the data in the text emanated from a newly appointed cleaner whilst that in the appendix came from a statistically sound survey, it would be more sensible to opt for the appendix. Data in one appendix can of course corroborate or contradict data in another appendix. What is the source of the data? How old is it? How reliable is it? Is the data quantitative or qualitative? What value can we place upon it? - are all worthwhile questions to ask.

3.17 Finally on this subject of appendix analysis, look for synergy by *cross analysis*. You can often gain valuable extra information by doing so. For example if Appendix 2 reveals that half our customers are female and Appendix 12 that female customers currently spend twice as much on our goods or services as males, then we can deduce that female customers are responsible for about two thirds of our turnover of £300,000 or approximately £200,000.

CASE APPENDICES - ANALYSIS/CROSS ANALYSIS

Appendix number	*What is it essentially saying?*	*How does it help us?*	*Which other appendices or text can it be related to?*	*If so what other extra information and insights does this reveal?*

Step 9. Re-consider your précis, marketing audit and SWOT analysis

3.18 Now is the time to recap on your work so far. It may well be that new knowledge acquired from your appendix analysis would warrant some modifications to your previous outputs. In some instances it may have given you fresh insights and in others, confirmed your views.

Step 10. Conduct a situational analysis and draw up a statement. Discuss with colleagues

3.19 The situational analysis can be both time consuming (depending on how well you did your marketing audit) but it is also rewarding. After a great deal of effort, you want to end up with a statement between half and one page long which puts the case study situation in a nutshell. It should leave you with a satisfying feeling of command.

8: The case study analysis methods recommended by the CIM senior examiner

3.20 Imagine you are a retail stores' group manager. You visit one of your hypermarkets and ask the manager 'What's the situation?' He or she might well reply - 'Well we've had a good month but that's down to the new city festival. Overall, we're down this year to date against last year, mainly on the premium brands. I'm worried about the high rate of pilferage and suspect the back stores have got a racket working. On the staff side, we're struggling a bit and I've worked it out that we've been two down on establishment on average this year. All in all, I reckon that we'll pan out about 98% of budgeted revenue this year but there'll be some compensation from costs of only 96%. We should just about hit targeted profit'.

3.21 You can see that the store manager knows the situation very well and has been able to sum it up in just a few sentences. However, to get there will have taken many hours of analysis and enquiry.

3.22 The *situational analysis* seeks to bring out the relevant relationships between the often overlapping and contradictory aspects of the SWOT. An example would be the importance of purchasing to marketing and corporate success.

3.23 The situational analysis builds on the marketing audit by adding a a time dimension by looking at likely future market trends and by looking for a prognosis (where is the company headed - glorious success, grim survival or somewhere in the middle ground). It establishes factual information and makes value judgements.

3.24 A situational analysis should cover at least the following issues, concentrating on the areas identified as important. You should have already covered these in your marketing audit, but need to revisit them together with your précis and SWOT in a grand summary.

External	*Internal*
Economic environment Market environment Competitive environment Technological environment	Sales Market share (if relevant) Profit margins Product range and development Price Distribution Promotion

3.25 However, before summarising you should add further analytical methods and models, wherever possible (eg product life cycle, diffusion of innovation, buyer behaviour models, product portfolio, customer portfolio, profit impact of marketing strategies), to establish understanding of the case material and gain fresh insights on the relationship between different pieces of information.

3.26 You should gain a thorough understanding of:

(a) buyer behaviour;
(b) competition and competitive strategies;
(c) distinctive competence.

3.27 This is the time to apply all your knowledge and use your full set of analytical tools, models and techniques, some of which are given for your convenience in the next chapter. The more perspectives you can bring to bear on the case then the greater will be your understanding and the higher your payoff in terms of examination marks. Take for example, buying behaviour models. You cannot know your markets without knowing your customers and understanding their buying behaviour. In the case study Euro Airport Ltd (June 1992) you would have learned a great deal by constructing a flow chart, depicting the stages through which a typical passenger goes from leaving work or home to arriving at the destination in a foreign country. At many of these stages lie opportunities for gaining, or losing, sales.

3.28 Remember that the objective of all this revising, reconsidering and further analysis is to give you a firm and clear command of the situation which you can express in not more than a single page statement. So let's hear it!

4 STEPS 11 TO 16: IDENTIFYING ISSUES AND DEVELOPING STRATEGIES

Step 11. Decide the key issues. Discuss with colleagues

4.1 Any good case study should yield, upon proper and thorough analysis, its key issues and any good examiner should set exam questions around these key issues in order to maintain good faith. So this is it. This is absolutely crucial to your exam success. Have you done your analysis thoroughly? If not, you have only yourself to blame if you haven't identified the right key issues and therefore the *likely exam question areas*.

4.2 In a retail situation you might have identified purchasing as a critical success factor, following analysis and discussion. A key issue might then be the method(s) of organising purchasing within the corporate and marketing plan. In Part E of this text you will be able to practise and test your ability to identify key issues in three actual exam case studies. Having identified the key issues we can now proceed to address these in our marketing plan.

4.3 As it can get out of hand (eg you could put forward 47 key issues just to be on the safe side) you should limit yourself to a maximum of *six*. Bearing in mind that the exam paper will normally contain three questions, you can see the wisdom in limiting yourself to six key issues. When deciding key issues, look for clues not only in the case study itself, *but also in the Candidates' Brief*. Try not to get carried away. By all means create a list of possible key issues, but then *reject* all those which are not key. You could use a *ranking technique* and you should 'parcel up' minor issues under a major heading eg:

- 4 Sales force effectiveness
- 6 Advertising constraints
- 8 Poor press relations (PR)

might then be parcelled up under the heading of *marketing communications* and allocated a ranking of 3.

Step 12. Develop a mission statement. Discuss with colleagues

4.4 The mission statement is an important part of strategy. It has an important role in providing a consensus between different viewpoints and a focus for business activity. It has been covered in detail in Chapter 1, Paragraph 3.65 of this text, but just to recap, look over the following paragraphs.

4.5 The mission statement is likely to have a degree of generality so that it can integrate various stakeholders' interests over a long period of time. Stakeholders could be defined as 'any group or individual who can affect or is affected by the achievement of an organisation's purpose'. (eg customers, government, employees).

4.6 Open objectives are appropriate for areas that are difficult to quantify or express in measurable terms, eg 'to be a leader in technology'. Open objectives can avoid over centralisation, opposition, rigidity to change and alerting competitors.

4.7 The mission is shaped by five key elements.

(a) The organisation's history.
(b) The current preferences of owners and managers (stakeholders).
(c) Environmental considerations.

(d) Resources.
(e) The organisation's distinctive competences.

4.8 An example of a mission statement is one adopted by Apple. 'Apple (computers) is not in the game or toy business but in the computer business. What Apple does best is to take a high cost ideal and turn it into a low cost, high quality solution.'

Note that there are two possible approaches to a mission. Here is an example.

Firm	Product view	Market view
Revlon	We make cosmetics	We sell hope
Xerox	We make copying equipment	We help improve office productivity

Step 13. Decide broad aims. Discuss with colleagues

4.9 Most people find it difficult to proceed directly from a mission statement into quantified and timescaled objectives. They are also perhaps overly concerned with the problems the company in the case study is facing.

4.10 For these reasons the step of deciding broad aims is often found to be very useful. You do not immediately have to decide by how much and when. For example, in the Brewsters case (December 1991) your broad aim might be to maintain sales, despite having to sell off a large proportion of your pubs, or to reduce your dependence on the UK market. In the Euro Airport case (June 1992) it might be to replace the loss of duty-free sales. In the Regional Railways (December 1992) case it might be to change staff attitudes towards customers from negative to positive.

4.11 Your broad aims must be consistent with your mission statement. (In fact, consistency throughout the different parts of your marketing plan is something you must aim for and continually check from now on.)

4.12 Generally speaking broad aims must be capable of *later* refinement into quantified and timescaled objectives, such as to increase sales (net of inflation) from the current £36m in 1992 to £63m by 1997.

4.13 However, this can be difficult in the case of a broad aim being for example 'to become more marketing orientated'. Nevertheless you could convert this into a marketing objective of 'to be fully marketing orientated by the end of 1997' and go on to suggest strategies and tactics by which this could be achieved. You could also say in what respects the company is not yet fully marketing orientated and the measures you would take at the end of 1997 to check whether your objective has been achieved.

4.14 The advantage of deciding broad aims before doing problem analysis is that you have the vision of your mission statement behind you, and are not held back by problems which upon subsequent analysis may turn out to be relatively minor.

Step 14. Identify and analyse major problems. Develop and analyse alternative solutions. Discuss with colleagues

4.15 You should now identify all the problems first and then decide which of these are relatively minor and which are major. Generally speaking your tactical plan will address the more minor, short term problems, whilst your strategic plan will focus upon the more major, long-term problems.

4.16 Having identified the major problems you must not immediately jump to ill-thought out solutions. The more responsible and managerial approach is to generate alternative solutions and then to evaluate each solution by examining its advantages and disadvantages, in order to arrive at the best selection.

4.17 A format for doing this is given on the next page and it is suggested you set yourself the task of analysing the six most important problems in this way, as a minimum. You should, of course, discuss your results with colleagues and be prepared to change your stance, given sufficient logical argument.

4.18 One way in which to decide which are the most major problems is to ask yourself 'Which of these problems most stands in the way of the achievement of my broad aims?'

Step 15. Develop quantified and timescaled objectives. Discuss with colleagues

4.19 Although modern marketing management must allow for some objectives which at first sight may be judged as qualitative, they should, if worked at, be capable of measurement over time. The hard business approach is that unless an objective can be measured over time, there is no accountability and no management objective, only a delusion.

4.20 The case study is difficult enough without making a rod for your own back unnecessarily. So choose your objectives carefully and do not parade too many in your answer. Remember that for each objective you need at least one strategy and for each strategy you need a set of tactics, a budget and a schedule. It is better to stick to key or main objectives and (only if you must) then use the subterfuge of sub-objectives to avoid over-complicating your plan.

4.21 Many people get confused between corporate objectives and marketing objectives, also between objectives and strategies, which is not surprising since most authors seem themselves confused or are at least incapable of writing clear differentiations.

4.22 It may help you to assume that corporate objectives are usually concerned with profitability, growth and risk reduction and to realise that all the functions are deployed strategically towards achieving these objectives.

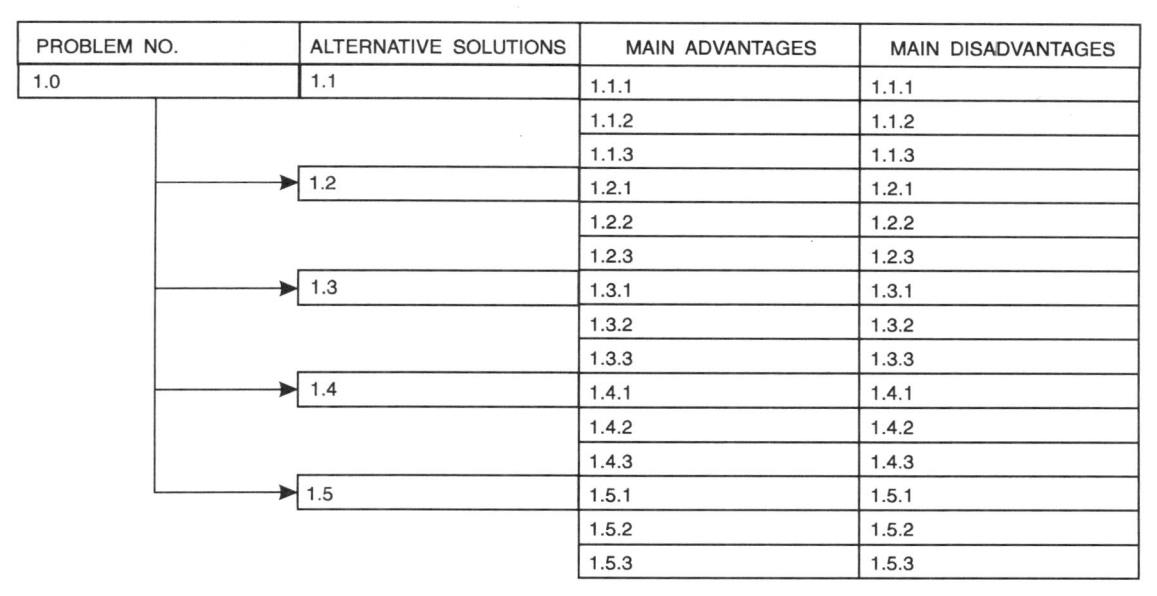

8: The case study analysis methods recommended by the CIM senior examiner

PROBLEM NO.	ALTERNATIVE SOLUTIONS	MAIN ADVANTAGES	MAIN DISADVANTAGES
1.0	1.1	1.1.1	1.1.1
		1.1.2	1.1.2
		1.1.3	1.1.3
	1.2	1.2.1	1.2.1
		1.2.2	1.2.2
		1.2.3	1.2.3
	1.3	1.3.1	1.3.1
		1.3.2	1.3.2
		1.3.3	1.3.3
	1.4	1.4.1	1.4.1
		1.4.2	1.4.2
		1.4.3	1.4.3
	1.5	1.5.1	1.5.1
		1.5.2	1.5.2
		1.5.3	1.5.3

PROBLEM NO.	ALTERNATIVE SOLUTIONS	MAIN ADVANTAGES	MAIN DISADVANTAGES
2.0	2.1	2.1.1	2.1.1
		2.1.2	2.1.2
		2.1.3	2.1.3
	2.2	2.2.1	2.2.1
		2.2.2	2.2.2
		2.2.3	2.2.3
	2.3	2.3.1	2.3.1
		2.3.2	2.3.2
		2.3.3	2.3.3
	2.4	2.4.1	2.4.1
		2.4.2	2.4.2
		2.4.3	2.4.3
	2.5	2.5.1	2.5.1
		2.5.2	2.5.2
		2.5.3	2.5.3

PROBLEM NO.	ALTERNATIVE SOLUTIONS	MAIN ADVANTAGES	MAIN DISADVANTAGES
3.0	3.1	3.1.1	3.1.1
		3.1.2	3.1.2
		3.1.3	3.1.3
	3.2	3.2.1	3.2.1
		3.2.2	3.2.2
		3.2.3	3.2.3
	3.3	3.3.1	3.3.1
		3.3.2	3.3.2
		3.3.3	3.3.3
	3.4	3.4.1	3.4.1
		3.4.2	3.4.2
		3.4.3	3.4.3
	3.5	3.5.1	3.5.1
		3.5.2	3.5.2
		3.5.3	3.5.3

Part C: How to analyse the CIM case study

4.23 For example, the marketing function can grow sales profitably, the production function can reduce costs, the finance function can manage funds more efficiently and the personnel function can recruit better people at less cost. In other words, all functions work together to achieve the corporate objective of profitable growth. Looked at from the viewpoint of corporate management the functions are means to ends and are therefore strategies. However, at functional level, the corporate strategies become objectives eg a marketing objective of increasing sales from X to Y by N date, whilst maintaining costs. The means by which the marketing function achieves a sales growth objective may be by introducing new products and/or entering new markets ie strategy (Ansoff), or indeed via the marketing mix (advertising, pricing etc) which are tactics to the marketing manager. Both strategies and tactics are means to ends, the difference is merely one of detail and the level at which you are looking from.

CORPORATE OBJECTIVES (SETTING)

Profitability	ROCE increase
Growth	Turnover, size, prestige
Risk reduction	Increase product base, customer base, market base

---

FUNCTIONAL OBJECTIVES ARE CORPORATE STRATEGIES

How is the marketing function deployed to meet corporate objectives? (Ask the same of production, finance and personnel functions.)

Say the marketing objective is to increase market share from X% to Y% by end of 19X9.

How is this done?
Devise a strategy

- new products
- new customers

These become the objectives for the following.

- New product development manager, to introduce 'N' new products by ....
- Sales manager, to obtain 'N' new customers by ....

TACTICS ARE DETAILS

Advertising objective	= To increase awareness from X to Y by ....
Strategy	= Press
Tactics	= Mirror, Times, 1 page black and white once monthly

Step 16. Consider alternative strategies and select those most appropriate. Discuss with colleagues

4.24 Please bear in mind the work 'select' and do not try to pursue every available strategy. Good marketing management is about strategic choice. Your starting point should be *Ansoff*. Leaving aside diversification for the moment, since this would normally involve corporate management, you need to ask yourself the following questions.

(a) Is the current market saturated, or is there room for greater market penetration?
(b) What opportunities are there for product development?
(c) What are the possibilities for market development?

4.25 The basic Ansoff analysis should of course be expanded to define which new products and which new markets should be developed and then into more detail such as:

(a) product modification;
(b) re-packaging;
(c) market segments;

(d) niche markets;
(e) positioning.

Your strategic choices should also be advised by competitor analysis.

5 STEPS 17 TO 23: DEVELOPING YOUR PLANS

Step 17. Draw up detailed tactical plans covering the marketing mix. Discuss with colleagues

5.1 Although some of the broader marketing mix decisions such as pull or push promotional policy, skimming or penetration pricing, overseas market entry etc, are quite rightly seen as strategic decisions by some authors, for the sake of simplicity we are treating the marketing mix plans here as tactical.

5.2 In the case study answers we will need to go into the tactical detail, since the senior examiner is on record as saying that his examination papers will contain a mix of strategic and tactical questions.

5.3 If you wish, you can in your marketing mix plans distinguish by headings between promotional strategy and promotional tactics, pricing strategy and pricing tactics and so on, but as was said earlier the distinction depends to some extent upon the level from which you are looking and you are likely to be placed in a more senior role than that of a manager of an element of a marketing mix (such as advertising manager, or sales promotion manager).

5.4 To help you in drawing up your detailed marketing mix plans, you will find a reminder of the normal types of decisions and considerations you need to identify, under each of the 4 P's, on the following page.

5.5 You should also look back to Chapter 1 Paragraph 4.30 for the general purpose screening model for new products. Also go back to Chapter 2 Paragraph 3.4 for the elements of the *promotional submix* (eg the mix elements for advertising, personal selling, sales promotion and PR).

5.6 Screening quite often crops up in exam questions and many students seem to lack knowledge of this important process. Screening of new product/service ideas or concepts can be seen as both part of the new product development plan and part of the marketing research process.

5.7 Finally, since case situations can cover services rather than products, you should consider the '7 P' approach to the marketing services, namely the 4Ps plus the extra 3 Ps of People, Process, and Physical evidence. These are described in Chapter 1.

5.8 Now carry on with your next task

PRODUCT SUBMIX

Product policies:
  product life cycle
  portfolio analysis
  product mix

Product strategy and tactics:
  branding
  new product development
  screening
  licensing
  organisational aspects

PRICING SUBMIX

Pricing policies:
  role of pricing
  approaches to pricing policies
  pricing and the PLC
  legal considerations

Pricing objectives

Pricing methods and tactics:
  experience and costs
  offensive pricing

MARKETING ELEMENTS - SUBMIX PLANNING

DISTRIBUTION SUBMIX

Distribution strategies and tactics:
  channels
  stock levels
  ordering systems
  speed of response
  dealer relationships
  depots/warehouses
  transportation

PROMOTIONAL SUBMIX

Promotional strategies and tactics:
  advertising
  sales promotion
  public relations
  personal selling

8: The case study analysis methods recommended by the CIM senior examiner

Step 18. Draw up a marketing research plan and MkIS (marketing information system)

5.9 Marketing research is usually dealt with separately by most authors since it does not easily fit into the standard planning outline of objectives, strategy and tactics.

5.10 Marketing research is, however, key to all the planning stages. It is needed for the adequate audit of the marketing environment prior to the formation of objectives. Internal data is used together with competitor information and market information when deciding objectives. Marketing research is also necessary to decide strategy (eg which new products and/or which new markets?). Finally, marketing research should be employed to decide the best marketing mix for given market segments and to check on the progress of the plan in achieving the objectives.

5.11 Because of its pervasive importance to marketing planning, marketing research (research into all aspects of marketing) often forms the basis of at least one of the examination questions. This can be in the form of an information specification eg 'what information is needed in order to determine the best means of entry into mainland Europe?' or an outline marketing research plan itself. Occasionally you will be asked to differentiate between information needed for a particular project or sub-plan and that which should be ongoing and part of the company's MkIS (marketing information system).

5.12 You also need to distinguish between:

(a) the detailed information sought ie the information specification, its type (product, market etc); and

(b) the method used (postal questionnaire, personal interview etc).

5.13 To help you with drawing up this sub-plan within your total marketing plan, a typical format is given below.

OUTLINE OF A MARKETING RESEARCH PLAN

(a) Research objectives.

(b) The information specification.

(c) Research methods - survey design - desk research, field research (postal, telephone, personal visit, observations).

(d) Questionnaire design - drafting, pilot testing.

(e) Respondent selection - sample size, sample frame, characteristics.

(f) Timing considerations - survey, report, decisions.

(g) Briefings - in-house and/or agencies.

(h) Analysis - method, staff.

(i) Report - format, writer, readers.

(j) Budget - costs of each plan element.

(k) Contingency - for overspend, delays, faults etc.

Step 19. Consider organisational issues and make recommendations for changes towards complete marketing orientation as felt necessary. Discuss with colleagues

5.14 You need to remember that the CIM case study is a test of all your marketing knowledge gained in previous studies. When auditing the organisation described in the case study you need to ask yourself questions such as the following.

(a) To what extent has this organisation adopted the marketing concept?

Notes *Part C: How to analyse the CIM case study*

(b) Do all functions in the company (not just marketing) accept the idea of customer sovereignty?

(c) To what extent does the company work together to satisfy customer needs?

(d) Is the marketing function on an equal footing alongside the other functions in the organisation or is it organisationally subservient?

(e) Is adequate marketing research being conducted to keep the organisation fully in touch with changing customer needs?

(f) Is the organisation structure flexible enough to respond to changing customer needs?

(g) To what extent does the marketing organisation reflect the importance of critical success factors in the particular market (such as in retail marketing - packaging, merchandising, point-of-sale)?

(h) Would the organisation benefit from a matrix approach?

(i) To what extent might brand managers, product managers or market managers be appropriate?

(j) Is the salesforce organisation properly aligned to customer buying behaviour, market segmentation etc?

5.15 By the use of these and other questions you might be able to identify ways in which the company could make organisational changes to gain greater competitive advantage and reap dividends in terms of increased sales and repeat business.

Step 20. Consider the organisation's culture and make recommendations for internal marketing programmes as felt necessary. Discuss with colleagues

5.16 This step is closely related to the previous one and both steps have been tested in recent examinations, so it would pay you to read up on marketing orientation, internal marketing (under TQM) customer care and relationship marketing. More books and articles are being published on these aspects, which are seen as intrinsic to modern marketing. Remember the CIM has to conserve its image as being at the cutting edge of marketing and all senior examiners reserve the right to test you on your knowledge of recent events in marketing development.

5.17 Any organisation can make cosmetic alterations, for example changing the title of the sales manager to sales and marketing manager but these do not themselves result in full marketing orientation. A change of culture will require total commitment from the top and often take several years of careful internal marketing planning and training. British Rail have brought about many improvements to their marketing mix but despite internal marketing, staff attitudes to customers still leave a lot to be desired.

Step 21. Consider the financial and human resource implications of your plans/recommendations. Discuss with colleagues

5.18 The CIM has in the past been criticised by industry for turning out marketers who are financially illiterate. For far too long it had been accepted that marketers, being creative, were therefore necessarily innumerate. In order to work effectively within the corporate team marketing managers and directors need to understand the basics of return on investment, cashflow and risk. They also require to be able to interpret a balance sheet and profit and loss account, at least as well as production and personnel managers.

5.19 The definition of marketing by the CIM ends with the word 'profitably'. No longer can marketers go on spending money in the hope of increasing market share without recognising the importance of a return on investment and that other projects within the company might return more profit at a lower risk and within a shorter period.

5.20 The CIM has made it clear that future members will need to provide evidence of financial literacy and that financial acumen will be tested in the case study.

5.21 As a minimum you will be expected to show the anticipated results of your proposals in terms of revenues, costs and gross margins. Hopefully you would also be able to demonstrate an understanding of how your plans might increase tensions on cashflow, affect rates of stockturn, require capital injections etc. A checklist of financial implications is given below for your convenience.

FINANCIAL IMPLICATIONS CHECKLIST

Capital investment	Stock
Risk	Liquidity
Revenue	Depreciation
Profit, profitability, break-even	Forecasting
Working capital	Budgets
Cash flow	Financial planning/organisation
ROI/ROCE	Financial control
Creditors/debtors	Costs-staffing etc

5.22 Equally you need to be able to show an appreciation of the human resource implications of your plans. Every proposed action will require time by people, time that may not be available. Proposed actions may demand from people skills or knowledge which they do not have.

5.23 Recruitment and training not only cost money but also take time and may not have the desired result. For every basic salary there are considerable related employment costs.

5.24 Changes in personnel have knock-on effects and may adversely affect team spirit and company culture. When proposing action you should at least indicate who is involved in taking it and who will monitor or control results.

Step 22. Assess costs and draw up indicative budgets. Discuss with colleagues

5.25 Within the four weeks time available to study the case, it should be relatively easy for marketers to acquire rough costs for advertising, market research, salaries, training etc.

5.26 You are not expected to be accurate beyond a 'ball park' figure. For example, it does not matter too much whether you indicate a cost of £1,000 or £1,500 per group discussion in a marketing research plan (they vary anyway) as long as you don't show £100 or £10,000.

5.27 The examiner does, however, expect you to have some knowledge of how to construct a marketing budget. Candidates who quote a total promotional budget of £100,000 appear to have plucked this out of the air. If this was supposed to cover everything from a series of exhibitions to an extensive TV advertising campaign they would reveal their ignorance. Far better to show the examiner that you know how this figure is built up viz:

	£'000	£'000	£'000
Literature	6		
Reps display materials	22		
Exhibitions	60		
Trade advertising	12		
		100	
Contingency reserve at 10%		10	
			110

5.28 Or if this were an advertising budget

	£'000	£'000	£'000
Local radio	10		
TV	-		
Press*	82		
Cinema	-		
Poster	8		
		100	
Contingency reserve at 10%		10	
			110

* Monthly 1 page black and white advertisements in the Daily Dozen (£42,000), and quarterly full page adverts in the Monthly Review (£40,000).

5.29 The typical contents of marketing budgets are given in Chapter 1, paragraph 3.55.

Step 23. Draw up schedules showing the timing/sequence of your plans/ recommendations. Discuss with colleagues

5.30 Far too many candidates lose valuable marks by failing to schedule their proposals. Others simply put timings such as X = 6 months, Y = 3 months, Z = 1 year, without indicating their sequence.

5.31 The easiest and quickest way to indicate schedules in the examination is by means of a Gantt chart similar to that shown below, which enables you to show activities, which are relatively short-term along with others which are ongoing. A modified Gantt chart for scheduling activities is shown below.

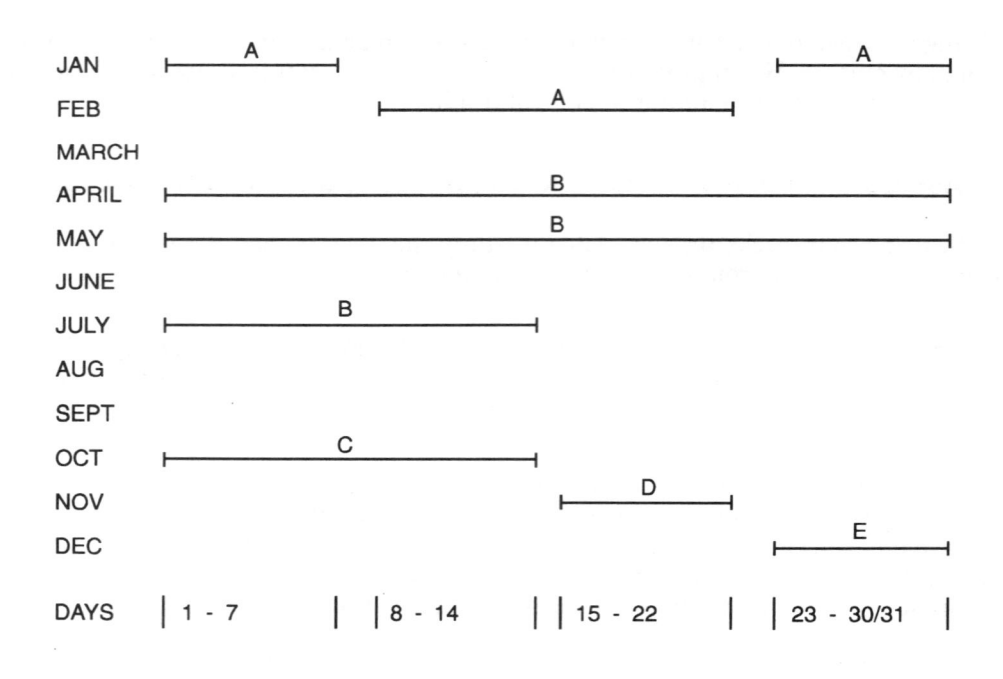

Month	Activity
JAN	A (days 1-7), A (days 23-30/31)
FEB	A (days 8-22)
MARCH	
APRIL	B (days 8-30/31)
MAY	B (days 8-30/31)
JUNE	
JULY	B (days 1-14)
AUG	
SEPT	
OCT	C (days 1-14)
NOV	D (days 15-22)
DEC	E (days 23-30/31)

DAYS: | 1 - 7 | | 8 - 14 | | 15 - 22 | | 23 - 30/31 |

Activity A = Product Development
Activity B = Launch Planning
Activity C = Pre-launch promotion
Activity D = Exhibitions and in-factory demonstrations
Activity E = Post-launch promotion

6 STEPS 24 TO 26: CONTROL AND CONTINGENCIES

Step 24. Specify review procedures and control mechanisms. Discuss with colleagues

6.1 Students' performance is generally weak in this area. If you excel here, this might identify you as a distinction grade graduate.

6.2 It is not enough to simply list items such as budgets, meetings, ratio analysis. You need to indicate clearly which budgets are used, which parts of the management accounting system are involved; which people should attend the meetings, when and for what purpose; and which particular ratios are important and so on.

6.3 Relevant material is covered in Chapter 1 of this text.

Step 25. Outline contingency plans. Discuss with colleagues

6.4 The CIM examiner reserves the right to introduce extra material into the actual examination paper. Since this right is not always exercised in recent examinations it is as well to think through this contingency.

6.5 What sorts of extra information might you, if you were the examiner yourself, introduce? Bear in mind this would have to be modest, fair and not over-demanding.

6.6 You should additionally consider one or two 'what if' scenarios which you could cover with an outline contingency plan in your standard answers. For example, what if the EU introduced new competition rules on mail services?

6.7 Good modern planning includes contingency planning and you need to show in a modest way that you have covered this in your thinking.

Step 26. Review your complete marketing plan

6.8 Does it fit together? Is it consistent? Does it cover everything? Which are the areas of weakness? Can you improve it?

7 STEPS 27 TO 28: THE EXAMINATION

Step 27. Draw up your examination plan

7.1 Now you are satisfied that your marketing plan is complete and satisfactory, it would be a sad folly if you had gone through all that effort simply to fail because of lack of examination technique and planning.

7.2 Examination planning should cover everything you need to do between now and when you finally put your pen down as the invigilator calls time in the examination hall. Many hardworking and clever people fail through lack of examination technique. This aspect is so important that it has been given a chapter to itself (Chapter 10). Please be sure to study it carefully and take the necessary action.

Step 28. Practise writing in true report style

7.3 Most of us have been conditioned at school, college and/or university to write essays for both assignments and examinations. However, essays are not the stuff of business communications. Business needs succinct, clear reports which take the minimum of time to assimilate, rather than elegant but wordy prose. Many candidates are unclear about what true business report style is, simply because they have not received any tuition during studies or training in this aspect.

7.4 Marketing managers need to be able to produce good business reports for their colleagues and seniors. You must demonstrate this ability in order to gain the CIM Diploma. Furthermore, you will find it is almost impossible to cover all the points you need to make when answering the case study questions, within the time available, when writing in essay style. So get some practice done. You will find further details on report style in Chapter 10.

Chapter roundup

- You have now reviewed the CIM examiner's recommended method.
- It covers everything from your mental state as you read the study from the first time to writing reports at the end.
- Help yourself succeed, and follow the method.

Chapter 9

ADOPTING THE ROLE AND CREATING THE PLAN

> **This chapter covers the following topics.**
> 1 Syndicates
> 2 Personalities and teamwork
>
> **Introduction**
> This is a guide to working in groups. There are benefits to be had from sharing insights.

1 SYNDICATES

1.1 This relatively short section is really aimed at getting the best out of syndicate work. Syndicates are an ideal way of enlarging individual perspectives, moderating excesses and producing results in more detail and of a higher quality than could normally be achieved by any individual working alone.

1.2 These benefits depend on the collective ability of the members of the syndicate to work as a team, to agree on a division of labour for the more menial and time consuming tasks, and, above all, to be organised and disciplined.

1.3 First of all, an individual syndicate member can adopt the role of *devil's advocate*, deliberately taking an opposing view to test the syndicate's logic. The role of devil's advocate can be adopted by each individual in turn, as can the adoption of the role specified in the candidates' brief. Other syndicate members can in discussion, adopt the role of the person reported to, the managing director, the financial director and so forth.

1.4 For maximum effectiveness a syndicate should elect a chairperson, for each session, and a spokesperson. Again these two roles should be passed round in turn.

1.5 The *chairperson's* job is:
 (a) to ensure the task is completed on time;
 (b) to maintain order; and
 (c) to arbitrate in the case of a dispute.
 It is not to steamroller his or her views on the syndicate.

1.6 Likewise, the *spokesperson's* job is to relay the syndicate's views objectively to the plenary assembly, not his or her own personal views.

1.7 There are occasions when the syndicate should work together (eg on the *mission statement*). At other times, individuals should work entirely on their own (eg *on the précis*) and sometimes the syndicate of eight persons, say, for example might be advised to split into four pairs to work on the SWOT analysis, for example.

Notes **Part C: How to analyse the CIM case study**

1.8 In the latter instance one pair could work on strengths, another on weaknesses, a third on opportunities and the fourth on threats. Very little is lost as a result, and a great deal is gained in the amount of items gathered. The team would, of course, come together to amalgamate their work at the end of the session.

1.9 Many syndicates leave the write-up for the presentation of their work to the very last minute and therefore often do not do themselves justice as a result. *It is strongly recommended that writing up is done as you go along* and this is particularly important when producing overhead projection transparencies.

1.10 Syndicates can also benefit by organising 'swap shops', between syndicate groups, to exchange work. This helps to avoid excessive note-taking during plenary sessions when all come together and encourages maximum debate.

1.11 Extra work outside course hours can also be conducted voluntarily within the syndicates. Alternatively, special assignments suggested by the case study tutor, can be accepted as extra workload.

1.12 Work allocated to syndicates can play to each syndicate's strengths, as can work shared among syndicate members. If a given syndicate contains a large number of people in marketing communications, it might be allocated the task of producing a promotional plan. If within a syndicate there is a person from an accounting background he or she might be asked to analyse the appendix containing the accounts.

1.13 This is not to absolve *individuals* from creating their own personal plans, but merely to make best use of limited syndicate and plenary group time. Individuals can and should sit in critical judgement of other people's contributions, accepting the best, rejecting the poorer and adding their own contributions.

1.14 Remember that while you can *prepare* with others, the exam is a test of *individual*, not *group* ability.

2 PERSONALITIES AND TEAMWORK

2.1 Syndicate members will get the best out of their team if they pull together, retain a sense of humour and recognise the value of interplay between personalities. Individuals should endeavour to categorise themselves eg as being too dominant or too quiet and attempt to overcome these faults in their own and the group's interests.

2.2 The following categorisation is offered for self-analysis and with the tiniest pinch of salt.

(a) The *Jumper*. Usually better qualified than the average, this person knows the best solutions instantly and feels that the development of alternative solutions and the weighing up of each solution's advantages/disadvantages before making a choice is a menial task suited to his or her less well qualified colleagues but unnecessary for someone of his or her acumen. 'It's obvious' is the catchphrase, delivered with thinly disguised scorn for those people who cannot see the argument (including the tutor). This person is impatient, quick-thinking and finishes the job in half the time, making other team members feel that it is they who are doing something wrong.

(b) The *Sitter*. This person finds it difficult to come to a decision and sits on the fence equivocating brilliantly on both sides. He or she seems to forget that the subject examined is 'Analysis and *Decision*'.

(c) The *Xerox*. With no strong personal views and no real inclination to hard work, this person copies other people's ideas - unfortunately often those of the Jumper. The Xerox is caught out by the exam questions which puts a slightly different slant on the matter and blindly copies out the pre-prepared answer notwithstanding.

(d) A *Tree* never sees the wood. This person tends to receive the case and plunge into analysis of all tables to the nth degree with calculator smoking. This person works hard and is extremely difficult to beat in discussion since he or she can bring more and more data to bear on the question, endlessly splitting hairs, crossing t's and dotting i's. This person can pass with honours if only he or she would sit back and review objectively what it is he or she is really trying to achieve.

(e) A *Blinker* sees things only from his or her narrow experience. This person tends to have one textbook approach for all situations, and adamantly sticks to this in face of all opposition or evidence to the contrary. This person worships Kotler, or Baker, or Smallbone, or Levitt, and apart from this one, all other authors are idiots not worth reading. Favourite catchphrases are 'I once knew a company which ...' and 'the company I once worked for (usually the Post Office as a Christmas temp) do it this way'. A favourite examination technique is to write out whatever pre-prepared views he or she has on the world, irrespective of the actual exam question or, for that matter, the case study.

Chapter roundup

- This chapter has endeavoured to give you some advice as to how to relate to your colleagues in the syndicates, and how you can get the most out of group work.

Part D
Examination techniques: planning your examination

Chapter 10

EXAMINATION TECHNIQUES: PLANNING YOUR EXAMINATION

> **This chapter covers the following topics.**
> 1 Preparing for the examination day
> 2 Report format
> 3 Examination day
> 4 What not to do
>
> **Introduction**
>
> The most thorough preparation beforehand will be wasted if your exam technique is poor. So don't spoil your chances by panic or a lack of foresight.

1   PREPARING FOR THE EXAMINATION DAY

1.1   As a professional marketing manager you should possess two attributes, namely to be able:

   (a)   to visualise the future; and
   (b)   to organise for it.

   Please apply these two attributes to preparing for your examination.

1.2   If you are typical of most candidates, you will have amassed a great deal of paperwork comprising your analysis and your complete marketing plan.

1.3   What you do now is to reduce it to manageable proportions. None of us likes to throw away the results of our hard work, but you can at least produce neat, concise summary sheets of each section. Relegate the remainder to the status of back-up detail, to be consulted and used only if needed. All your work should be placed in an A4 ring binder and indexed for quick and easy access. The best way to index it is to use the framework for your marketing plan since this is the most logical and practical access system for your exam and you are already familiar with it.

1.4   An outline for your index is suggested overleaf but however you organise your ring binder, be familiar with it. Know exactly where everything is and how to locate it quickly.

> EXAMINATION RING BINDER INDEX: SUGGESTED FORMAT
>
> (a) Analysis
>
>   (i) Précis
>   (ii) Marketing audit
>   (iii) SWOT analysis
>   (iv) Appendix analysis
>   (v) Situational analysis
>   (vi) Problem analysis
>   (vii) Key issues
>
> (b) Mission statement/broad aims
>
> (c) Objectives
>
> (d) Strategies
>
> (e) Tactics/marketing mix
>
>   (i) Product/service plan, packaging
>   (ii) Pricing
>   (iii) Promotion
>
>   (1) Advertising
>   (2) Sales promotion
>   (3) Selling
>   (4) PR
>
>   (iv) Place - Distribution
>   (v) People
>   (vi) Process
>   (vii) Physical evidence
>
> (f) Organisation/internal marketing
>
> (g) Budgets/financial and human resources
>
> (h) Scheduling
>
> (i) Control
>
> (j) Contingencies
>
> (k) Ready reckoner (see Paragraph 1.12)

1.5 You will need at least 42 hours to apply the 28 step approach recommended in this text to the actual examination case. You have about four weeks to do this; let us say this works out at 12 hours a week. You must find the time and plan it out properly.

1.6 Take a copy of the case study - ideally you should enlarge this from A5 size pages to A4 to allow you space to make notes.

1.7 The principles of marketing planning and control should also be applied to your examination scripts. In the Chartered Institute of Marketing's (CIM) major case study examination there are usually three or four questions each scoring a different percentage of marks eg 20%, 30%, 50%, or 15%, 15%, 30%, 40%. Your time needs to be apportioned accordingly.

1.8 A spatial control as well as a temporal control is recommended. How long does it take you to write an A4 page, legibly in essay style and report style? Make allowances for fatigue setting in part way through a three hour paper. For example, you may find you can write a legible A4 page in essay style, in ten minutes, when you are fresh but this increases to twelve minutes when fatigued. The figures for report style become five minutes and six minutes respectively.

10: Examination techniques: planning your examination

1.9 You can now calculate the number of pages you should target for any given question (after deducting thinking and planning time) and pencil in a 'spatial control' on your script paper. A three part report for 30% of the market might be allocated a total time of 50 minutes, of which 15 minutes is allocated to thinking and planning, and five minutes for checking what you have written. This leaves 30 minutes for report style writing when fresh, which equals six pages or two pages for each section of your report.

1.10 This sort of planning can of course be conducted before you enter the examination hall to avoid unnecessary waste of precious examination time.

1.11 In the examination room itself, use the following 'ready reckoner' to quickly allocate time proportionately to question marks. Have a copy of this ready reckoner handy in your ring binder and indexed.

1.12 This table shows how many minutes to allocate to each question in a three hour exam, based on the number of marks per question.

Marks	Minutes
5	9
10	18
15	27
20	36
25	45
30	54
35	63
40	72
45	81
50	90
55	99
60	108
65	117
70	126
75	135
80	144
85	153
90	162
95	171
100	180

1.13 Think through and prepare your ancillary equipment for the examination.

(a) Your exam entry documentation.

(b) Pens and pencils, pencil sharpener.

(c) Calculator. Your calculator needs to be silent and should not require mains electricity. You are not likely to need it if you have thoroughly prepared your analysis, but take one in case.

(d) Rubber/White 'Tippex' fluid.

(e) Stencils for drawing organisation charts, boxes, or anything that may help you to save time as well as being neat. If you pre-prepare charts do them in black ink on a white background and on an A4 sheet. If you slide these behind your CIM exam script paper you will find they show through sufficiently well for you to copy neatly in double quick time.

(f) Blanks of charts - organisation, Gantt schedules, graphs, pie charts etc in black ink on white paper.

(g) Ruler.

(h) The case study itself.

(i) Indexed ring binder.

Notes Part D: Examination techniques: planning your examination

  (j) Sweets?

  (k) Watch/clock.

  (l) Marketing text book. Although you will not have time in the exam to keep looking things up, it is as well to take this tutorial text with you as an insurance policy. Be reasonably familiar with its index and layout.

1.14 Check where the examination centre is and estimate how long it will take you to get there. Allow for contingencies like traffic and parking delays. *You will not be allowed into the exam hall more than 15 minutes after the start.*

1.15 Plan to get there early so that you do not put undue pressure on yourself.

1.16 Plan to get to bed early the night before the examination day and to dress comfortably for the weather.

1.17 Remember that space (ie the desktop and around the desk) will probably be extremely limited.

Consultant's analysis

1.18 You should consider purchasing one of the consultant's analyses advertised in *Marketing Success*. These cost around £12.

1.19 You would normally receive this analysis about two weeks before the examination. Whilst it should not of course *substitute* for your own analysis, it can rather act as a check on what you have done and hopefully add additional perspectives, which can be particularly useful if you have not been working with a syndicate group.

1.20 Copies of all consultants' analyses are lodged by the CIM and cannot be copied out in the exam without risk of failure, not that there are exam questions based solely on analysis. They are generally the work of a team of experienced marketing lecturers but you must realise that whilst the work is professional, it will have been produced within a very short lead time and it is not intended to be perfect.

2 REPORT FORMAT

2.1 Report style is always mandatory for the major case study, and is often mandatory or recommended for the mini-case studies as far as the CIM is concerned. You are being examined in Marketing Management and busy managers do not thank you for wasting their time by using too many words to get to the point in essay format, when report format will convey information not only more quickly but more clearly. The use of charts of diagrams is also recommended wherever possible.

2.2 Many of the questions related to planning will require costing and activity scheduling in the answers to score good marks.

2.3 Many candidates are unclear about report style and use a quasi-report style which is really an essay split into sections under headings rather than true report style. Here are a couple of examples. The sections addressed by each relates to the criteria on whether to launch product A.

10: Examination techniques: planning your examination

Quasi-report style: WRONG

'The first criterion is whether this will be profitable over the estimated life cycle of product A. Another criterion which is related to the first criterion is that of estimated volume sales at the proposed price. A third criterion which needs to be considered when deciding whether or not to launch Product A is....'

Report style: RIGHT

(a) Decision criteria in rank order

   (i)   Profit (ROI) over product life cycle
   (ii) Sales volume at proposed price
   (iii) ...

Question structure

2.4 Try to structure your answers in the same way in which the question is structured so that there is no doubt as to which parts of your report relate to which parts of the question. An example of how to do this against the CIM December 1995 paper follows.

Example

2.5

Based on the data you have collected and further consultations with Interbrew and various customers, you have decided to approach the strategic marketing presentation in three parts.

Your presentation, *in report format*, will cover the following:

1. Propose a clear position for Leffe in the UK market. Describe the rationale behind your decision and explain the brand attributes and values that will be required to establish Leffe as a unique offering against the competition.

2. Produce a strategic marketing plan for Leffe. Your plan should explain how you will achieve the positioning proposed for the brand by 2000. The plan should include all aspects of the marketing activity except promotional plans (see question 3).

3. Based on market position and strategic marketing plans for Leffe, produce a strategic promotional plan for the Leffe brand. This plan will form the basis of a subsequent presentation to Interbrew and should cover the next ten years of Leffe's development in the UK market.

Notes **Part D: Examination techniques: planning your examination**

2.6 A specimen layout of the report asked for in 2.5 is given below

> LEFFE
>
> FROM: James Burgess
>
> SUBJECT: Presentation on the strategic marketing of Leffe for the divisional board meeting
>
> DATE: December 1995
>
> CONTENTS
>
> (a) *Positioning*
>
>   (i) Proposed positioning for Leffe in the UK market
>   (ii) Rationale for proposition
>   (iii) Brand attributes and values required
>
> (b) Strategic marketing plan (excluding promotional plans)
>
>   (i) Environmental analysis
>   (ii) Marketing objectives
>   (iii) Marketing strategy
>   (iv) Marketing mix programmes (excluding promotion)
>   (v) Budgets and controls
>
> (c) Strategic promotional plan
>
>   (i) Promotional objectives
>   (ii) Promotional strategies
>   (iii) Promotional mix
>   (iv) Promotional budgets and controls

Succinct writing

2.7 Practice writing succinctly. Critically review your own wording. In fact 'staccato' style is often more appropriate than long sentences.

Example

2.8 Consider the following actual extract from an exam script for the June 1992 exam paper.

> (a) Proposals for change in the organisational structure.
>
> (b) Creation of 'strategic business units' centred around each terminal
>
> This would allow each terminal to be represented at board level with each managers having his own operational and commercial staff beneath him. This will involve a huge restructuring of the organisation and individual job roles/responsibilities, however this move is necessary in order that commercial and operations staff work alongside each other and cooperate to solve problems in the most effective way, to the benefit of EAL in serving the needs of its customers. All commercial versus operations conflicts would be solved lower down the hierarchy which will in turn be flattened out as a result of restructuring. Each terminal general manager must have beneath him his appropriate support staff for his commercial and operations roles eg catering manager, retail operations manager, quality control engineers.'
>
> Total words = c 140
>
> Total time = 8 minutes

10: Examination techniques: planning your examination *Notes*

2.9 Keeping the same heading we might change the section to read as follows.

> Each terminal to become an SBU under a general manager with his own support staff (catering, retail operations, quality control etc).
>
> BENEFIT
>
> Although requiring much restructuring and reformulation of job descriptions:
>
> (a) commercial and operations staff would work together in meeting the needs of the customer;
> (b) all commercial v operations conflicts would be solved lower down the hierarchy;
> (c) each terminal would be represented at board level.
>
> Total words = c 70
>
> Total time = 4 minutes

2.10 Quite apart from the re-wording which cuts the original word length in half, it is easier to understand and mark. If this saving was replicated throughout the paper there would be at least an extra hour to make extra points and gain extra marks.

2.11 You really do owe it to yourself to work at this if you are the sort of person who writes 'quasi-essays' instead of reports. Not only will you be much more likely to pass the examination but you will also become a more effective communicator for your company.

3 EXAMINATION DAY

3.1 Hopefully, you will have gone to bed the previous evening, risen early, gone through your normal ablutions and breakfast routine and are now feeling organised.

3.2 Check through your exam kit once more and pack it in your brief case if you have not already done so.

3.3 Allow yourself the luxury of a short walk round the block to clear your head and make you feel good.

3.4 Psychology is important. Tell yourself that you are well prepared, you are intelligent, you have a track record of success. Look forward to performing well.

3.5 Try not to feel nervous (although some nerves are normal and can enhance performance). Remember that the examiners want you to pass - all you have to do is to give them sufficient excuse.

3.6 In your mind's eye, imagine yourself in the exam room. Imagine yourself sitting there calm and organised whilst others are fussing about, all 'uptight'. Don't feel intimidated if you see other examinees entering the hall with the equivalent of the Encyclopaedia Brittanica as their case ring binder. Instead, anticipate a glow of satisfaction and superiority once the exam has started and you can see and hear the endless shuffling of mountains of paper.

3.7 Always make it a point of honour not to be the first to start writing. Do all your thinking up front. Plan your answers. Make sure you have read the questions properly and understood them and any instructions.

3.8 Plan your time and stick to it. Allow adequate time for checking. If you have really thought through and planned your answers thoroughly, all the hard work is done. You know you will pass. All you need to do now is to put the flesh on the bones.

Notes *Part D: Examination techniques: planning your examination*

4 WHAT NOT TO DO

4.1 Please do not:

(a) write out the questions;

(b) write a lead sheet for each section of the report (just do one at the beginning);

(c) repeat information from the case (your reader will know this);

(d) write lengthy introductions, current situations, executive summaries, background information or other time wasting waffle - get straight down to business;

(e) answer only part of the question (a good technique is to pencil in the key words in the question at the start of each answer and stick rigidly to these);

(f) write endless assumptions;

(g) submit uncalled for SWOT analyses.

4.2 Hopefully you will find the following guide to examination failure both instructive and amusing.

HOW NOT TO PASS EXAMS
SOME KEY RULES

(a)	Play it by ear	'Candidates don't plan to fail, they fail to plan'
(b)	Don't revise	Do not have a revision plan either
(c)	Aim to just pass	That way you won't waste effort
(d)	Have no exam technique	Exams are bad enough without having to think about techniques
(e)	Do not anticipate questions	You may get it wrong
(f)	Do not read previous papers or exam reports and avoid any student aids like the plague	*You're* no wimp
(g)	Just do the first five questions	They're all as bad anyway
(h)	Write what you want to say. Don't worry about the question	It's more interesting
(i)	Ignore instructions	They only put you off
(j)	Do not check the time	Whilst you're doing this you could write a few more words
(k)	Never check your answers	There'll only be a few minor errors
(l)	Always start with an introduction and finish with a summary	That way you can forget about the middle
(m)	When in doubt - waffle	It will probably con the marker into thinking you know what you're talking about.
(n)	Write illegibly, especially the words that really matter	The examiner will always give you the benefit of the doubt
(o)	Do not structure your answers when it is a multi-part question	Let them guess which part belongs to which - it's what they are paid for isn't it?
(p)	If it is a two-part paper do the last bit first	It shows initiative - makes you stand out from the crowd
(q)	Arrive late and leave early	What's a few minutes between friends
(r)	Be disorganised	You can always ask the invigilator if you can borrow his/her pen, and for the odd toilet break or two

(s) Have just a little drink before the exam	It helps you to relax doesn't it?

(t) Don't bother to put the question numbers down	Well it should be obvious shouldn't it and you never know your luck!

(u) Tell the examiner what a hard life you've had and don't forget the good wishes for Christmas, Easter, the hols etc.	Should earn you a few 'Brownie points'. Well they're only human aren't they?

If all else fails - ignore the above - do not take any action, do not change your ways one iota.

Chapter roundup

- You have by now learned the Senior Examiner's recommended method to approach this paper, and you have revised some analytical techniques.

- You have also been instructed in exam technique. And, should you intend to fail, perhaps for the pleasure of retaking the case study, we have even told you how to manage that as well.

- Now it is time for you to practise some real cases.

Part E
Learning from experience: ensuring you pass

Chapter 11

INTRODUCTION TO PAST CASES

> **This chapter covers the following topic.**
> 1 Practice on previous cases
> 2 Your first steps

1 PRACTICE ON PREVIOUS CASES

1.1 There is no better way to prepare for your examination than to practice on actual previous case studies used for CIM exams. This means systematically analysing the case study using the methodology described in Chapters 8 and 9 and then tackling the actual exam questions set using the techniques given in Chapter 10.

1.2 You will then see for yourself how the methodology and techniques work to ensure you pass. This will build up your confidence and of course your expertise. It will help you to avoid making costly errors in the examination paper and to make best possible use of the limited time available.

1.3 To make it easier for you we shall, after each stage of your analysis, give you examples of other students' analyses. These are not necessarily the best examples or in any way perfect analyses but rather the sort of acceptable standard you would normally get from a syndicate working under pressure.

1.4 Remember there is no one correct answer. Different people interpret the same data in different ways. The purpose of the analysis is to widen your perspectives so as to better understand the case situation and to identify its key issues.

1.5 The senior examiner in his Examiner's Report states 'A good case study should, given competent and thorough analysis, yield its key issues. These key issues should normally be the basis on which the examination questions are set, so as to preserve the integrity of the case'.

1.6 The first case study you are recommended to practice on is *FirstrATE Europe* as set for the CIM June 1995 examination and based upon the threats to an old-established organisation by advances in technology increased competition, and the after-effects of radical organisational change.

1.7 The first step is of course to read the case study which is presented on the following pages exactly how you would have received it through your letter box about four weeks before the exam.

Part E: Learning from experience: ensuring you pass

2 YOUR FIRST STEPS

2.1 You should now turn to Chapter 8 paragraphs 2.1 to 2.19 of this Tutorial Text for full details of how to conduct Steps 1 to 5 of the analysis namely:

(a) read the case;
(b) after an interval re-read the case;
(c) reflect on the instructions and candidates' brief;
(d) think yourself into the role and the situation;
(e) re-read the case and write a précis.

(NB. Most students need between three and six hours to complete these steps.)

2.2 Good luck!

Chapter 12

GRAVESEND TOWN CENTRE: CASE STUDY DOCUMENTATION

> **This chapter includes the case study information sent to candidates.**
> 1 Candidates' brief
> 2 Gravesend Town Centre: text
> 3 Appendices to Gravesend Town Centre: Bill's file contents

INTRODUCTORY NOTE

The first practice case is Gravesend Town Centre. It concern services in the public sector, so you need to think in terms of the 7P approach to the marketing mix for services and the wider target audiences associate with marketing in the public sector.

The Senior Examiner took the unusual step of issuing a special message to all students which was circulated with the case study and which is reproduced below.

Introduction

'As you receive your copy of the case study for the forthcoming examination I thought it would be worthwhile writing to you before you begin your preparation on the current case.

A case study examination is a new style of examination for most candidates and those who have not sat case exams before need to prepare carefully both before the examination and on the day itself. The case study, unfortunately, has a low pass rate - not because it is more difficult but, perhaps, because it is different!

Any wise marketer always learns from the mistakes of others. I urge you to read this paper carefully. You can avoid the most common mistakes made by previous candidates when you sit your examination next month.

As you begin your preparation this month you should think about the following points. Together these account for the majority of the failing scripts - every year!'

Do you know what the case study is looking for?

The Analysis and Decision (A&D) case study, as with all Diploma subjects, is testing your ability to apply the marketing theory that you possess. The examination is not a simple test of knowledge. To be sure of a pass in this case study you will need to convince the examiner not that you know (for example) what the Ansoff Matrix is but how you would apply it in the confines of the case study. Do you know what 'market penetration' means? Can you explain it in terms of the marketing mix required to implement it? The same applies to any models you think may be relevant.

The second problem candidates face is separating *analysis* from *decision*. Some marks will be acquired in the examination for analysis of case material but certainly the majority of the marks will be reserved for clear recommendations of action. It is always sad to see answers containing four of five pages of detailed SWOT or PEST analysis that might, at best, acquire 5 marks. The time spent writing out detailed analysis could often be much better employed justifying recommendations for marketing objectives, strategy evaluation and strategy choice with justifications where far greater marks can be obtained.

Part E: Learning from experience: ensuring you pass

Do you understand marketing?

The very core of marketing is the customer. The customer is the reason for an organisation's existence and customer satisfaction is the source of the organisation's profits.

Following this basic tenet of marketing, any strategy document needs to be based on an understanding of customer needs. Far too many papers are presented that ignore customer needs completely, preferring to identify short-term methods of selling more products. The resulting 'product push' or sales plans regularly fail to achieve a pass grade.

Do you understand what the customers in the case want? Can you differentiate between product features and benefits? Can you identify what makes the customers buy?

Remember too that, unlike other Diploma subjects, the Analysis and Decision case study has no set syllabus. Questions can span the subject matter of the entire Diploma syllabus (Planning and Control, Communications Strategy, International Strategy) and the full range of CIM Certificate and Advanced Certificate are all assumed knowledge.

Do you understand strategy?

Can you spot the difference between a strategy and a tactic? Remember that this is an examination of your ability to apply *Marketing strategy* to the organisation described in the case. Quite simply there are more marks to be obtained by your recommendations on the strategic issues (segmentation, differentiation, positioning, targeting, strategy evaluation, strategy choice etc) than there are to be gained from long explanations of the marketing mix.

Secondly, strategy is by its very nature longer term. You will normally be given a time frame in the case (often 5 years or longer) within which to base your answers. Short term plans, 1-2 years, are much more tactical in nature and tend not to gain pass grades. To be sure of success you must be thinking in the longer term.

Do you understand your role?

In each case study you will be given a clear role to play. You may be asked to assume the role of Chief Executive, Director, Marketing Manager or external consultant. It is important that you answer the case questions from that role consistent with the terms of reference that would normally apply in that role. For example, if you are placed in the role of marketing manager you can question certain aspects of the organisation (for example the mission statement if provided) but you cannot be expected to change them If, for example, you are placed in the role of external consultant you can advise the organisation but you have no executive control.

Can you present your answer in a definite structure?

You do not know the questions until the day of the examination but you may be able to see the areas that the questions will address. You are required to lay out your answer in report format. That is, you should work to construct a logical sequence to your thinking and use appropriate headings/sub-headings. There are a number of recommended approaches to the problem, you should choose one that suits you best. At the very least you should have very clear ideas to these two questions before the examination day.:

(a) What is wrong in the situation described?
(b) What are you going to do to put it right?

Are you presenting your own work?

The Analysis and Decision examination is a test of *your* ability to apply marketing strategy. Only work which is clearly the individual work of the candidate will be marked.

A number of candidates prepare for the case study examination in groups. This is encouraged. Unfortunately, too many students then simply copy down the group answers prepared before the examination and hope that this will be enough to pass. Such papers are quite easily identified by the examiners and they are normally *failed en masse*.

By all means use the strength of the group to make sense of the case study but be careful to develop and present your own solutions, in your own words, if you wish to pass.

The *additional information* is presented on the day of the examination precisely for the purpose of discouraging pre-prepared answers. The additional information will be extremely difficult to predict and will force you to think independently about the case organisation's strategy. *The additional information can be assessed separately and can account for up to 20% of marks awarded - do not ignore it.*

Are you prepared for examination day?

Finally it must be said that any amount of good preparation can easily be destroyed by bad examination technique on the day. If you have taken a 'mock' examination of a previous case study as part of your preparation you will know how difficult it is to read and understand the question, plan your answers and write down all you need to say - in just three hours. If you have not tried to do this under 'mock' examination conditions be warned that probably one third of all failures are caused by bad time management.

When you arrive in the examination room you should spend at least the first 20-25 minutes reading the question and planning your answers before you start writing. You should:

(a) read the questions and the additional information;

(b) understand what the additional information means;

(c) understand what the question are asking - precisely;

(d) plan your answers to each of the questions (based on your preparation but now incorporating the additional information);

(e) plan your time, by question, according to the marks allocated to each question.

Only when you are clear what you want to say and how you are going to say it should you start writing.

I and my examiners wish you every success.

Paul Fifield

Note that the paragraph numbers here have been inserted by BPP for ease of reference. You are unlikely to find such a numbering system in the case itself.

We will remind you of the essentials for each step/stage in panel form as before. Here we go then.

> CONSULT THE GUIDANCE NOTES IN
> CHAPTER 8 PARAGRAPHS 2.1 TO 2.19
>
> **STEP 1 READ THE CASE**
> **STEP 2 AFTER AN INTERVAL RE-READ THE CASE**
> **STEP 3 REFLECT ON THE INSTRUCTIONS AND CANDIDATES' BRIEF**
> **STEP 4 THINK YOURSELF INTO THE ROLE AND THE SITUATION**
> **STEP 5 RE-READ THE CASE AND WRITE A PRÉCIS IN NO MORE THAN 2 A4 SIDES**
>
> ALLOW YOURSELF BETWEEN 3 AND 6 HOURS FOR THESE STEPS

1 CANDIDATES' BRIEF

1.1 You are Bill Morrison, an independent marketing consultant specialising in marketing strategy assignments. You have been engaged by Brian Richmond, Town Centre Manager for Gravesham Council.

Part E: Learning from experience: ensuring you pass

1.2 You have long experience in marketing consultancy with a client list that spans a number of industry sectors. You have worked with clients in retailing, telecommunications, financial services, hotels, manufacturing and IT. This is the first time that you have been awarded an assignment in the public sector. The client was keen to recruit a consultant with strategic marketing expertise rather than experience in planning or town centre management in order to get a fresh and creative approach to the problem.

1.3 You have met with your client and collected all the information available on Gravesend Town Centre. You are to prepare a report of your initial recommendations to be presented to the Town Centre Manger and the Town Centre Initiative Steering Group on 14 June.

2 GRAVESEND TOWN CENTRE: TEXT

2.1 Bill Morrison walked into his office, automatically flicking on the light switch with his left hand. He dropped his briefcase on his desk with a dull thud and shrugged his coat off, laying it across the back of one of the chairs facing his desk. Running his hand through his damp hair, he crossed to the window and looked out. It was already getting dark on a wet, windy February afternoon. The rain suddenly hammered against the window panes as a squall of wind brought it against the side of the building. He watched as it formed into rivulets and they ran silently down the glass. It was depressing and he was depressed.

2.2 With a rather heartfelt sigh, he turned back to his desk, switching on the angle-poise lamp as he sat down. It had been an irritating drive down from the Midlands, long delays and a couple of hold ups on the M1 and M6 motorways. Perhaps it was some consolation that, for a change, the M25 motorway had been trouble-free as he had driven round the north of London and across the Dartford Bridge. But it was not the drive that had depressed him, it was what he had gone to see. He had driven north early the day before to look at what had happened to the once prosperous town of Dudley, situated on the south-west side of that sprawling conurbation in the middle of England called Birmingham. He had gone to see what can happen to a town centre when a large out-of-town shopping centre opens nearby. He had not liked what he had found.

2.3 Three weeks earlier, he had been delighted when his marketing consultancy, Fleetwork Marketing had been asked by the Economic Development Office of nearby Gravesham Borough Council to undertake a long-term strategic marketing study as part of Gravesend's Town Centre Initiative - a joint endeavour between public and private sector, bringing together the Borough council itself and Kent County Council on the one hand and retail organisations like Marks & Spencers and Boots on the other. Living nearby, in the village of Hook Green, he was aware that the Town Centre Initiative had put a lot of effort into sustaining Gravesend town centre and relished the chance to contribute his own knowledge and marketing experience.

2.4 Like anyone else, he had been conscious of the growth in out-of-town shopping centres during the *laissez-faire* days of the 1980s, but they had never particularly affected him. He had visited the vast Lakeside shopping complex on the other side of the Thames on a couple of occasions but had never really stopped to think about the effect such concentrated shopping precincts have on nearby towns and communities.

2.5 As his investigations had progressed, he had become familiar with names like Meadowhall near Sheffield and the Metro Centre near Newcastle. But the example that everyone seemed to quote was the Merry Hill Centre near Dudley. In the end, he had determined to see for himself, hence his visit the day before. It had been worse than he had imagined.

2.6 Apparently, Dudley council had approved planning permission for one million sq ft (92,900 sq metres) of retail shopping to be developed at Merry Hill, just two and a half miles (4 km) from Dudley Town Centre, in 1986. The new mall was opened three years

12: Gravesend Town Centre: case study documentation

later, in 1989, with free car parking for 10,000 cars and its own monorail with three stations. While no doubt the UK recession of the early 1990s and other factors had played their part, the overall effect on Dudley was devastating. Within four years all the town's major retailers, including British Home Stores, C&A, Littlewoods, Currys, Marks & Spencer, Next and Burtons - who had shops on Dudley's Market Place - had moved out. Tesco abandoned its 70,000 sq ft supermarket site and Sainsbury's did the same with their supermarket site in the once-thriving Trident Centre. Even Cooks department store, once a Dudley landmark, had shut. As 70% of its high-class shopping disappeared, rents plummeted by over 25% and only the amusement arcades, cheap markets and discount or charity shops could be induced to take up the vacant spaces as local independent shops closed down in response to the dramatic loss of shoppers and the absence of passing impulse purchasers.

2.7 As he had walked through the centre of Dudley, Bill had felt a real sense of loss. Many shops were boarded up, or had been taken over by low-value, second-hand goods sellers. 'To Let' and 'For Sale' signs sprouted from ground and first floor windows and the streets were strangely quiet and empty. It was, as he had read, what the Americans call 'doughnutisation'- trust them to come with a word like that, he had thought at the time. But now that he had seen it, he supposed it did capture something about the hollowing out of an entire town centre and the fact that all the 'dough' had moved to an outer ring.

2.8 Perhaps most of all, it was the scale, speed and completeness of the transformation that had shocked him. A once proud town centre now sadly decaying, while only a couple of miles away, cars and shoppers streamed in and out of what he suddenly felt was a garish neon-lit symbol of the consumerist 1980s. His problem, and what was depressing him, was the Gravesend might just be heading for the same destiny.

2.9 The enthusiasm for out-of-town shopping centres had waned after the 1980s as the impact they made became clear. The government's Department of the Environment, which had previously allowed market forces to work relatively unchecked, issued a new Planning Policy Guidance Document on Town Centres. This new guidance expressed the need to secure what it called 'the vitality and viability of town centres' and pointed out what planners should consider when looking at an application for an out-of-town centres. While 'it is not the function of the planning system to preserve existing commercial interest', it was important to ensure that 'the effects of competition should not be such as to deny access to retail facilities for significant sectors of society'. It even stressed that town centres should continue to offer 'a sense of place and community identity'. Much of this change of approach was also a response to the uncounted impact of the extra traffic flows that out-of-town centres tended to generate, the resulting extra pollution, the impact on people's health and perhaps particularly the social problems created for those without cars as well as the elderly and the disabled.

2.10 Bill knew the problem facing Gravesend was not only a local one. Out-of-town shopping and its effects on urban centres was an international problem. In 1992 the French Prime Minister, Edouard Balladur, announced a ban on all new out-of-town stores, particularly those near small rural towns until the Minister for Corporate and Economic Development has assessed their impact on 'the social fabric of rural communities'. In the United States the development of 'shopping malls' has slowed dramatically and commentators are busy trying to predict the next great leap in shopping fashion.

2.11 Bill got up and walked round his desk toward the maps on the facing wall that showed the whole area around Gravesend. He had persuaded the architect across the road to enlarge the maps for him, on his specialist photocopier, as soon as the consultancy had won the assignment. Perhaps for the hundredth time he stood a few feet away from them and took it all in.

2.12 Gravesend lay on the south side of the river Thames, opposite the port of Tilbury on the other shore. A dotted line showed where a passenger ferry still crossed the expanse of river between the two towns. The area covered by Gravesham Borough Council was shaped like a triangle, with one of its three sides running along the Thames and the other two meeting in an acute angle pointing due south. Dominated by the town of

Gravesend at the top, with a population of 56,000, the triangle spread far enough south to include around 20,000 acres of unspoiled north Kent country-side, much of which was designated as an Area of Outstanding Natural Beauty. To the west was the smaller town of Northfleet and so compact was the nature of Gravesham that eight per cent of the borough's total population of 92,000 resided within the two urban areas of Gravesend and Northfleet. Further west was Swanscombe, before you reached the M25 perimeter motorway around London - just ten minutes drive away. On the other side of the motorway was the town of Dartford which gave its name to the northbound tunnel under the Thames, and the southbound bridge over it, that between them provided the M25 with its Thames crossing. To the east, about 20 minutes drive away were Rochester, Gillingham and Chatham - the Medway towns - spread along the banks of the River Medway that joins the mouth of the Thames estuary some 20 miles downstream. The borough was intersected by the main A2 trunk road which connected London in the west with the Channel ports of Dover and Folkestone to the south east.

2.13 Bill knew the whole area was steeped in history. His mind flicked through the claims that Gravesend had on it. As he did so, he had a strange sense of history repeating itself. Gravesend had had its 'ups' and 'downs' through the ages but, overall, it felt as if the 'downs' had been more serious than the 'ups'!

2.14 The town's market charter dates from the 13th century and a weekly market still flourished to this day. During the 16th century, in Tudor times, Gravesend had a population of about 2,000 and was incorporated within the area covered by the Elizabethan Port of London. While the French port of Calais remained in English hands, the town flourished since travellers came though Gravesend on their way to Dover. When Calais was lost to the French in 1558, there was an abrupt halt to this traffic and the town's trade suffered badly. Matters were only made worse when the plague hit Gravesend in 1563, killing 247 people, over 10% of the population.

2.15 During Elizabethan times, Crown officials were stationed in the town to search for illegal imports, fugitives wanting to cross the Channel to the Continent and, of course, to collect taxes and dues. A pub, The Three Daws, built in 1565, still stands on the Gravesend waterfront. It had harboured smugglers through several centuries, and later hid those trying to avoid the notorious press-gangs of the 18th century, who pressed ignorant citizens into joining the Navy.

2.16 In fact, Gravesend had remained the main customs house for the Port of London and ships were obliged to stop at Gravesend on their way up the Thames to await the visit of the customs officers known as Searchers. This provided work of every sort for the townspeople, especially the waterferrymen who rowed between the moored ships carrying passengers, supplies and busy officials. Unfortunately, when the new docks were built in London itself, during the early 19th century, the Customs Office moved to London in 1825 and thereafter ships by-passed Gravesend on their way up the river. What seagoing traffic there was, tended to be outward bound emigrant ships which only stopped briefly at Gravesend pausing, before their lengthy sea crossings, to take on last minute supplies or to hove-to while they awaited better weather.

2.17 However, coincidentally, Gravesend was developing a reputation as one of the first seaside resorts in Europe. Close to the ever-growing population of the capital, bathing machines had been installed at Gravesend as early as 1796, and what was later to become the Clifton Hotel offered 'Warm and Cold Salt Water Baths' for those who chose not to bathe in the river. Pleasure steamboats brought visitors from London out to Gravesend in the early 19th century to see the zoological gardens, listen to a resident band and enjoy the bracing air, and the Town's waterferrymen found new work bringing the steamboat's passengers ashore. When the town council proposed, in 1831, to build a pier which would enable passengers to come directly ashore, whatever the tide, the waterferrymen expressed their violent opposition. When the necessary Bill for building the pier was passed in the House of Lords on 22 June 1833, the waterferrymen rioted and local troops had to be brought in to restore order. Unfortunately, the new pier, called Town Quay Pier, completed by the council in 1834, soon faced competition from a new private pier - The Royal Terrace Pier - which charged users less. This cut-throat competition and the overall cost of building the Town Quay Pier eventually bankrupted the town's Corporation. For the waterferrymen, and therefore much of the towns prosperity, things went from bad to worse. The cross-river ferry between Gravesend and Tilbury was taken over by The London, Tilbury and Southend Railway Company in 1852. To add insult to injury, they immediately introduced paddle steamboats and then built yet another pier, with a rail link, at West Street in Gravesend. By the time that the Tilbury docks were completed in 1886, there were few waterferrymen left, although the Town Quay Pier and the Royal Terrace Pier still existed, in various states of repair, and added to the interest of Gravesend's riverside.

2.18 These effects on the town's main source of employment were, however, mitigated by its new-found role as a holiday resort. In 1844, no less than one million visitors came to Gravesend during the holiday season. But, here again, the continuing extension of the railways meant that, soon afterwards, fashionable visitors moved on to new resorts further afield, like Southend and Margate. In the meantime, Gravesend evolved into a popular resort for the lower and middle classes, who either came just for the day or stayed in lodging houses in the town. Nevertheless, Gravesend's Rosherville Gardens, which boasted a bear pit, an aviary and a monkey cage, could still attract up to 30,000 visitors on a Bank Holiday weekend and remained popular until the end of the 19th century. However, the wider attractions of local tea gardens serving fresh shrimps and watercress (both local produce) and the panoramic views from nearby Windmill Hill failed to attract visitors toward the end of the century as the river became too dirty to bathe in (or to fish for shrimps) and the endless progression of the railways made yet newer destinations the latest and most fashionable holiday resorts.

2.19 Typically, thought Bill, economic cycles sweep all before them. In fact, once again most of the economic functions of the Thames river were now controlled from Gravesend, with the headquarters of the Port of London Authority, Thames Navigation Services, the Sea and River Pilots and the Customs & Excise for the south-east region, as well as other associated maritime activities currently located in the town. Not only had this historical area of activity returned, but also the river Thames had been cleaned and was suitable for leisure activities, including fishing, once more. What is impressive is the resilience that a local community has. Noticing that time had sped past as he recalled the past, he realised that it was completely dark outside and that he had rather distractedly said good-night to his secretary as she left for the weekend while he was in the middle of his reverie. Sensing every more strongly that he was just a part of Gravesend's history he walked across to his drinks cupboard. It was already 6.30 and he could hear the swish of tyres on the wet road outside. Happy to stay in the warm, well-lit space of his office, he poured himself a single measure of Scotch Whisky. Spinning the glass absent-mindedly in his hand, he looked back at the map. 'Am I', he wondered, 'just another small part of the endless evolution of a community?' 'Did anyone think about Gravesend and a "product" or a "service" before? Or did everyone just react to what was happening to them after the event?' He took a sip of his whisky and allowed himself to drift with time again. After all, it was Friday evening!

2.20 Who else was involved with Gravesend? The literature said that Charles Dickens was a local. In fact, Charles Dickens had honeymooned in the nearby village of Chalk and then lived for most of his life in Gads Hill Place, just outside the town. Unfortunately, he had not thought too much of the Gravesend of the time, thinly disguising it as Muggletown in *The Pickwick Papers*! Apart from Charles Dickens, the other two names associated with Gravesend were General Gordon, who had lived there before going to the Sudan to meet his death and Pocahontas, the native American princess who had married an Englishman and visited England in 1616. She and her husband had arrived in Gravesend to return to Virginia in 1617, but she had fallen ill and died before they sailed. Sadly thought Bill, nobody quite knew where she was buried and so, although the Disney film about Pocahontas, released in 1995, had dramatically increased the number of visitors to Gravesend and put the town on the American Heritage Trail (designed for American tourists), there was some doubt about how long the connection would remain a tourist attraction.

2.21 As far as the town itself was concerned, Bill knew that due to a series of fires in the 18th and 19th centuries, many of Gravesend's oldest buildings were destroyed so its finest buildings today tend to be Victorian, built as the town expanded rapidly in the middle and late 19th century. As a shopping centre, it was fine. Major retail stores in the town included W H Smith, boots, Marks & Spencer, British Home Stores, Mothercare, Woolworths, Debenhams and Argos as well as the two supermarkets, J Sainsbury and Tesco. Just beside the town centre, Asda and Great Mills had opened large stores, along with B&Q, Comet, Halfords, PetCity and Fads. The Anglesea Centre within the town had twenty shops, including a Safeway supermarket.

2.22 Bill had also looked closely at patterns of employment and knew that local industry was concentrated in a half mile strip that ran along the river's edge. Here well known names such as Blue Circle, Scott, AEI, GEC, Brittania Refined Metals and Rodenstock manufactured products as diverse as electric cables, refined metals, cement, paper tissue and optical lenses. There were several important riverside wharves with modern cargo and storage facilities on this section of the river. The resident workforce in the borough was 45,000 with some 22% of the employment being in the manufacturing sector while 66% were in the service sector and a further 7% in construction. Unlike the rest of Kent, Gravesend also had a rich cultural mix. It has an ethnic population of approximately eight thousand, drawn mainly from the Indian Sub-continent and predominantly Sikh by religion. This significant minority had its roots in the Punjab, in India, and offered an important diversity and character to the town.

2.23 Gravesend itself was less than an hour away from the port of Dover and Gatwick airport by road, and 45 minutes from Central London by train. Rail services were also frequent with Gravesend having four trains an hour into Charing Cross for most of the day and because the Gravesham area was served by two main train routes, it was possible to catch services to other central London termini - Waterloo, Cannon Street and Victoria as well as Charing Cross. In fact today about half the local workforce commuted to jobs in central and south east London.

2.24 Bill remembers only too well what Gravesend had been like at the start of the 1990s. Heavy traffic in the town centre, lack of easy parking and the draw of the newly opened Lakeside shopping centre across the Thames had left shoppers and shopkeepers alike in dismay. In the last 1980s council and local commercial interest united and, galvanised by the Marks & Spencer roadshow 'Going to Town', initiated the Town Centre Initiative in 1992 which proposed pedestrianising parts of the shopping centre. Coincidentally, a new role was emerging elsewhere, that of Town Centre Manger. The London Borough of Redbridge had appointed the first one in the UK, in 1986, as an idea that had grown in the United States during the 1960s and 1970s spread to England. By 1992, the number of Town Centre Managers in the UK had reached 45 with Kent County Council playing a leading role in promoting the idea. By 1995 there were 14 Town Centre Managers in Kent alone. The Gravesend scheme was started in early 1991 and was one of the first. In February 1991, the Gravesham Borough Council launched a booklet calling for intensive town centre improvement and in September 1992 a Town Centre Initiative for Gravesend was created, jointly supported by Gravesham Borough Council, Kent County Council and the local private sector including the Gravesham Chamber of Trade and Industry. Boots and Marks & Spencer added their weight to the initiative as they had done in other towns in the UK. Because of the joint nature of the way in which the initiative was planned, a large number or working groups were set up, involving 60 people drawn from a wide range of interests. Together these groups looked at every aspect of the town centre. The Town Centre Initiative (TCI) came up with an eight point plan.

1	A safe, clean town centre designed for pedestrians
2	Well-signposted access routes
3	Attractive and reasonably priced parking
4	Good public transport
5	More jobs in the town centre itself
6	Comprehensive improvements to selected areas of the town
7	Promotional events and activities
8	Greater emphasis on the town's major asset - the riverfront

2.25 Between 1992 and 1995 some £1 million had been invested by the Borough council in environmental improvements and the partnership created between the public and private sector had paid dividends. Local traders had become sufficiently involved to create two groups - one for independent retailers and one for the large multiples. The newly appointed Town Centre Manager, who was a former town centre retailer himself and a former president of Gravesham Chamber of Trade and Industry, was welcomed by traders in Gravesend, both large and small, and acted as a focal point for concerns, ideas and promotional activities.

2.26 While the real role of a Town Centre Manager was still emerging, it soon became clear that it involved the co-ordination, motivation and organisation of different participants and an ability to act as the town centre's 'champion' rather than the job of direct control. It also became apparent that changing the way a town centre works is not a job for one person, and that just appointing a manager was not a substitute for gaining everyone's commitment and involvement.

2.27 The result had been a very different town centre with attractive street lighting, repaved streets and pavements, cast iron name plates for streets, tubs of flowers, new signposting, large scale pedestrianisation and easy and abundant parking (some of it free) with four clearly identified 'gateway' access routes to the centre. Good lighting and video camera surveillance was provided in car parks, street and pavement cleaning was made a priority, environmental improvements were made to buildings and public areas, new bus shelters and public seating were added, buildings were re-furbished, a 'hit-squad' dealt with graffiti on walls and illegal posters, while changes were made to the highway network to improve traffic flow. Apart from financial contributions from retailers Marks & Spencers and Boots, the industrial company Blue Circle Industries and the owners of both the Anglesea and St George's shopping centres contributed funds. Several companies committed resources in terms of staff secondments while others such as the Halifax Building Society (a savings and loans society), the TSB and Midland Bank, and three national supermarket chains (Safeway, Sainsburys and Tesco) contributed to specific projects such as the refurbishment of the market place and the paving of the pedestrian centre of the town.

2.28 The TCI continued with a Steering Group and five working groups whose membership was drawn from both the public and private sector: the TCI's five working groups were Access and Transport; Environmental Improvements; Environmental Maintenance; Promotions and Events; and Quality of Life/Security. The developing success of the TCI and the ability this brought to enter into a dialogue with the various bodies involved led to the formation of two new retail groups in Gravesend. The 'Retail Strategy Group' representing the multiple retailers and the 'Business in Gravesend - Action Group' representing independent retailers. The TCI also encompassed representatives from schools, community groups and special interest groups.

2.29 While the success of the initiative was recognised, referred to and learnt from by towns elsewhere in the UK, more change was on its way. The 'Thames Gateway' was the name created in 1994 by the government for its future vision for the area along the Thames to the East of London. Extending from Docklands, in London itself, the area stretched to Tilbury on the north side of the Thames and to the mouth of the river on the south side. Gravesend was one of many towns within this area. Identified as an area which presented very real opportunities for growth, the *Regional Planning Guidance for the South East 1994* stated that 'this part of London, South Essex and Kent has the capacity over the longer term...to accept significant levels of housing and employment development, alongside improvements in environmental quality'. It was foreseen that it would 'benefit particularly from planned transport infrastructure investment' and that its location 'close to the heart of London, yet well related to the Channel Tunnel and the improving links to the expanding continental markets, creates the potential to attract higher levels of investment'.

2.30 The end to the controversy over the siting of the Channel Tunnel Rail Link (CTRL) was to bring Gravesend close to the heart of these infrastructure developments. Ebbsfleet, an area between Northfleet and Swanscombe, just a few miles to the west of

Gravesend town centre was chosen as the site for a new International and Domestic Passenger Station on the CTRL.

(a) Announced in August 1994, and to be called Ebbsfleet International Station, it was seen by both national and local government as a unique opportunity for a new focus of growth in the entire South East. In particular, it was seen as a new employment centre, bringing local job opportunities for those in the area who had to commute into London to find work. It was also seen as providing a 'major contribution to the regeneration of the Dartford/Gravesend area' because it would be the sort of development that can underpin 'a quality housing market, necessary for securing lasting regeneration'.

(b) Close to Ebbsfleet was a site known as Eastern Quarry which had 250 hectares (620 acres) of developable land and government planning guidance saw this as a suitable site for the creation of a 'high quality, compact, mixed use development in the form of an "urban village"' although work would not commence until 2005.

(c) North of Ebbsfleet, two other development, Greenhithe Waterfront and Swanscombe Peninsula, would be additional housing areas. Work on Greenhithe would begin in 1997 and be completed by around 2005. Building on Swanscombe Peninsula, jutting out into the Thames, would begin in 2003 with probable completion by 2005. Overall the Government foresaw around 30,000 new houses could be built in the Dartford and Gravesend area, nearly one third of all new residential development in the Thames Gateway. Some 45,000 jobs are envisaged in this area.

2.31 Apart from housing, the siting of both a new campus for Greenwich University and the creation of the London Science Park at Dartford, as well as the continuing development of nearby Crossways, the largest mixed use business and distribution park in the UK, meant that forces and pressures for change were likely to be considerable. The new station at Ebbsfleet, which would become operational along with the rest of the CTRL in 2002, was seen as a place where many of those arriving from the continent would 'choose to leave the train ... rather than going into central London. For many, Ebbsfleet will become the main gateway to London and the rest of the country'. The station would have regular direct services via Lille to Paris and Brussels with a journey time of 2 hours 15 minutes to Paris and about 1 hour 55 minutes to Brussels. Separately, the domestic service from the station would run to St Pancras in London with an expected journey time of just 17 minutes.

2.32 In order to take forward the Government's framework plan for Thames Gateway a new partnership was formed between the Dartford and Gravesham Borough Councils. Kent County Council, Blue Circle Industries (the major landowner) and the University of Greenwich. The partnership published its long term vision for Kent Thameside which took a 20-30 year perspective and was widely welcomed locally. One of its five basic themes was to ensure that the town centres of Dartford and Gravesend 'keep their traditional range of shopping, commercial premises and entertainment venues.' And that, thought Bill as he looked at his watch and noticed it was already 8.30, was the problem.

2.33 In 1990, despite opposition from Gravesham Borough Council, planning permission had been granted by the Government for the development of 150,000 square metres of retailing floor space in Dartford just five miles down the road from Gravesend Town centre. Sited in the dramatic setting of a vast former chalk pit, it was called *Bluewater* and would be the largest out-of-town shopping centre in the UK. The anchor stores of John Lewis Partnership, Marks & Spencer and House of Fraser have been secured. Building work started in 1995 and the centre is due to open during 1998. It was expected that 5,000 new jobs would be created at Bluewater.

2.34 Whatever way you looked at it, thought Bill, things happen to Gravesend! Now it faced yet another longer term threat to its vitality as a community and a potentially serious one at that. And he was trying to think of a solution. He had four weeks before the presentation that he had to make on 14 June and he would need all the time he could find. What, he wondered, would be the shape of the strategic plan he had to prepare?

How much was a town centre like Gravesend at the mercy of external forces, many of which, as in the past, were outside its control? Or could it take a positive lead and shape the effects to its own advantage?

2.35 Bill had an impressive client list and had helped many organisations to develop their marketing strategies. He tended to work for clients in a range of industrial sectors but had never before tackled a situation like this. He had tendered for the contract because he was interested in his local area. The Town Centre Manager had been instrumental in awarding Bill's company with the contract precisely because he had no previous experience in town planning issues so would be forced to fall back on basic marketing strategy principles. The client has faith, thought Bill, although now that he had started to dig into the problem he was starting to wonder how he could apply his strategic marketing skills to Gravesend.

2.36 Bill was never keen to work weekends but thought that if he took the file home he might gain a fresh perspective. He quickly looked through his file to make sure everything was in there ... .

Part E: *Learning from experience: ensuring you pass*

3 APPENDICES TO GRAVESEND TOWN CENTRE: BILL'S FILE CONTENTS

Ref	Subject matter	Paragraph
A	Client letter	3.1
B	Key retailer profiles	3.2
C	Location maps (4)	3.3
D	Gravesham Household Expenditure Survey, 1993	3.4
E	Customer Needs Survey, 1993	3.5
F	Town Centre Initiative Vision - ten point plan	3.6
	- steering group structure	3.6 (a)
G	Thames Gateway - selected maps and tables	3.7 (b)
H	The Channel Tunnel Rail Link	3.8
I	Bluewater	3.9

Appendix A: Client letter

3.1

Gravesend Town Centre Initiative
Windmill House, Cygnet Street, Gravesend, Kent. DA12 2AB

To: Mr W Morrison
Managing Director
Fleetwood Marketing Ltd
37-29 Western Road
Dartford, Kent DA1 3GQ

19 November 1995

Dear Bill

Re: Marketing Strategy - Gravesend Town Centre

I am pleased to be able to write and confirm officially that Fleetwood Marketing has been selected to help the steering group develop a marketing strategy for the longer term development of Gravesend town centre.

As I told you over the telephone, the group was particularly impressed by your work with previous clients and the fact that you have not worked on this type of project before suggests that you will be able to help us develop some good ideas based on solid marketing principles rather than conventional wisdom. I am looking forward to your initial report on June 14.

As agreed, your report which you will be presenting to the steering group in June will cover our initial planning period up to 2005.

Gravesend town centre is under threat from the combination of the shift to out-of-town food retailing and two regional shopping centres on its doorstep - Lakeside and the proposed Blue Water Park. Change in the town is inevitable. The town centre's competition is well managed, is marketing driven and has large promotional budgets. Gravesend has begun to fight back by setting up a Town Centre Management initiative and has successfully completed some major environmental and security driven projects. However, some vital questions remain unanswered ie:

(a) What is/will be its new market position, is there a niche market it can develop?
(b) Who will be its target markets and what are their needs?
(c) How can their needs be met?
(d) If new retailers need attracting to the town, what promotional strategy does it follow?
(e) Is the current management marketing driven? If not, how will it need to change etc, etc.

In other words, a marketing plan is missing.

This is, of course, just our thinking around the problem and, as you know, we are not trained marketers. You will no doubt have your own ideas as to the nature of the problems which we face and how we should go about solving them.

To compound the problem, any planning authority only has certain powers. We can plan - pedestrianisation, cleaning, compulsory purchase etc. We can stop people doing certain things but we cannot specify or reject certain shops from setting up business. We can offer grants to attract certain businesses but funds in this area are severely limited. Out-of-town shopping centres can negotiate as landlords to attract certain businesses in a way that we cannot. Anything we may want to do will have to be done by consultation and negotiation. Some funds may be available for promotional purposes but again we rely on businesses to promote themselves.

I have enclosed:

(a) Gravesend Town Centre Initiative Annual Review 1994
(b) A Customer's Needs Survey 1993
(c) Gravesham Household Expenditure Survey.

I look forward to seeing you on 14 June.

Yours sincerely

Brian Richmond

Brian Richmond, Town Centre Manager

Part E: Learning from experience: ensuring you pass

Appendix B: Key retailer profiles

3.2

	MULTPILE RETAILERS*	
	Argos	Discount catalogue outlet - wide range of products
	Asda	Supermarket, mainly food
	B&Q	Discount home maintenance and decoration products
	Boots	Pharmacy and cosmetics
	British Home Stores	Variety store, clothing and household goods
	Comet	Discount domestic electrical products
	Debenhams	Variety store, clothing and household goods
	FADS	Home decoration
	Great Mills	Discount household and home maintenance products
	Halfords	Motoring and cycle products
	House of Fraser	Variety store, clothing, fashions and household
	John Lewis	Variety store, clothing, fashions and household
	Marks & Spencer	Clothing and chilled food
	Mothercare	Children and baby products
	PetCity	Pet products
	Safeway	Supermarket, mainly food
	Sainsbury	Supermarket, mainly food
	W H Smith	Specialist stationery, books, greeting cards and records (audio)
	Tesco	Supermarket, mainly food
	Woolworth	Video, records (audio), clothing and toys

* Multiple retailers are outlets that form part of a national chain. These stores often have outlets in most important shopping areas in the UK.

Appendix C: Location maps

3.3 (a)

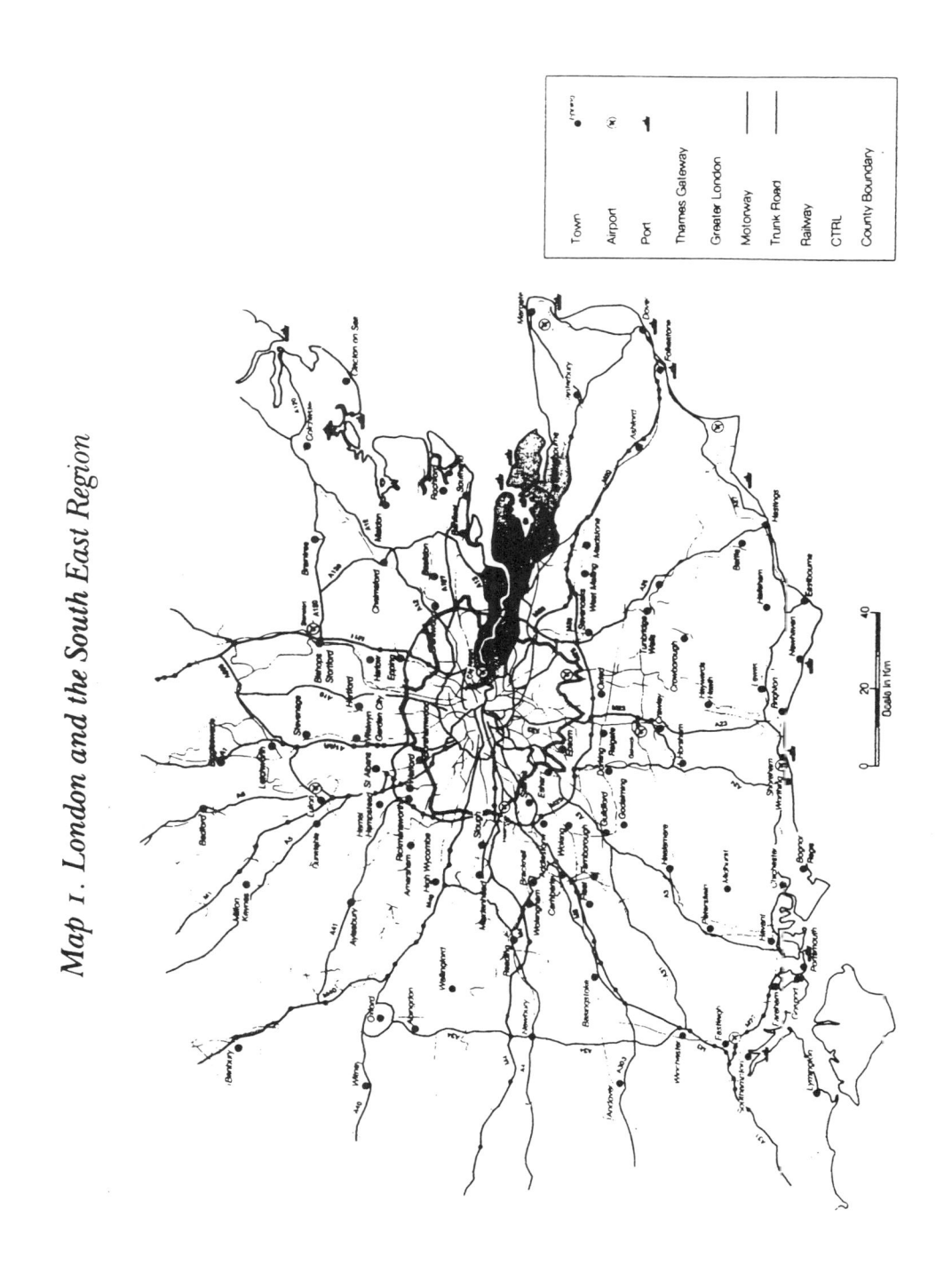

Map 1. London and the South East Region

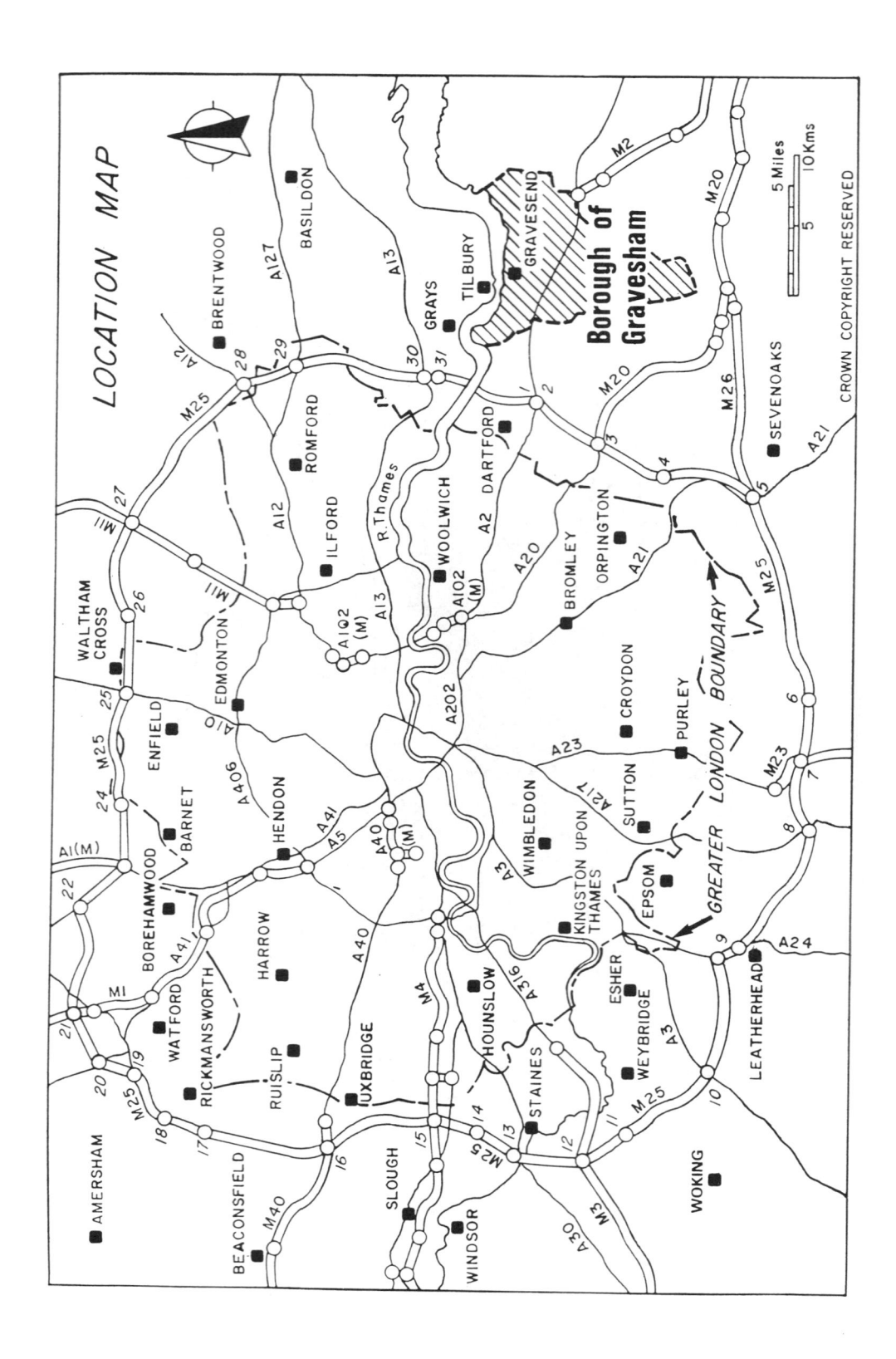

Part E: Learning from experience: ensuring you pass

LOCATION MAP

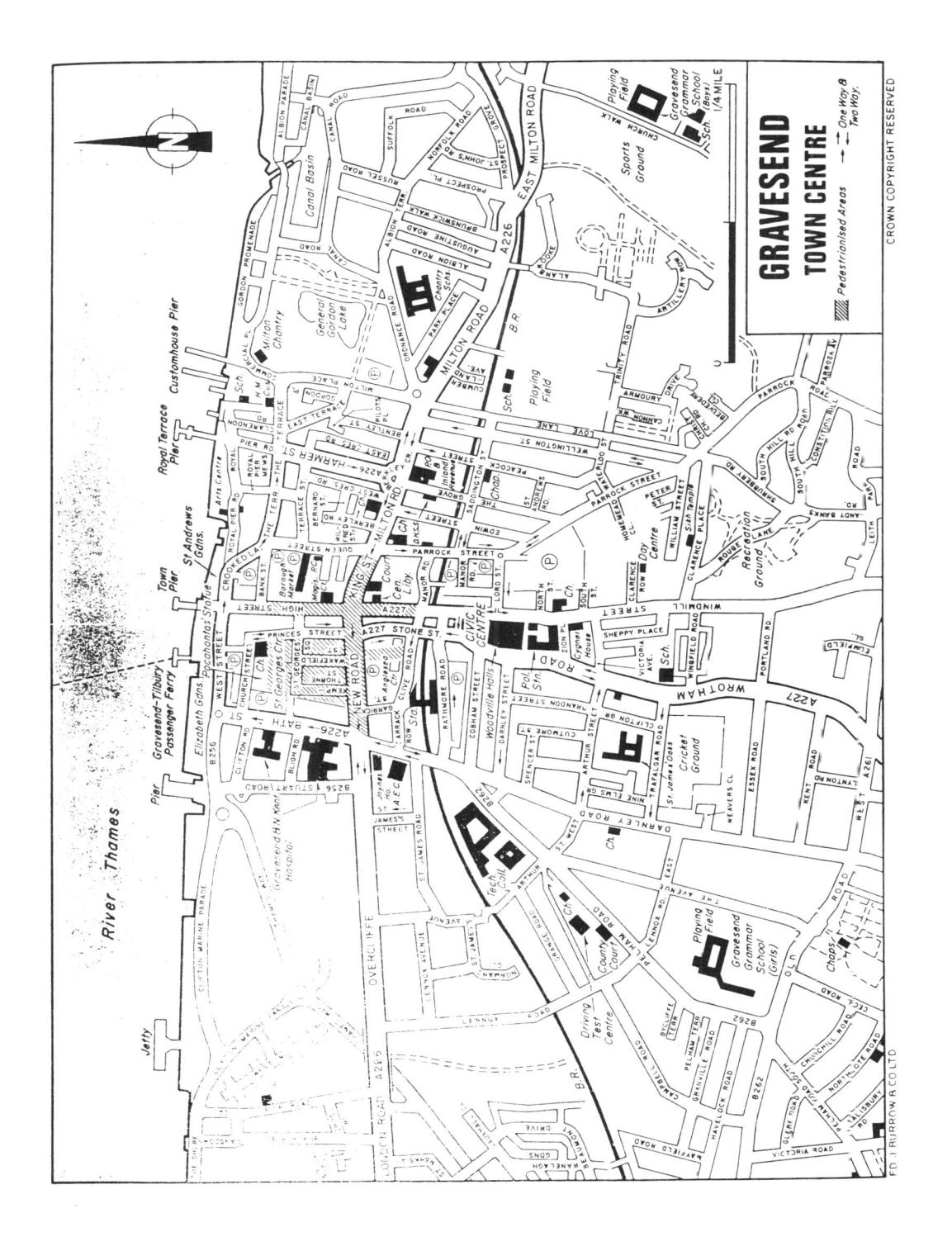

12: Gravesend Town Centre: case study documentation

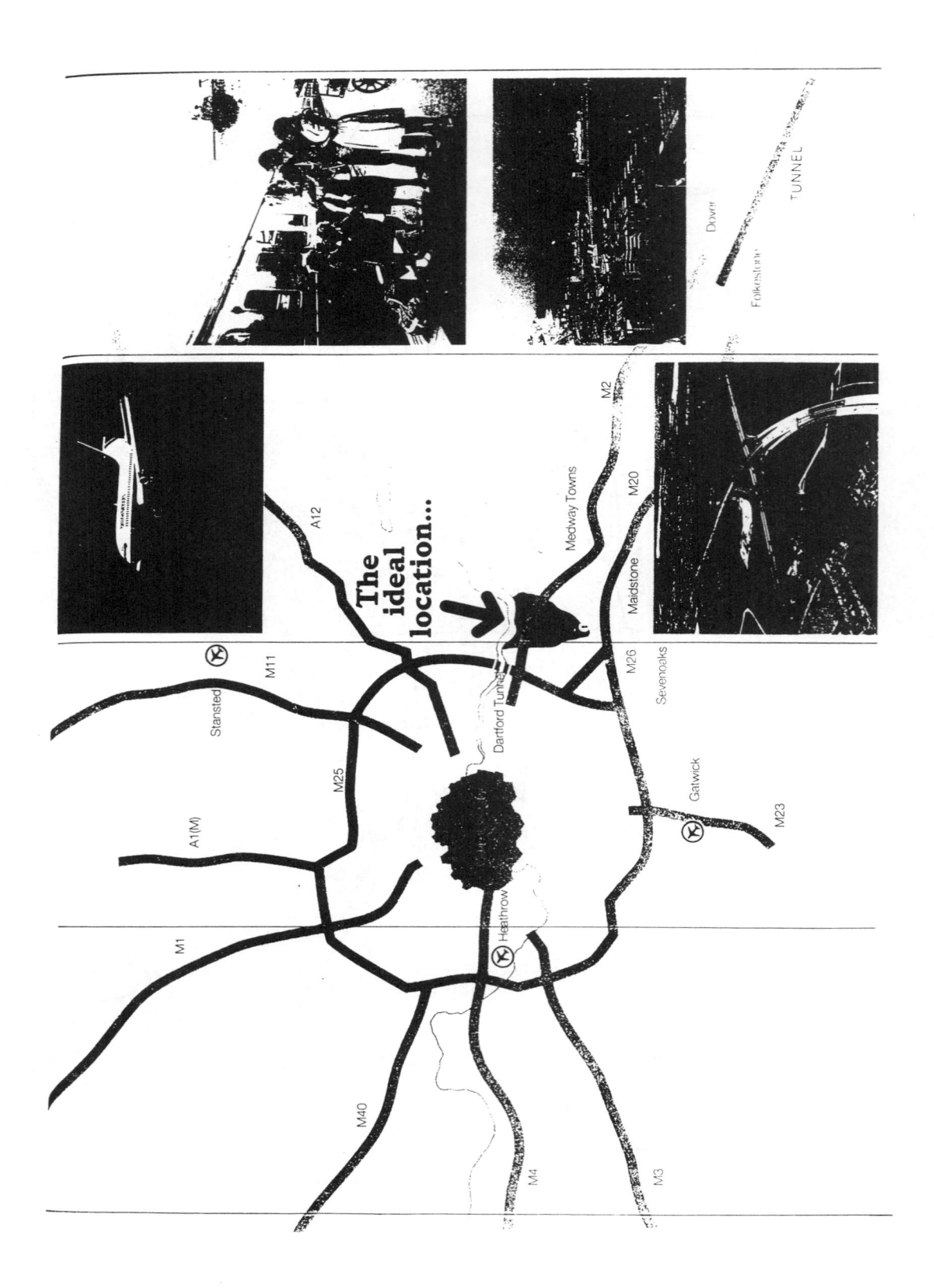

Notes   *Part E: Learning from experience: ensuring you pass*

Appendix D: Gravesham Household Expenditure Survey, 1993

3.4

GRAVESHAM

HOUSEHOLD EXPENDITURE 1993

A Profile of Gravesham Residents

> Contents
> (a) Introduction
> (b) Demography
> (c) Socio-economic status
> (d) Household expenditure
> (e) 'Mobile' household expenditure
> (f) Placement of 'mobile' expenditure
> (g) Summary

(a) *Introduction*

This document offers a brief profile of Gravesham's population, including local buying behaviour patterns, purchasing power and general economic status.

Designed to be of use to both current and potential town centre retailers, the information contained can help existing retailers decide on expansion plans or the planning of future product ranges.

It also enables prospective new retailers to Gravesham to make an informed decision on whether to locate here.

Market research data has established that local purchasing power is significantly higher than National averages. This factor, enhanced by an effective Town Centre Initiative partnership between the private and public sectors and backed up by the advantages of good transport links (and town centre car parking) makes Gravesham a good retail location.

(b) *Demography*

(i) The following two tables give the predicted actual numbers and proportions of males and females in certain age ranges over the next decade residing in Gravesham.

Numbers

Age range	1991 M	1991 F	1996 M	1996 F	2001 M	2001 F
0-14	8,800	8,600	9,000	8,700	9,200	8,800
15-24	6,600	6,800	5,600	5,600	5,100	5,200
25-44	13,700	12,900	13,700	12,500	13,400	11,900
45-59/64	10,600	8,300	10,900	8,900	10,700	8,800
60/65+	5,800	10,500	6,200	10,700	6,500	10,800
Total	45,500	47,100	45,400	46,500	44,900	45,400

	1991	1996	2001
Total M+F	92,600	91,400	90,300

Present proportion (%) Gravesham

Age range	1991 M	1991 F	1996 M	1996 F	2001 M	2001 F
0-14	19.3	18.3	19.8	18.7	20.5	19.4
15-24	14.5	14.4	12.3	12.0	11.4	11.5
25-44	30.1	27.4	30.2	26.9	29.8	26.2
45-59/64	23.3	17.6	24.0	19.1	23.8	19.4
60/65+	12.7	22.3	13.7	23.0	14.5	23.8

(ii) By way of comparison, a similar table giving the percentage proportions for England and Wales is given below.

Present proportion (%) England and Wales

Age range	1991 M	1991 F	1996 M	1996 F	2001 M	2001 F
0-14	20.0	18.1	20.7	18.9	20.9	19.1
15-24	14.8	13.5	12.9	11.8	12.7	11.6
25-44	30.2	28.6	30.0	28.5	29.4	27.9
45-59/64	21.9	16.2	23.1	17.8	23.8	18.6
60/65+	13.1	23.6	13.2	23.1	13.3	22.8

(iii) Broadly, the trends for Gravesham mirror those for England and Wales, although there are clearly differences in detail.

(iv) The most significant feature of these statistics is that over the forecast period the numbers and proportion of people of working age in the youngest age groups tend to decrease, particularly so for those up to 24.

(c) *Socio-economic status*

(i) *Socio-economic groups.* The diagram below depicts a comparison of the proportions of socio-economic groups in Gravesham with the relevant proportions for Kent and Great Britain.

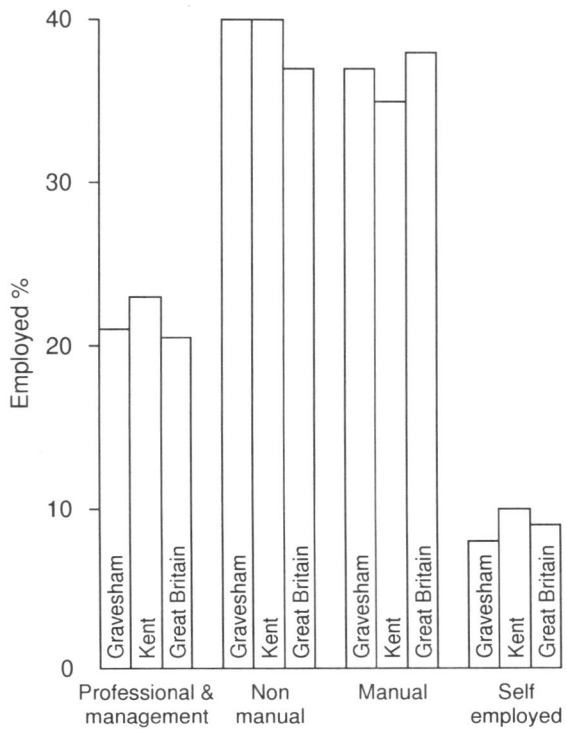

(ii) The proportion of manual workers, whilst higher than that of Kent, is lower than the national average.

(iii) At the other end of the skill range, the proportion of professional and managerial workers, which is lower than that for Kent, is slightly higher than the national average.

(iv) It will be noted that the data is derived from the 1981 Census. Whilst there is some reason to believe that the proportion of socio-economic groups for Gravesham have since shifted in favour of the more skilled groups (eg professional and managerial workers) detailed confirmation of the extent that the relationship with regional and national trends must await the publication of the 1991 census in 1993.

Part E: Learning from experience: ensuring you pass

(v) *ACORN profile: households*

The profile categorises housing stock according to certain criteria, viz

		1990 Gravesham households
A	Agricultural areas	0
B	Modern family housing, higher incomes	8,268
C	Older housing of intermediate status	4,744
D	Older terraced housing	1,783
E	Council estates - category I	4,718
F	Council estates - category II	3,319
G	Council estates - category III	1,550
H	Mixed inner metropolitan areas	1,755
I	Higher status non-family areas	922
J	Affluent suburban housing	5,476
K	Better off retirement areas	149

(vi) Whereas the proportion of privately owned (or rented) housing in Gravesham is similar to the national average (70.7% against 70.3%) the combined proportion of housing categorised either as *modern family housing, higher incomes* or as *affluent suburban housing* is distinctly *better* than the national average (42.1% against 32.1%).

(vii) Similarly, whereas the proportion of *council housing* in Gravesham is close the national average (29.3% against 29.7%), the proportion of *category I* is rather better than the national average (14.4% against 12.6%).

(d) *Household expenditure*

(i) The following table gives a comparison of the estimated *actual weekly expenditure* pattern of the 33,043 households in the Borough with notional estimates of a similar number of households based on national and regional expenditure patterns.

	National £	Rest of south east (ROSE) £	Gravesham(1) £	Gravesham(2) £
Housing	1,227,000	1,552,000	1,306,000	1,319,000
Fuel, light and power	348,000	357,000	359,000	354,000
Food	1,321,000	1,446,000	1,441,000	1,448,000
Alcohol	310,000	299,000	330,000	341,000
Tobacco	152,000	134,000	165,000	168,000
Clothing and footwear	492,000	536,000	531,000	546,000
Household goods	618,000	730,000	655,000	669,000
Household services	323,000	401,000	332,000	338,000
Personal goods and services	275,000	313,000	294,000	299,000
Motoring	922,000	1,079,000	1,058,000	1,095,000
Travel	169,000	200,000	185,000	193,000
Leisure goods	341,000	411,000	380,000	398,000
Leisure services	614,000	751,000	658,000	652,000
Miscellaneous	28,000	30,000	33,000	35,000
Total	£7,140,000	£8,239,000	£7,737,000	£7,855,000

Gravesham (1) - based on distribution of type of household
Gravesham (2) - based on distribution of socio-economic group of head of household

Source data: Expenditure patterns household survey 1988/89.

(ii) The two estimates of expenditure patterns of Gravesham residents, derived via two somewhat different routes, agree well with one another.

(iii) The total expenditure of Gravesham residents is noticeably higher than the national average but rather less than that of Rest of South East (ROSE). This might be seen a confirmation of the commonly held subjective view of Gravesham, ie situated in the prosperous South East but one of its poorer relations. One feature worthy of note, though, is that about one half of the difference between Gravesham and ROSE can be accounted for by lower expenditure on housing in Gravesham. This does lend substance to the view that in the context of the South East, Gravesham is one of the more competitive housing areas.

(iv) Similar to the expenditure levels on housing, Gravesham residents spend more than the national average on household goods, but less when compared with ROSE.

(v) The other interesting point to note is that when examining clothing and footwear, Gravesham residents not only spend more than the national average but compare favourably with ROSE.

(e) *'Mobile' household expenditure*

(i) The categories of expenditure listed in the table under (d)(i) each have several elements of expenditure within them. The title of this section is used to indicate those elements of expenditure where there can be considerable variation in the place where the expenditure is made, ie locally or outside the immediate area. For the purpose of this definition, most housing costs, fuel light and power, and food expenditures are, for example, termed wholly local expenditures; whereas household goods expenditure, which can be made either locally or elsewhere, is designated 'mobile'. The distinction is necessarily somewhat arbitrary.

(ii) Mobile expenditure is of crucial importance in considering the competitiveness of the Borough's shopping facilities, particularly those of Gravesend town centre, and therefore relates most directly to the Town Centre Initiative.

(iii) A table similar to that of paragraph (d)(i) has been compiled but restricted to mobile expenditure.

'Mobile' household expenditure

	National £	Rest of south east (ROSE) £	Gravesham £
Housing			
Repairs, maintenance and decoration	186,000	159,000	201,000
Food			
Meals bought away from home	275,000	616,000	301,000
Clothing and footwear			
All types	429,000	636,000	531,000
Household goods			
Furniture	163,000	180,000	176,000
Floor coverings	83,000	107,000	80,000
Soft furnishings	41,000	54,000	47,000
Gas and electrical appliances	107,000	114,000	119,000
China, glass, cutlery, etc	64,000	77,000	69,000
Personal goods and services			
Leather and travel goods	73,000	74,000	75,000
Motoring			
Net purchase of motor vehicles	468,000	550,000	559,000
Leisure goods			
Television, video, Hi-Fi etc	120,000	144,000	135,000
Sports goods	17,000	18,000	22,000
Optical and photographic goods	26,000	35,000	31,000
Leisure services			
Cinema admissions	5,000	5,000	6,000
Theatres, sports events, etc	67,000	78,000	73,000
	2,124,000	2,447,000	2,425,000

Gravesham data based on distribution of type of household.
Source data - ibid

(iv) The national, ROSE and Gravesham total 'mobile' expenditure are all around 30% of the relevant total weekly expenditures, ie are very significant both in total amount and proportion.

(v) Whereas the expenditures in various elements are somewhat variable, the overall picture is that the total Gravesham 'mobile' expenditure is well up to the level of ROSE and rather more than the national average.

(f) *Placement of 'mobile' expenditure* (by customers in the Gravesend Town Centre catchment area).

(i) In December 1992, as part of the Gravesend Town Centre Initiative, a survey was conducted into the needs and expectations of local residents regarding the provision of shopping facilities in Gravesend. The study consisted of a representative sample of households in the catchment area (10 mile radius of the town centre, south of the Thames).

(ii) The survey found that for non-food shopping, 79% of respondents said they shop at Gravesend, with 65% shopping there at least once a week. Of shopping centres that are visited on a weekly basis, Gravesend is by far the most popular. Its closest competitor in this respect is Chatham, with only 9% of respondents visiting on a weekly basis.

(iii) Although the study shows a high level of respondents shopping at Gravesend town centre for non-food goods, it does not, however, elicit precise information on the proportion of expenditure spent.

(g) *Summary*

(i) The distribution of Gravesham residents by age and by sex is close to the national averages.

(ii) The predicted trends in age and sex distribution for the next decade show an 'ageing' populating brought about by decreasing proportions of younger age groups. This again corresponds closely with national trends.

(iii) In the proportions of socio-economic groups, ie managerial and professional, non-manual and manual workers, Gravesham is quite close to the national averages.

(iv) The quality of housing in Gravesham is significantly better than the national norms in both the private and the public sectors.

(v) The aggregate sum of weekly household expenditure and the amounts of individual types of expenditure made by Gravesham residents are significantly higher than the notional sums based on national averages.

(vi) Whilst the aggregate sum of weekly household expenditure is less than the notional sum based on expenditure in Rest Of South East (ROSE), a large part of the difference can be explained by lower expenditure on housing and household goods by Gravesham residents.

(vii) Gravesham residents spend more than the national average on clothing and footwear and compare favourably with ROSE in this respect.

(viii) The aggregate sum of weekly 'mobile' household expenditure by Gravesham residents is significantly higher than the notional sum based on national averages and is on a par with the notional sum based on expenditure by ROSE.

Appendix E: Customer needs survey

3.5 Customer needs survey: Summary report March 1993, prepared by Economic development - Gravesham Borough council on behalf of Gravesend Town Centre Initiative).

(a) CONTENTS

- (b) Introduction
- (c) Methodology
- (d) Where and why do people prefer a particular shopping centre
  - (i) Main centres visited
  - (ii) Frequency of visiting
  - (iii) Changes in non-food shopping habits
  - (iv) How do shoppers rate Gravesend as a Town Centre
  - (v) Differences between 'preferred' and 'visited' shopping centres
  - (vi) Preferred times for visiting Gravesend
  - (vii) Preferred mode of travel to Gravesend
  - (viii) Environmental improvements
  - (ix) Local awareness and advertising:
    - (1) Local radio
    - (2) Local newspapers
    - (3) Advertising seen
- (e) Customer profiles
  - (i) Socio-economic groups
  - (ii) Income groups
  - (iii) Age groups
  - (iv) Is there a typical Gravesend shopper?
- (f) Shopping centres used for food shopping

(b) *Introduction.* In December 1992 The Gravesend Town Centre Initiative, (GTCI), a public and private sector partnership, commissioned Benchmark Research Ltd, to conduct a study into the needs and expectations of local residents regarding the provision of shopping facilities in Gravesend. This research was intended to act as a basis for developing a strategy to create a more popular and commercially successful shopping and leisure environment.

(c) *Methodology*

(i) A 1% sample of households in the catchment area (10 mile radius of the town centre south of the Thames), was considered statistically significant. The research comprised 550 house-to-house interviews. This choice of information gathering was preferred over telephone interviews and postal research due to the speed of the response, as well as the quality afforded by this method. House to house calling was also thought to give greater accessibility to the target respondents than telephone research.

(ii) Fieldwork was conducted from 25th November 1992 to 15th December 1992 and from 4th January 1993 to the 13th January, fieldwork being suspended over the Christmas period to avoid extraordinary shopping patterns.

(iii) 33% of the respondents were interviewed at the weekends. Of the remaining 369, 40% were interviewed in the morning, 55% in the afternoon and 5% in the evening.

(iv) The variables that affected the sample structure were these.

1. Population distribution
2. Socio-economic characteristics
3. Travelling distance from Gravesend
4. Proximity to alternative shopping centres

DARTFORD
SWANSCOMBE
DARTFORD BOROUGH COUNCIL
Hextable
Swanley Village
Sutton at Hone
South Darenth
Horton Kirby
Longfield
Hartley Wood
New Ash Green
Fawkham Green
SEVENOAKS DISTRICT COUNCIL
Farningham
Eynsford
Lullingstone Roman Villa
Brands Hatch Motor Racing
West Kingsdown
Stansted
Wrotham
Borough Green
M25
M20
M26
A20
A225
A226
A227
GRAVESHAM
KEY
Motorway
'A' Roads
Other Roads
Proposed New Roads
CTRL
Business Parks
Historical Buildings
Castles & Forts
Parks & Open Spaces
Designated Areas of Outstanding Natural Beauty
Based upon the Ordnance Survey map by Cook, Hammond & Kell, Ltd with the permission of the Controller of Her Majesty's Stationery Office. Crown Copyright reserved.
Published by Gravesham Borough Council
PRINTED IN ENGLAND BY COOK, HAMMOND & KELL LTD

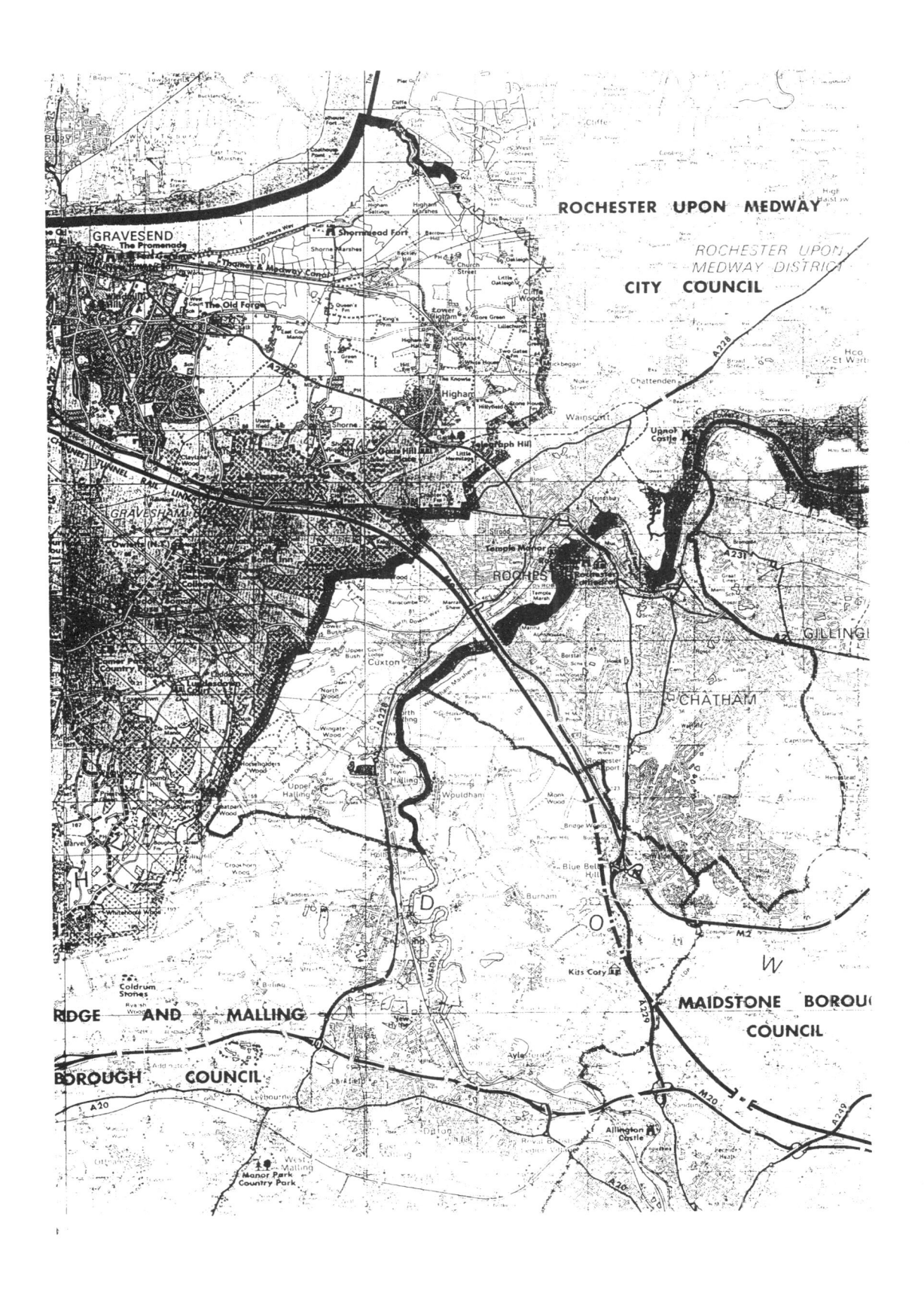

12: Gravesend Town Centre: case study documentation

Notes   Part E: *Learning from experience: ensuring you pass*

(v) Addresses were randomly selected by Gravesham Borough Council and formed the basis of the research sample. Neighbourhoods were selected with the underlying desire to gain cross section of the socio-economic groups. Distance to Gravesend as well as to other major shopping centres is a further consideration that is addressed through the use of the 'zoning system' described above.

(vi) Some households within the immediate vicinity of Dartford, Gillingham and Chatham were excluded. This allowed the research to focus more clearly on the important 'floating' shoppers living in the area between the A2 and the M20. It was recognised that these people represent a group of strategic interest to the GTCI as well as being able to provide useful feedback on the Dartford and Gillingham/Chatham shopping areas.

(d) *Where and why do people prefer a particular shopping centre?*

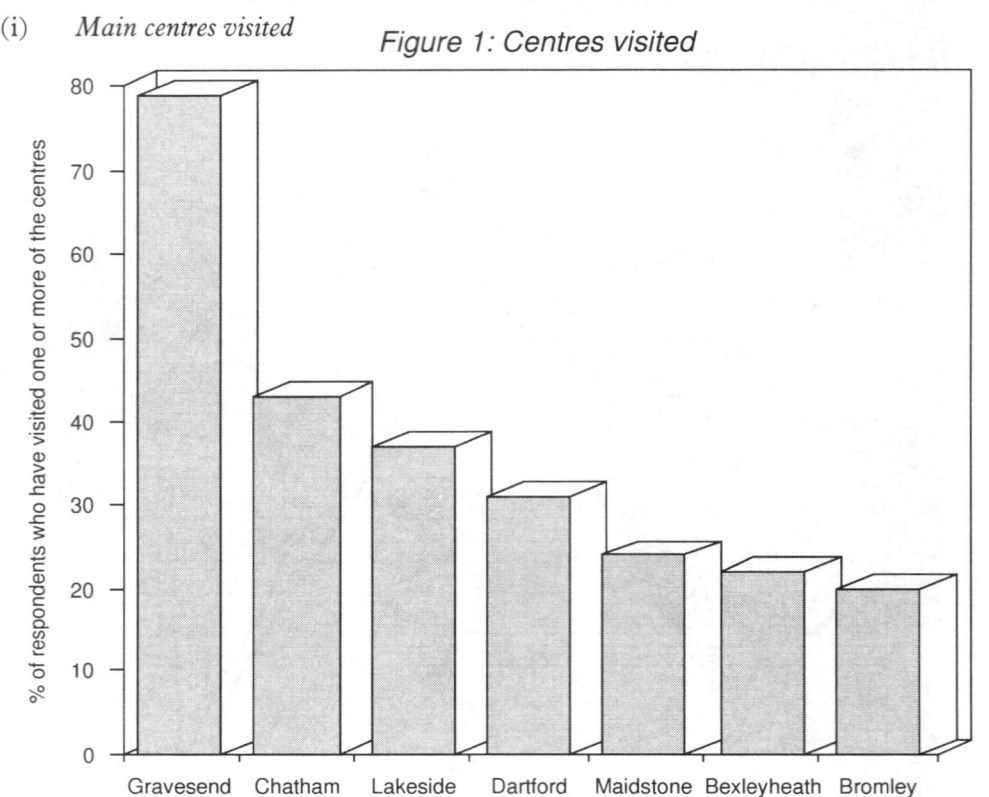

(i) *Main centres visited*

Figure 1: Centres visited

[Bar chart showing % of respondents who have visited one or more of the centres:
Gravesend ~78%, Chatham ~43%, Lakeside ~37%, Dartford ~31%, Maidstone ~24%, Bexleyheath ~22%, Bromley ~20%]

Gravesend is clearly the most visited shopping centre, a full 35% above Chatham. Chatham is the second most visited centre with Lakeside third.

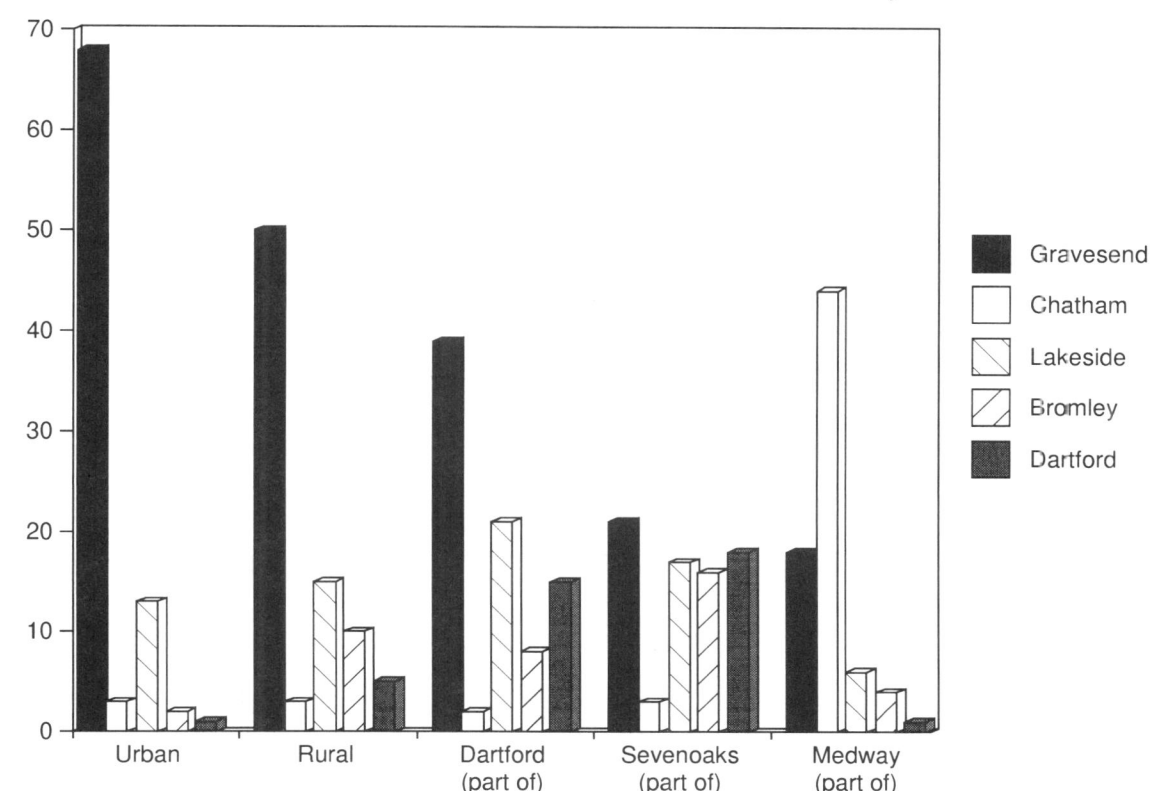

Figure 2: Gravesend town centre catchment area: centres visited by zones

Of those responding to the questionnaire, 68% of the Gravesham urban area and just under 50% of the Gravesham rural areas shop in Gravesend. Chatham is the second most popular shopping area with 44% of respondents choosing to shop there. It is not surprising that it attracts large numbers of respondents from the Medway area. Lakeside and Dartford are the next most important shopping centres with 37% and 31% respectively saying that they visited these centres. Lakeside attracts relatively large numbers from the Gravesham rural area (52% of respondents from this area) and to a lesser extent from areas within Dartford and Sevenoaks.

(ii) *Frequency of visiting*

(1) 65% of respondents shop at least once a week. Of the centres that are visited on a weekly basis, Gravesend was by far the most popular with 43% of all respondents shopping there at least once a week. Its closest competitor in this respect is Chatham, with only 9% of respondents visiting on a weekly basis.

(2) Gravesend's popularity can perhaps be explained by the geographical distribution of the sample, which is centred on the Gravesend rural and urban areas and who are most likely to shop at their nearest centre. Shoppers are also most likely to shop locally for non food products that they need on a regular basis. For higher value goods purchased less regularly, shoppers will be prepared to travel further afield to increase the element of choice.

(iii) *Changes in non-good shopping halls*

(1) Variation in peoples' choice centre for non-food goods was found to be very low, with only 18 of respondents saying that they had changed their shopping habits in the last 12 months. Bearing this small proportion in mind, it is however interesting to note that Gravesend featured highest in the list of centres no longer visited. 5 of respondents who had changed their shopping centres I the last 6 months, said that they no longer used Gravesend. Chatham also fared poorly in this respect, with 4 of respondents who had changed their habits, ceasing to shop there.

Part E: Learning from experience: ensuring you pass

(2) The key variables including the decision to change shopping centre were: 'ease of access to the centre', 'difficulty in parking', 'distance from the centre' and 'low quality of shops'.

(iv) *How do shoppers rate Gravesend as a town centre?*

Figure 3: Gravesend's ratings

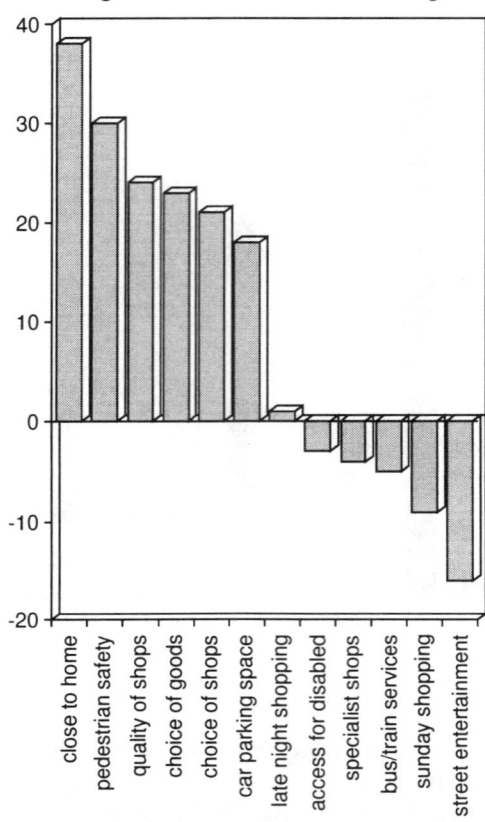

+100 = good +50 = quite good 0 = neither good nor bad
-50 = quite bad -100 = very bad

Shoppers considered Gravesend's key feature as its proximity to home scoring just under 40. Pedestrian safety and choice of goods both achieved mean scores of just over 25. Choice of shops features only fourth in relation to the town's strengths with a low score of 24. Specialist shops, bus/train services, ability to shop on Sundays and in particular street entertainment were considered poor.

(v) *Differences between 'preferred' and 'visited' shopping centres*

In order to evaluate the strengths and weaknesses of Gravesend town centre compared with its competition, questions were asked on how shoppers rated their 'preferred' centre. By comparing these answers with the rating for Gravesend key issues begin to emerge.

(1)

Figure 4: Comparison of Gravesend's rating with preferred centre's factors of importance

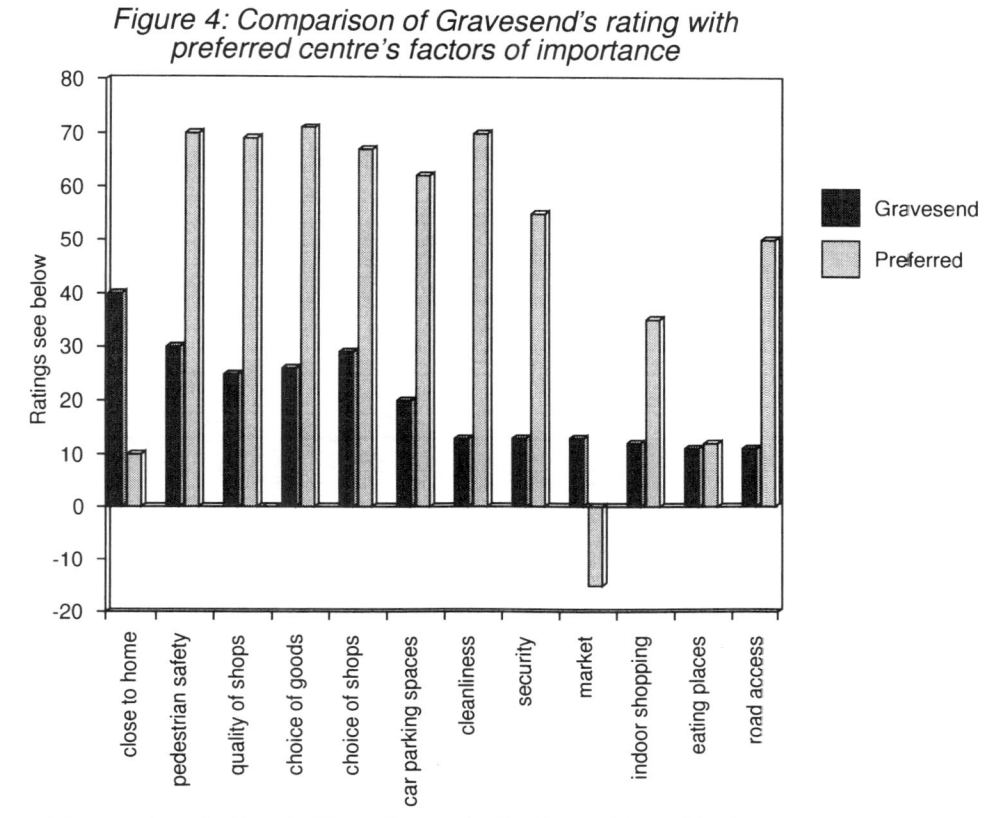

+100 = very important/good +50 = quite important/guide good 0 = neither important or unimportant/neither good nor bad -50 = quite important/quite bad -100 = not at all important/very bad

Figure 4 compares the factors that are important when choosing a shopping centre with the ratings of Gravesend town centre. Clearly there is a gap between what shoppers require and what Gravesend is currently offering. It can also be seen that there is a package of factors that are of almost equal importance: cleanliness (71.2); choice of goods (70.5); pedestrian safety (69.9); quality of shops (67.9) and choice of shops (67.2).

(2)

Figure 5: Comparison of Gravesend's ratings with preferred centre's factors of importance

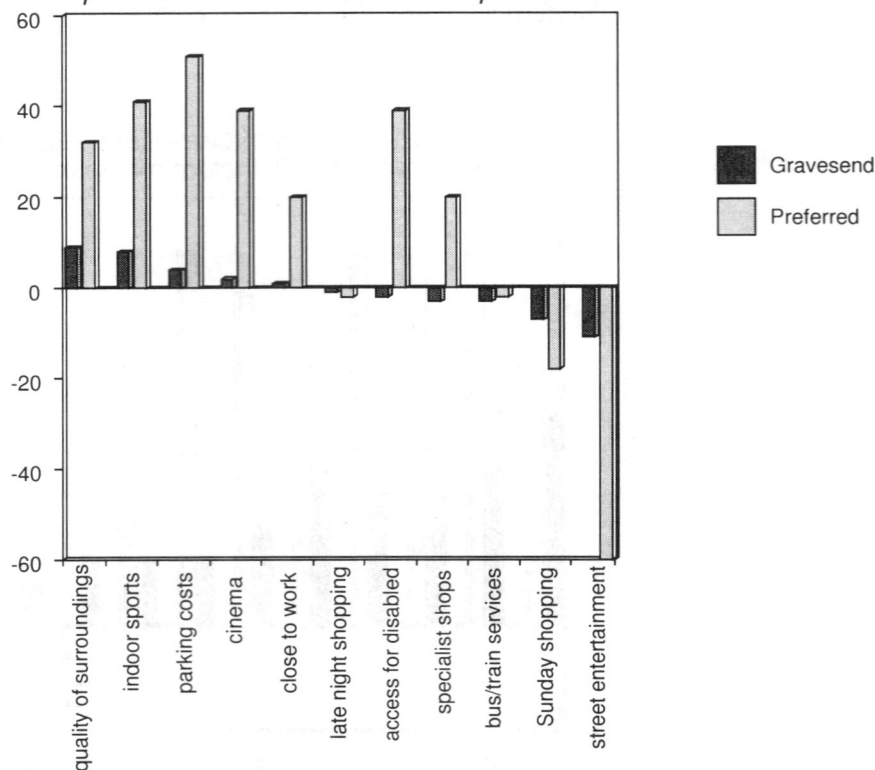

[Bar chart comparing Gravesend and Preferred ratings across factors: quality of surroundings, indoor sports, parking costs, cinema, close to work, late night shopping, access for disabled, specialist shops, bus/train services, Sunday shopping, street entertainment]

+100 = very important/good +50 = quite important/guide good 0 = neither important or unimportant/neither good nor bad -50 = quite important/quite bad -100 = not at all important/very bad

Figure 5 similarly compares the factors that are not important: street entertainment, indoor sports, cinema, close to work and Sunday shopping were all areas seen to be of little importance.

Although a question was put to those who are currently visiting Gravesend town centre on ways in which they thought the town centre could be improved only 44% had any definite answers. However, out of those who did the largest proportion (18%) mentioned 'choice of shops'. Obviously this is too small figure to make any meaningful analysis.

(vi) *Times when Gravesend is visited*

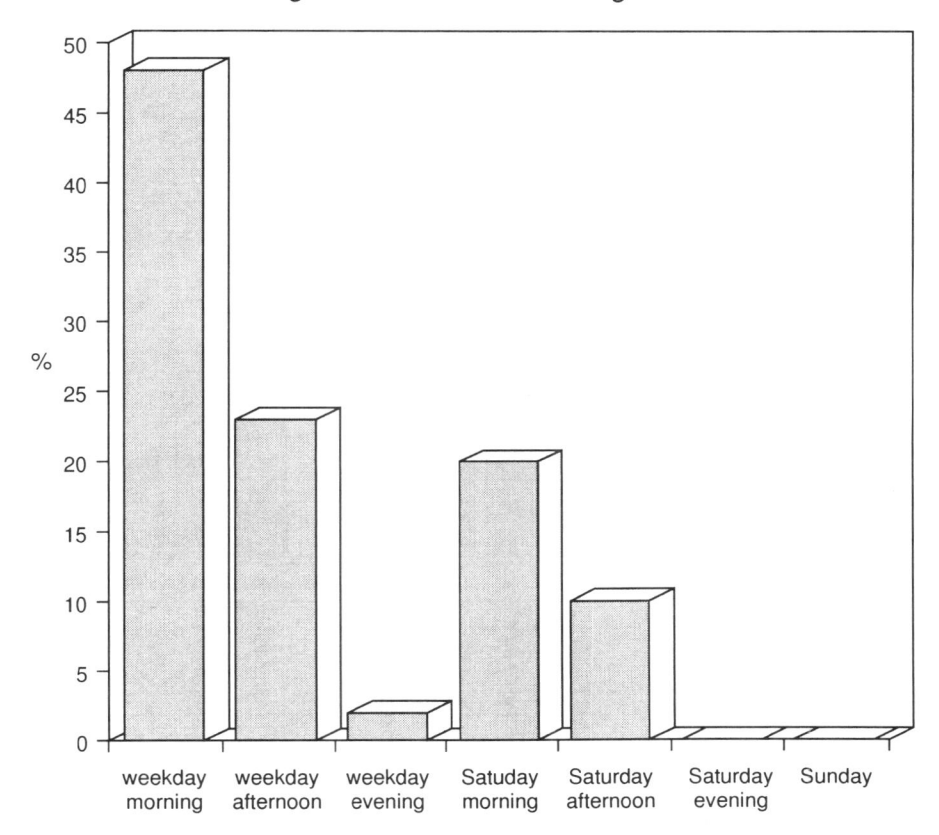

Figure 6: Gravesend visiting times

[Bar chart showing percentages for: weekday morning (~48%), weekday afternoon (~23%), weekday evening (~2%), Saturday morning (~20%), Saturday afternoon (~10%), Saturday evening (0%), Sunday (0%)]

(1) 48% of Gravesend shoppers favoured weekday mornings as their shopping time (for non food shopping), with 'convenience' (58%) and a 'wish to avoid busy periods' (16%) as the most important influences.

(2) Untypically, the second most popular time for non-food was weekday afternoons, not Saturday mornings, as with other centres, perhaps reflecting the high proportion of retired and unemployed people shopping at Gravesend. Once again 'convenience' and the desire to avoid the busy periods were given as reasons for these shopping patterns. The availability of time through shift work or flexitime was also given by 21% of the respondents as the reason for this preference.

(3) Only 9% of respondents suggested they prefer an alternative time to shop other things being equal.

(vii) *Preferred mode of travel to Gravesend*

Using a car/van was the preferred mode of transport for non-food shopping in Gravesend for 74% of respondents. Using the bus or reaching the centre by foot were preferred by 17% and 11% of respondents.

(viii) *Environmental improvements*

Figure 7: Importance of factors for improving the town centre's environment

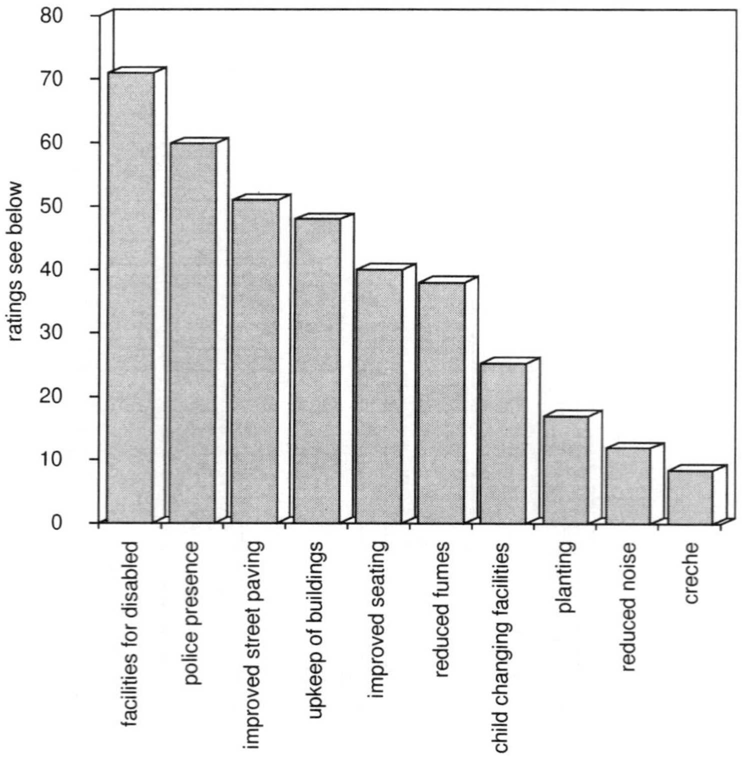
80
70
60
50
40
30
20
10
0
ratings see below
facilities for disabled
police presence
improved street paving
upkeep of buildings
improved seating
reduced fumes
child changing facilities
planting
reduced noise
creche

+100 = good +50 = quite good 0 = neither good nor bad -50 = quite bad -100 = very bad

Interestingly respondents gave the improvement of 'disabled facilities' a high score of just over 71, 'police presence' was given the second highest score of 59.8, although it seems that 'baby changing facilities' with a score of 25.2 are needed the town there is little demand for a 'Crèche', it scoring only 8.4.

(ix) *Local awareness and advertising*

(1) *Local radio*

Figure 8: Radio stations listened to: By age group

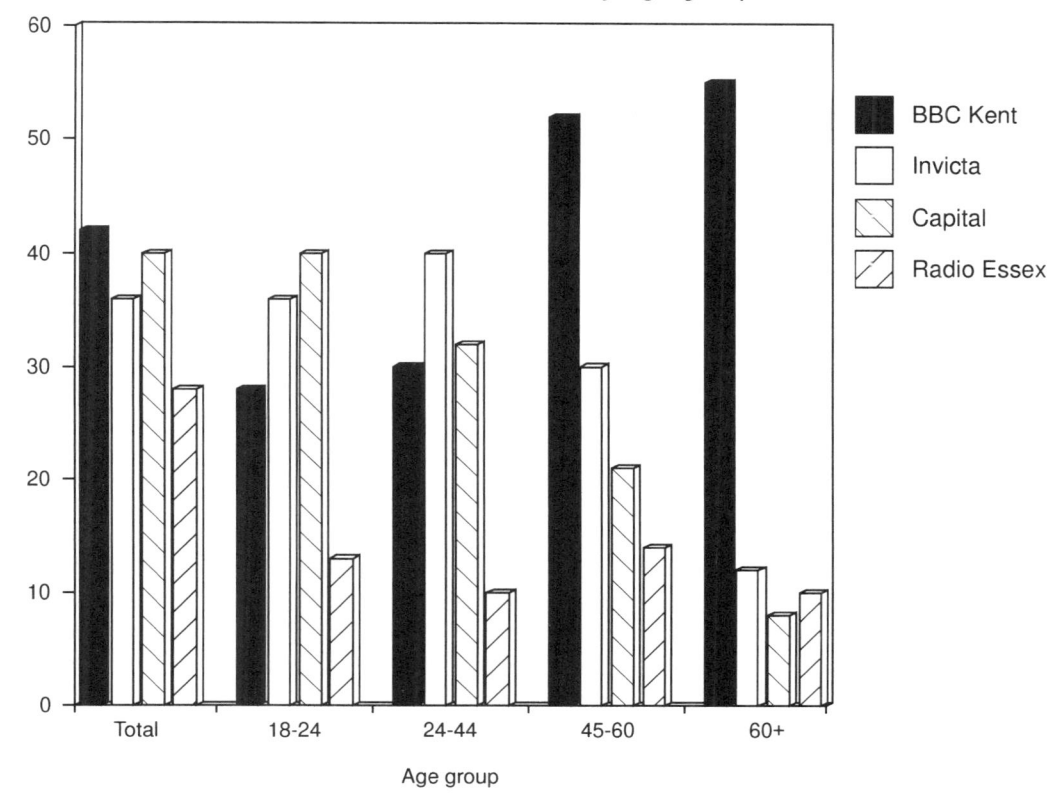

Local radio stations provide a useful target audience for the surrounding community. Of the local radios, BBC Kent and Invicta were found to be the most popular. They are listened to by 32% and 18% of respondents respectively with a further 11% of respondents listening to Capital. It is significant that Invicta and Capital both have much younger listeners than Radio Kent. Whilst listeners of the first two are dominated by the 18-24 and the 25-44 year old brackets, Radio Kent listeners tend to be primarily in the 46-60 and 60+ age groups.

(2) *Local newspapers*

Figure 9: Newspapers read

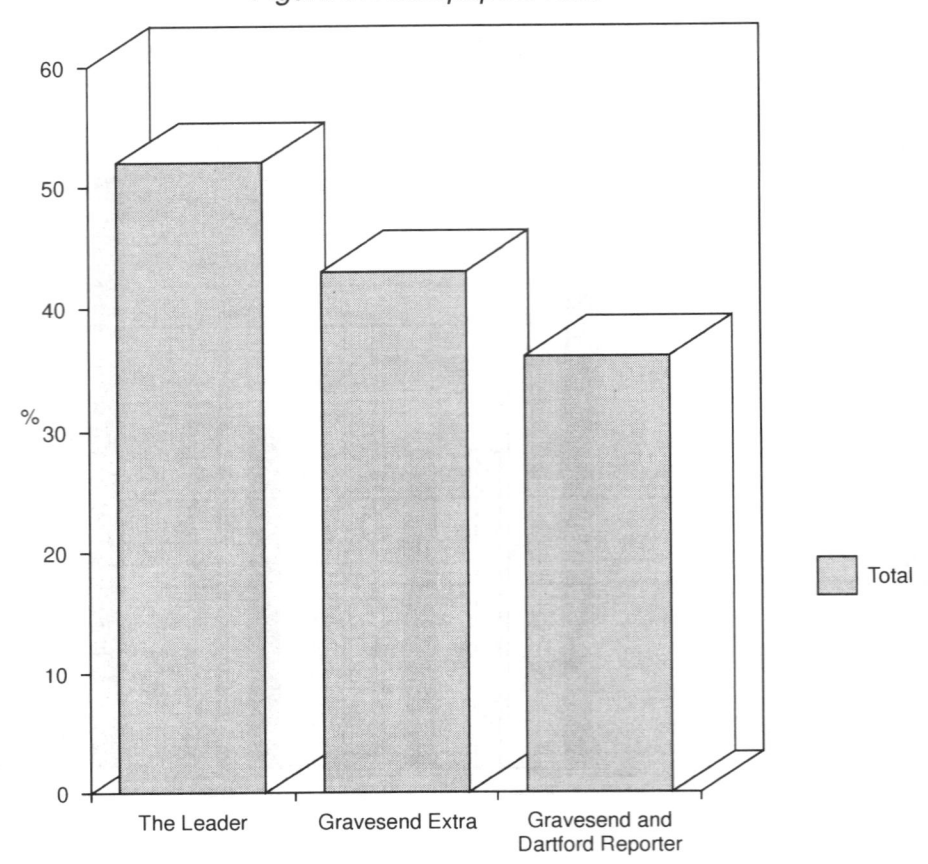

- Of the local newspapers, the most popular were 'The Leader' (read by 52% of the respondents) the 'Gravesend Extra' (43%) and the 'Gravesend and Dartford Reporter' (36%).
- The 'Leader' is the most popular local newspaper in the urban area (87% of urban respondents) closely followed by the 'Gravesend Extra' (77%) and the 'Gravesend and Dartford Reporter' (57%).
- The 'Gravesend and Dartford Reporter' was the most popular newspaper in the rural area (69% of the rural respondents) followed by the Gravesend Extra' (58%) and the 'Leader' (40%).

(3) *Advertising seen*

- One third of all respondents could recall recent advertising for shopping centres, an encouragingly high figure.
- Only 6% of these people however, cited Gravesend as being the subject of such advertising, with Lakeside having the highest profile by far with 63% of people who recalled an advertisement of this nature remembering the centre.
- In view of this low level of general awareness perhaps Gravesend town centre could benefit from a promotional campaign aimed at improving consumer awareness.

(e) *Customer profiles*

  (i) *Socio-economic groups*

Figure 10: Preferred centre: socio-economic groups

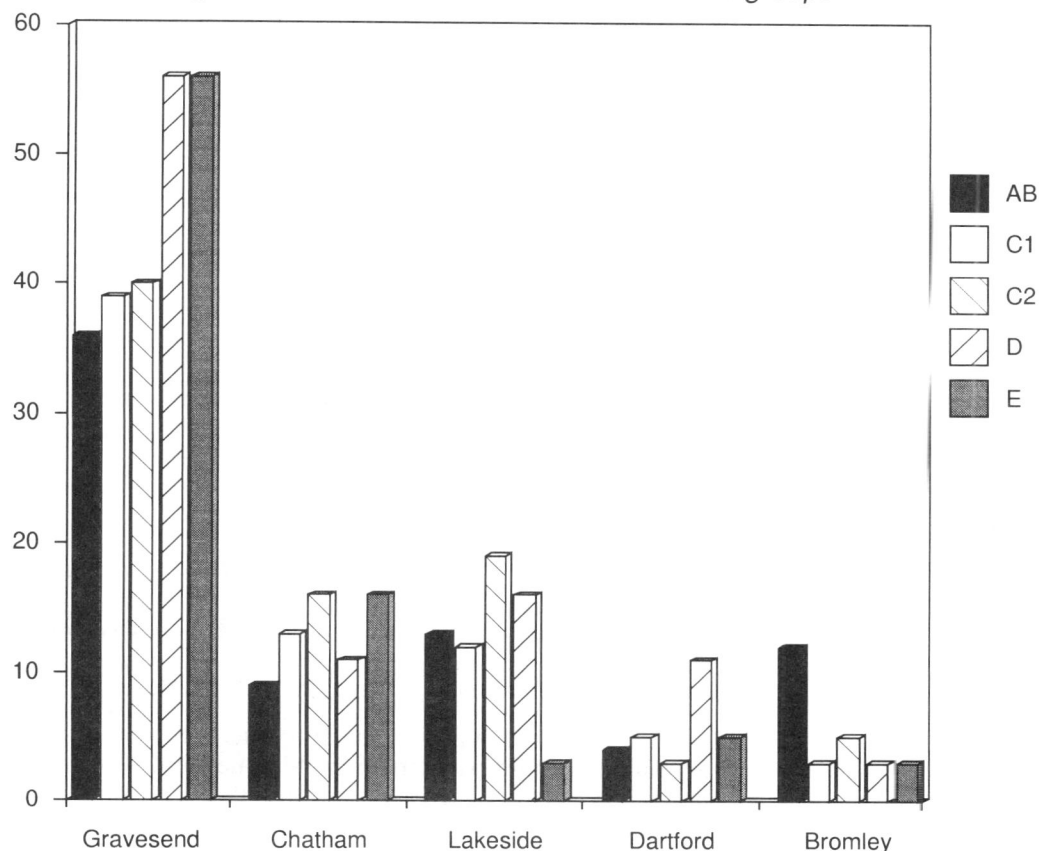

56% of both the D & E socio-economic groups prefer to shop in Gravesend while only 36% of the AB group prefer Gravesend. The pattern seems to be that the higher socio-economic groups are more discerning in their shopping preferences while the lower groups are not.

(ii) *Income groups*

Figure 11: Preferred centres: income groups

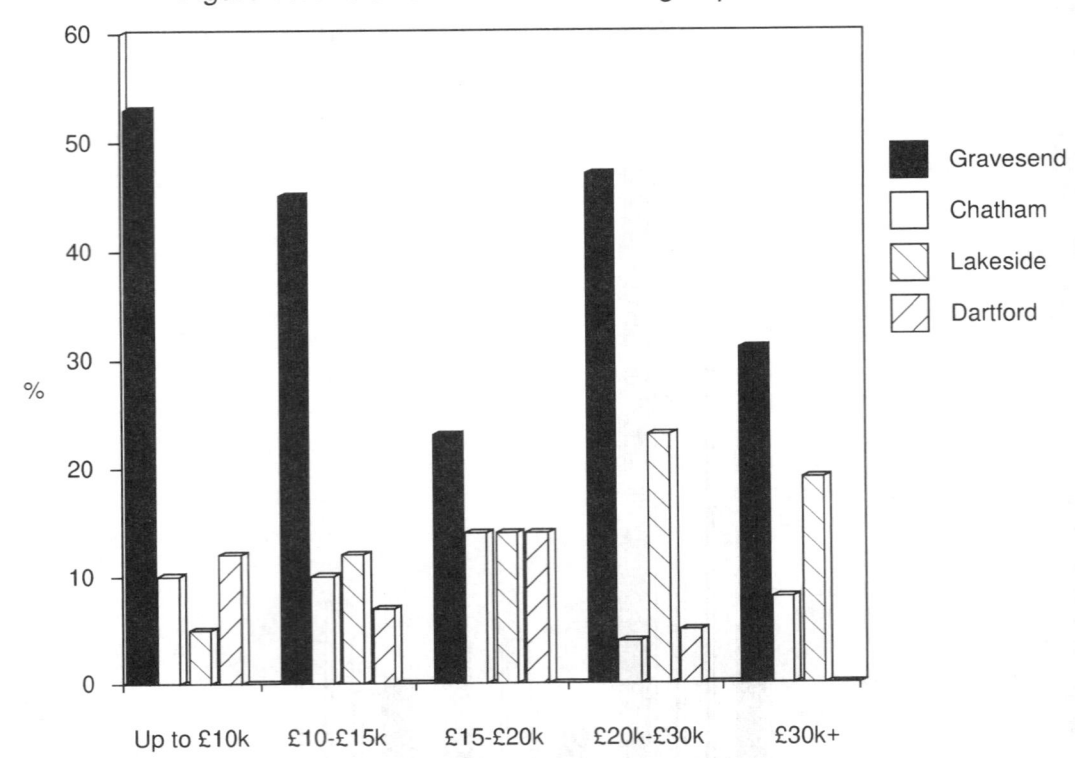

It must be noted when examining income groups that only half of the respondents would participate in this question. Nevertheless, a pattern does emerge: as income increases so does the preference to shop at Lakeside. Although this pattern is present in the £20k-£30k income group there is a larger proportion who prefer to shop at Gravesend.

(iii) *Age groups*

Figure 12: Preferred centres: age groups

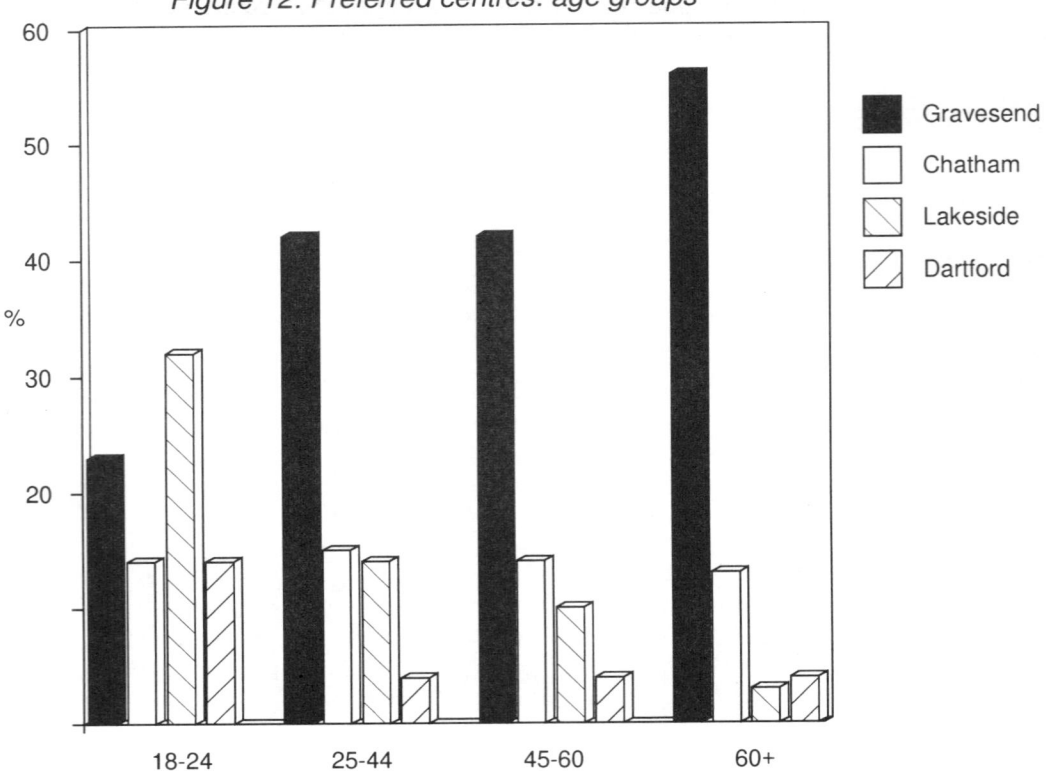

Figure 12 clearly shows that the older age groups prefer to shop at Gravesend while the young prefer Lakeside, although there is still a large proportion of the 25-44 age group who prefer Gravesend.

(iv) *Is there a typical Gravesend shopper?*

From the survey it appears that the most common profile of the Gravesend shopper appears to be someone of relatively low socio-economic standing, earning less than £10,000, 60+ years of age and living in the urban area. This is probably common to most town centres. Of interest is the strong showing of groups C1 and C2 earning between £20,000 - £30,000 aged between 25-44, living in the urban area. The young and the more affluent members of the community prefer Lakeside.

(f) *Shopping centres used for food shopping*

(i) Gravesend fared favourably when compared to other shopping centres for 'bulk food' shopping. 63% of respondents ranked it either first or second as their preference for bulk food shopping. Its closest competitors were Chatham and Lakeside (Thurrock) which were ranked first or second by 26% and 17% of respondents respectively.

(ii) Saint George's in Gravesend was found to be the most popular centre for food shopping with just 10% of those who expressed a preference identifying it as their favoured shopping centre. Its closest competitor in the locality was Pepperhill, which enjoyed similar levels of popularity to Saint George's and was recognised by respondents as being an area of growth. The threat that it poses to Saint Georges, Gravesend, should therefore not be underestimated with its geographical location suggesting that it is more likely to steal the more affluent shoppers with their own transport.

(iii) The key factors that influence the choice of centre for food shopping were the presence of a wide variety of products and competitive pricing with mean scores of 84.3 and 76.6 respectively. Accessibility to good parking facilities, particularly adjacent free parking was also cited as being a significant influence on choice of good shopping centre, a clear benefit of the 'out of town' centres such as Pepperhill.

(iv) The importance of parking as an influence on choice of food shopping centre reflects the very high number of respondents that use a car or van as the mode of transport for food shopping. (Fully 77% of respondents travelled as a driver or passenger or a car or van.) This emphasis on private transport is also reflected by the fact that availability of good public transport was found to be the least important influence on choice of food shopping centre.

(v) *Frequency of food shopping for food and groceries*

(1) 77% of respondents indicated that they shop for food and groceries once a week with a further 26% undertaking food shopping twice a week. Just 20% of respondents food-shopped once every two weeks.

(2) It has already been pointed out that food-shoppers in Gravesend conform to the tendency of shoppers in other centres in their preference for car and van transport, favoured by 77% of respondents. Buses were the next most important mode of transport to and from food stores.

This section related to question 24 on the questionnaire in which respondents were asked the two stores most frequently visited for food and groceries. Two different answers may be given for each of these two shops. Thus the % figure given may not add up to 100%, as respondents could choose more than one answer.

Notes   Part E: *Learning from experience: ensuring you pass*

Appendix F: Town Centre Initiative Vision

3.6   This is a joint initiative between Gravesham Borough Council, Gravesham Chamber of Trade and Commerce in partnership with Kent County Council.

(a)

OUR 10 POINT PLAN

1. Revitalised High Street: the historic core of the town, containing some of the Borough's oldest buildings. Its physical and economic revitalisation is of high priority.

2. Regenerated Harmer Street: originally intended as part of a much larger scheme, this impressive street was built in 1836. Many buildings have been or are being restored to their former glory as a result of IMPACT grant aid, and ultimately it is intended to provide relief from through traffic.

3. Improved Riverside: Gravesend's historical development is bound up with the River Thames which provides the town with its unique character and flavour. New uses such as recreational and residential are being encouraged adjacent to the river in place of industry. Improved public access between the river and the town centre will be sought.

4. Improved Public Transport: many visitors and residents travel to and from the town centre by train, bus, taxi and ferry. Passengers' ease of access to the shopping centre is a priority.

5. Attractive Pedestrian Areas and Spaces: help to create prosperous town centres. Main town centre shopping streets will be enhanced with paving, trees and seats, improved cleansing and maintenance, floral displays and entertainments.

6. Thriving Shopping Centre: the key to growth in employment and prosperity. Gravesend's main assets such as ease of access and parking, variety of services and trades will be promoted.

7. Changes to the Highway Network: Gravesend town centre enjoys relatively easy access, without problems of traffic congestion. Opportunities for traffic management and limited new road building do exist together with improved signposting. This will further enhance the town's environment for pedestrians and ease vehicle passage, while maintaining easy access to the shopping core.

8. New Market Square: land to either side of Bank Street has been acquired by the Council to ensure co-ordinated enhancement. A high quality appearance to the site will improve the entrance to shopping areas and prospects for The Market.

9. Attractive and Secure Car Parks: encourage shoppers and visitors, and cater for town centre work force. Their appraisal to ensure adequate provision and enhancement to make them more inviting is a priority.

10. Redeveloped Vacant Sites: increasing the town centre's potential by ensuring that the whole area contributes to its performance. Vacant sites will receive special attention.

12: Gravesend Town Centre: case study documentation

(b)

Top row (stakeholders):
- Town Centre Businesses
- 'Businesses in Gravesend Action Group'
- 'Chamber of Trade'
- 'Commercial Strategy Group' (North Kent)
- 'Retail Strategy Group' (Multiples)
- Schools
- Community Groups
- Special Interest Groups

Middle: Private sector co-ordinator & Public sector co-ordinator

Bottom row:
- Chair
- Steering Group
- Access and Transport
- Environmental Improvements
- Environmental Maintenance
- Promotion & Events
- Quality of Life/Security

Notes *Part E: Learning from experience: ensuring you pass*

Appendix G: Selected maps and tables

3.7 (a) *Thames Gateway definition of the area*

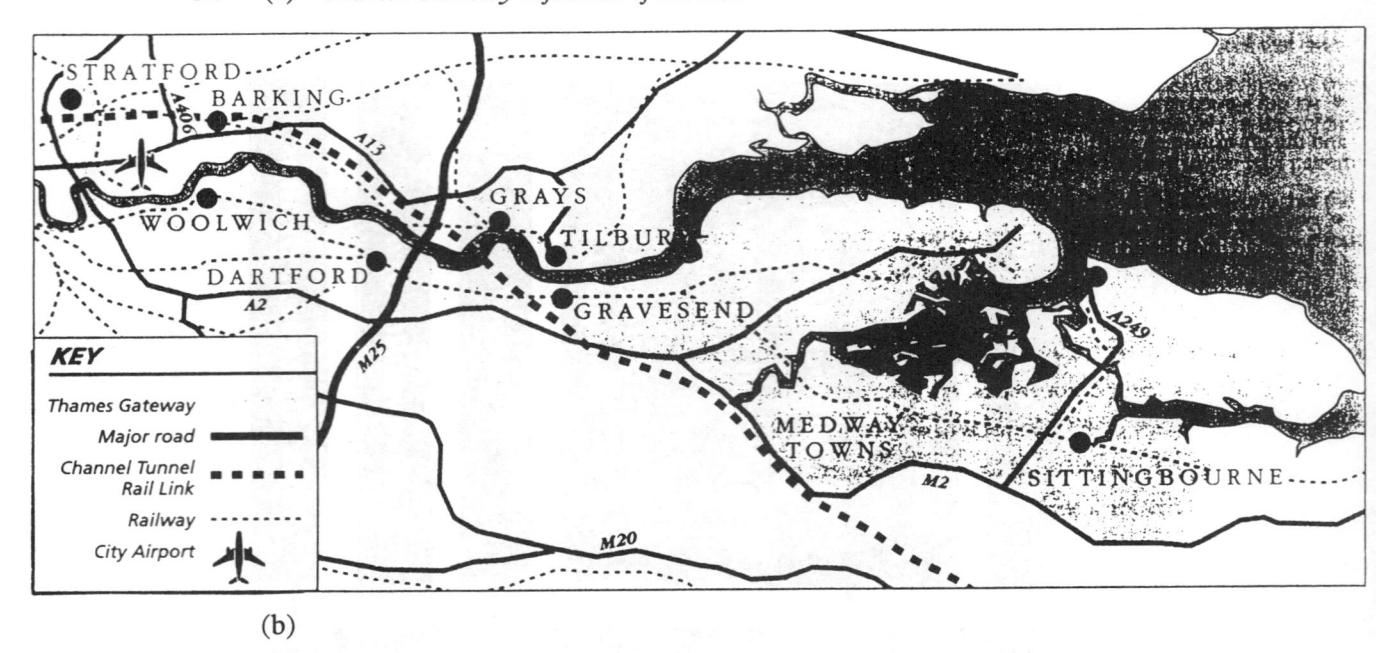

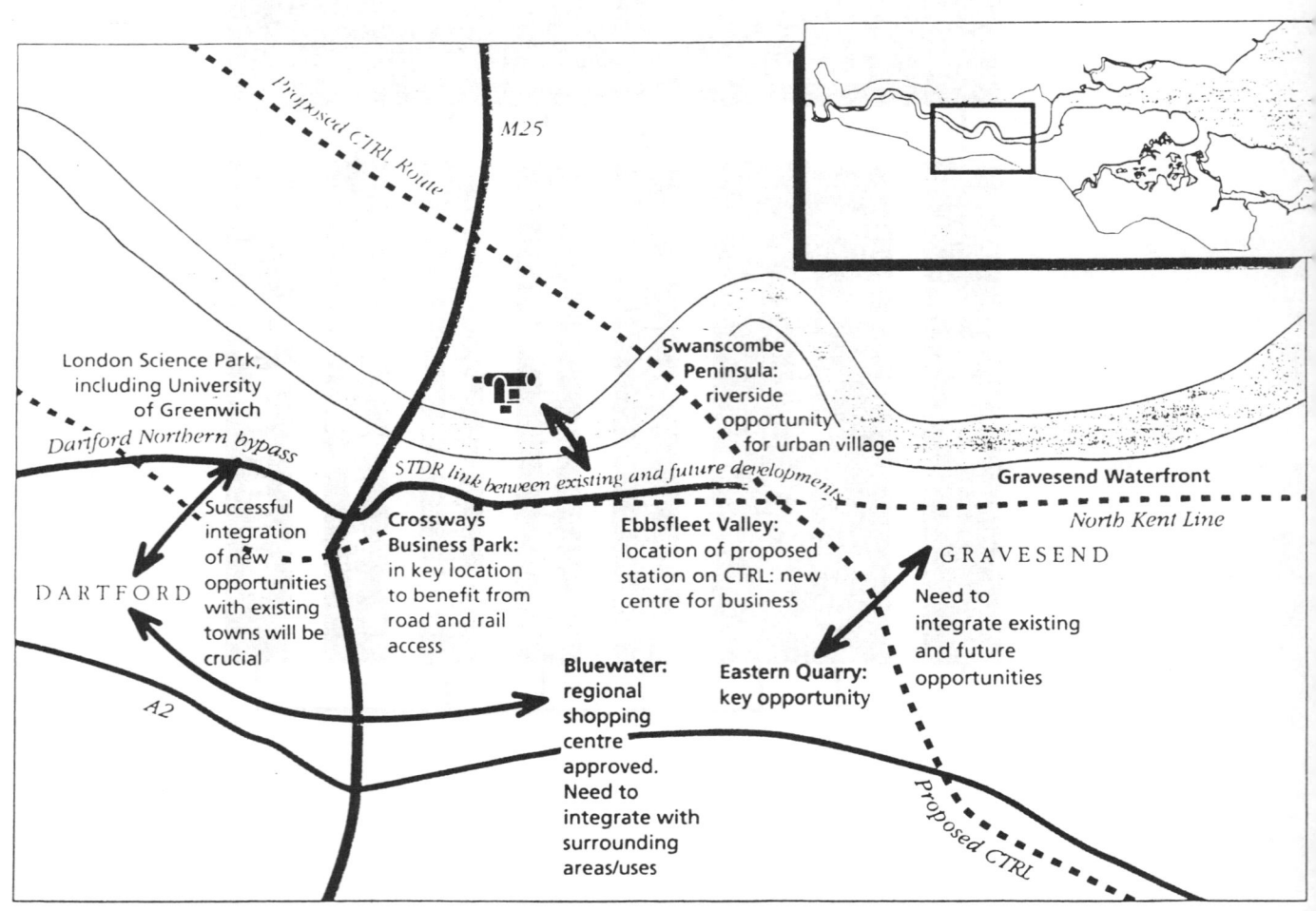

KEY
- Thames Gateway
- Major road ———
- Channel Tunnel Rail Link ▬ ▬ ▬
- Railway - - - - -
- City Airport ✈

(b)

(c) *The facts, the figures ... the future*

A cross-section of statistics from the 1991 Census (shown below) tells us little that is unexpected about the Kent Thames-side area.

Indicators of relative prosperity - owner occupation, unemployment levels, types of employment and car ownership - all show Kent Thames-side lagging behind similar figures for Kent as a whole and, in many respects, below the national average.

1991 Census profile

	Thames-side %	Kent %	Great Britain %
0-15 year olds	20.4	20.1	20.1
Working age	62.5	60.7	61.2
Pensionable age	17.1	19.2	18.7
Employed in manufacturing	16.3	14.	17.8
Professional and technical	29.5	38.5	38.1
Skilled manual and non-manual	48.4	41.8	40.4
Unemployed	8.0	6.8	7.9
Owner occupiers	68.6	73.9	66.3
Ethnic minorities	7.7	2.3	5.5
Car owners	69.6	73.3	66.6
College students	17.9	23.9	24.6
With degrees	3.9	6.1	7.2

But what such figures do *not* reveal is the potential of the area to begin to redress the balance in a big way: to provide more jobs, to provide more quality homes and to transform the physical appearance of the less attractive parts of the area.

Today, as the table (below) illustrates, large numbers of Kent Thames-side residents travel out of the area to their place of work. That could all change. In the *Vision of Kent Thames-side* of the future described on the following pages, sufficient land could be made available to create well over 50,000 new jobs by 2020.

17,000 commute into Kent Thameside

22,700 commute out to London and beyond

12,600 commute out to Bexley and the rest of Kent

This does not mean that the area is going to be swamped with new offices and factories: far from it.

Kent Thames-side is a big place with plenty of space for a variety and mix of developments as well as new parks and green areas. The Vision estimates that there is also room for over 26,000 new homes to be built by 2020 with space for up to another 4,000 soon after. This represents over a 50% increase in the number of homes in the area.

The actual increase in the number of people, however, will be far less dramatic. This is because the average number of people living in each home will be less than it is today.

This is no surprise. Over the years, there has been a steady decline nationally in average household size - a result of more people living on their own for longer before they get married, more divorced families, and more elderly people living longer.

This trend is set to continue. Recent figures issued by the Government forecast that a slightly rising population combined with a continuing decline in average household size will result in the number of households in England going up by almost a quarter by 2016. The rate of increase in Kent is expected to be at, or slightly above, the national average.

In all, the Vision foresees the use of over seven square miles for new development and the provision of open space. To put this figure into perspective, the total development potential of London Docklands is less than four square miles.

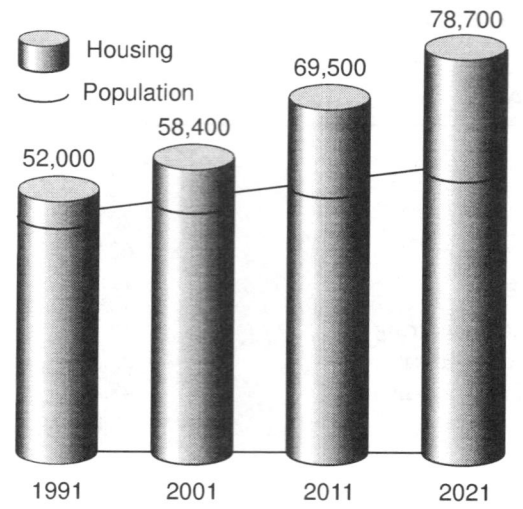

Notes   **Part E: *Learning from experience: ensuring you pass***

Housing and population growth envisaged in Kent Thames - side

Values shown: 52,000 (1991); 58,400 (2001); 69,500 (2011); 78,700 (2021)

Various assumptions are made in the chart below about the timing of development in each of the main development areas.

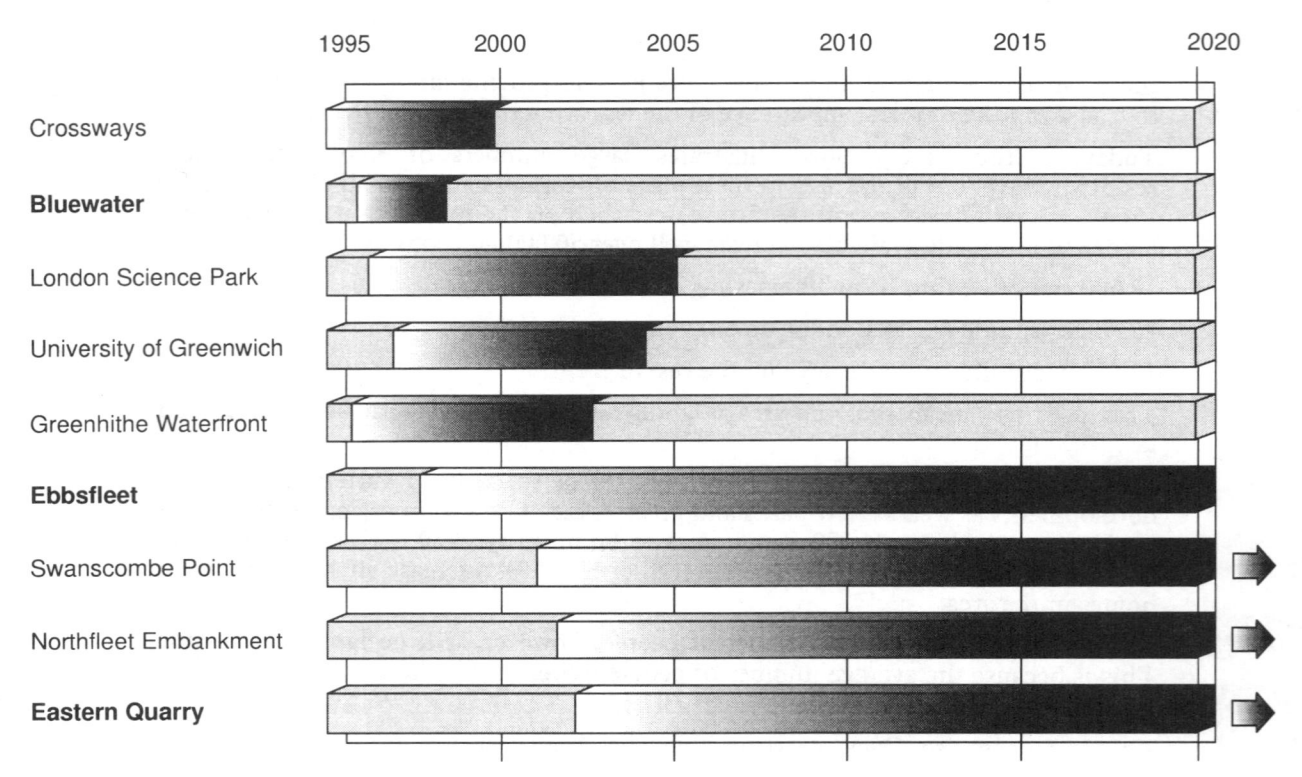

Development timing chart (1995–2020) for:
- Crossways
- **Bluewater**
- London Science Park
- University of Greenwich
- Greenhithe Waterfront
- **Ebbsfleet**
- Swanscombe Point
- Northfleet Embankment
- **Eastern Quarry**

Crossways

The remaining two-thirds of the business park development is completed during 2002. The completion of Crossways dovetails with the availability of the first new commercial properties around the new International and Domestic Passenger Station at Ebbsfleet.

Bluewater

Work on the new regional shopping centre begins in the latter part of 1995. The centre opens during 1998.

Science Park

The Science Park project kicks off in 1995 when work starts on the Business Innovation Quarter. Development continues through to 2010.

University of Greenwich

Infrastructure work begins in 1995 followed by the first buildings in 1998. The first students arrive in 2000. Completion of the campus takes a further six years, finishing in 2006.

Greenhithe waterfront

Work commences in 1997 on the urban village centred on the redevelopment of the area about the Empire Paper Mills. It takes eight years, through to 2005, to be completed.

In the meantime, the infilling of the small sites between Crossways and Greenhithe Village has occurred, work on the first one commencing in 1996.

Ebbsfleet

In 1998, a year after work has started within the valley on constructing the Channel Tunnel Rail Link, work begins on the new urban village at Springhead. This takes about seven years, finishing in 2006.

Meanwhile, building work on commercial properties around the new station begins in 2000. The first are completed at the same time as the station opens in 2002.

The development of Ebbsfleet is completed in 2020.

Swanscombe Peninsula

In 2003 development of the urban village, centred on the Empire Paper Mills in Greenhithe Waterfront, extends into the west part of Swanscombe Peninsula and is subsequently completed in 2005.

Development of the second new urban village, towards the Point, also commences in 2003, now that the construction of the Channel Tunnel Rail Link through the area has been completed and construction traffic can gain access to the site of the urban village. The urban village is completed in 2011.

From 2003, the gradual redevelopment of some of the old industries near Britannia Metals also begins and continues to 2020 and beyond.

Northfleet Embankment

Following the opening of Ebbsfleet International Station, the potential of this nearby area for quality residential development is soon appreciated. From 2004 onwards, there is gradual redevelopment continuing to 2020 and beyond.

Eastern Quarry

The taking of chalk from the quarry continues for some years to come, but in 2005 building work begins at the eastern end. Development of the entire quarry continues beyond 2020.

Part E: *Learning from experience: ensuring you pass*

Appendix H: The Channel Tunnel rail link

3.8

(a)

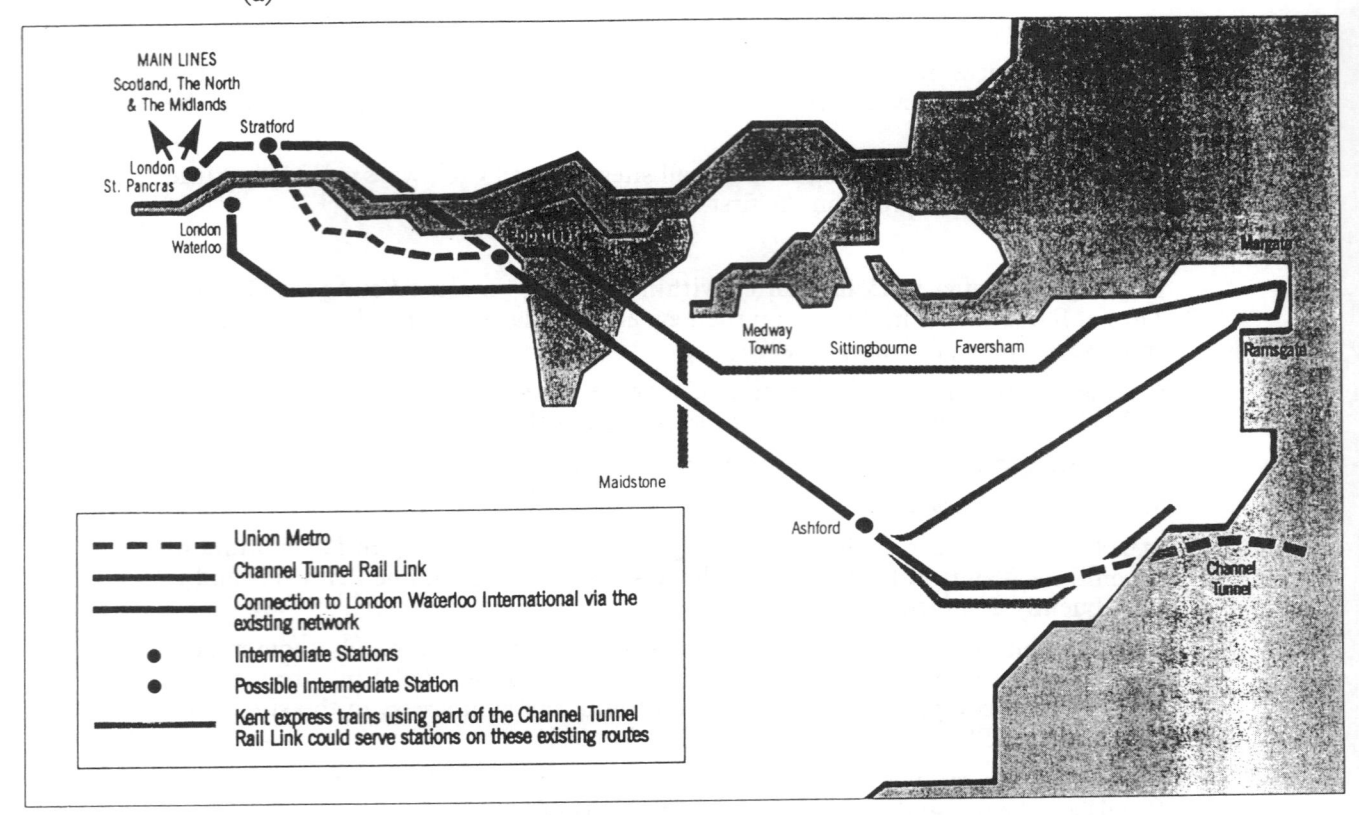

FIGURE 1 : GRAVESHAM & THE RAIL LINK

(b)

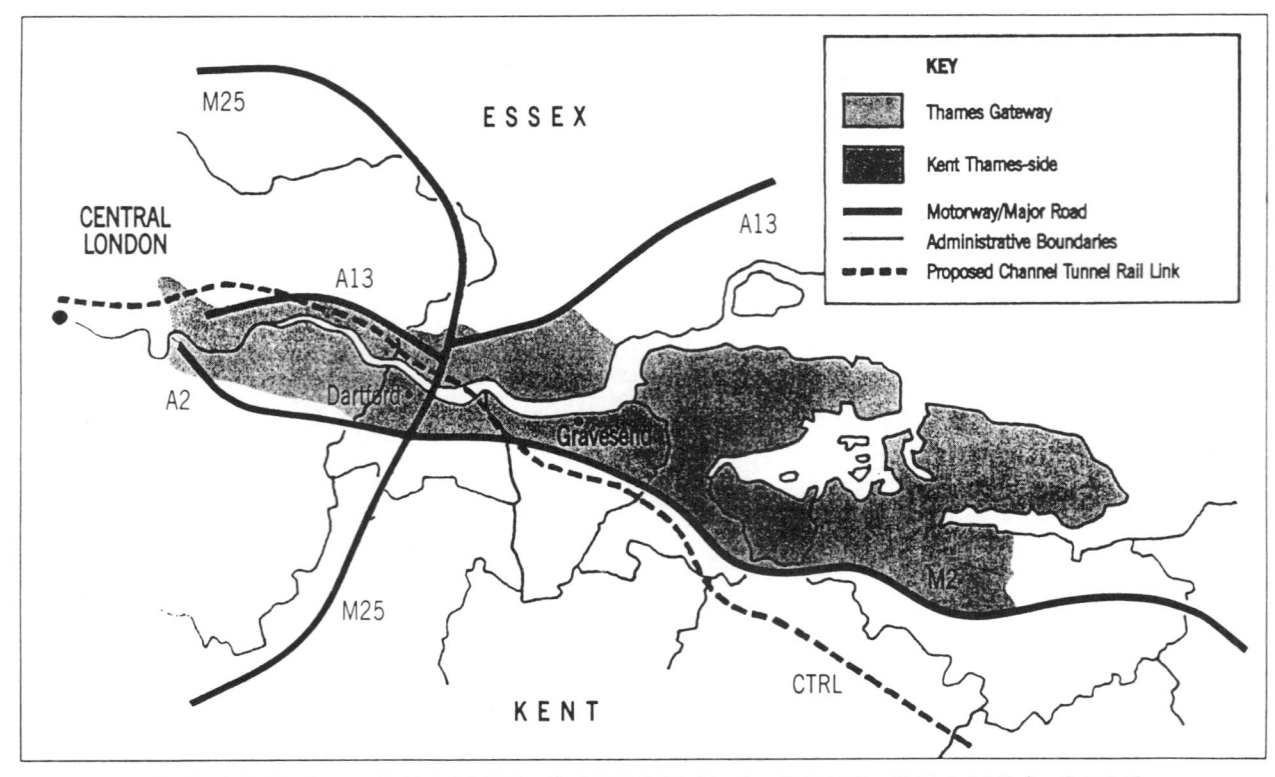

FIGURE 2 : THAMES GATEWAY & KENT THAMES-SIDE

12: Gravesend Town Centre: case study documentation Notes

(c)

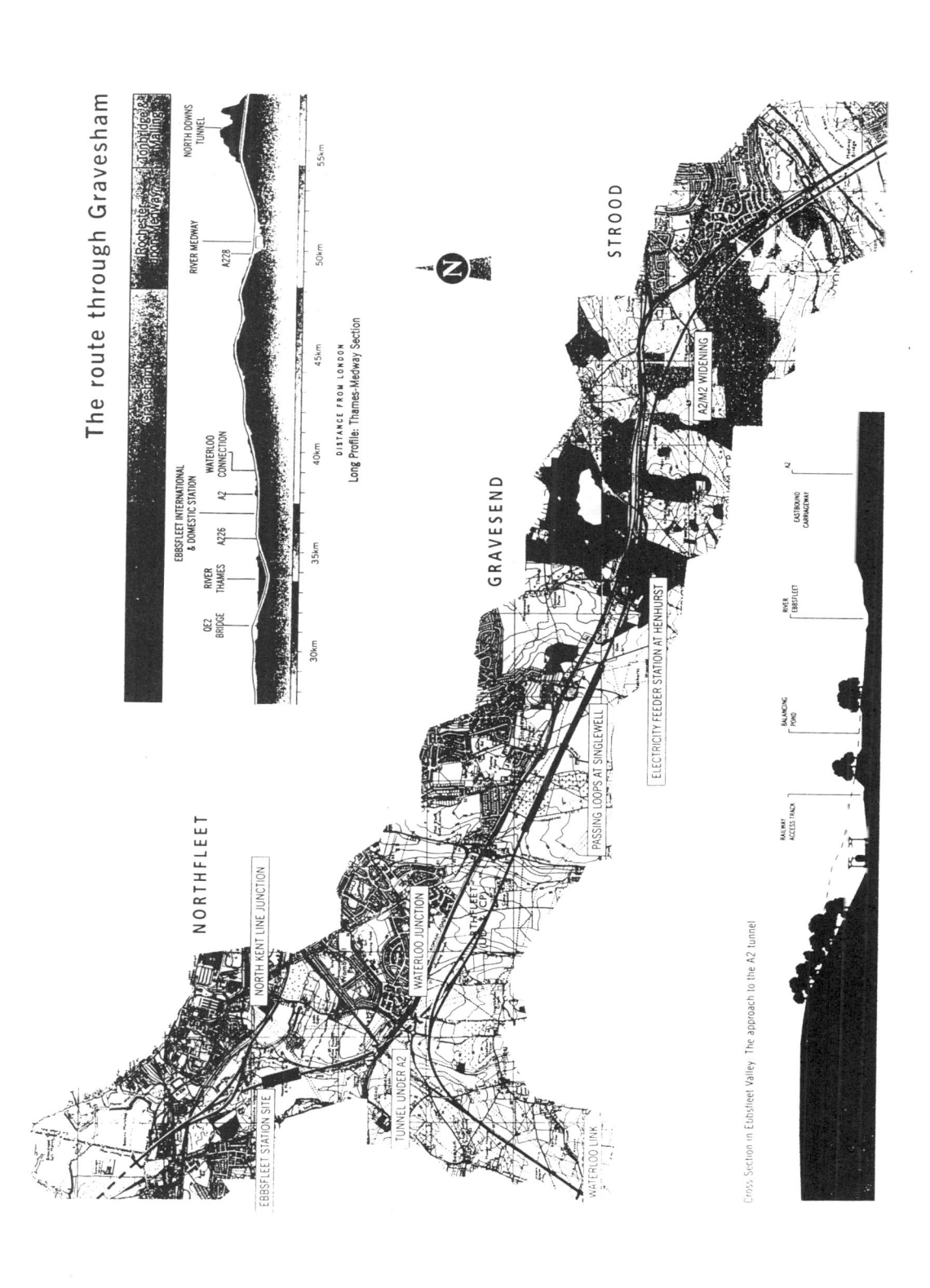

The route through Gravesham

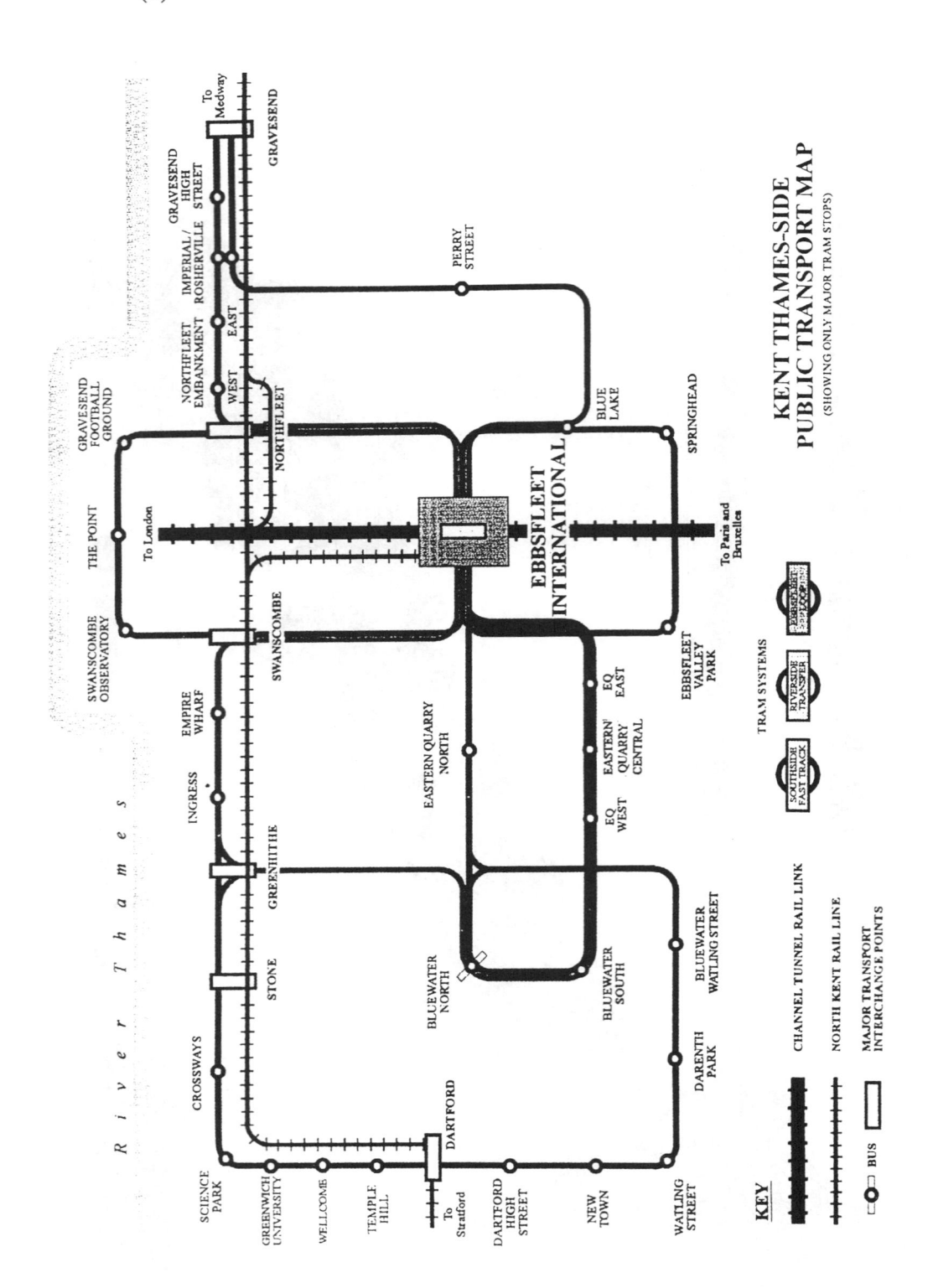

Part E: Learning from experience: ensuring you pass

(d)

12: Gravesend Town Centre: case study documentation Notes

Appendix I: Bluewater

3.9

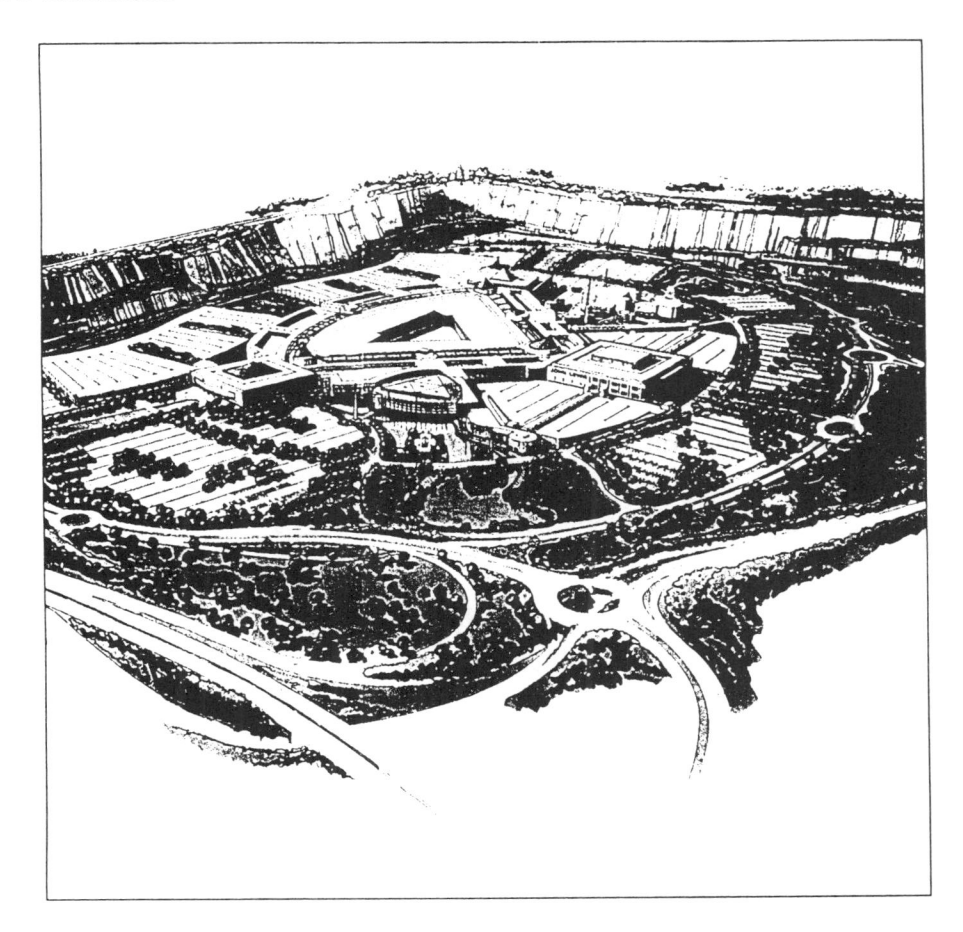

Construction of this 150,000 m² shopping centre in the dramatic setting of Western Quarry, a former chalk pit, is due to commence this year. Containing over 300 shops, the centre will bring quality shopping to local residents and the wider area.

The centre is being developed by Lend Lease, an Australian company with a world-wide reputation for high standard developments.

Leisure provision will also form an important part of the centre. A multiplex cinema, a fitness centre and restaurants are amongst the facilities that will add life to the centre even outside normal shopping hours.

Improvements to be made to the A2 and Bean Road will aid access to Bluewater as well as generally improve traffic flows in the area.

5,000 new jobs are expected to be created at Bluewater. The centre is due to open in 1998.

Chapter 13

GRAVESEND TOWN CENTRE: PRÉCIS, MARKETING AUDIT, SWOT

> **This chapter covers the following topics.**
> 1. Introduction
> 2. Sample précis
> 3. Marketing audit checklist
> 4. Marketing audit 1
> 5. Marketing audit 2
> 6. Marketing audit 3
> 7. SWOT analyses

1 INTRODUCTION

1.1 Having now completed your précis you can now compare it with the specimens which follows.

1.2 None of the three specimens have been structured, probably because untypically the text of case study itself is unstructured. All three précis are also very brief, perhaps reflecting the amount of peripheral information in this particular text. Compared to normal standards, at first sight, these three examples appear minimal and unsatisfactory.

1.3 However, on closer examination these specimens exhibit a great deal of consistency and might be said to summarise the Gravesend situation rather well. Succinctness is an asset provided nothing substantial is omitted. All three samples paint a picture of Gravesend in its regional setting and end with the threat to continued prosperity of its town centre caused by Bluewater.

1.4 *Sample précis 1* includes some information derived from an analysis of the appendices and refers albeit briefly to Gravesend's early history. *Sample précis 2* is the shortest of the three and dwells rather more on recent improvements to the town centre. *Sample précis 3* is the only one to cover your role and the Channel Tunnel link and ends with a description of data available in the appendices.

1.5 So now how does your précis compare? In what respects is it better than these samples and in what is it deficient?

2 SAMPLE PRÉCIS

2.1 *Sample précis 1 by Tara Becket, Maggie Law, Marie Lock, Simon Scard, Purnima Tailor*

Gravesend, the featured town centre, dominates the Borough of Gravesham situated alongside the River Thames. The borough extends south from Gravesend at the top comprising of 20,000 acres of unspoiled North Kent countryside, renowned for being an area of outstanding natural beauty. Gravesend can be described to be in a prime location with adequate transport infrastructures. The A2 trunk road which intersects the Borough of Gravesham has led to Gravesend being less than half an hour away from the Port of Dover and 45 minutes from central London by road and rail.

Despite Gravesend being a victim of economic cycles, the town's market still flourishes today from the date it started in the 13th century. The town has historical tales to tell from Elizabethan times and fine Victorian buildings still remain today with the Royal Terrace Pier adding to the interest of Gravesend's riverside. The town is fascinating itself, being associated with the writings of Charles Dickens and being associated with two other famous names, General Gordon and Pocahontas.

Gravesend has a current population of 56,000 with the possibility of 30,000 houses being built in the Dartford and Gravesend area. With a resident workforce of 45,000 of which 22% are concentrated in the manufacturing industry estate running along the river's edge, 66% of the workforce are in the service sector, who either work in Gravesend or commute into London. Unlike the rest of Kent, Gravesend has a rich cultural mix, with a substantial Sikh community.

The Gravesend Town Centre Initiative, which started in February 1991 in order to instigate intensive town centre improvements, was supported by Gravesham Borough Council, Kent County Council and the local private sector. The eight point plan (Appendix 1, Chapter 27 paragraph 3.1), which was designed to improve Gravesend town centre for transport, parking and access, involved a sum of £1 million from the partnership. The major stores of M&S, Boots with Blue Circle industries also contributed funds for the town centre development and the results have created an attractive, flowering and accessible shopping environment. Gravesend town centre offers a range of stores including the anchor stores of John Lewis and Debenhams and various of the chain stores familiar to every high street.

A recent study on behalf of the Town Centre Initiative defined the typical Gravesend shopper as someone of a relatively low socio-economic standing earning less than £10,000 and is more than 60 years of age. 56% of both the D and E socio-economic groups prefer to shop at Gravesend. (D comprises at those with a fixed income or unskilled workers, whilst E is made up of pensioners, students and the unemployed.)

Dartford and Gravesend are already affected by the out of town centres such as Lakeside. Thus the current plan of the construction of Bluewater, a major 150,000m^2 shopping centre, implies a certain threat to Gravesend.

2.2 *Sample précis 2 by Georgina Little, Katie Hallam, Anna Peluso*

Gravesend is situated on the south side of the Thames and is part of the Kent County Council. It has a strong historical background dating from the 13th century. Gravesend was once a popular town but has since faced a number of threats, causing it to deteriorate. This fact has been recognised and some steps have been taken to try to build up the town centre in an attempt to make it a more attractive place to shop and attract new business. In 1992, the Town Centre Initiative (TCI) began which initially involved an eight point plan, developing into the current ten point plan. Already, £1 million has been invested by the Borough Council to aid improvements in partnership with the public and private sector. Local traders created two groups, one for independent retailers and one for large multiples. A number of physical improvements have already been made, namely:

(a) attractive street lighting;
(b) re-paved streets and pavements;
(c) cast iron name plates for streets;
(d) flowers;
(e) easy and abundant parking;
(f) video camera surveillance in car parks.

Notes   **Part E: Learning from experience: ensuring you pass**

The current retailers and banks have funded pedestrianisation in the town centre. All these changes are in response to threats from Lakeside - the out of town shopping centre, and soon to be completed Bluewater. Further developments of the CTRL and an urban village are currently being planned

2.3 *Sample précis 3*

I am Bill Morrison, independent marketing consultant specialising in marketing strategy. My client is Brian Richmond, Gravesend Council's Town Centre Manager. I need to report on initial recommendations to client plus the Town Centre Initiative (TCI) Steering Group on 14th June 1996.

I have recently been to Dudley to see for myself the effects a large out-of-town shopping centre can have on nearby towns and communities.

Gravesend, which lies on the south side of the river Thames opposite the port of Tilbury, is less than an hour away from the port of Dover and Gatwick Airport by road and central London by train. It is a town with an interesting history with a record of substantial environmental improvements in recent years owing to investment and the TCI. Furthermore Gravesend features in the 'Thames Gateway' ambitious regional development plans and is close to the agreed site for the Channel Tunnel Rail Link as well as a proposed new development of 30,000 new houses and other initiatives.

Unfortunately this rosy scenario of a prosperous future for Gravesend is threatened by a huge new out-of-town shopping/entertainment centre called Bluewater, only five miles away on which the building has already started for completion in 1998. This is in addition to Lakeside, a vast shopping centre across the Thames, opened about five years ago.

The TCI has a Steering Group and five working groups with memberships drawn from both the pubic and the private sectors.

The Thames Gateway plan will be progressed through a new partnership between the Dartford and Gravesham Borough Councils, Kent County Council, Blue Circle Industries (the major landowner) and the University of Greenwich.

Information currently available to me apart from a myriad of maps, includes key retailer profiles, customer needs/household expenditure surveys 1993, details of the TCI ten point plan and steering group structure and some sketchy information on the channel tunnel link and Bluewater development.

3   MARKETING AUDIT CHECKLIST

Checklists

3.1   Before doing the audit proper you might like to try the information checklist mentioned in Chapter 8 Paragraph 3.7 and the checklist format in Chapter 1, Paragraphs 2.8 and 2.9. You should use this checklist to determine the information we have on Gravesend Town Centre and the information we do not have. You could use a tick to show the information we have and a cross(X) to show the information we do not have (and which might then form the basis of your MkIS/MR recommendations later on in your plan). Further refinements might be to use P for information we have in part only and NA for *not applicable*. Really organised students might like to note the page numbers on which items ticked or marked P occur. It is easy for people to panic when they realise how little information the case study gives them. However, in real life we often take decisions based on inadequate information: the important thing is to recognise this and make reasonable assumptions. Having done this operation you might like to compare your results with those of the syndicate which follows, noting that there are likely to be some discrepancies, since this exercise is partly judgmental.

It might also be revealing for you to compare this checklist with those done for FirstrATE and Leffe, so as to achieve further insights into the differences between the marketing of services and products and between the private and public sectors.

Internal

3.2 (a) *Current position*

    (i) *Performance*

        P   Total sales in value and in units
        X   Total gross profit, expenses and net profit
        X   Percentage of sales for sales expenses, advertising etc
        P   Percentage of sales in each segment
        X   Value and volume sales by year, month, model size etc
        X   Sales per thousand consumers, per factory, in segments
        X   Market share in total market and in segments

    (ii) *Buyers*

        P   Number of actual and potential buyers by area

        ✓   Characteristics of consumer buyers, eg income, occupation, education, sex, size of family etc

        P   Characteristics of industrial buyers, eg primary, secondary, tertiary, manufacturing; type of industry; size etc

        NA Characteristics of users, if different from buyers

        P   Location of buyers, users

        P   When purchases made: time of day, week, month, year; frequency of purchase; size of average purchase or typical purchase

        X   How purchases made: specification or competition; by sample, inspection, impulse, rotation, system; cash or credit

        P   Attitudes, motivation to purchase; influences on buying decision; decision making unit in organisation

(b) *Products*

    (i) *Gravesend Town Centre*

        NA Quality: materials, workmanship, design, method of manufacture, manufacturing cycle, inputs-outputs

        P   Technical characteristics, attributes that may be considered as selling points, buying points

        NA Models, sizes, styles, ranges, colours etc

        P   Essential or non-essential, convenience or speciality

        P   Similarities with other company products

        P   Relation of product features to user's needs, wants, desires

        P   Development of branding and brand image

        P   Degree of product differentiation, actual and possible

        NA Packaging used, function, promotional

        P   Materials, sizes, shapes, construction, closure

    (ii) *Competitors*

        P   Competitive and competing products

        P   Main competitors and leading brands

        P   Comparison of design and performance differences with leading competitors

        P   Comparison of offerings of competitors, images, value etc

    (iii) *Future product development*

        P   Likely future product developments in company
        P   Likely future, or possible future, developments in industry
        P   Future product line or mix contraction, modification or expansion

(c) *Distribution*
   (i) *Gravesend Town Centre*
   - P   Current company distribution structure
   - P   Channels and methods used in channels
   - P   Total number of outlets (consumer or industrial) by type
   - X   Total number of wholesalers or industrial middlemen, analysed by area and type
   - P   Percentage of outlets of each type handling product broken down into areas
   - X   Attitudes of outlets by area, type, size
   - P   Degree of co-operation, current and possible
   - P   Multi-brand policy, possible or current
   - X   Strengths and weaknesses in distribution system, functionally and geographically
   - NA   Number and type of warehouses; location
   - P   Transportation and communications
   - NA   Stock control; delivery periods; control of information

   (ii) *Competitors*
   - P   Competitive distribution structure; strengths and weaknesses
   - P   Market coverage and penetration
   - NA   Transportation methods used by competitors
   - NA   Delivery of competitors
   - P   Specific competitive selling conditions

   (iii) *Future developments*
   - P   Future likely and possible developments in industry as a whole or from one or more competitors
   - X   Probable changes in distribution system of company
   - P   Possibilities of any future fundamental changes in outlets

(d) *Promotional and personal selling*
   (i) *Gravesend Town Centre*
   - NA   Size and composition of sales force
   - NA   Calls per day, week, month, year by salesmen
   - NA   Conversion rate of orders to calls
   - NA   Selling cost per value and volume of sales achieved
   - NA   Selling cost per customer
   - P   Internal and external sales promotion
   - NA   Recruiting, selection, training, control procedures
   - NA   Methods of motivation of salesmen
   - NA   Remuneration schemes
   - X   Advertising appropriation and media schedule, copy theme
   - X   Cost of trade, technical, professional, consumer media
   - X   Cost of advertising per unit, per value of unit, per customer
   - X   Advertising expenditure per thousand readers, viewers of main and all media used
   - X   Methods and costs of merchandising
   - X   Public and press relations; exhibitions

13: Gravesend Town Centre: précis, marketing audit, SWOT

  (ii) *Competitors*

　　P　Competitive selling activities and methods of selling and advertising; strengths and weaknesses

　　P　Review of competitors' promotion, sales contests etc

　　P　Competitors' advertising themes, media used

  (iii) P *Future developments* likely in selling, promotional and advertising activities

(e) *Pricing*

  (i) *Gravesend Town Centre*

　　X　Pricing strategy and general methods of price structuring in company

　　X　High or low policies; reasons why

　　X　Prevailing pricing policies in industry

　　X　Current wholesaler, retailer margins in consumer markets or middlemen margins in industrial markets

　　X　Discounts, functional, quantity, cash, reward, incentive

　　X　Pricing objectives, profit objectives financial implications such as breakeven figures, cash budgeting

  (ii) *Competitors*

　　X　Prices and price structures of competitors
　　P　Value analysis of own and competitors' products
　　X　Discounts, credit offered by competitors

  (iii) *Future developments*

　　X　Future developments in costs likely to affect price structures
　　X　Possibilities of more/less costly raw materials or labour affecting prices
　　P　Possible price attacks by competitors

(f) *Service*

  (i) *Gravesend Town Centre*

　　P　Extent of pre-sales or customer service and after-sales or product service required (by products)

　　✓　Survey of customer needs

　　NA　Installation, deduction in use, inspection, maintenance, repair, accessories provision

　　NA　Guarantees, warranty period

　　P　Methods, procedures for carrying out service

　　NA　Returned goods, complaints

  (ii) *Competitors*

　　P　Services supplied by competing manufacturers and service organisations

　　NA　Types of guarantee, warranty, credit provided

  (iii) X　Future possible developments that might require revised service policy

External

3.3 (a) *Environmental audit - national and international*

　　P　Social and cultural factors likely to affect the market, in the short and long term

　　P　Legal factors and codes of practice likely to affect the market in the short and long term

　　P　Economic factors likely to affect market demand in the short and long term

Part E: Learning from experience: ensuring you pass

- X Political changes and military action likely to impact upon national and international markets
- X Technological changes anticipated and likely to create new opportunities and threats

(b) *Marketing objectives and strategies*

- P Short-term plans and objectives for current year, in light of current political and economic situation
- P Construction of standards for measurement of progress towards achieving of objectives; management ratios that can be translated into control procedures
- P Breakdown of turnover into periods, areas, segments, outlets, salesmen etc
- P Which personnel required to undertake what responsibilities, actions etc when
- P Review of competitors strengths and weaknesses likely competitive reactions and possible company responses that could be made
- X Long-term plans, objectives and strategies related to products, price, places of distribution, promotion, personnel selling and service.

3.4 You are now ready to conduct the marketing audit proper, systematically working your way through the environmental audit, to the marketing functions audit and the other functional audits (financial, production and personnel).

CONSULT THE GUIDANCE NOTES IN
CHAPTER 8 PARAGRAPHS 3.1 TO 3.8

STEP 6 CONDUCT A MARKETING AUDIT

ALLOW YOURSELF ABOUT THREE HOURS FOR THIS STEP

3.5 Have a thoughtful and *critical* look now at the marketing audits submitted below. Both audits are quite good in their different ways.

(a) That done by Georgina Little, Katie Hallam and Anna Peluso is nicely succinct but perhaps too much so.

(b) That done by Tara Beckett, Maggie Law, Marie Lock, Simon Scard and Purnima Tailor is a great deal more extensive as regards the 'PEST' analysis. The competitor pie chart is a useful adaptation of Figure 1 in Appendix 5 of the case.

3.6 Neither of the two syndicates produced a human resources or financial audit. Did you? If so you may find a pay-off as you proceed. A production audit was of course not applicable.

3.7 Marketing audit 3 by a CIM Intensive Diploma course syndicate is an interesting hybrid which starts with a detailed audit of stakeholders and ends by auditing human resources, financial resources, assets and markets in terms of *strengths* and *weaknesses*. It is certainly different. You must make up you own mind whether it adds substantially to audits 1 and 2.

4 MARKETING AUDIT 1 (by Georgina Little, Katie Hallam and Anna Peluso)

External/environment

Macro environment

4.1 *Political, legal and fiscal:* government housing development and the channel tunnel.

4.2 *Economic*

(a) *Household expenditure.* The total expenditure of Gravesham residents is noticeably higher than the national average, but rather less than the rest of South East (ROSE). Gravesham residents not only spend more than the national average on footwear and clothing, but compare favourably with ROSE. Does Gravesham provide the facilities for this, or are they forced to shop elsewhere? Gravesham residents spend more than the *national* average on household goods, but less than ROSE.

(b) *Unemployment.* The majority of people commute to London to work. It is foreseen that 45,000 jobs are envisaged in this area through developments commencing in 1997 and completing in 2005.

4.3 *Socio/cultural*

(a) *Demographic trends.* The predicted trends in distribution for the next decade show an ageing population bought about by decreasing proportions of younger age groups. The total population in the area is predicted to drop by 1,100 people (by the year 2001).

(b) *Lifestyle:* Retired 60+, social class D and E; and 25-44, social class B, C1 and C2.

(c) *Attitudes:* Gravesend is thought of a rundown, uninteresting, and with poor shopping facilities.

(d) *Religion.* Mixed cultural base, an ethnic population of approximately 8,000 with a high proportion of Sikhs.

4.4 *Technological* innovation and technological change includes CTRL development at Ebbsfleet.

Market environment

4.5 *Competitors*

(a) *Numbers:* the major competitors are Lakeside and the soon-to-built Bluewater.
(b) *Strengths:* good product offering and extensive services.
(c) *Weaknesses:* lack of individuality/character.

4.6 *Customers*

(a) *Needs and wants:* Gravesend customers require better retail outlets, more product variety and a more pleasant, user friendly centre.

(b) *Brand loyalty, in terms of the shopping centre:* since expenditure on footwear and clothing is high from the Gravesham area, but Gravesend does not cater for this, consumers are forced to shop elsewhere.

4.7 *Distributors and physical logistics.* The Town Centre Initiative has ensured that there are good transport links which enable Gravesham to be a good retail location.

Internal environment

Marketing activity

4.8 *Marketing mix*

(a) *Product:* retail outlets offer a limited product range.

(b) *Promotion:* there is very little promotion of the town centre, due to the lack of advertising.

(c) *Place:* existing history.

(d) *Price:* what is the cost of Gravesend of being a good town centre?

Part E: Learning from experience: ensuring you pass

4.9 *Planning systems*

(a) *Current strategies and tactics.* The Town Centre Initiative has already been developed.

(b) *Effectiveness and efficiency.* The Town Centre Initiative has set the ball rolling and has set a precedent for change. However, this is not enough. The Thames Gateway plan is moving slowly but is based on long term objectives.

5 MARKETING AUDIT 2 (by Tara Beckett, Maggie Law, Marie Lock, Simon Scard, Purnima Tailor)

Masco analysis

Politics

5.1 The attitudes and reactions of people, social critics and government all affect the political environment.

5.2 The government's vision for the *Thames Gateway* (announced in 1994), which covered the area along the Thames to the East of London, will create many opportunities for the city of Gravesend.

(a) The government cited the Thames Gateway as *having capacity over the longer term.*

(b) Such benefits will *include significant levels of housing and employment development, alongside improvements in environmental quality.*

5.3 Gravesend will also benefit from the related investment in the Gravesend infrastructure. The decision to locate one of the Channel Tunnel's international domestic passenger stations in Ebbsfleet, which is just a few miles away from Gravesend, should provide further emphasis for growth in the region. Certainly the decision will bring in employment opportunities, especially for those who will now commute to work. It is also seen to provide *major contribution to the regeneration of the Gravesham area.*

5.4 A further opportunity lies in the recent approval of planning permission for the development of urban villages in Eastern Quarry, Greenhithe Waterfront and Swanscombe peninsula. Such villages will add around 30,000 new houses to the Gravesend area, adding to the emphasis for an attractive town centre sopping environment.

5.5 The partnership between Dartford and Gravesham Borough Councils, Kent County Council, Blue Circle Industries and the University of Greenwich has been formed with the aim of implementing the Government's framework for the Thames Gateway. One of the themes was to ensure that Gravesend keeps its traditional range of shopping commercial premises and entertainment venues. But this objective must surely be questioned as there is no doubt that development of the town centre lies as the only way ahead for its long term survival.

5.6 In 1990 the government approved planning permission for the development of the Bluewater out-of-town shopping centre; this went ahead despite opposition from Gravesham Borough Council. Surely, this is the biggest threat to Gravesend town centre.

5.7 Recent hope on the political front lies with Labour's leaked *tax suggestions.*

(a) A new government might impose a levy on out-of-town parking spaces, with the aim of discouraging motorists from using them. This possibly indicates Labour's support for town centres such as Gravesend as they view out-of-town shopping centres as: 'loosening the social fabric of our cities, towns and villages'.

(b) Labour also proposes to use such revenues perhaps to subsidise the rates charged on small businesses within town centres, but this may be too late for Gravesend.

(c) The financial resources of Gravesham Borough Council are severely restricted and thus the scope for improvements will be severely restrained. Government spending controls might make this position worse.

Legal

5.8 There is an abundance of legislative controls that are concerned with issues relating to retailing. Such controls are also influenced by legislation from the European Union. Retailers not only have to comply with specific legislation such as the Food and Safety Act 1990, Health and Safety at Work Act 1974, Building Act 1984, the Town and Country Planning Act, but also with employee regulations such as the Employment Act and Young Persons Employment Act, and, in more recent times with the advent of the trend towards Sunday shopping, the Sunday Trading Act.

5.9 This legislation must be complied with in full, as businesses are liable to be prosecuted for contravention. The enforcement authority for the majority of this legislation applying to business is the local authority. They have the power to visit retailers and inspect their premises and documentation to obtain the information they require. In the case of Gravesend Town Centre, the local authority is the Gravesham Borough Council and it would be the environmental Health Officers employed by Gravesham that would ensure that the standards required by the legislation are upheld.

5.10 Advice can be obtained from the local authority for complying with this legislation. Small retailers are recommended to find out the legislative requirements before commencing on their venture as their budget could increase drastically, just to comply with the current legislative standards.

5.11 Legislation affecting businesses has steadily increased over the years. The purposes of the legislation are:

(a) to promote competition;

(b) to prevent unfair competition;

(c) to protect consumers from unfair business practices;

(d) to protect the larger interest of society against unbridled business behaviour.

Environment

5.12 Environmentalism features organised movements of concerned citizens and governments to protect and enhance people's living environment. Such environmentalists focus on marketing's impact on the environment and the costs of serving these needs and wants.

5.13 In context, the environmental issues in and around Gravesend Town Centre have clearly improved in recent years as a result of the *Town Centre Initiative*. General improvements to buildings, pavements, and the surrounding gardens have reportedly removed the 'eyesores' from the town.

5.14 The Town Centre itself is now pedestrianised, improving the air quality. In fact, £1m has now been spent on environmental improvements in and around the town centre.

5.15 Although many of the town centre buildings are Victorian, and therefore protected against any structural changes without authorisation, there are many derelict, redundant properties throughout the town centre. A situation that needs monitoring and controlling is the rise in acts of vandalism and graffiti; such acts of hooliganism can severely detract from an image of a town centre.

5.16 The environmental protection that has been provided in Gravesend Town Centre would have been impossible without the support and financial backing of a number of key businesses within the area. This support needs to continue to ensure the prosperity of the town centre.

Social and demographic changes

5.17 Over the next decade, the Gravesham population structure will change substantially. The main feature of change will be an increase in 60-65 year old women. A slight decrease is expected in the 25-44 age group, whilst there is an increase in 0-14 year olds.

5.18 Demographic changes have powerful effects upon many aspects of economic life. For example, there is an increase in the number of car owners; this affects people's ability to commute into town and other shopping centres. There are a number of developments that may produce a major shift in the profile of consumer demand.

  (a) There is an increase in the number of working women in either full or part time employment. This means there is an increase in spending, since both partners in a household are earning.

  (b) Due to the increase in younger population, the dominant role of fashion leads to brand loyalty, causing an increase in spending and more 'material' lifestyle.

  (c) The trend towards an ageing population in Gravesham means that mobility may be restricted to town centres, since travelling to out of town shopping areas can be expensive and too daunting.

  (d) Over the past two decades, there has been a significant, general change in eating habits. Overall, people of all age groups tend to eat out. Also there has been a trend in healthy eating which allows for growth in this section.

  (e) Due to other modes of transport, such as trains and buses, mobility is increased, so residents are able to commute to places such as London, where shopping facilities are extensive and of a wide variety.

  (f) Overall people are making more of an effort to increase their leisure time, therefore allowing greater time to shop.

Economy

5.19 The past twenty-five years have seen a remarkable growth in service industries in the developed countries of the world. Many such countries, including Britain, have ceased to be manufacturing based and are now service-based economies.

5.20 More and more shopping centres are developing out of town and away from the inconvenience of the High Street with its car parking restrictions and declining facilities. It was revealed in a Boots Survey (1995) that 31% of total sales now occur in out of town sites.

5.21 Following five years of low activity, the economy is now picking up and jobs are becoming more secure, with the unemployment rate decreasing to 9% in March 1996. Unemployment fell by 20,100 in May to 2.7 million - a 26 month low. Official figures show that long-term unemployment, too, is now falling.

5.22 A surge in the rate of start-ups of small business in the 1980s created around 350,000 jobs, at a time when most big firms were shedding labour. British companies are now emerging from their second recession in ten years in surprisingly good condition; however, many people still believe that the idea of boom sounds far-fetched.

5.23 A GDP growth of 3% was forecast for 1997, at an average of $3^{1}/_{4}$% in 1995 and 1996. Retail sales have expanded by 4% in the 12 months to April 1995. Consumers do not seem yet to have been affected by the tax rises and the introduction of VAT on domestic fuel, despite initial fears that their purchasing power was being diminished.

5.24 Inflation stands at 2.5% and the government is determined to get public finances under control by maintaining a tight grip on public spending. The public sector borrowing requirement seems to be less than forecast in last November's budget (£9.8 billion in 1993/94 and £37.9 billion in 1994/95); however, the Treasury is under pressure from backbenchers to use this cushion to cut taxes and so boost the government's popularity. The fight against inflation continues and economists are forecasting that it will rise only to 3.2% in the 4th quarter of 1995, well within the government's 1-4% target.

Technology

5.25 Relevant to economic developments are the underpinning technology skills and equipment, affecting the way an economy's resources are converted into outputs. Technological developments can and do affect marketing. Moving from an industrial society to an information society is aided by modern technology. The wide use of computers has fed down to the High Street, noticed clearly with such things as Automatic Teller Machines and computerised information screens.

5.26 In relation to Gravesend Town Centre, it would clearly not be acceptable to have complete automation within the centre. Some personal contact with advisers and sales assistants is not only suitable but reassuring. But to ignore technology completely would be foolish, as it would not take long for the city centre to look out-dated, especially compared to the Bluewater site, and even inappropriate for the requirements of its customers. Thus, a good mix of technology and reliability would create a well balanced and enjoyable atmosphere that will be required to entice customers to shop and shop again.

5.27 Individual retailers will be encouraged to introduce automatic doors, electronic point of sale (EPOS) terminals and even escalators and lifts. The Town Centre will find wide-scale surveillance not only ensures consumer security in the town centre but in the car parks as well.

5.28 Recent developments have allowed both retailers and town centre planners to benefit from electronic traffic flow analysis. This will allow both groups to target both 'hot' and 'cold' areas in terms of throughflow of consumers in the city centre.

5.29 A potential technological threat that needs to be highlighted is the trend towards home-shopping. Not only is such a service offered on satellite television, but also retailers will be soon offering their products on the Internet. Although such services will never replace the retail store, such advances must surely be carefully monitored.

Micro market analysis

Competitors

5.30 The main competitors are as follows.

(a) Bluewater
(b) Lakeside, Thurrock
(c) London city centre
(d) Home shopping (catalogues, directories, internet, cable TV)
(e) Other local town centres: see pie chart below.

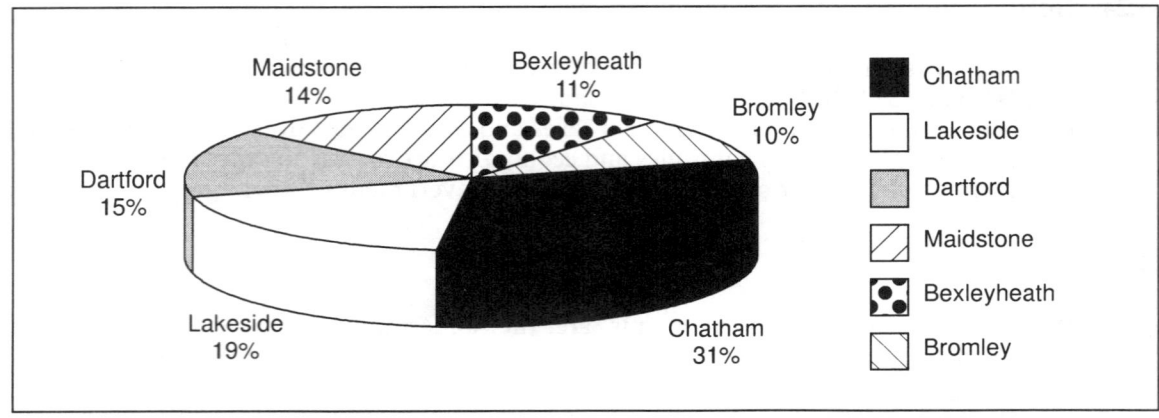

Shopping centres visited

Customer needs survey

5.31 In a survey undertaken by Gravesend Town Centre Initiative, Gravesend has the largest market share of shoppers, followed by Chatham with less than two thirds of Gravesend and, thirdly, Lakeside in Thurrock.

Customers

5.32 The following data relates to customers.

(a) 50% of people from rural areas shop in Gravesend.

(b) The typical shopper is 60 or over, and from the urban area.

(c) 43% of residents of Gravesend shop weekly.

(d) 48% of shoppers prefer to shop on weekday mornings.

(e) A growing trend towards bulk shopping is apparent in the town centre.

(f) There is a strong showing of groups C1 + C2 earning between £20,000 - £30,000 aged between 24-44 living in the urban areas who could be potential customers.

Services facilities

5.33 *Retail*

(a) Three major retail stores (John Lewis, M&S, Boots).
(b) Lack of fashion retailers to attract fashion-conscious 25-40 year olds.
(c) Lack of financial services.
(d) Low priority given to restaurant and other food retailers.

5.34 *Non-retail*

(a) Pedestrianised area.
(b) Concentrated area of shops.
(c) Car parking facilities available.
(d) Other public amenities, available.

6 MARKETING AUDIT 3 (by a CIM ID Course syndicate)

Stakeholders

The market place

6.1 *Customers*. The list below identifies what major customers expect from Gravesend.

(a) Retailer strategy group (multiples, including banks)

(i) Continued flow of high spending consumers
(ii) Ease of trading environment
(iii) Competitive rentals

13: Gravesend Town Centre: précis, marketing audit, SWOT

(b) Big action Group (independents)
   (i) Continued flow of high spending consumers
   (ii) Ease of trading environment
   (iii) Competitive rentals

(c) Local employers
   (i) Work force
   (ii) Profitable business
   (iii) Low costs
   (iv) Favourable trading conditions

(d) Employees
   (i) Job security
   (ii) Quality of life
   (iii) Career prospects

(e) St George's Centre/Anglesea Centre
   (i) Continued flow of high spending consumers
   (ii) Ease of trading environment.
   (iii) Competitive rentals
   (iv) Easy access, parking, security etc

(f) Greenwich University and Science Park: Crossways Business Park
   (i) Student population
   (ii) Need to attract appropriate staff
   (iii) Skilled workforce, educational connections

(g) Gravesham population; Sikh community; Eastern Quarry urban village
   (i) Positive retail experience
   (ii) Choice of shopping, quality
   (iii) Bus/trains
   (iv) Street entertainment
   (v) Sunday shopping
   (vi) Cultural sensitivity
   (vii) Safety

(h) Schools
   (i) Safety, cleanliness, new residents with young families
   (ii) Learning environment

(i) Tourists and tourist industry
   (i) Interesting venues
   (ii) Value for money
   (iii) Leisure activities
   (iv) Transportation, easy access
   (v) High service levels
   (vi) Cultural sensitivity
   (vii) Hotels, restaurants
   (viii) Tourist-friendliness

(j) Service industries (professional services, technical support)
   (i) Vibrant economy
   (ii) Communications infrastructure

6.2 *Competitors' objectives*

(a) Out-of-town shopping centres(OOTSC's): Bluewater Park/Lakeside/Pepperhill
   (i) Continued flow of high spending consumers
   (ii) Ease of trading environment
   (iii) Competitive rentals
   (iv) High St retailers
   (v) Ease of access
   (vi) Promotion to increase local awareness

(vii) Growing market for out-of-town shopping

(b) Other towns: Northfleet, Chatham, Dartford, Croydon, London West End

(i) Defend position against out-of-town shopping
(ii) Retain local market
(iii) Retain residents
(iv) Create distinctive identity

6.3 *External stakeholders' objectives are as follows.*

(a) Government

(i) Seen to be successful
(ii) Job and housing creation
(iii) Election victory
(iv) Thames Gateway's success
(v) Success of Channel Tunnel Rail Link (CTRL)
(vi) Conservative voters' values
(vii) Encouragement of enterprise and wealth creation

(b) Kent County Council

(i) Regional development, whilst respecting local community integrity
(ii) Exploitation of international opportunities arising from CTRL development

(c) Gravesham Borough Council

(i) Meeting local community. Needs
(ii) Maintenance of cultural sensitivity
(iii) Balance of borough town needs

(d) Port of London Authority, Thames Navigation Services, Sea and River Pilots

(i) See River Thames as thriving waterway
(ii) Skilled work force
(iii) Local employer needs

(e) CTRL consortium

(i) Integrated transport system
(ii) Local community acceptance
(iii) Attractive local area
(iv) Leisure industry links

(f) Financial community

(i) Good ROCE
(ii) Economic stability
(iii) Encouragement of new business opportunities

(g) Building and land developers: benign local planning regulations

(h) Transport Agencies ie Highways/Railtrak, bus operators: develop own transport attractiveness.

6.4 *Internal stakeholders' objectives*

(a) Retailers

(i) Satisfied customers
(ii) Customers with high disposable incomes
(iii) Low costs
(iv) Continued flow of high spending consumers
(v) Ease of trading environment
(vi) Competitive rentals.

(b) Property owners, especially Blue Circle Industries

(i) Sustained and long term income
(ii) Development opportunities

(c) Bill
  (i) Success from a difficult contract
  (ii) Avoid 'doughnuting' Gravesend

(d) Brian
  (i) Coordination of multiple interest groups
  (ii) Facilitate the workings of a complex DMU
  (iii) Clear role for future

(e) TCI group
  (i) Prosperous town
  (ii) Long term growth and stability

(f) New partnership re Thames Gateway (DBC, GBC, BCI)
  (i) Local support for 20-30 year plan
  (ii) Keep traditional commerce going
  (iii) maintain government support
  (iv) Environmentally sensitive exploitation of opportunities

Resources

6.5 *Men and women*

Staff skills	Strengths	Weaknesses
(a) Brian Richmond. TCM	• Commercially aware • Tactically active • Local knowledge • Local support • Proactive	• Lack of committed resources • Questionable power base • Evolving job role • Influence-dependent
(b) TCI working groups (60 people)	• Local knowledge • Experts in field • Local commitment • Vested interest • Commercial skills • Large cross section of community	• No goal congruence • Limited budget • Reliant on industry sponsorship • May have limited influence in own organisation • Conflict: public/private interests • Market driven vs own interests? • Activity to date is tactical • Evidence of success or was it Richmond?
(c) Economic development office	• Appointed me?	
(d) Major local sponsor	• Is there one?	• Don't appear to have one
(e) Staff costs	• External secondments	• Internal costs? • Who is fitting the bill? • What pool of financing? • What is the 'organisation'?

Part E: Learning from experience: ensuring you pass

6.6 Money

Staff skills	Strengths	Weaknesses
(a) Local income vs expenditure	Current levels	Minimal control: demand-led
(b) Long term availability	Major retailers/investors on board	• May pull out • No respectors of local impact • Depends on sustained trading
(c) Financial backing	Local business and local government	• Limited availability (£1m/3years) • No detailed information questionable loyalty • No long term commitment
(d) Access to funds	• Grants available • Project may merit Millennium funding	• Restricted • Unknown

6.7 Materials

Staff skills	Strengths	Weaknesses
(a) Relations with suppliers	• Good at the moment: the TCI is working • Groups/RSG/BIG-AG	• Different sub-groups: own agendas? • Loyalty not guaranteed

(b) Foot flow and product movement	63% of MR sample choose Gravesend	• 26% Chatham
		• High mobile spending element
		• Pepperhill is increasing in population
		• Competition with OOTSC's
		  - only 36% ABs prefer Gravesend
		  - 56% DEs

(c) Costs and availability		• Rental levels/space availability not known
(d) Distribution channels and effectiveness	Currently good range of shops: Marks & Spencer, John Lewis Partnership etc	• John Lewis Partnership, HoF enticed into new Bluewater park • Access is poor - parking, public transport • Poor range of quality and specialist shops

6.8 Property (machines)

Staff skills	Strengths	Weaknesses
(a) Spare capacity	• Some space for additional development/vacant shops	• Limited funds available to attract new clients • Cannot dictate which types: need for consultation/negotiation
(b) Utilisation		Mix of outlets by type (clothing/food-non-food) not known in detail
(c) Quality control	• Planning guidelines could offer some control on quality? • Parliamentary planning Guidance note 6 (1995) re viability of town centres	• Falling rent may attract less desirable outlets • Outside your control?
(d) Technology		Impact of car ownership growth: access to alternative markets (ie OOTSC's) and need for parking/congestion-free routes

Notes **Part E: Learning from experience: ensuring you pass**

6.9 *Markets*

Staff skills	*Strengths*	*Weaknesses*

(a) Image and reputation	• Well visited by locals (close to home)
	• Historic buildings (some)
	• History: Pocahontas/ Dickens/Gordon/ smuggling
	• Repackaging: cameras/lights/flowers
	• Near to areas of outstanding natural beauty
		• High unemployment/ageing population
		• 1993 survey identified:
		  - poor choice of shops/goods
		  - poor cleanliness
		  - lack of facilities for disabled
		  - lack of police presence etc
		• Poor reputation with the young (Lakeside preferred)
		• Poor awareness of image

(b) Market shares	• 35% locals prefer to go to Chatham/Lakeside • 77% of Gravesham shop once a week in Gravesend	• 52% Rurals visit Lakeside • Gravesend only chosen for low-value items • 36% ABs shop in Gravesend • As income increases, so does propensity to shop elsewhere • Profile: < £10K pa 60+ Urban dweller

(c) Quality of market information	• Population figures useful
	• Reasonable sociodemographic data, ACORN profiles
		• Shopper research
		  - dates from 1993
		  - limited sample (1%) a typical
		  - 10 miles radius of TC
		  - lack of benchmark data

(d) Customer loyalty	65% shop at least once a week - 43% at Gravesend > once a week
	• Gravesham shoppers all more likely to shop locally
	• Few change shopping habits
		• Notably those who changed moved from Gravesend because of:
		  - parking
		  - proximity to centre
		  - low quality shops

(e) Strength of marketing function	• Recognition of the need for marketing strategy as opposed to tactics	• Little knowledge and few resources • No details of any key players other than Richmond - need more than one person • Need for education on marketing • Poor awareness - no evidence of promotion • No strong branding of Gravesend's name (!!) in UK

7 SWOT ANALYSES

7.1

CONSULT THE GUIDANCE NOTES IN CHAPTER 8 PARAGRAPHS 3.9 TO 3.13
STEP 7 DO A SWOT ANALYSIS
ALLOW YOURSELF ABOUT THREE HOURS FOR THIS STEP

7.2 Look now at the three SWOT analyses conducted by students/syndicates which follow and see how these compare with yours.

7.3 The first example is very good, but it is not referenced or scored. The further issues arising are interesting and pertinent.

7.4 The second sample takes a similar approach and both confirms and builds on Sample 1 but then lacks categorisation, references and scoring.

7.5 The third sample is structured by the marketing mix for services and incorporates degrees of importance (high, medium or low) but again lacks references and does not cover opportunities and threats.

7.6 How did yours compare? Did yours include the ingredients of categorisation, referencing, scores and degrees of importance? If so - go to the top of the class.

SWOT analysis 1 by Tara Beckett, Maggie Law, Marie Lock, Simon Scard, Purnima Tailor

7.7

Strengths	*Weaknesses*
• Prime location • Large catchment area • Current retail mix/anchor stores • Pedestrian town centre • History/traditions • Town market • Area of outstanding beauty	• Bad reputation • Poor town infrastructure • Inadequate local transport facilities • Lack of advertising • Dispersal of stores • Cultural diversity of the local population causes some fragmentation of the market, perhaps • Inflexible shopping hours, no late night shopping and closure on Sundays • Lack of C1 and C2 shoppers • Lack of clothes stores/music stores/restaurants • Lack of street entertainment
Opportunities	*Threats*
• Anchor stores' financial involvement • Economic environment is strong for developments • Demographic trends indicate a rise in disposable incomes and increased spending on leisure and recreational activities • Government legislation preventing the building of further out-of-town shopping centres • Channel Tunnel/visitors passing through • New residential developments • University housing developments • Town and Riverside developments • Town centre manager's role	• Lakeside, Thurrock • Other town centres • Bluewater • Central London • Increased mobility of the local population • Home shopping • Easier access to European towns

Part E: Learning from experience: ensuring you pass

7.8 *Further issues arising*

(a) We need to develop the concept of *relationship marketing* within the TCI as the TCI needs a marketing focused approach. This will enhance frequent shopping, encourage loyalty and improve the image of the town centre.

(b) Further potential exists with the relationship between the *TCI and the retailers*, to build on the success of the town centre and develop strategic alliances to improve the provision of services.

(c) The development of Bluewater may cause Gravesend Town Centre to lose market share (ie of shoppers coming to visit).

SWOT analysis 2 by Jonathan Avery, Jonathan Hurry and Stephen Hoy

7.9 *Strengths*

(a) Location
   (i) S/E; prosperous communities
   (ii) Socio-demographics of population - high disposable incomes
   (iii) Centre for several shopping communities
   (iv) High demand for housing - very high potential growth area
   (v) Most frequently visited shopping centre in the region
   (vi) Proximity to Gatwick airport and Dover
   (vii) Expanding continental market presence due to Channel Tunnel

(b) Historical connections (marketing potential): architecture/leisure amenities

(c) Commitment from large retailers and commercial enterprises
   (i) *Chambers of commerce*: involvement
   (ii) *Retail strategy group*: multiples
   (iii) *Business in Gravesend*: small independents

(d) Presence of 'blue chip' companies within area

(e) Town Centre Initiative package - £1million

(f) Strong local customer base

(g) Centre of several shopping communities

(h) Secure shopping centre and abundant parking facilities

(i) Prominent police and security presence within area

(j) Pedestrianised location: aesthetically pleasing; security minded; clean

(k) Recognition of problem - consultants' involvement

7.10 *Weaknesses*

(a) Relatively poor catchment area for 'locking in' customers: 50% of residents commute to London; shopping habits will also follow this pattern.

(b) Poor choice/quality of shops
   (i) Lack of speciality shopping
   (ii) No Sunday/late night shopping
   (iii) Minimal levels of choice of shopping environment
   (iv) Disabled access

(c) *Transport linkages*
   (i) Not accessible from the M25
   (ii) Ease of access to Lakeside

(d) Out of town developments
   (i) Well managed
   (ii) Large promotional budgets

(e) Underresourcing of developments

(f) Slow and bureaucratic decision-making processes

(g) Restrictions on shop allocation - unlike large out of town (OOT) shopping

(h) Large scale decrease in passing trade and impulse purchases

7.11 *Opportunities*

(a) Exploitation of historical assets: possibilities for tourism

(b) New housing developments - channel tunnel and commuters - 30,000 homes and 45,000 jobs

(c) Linkages with Crossways, the largest business and distribution park in the UK

(d) Growing disenchantment with OOT shopping
- (i) Increasing restrictions on planning and development
- (ii) Customers are willing to travel for high quality goods

(e) Growth in 25-40 year old age group, with increasing disposable income

(f) Possibilities of marketing to local ethnic groups

(g) Thames Gateway
- (i) New jobs and housing being brought to the area
- (ii) Improved transport links

(h) Increase the utilisation of promotional events and activities

(i) Increased emphasis on the riverfront as a developmental opportunity

7.12 *Threats*

(a) Ageing population - provision of suitable services required

(b) Bluewater development

(c) Potential scale and speed of town centre decline

(d) Popularity of Lakeside

(e) Increasing centralisation of shopping habits: 'doughnutisation'

(f) Environmental impact of increasing customer flow through area
- (i) Transport problem
- (ii) Pollution
- (iii) Social problems for those without cars or the elderly; inaccessiblity

(g) Loss of 'cornerstone retailers'. This substantially undermines the town centre's attractiveness to new investors.

Part E: Learning from experience: ensuring you pass

SWOT analysis 3 by a CIM ID Course syndicate

7.13

	Performance					Importance		
	Strength		Neutral	Weakness		High	Medium	Low
	Major	Minor		Minor	Major			
Product								
Public services			X			X		
Land and buildings				X		X		
Infrastructure		X				X		
History		X					X	
Waterfront	X					X		
Proximity to A2/M25/Ports	X					X		
Safety			X			X		
Two shopping centres				X			X	
Weekly market		X				X		
Place - 'Pull Factor'								
Riverfront			X				X	
Shops				X		X		
Leisure/recreation				X			X	
Work			X					X
Administration			X				X	
Events					X	X		
Worship			X					X
Eat				X			X	
Household		X				X		
Price								
Shopping costs			?			X		
Rents and rates			?					X
Council tax			?					X
Government funding				X		X		
Access costs				X		X		
Business investment		X				X		
Labour rates			X			X		
Promotion								
£1m spent on env uplift		X				X		
Local advertising					X		X	
Other advertising					?	X		
People								
Contractors								
Direct sales staff			?			X		
Welfare organisations			?				X	
Education			?					X
Tourism/leisure staff			?			X		
Transport			?			X		
Modifiers								
Chamber of commerce		X					X	
Local bureaucracy			?				X	
Information services	X						X	

13: Gravesend Town Centre: précis, marketing audit, SWOT

	Performance					Importance		
	Strength		Neutral	Weakness		High	Medium	Low
	Major	Minor		Minor	Major			
Influencers								
TCM	X					X		
Existing business managers		X					X	
Investors and landlords			?				X	
Retail strategy groups		X				X		
Isolateds								
Consultants		X						X
Researchers				X				X
Utilities			X					X
Employers			X			X		
Lobby groups			?				X	
Physical evidence								
Pedestrianisation		X				X		
Lighting		X				X		
Security		X				X		
Cleanliness			X			X		
Car parking		X				X		
Aesthetics		X				X		
Process management								
Access		X				X		
Availability				X		X		
Quality				X		X		
Choice					X	X		
Bureaucratic procedures			?					X

317 BPP Publishing

Notes Part E: Learning from experience: ensuring you pass

Chapter 14

GRAVESEND TOWN CENTRE: ANALYSES OF APPENDICES

> This chapter covers the following topics.
> 1 Your own analysis
> 2 Appendix analysis 1
> 3 Appendix analysis 2

1 YOUR OWN ANALYSIS

> CONSULT THE GUIDANCE NOTES IN
> CHAPTER 8 PARAGRAPHS 3.14 TO 3.17
>
> STEP 8 CONDUCT ANALYSES/CROSS ANALYSES OF APPENDICES
>
> ALLOW ABOUT 2 TO 3 HOURS FOR THIS STEP

1.1 To help you refer back to the relevant appendix, the table below lists Bill's file contents.

Ref	Subject matter	Chapter 12 Paragraph
1A	Client letter	3.1
B	Key retailer profiles	3.2
C	Location maps (4)	3.3
D	Gravesham Household Expenditure Survey, 1993	3.4
E	Customer needs survey, 1993	3.5
F	Town Centre Initial Vision - ten point plan	3.6
	- steering group structure	3.6
G	Thames Gateway - selected maps and tables	3.7
H	Channel tunnel Rail Link	3.8
	Bluewater	3.9

1.2 Having done your own analyses, you can now compare these with the specimens which follow.

(a) The first appendix analysis has the benefit of being succinct and simple to understand but is largely descriptive.

(b) The second specimen is much better don't you think? With its greater detail and especially the cross-relating with other appendices, you emerge with much clearer insights of the key issues and also gain strong clues as to possible exam questions.

(c) In comparing the different approaches with your own, the end result is what really matters. You should be following the process of data → knowledge → analysis → understanding → decision.

2 APPENDIX ANALYSIS 1

2.1 *Appendix 1: Client letter*
   (a) This tells me some vital questions which the TCI want me to answer.
   (b) It indicates that they are looking for a marketing plan.
   (c) It points out limitations in implementation: I can only persuade, consult and negotiate.

2.2 *Appendix 2: key retailer profiles:* This is essentially a list of multiple retailers - the key ones, with very brief details of their nature and product ranges.

2.3 *Appendix 3: Location maps (4)*
   (a) London and South East region
   (b) M25 and the Borough of Gravesham
   (c) Gravesend town centre - street map
   (d) Gravesend/Gravesham relative to London and Heathrow/Gatwick and Stanstead airports.

2.4 *Appendix 4: Gravesham Household Expenditure Survey - 1993*
   (a) This is a detailed statistical document covering the demography, social classes, household expenditure patterns, 'mobile' household expenditure and its placement.
   (b) Mobile expenditure refers to items (eg consumer durables) where there can be considerable variation in the place of purchase.

2.5 *Appendix 5: Customer Needs Survey - 1993:* an even more detailed document in three main sections: 1 Where and why do people prefer a particular shopping centre, 2 Customer profiles; 3 Shopping centres used for food.
   (a) Section 1 covers main centres visited, frequency, change in non-food shopping habits, attitudes towards Gravesend, differences between 'preferred' and 'visited' shopping centres, preferred items and modes of travel, environmental improvements and local awareness/advertising.
   (b) Section 2 covers social class, income, age and the typical Gravesend shopper.
   (c) Section 3 covers shopping centres used for food.

2.6 *Appendix 6: TCI vision*
   (a) This simply lists the ten point plan.
   (b) This gives the steering group structure.

2.7 *Appendix 7: Thames Gateway*
   (a) This gives maps of defining the area and major features.
   (b) This gives details of housing, population and commuting patterns.
   (c) This schedules major future developments.

2.8 *Appendix 8: Channel Tunnel Rail Link:* consists really of four maps positioning the link vis a vis the motorways, the mainline railways, the route through Gravesham, bus and tube lines.

2.9 *Appendix 9 - Bluewater:* An artist's impression of the site plus very brief description.

3 APPENDIX ANALYSIS 2

3.1 Consult the table in Section 1 of this chapter for where to find the Appendix in the case study documentation. The paragraph references refer to the main text of the case, in Chapter 12.

Part E: Learning from experience: ensuring you pass

Appendix number	What is it saying?	How does it help us?	Which other appendices or text can it be related to? (Chapter 12)	If so what extra information insights does this reveal?
Appendix 1	Letter from TCI manager setting out my brief = my plan, various strategic issues, organisational/implementation issues.	Clarifies what I need to do and the problems I face.	The Candidate's Brief and text generally.	Confirms that I need to produce a complete marketing plan addressing specified strategic issues and implementation. Gives strong points towards the sort of exam question I can expect.
Appendix 2	Lists the major food/non food multiple retailers you would expect to find in the most important shopping areas.	• Tells me the type and product range of the various multiples. • Helps to target key multiples for retention and/or wooing to set-up in Gravesend TC.	Apps 4, 5, 6, 9 Test [p 11] para 2.30-2.33	Gravesend must offer incentives to multiples to open/stay in the TC. Already Bluewater has attracted, M&S, John Lewis and the House of Fraser.
Appendix 3	Gives four maps locating Gravesend to London and M5, and to Heathrow, Gatwick and Stanstead airports. Includes a street map of the TC	Gives me a good feel for Gravesend's favourable geographical location.	Apps 5, 6, 7, 8, 9	• Shows opportunities for future exploitation of industrial development and tourism. • Relates to TCI plan points 4 and 7 in creating easy access.
Appendix 4	Give household expenditure for Gravesham Borough on all major food and non-food categories of goods and services. Also population/demographic data and 'mobile' H/H expenditure.	Very useful for comparison with national/regional data, for planning resources and for developing positioning/segmentation strategies.	Just about all really	Expenditure per H/H × no of H/H = spend and is the major attraction for businesses of all sorts to set up in Gravesham. Can market Gravesend more accurately and positively.

14: Gravesend Town Centre: analyses of appendices

Appendix number	What is it saying?	How does it help us?	Which other appendices or text can it be related to? (Chapter 12)	If so what extra information insights does this reveal?
Appendix 5	This is a summary report of a Customer Needs Survey conducted in 1993 by the Economic Development Unit of Gravesham BC.	Being a summary report means that further details will be available. Whilst being a description of the facts of buying behaviour rather than establishing need, it does tell me that Gravesend is the most visited centre with Chatham second and Lakeside third. The key variables inducing centre switching were access, parking, distance and shop quality. There is a gap between what shoppers require and what Gravesend is currently offering. The typical Gravesend shopper is D/E, 60+, living in the urban area and earning <£10K. Awareness of Gravesend TC is to low. Local radio and local newspapers offer good reaches.	Apps 1, 2, 3, 4, 6, 9	The situation is correctable in the longer term. Gravesend town Centre can be made more attractive and to wider target markets, also better known. It has important implications for the Town Centre Initiative and particularly for wooing further investment.
Appendix 6	Gives me the TCI Vision, 10 point plan and structure to which my marketing plan will have to relate.	Will help me to key in to the corporate plan and to address the interests of the major stakeholders.	Apps 1, 5, 7, 8, 9	The TCI cannot proceed in a vacuum and has to react to external developments and changes in the macro-environmental factors, and competition.

Part E: Learning from experience: ensuring you pass

Appendix number	What is it saying?	How does it help us?	Which other appendices or text can it be related to? (Chapter 12)	If so what extra information insights does this reveal?
Appendix 7	Defines the geographical area of the Thames Gateway and locates the proposed developments. Also schedules developments and gives population and commuting data.	• Helps me in developing longer-term strategy. • Gravesend Waterfront could be a tourist attraction with implications for the TCI.	Apps 1, 3, 4, 6, 8, 9	My marketing plan will have to take these longer-term developments into account since they will affect total demand segmentation, positioning and promotional strategies.
Appendix 8	Shows me how the Channel Tunnel Rail Link will be sited relative to Gravesham, Gravesend, the Thames Gateway, London and South East. Shows related infrastructure - road, rail and bus.	Indicates the possibilities of integrating Gravesend access improvement plans with Ebbsfleet International Station on the CRTL.	Apps 1, 3, 6, 7 Text [p 11] para 2.30-2.33	Could provide a powerful incentive when linked with Gravesend Waterfront for tourists to drop off. Adds further stimulus to the TCI and its marketing.
Appendix 9	• Gives a picture of the Bluewater site and brief details.	Reminds me of this major threat to the Town Centre Initiative and the need to develop an effective competitive strategy.	Appx 1, 2, 3, 4, 5, 6, 7, 8 Text [p 11] para 2.30-2.33	Reminds me that this is the major short-term strategy issue. What can I learn from the Lakeside experience?

Chapter 15

GRAVESEND TOWN CENTRE: SITUATIONAL ANALYSIS, KEY ISSUES, MISSION STATEMENT, BROAD AIMS, MAJOR PROBLEMS

This chapter covers the following topics.

1. The steps you should take
2. Situational analyses
3. Decide key issues
4. Mission statement and broad aims
5. Major problems

1 THE STEPS YOU SHOULD TAKE

1.1 It is now time to move on to the next two steps.

CONSULT THE GUIDANCE NOTES IN CHAPTER 8 PARAGRAPHS 3.18 TO 3.28
STEP 9 RECONSIDER YOUR PRÉCIS, MARKETING AUDIT AND SWOT ANALYSIS STEP 10 CONDUCT A SITUATIONAL ANALYSIS
ALLOW BETWEEN 2 AND 3 HOURS FOR COMPLETING THESE STEPS

1.2 When you have completed your situational analysis please compare it with the four specimens which follow.

2 SITUATIONAL ANALYSES

2.1 You will note come inconsistencies in the analysis which follows. Some candidates find it extremely difficult to condense the case situation into a few paragraphs after all their analytical efforts. Three of the four samples have been expressed in bullet point style and only one in written statement format. Which do you prefer for this particular exercise? As Bill Morrison, which format is most suitable for his written report and/or a possible verbal presentation?

   (a) *Situational analysis 1* is extremely brief and the first paragraph is not particularly helpful.

   (b) *Situational analysis 2* covers more ground but it more like a list of weaknesses.

Part E: Learning from experience: ensuring you pass

(c) *Situational analysis 3* is far more optimistic, but is improving the aesthetic elements of the town centre, combined with attracting new retailers and retaining the existing mix, the only/best solution, particularly if the existing mix is unsatisfactory?

(d) *Situational analysis 4*, whilst not in bullet-point format, follows a structure of PAST → PRESENT → CHANGE → FUTURE → THE TASK FACED. It smacks of a greater degree of command that the others, don't you think?

2.2 Well how did yours compare? Hopefully quite well! By way of interest and further comparison, some of the extra analysis and use of models produced by a syndicate in pursuance of its situational analysis follows.

2.3 *Situational analysis 1*

- The commission handling the Thames Gateway project has restricted the scope of changes that could be implemented by Gravesend over the next twenty to thirty years. The Commission's main priority appears to be to ensure that Gravesend remains to '...keep the traditional range of commercial premises'.
- The previous investment co-ordinated by the Town Centre Initiative successfully addressed the problems faced during the period 1992 to 1995. However, the external threats which have now emerged present different problems which require new solutions.
- The most significant problem faced is the development of an out-of-town sopping centre at Bluewater only five miles away, which opens in 1998.
- The successful implementation of strategies will require not only the assistance of town centre retailers but also a restructuring of the TCI Steering Group to improve the decision making process.

2.4 *Situational analysis 2*

The key elements are as follows.
- Competition from out of town shopping centres is increasing.
- Reduction in number of shoppers spending money in the town centre.
- Falling retailer turnover decreases the town centre's attractiveness, starting a vicious circle of events.
- Gravesend faces a period of extensive environmental change.
- The town centre has a poor image.
- There is a lack of marketing orientation
- The TCI lacks the structure for effective planning, implementation and control.
- Over-reliance on local shoppers and C_2 DE blue-collar workers plus elderlies with income less than £10k.
- Gravesend is largely product-led and not specifically customer focused.
- Funding is limited.

2.5 *Situational analysis 3*

- Gravesend is on the verge of a new phase of prosperity in its history.
- There is potential for rapid growth.
- The business opportunities must be exploited before the window closes.

- We can build on the foundations laid out in the Ten Point Plan and develop the hidden potential of Gravesend as a thriving market town within the Borough of Gravesham.

- Having examined the macro-environment including the PEST factors, the competition and our strengths and weaknesses, the situation overall is favourable.

- However, the TCI Steering Group has recognised that a major threat to future prosperity lies in the completion of Bluewater. Lakeside has already damaged Gravesend's town centre shopping by attracting the younger population and is intending to spend £1.6m pa to attract even more shoppers.

- We need to continue to improve the aesthetic elements of the town centre so as to make it a more relaxed and pleasant place in which to stop.

- We must also identify and satisfy the needs of the target market by retaining the current retailing mix and attracting new retailers into the portfolio.

- Funding is limited.

2.6 Situational analysis 4

Since 1992 when the Gravesend TCI was initiated to fight of the threat from the Lakeside shopping centre across the Thames. Gravesend TCI has enjoyed a measure of success in retaining shoppers. Improvements include aesthetics, safety, easier access and parking.

Forthcoming changes in the external environment, including the Thames Gateway developments and the Channel Tunnel Rail Link, offer the prospect of an even more prosperous future.

However, in 1998 a new combined shopping and leisure centre called Bluewater is due to open only five miles away from Gravesend's town centre. It will contain over 300 shops (including Marks and Spencer, John Lewis and the House of Fraser). Leisure provision will include a mutiplex cinema, a fitness centre and restaurants to add life to the centre outside normal shopping hours

All of these changes have led to the Economic Development Office of Gravesham Borough Council to ask my marketing consultancy (Fleetwood Marketing) to undertake a study of long-term strategic marketing a part of the Gravesend Town Centre Initiative (TCI).

My brief has been clarified by the Town Centre Manager on behalf of the TCI Steering Group as being to develop a strategic marketing plan which includes defining the target markets and their needs; repositioning as necessary to suit; the promotional strategy required; and how to achieve a more marketing-driven management. A further problem I need to address in my recommendations for implementation is the lack of power in this public sector situation and the need to do everything by consultation and negotiation.

Ideally, further research on buying behaviour is required prior to confirming segmentation and positioning strategies in support of the marketing objectives I intend to set for the Gravesend Town Centre.

2.7 Further analysis/models used by a CIM ID Course Syndicate for its situational analysis are offered below.

Part E: Learning from experience: ensuring you pass

(a) *Understand the total product (Town Centre) and how/where to differentiate*

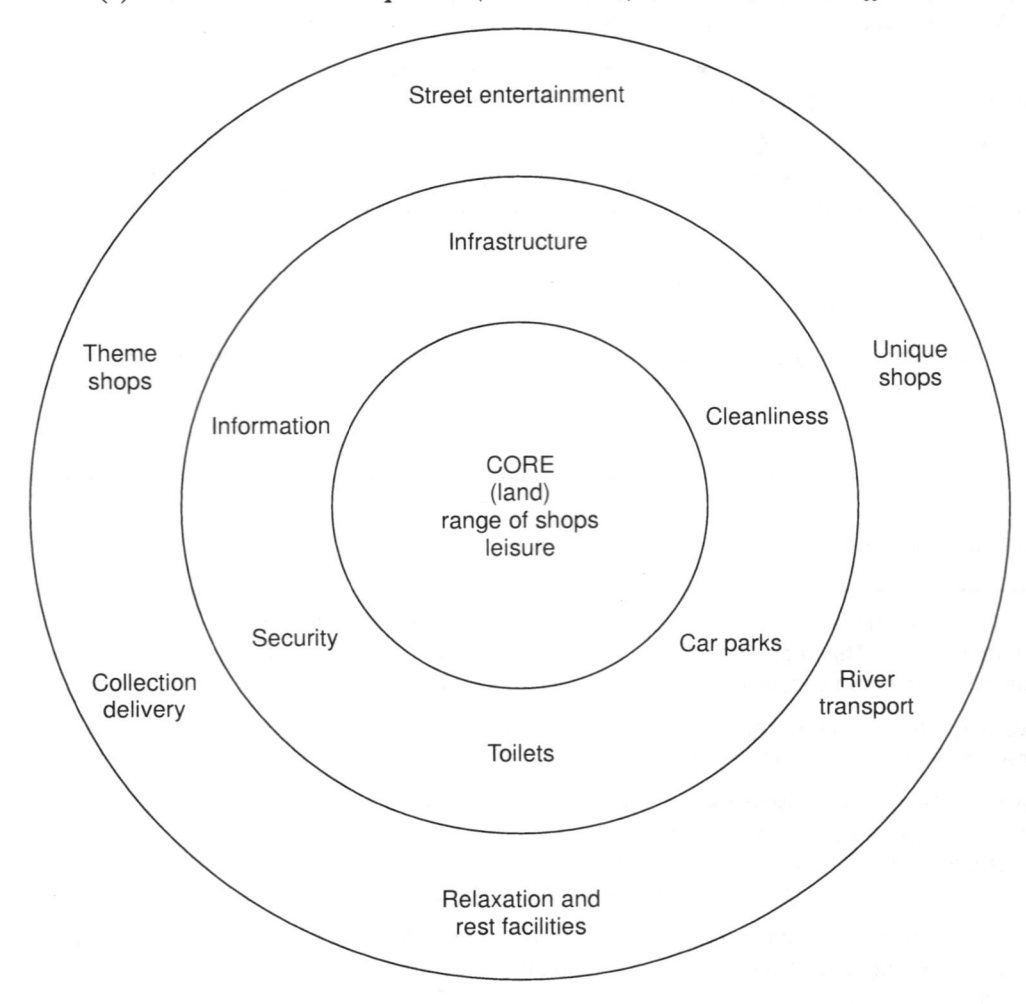

Outer ring: Street entertainment, Theme shops, Unique shops, Collection delivery, River transport, Relaxation and rest facilities

Middle ring: Infrastructure, Information, Cleanliness, Security, Car parks, Toilets

Core: CORE (land) range of shops leisure

(b) *Product life cycle - shopping phases*

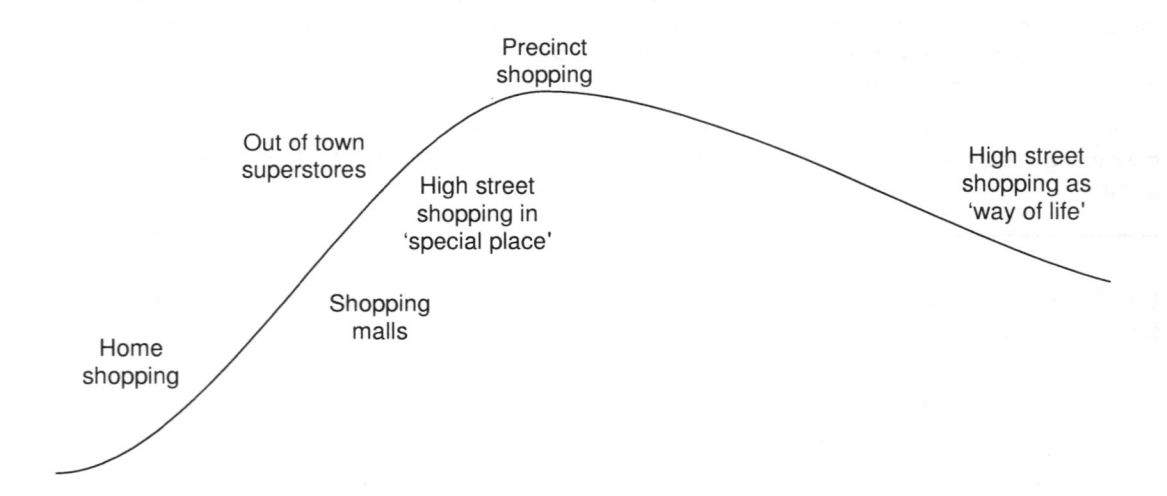

Curve stages (left to right): Home shopping, Out of town superstores, Shopping malls, High street shopping in 'special place', Precinct shopping (peak), High street shopping as 'way of life'

BPP Publishing 326

(c) *Levels of place marketing*

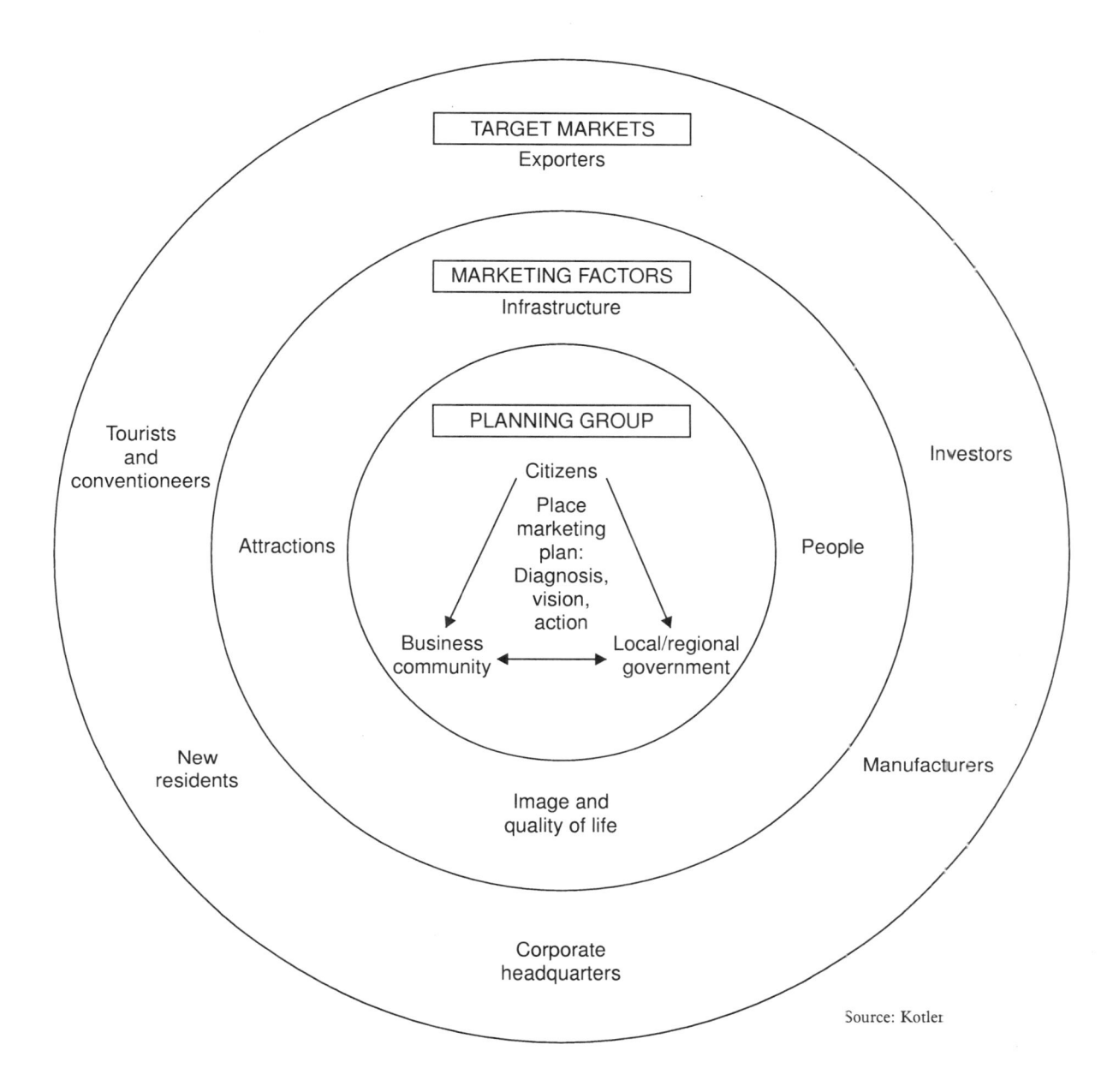

TARGET MARKETS: Exporters, Tourists and conventioneers, New residents, Corporate headquarters, Manufacturers, Investors

MARKETING FACTORS: Infrastructure, Attractions, Image and quality of life, People

PLANNING GROUP: Citizens, Business community, Local/regional government — Place marketing plan: Diagnosis, vision, action

Source: Kotler

(d) *Competitive structure of industry - Gravesend*

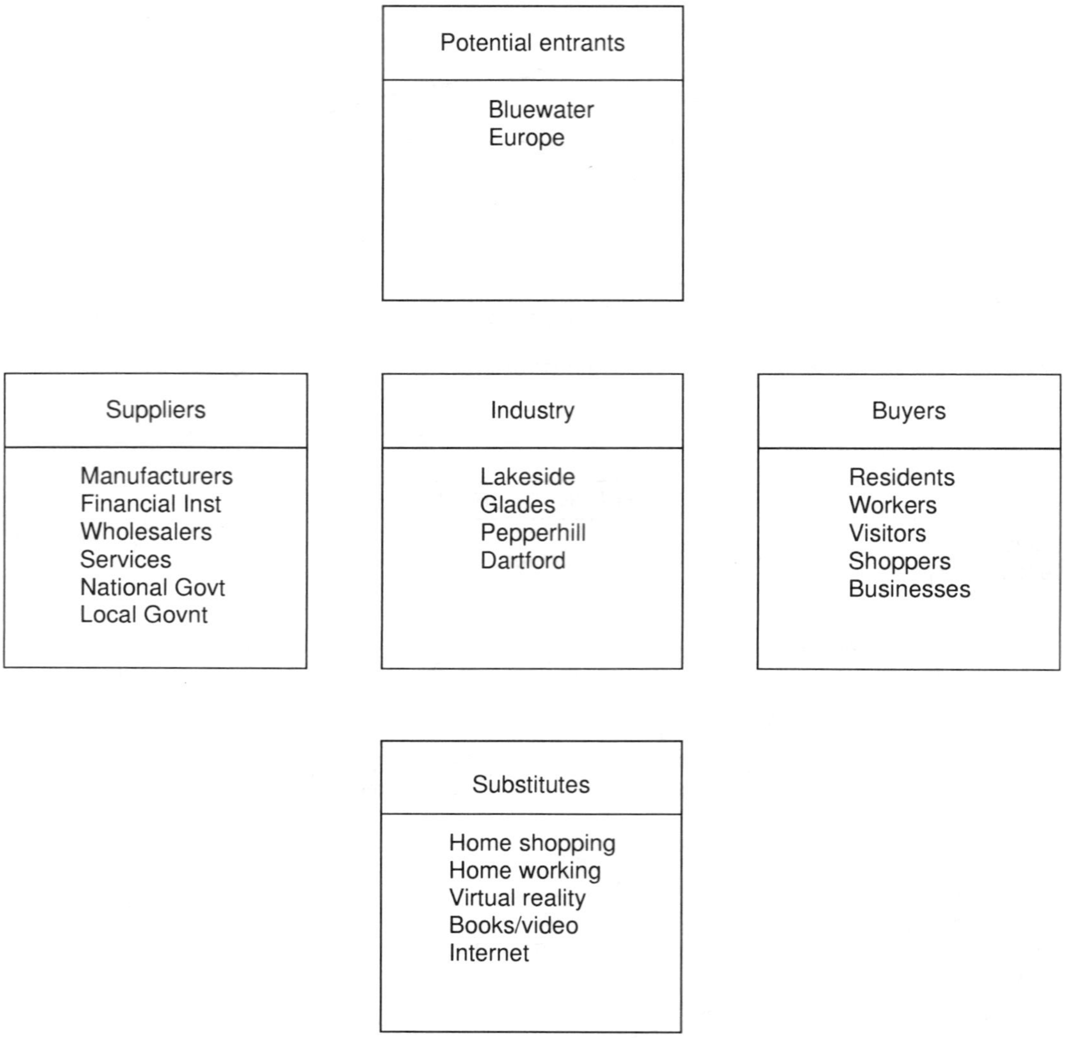

Potential entrants
Bluewater
Europe

Suppliers
Manufacturers
Financial Inst
Wholesalers
Services
National Govt
Local Govnt

Industry
Lakeside
Glades
Pepperhill
Dartford

Buyers
Residents
Workers
Visitors
Shoppers
Businesses

Substitutes
Home shopping
Home working
Virtual reality
Books/video
Internet

(e) *Conflicts of interest*

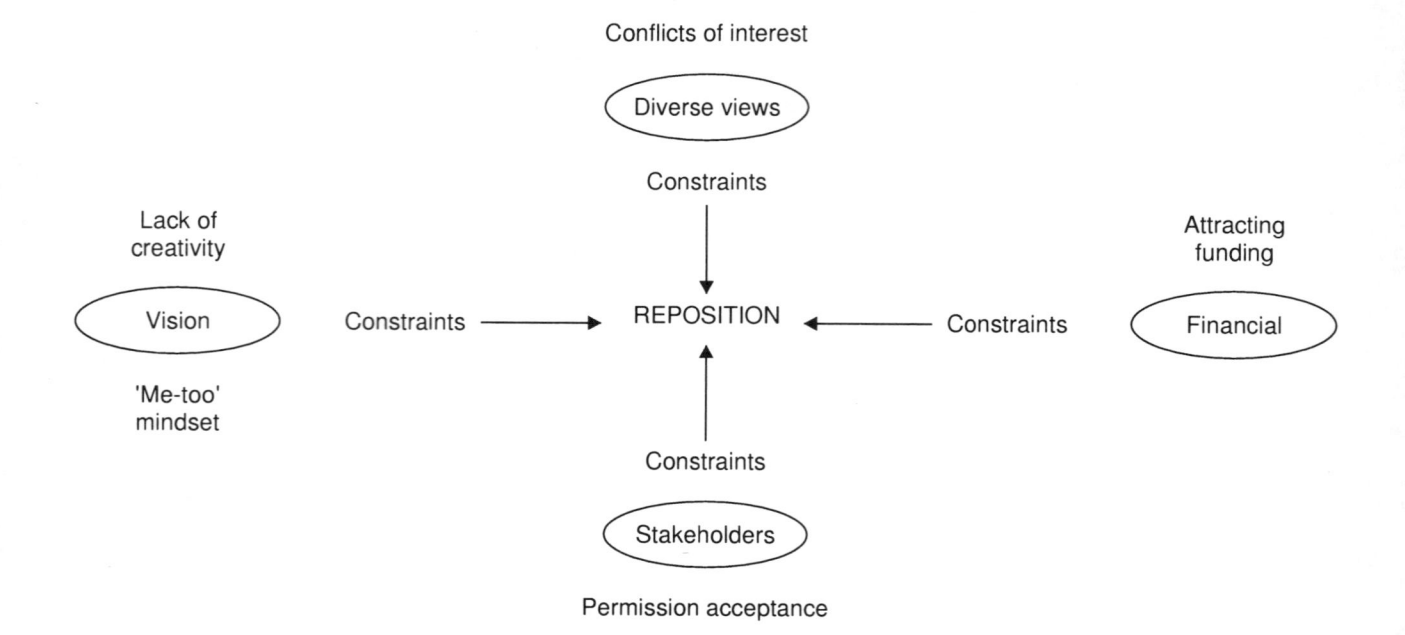

Conflicts of interest
- Diverse views → Constraints → REPOSITION

Lack of creativity / 'Me-too' mindset
- Vision → Constraints → REPOSITION

Attracting funding
- Financial → Constraints → REPOSITION

Permission acceptance
- Stakeholders → Constraints → REPOSITION

15: Gravesend Town Centre: situational analysis, key issues, mission statement, broad aims, major problems

(f) *Other stakeholders*

```
                        Employers
         Impact                      Impact

National/local                              Services
government
                    FOCUS
                    TOWN
                    CENTRE
Employees                                   Housing

         Impact                      Impact
      Pressure groups            Residents
```

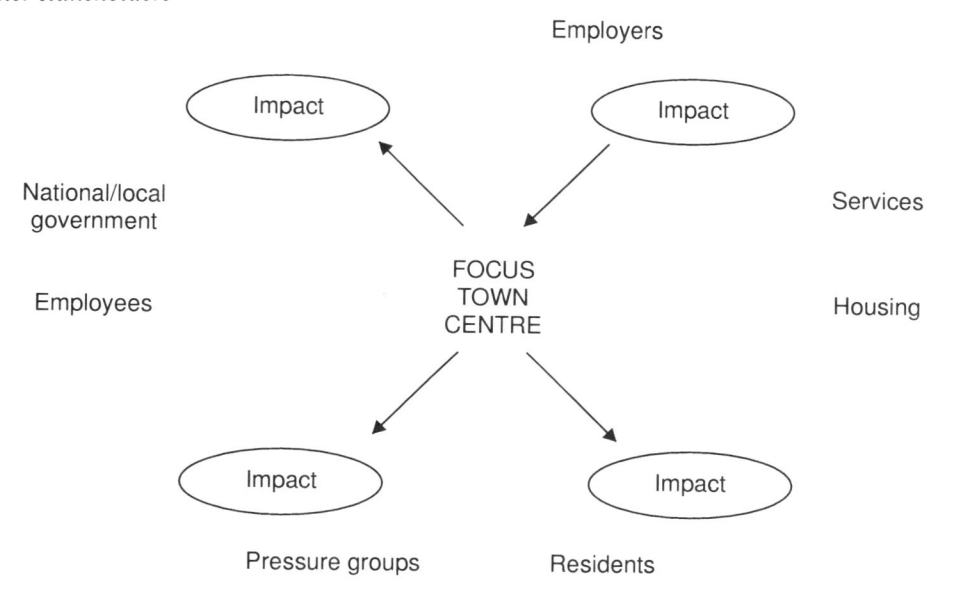

(g) *Gap analysis: Mobile household expenditure figures using selected mix*

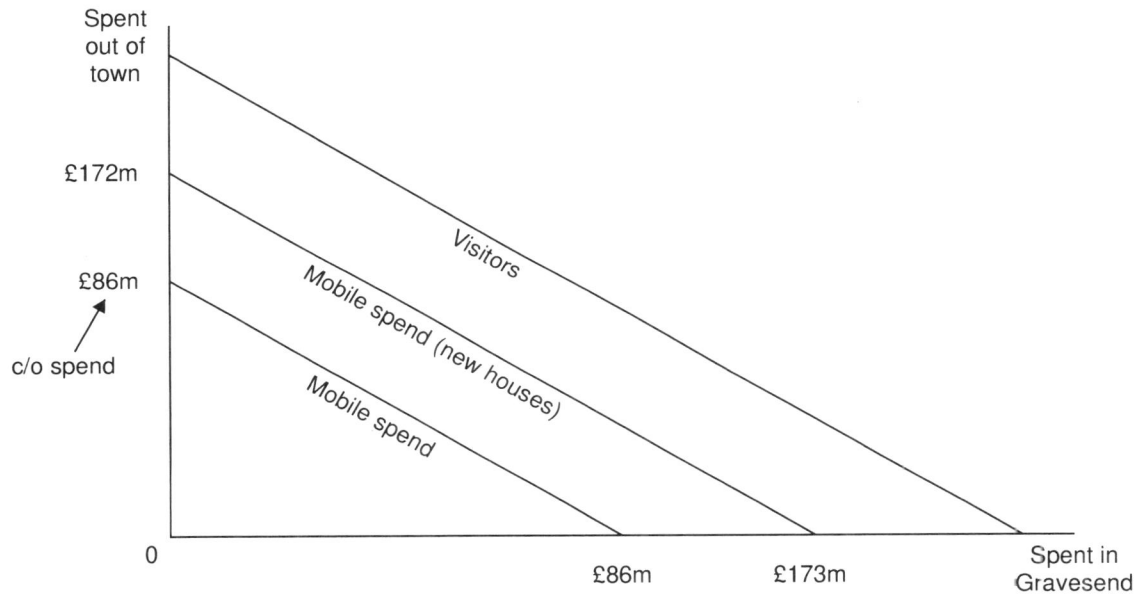

Spent out of town

£172m

£86m
↑
c/o spend

Visitors
Mobile spend (new houses)
Mobile spend

0   £86m   £173m   Spent in Gravesend

If we assume that current household expenditure is 80% out of Gravesend and 20% in, currently £68m is spent out of Gravesend and £17m in. (Household expenditure is currently £115m on selected mix, growing to £269m after the extra 30,000 houses are built.)

Mobile Gravesend exp

Fixed Gravesend exp

Part E: Learning from experience: ensuring you pass

3 DECIDE KEY ISSUES

> READ THE GUIDANCE NOTES IN
> CHAPTER 8 PARAGRAPHS 4.1 TO 4.3
>
> **STEP 11 DECIDE THE KEY ISSUES**
>
> ALLOW 1 HOUR TO 1½ HOURS FOR THIS STEP

3.1 You are reminded that the next step is the most important one, since it has the most bearing on the likely examination areas.

3.2 You are also reminded to limit these to a *maximum of six* and that you might like to construct a list of candidate key issues which could then be ranked, as a way of doing this exercise.

3.3 Remember also the technique of parcelling up several minor issues into one major issue as described in Chapter 8 paragraph 4.1.

3.4 Now that you have completed this crucial exercise, please compare your conclusions with those produced by four separate sources as given on the next page.

3.5 You will note a reassuring degree of unanimity in these four separate sources. Syndicate (B) could have 'parcelled' item 5 under item 6, don't you think?

3.6 *Gravesend Town Centre key issues*

Syndicate A1	*Syndicate B1*
1 Lack of marketing plan 2 How to implement recommendations 3 Making management more marketing driven 4 Increasing awareness 5 Re-positioning 6 Target market identification	1 Lack of marketing orientation/strategic vision 2 How to control the plan (large number of stakeholders) 3 How to respond to competition 4 Best ways of exploiting infrastructure changes 5 Lack of resources - expertise, funding etc 6 Adapting to constantly changing buying behaviour
Syndicate A2	*Syndicate B2*
1 Producing a viable marketing plan 2 Lack of up to date MR 3 Attracting new investment 4 Managing change 5 Re-positioning the retail portfolio 6 Changing perceptions	1 Selling the marketing plan 2 Re-structuring the TCI 3 Obtaining support and funding 4 Developing a competitive marketing strategy 5 Achieving control 6 Internal marketing

4 MISSION STATEMENT AND BROAD AIMS

> CONSULT THE GUIDANCE NOTES IN
> CHAPTER 8 PARAGRAPHS 4.4 TO 4.14
>
> **STEP 12 DEVELOP A MISSION STATEMENT**
> **STEP 13 DECIDE BROAD AIMS**
>
> ALLOW ABOUT AN HOUR FOR EACH OF THESE STEPS

4.1 Remember that there should be consistency between your mission statement and your *broad aims*. Also try to limit the latter for *four* bearing in mind the need to convert these into quantified and time-scaled objectives at a later stage.

4.2 In this particular case, a mission statement has not been provided although Appendix 6 is title 'towards a VISION'. You might feel you have to take this into account when deciding upon your mission statement and your broad aims.

4.3 Having completed these two steps, you can now compare your results with those of the syndicates which follow.

4.4 *Syndicates' mission statements*

Syndicate A	To provide an attractive, safe environment for the community to live and work in. To make a significant contribution to the economy of the area through increased employment in retail, entertainment and leisure by offering a wide rage of facilities both for business and service providers, and achieving sustainable growth.
Syndicate B	Gravesend's mission is: - To attract investments into the area encouraging the long-term economic viability of the town and the individual businesses within - To offer a diversity of shopping attractions and a variety of entertainments - To ensure a sense of 'place and community identity' by providing a focal point for the local and wider communities
Syndicate B1	To enhance the vitality and prosperity of Gravesend Town Centre by making it the first choice for quality consumer services for customers and potential customers. To do this whilst preserving a sense of community and care for the environment as well as a spirit of co-operation between all its publics.
Syndicate C	Gravesend TCI is dedicated to redeveloping the town centre in order to become a centre of excellence and vitality. Tourism, retailing, business and entertainment will be developed for the benefit of the local community and our customers elsewhere in the UK and overseas. Gravesend will become and remain a safe prosperous and healthy environment whether you live, work or visit here.
Syndicate D	To preserve and develop the town's unique heritage whilst providing shopping leisure, transportation and hospitality facilities to meet the needs of residents and visitors.

4.5 (a) *Reminder of contents.* A mission statement should:

    (i) offer a statement of the organisation's purpose;

    (ii) state what the organisation wants to accomplish in the larger environment;

    (iii) indicate the particular customer groups to be served, their needs and the technologies to be utilised.

Notes Part E: Learning from experience: ensuring you pass

       (b) *A clear mission statement:*

           (i)   guides people in the organisation so they can work independently and yet collectively;

           (ii)   should not be too narrow or too broad;

           (iii) should be specific, realistic and motivating.

4.6   Other mission statement assessment criteria might be listed as follows.

       (a) Generality versus limited focus (ie balance)
       (b) Longevity
       (c) Purpose
       (d) Audiences - stakeholders
       (e) Clarity - what business are we in? Boundaries (geographical, product areas)
       (f) Brevity
       (g) Ease of memorisation
       (h) Credibility
       (i) Consistency - with broad aims

Broad aims

4.7   A consensus of the above five syndicates' broad aims is given below.

1	To achieve a sustainable competitive advantage for Gravesend which will ensure its long term survival for the benefit of business and residents.
2	To increase the level of external funding and total funding
3	To increase the per-capita spend per visitor and the total number of visitors
4	To promote the benefits of a thriving town centre to all our stakeholders
5	To preserve and develop the town's unique heritage whilst providing shopping leisure, transportation and hospitality facilities to meet the needs of residents and visitors.

4.8   You will note that there is a good degree of consistency between these syndicates' mission statements and the broad aims arrived at by consensus. Interestingly, Syndicate D's mission statement was felt by the majority to make a very good broad aim and so this was adopted by popular demand. However, broad aim number 5 does not lend itself so well as the other four to conversion into a quantified and time-scaled objectives, does it?

5   MAJOR PROBLEMS

CONSULT THE GUIDANCE NOTES IN CHAPTER 8 PARAGRAPHS 4.15 TO 4.18
STEP 14 IDENTIFY AND ANALYSE MAJOR PROBLEMS
ALLOW BETWEEN 2 AND 3 HOURS FOR THIS STEP

5.1   Remember to restrict yourself to six major problems in rank order.

5.2   Do not worry if your major problems relate closely with the key issues. This is quite usual.

5.3   Having done this, you can now compare your items/rankings with those of eight syndicates provided below.

5.4   *Gravesend Town Centre: major problems*

	Item	A1	B1	C1	D1	A2	B2	C2	D2
1	Combatting competition from Lakeside and Bluewater	1	3	3	2	1	1	4	1
2	How to make the management more marketing led		1	6					4
3	How to implement and control the new marketing plan		2	5					6
4	Developing a new corporate identity to satisfy all stakeholders					3			
5	Assessing the impact of environmental changes				5		4	1	
6	How to preserve the town's unique heritage whilst developing				6			2	
7	Obtaining more favourable awareness from target markets		5		3				5
8	Retaining current customers whilst gaining new ones	4			1	5			2
9	Attracting new retail and leisure outlets to the town centre	5	4			6			
10	How best to exploit opportunities arising from the Thames Gateway				4			3	
11	Quantifying and timescaling objectives	2		1		2	3		3
12	Re-defining target markets and repositioning	6	6	2		4	2	5	
13	Lack of up-to-date MR			4			6	6	
14	Lack of adequate funding	3					5		

5.5   You may note that the list is rather long and the consensus less certain than that shown for the Leffe case. This may be because students find services marketing and the public sector more complex and ephemeral than say private sector manufactured goods. However, how to combat competition is clearly the number 1 problem followed by quantifying and timescaling objectives.

5.6   Please remember that whatever you have listed on your own problem sheet should be addressed in your marketing plan.

Chapter 16

GRAVESEND TOWN CENTRE: OUTLINE MARKETING PLANNING

> **This chapter contains the following guidance and plans.**
> 1   Introduction: approaching a marketing plan
> 2   The steps you should follow
> 3   Sample outline plan 1
> 4   Sample outline plan 2
> 5   Sample outline plan 3

1   INTRODUCTION: APPROACHING A MARKETING PLAN

1.1   We are now at the crunch decision stage namely that of drawing up a *complete* marketing plan starting with objectives, progressing through strategy and tactics (including market research) and covering the organisational, financial and human resource aspects. You will also need to schedule, decide review and control mechanisms, and consider contingency action. (All these items are covered in the notes given in Chapter 8, paragraphs 4.19 to 6.8 for Steps 15 to 26. You will need 15 to 18 hours to do a reasonably thorough job. Relevant examples are given in the next chapter.)

1.2   Remember that you will not be tested on your analysis in itself in the examination room. The purpose of your *complete* plan is to cover and prepare for all potential exam questions.

1.3   Experience shows that syndicates starting on the plan and working against time get bogged down on objectives for far too long, getting mixed up over *corporate objectives* and *marketing objectives*, and then between objectives, strategy and tactics. Tempers can get frayed and confidence lost. A technique we have successfully used to overcome this problem is to get syndicates to blitz through an *outline* plan first, taking a maximum of *one hour* to do this. You can then look at this outline to see that it is reasonably consistent and logical before committing yourself to detail. In this way you see the plan as a whole, whereas if you get straight into the detail you may never see the wood for the trees and never get to the end of your journey. What you are doing is creating a *framework* or a *skeletal plan*.

1.4   A useful analogy here is to consider a drawing or a painting. The artist does not normally paint a landscape by immediately painting leaves or blades of grass in great detail. He/she would consider first what proportion of the landscape is to be devoted to sky and what to land; whether the sky is to be cloudy and the land hilly; whether to depict some trees and meadows etc. Having then visualised the painting as a whole and put in the rough parameters, more detail would be added in the sure knowledge that it fitted into the setting. Consider the following two syndicates' work after one hour.

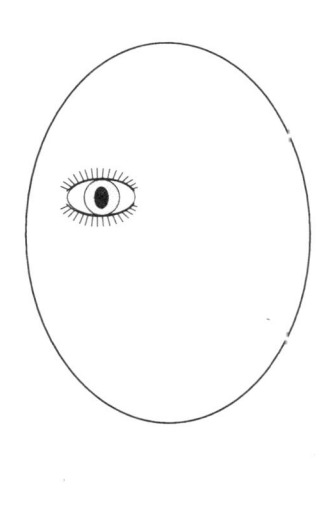

1.5 Syndicate B started with a head and went into great detail on the eye, debating how many eyelashes should be shown, their length, the position of the pupil, the shade of colour etc. They never completed the skeleton.

1.6 Syndicate A visualised their skeleton as a little girl. After one hour they produced a complete skeleton. they then split up to make best use of limited time, one pair to do the detail on the head, another pair the legs, a third pair the arms and a fourth pair the body. After a few more hours, they brought these parts together in the sure knowledge that they would fit.

1.7 If this syndicate had used division of labour without agreeing the skeleton first they might have produced a 'Frankenstein' monster, rather than the perfectly symmetrical little girl they had finished up with.

1.8 Please use this technique now. Produce an outline plan first taking only about one hour. Force it through, do not hover or vacillate over the detail. If it is only rough you can always adjust it later to gain better cohesion and consistency, before doing the detail.

1.9 Having done it, compare it with the very rough outline plans produced by two syndicates in about the same time in the pages which follow. These may not be satisfactory but at least the syndicates got there and they all felt a lot better and more in command after the exercise, even though they realised a lot more work needed to be done.

Part E: Learning from experience: ensuring you pass

2 THE STEPS YOU SHOULD FOLLOW

2.1 These are of course the same as for the detailed marketing plan and are given below for your convenience.

CONSULT THE GUIDANCE NOTES GIVEN IN CHAPTER 8 PARAGRAPHS 4.19 TO 6.8
In outline only
STEP 15 DEVELOP QUANTIFIED, TIMESCALED OBJECTIVES **STEP 16 CONSIDER ALTERNATIVE STRATEGIES. SELECT THOSE MOST APPROPRIATE** **STEP 17 DRAW UP DETAILED TACTICAL PLANS COVERING THE MARKETING ORIENTATION** **STEP 18 DRAW UP A MARKETING RESEARCH PLAN** **STEP 19 CONSIDER ORGANISATIONAL ISSUES, CHANGES AND MARKETING ORIENTATION** **STEP 20 CONSIDER ORGANISATIONAL CULTURE AND NEED FOR INTERNAL MARKETING** **STEP 21 DETERMINE THE FINANCIAL/HR RESOURCE IMPLICATIONS OF YOUR PLANS** **STEP 22 ASSESS COSTS AND DRAW UP INDICATIVE BUDGETS** **STEP 23 DRAW UP SCHEDULES GIVING TIMINGS/SEQUENCE OF ACTIONS** **STEP 24 SPECIFY REVIEW PROCEDURES AND CONTROL MECHANISMS** **STEP 25 DRAW UP OUTLINE CONTINGENCY PLANS** **STEP 26 REVIEW YOUR COMPLETE MARKETING PLAN**
YOU WILL NEED ABOUT ONE HOUR TO DO YOUR OUTLINE

2.2 Having completed your outline plan you might like to compare your thoughts with the specimens which follow produced by CIM ID course syndicates. These are not at all bad are they?

2.3 Please then flesh out your own outline plan in more detail before looking at the detailed planning example by Jonathan Avery, Jonathan Hurry and Stephen Hoy which follows in the next chapter.

3 SAMPLE OUTLINE PLAN 1

Vision

3.1

Our vision is to reduce reliance upon the spending power of the existing community by becoming a leading leisure environment into the new millennium. We will draw on and exploit our natural assets including the waterfront proximity and cultural heritage, in order to serve the needs of our stakeholders.

Mission

3.2

Our mission is to provide the environment and infrastructure which will attract and enable the business community to add value to their customers for the mutual benefit of the community and all its stakeholders.

Corporate objectives and strategy

3.3 (a) Focus on product development to deliver an additional £56m to cover the planning gap by the year 2005.

    (b) Develop a new waterfront complex.

3.4 *Background*

    (a) Gravesend Town Centre (GTC) is in decline as a result of the increased popularity of out of town shopping.

    (b) GTC needs to attract new businesses and consumers.

    (c) We suggest a three tier strategy: market penetration, market development and product development.

Marketing objective and strategy

3.5 *Marketing objective*: attract 60 new businesses with a combined potential turnover of at least £56m.

3.6 *Marketing strategy*

    (a) Segmentation

        (i) Criteria (from GE matrix)
        (ii) Restaurants
        (iii) Specialist quality clothing retailers
        (iv) Sport/leisure retailers
        (v) Restaurant:

            (1) Turnover approximately £1m
            (2) Circa 100 seat capacity
            (3) Bistro/wine bar
            (4) European/specialist
            (5) Brunch, lunch, evening
            (6) Possibly themed eg Fatty Arbuckles

    (b) Targeting - undifferentiated

    (c) Positioning

        (i) Restaurants: up market, romantic and family
        (ii) Fashion outlets: exclusive/high fashion
        (iii) Sports goods: specialist/high quality

Marketing tactics

3.7

Product Public services - passenger ferry Infrastructure - Ebbsfleet/tram Safety/security - police, CCTV, lighting History	Place Waterfront
Promotion PR (eg Money programme) Lobbying Trade promotion Advertising (esp trade advertising) Consumer promotions?	Price Including service Access cost
Physical evidence Street signs/nautical design Process management Easy local operating conditions Specific restrictions Planning permission	People Chamber of commerce TCI drive Account manager

3.8 *Controls*

    (a) Budgets
    (b) Salesperson £50k
    (c) Direct mail £15k
    (d) Trade show/exhibition £15k
    (e) MR before implementation £20k
    (f) MR after implementation £20k

3.9 *MkIS components*

    (a) Retailer perceptions
    (b) Monitor press cuttings
    (c) Hit rates on retailers
    (d) Benchmark vs other clean, safe leisure environments
    (e) Attitude monitoring
    (f) Stakeholder perceptions

4 SAMPLE OUTLINE PLAN 2

4.1 Contents

1	Background/current situation	
2	Corporate objectives	- Vision
3	Market objectives	- Long-term - Medium-term - Short-term
4	Strategies - Positioning - Segmentation - Brand identities	- Targeting
5	Tactics	7P's
6	Budgets	
7	Timetable	
8	Control	
9	Contingencies	

Strategic alternatives

	Existing products	New products
Existing markets	*Short term penetration* Existing customers from Bluewater etc	*Product development* More leisure: restaurants Service/quality Family pubs in nautical zone
New markets	*Market development* Change retail leisure mix New customers Push strategy Me-too Medium term mix development	*Long term diversification* Fun fairs Piers Tourism Marina Historical differentiation

Notes   **Part E: Learning from experience: ensuring you pass**

Strategy evaluation

4.2   *The town's criteria for evaluating strategy*

    (a) Improve waterfront
    (b) Additional jobs
    (c) Better facilities
    (d) Civic pride
    (e) Change image

4.3   *Business criteria for evaluating strategy*

    (a) ROCE
    (b) Growth market
    (c) Access to potential market
    (d) Infrastructure
    (e) Access to funding (eg Millennium fund)
    (f) Low rents/rates

4.4   *G E Matrix*

GE matrix

Attractiveness to Town: High | Medium | Low
Attractiveness to business: High | Medium | Low

- High/High–Medium: Waterside development; Change mix
- Medium/Medium: Penetration (existing)
- Low/High: Market development; Me-too

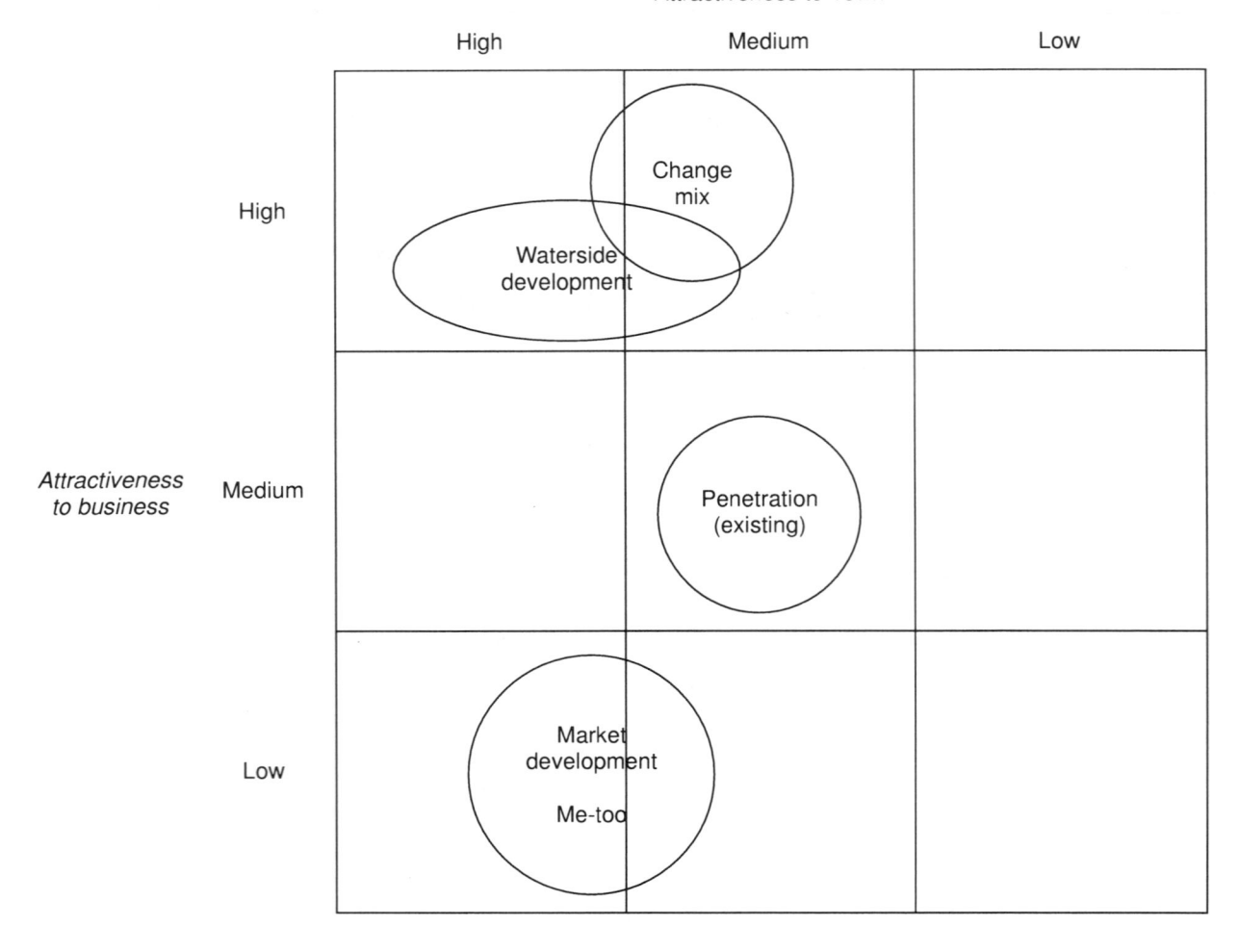

4.5   *Strategy*

    (a) Long-term: reposition Gravesend with leisure/waterside activities.
    (b) Medium term: Increase local amenities pubs, restaurants.
    (c) Short-term: maintain existing local retail/leisure interests

16: Gravesend Town Centre: outline marketing planning

4.6 *What is vision/role of the town?*

   (a) 'Blackpool of the South'

   (b) 'Through innovation, creativity and local partnerships to be recognised as the family fun capital of the South East'.

4.7 *Vision: positioning*

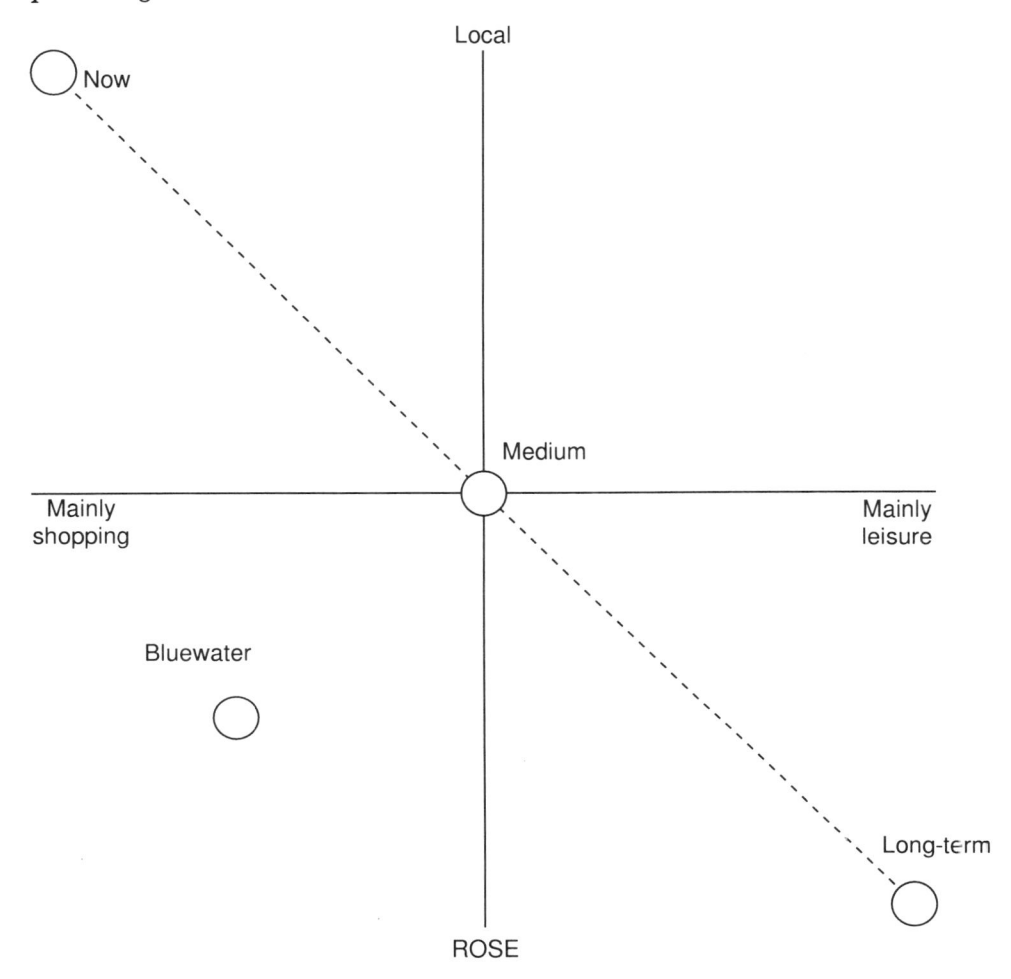

```
                        Local
           ○ Now
            ╲
             ╲
              ╲
               ╲
                ╲
                 ╲     Medium
    Mainly        ○              Mainly
    shopping      ╲              leisure
 ─────────────────┼──────────────────
                   ╲
                    ╲
         Bluewater   ╲
           ○          ╲
                       ╲
                        ╲
                         ╲  Long-term
                          ○
                        ROSE
```

4.8 *Corporate objective*

   (a) To generate 200 new jobs in the town centre by the year 2000

   (b) To increase cash expenditure in the town centre from £82m to £98m by year 2000, £110m 2010, £125m by 2015.

   (c) To attract £30m + inward investment before year 2000.

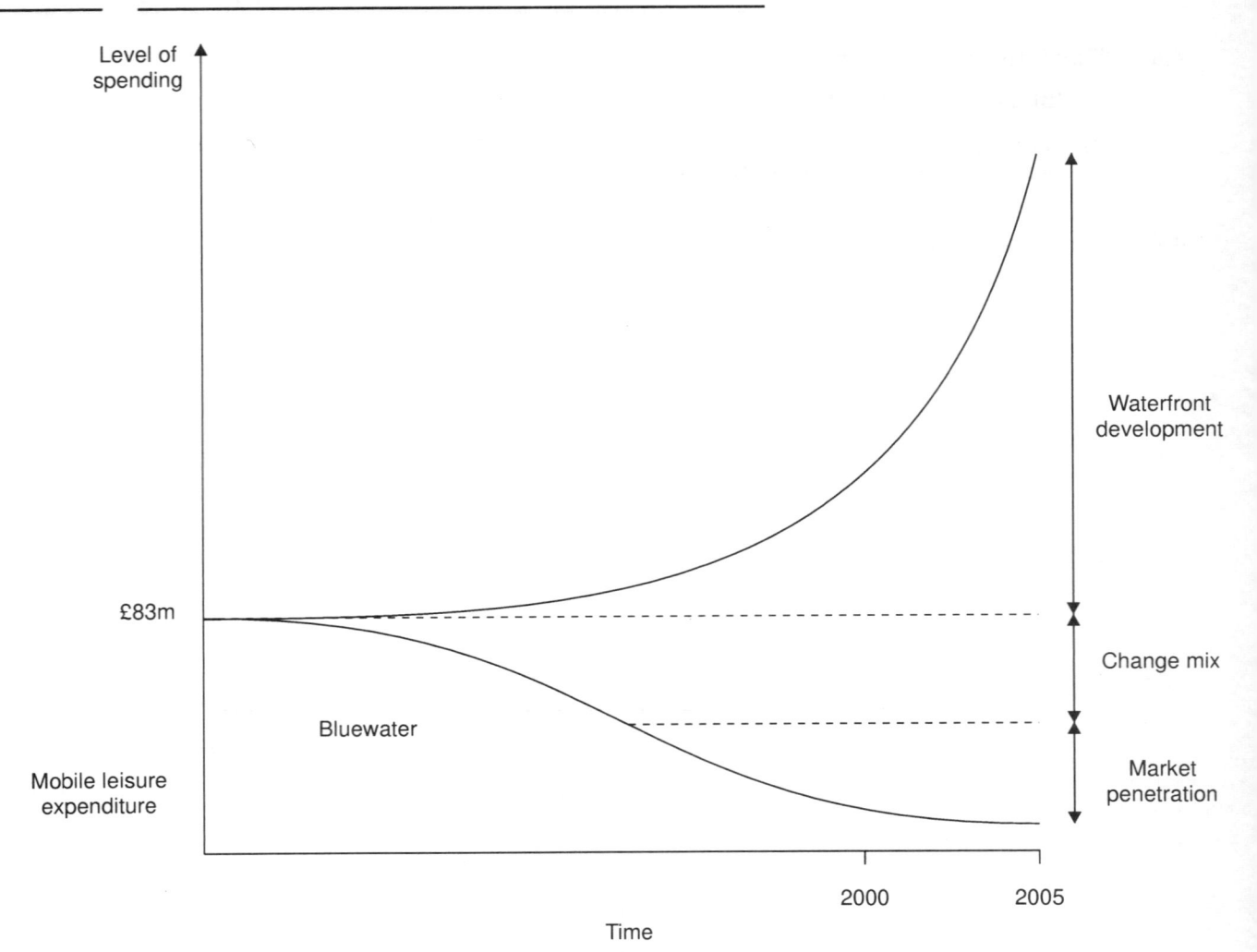

Notes   Part E: Learning from experience: ensuring you pass

Level of spending

£83m

Mobile leisure expenditure

Bluewater

Waterfront development

Change mix

Market penetration

2000   2005

Time

Business interest

(d) *Positioning*

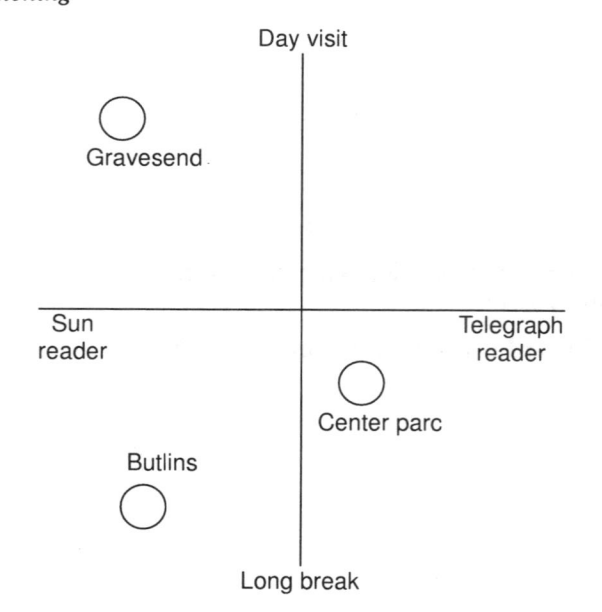

Day visit

Gravesend

Sun reader — Telegraph reader

Center parc

Butlins

Long break

4.9 *Brand values - product*

    (a) Family
    (b) Fun
    (c) Nautical
    (d) Clean
    (e) Value

4.10 *Brand positioning*

    (a) All inclusive
    (b) Day out
    (c) Accessible
    (d) Safety

4.11 Tactical implementation of the mix by segment follows in the tables on the next two pages. These lead into the budgets provided.

MARKETING MIX BY SEGMENT

	Product	Place	Price	Promotion	Physical evidence	Process	People
Investors/ business	Planning permission Strategic plan phased and agreed in advance	Access Infrastructure Proximity Retail development Continuation of integrated transport Cooperation with and complementary to Bluewater	Attractive rents/ rates Local council development corporation offers Negotiation	Fixed rates Rental holidays Collateral signage Direct selling to targeted firms	Clearance plus development of site More town centre hygiene Continued emphasis on hygiene, look and feel	Security	Quality and enthusiasm of local workforce Quality of local administration/ council Training initiatives Advance recruitment
Consumers	Fun Good leisure retail mix interesting retail Direct mail Radio TV	Access Infrastructure Buses Trains Parking Free travel Bluewater-Waterside pass Parking	Attractive Value for money Family cards Bluewater tokens Possible promotions at TC shops	Fun capital 'Extend your shopping trip' Radio TV Mail	Riverside location Attractive packaging Develop corporate standards and plan	Flexible retail plus opening hours Local corporation development and agreements	Jobs (full and part time) Community spirit Civic pride Local PR and advertising

16: Gravesend Town Centre: outline marketing planning

MARKETING/INVESTMENT BUDGETS

	Product	Place	Price	Promotion	Physical evidence	Process	People
Investors Business	Outline planning report £50k	Extension of tram to waterside £2.5m	Rates subsidies £500k pa	Brochure, collateral and signage £75k	Site clearance £1.5m	Security £50k	Training initiatives £250k Donation to colleges
Consumers	High street rejuvenation £1.5m	Access £200k (Bluewater promotions)	Value for money £250k (Discount cards promotions)	'Fun capital;' £3m	Location See 'product'	Retail and opening hours	Jobs Civic pride £75k (Local PR plus advertising)

4.12 *Financials*

	£
One time fixed costs	
Waterside development corporation (including brochures and signage)	200,000
High street rejuvenation	1,500,000
Tram extension	2,500,000
Site clearance	1,500,000
Training initiatives	250,000
	5,950,000
Annual or recurring costs	
Product	50,000
Place	200,000
Price	750,000
Promotion	3,075,000
Physical evidence (in 'product')	
Process	50,000
People	75,000
	4,200,000

4.13 A summary Gantt chart outlining timescales is offered below.

Activity	96	2000	2010	2015
Committee formed	⊢–⊣			
Tenders response	⊢––⊣			
Raise investment	⊢––––––⊣			
Site clearance	⊢–⊣			
Development	⊢–––––––––––––––⊣			
Job creation	⊢–––––––––– - - - - - - - - - ⊣			
Opening	⊢–⊣			
Town development (phase 2)	⊢––––––––––––––––––––––⊣			

4.14 *Tracking studies to monitor implementation are these.*

How many people?
Where they come from?
How much do they spend?
Number of visits per year
Repeat visits

- Consumer survey
- User groups
- Direct mail
- Coupon response

4.15 *Recommendations*

(a) The plan is accepted as the way forward to regeneration.

(b) Nominate a steering group/development corporation.

(c) Appoint a marketing consultant. Fleetwood can develop detailed elements of the plan.

5 SAMPLE OUTLINE PLAN 3

5.1 (a) *Vision*. To reposition Gravesend as a maritime heritage centre.

(b) *Mission*. To establish Gravesend as a thriving centre, creating long term jobs and economic stability/vitality

(c) *Position*

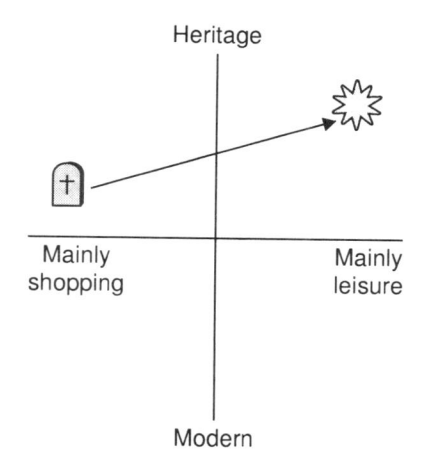

[Positioning chart with axes: Heritage (top) / Modern (bottom), Mainly shopping (left) / Mainly leisure (right). Arrow moves from a gravestone symbol on the shopping side toward a star in the upper-right Heritage/leisure quadrant.]

(d) *Brand values*

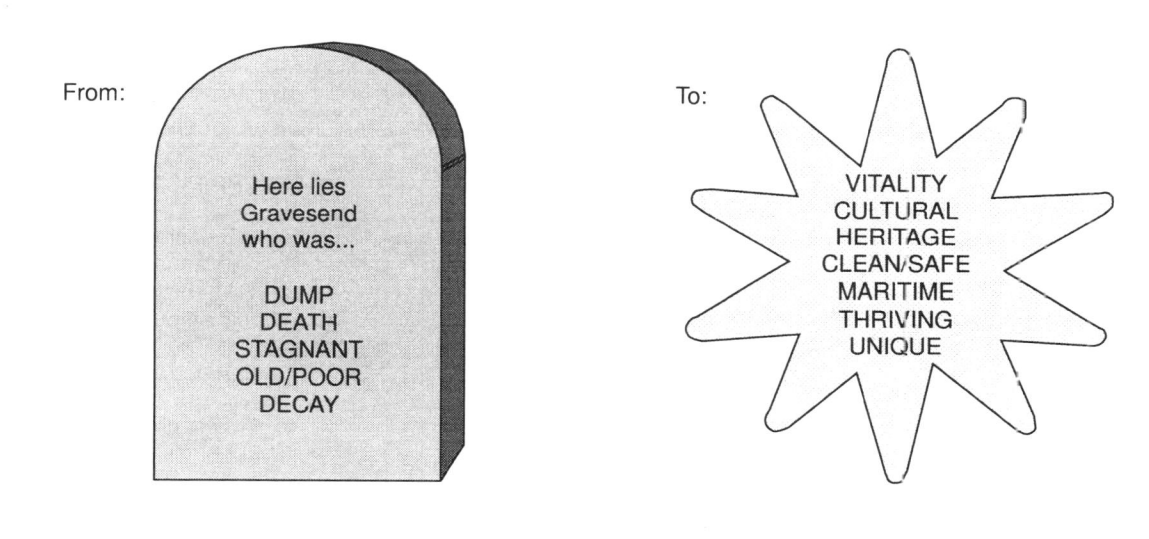

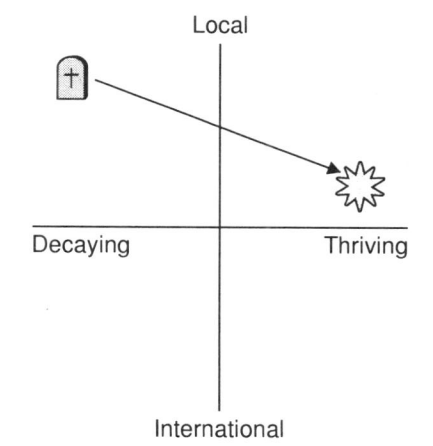

From:
Here lies Gravesend who was...
DUMP
DEATH
STAGNANT
OLD/POOR
DECAY

To:
VITALITY
CULTURAL
HERITAGE
CLEAN/SAFE
MARITIME
THRIVING
UNIQUE

[Positioning chart with axes: Local (top) / International (bottom), Decaying (left) / Thriving (right). Arrow moves from a gravestone symbol on the Local/Decaying side toward a star in the Thriving area just below the horizontal axis.]

Objective

5.2 To increase the total expenditure in Gravesend Town Centre from £250m to £400m by the year 2005.

Notes   *Part E: Learning from experience: ensuring you pass*

Strategies

5.3 (a) *Short-term market development plus penetration.* Attract new shops (quality/independent)

(b) *Medium-term: product development.* Attract waterfront leisure service providers.

(c) *Long-term.* Attract investment in River Heritage Project.

(d) The following marketing plan is for the above River Heritage strategy only.

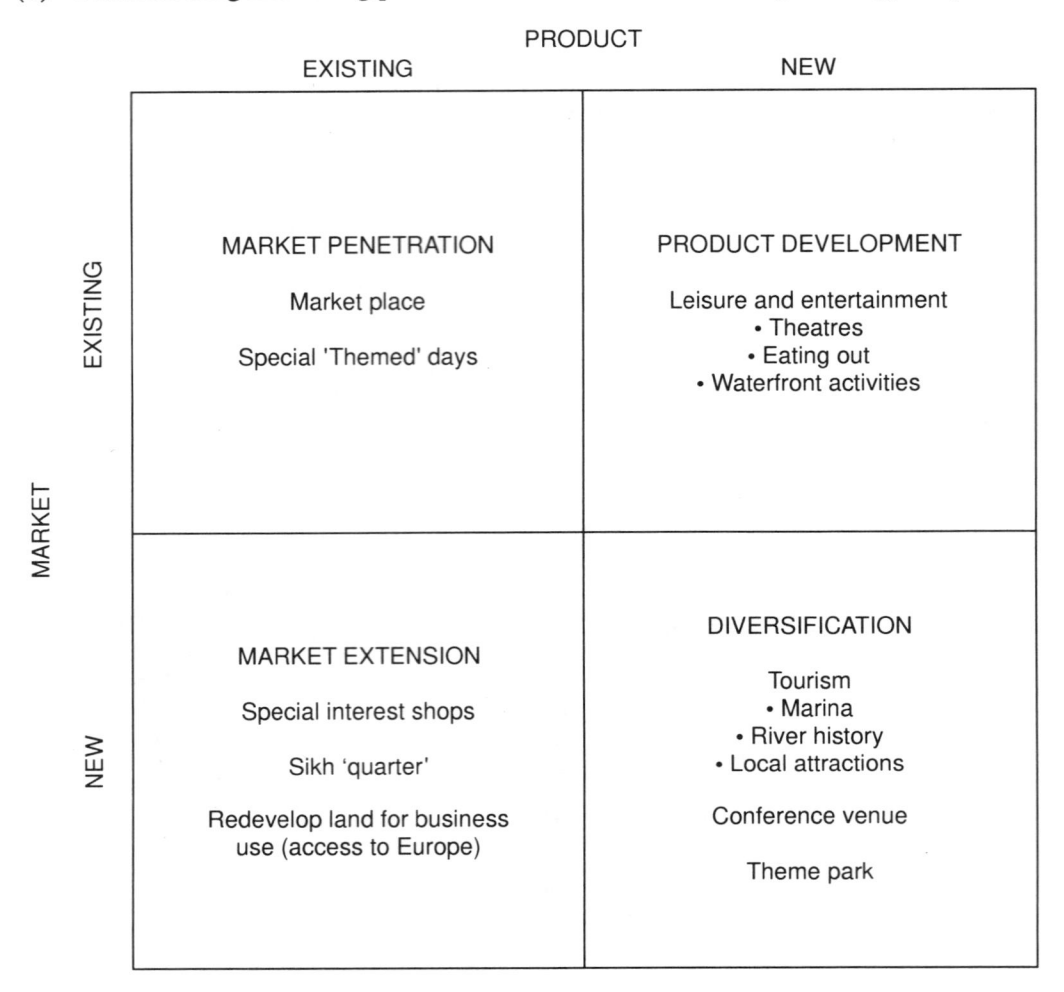

PRODUCT

	EXISTING	NEW
MARKET EXISTING	MARKET PENETRATION Market place Special 'Themed' days	PRODUCT DEVELOPMENT Leisure and entertainment • Theatres • Eating out • Waterfront activities
MARKET NEW	MARKET EXTENSION Special interest shops Sikh 'quarter' Redevelop land for business use (access to Europe)	DIVERSIFICATION Tourism • Marina • River history • Local attractions Conference venue Theme park

5.4 *The planning gap*

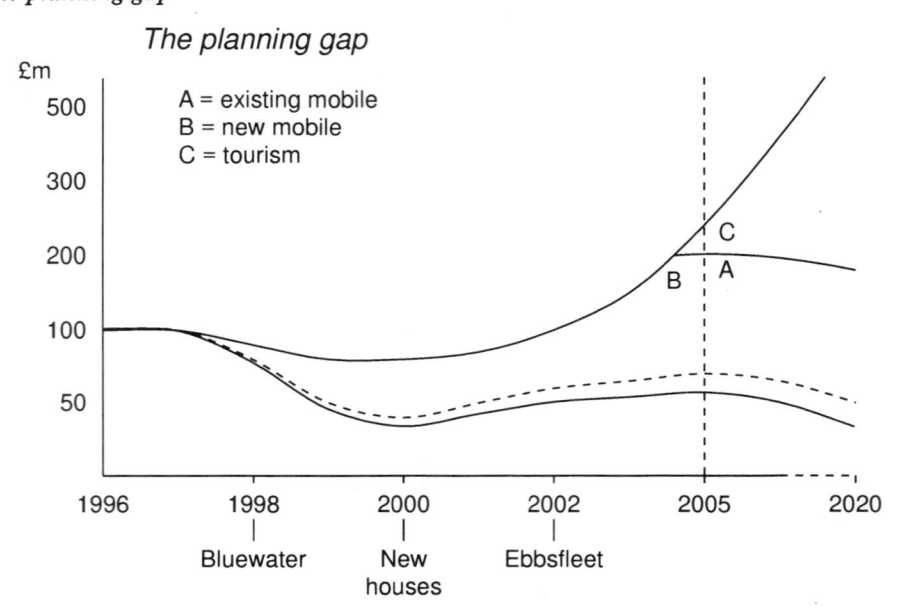

The planning gap

£m

A = existing mobile
B = new mobile
C = tourism

1996 1998 2000 2002 2005 2020
      | | |
   Bluewater New Ebbsfleet
              houses

16: Gravesend Town Centre: outline marketing planning — Notes

5.5 Increasing consumer expenditure

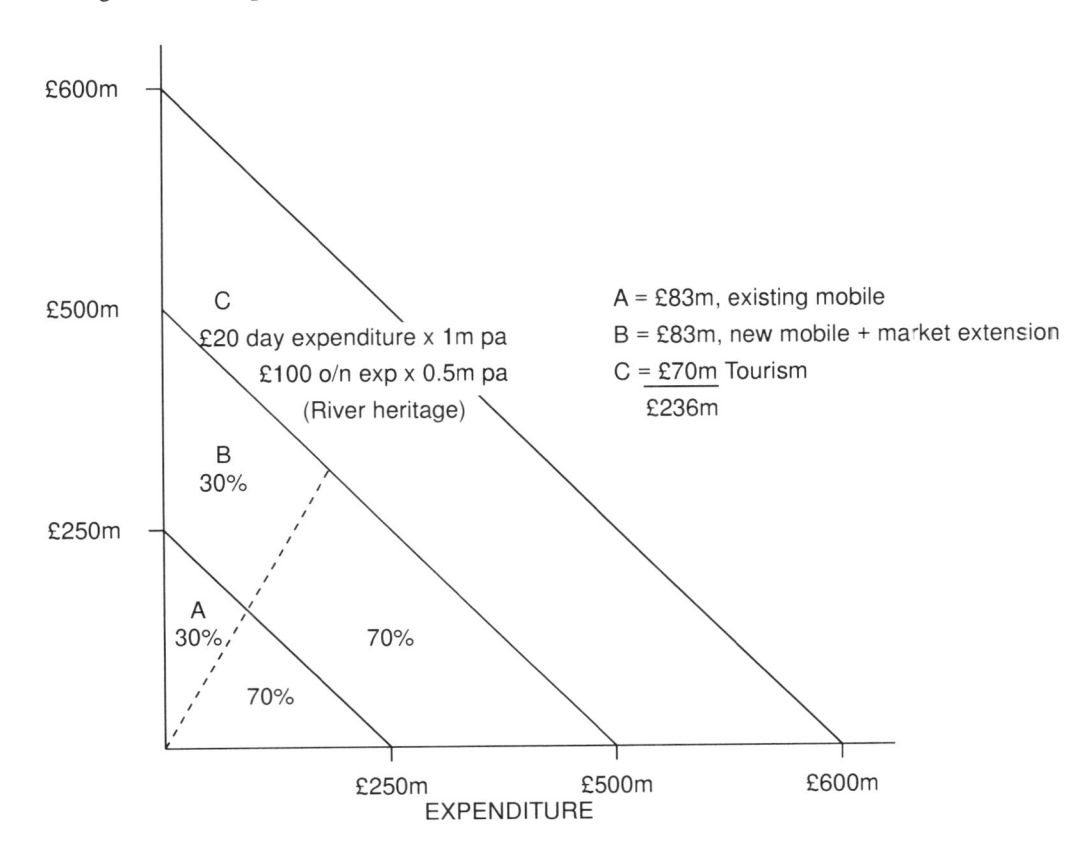

```
£600m |\
      | \
      |  \
£500m |C  \
      |£20 day expenditure x 1m pa     A = £83m, existing mobile
      |£100 o/n exp x 0.5m pa          B = £83m, new mobile + market extension
      |(River heritage)                C = £70m Tourism
      |B                               ─────
      |30%                             £236m
£250m |A
      |30%/    70%
      |   /70%
      └─────────────────────
         £250m   £500m   £600m
              EXPENDITURE
```

5.6 Criteria for strategic choice

Criteria for choice

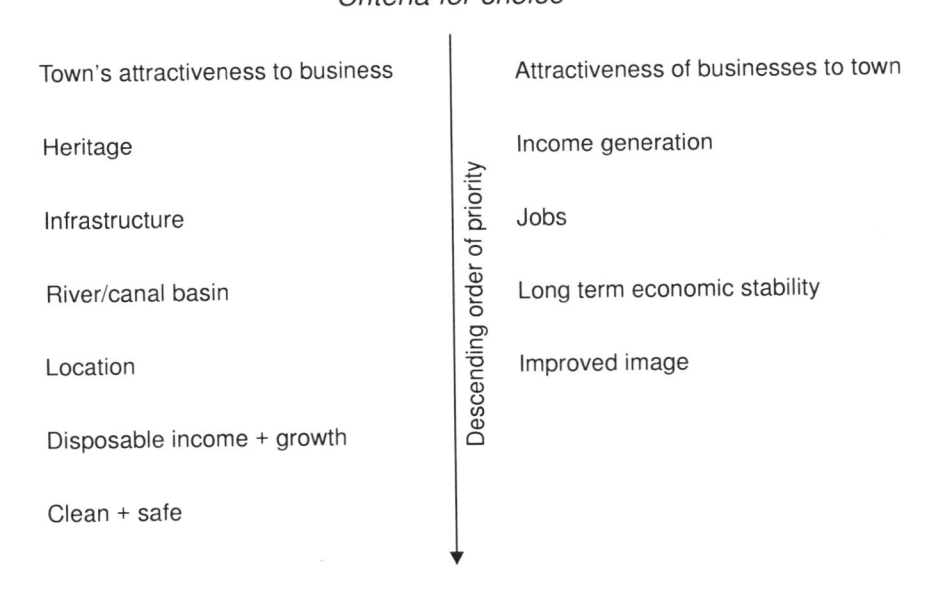

Town's attractiveness to business	Attractiveness of businesses to town
Heritage	Income generation
Infrastructure	Jobs
River/canal basin	Long term economic stability
Location	Improved image
Disposable income + growth	
Clean + safe	

↓ Descending order of priority

Part E: Learning from experience: ensuring you pass

5.7 Applying these criteria leads us to a grid on which the attractiveness of various strategic ideas can be mapped.

	Business's attractiveness to town		
	High	Medium	Low
High	• River heritage • Waterfront leisure • New shops	• Foreign/UK Gateway	• Business use
Medium	• Conference venue	• Theme days • Market square	
Low		• Entertainment	• Theme park • Sikh quarter

(Y-axis: Town's attractiveness to business)

Segmentation

5.8 Subject to appropriate research findings our approach to segmentation suggests a differentiated strategy with a separate mix for each segment (our strategy is to attract investment in each project).

5.9 *Segments*

(a) Investment institutions

(i) Millennium fund
(ii) Government Funding
(iii) Lottery
(iv) EU
(v) Private investors

(b) Property developers

(c) Tourist service providers

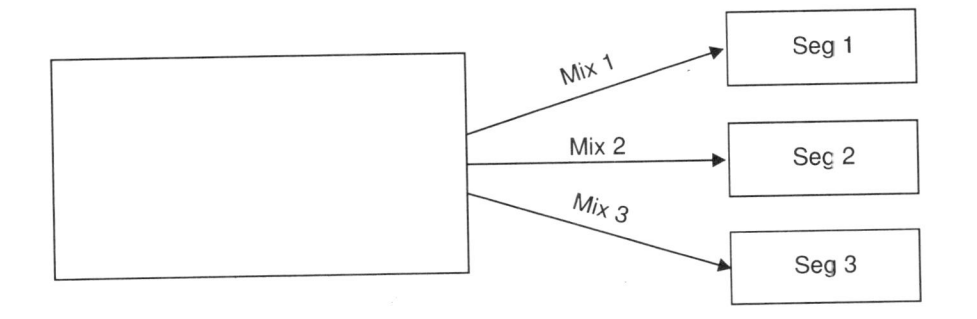

16: Gravesend Town Centre: outline marketing planning

```
┌──────────┐  Mix 1  ┌──────┐
│          │────────▶│ Seg 1│
│          │         └──────┘
│          │  Mix 2  ┌──────┐
│          │────────▶│ Seg 2│
│          │         └──────┘
│          │  Mix 3  ┌──────┐
└──────────┘────────▶│ Seg 3│
                     └──────┘
```

5.10 *Product*: an investment opportunity?

    (a) Name change - to be researched and considered
    (b) Hygiene work (TCI 10 point plan etc)
    (c) Defined business strategy/investment package

5.11 *Price*: the cost to investors

    (a) Attractive rates/holidays
    (b) Availability/accessibility of government/grant funding

5.12 *Place*

    (a) Infrastructure - maintain/improve/accessibility
    (b) Available space
    (c) Riverfrontage

5.13 *Promotion*

    (a) Business-to-business

        (i) Personal selling
        (ii) Direct mail lead generation
        (iii) Public relations
        (iv) Marketing 'suite'

    (b) Improve image/brand values

    (c) Brochure (POS)

    (d) Video (now) and multimedia/(in future)

    (e) Internal marketing

5.14 *Processes*

    (a) Planning permission availability
    (b) Reduce bureaucracy

5.15 *People*

    (a) Identify skills in TCI/council and re-organise
    (b) Appoint marketing development manager

5.16 *Physical evidence*

    (a) TCI activities
    (b) Marketing suite access

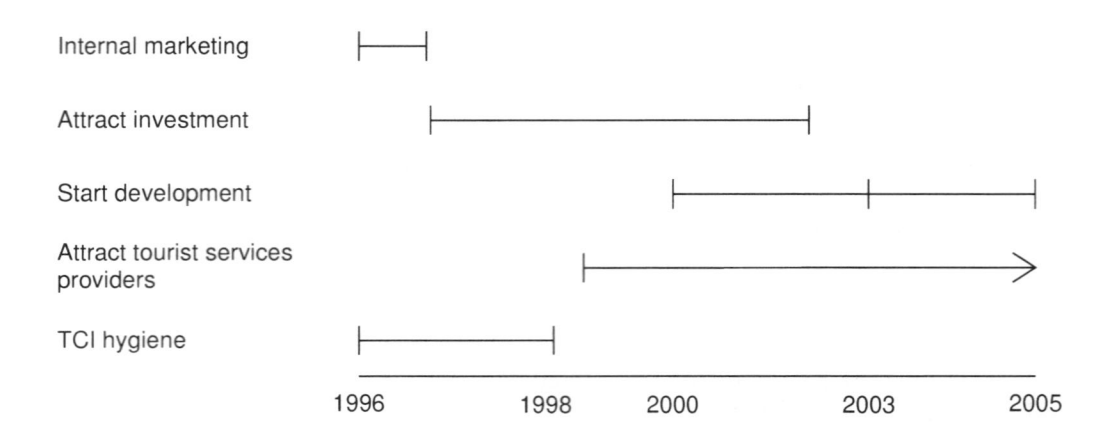

```
Internal marketing          |—|
Attract investment                |————————————|
Start development                      |—————————|————|
Attract tourist services
providers                          |————————————————————>
TCI hygiene             |—————————|
                     1996       1998      2000     2003    2005
```

5.17 *Budget*

In recognition of the limited resources available, low cost activities are mainly suggested.

	£
Personal selling (administration and support)	20,000
Limited direct mail	15,000
PR and internal marketing	5,000
POS - Brochure	5,000
- Video	10,000
Internal marketing	5,000
Marketing manager	50,000
Marketing suite	100,000
Research	20,000
TCI 'hygiene' activities	1,000,000
Consultants' fees (initial)	12,000
	1,242,000

5.18 *Controls*

(a) Annual review of income generated against target

(b) Management/review of budgets spend vs forecast

(c) Image development - awareness

Qualitative research } Use an agency and offer questionnaires to visitors
Quantitative research   to the marketing suite

(d) Number of investors attracted each year.

(e) Number of visitors to marketing suite and overall trends of visitors to the town.

Chapter 17

GRAVESEND TOWN CENTRE: DETAILED MARKETING PLANNING

> **This chapter contains the following information and plans.**
> Introductory note to detailed plans by Jonathan Avery, Jonathan Hurry and Stephen Hoy
> 1 Introduction and mission
> 2 SWOT analysis
> 3 Segmentation strategy
> 4 Positioning strategy
> 5 Growth strategy
> 6 Marketing objectives
> 7 Marketing mix
> 8 Marketing implementation
> 9 Conclusions
> 10 Appendices

INTRODUCTORY NOTE TO DETAILED PLANS BY JONATHAN AVERY, JONATHAN HURRY AND STEPHEN HOY

At this point we need to advise that whereas a complete marketing plan is intended to cover you for all eventualities, it cannot of course provide all the detail that might be needed for a specific examination question. You will therefore have to add detail as required in the examination itself. Moreover, the CIM reserves the right to introduce additional material to you in the examination hall and normally will do so.

However, in anticipation of examination questions signalled in the case study, some syndicates will prepare extra material on, say, organisations for financial implications or marketing research. You have already been introduced to this idea in previous chapters.

The work done by Jonathan Avery, Jonathan Hurry and Stephen Hoy has been included as a reasonably good effort to develop a creative and convincing marketing plan although it could of course be improved by the addition of a marketing research plan and marketing budgets. See previous outline plans.

Hopefully, this detailed plan combined with the three sample outline plans already reviewed will stimulate your own ideas and confidence in tackling your first *mock exam* coming up in the next chapter.

Gravesend
your first port of call...

@kaiZen
marketing consultants

Jonathan Avery, Jonathan Hurry, Stephen Hoy

Fleetwood Marketing Ltd
37-39 Western Road
Dartford
Kent, DA1 3GQ

7 June 1996

Brian Richmond
Town Centre Manager
Gravesend Town Centre Initiative
Windmill House
Cygnet Street
Gravesend
Kent, DA12 2AB

Dear Brian

Re: Marketing Strategy - Gravesend Town Centre

Following your letter of 19 November 1995 I would like to thank you for choosing Fleetwood Marketing to provide a long-term marketing strategy for the development of Gravesend Town Centre.

As discussed, the redevelopment of the Gravesham district and Gravesend Town Centre is not a one-shot overnight process, and therefore I have decided a specific Marketing Group that will initiate and nurture a redevelopment process that will be structured to become self-supporting well within the ten year period of our suggested marketing plan. The three-man team responsible for this task will take its name from the Japanese principle of continuous improvement and thus will be called 'KAIZEN'.

Enclosed with this letter I am pleased to submit a proposed marketing plan by the 'Kaizen' team who will be presenting their findings to yourself and your colleagues on the TCI project on Friday 7th June.

I feel confident that Fleetwood Marketing and Kaizen team can deliver the results Gravesend TCI and its private sector partners are seeking from this active redevelopment project.

If you have any further queries regarding Fleetwood, the Kaizen team or their proposed plan, please feel free to contact me at your convenience.

Yours sincerely,

Bill Morrison

Bill Morrison

CONTENTS

		Para ref
1	**Introduction and mission**	1.1 - 1.4
2	**Environmental and SWOT analysis**	2.1 - 2.2
3	**Segmentation strategy**	3.1 - 3.3
4	**Positioning strategy**	4.1 - 4.3
	• Competitors positioning	4.4 - 4.6
	• Gravesend Town Centre positioning	4.7 - 4.8
5	**Growth strategy**	5.1
	• Year 1: Market penetration strategy	5.2
	• Years 2-5: Product development strategy (5.3)	5.3
	• Years 6-10: Market development strategy	5.3
6	**Marketing objectives**	
	• Year 1: Consolidation	6.1
	• Years 2-5: Developing retail/leisure mix (6.2)	6.2
	• Years 6-10: Marketing objectives	6.3
7	**Marketing mix**	
	• Product	7.1 - 7.4
	• Place: Gravesend initiative land zoning scheme	7.5 - 7.7
	∘ Retail development zone	7.8
	∘ Tourism/cultural development zone	7.9 - 7.10
	∘ Leisure development zone	7.11 - 7.12
	∘ Shaping the product to reflect target market needs	7.13
	• Corporate identity	7.14 - 7.16
	• Promotional activity	
	∘ Stage 1: Consolidation	7.17
	∘ Stage 2: Attracting new customers and investment	7.18
	∘ Local level promotional activity	7.19
	∘ Awareness campaigns	7.20 - 7.22
	∘ Stimulating investment: business/retail	7.23
	• Promotion: providing for the future	7.24
8	**Marketing implementation**	
	• Year 1-5; Gravesend Initiative	8.1
	• Year 6-10: The changing role of the TCI	8.2
	• Funding	8.3
9	**Conclusions**	

1 INTRODUCTION AND MISSION

1.1 Gravesend is on the verge of a new phase of prosperity in its history.

1.2 There is potential for rapid growth and the cultivation of business opportunity. In unison with Gravesend Town Centre initiative, Kaizen believe that this opportunity must be seized before the strategic window closes. We must build on the foundations laid out in the ten point plan, and develop the hidden potential of Gravesend as a thriving market town in the Borough of Gravesham.

1.3 The following marketing plan identifies existing shoppers as relatively content with the retail mix currently offered, but they only account for a small proportion of Gravesend's catchment area. It is essential, therefore, to increase the number of people visiting and spending in Gravesend in order to support the improvements already under way as part of the Town Centre Initiative.

1.4 The essential factors to ensure the long-term growth of Gravesend Town Centre are embodied in the following mission statement.

> Our mission is to create an environment to attract investment from local and national companies who will create a diversified retail/leisure mix that will cater for the needs of potential users.

2 SWOT ANALYSIS

2.1 Following a detailed SWOT analysis, it is clear to Kaizen that the main problem threatening the growth of Gravesend Town Centre is its current retail/leisure mix. The potential for growth in various markets must be realised by Gravesend Town Centre. An opportunity to create a multi-segmented town centre will allow for different customer groups to be targeted.

2.2 *Tutorial note.* The underpinning environmental and SWOT analysis for this plan can be found in Chapter 13, paragraphs 7.9 to 7.12.

3 SEGMENTATION STRATEGY

3.1 When considering the demographic diversity of Gravesend, and in line with the aims and objectives of the Gravesend TCI, Kaizen recommend that the target market is segmented into four primary groups.

   (a) Each of these four groups will be targeted with their own individual marketing tactics tailored to suit best their particular needs.

   (b) This approach also has the benefit of enabling an incremental marketing strategy to be implemented as resources become available.

   (c) Thus the process of continuous improvement will be supported as new investment becomes available to complete the next stage of the proposed ten year plan.

3.2 The 'Catchment Area' is defined as 'within ten miles of Gravesend Town Centre'. Broad target segments are described below.

Table 1

Residents*	Those people already living within the catchment area.
Visitors	Those people who travel into or through the catchment area and whose stay is considered only temporary. Visitors may be frequent or irregular but often.
Tourists	Those people who visit the catchment area for the purpose of tourism. These tourists are considered irregular and infrequent visitors.
Industry	Any organisation that could potentially carry on its business from within the catchment area. This segment would include retailers, service businesses and 'clean' or blue-chip manufacturers

* As described in the environmental and SWOT analysis section of this report, Gravesend has a demographic profile of active shoppers with higher proportions of older and younger people in comparison with the UK as a whole. Although existing residents will cover the whole age range, clearly it is important to cater for the older generation's shopping habits, whilst implementing a structure that serves the younger generation's preferences; the creation of an infrastructure for the younger markets being the main thrust of Kaizen's marketing plan.

3.3 Within these broad segments, further sub-segments have been identified as key target groups for Kaizen's strategy.

(a) *Residents*: target non-users

   (i) Emphasise the 18-24 age group
   (ii) Do not alienate existing customers

(b) *Visitors*

   (i) Extend catchment area to Greater London
   (ii) Target 'affluents' (attract mobile expenditure)

(c) *Tourists*: the tourism 'mix' will feature a leisure orientation rather than culture. Gravesend has a limited capacity for long-stay tourists and thus marketing will focus on leisure facilities targeting appropriate potential consumers. This segment will thus include young affluents and keen hobbyists.

(d) *Industry*: small businesses and national companies as sources of potential growth and investment funding for TCI initiatives.

4 POSITIONING STRATEGY

4.1 The key to Kaizen's positioning strategy is one based entirely on realistic principles rather than idealism. With the advent of various 'out-of-town' retail parks emerging within easy reach of Gravesend Town Centre, a superficial analysis would probably suggest a style of competitive frontal attack on these centres in order to bring trade back to the Town Centre. Kaizen believes that this is not the solution to the problem. It is very short-termist and over the long term would help neither the retail parks nor the Town Centre, as profits are competed away and consumers are aggressively targeted for their trade.

4.2 Kaizen are convinced that the Town Centre is *not* able to compete equally with the retail parks, partly because it cannot afford the finance required, and therefore should seek to work *with* its environmental threats, not *against* them. This philosophy runs throughout the report and is the basis for both Kaizen's marketing strategy and the tactics detailed later in this report.

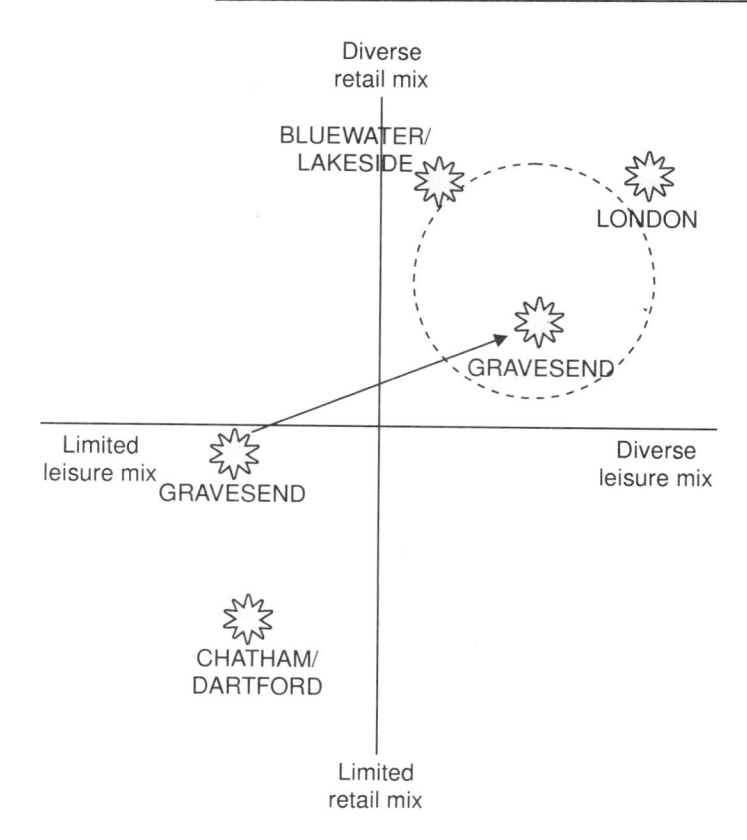

17: Gravesend Town Centre: detailed marketing plan

```
                    Diverse
                    retail mix
                         │
           BLUEWATER/    │
           LAKESIDE ✦----│----✦
                     ╱   │    LONDON
                   ╱    ✦
                 ╱    GRAVESEND
                ╱      │
    Limited   ╱        │            Diverse
    leisure ─✦─────────┼──────────  leisure mix
    mix    GRAVESEND   │
                       │
                      ✦
                   CHATHAM/
                   DARTFORD
                       │
                    Limited
                    retail mix
```

4.3 The positioning map above shows where Gravesend's desired position should be. Positioning Gravesend Town Centre will follow a concurrent three-stage process over one, two-to-five and six-to-ten years. During these periods, Gravesend Town Centre will be focusing on different aspects of its growth areas, with the introduction of Town Centre zones as described in the growth strategy section of this report.

Competitors' positioning

4.4 Clearly, all other towns in the near vicinity of Gravesend, and those representing key alternatives to Gravesend as places for shopping, or visiting as business locations are the prime competitors of Gravesend's Town Centre Initiative.

4.5 *London* itself is within easy reach and thus represents an important competitive consideration to Gravesend TCI's positioning. Whilst London offers a large city's diversity and facility to shoppers, tourists and industry, it is expensive and inflexible for industry, and tourists and shoppers have to travel across the city to reap the benefits of its variety. Travel in London is not only slow, but can be costly too, and shoppers and tourists have to fight off the crowds to get wherever they are heading.

4.6 Smaller local towns are not well represented statistically as preferred locations for trade (business and personal) in comparison to Gravesend, and are not seen as possessing the potential for growth that could provide direct competition to Gravesend as it develops over the proposed ten-year period.

Gravesend town centre positioning

4.7 Kaizen believe that in the short-term Gravesend Town Centre should be seeking to position itself as a *New Town* with *rich historical values*. With the facilities of a new town such as the wide retail base and considerable leisure opportunities, coupled with the cultural promotion of its history, Gravesend could offer attractions for all ages and types of people within easy reach of the large population pool of Greater London. Thus for the town centre itself, Kaizen propose a *cultural* and *leisure* positioning strategy, with a retail focus on small independent specialists to boost activity levels and cash generation.

4.8 Over the long-term, this inwardly focused positioning strategy should extend to what Kaizen have described as the 'Gravesham Initiative' which seeks to place Gravesend Town Centre as a complement to the out-of-town retail parks and alternative leisure facilities within Gravesham as a whole. Positioning Gravesend as the focus of the much larger and more diverse industrial and commercial base of Gravesham will identify greater possibilities for attracting custom to the town centre: those seeking to invest or locate in Gravesham might consider the principal town of Gravesend as an ideal place to operate from or live within.

5 GROWTH STRATEGY

5.1 To reposition Gravesend successfully, Kaizen have developed the following marketing aims.

(a) The creation of a diverse retail and leisure mix, located in an attractive environment, which will make Gravesend the focal point for the area.

(b) The encouragement of new investment to create a differentiated retail/leisure mix.

(c) The targeting of existing residents, visitors (floating shoppers and commuters) and tourists (of limited nature), with special emphasis on winning back 18-24 year olds.

(d) To rejuvenation of the non-retail element to make Gravesend a thriving hub outside shopping hours.

(e) The attraction of new business to the region to ensure sustained growth.

(f) The creation of brand values.

5.2 The marketing aims outlined above will be realised through the implementation of an aggressive growth strategy, outlined below in Figure 2.

	CURRENT PRODUCTS	NEW PRODUCTS
CURRENT MARKETS	Market Penetration strategy Year 1 Increase usage from existing customer base	Product development strategy Years 2-5 Create differentiated retail/leisure mix
NEW MARKETS	Market development strategy Years 6-10 Sustain growth by encouraging new development	Diversification strategy

Year 1: Marketing penetration strategy

5.3 Completing the rejuvenation of Gravesend Town Centre, as advocated by the 10 point plan, is vital to the long-term success of this project. Potential investors will only be lured once there is an attractive environment in place for them. Whilst the environmental infrastructure work is taking place, Kaizen plans to implement marketing tactics which will increase usage from the existing customer base, and will convert non-users.

Years 2-5: Product development strategy

5.4 Once the infrastructure is in place, the quest to attract private investment to create a differentiated retail/leisure infrastructure begins. Investment will improve the existing facilities, hence increasing their appeal to a larger audience.

Years 6-10: Market development strategy

5.5 Once the revitalisation of Gravesend is completed, the long-term focus shifts to sustaining growth and development in the Borough of Gravesham and the surrounding area. Integration with future developments (see Table 2) will allow a revitalised Gravesend to flourish. Resources from the various developments in the surrounding area need to be pooled, so that by working together, a more alluring proposition can be created to attract new investment into the Borough.

Table 2: Development opportunities

Crossways - Business Park
Science Park
University of Greenwich
Greenhithe, Ebbsfleet & Swancombe - Urban Villages
Northfleet Embankment & CTRL Station
Eastern Quarry

6 MARKETING OBJECTIVES

Year 1: Consolidation

6.1 Complete the 10 point plan and commit existing resources to short-term promotional activity, for example a *Maritime Festival* and a *Christmas Shopping Extravaganza*.

Year 2-5: Developing the retail/leisure mix

6.2 (a) Retain 90% of existing national multiples

(b) Retain 60% of existing independent stores

(c) Target existing vacant (June 1996) units

  (i) Year 2: 30% occupied
  (ii) Year 3: 60% occupied
  (iii) Year 4: 85% occupied
  (iv) Year 5: 100% occupied

(d) Achieve the following increase in expenditure on leisure (per capita, from catchment area based on 1996 figure).

  (i) Year 2: + 10%
  (ii) Year 3: + 30%
  (iii) Year 4 + 60%
  (iv) Year 5: + 100%

Notes | Part E: Learning from experience: ensuring you pass

Objectives: Years 6-10

6.3 (a) Objectives for this period will depend on the investment secured in years 1-3 and initial projections will be made in year 4.

(b) 40% of local companies (retail and other) should be persuaded to contribute to the development fund required to implement promotional activity.

7 MARKETING MIX

Product

7.1 Gravesend as a product can be illustrated on three different levels: core, actual and augmented. Repositioning Gravesend will entail elevating its core product to create a diverse retail/leisure mix which will satisfy the needs of residents', customers' and businesses.

7.2 Before the *core product* can be shaped, Gravesend town centre needs to be rejuvenated. Currently the packaging of the augmented product is inadequate to attract the investment and consumers, that will help generate the actual product. Realisation of core product benefits will only occur when there is an attractive environment in place.

7.3 Development of the *augmented product* through completion of the 10 Point Plan is the basis for Kaizen's incremental growth strategy. The key areas of the 10 Point Plan are outlined below.

(a) Attractive pedestrian areas, open spaces and street furniture
(b) Attractive and secure car parks
(c) Regeneration of High Street and Harmer Street
(d) Redevelopment of vacant sites
(e) Improved riverside - clean water suitable for watersports
(f) Public utilities - phone, toilets
(g) Tourist office/Bureau de change

7.4 Once environmental improvements are complete, the infrastructure can be fully utilised to pursue the initial penetration strategy. As Gravesend attracts more customers and investment, the *actual product* will be exposed to a snowball effect that continuously strengthens the core product.

Gravesend initiative land zoning scheme

7.5 Once the infrastructure is in place, Kaizen propose that creative land zoning can add further value to the three levels of product described above. A framework has been designed to develop the existing product, through zoning, helping it to increase penetration in a diverse target market.

7.6 Land zoning aims to leverage the existing physical attributes of the town centre to create a framework for future development in the area. Encouraging clustering of related retail and non-retail functions, it creates a focus-point in the town for the various target market groups. Each zone has been developed to maximise synergy between the target leisure/retail mix, and its natural surroundings.

7.7 Providing a planned structure for the town centre allows for easier management of long term development. Potential investors can be encouraged to locate in zones that best suit their business, therefore not conflicting with existing retail/leisure mix that is already sited. Appendix 1 illustrates how the town centre will be divided to create the zones described below.

17: Gravesend Town Centre: detailed marketing plan

Retail development zone

7.8 The development of retail functions will be restricted to within a quarter mile radius of the High Street. The suggested zone stretches from Harmer Street (East) to Bath Street (West). Within this identified zone, an attempt will be made to further segment retail development. Mainstream national multiples and independent retailers will be encouraged to locate in the central pedestrainised area. Specialist stores, carrying a more exclusive product range, will be encouraged to situate on the regenerated Harmer Street. This impressive street which was built in 1836, offers a prestigious backdrop for Gravesend's niche retail element. As Harmer Street is intended to provide relief from through traffic it is an ideal location for specialised retailers because they will be highly visible to the passing traffic. Such a presence should stimulate the perception of a diverse retail mix in Gravesend.

Tourism/cultural development zone

7.9 Gravesend *heritage* is another well-documented resource that can be leveraged to attract visitors to the town. A small area running west, from the Arts Centre, to HM Customs House, has been identified as a development zone for tourism and culture. The waterfront has a long association with HM Customs, and was once the haunt of notorious smugglers. This heritage, combined with the Arts Centre, make it an ideal base for the proposed tourist centre.

7.10 Kaizen realises that there is limited potential in attracting long-stay tourism to the town. However, there is potential within the development of leisure facilities which will inherently attract passing enthusiasts from around the country.

Leisure development zone

7.11 (a) *Watersports*. The first zone is located east of Custom House Pier: the area has been allocated for the development of watersports activities along Gordon Promenade. This scheme will also earmark the Canal Basin as a potential future development site for a marina.

   (b) *Leisure*. The second zone will be created along West Street, between St Andrews Gardens and Elizabeth Gardens. The development of bars, restaurants and nightlife will be encouraged along the bank of the River Thames, to add a distinctly cosmopolitan flavour to Gravesend. The vicinity of the technical college was taken into consideration when making this decision, as the student population do not currently appear to be well catered for.

7.12 By the end of Year 5 the development of Gravesend's retail/leisure mix will be completed. Our aim is to create a diverse environment that will satisfy the needs of the identified target markets through *mass customisation*.

Shaping the product to reflect target market needs

7.13 The table below typifies the investment in retail/leisure functions Kaizen believe is necessary to attract the target markets.

   (a) *Residents*
      (i) Core retail - retention of anchor stores; more national multiples
      (ii) Nightlife, bars and clubs

   (b) *Visitors*
      (i) Specialist shops, boutiques, antiques shops, specialist sports shops etc
      (ii) Leisure activities, sports, bars, restaurants

   (c) *Tourists*
      (i) Tourist office
      (ii) Bureau de change

(iii) Accommodation and restaurants
(iv) Public amenities
(v) The diverse leisure facilities already suggested

Corporate identity

7.14 Corporate imagery can be a valuable marketing tool when it is attractive, distinctive and memorable. Kaizen are committed to creating a corporate identity for Gravesend that will build a unique image of the town in the mind of the target markets. The introduction of a new identity will help increase stature and credibility, whilst acting as the springboard for the launch of an intense promotional campaign.

7.15 Kaizen has leveraged Gravesend's physical location on the River Thames and some of the images associated with its heritage, to create a corporate identify (see Appendix 2).

To communicate Gravesend's brand values effectively, Kaizen have developed an individual branding for the retail and leisure elements of the service mix, which are positioned underneath the umbrella branding. Examples are offered in Appendix 2.

(a) *Umbrella branding*. '*Gravesend - your first port of call*'. Borrowing from the heritage of the River Thames, Gravesend's identity reflects its brand values and positioning.

(i) The galley symbolises passage to the new world, an image associated with hope and a fresh start.

(ii) '*Your first port of call*', emphasises that Gravesend has a diversified retail/leisure mix that is likely to appeal to everyone.

(b) *Product branding*.

(i) Gravesend shopping centre: '*seek out the smugglers cove*'. In the past 'searchers' from Customs House used to check all the passing sea traffic for smugglers stashing their valuable hoards. The creative branding, '*Seek out the smugglers' cove*', indicates that the retail outlets in Gravesend are valuable, like the hidden treasure sought by the 'searchers'.

(ii) Gravesend leisure facilities: '*discover the new world*'. The leisure branding highlights the development of new facilities that previously were not part of Gravesend's service mix.

7.16 Corporate colours, type faces, logos and brandings, will be used consistently throughout Gravesend's promotional campaigns. The distinct image will feature everywhere from corporate stationery, right down to street level advertising.

Promotional activity

Stage 1 consolidation

7.17 Kaizen propose a series of events in 1996 to launch the Gravesend Initiative and the new corporate identify. It is crucial that the TCI shows immediate commitment to the project to ensure that our anchor retailers do not lose confidence. The aim is to bring people back to the town centre and let them discover the strong retail mix that already exists. These events include the following.

(a) *Maritime festival/regatta - July 1996*. This will:

(i) stabilise the current customer flow and create a 'feel good factor';
(ii) promote confidence in Gravesend (existing retailers and potential investors);
(c) attract local residents who would not normally visit Gravesend.

(b) *Christmas shopping extravaganza - December 1996*. This will:

(i) boost awareness, and ensure people do not forget about Gravesend;
(ii) promote Gravesend as an alternative to the busy regional centres for last minute shopping

17: Gravesend Town Centre: detailed marketing plan

Attracting new customers and investment

7.18 Hopefully the renewed interest in Gravesend created by activity in Stage 1, and the completion of the 10 Point Plan will act as a catalyst for new customers and investment. The aim of Stage 2 is to build on these achievements and further enhance the actual product. Promotional activity intensifies at this stage to combat the launch of Bluewater.

Local level promotional activity

7.19 Gravesend town centre will become the focus for relationship marketing and retention exercises to gain customer loyalty from the existing users.

(a) Promotional activity within the town centre will allow local events to be communicated through official banners and poster sites, sporting the Gravesend Initiative's corporate identity. The adverts will appear regularly in prime sites such as the main pedestrianised shopping street, Harmer Street and the riverfront.

(b) The aim of this activity is to build a rapport with the local community and keep them informed about 'what's on' in the town. As the retail/leisure mix diversifies, special events should become more frequent.

(c) This method of communication gives local businesses a chance to advertise free of charge, therefore encouraging them to launch special promotions that will in turn attract more customers to the town centre. Grass roots promotions will be complemented with sponsorship of the 'What's On' section in the local newspaper.

(d) As the retail/leisure mix spreads into the allocated zones, customers will be able to navigate their way round the town using maps and extensive sign-posting. Small information kiosks located at frequent intervals in each zone provide the customer with information about the stores, and leisure amenities and their location.

Awareness campaigns

7.20 Promotional activity designed to boost awareness across a wider area serves two purposes.

(a) It should attract more visitors to the town, challenging Lakeside and Bluewater.

(b) It should encourage investment.

7.21 *Editorial/advertorial.* Coverage of Gravesend's revitalisation in a variety of local/national newspapers and business magazines should help target customers from further afield and investors. Editorial is a more appropriate approach than mass market advertising, because it is cost effective, and carries the endorsement of the publication it appears in. A media pack will be designed and sent to the media, containing history, target markets, competitive advantages, future developments, incentives etc. Advertorials in local newspapers can also be utilised to welcome new retailers to the town, emphasising a close knit community.

7.22 *Cross advertising campaigns.* Businesses in Gravesend will be given the opportunity to participate in cross advertising campaigns that will be jointly funded by the TCI. Mutual benefit is created for both parties through this association. These activities provide an opportunity for small businesses to advertise using media that previously they could not afford. Gravesend benefits from the association with the retailer, by communicating their message to the retailer's target audience. Using this method of advertising, Gravesend can have a considerable impact on a variety of different target markets. This tactic is also valuable for communicating the diversified service mix available in Gravesend. Cross advertising can be applied to the local press, or radio, all adverts will be produced by the retailer, and tagged with the relevant Gravesend product branding.

Stimulating investment: business/retail

7.23 The initial promotional activity and infrastructure work are designed to rebuild confidence in Gravesend as a centre for retailing and leisure activities. The enthusiasm created by these events needs to be built on by creating an attractive proposition for new retailers. Kaizen propose the following incentives are utilised.

(a) *Rates holiday*: various financial incentives can be used to encourage entrepreneurs and national companies to locate in Gravesend.

(b) *Professional sales approach*: targeting national retailers to promote Gravesend.

(c) *Advice line for small businesses*: designed to encourage local business start-ups in the town. The telephone help line can advise potential advisers about the promotional and financial incentives on offer and help them find a suitable location for their business. Encouraging small business will help create a diversified retail/leisure mix that cannot be imitated by the regional centres.

Promotion: providing for the future

7.24 The networked group will operate under separate corporate identity, to encourage relocation in the area through active promotion and hard selling. Working under the slogan, '*Navigating business into the 21st Century*', the Gravesham Initiative should consider using the following tools.

(a) *Networking* with government bodies and regional development organisations in an attempt to gain funds and recommendations. Other opportunities exist for developing strong links with the public utilities companies (BT, regional electricity, water and gas), as they will also benefit from relocation in the area. Under similar circumstances these organisations have been influential in attracting investment and providing funding for promotional work.

(b) Positive editorial coverage in the location journals, which are published around the world, should also be sought after. Publications like these can stimulate interest for an area when a company is considering where to locate.

8 MARKETING IMPLEMENTATION

8.1 *Year 1-5: Gravesend Initiative*. Implementation of marketing activities throughout this period are illustrated in Appendix 3. Kaizen suggest that the TCI designs an internal marketing programme to complement the external programme that has been outlined in this document. The content of the plan needs to be effectively communicated to key members of the TCI so that all those involved understand what is trying to be achieved.

8.2 *Years 6-10: The changing role of the TCI: 'Architect' to 'lead operato'r to 'caretaker' over 10 years.*

(a) All the initiatives in the area will need to work together to ensure long-term growth. Individual resources should be focused through the development of a working group to co-ordinate growth in the region. A repositioned Gravesend could become the focus point for sustaining long-term growth if it can be moulded into an asset that will complement the future developments (see Table 2).

(b) A network needs to be created to ensure that the resources of all the developments are pooled, to attract investment into the area.

(i) The Gravesend Town Centre Initiative could act as the *architect* in the development of such a network.

(ii) Having established this network, the TCI's role will evolve into one of *lead operator*, where the promotional effort is coordinated to run smoothly for the benefit of everyone. Producing synergy from coordinating the different future development programmes will create a unique marketing advantage where any individual organisation can position itself as part of the whole under the corporate brand. The overall aim is to create a 'focus-point marketing culture' where the individual contributors within the network

work together to develop a single focus (sustainable growth for Gravesham) regardless of their own individual objectives.

(c) This sustainable growth for Gravesham should be seen as beneficial to all parties involved, and therefore it is the role of the TCI as network caretaker to communicate this message clearly.

8.3 *Funding*

(a) Current resources available will be committed to completing the activities for year 1. Funds need to be allocated for promotional activity for years 2-5 from local and regional budgets.

(b) Kaizen's proposal incorporates the creation of a self-supporting network that will take ownership of development opportunities, and thus funding the tactics required to realise these opportunities.

9 CONCLUSIONS

Gravesend needs to weather the storm before it can realise its full potential. This report illustrates the opportunities available to Gravesend to ride the crest of the wave of new business opportunities into the next century.

10 APPENDICES

10.1 *Appendix 1*

Kaizen produced a suggested touring map identifying the overlapping zones for retail, leisure, culture and tourism. This is reproduced on the following page.

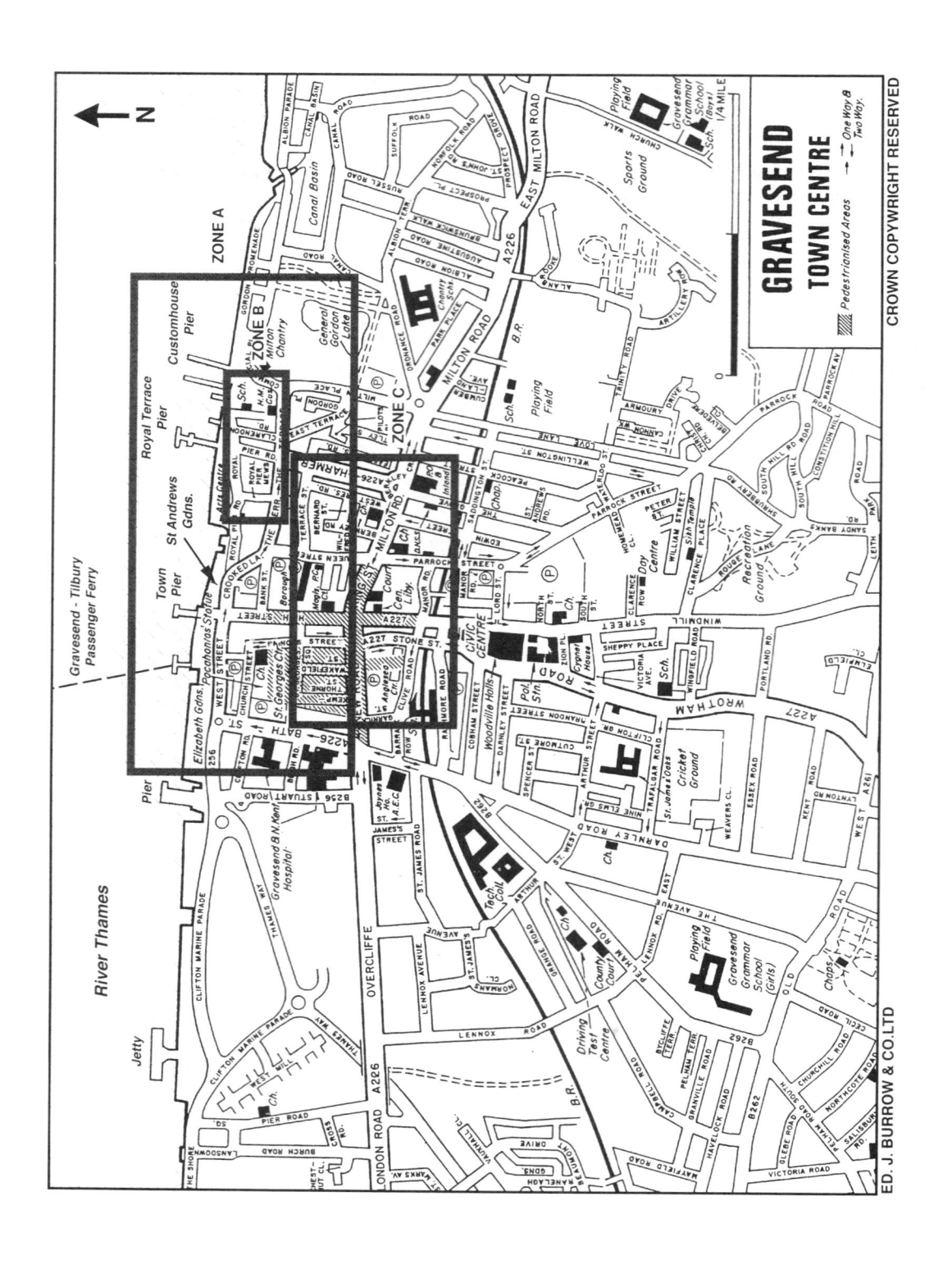

Part E: Learning from experience: ensuring you pass

17: *Gravesend Town Centre: detailed marketing plan*

10.2 *Appendix 2: promotional material*

369 BPP Publishing

Part E: Learning from experience: ensuring you pass

10.3 *Appendix 3: Gantt chart*

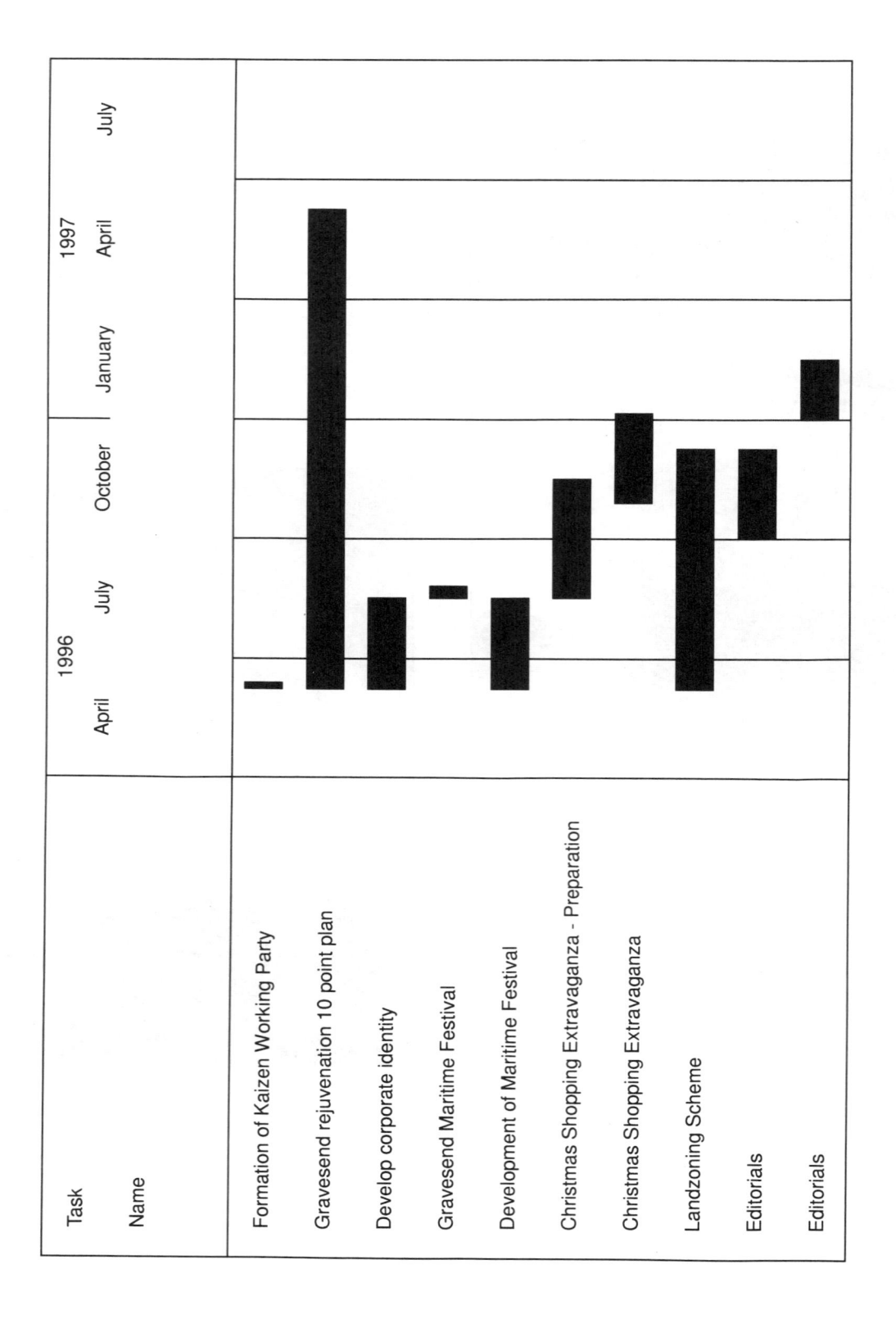

Task Name	April 1996	July	October	January 1997	April	July
Formation of Kaizen Working Party	▬					
Gravesend rejuvenation 10 point plan	█████████████████					
Develop corporate identity		▬▬				
Gravesend Maritime Festival		▪				
Development of Maritime Festival		▬▬				
Christmas Shopping Extravaganza - Preparation			███			
Christmas Shopping Extravaganza			▬▬			
Landzoning Scheme	█████████					
Editorials			▬▬			
Editorials				▬▬		

Chapter 18

GRAVESEND TOWN CENTRE: THE EXAMINATION PAPER, EXAMINER'S REPORT AND INDICATIVE MARKING GUIDES

This chapter contains the following.

1   The examination paper
2   Examiner's report
3   Indicative marking guides
4   A final word

GRAVESEND TOWN CENTRE

THE EXAM QUESTIONS ARE ON THE NEXT PAGE

DO NOT LOOK UNTIL YOU ARE READY TO SPEND
THREE HOURS ON DOING THESE AS A MOCK EXAM

Part E: Learning from experience: ensuring you pass

1   THE EXAMINATION PAPER

Additional information to be taken into account when answering the questions set

---

Gravesend Town Centre Initiative
Windmill House
Cygnet Street
Gravesend
Kent, DA12 2AB

5 June 1996

Mr W Morrison
Managing Director
Fleetwood Marketing Ltd
37-39 Western Road
Dartford
Kent, DA1 3GQ

Dear Bill

As a response to your phone call I have spoken to some of my contacts. It seems that your concerns about competitive activity were well founded.

You asked me to find out what the major out-of-town shopping centres are investing in promotion. It would seem that Lakeside spends £16 million per annum and Bluewater is planning to spend £2.0 million per annum when it gets going. I also hear that Lille and Calais will be spending up to £1.0 million between them on promotion aimed at attracting shoppers from London and the South East as soon as the Channel Tunnel Rail Link (CTRL) is operating.

As you know, there is no way that we can compete with that sort of promotional spend - at least not directly. I hope that your presentation on the 14th will help us deal with the sort of competition that will be facing us soon.

Yours sincerely,

Brian Richmond

Town Centre Manager

Based on the data you have collected you have decided to approach the presentation to the Town Centre Initiative Steering Group in three parts. Your report, in *report format*, will cover the following.

Question 1 - (30 marks)

Identify the uncontrollable elements of the environment that are likely to have significant impact upon Gravesham's strategic marketing plans. How and to what extent can such important environmental factors or trends be forecast?

Question 2 - (40 marks)

Produce a strategic marketing plan for Gravesend Town Centre for the planning period to 2005.

Question 3 - (30 marks)

As the Town Centre Management has no direct control over events, explain how the strategic marketing plan might be implemented and controlled with and through the key parties.

2 EXAMINER'S REPORT

General comments

2.1 Although this case produced a slightly better overall pass rate than the previous case (Leffe), results are still generally disappointing. Too many candidates are still failing to demonstrate their ability to apply the most basic of marketing principles.

2.2 The Gravesend case found too many candidates unable to address the questions posed on examination day. Work prepared before the examination was too often regurgitated without taking account of the marks allocated on the paper.

2.3 The list of reasons for failure in the case were (yet again)

(a) failure to answer the question posed on the day;
(b) regurgitation of case material;
(c) presentation of prepared answers regardless of questions set;
(d) lack of knowledge on strategic marketing issues;
(e) inclusion of irrelevant data, numbers and SWOT analyses;
(f) ignoring the additional information;
(g) poor time management.

2.4 The last point requires special mention. In this case the questions carried marks of 30:40:30. Question two was rightly anticipated by most candidates but was often answered as if it carried 80% of the marks. Question one was often answered quite superficially and question three either ignored or covered in two or three pages.

2.5 Examiners try hard to award marks but to do so we need something to mark! Time management is a critical skill for the practising marketer - not just useful to pass exams.

Question 1 (30 marks)

> Identify the uncontrollable elements of the environment that are likely to have a significant impact upon Gravesham's strategic marketing plans. How and to what extent can such important environmental factors or trends to be forecast?

2.6 This question (like question 3) proved difficult for candidates who had only prepared a strategic plan before the examination. Those who had succeeded in understanding the Gravesend situation managed quite well.

2.7 The question was looking for three things.

(a) Identifying the uncontrollable elements.
(b) Show why/how they affect Gravesend.
(c) How can these be forecast.

2.8 Candidates who thought this simply meant writing out the PEST/SWOT they had prepared for the strategic plan tended to fail this question.

2.9 The main problems encountered on this question were:

(a) listing all factors, not just those that are uncontrollable;
(b) citing the main PEST headings and not going beyond these to consider (eg competition, customers etc);
(c) failing to justify the factors by explaining how they are important to Gravesend;
(d) covering the forecasting element in less than half a page;
(e) ignoring the forecasting element altogether.

Notes   Part E: Learning from experience: ensuring you pass

Question 2 (40 marks)

> Produce a strategic marketing plan for Gravesend Town Centre for the planning period to 2005.

2.10 Most candidates had properly forecast this question. Having been asked so many times in the past, this question is beginning to focus attention on the contents of a strategic marketing plan and generally the structures (if not the contents) of plans are improving. Unfortunately, for some candidates it is obviously the only thing that they prepare. In this case, the strategic marketing plan attracted only 40% of the marks and too few candidates modified their approach accordingly.

2.11 One by-product of an easily predictable question is the reliance on group preparation or even completely pre-prepared answers simply copied out on the day of the examination. Such collusion is easily spotted by examiners and always rewarded with a fail grade. Remember, you can prepare with others but the examination is a test of individual, not group, ability.

2.12 SWOT and PEST analyses continue to take up pages of examination scripts (despite question one) but still attract relatively few marks because they are not applied to strategic action and recommendations.

2.13 The major problems in answers to this question centred around the following.

(a) Concentration on tactics rather than longer term strategy.

(b) Application of the 4Ps rather than the services mix.

(c) Inadequate understanding of targeting and positioning.

(d) Failure to identify target markets thereby producing a wide range of conflicting objectives and actions.

2.14 The major comment from examiners is that while many candidates can identify strategic alternatives by using Ansoff/Porter, far too few seem capable of making an informed choice. Suggesting Gravesend should do everything simply shows an inability to come to grips with the core problem.

Question 3 (30 marks)

> As the Town Centre Manager has no direct control over events, explain how the strategic marketing plan might be implemented and controlled with and through the key parties.

2.15 This question proved the downfall of far too many candidates. Even allowing for thinking and planning the answer, 30 marks should justify close to 45 minutes writing time. Examiners offered just two or three pages found it difficult to award pass marks.

2.16 Despite the attention paid to the implementation and control aspects of marketing strategy over recent years, not enough preparation is being made in these important areas. Strategic marketing planning is not an academic exercise. The difference between a theoretical exercise and company success is implementation and control. Too many candidates failed to demonstrate their ability to the examiners' satisfaction.

2.17 Future papers will monitor progress in this area.

18: Gravesend Town Centre: the examination paper, examiner's report and indicative marking guides

2.18 The third part of this question was answered particularly badly. All marketing depends on the marketers' ability to achieve marketing objectives through others - inside the organisation as well as outside! While a large number of candidates did not demonstrate this ability, other misinterpreted the question and produced a communications plan - still others ignored it completely.

Conclusions

2.19 Gravesend again proved to be a difficult case for many candidates.

2.20 Too many candidates focus their preparation on the strategic marketing plan as if marketing strategy is little more than filling in words under a set of agreed headings. Questions one and three exposed those candidates who had taken this 'tick-box' approach and, as a result, were unable to think more creatively around the problem on the day of the examination.

3 INDICATIVE MARKING GUIDES

3.1 *Overview*
   (a) (i) The case study presented for this examination is completely undisguised and the data and research figures presented have been reproduced unchanged from the original sources. Only names have been altered. The case is both topical and immediate. It describes the real situation faced by Gravesend now.

   (ii) From early discussions with candidates and tutors, many were originally surprised by the topic of the case study diverging as it does from the more 'normal' subject matter of marketing problems. Despite the unusual nature of the case, the organisation described is facing classic marketing problems and needs a clear strategy for the future.

   (b) *Key points*

   (i) Gravesend has been hit by competition from Lakeside and now contemplates the imminent opening of the biggest out-of-town retail development in Western Europe - on its doorstep.

   (ii) Town centres worldwide have been devastated by out-of-town developments.

   (iii) The town centre provides a wide range of benefits.

   (iv) Gravesend has a wide range of 'customers' with different needs. Some degree of trade-off or compromise will be required.

   (v) The planning period in the case is given as 10 years but traditionally planning needs to extend well beyond this.

   (vi) Gravesend exists to meet social as well as commercial needs.

   (vii) The Town Centre Manager has little direct control over events or what happens in Gravesend. He must work through others to achieve his aims.

   (viii) Besides seeing all the environmental factors as threats, they can be seen as opportunities too. For example, the millions of visitors coming to Bluewater could be given a reason for visiting Gravesend while they were there.

   (c) *The answers*

   In awarding marks in this case, the key points are as follows.

   (i) We are looking for application, not just the statement of theory.
   (ii) We are assessing marketing answers, not product-led sales answers.
   (iii) We are assessing marketing strategy, not tactics.
   (iv) The answer must be practical given the case situation.
   (v) The 'acid test' remains, would you give this person a job as a marketer?

Part E: Learning from experience: ensuring you pass

(d) *The additional information*

(i) The additional information was offered to candidates to present a clear picture of the type of competition they would be facing from the main centres close to them.

(ii) For the unwary it provides a possible parity spend figure. For the better students (they will ignore the parity trap) it will encourage them to offer practical solutions for Gravesend to counter this competitive activity without spending this type of money.

(iii) The only way of facing this type of competition is by being different.

Question 1

3.2 *Question 1 (30 marks).* ('Identify the uncontrollable elements that are likely to have a significant impact upon Gravesham's strategic marketing plans. How and to what extent can such important environmental factors or trends be forecast?')

(a) *Approach*

(i) This question ought to have been covered by the candidates' case preparation under the heading of marketing audit or SWOT.

(ii) We are not interested here in the complete SWOT analysis, of course, but only in the *external/uncontrollable* elements of the analysis.

(iii) A simple list (without explanation of how these factors are likely to affect the strategic marketing plans) will be insufficient.

(iv) Part two of the question asked 'how and to what extent' these factors or trends 'can be forecast'.

(b) *Good answers* will begin with a fairly detailed analysis of the uncontrollable factors likely to influence the marketing plans. These factors should be captured by the four major headings.

(i) Environmental factors - business and political eg:

(1) CTRL;
(2) University of Greenwich.

(ii) Environmental factors - social and political eg:

(1) mix of residents;
(2) Thames Gateway;

(iii) Market factors - customer needs

(1) Shoppers, residents, visitors, business people
(2) Needs:
- shopping
- recreation and social
- parking and transportation
- safety and security

(iv) Competitive factors eg:

(1) Lakeside, Bluewater, Calais, London
(2) Other forms of competition
(3) Competitive activity, eg
- product offer
- activity and promotion
- price
- management
- environment

(v) Part two of the question is covered with forecasting environmental factors. Better answers will consider some methods of forecasting, eg:

(1) expert opinion, eg Delphi method
(2) travel extrapolation, eg linear programming
(3) trend correlation, eg identify lead and lagging indicators for change

(4) dynamic modelling, eg computer models for forecasts
(5) scenario planning, eg build multiple scenarios plus probability

(vi) Good answers will discuss further around the subject and discuss what the organisation might do to create a system for environmental analysis and forecasting. Such a system consists of two elements.

(1) Elements concerned with the generation of up-to-date database.

(2) Elements concerned with the dissemination of the information to decision makers.

The discussion might further consider the possibility of setting up a dedicated unit with specific responsibility for environmental monitoring (this need not be expensive - could be one person or external body). Discussion may move into broader issues of the marketing information system required by the organisation.

Best answers will identify:

(1) uncontrollable elements;
(2) how can these be forecast

Question 2

3.3 *Question 2 (40 marks)* (Produce a strategic marketing plan for Gravesend Town Centre for the planning periods to 2005.)

(a) *Approach*

(i) This question is similar to those asked in previous papers, but this time carries only 40% of the marks. Implementation and control aspects have been covered in Question 3. This question should have been predicted by candidates so marks should not be awarded too easily. Also, given that developing a strategic marketing plan is what candidates should have spent a proportion of the past four weeks doing, we can be demanding.

(ii) Models will be popular, of course, but should only be used as a guide to strategic recommendations that must be firmly linked to Gravesend's particular situation. (*Note*. In an open book examination no marks are gained for simply copying models out of books.)

(iii) Question 2 builds on question 1 and the plan should grow out of the environmental analysis. The question is asking for:

(1) a strategic marketing plan
- what needs to be done?
- how should they do it?

(2) for Gravesend Town Centre

(3) for the period 1996-2005

(iv) It is reasonably clear from the case that Gravesend is very unlikely to be able to compete with direct competition (Lakeside, Bluewater etc) unless it can be different. Positioning, based on an understanding of the target market (customers) will be essential.

(b) *Good answers*. We can expect to see a logical sequence of steps that might look like the following.

(i) Current situation
(1) What is going on?
(2) What is the problem?

(ii) Corporate objectives/mission statement
(1) What business are we in?
(2) What do we want to achieve?

(iii) Target market
(1) Who are we aiming at?

(2) What are key needs/want/motivators?
(3) Segmentation
(4) Other 'stakeholders' and their interests

(iv) Marketing objectives

(1) What should we be trying to do?
(2) Quantifications
(3) SMART

(v) Targeting and positioning

(1) How do we differentiate Gravesend Town Centre?
(2) How do we position Gravesend Town Centre in the customers' minds?
(3) Key 'product-market matches'?

(vi) Marketing strategy

(1) What are the alternatives?
(2) Which route is best
(3) Why?
(4) Porter/Ansoff/GEC/ADL models - if relevant
(5) SWOT analysis as strategic framework

(vii) *Marketing programmes (test for rigour as a mix)*

(1) Product policy:
- outlets, services, mix
(2) Pricing policy:
- relating to competition and position
(3) Distribution policy:
- location fixed, layout suggestions;
- local environment.
(4) Customer service:
- relate to position
(5) Process policy
(6) People policy
(7) Promotional policy:
- related to position and additional information

(c) *Best answers will*:

(i) briefly state situation and corporate objectives/mission statement;
(ii) identify target market(s) and position Gravesend Town Centre;
(iii) show marketing objectives;
(iv) show marketing strategy - alternatives and selection;
(v) show marketing programmes (7Ps).

3.4 *Question 3 (30 marks)* ('As the Town Centre Manager has no direct control over events, explain how the strategic marketing plan might be implemented and controlled with and through the key parties.')

(a) *Approach*

(i) This question can be expected to cause candidates some problems for two reasons.

(1) A final question carrying 30% of the marks will defeat the bad time managers (ref Leffe case): remember that 30% of the marks should represent something like 45 minutes writing time!

(2) Implementation and control is often badly dealt with.

(ii) Both A&D and P&C papers have been stressing the importance of good implementation and control of strategic plans. This is the first time that an A&D question has been directed to the topic.

(iii) An additional feature for the Town Centre Manager is that he has no direct control over the town centre so must find other ways of ensuring implementation.

(iv) Financial resources are also limited.

- (b) *Good answers* will build on the answers to question 1 and question 2 and should cover the following, described (c) and (d) below.

- (c) *Part one* asks for methods of implementation and control of the marketing plan. The main points that might be covered include the following:

    (i) Barriers to implementation

    (1) Environmental problems (discussed in Question 1)

    (2) Organisational problems
    - Organisational culture
    - Skills and experience
    - Organisational structure and design
    - Resources

    (3) Marketing problems
    - Marketing culture
    - Marketing expertise
    - Information

    (ii) Drivers for implementation

    (1) Environmental change (discussed in Question 1)

    (2) Customers' expectations
    - Constant change
    - Innovation

    (iii) Discussion of how barriers will be overcome to implement successfully the plan proposed.

    (iv) Control systems

    (1) Measurements selected
    - Normally cover quantity, quality or cost
    - What is best for Gravesend?

    (2) Controls are managed through a blend of financial and non-financial measures

- (d) *Part two* of the question seeks an answer to how this is done without direct control over the key elements of the marketing mix. Answers to this section will vary according to the recommendations made in Question 2. Depending on the position proposed and the actions required the following should be noted.

    (i) Financial resources are limited

    (1) Gravesend cannot compete at the same A&P levels as Lakeside and Bluewater.

    (2) Gravesend Town Centre has only limited powers.

    (3) Local shop managers have only limited funds.

    (ii) A strategic alliance is required

    (1) This requires common vision.
    (2) Synergies in the alliance.
    (3) Collaborative not competitive marketing within the town centre.

    (iii) Identification of 'key parties'.

    (1) Relate to proposed strategy
    (2) Who are key parties/partners?

    (iv) Aspects of internal marketing may apply.

    (v) What is the role of the Town Centre Manager? A marketing function for the town centre 'organisation'?

(vi) Information is essential to the process.

    (1) Collaborative marketing requires:
- consultation
- agreement
- a common ownership of the plan

    (2) A strategic plan cannot be 'imposed' on others

    (3) McKinsey '7S' model may be relevant, if applied.

(e) *Best answers will cover*

    (i) implementation;
    (ii) control systems;
    (iii) working through key parties.

4 A FINAL WORD

4.1 Well, how did you get on with your first mock exam? If you are dissatisfied with your performance please do not despair.

(a) Read the consultants' analysis in the next chapter, which is particularly relevant to your analytical skills.

(b) Try the next two cases, *Mistral* and *Sentinel Aviation*

Chapter 19

CONSULTANTS' ANALYSIS OF GRAVESEND TOWN CENTRE

> **This chapter contains an analysis of Gravesend Town Centre by Northern Consultancy Associates.**
>
> 1   How to use this analysis
> 2   Strategic considerations
> 3   Customers/markets
> 4   The offering
> 5   Promotion
> 6   Planning
> 7   Tackling the exam
> 8   Food for thought
>
> The address of Northern Consultancy Associates is 8, Church Chare, Ponteland, Newcastle-upon-Tune NE20 9XT. Phone 01661 820633 (administrative queries only).

1   HOW TO USE THIS ANALYSIS

1.1 It is intended that this analysis be used in conjunction with a copy of the *Gravesend Town Centre* case study obtained from the Chartered Institute of Marketing. It is designed for students preparing for the Institute's Analysis and Decision examination, but may be of value to other users. The following comments are intended for those taking the CIM examination.

1.2 This document was designed to help you think through the problem areas confronting you as *Bill Morrison*, independent marketing consultant engaged by Brian Richmond, Town Centre Manager for Gravesham Council. Its purpose is to save you valuable study time. However, we do not point to a particular solution, and this analysis is *not* an examination answer.

1.3 You are likely to have to make firm recommendations at the time of the examination. Make these, with appropriate justification, without regurgitating tracts of the case study itself, or this analysis.

1.4 You must answer the questions that are set for you. Do not allow preconceived notions to deflect you from this task. You must adopt a report style in the examination. Not only will this be required by instructions given, it will aid clarity of thought and save you time. Please read carefully our comments in this document on examination technique.

1.5 You have been asked to prepare a report of your initial recommendations to be presented to the Town Centre Manager and the Town Centre Steering Group on 14 June. That is your opportunity to put forward your views as to what strategy should be Despite that expectation, you must address the specific questions asked during the examination.

Part E: Learning from experience: ensuring you pass

1.6 You must use the information given in the case study. You will, however, be given additional information during the examination itself, and it is important that you incorporate it in your answer.

1.7 This document will be lodged with the Chartered Institute of Marketing's examiners. You will not gain marks by simply copying sections of it. Use it instead to arrive at and justify recommendations.

1.8 This publication is of necessity produced at great speed, but with every possible care. However, all material should be carefully scrutinised before basing recommendations on it as errors are not impossible.

2 STRATEGIC CONSIDERATIONS

The process

2.1 Whenever one approaches a case study it is necessary, after analysing it, to decide on the basic strategy that the organisation should follow. A strategy is a long term/important decision which will determine that the organisation is moving in the right direction. Then the tactics or operating plans can be determined coherently following the overall direction which is laid down for the organisation. It is often said that strategic decisions ensure that the organisation does the right thing, whilst operating plans concentrate on 'doing things right'.

2.2 It must also be understood that strategies exist at different levels in the organisation and are hierarchical. Thus there will be a corporate strategy which will help determine the marketing strategy which itself will constrain/direct the advertising strategy. Similarly, the strategy of the corporate headquarters will to an extent determine that of its subsidiaries.

2.3 Since case studies are complex it is considered desirable to adopt a specific process to assist in drawing up a strategy. You may have met this before, but it is important enough to outline here before considering the specific case.

The mission

2.4 Here one decides the basic business the organisation is in. It is expressed fairly broadly so as not to constrain subsequent thinking. It takes into account customer need, the organisation's distinctive competences and any basic history/philosophy that may have become integral to the organisation.

Objectives

2.5 If asked to prepare a plan at any level you should specify objectives, and at least some of these should be quantified (eg sales, market share, percentage profit).

Analysis or audit

2.6 This is the basis of any proposals and much of this analysis is to assist you in making such an audit (ie the selection of strategies and plans is left to you). Basically internal factors are considered (strengths and weaknesses) and external factors (opportunities and threats). Such an exercise is known as a SWOT analysis.

Strategy selection

2.7 Your analysis has outlined your current position and prospects; your objectives have stated where you wish to be in the future. Your strategies will reflect the amount of change required if the organisation is to meet its objectives. If the current situation is very inadequate than a dramatic change is required; if it is slightly inadequate then slight changes may be required. Usually the greater change in direction, the greater the risk.

2.8 Ansoff specified some broad alternatives strategies, most appropriate in growth situations, on the basis of a combination of existing or new products, or existing or new markets.

(a) *Existing product/existing market* - market penetration

(b) *Existing product/new market* - market development strategy

(c) *New product/existing market* - product development strategy

(d) *New product/new market* - diversification strategy

2.9 Porter proposed three alternative generic strategies.

(a) *Overall cost leadership* - a large market share tends to follow from this strategy.

(b) *Differentiation* - differentiate the offering to offer some customer benefit eg style, quality, technology.

(c) *Focus* - really about market segments. Clearly identify those customers whom you can satisfy most effectively.

2.10 Critically, Porter argues that an organisation must determine its generic strategy, its strengths within that strategy and outpoint its competitors in that area if it is to succeed. Having studied and analysed the case you must make decisions on strategies. Only then can you formulate plans for your marketing mix elements which are coherent and compatible.

Strategic considerations in this case

2.11 This is an unusual case in that it does not deal with what might be considered a 'normal' product or service but with a conglomeration of services that is Gravesend Town Centre, how to protect its current position and indeed promote it in the face of perceived threats. Moreover, the Chief Examiner has taken the unusual step of providing an accompanying leaflet to guide you. Let us first of all say we agree fully with the statements made about your approach to the examination. In each analysis a section is devoted to tackling the exam (Section 7 in this analysis). There is much similarity in our approaches. However, the examiner stresses generally the importance of a strategic approach in the Analysis and Decision examination. This would appear to be particularly true in this case as there is less scope for the normal mix elements (eg place and price) and therefore it is important that you give full consideration to strategy at this point although many of the issues raised will be explored fully later.

2.12 In this case you are in the role of consultant; therefore you will be able to advise but have no executive control. You will be expected to make recommendations or provide options but the person to whom you are reporting, Town Centre Manager, himself has not executive powers (he describes himself as a co-ordinator/motivator/organiser). Your reports will provide him with arguments with which to persuade people and therefore the justification of your proposal can be seen as particularly important. Moreover it is your brief to make recommendations concerning Gravesend Town Centre, but this cannot be divorced from the surrounding areas, nor from regional initiatives (eg Thames Gateway). You are becoming involved in a typical local government network and much bureaucracy is threatened. This is considered more fully in paragraphs 6.1 to 6.9 (covering organisation and implementation).

2.13 Given the unusual nature of the case, is the basic strategic process of any value? Gravesham Borough Council will almost certainly have a broad mission, but may not have one for Gravesend Town Centre. You should draft one and quotes from documents such as the DoE Planning Policy Guide may help you, eg 'Sense of place and community', 'vitality and viability'.

2.14 It is difficult to quantify objectives although Gravesham will undoubtedly have other pertinent objectives such as a healthy industrial and employment base supporting a level of housing development which itself supports the retail outlet within the town. Some quantification here may be possible. Your brief is to focus on the town centre itself and your objectives will depend to an extent on the strategies you perceive to be necessary. Planning is an iterative process. You may wish to attract a certain percentage of shoppers by area to Gravesend, and possibly a certain minimum of tourists.

2.15 Those objectives which are reasonable and achievable will be determined by your analysis. You may be asked to prepare specifically an analysis within the examination. It helps the examiner if you use a framework to do this, and a SWOT has already been mentioned. An alternative is the PEST analysis whereby one considers political, economic, social and technological factors affecting an organisation. These are external issues and basically an explosion of the external/uncontrollable categories (opportunities/threats) within the SWOT. It may be relevant to mention a feasibility study here. Tourism is an issue in this case, and feasibility studies are frequently commissioned. Basically the consultant would analyse the situation from a tourism perspective and then consider various options and their feasibility. In other words of you have prepared yourself as suggested do not be worried by this term if it is introduced.

2.16 Note that we do not provide a comprehensive SWOT or PEST within this analysis. Remember the examiner sees this analysis, and such a list would not be in your best interest, but you must prepare a SWOT fully.

2.17 As a guide, however, retail support in the TCI is an obvious strength, the relatively small population base in Gravesend, and indeed Gravesham is a weakness. Several opportunities exist such as the CTRL and tourism. The obvious threat is Bluewater. Remember to provide your SWOT and do not be too mechanistic.

2.18 Some items do not clearly fit into any category, for example good road access could help people shop in Gravesend but could equally allow people to exit to Bluewater. Do not be afraid to expand and debate qualitative issues outside the SWOT structure.

2.19 You will ultimately need to propose strategies and here it is up to you to make decisions. Ansoff can assist us here. We shall see in Section 4 that the product offering is complex, but the range of retail outlets is clearly central. Are you trying to maintain this, to amend it or increase it? Alternatively you could propose an entirely new offering in the form of tourism. You can propose staying with the same market profile in demographic terms, adjusting it to an extent and/or going for a new group of customers, the tourists. From Porter's model, differentiation and focus seem important. How can you best gain a competitive advantage over competition such as Bluewater and which target markets are likely to appreciate it the most?

2.20 Whatever strategies you select, and there is likely to be more than one, you must provide justification. This indeed is a key advantage of a SWOT. Even if you are not asked a specific question on analysis, you can always use it to justify proposals, eg strategy or option A is proposed because it capitalises on strengths (a) and (b), also on opportunity (c) and offsets threat (d), and so on. A prepared SWOT can be used for many purposes in the examination.

3 CUSTOMERS/MARKETS

Categories of goods and shoppers

3.1 Classical marketing theory recognises classes of goods that mirror particular types of decision making in customers.

(a) *Convenience goods.* Products that are bought regularly. Little or no thought is given to the decision making process, and ease and convenience are the most important aspects of shopping behaviour.

(b) *Shopping goods.* Products that represent some risk to the customer, either in financial or other terms, and where the customer will 'shop around'.

(c) *Speciality goods.* Products where there is such an established niche, that no other brand or product will be considered. This type of product will frequently be upmarket - the customer 'will not consider any substitute'.

3.2 These categories apply equally well to particular shops, or chains of shops, or even shopping centres and towns. Apart from food being bought for special occasions, food shopping has to be done regularly, and there is a high convenience factor. Gravesend has leading national supermarket groups (Safeway and Sainsbury's) and has good parking facilities. Unlike other shopping food shopping, requires adjacent parking rather than near parking. We note that in the survey 63% of respondents rank Gravesend as first or second for food shopping. It is also worth noting that 58% of non food shoppers cite convenience as a reason for their choice of Gravesend.

3.3 Figure four from the *shopper survey* gives a positive rating for car parking, but the 'preferred' figure at around 70% is so high that there is no room for complacency here. Figure 4 also shows Gravesend rating fairly highly for being close to home, and higher than the 'preferred' centre so that it would appear to be convenient for most of its customers. Choice of goods and choice of shops are rated positively, but in the twenties, and below the preferred score. It is not entirely clear where the preferred score comes from. Since Gravesend is preferred to the other centres, for example in figures 10 and 11, the preferred score does not appear to relate to another specific centre, but represents a measure of 'ideal' as indicated by a score for importance.

3.4 The choice seems to be reasonable, but there seems to be a lack of facility that would attract people to make a special trip. There may be a lack of speciality shops.

3.5 For shopping goods such as clothes, household goods etc, the major chains are represented in Gravesend, thus providing the shopper with a reasonable choice of mainstream products. If this choice started to be reduced, the attractiveness of the centre would be affected. Thus, for an individual retailer, it is not necessarily desirable if a competitor pulls out, as the general area then loses its attractiveness. This is the nature of the collapse at Dudley, which so haunts you as Bill Morrison, marketing consultant.

3.6 Gravesham shoppers spend more than the national average on household goods but less than the rest of the south-east, but spend more than both national and rest of the south-east on clothing and footwear.

3.7 In the survey on household expenditure, 'mobile' expenditure is more than the national average, and well up to the rest of the south-east. This expenditure would represent shopping goods and speciality goods.

Identity of current shoppers

People in the catchment area

3.8 The nature of the catchment area gives us a good idea of the potential market for shoppers. The profile of Gravesham residents provided in the case study is useful in this respect. The demography is unremarkable, and shows an ageing population. Note that in the demography tables there are age groups shown as 45-59/64 and 60-65 plus. This reflects the current retirement ages in the UK of 65 for men and 60 for women. This difference is set to be eliminated in the future, and in any case is slightly misleading, as actual retirement ages average lower than these points.

3.9 The Household Expenditure survey shows that there is a higher proportion of professional and managerial workers than the national average, although this proportion is lower than the surrounding Kent area. The figures are from the 1981 census, and it is thought that more up to date information will reveal that these categories of socio-economic groups have increased as a proportion of the Gravesham population. Of particular significance is the combination of facts revealed by the distribution of households according to ACORN group (ACORN records the housing status of neighbourhoods). A higher proportion than the national average live in the higher categories of housing, but the household expenditure shown in section four reveals less than the normal proportion of expenditure for the south-east spent on housing. This means that house prices are likely to be below the average for the south-east, and more discretionary income is left that can be spent in shops.

3.10 The proportion of working people in younger age groups is stated as set to decrease. This is not inaccurate in itself but may not reflect some significant developments. Developments at Greenhithe and Swanscombe will be mainly outside the Gravesham boundaries, but well within the shopping catchment area. These are on the Dartford side of Gravesend, but figure two in the shopper survey shows that Gravesend is the preferred centre even for residents of part of Dartford. In addition, there will also be a substantial development at Eastern Quarry.

3.11 The net effect of these development will be the creation of 30,000 new homes, and the related expenditure especially on household items such as furniture, decorating materials etc. The age structure of shoppers will also be affected, as many of the houses will be taken up by young families. The total shopping population as well as the number working in the area will increase. Note that the Bluewater development is likely to come on stream before most of these developments will have been completed.

3.12 The new Greenwich University campus will inject further spending power into the area, and create further employment.

Characteristics of the shoppers

3.13 The case study appears to answer the question 'Is there a typical Gravesend shopper'. The profile is given of someone of relatively low socio-economic standing, over 60, and living in the urban area, and shopping through the week, but also noting that there is a strong showing of groups C1-C2 earning between £20,000 and £30,000 aged between 25 and 44 and living in the urban area, and it is stated that the younger and more affluent members of the community prefer Lakeside.

3.14 The foregoing can be a misleading interpretation of the data. Whilst it is true that a higher proportion of poorer, lower socio-economic groups and older urban dwellers prefer Gravesend than in the other groups, *Gravesend is still clearly preferred by the majority of people in the other groups*. The one exception is for age, where Lakeside gets the highest preference rating for people in the 18-24 age group. For those having difficulty in distinguishing separate bars in the charts, the order across by centre in the chart is the same as the order down in the key at its right hand side.

3.15 Thus, currently it is unlikely that the profile of the Gravesend shopper is predominantly older, poorer and urban *but that could become the case, if the other groups are lured away. That they less strongly prefer Gravesend shows that this threat is at least a possibility.*

3.16 A final point in this section is that the nature of the shopper is partly an uncontrollable factor in that it is determined by the nature of the catchment area etc, but it is also something that can be influenced as a result of specific actions designed to attract particular groups.

19: Consultants' analysis of Gravesend Town Centre

Range of target markets

3.17 So far we have concentrated on shoppers. There are, however, other 'publics' that will be extremely important in the marketing of Gravesend town centre. Vital amongst these are the retailers.

3.18 The Town Centre Initiative has been an exercise in co-operation between retailers in Gravesend, Gravesham Borough Council, Kent County Council and Gravesham Chamber of Trade and Industry. This has already produced good results, and it would be hard to see any recommendations not to build on this. However, there will also be a need to co-operate with and promote to head offices of multiple retailers as well as local branches.

3.19 Links are at present with retailers who are already in the town centre. Target markets could include retailers who are not represented in the town, but might be persuaded to come in eg House of Fraser and John Lewis, who sell clothing and household goods, categories where we know there is a substantial market in the Gravesham area. These two particular retailers already seem to be committed to Bluewater, but others exist. Similarly, if the nature of the town is to change and other forms of shopping are to be encouraged, specific types of retailer could be targeted. Thus if tourism (discussed elsewhere) is encouraged, more specialist types of shops might be encouraged, and the shopping pattern might shown an increase in weekend shopping. This would mean that for the first time, the target markets could extend beyond the immediate area of Gravesham.

3.20 Other economically significant bodies such as employers and bodies involved in regional or national planning issues might also be included in the list of target markets.

4 THE OFFERING

The current position

4.1 Gravesend Borough Council no doubt considers it offers a range of interlinked amenities, a range of industry and attractive industrial sites. Evidence from the profile of Gravesend residents also suggests good quality housing at reasonable prices. It also has a healthy mix of retail outlets set in increasingly attractive surroundings. The support indicated from government is encouraging. Its Regional Planning Guide for the South East proposed the Thames Gateway which promises investment in employment, housing and transport infrastructure. Gravesham must try to ensure that this is spent in a manner which helps its interests as much as possible. It will be assisted in this by the formation of the Kent Thameside Partnership including Gravesham, Dartford and the Kent county council among others. In addition to all of this is the development of the CTRL alongside the A2.

4.2 More important, the Ebbsfleet International Station may bring many visitors to the area and will allow much more rapid commuting to London (17 minutes). Whilst there is a desire to increase employment in Gravesham, commuters also spend in the area and are a potential source of retail strength.

4.3 Your brief lies mainly in the retail sector. We are given some information on outlets in Gravesend within the text; some within the town in St George's and Anglesea Centre, others 'just beside the town'.

Town centre	*Nearby*
Sainsbury	Asda
Tesco	B&Q
British Home Stores	Great Mills
Marks & Spencer	FADS
Argos	Comet
W H Smith	Pet City
Mothercare	Halfords

Part E: Learning from experience: ensuring you pass

Woolworth
Boots
Safeway

4.4 Whilst St George's and Anglesea Centre can be found on the town map, the location of the 'others' would be interesting. Could these be at Pepperhill described as 'in the locality'? The location of Pepperhill would be nice to known. All these shops are listed in the appendix: Key Retail Profiles. Also listed are House of Fraser and John Lewis which we know are committed to Bluewater but apparently *not* in Gravesend. These are large, quality department stores only matched in type by Debenham's within Gravesend; moreover the image of the former two may be considered higher. The will clearly be a draw to normal Gravesend shoppers.

4.5 How do people currently view Gravesend as a shopping centre? For this we need to consider the survey provided for you as an appendix. Many more have visited Gravesend and more of the sample shop in Gravesend than elsewhere from all 'zones' except Medway. What are the reasons for this? Figure 3 gives a guide here with Gravesend's proximity to home, and the quality/range of shops and goods also showing some strength. You should note, however, that the best averaged score was 40, less than 'quite good', therefore there is no cause for complacency. This is reinforced by figures 4 and 5, although here in particular it would have been beneficial to see the questionnaire used. Here shoppers were asked to compare Gravesend to their preferred centre. However, for most, Gravesend is the preferred centre and therefore in effect these respondents would be rating against an 'ideal' centre. This explains the choice in the rating scale between good/important. Thus a Gravesend shopper may see the choice of shops (fig 3) as quite good but fell it is very important (fig 4). If measured against an ideal by the majority of the survey Gravesend is bound to suffer. Thus it is important not to over react to figs 4 and 5, but much useful information is contained. It can be argued that Gravesend's stronger areas (fig 3) are those seen as most important, even though the preferred score is higher. Gravesend seems to score higher than competitors on important areas, so the preferred score represents an ideal, but it can also be argued that Gravesend must do better here. One worry from fig 4 is that whilst the main reason given for shopping in Gravesend is proximity to home, this is considered relative unimportant when thinking of either the preferred or the ideal centre. This suggests that current shoppers would not be deterred from going to Bluewater.

4.6 It could also be said that in action terms lower scoring items such as access for the disabled and parking costs are important issues. The detailed interpretation of the survey and appropriate action must be considered by you. However, parking issues and choice of shops do seem important. The test suggests that Gravesend has improved in these respects in recent years. This must continue and shoppers need to be convinced it is happening.

4.7 This section began by mentioning the support the Borough council was receiving. The assistance Gravesend itself is receiving through the TCI should be mentioned here. To this point it has been a real strength.

Product positioning

4.8 In order to propose an appropriate product position we need to consider the competition. Unfortunately there are some gaps in our knowledge here. It would be nice to know of the range of shops in Dartford and Chatham. More important would be detail on Lakeside if we are to anticipate likely reaction to the opening of Bluewater. It is north of the river but where? In the food survey Thurrock is mentioned. Thurrock seems an ill defined area around Grays, (just readable in the Gravesham map). It seems likely that Lakeside is near the M25 and this is supported by fig 2 showing that more from the Dartford region shop there than from other zones. Incidentally the inevitable loss of colour in the bar charts makes them difficult to interpret. It is a reasonable assumption that Lakeside is the central bar. Therefore there does seem to be an error in the relevant comment stating that 52% of the rural Gravesend shoppers went to

Lakeside. This would seem a very worrying statistic. Again make a clear statement of your interpretation/assumption.

4.9 Despite the lack of firm information, however, you are able to infer quite a lot concerning Gravesend's competitive position from the survey. Whilst the composition of the sample must be remembered, Gravesend is clearly the town most frequently visited and in fig 2 it is the most frequently visited shopping centre. Moreover this includes those responding from the Dartford and Sevenoaks zones. Probably the most heartening is the frequency of visiting; 43% shop in Gravesend once a week compared with 9% in Chatham. Add to this the food survey where 63% place Gravesend first of second and this does seem important. This suggests that a majority of respondents definitely perceive Gravesend as an attractive shopping centre for food and probably the moderately expensive non-food items; they may search further afield for specific and important goods. Gravesend must seek to maintain this patters. It is interesting to note from the food survey the importance of *adjacent* parking. Major centres like Bluewater have been less attractive or supermarkets as they have not been able to provide specific parking for supermarket shoppers, who may have to wheel trolleys large distances. Bluewater may be planning to overcome this and the position should be monitored. It seems critical that Gravesend provides appropriate parking to retain regular shoppers; whilst parking can be seen on the town map its precise proximity to supermarkets cannot be judged.

4.10 In all talk of *positioning* of course the general development of *Bluewater* must be monitored. One matter of concern may be the attitude of retailers on the TCI as Bluewater opens. It is one thing for Marks and Spencer to provide funds to Gravesend to promote the town centre, but if this is to compete with Marks and Spencer Bluewater they may be less keen. Of course, the Gravesend manager has a vested interest in the town centre, but funds may reduce.

4.11 In all talk of *competition* the convenience of reaching various centres needs consideration. You must familiarise yourself with the maps in the case, and as Bill Morrison you should think through the spatial considerations. The town planners may need consultation on this. There are actual distances and there is the *perceived* distance/convenience to the individual. For example, historically in this area the Thameside towns have been linked by the local railway and the A226. To what extent do local inhabitants see the A2/M2 and M25 as being for 'others'? Can the historic link be maintained by improved transport links along the coast. The Thames Gateway funding may be available for this.

4.12 On a broader scale, what will the impact be of the improved links with London? Is this an opportunity or a threat? Also planners may have a view on the size of Gravesend and its current shopping centre. There seems to be a critical mass in these matters. For example, the Metro Centre is mentioned in the case. Situated in Gateshead, it has destroyed shopping in that centre, but not in nearby Newcastle, the regional centre. Will Gravesend follow Gateshead and Dudley, or does it have the strength to survive.

4.13 You may propose surveys to investigate these issues, but really you must make assumptions. Basically you must show you have not ignored them.

Tourism

4.14 It is clear that you, Bill Morrison, are aware of the history of Gravesend and must be considering its potential as a Tourist attraction to add to the offering already discussed. You should list out the historical facts provided and consider the best means of capitalising on them. Certainly Gravesend has an interesting history connected with the river and plans to improve its waterfront are already part of the TCI's 10 point plan. This proposed development echoes many riverside developments nation-wide and dovetails with wider plans for development further upstream eg Greenhithe waterfront and Northfleet embankment. These plans will lead to general upgrading of the area with urban villages and good quality residential property. The Gravesend waterfront development specifically will make the town more pleasant to visit and as it is close to the main shopping centre it must benefit retailing. The real aim of tourism is to attract additional visitors by making them aware of the current attractions and developing new ones. You must think how this can be done.

4.15 Doubtless you will wish to capitalise on the history of the customs houses and smuggling. Some form of maritime museum may be feasible. You may be able to co-ordinate this with current commercial activities in Gravesend eg Port of London Authority and the regional customs and excise. The attraction of visitors to current workplaces is thriving and known as Industrial Tourism, and may be worthwhile here. Then there is the river itself, now clean, with at least three piers, and once cross river passenger ferry. How do you capitalise on this? Finally there are the links with famous personalities. From the town map we can see General Gordon Gardens and the Gordon promenade, also the Pocahontas statue. The film Pocahontas encouraged tour operators to place Gravesend on the American Heritage Trail without any effort on the town's part. Surely now is the time to be more proactive. There is also the Dickens connection. If a more substantial connection is required perhaps a Dickensian trail throughout Kent is possible. Could a historian from a local university help develop relevant details of these personalities and their links with Gravesend?

4.16 A further consideration is the general beauty of the area. The map of Gravesham shows country parks, castles and other historic buildings. The possibility of a package is clear.

4.17 The greater tourism opportunity however must lie in the development of Ebbsfleet International Station. It is anticipated that many European visitors may wish to disembark here before moving on to the rest of England. How can Gravesham persuade them to do this and what infrastructure will be necessary. Kent itself is a beautiful county and visitors are centrally situated with Canterbury to the east, London to the west and attractions such as Leeds Castle to the south.

4.18 Note that Ebbsfleet is just over the local boundary into Dartford (indeed many of the developments are in that borough council). Cooperation with Dartford is essential and has begun with Kent Thameside. It does mean however that control of plans will be even more complex. Remember, however, that from the visitor's viewpoint boundaries are meaningless. Wherever the hotel, if Gravesend is the most interesting local town it will be visited. Nevertheless, you may wish to encourage hotels in Gravesham; another target market?

4.19 If you decide to promote tourism, you must begin to think positively of plans to proceed. Make them realistic, prioritise them, and ensure they are lively and interesting for the examiner. Remember the need for co-ordination and for planning permission. You cannot rush these matters. Also who will co-ordinate and implement this? Does Gravesend need a Tourism Manager?

5 PROMOTION

5.1 It is vital that promotion fits in with chosen strategy - promotional decisions should not be made in isolation. This allows the clear definition as to *who* to aim at, and *what* communication objectives have to be met. In turn, this helps inform what budget is required.

5.2 Just as promotion is part of the marketing mix, there is also a balance to be sought in different types of promotion - the Promotional Mix. This includes publicity (news coverage that is 'free' in terms of cost for time or space), advertising, personal selling, mailshots and sales promotion. The balance will be affected by the nature of the target market, and the communication task. Thus, personal contract might be the most important variable in persuading a large retailing organisation to locate in Gravesend, but publicity and advertising might be more suitable for creating shopper awareness.

5.3 Advertising media can be chosen on their ability to carry a particular type of message, and on the cost effectiveness in reaching a particular audience. We can apply this to the media details given in the case study. Capital Radio covers the London area, and would have a huge number of listeners. This would mean that its charges might be quite high, and if many of its listeners are not in the shopping catchment area it might not represent good value. Advertising is not allowed on BBC radio. Invicta has a high coverage in the younger age groups - this would be important if an objective is to gain greater awareness in this age group. Radio is generally thought to be effective in increasing awareness, but there is a limit to the information content it can convey. Depending on the nature of the communications objective this mayor may not be a factor in the choice.

5.4 Similar consideration apply to newspapers. The most secure market at the moment might be older, less well off and urban. Invicta radio has a young audience. The Gravesend and Dartford Reporter does best with rural readers, whilst the Leader is most popular in urban areas.

5.5 One third of all respondents in the customer needs survey could recall recent advertising for shopping centres, but of these, only 6% cited Gravesend as the subject of such advertising. This compares with the 63% of Lakeside. The proportion of respondents overall citing Gravesend is 6% of the third who recall *any* advertising in other words, just under 2% of all respondents. This is negligible. Indeed it is so small that it could even have resulted from confusing other advertising with that for Gravesend. This indicates that Gravesend is not spending enough in comparison with competitors, and perhaps not spending it well.

5.6 It is possible that more professional and cost-effective advertising could be created by engaging the services of an advertising agency. Since the bulk of the agency's income would derive from commission from the media (typically 15% of the amount spent on the media) this need not be an expensive option (direct expenditure on the media without an agency would not produce any commission). For very low expenditure, commission would be too low to cover an agency's costs and therefore there would be a higher fee, which might in those circumstances make the use of an agency a practical proposition.

5.7 A considerable selling effort might be required to persuade the various members of the Town Centre Initiative to contribute funds for promotion. Your recommendations as consultant should carry some weight in this respect however.

5.8 The adoption of a professional approach becomes even more important when considering other target markets which you will wish to approach. Industry, government agencies and hotel groups have all been mentioned in this analysis. Different media, including the personal approach, will be necessary here, but also some rational, image building advertising might be required in leaflets or appropriate periodicals.

5.9 The need for alternative approaches becomes even more important if tourism is considered a serious option. Whilst Gravesend has always been a respected shopping area in the district, the notion of it as a tourism/leisure attraction is new. Persuasive and informative material must be prepared detailing activities and events. Local media (eg newspapers and radio) would again be involved to attract the local visitor. Day visitors could also be attracted from the south east region and media covering that wider area must be considered. National media often has the facility to advertise on a regional basis but cost now becomes a factor.

5.10 Tourism promotion can also be assisted by the ETB and BTA. The English Tourist Board (ETB) is responsible for promoting attractions within England to that market. There are regional tourist boards operating within it and they have Tourist Information Centres at strategic point. This is a key means of inexpensive distribution of leaflets and brochures. Likewise the British Tourist Authority (TBA) has offices overseas and responsibility for promoting British attractions there. Which national markets will you be targeting? Obviously timing is important here and at the appropriate point to must approach and convince these organisation of the attractions of Gravesend. Would presentations at appropriate conferences be useful here?

6 PLANNING

General

6.1 In many cases CIM Analysis and Decision candidates are expected to be in a position to produce a detailed marketing plan. In your role as Bill Morrison, your initial brief is to prepare *initial recommendations* to the Town Centre Manager and the Town Centre Initiative Steering Group on 14 June. This, together with the lack of information that is sometimes contained in case studies, means that all the recommendations cannot be fully detailed. This is no excuse for 'waffle' and you will not doubt be expected to be as specific as possible. You have been retained as a consultant with the aim that you are able to produce recommendations that can be acted upon.

6.2 What you have to produce may be a recommended marketing strategy. What might it contain? First of all there might be an audit of the current situation. This analysis will help you do that. Some of the major issues in the current situation might be summed up in a PEST or STEP analysis (Social, Technological, Economic and Political factors), and a SWOT analysis (Strengths, Weaknesses, Opportunities and Threats). SWOT analysis is normally applied to an organisation, but there is no reason why it cannot be applied to a place.

6.3 Next you will need to specify objectives. Unlike some other case studies, at this stage you are not in a position to specify objectives in sales and profit and loss terms, but nevertheless you cannot make well directed and co-ordinated recommendations unless you are clear what you are trying to do. Firstly you may have a limited number of broad objectives, which are likely to centre on countering certain threats and/or taking advantage of certain opportunities. When you have developed broad strategies, you can then specify more detailed objectives. For example, if you intend to achieve certain overall results with part of the target market, that might allow you to produce more detailed promotional objectives that help make progress towards your overall goals. You will certainly have to identify and choose appropriate target markets. You should consider to what extent your market will consist of existing customers, new customers, or a mix of both. Being realistic, Bluewater will probably take away some business but given your chosen strategy, you may wish to make estimates of the extent to which that might be made up for, or more than made up for by visitors and tourists, and new residents in the area.

6.4 You do not have a *budget* to work to, but will help to be able to indicate how ambitious the spending needs to be, and from where the money will come. You will need to be realistic - it would be likely that money would come from a combination of the bodies involved in the Town Centre Initiative. You may wish to consider whether your brief covers narrowly and literally the town centre, or more generally Gravesend. Certainly developments are possible on the edge of the river that could involve visitors to areas of interest or even new specific ventures such as factory shops. We are not told exactly where Pepperhill is, but we know that it enjoyed similar levels of popularity to St George's, and respondents in the shopping centre felt that it could be an area of growth - should that be encouraged? Would such a policy alienate any of the existing retailers in the centre of town? If success is gained for Gravesend, it will be almost impossible to share it equally. Tough decisions may have to be made and great diplomacy employed. In your role as consultant you may be able to be more direct than would be possible for your client.

6.5 Initial recommendations are likely to be less detailed than an annual marketing plan, but you should still have in mind a time scale for major activities to take place in, and what key measures would indicate how well or badly progress was going. If it is essential to collect further information this might also be indicated.

Organisation and implementation

6.6 Most marketing recommendations are made in an environment where there is a single organisation with specialised staff and an organisation structure. That is not the case here, and it creates further problems. Timing is a key aspect of implementation, but so too is definition of responsibility.

6.7 The Town Centre Manager does not have direct control, but rather acts as a co-ordinator. Success so far indicates that the co-ordination is possible, and it has resulted in a ten point plan. There is an overall steering group, and five working groups. Can all the actions you recommend be dealt with and implemented by the working groups - access and transport, environmental improvements, environmental maintenance, promotions and events and quality of life/security? Which tasks would go where? Would any additional/alternations be required?

6.8 You are providing recommendations now. How will the planning process be conducted in the future? Presumably the Steering Group would have the main responsibility for planning, but would need to involve the workings groups and the various groups who have an involvement in the Town Centre Initiative. It might be useful to be able to recommend how these bodies would be involved in a future planning *process*. For that you indicate who and when in future would the activities described in section (a) of this part of the analysis be done.

6.9 The letter from Brian Richmond shows that he has limited powers. He cannot specify or reject particular retail outlets. Grants can be given on a limited scale. The wider partnership in response to Thames Gateway, and the implications of tourism, may indicate that a wider vision is required than has been the case up to now.

7 TACKLING THE EXAM

7.1 Most readers who use this analysis are preparing themselves for the Chartered Institute of Marketing's Analysis and Decision examination, and the following remarks are intended for them. Most of the points, however, are of widespread application.

Answering the question

7.2 The fact that the examination is 'open book' emphasises the need to answer the questions that have been set, and not simply to copy prepared answers. Irrelevant material wastes time, and gains no marks.

7.3 You will, of course, have decided what you would recommend generally, and have prepared some detailed plans. To be able to refer to this material and use it to directly answer the questions, it is a good idea to break it into very small sections.

7.4 Whatever you do, you *must* lay out your answer in such a way that you clearly label each question number. It is fatal to just write a general report, and expect the examiner to try to tease out which part refers to which question.

7.5 We cannot emphasise too strongly that this analysis is not an examination answer, but instead it is provided to help you make the most of your study time, so that you are well prepared for the examination. Copies of the analysis are lodged with the examiners.

7.6 We do not recommend working with others on a *group approach* prior to examinations. Although this may be helpful in some circumstances, there is an increased risk of regurgitating material that is not properly understood, and which is not related to answering the question.

Part E: Learning from experience: ensuring you pass

Time management

7.7 You should have to work hard for the whole of the examination period, but the questions are such that they can be finished. Failure to answer part of the examination simply throws away marks. If you spend ages making an over elaborate answer to part of the paper, it will never make up for part which is complete or skimped.

7.8 You should allocate time to the questions roughly in proportion to the marks available. Any other approach is taking a gamble.

7.9 In the examination room you will find that many candidates will be writing furiously from the second the examination starts. Don't do it! Give yourself sometime to plan your answer. Anything from ten to twenty minutes would be reasonable. At the end try to have a few minutes available for checking. You must therefore divide your time between the question after this general time has been taken into account.

Report style

7.10 Many students, particularly those who have been used to writing essays as the basis for assessment, find difficulty in writing reports. There is not an option, the examination must be written in report style, and ideally you will have practised writing reports.

7.11 We do not recommend the style of this analysis as the model for an examination report. Inevitably, it must be more discussive than required in the exam, where alternatives might be written in list form, and 'bullet points' might be used to justify a recommendation.

7.12 Your report has to have a structure, with large divisions further subdivided into smaller ones. The divisions could be entirely number based, eg 1, 2, 3 etc for major divisions, with further numerical divisions eg 1.1, 1.2 etc and then 1.2.1, 1.2.2 etc. Further numerical divisions might become cumbersome, and letters might be used at the next stage. Alternatively a combination of letters and numbers might be used, eg 1, 2, 3 for major sections, with (a), (b), (c) for subsections and Roman numerals for further subdivisions. At all times it must be clear to the reader what the headings and subheadings are.

7.13 A good report style will make your points clear to the examiner, will help you to think clearly, and will save you time.

Assumptions

7.14 There are some judgements in any case study that can be calculated or derived from the given 'facts'. Others must be inferred. Reasonable but 'unprovable' assumptions should be clearly stated as assumptions. As in real life, evidence is sometimes contradictory. If you find this, decide what view you are accepting and state it clearly.

Extra information

7.15 You *will* receive some additional information in the examination room. Whilst this is highly unlikely to overturn your preparation you *must* make an effort to take it into account, and incorporate its effects into your answer. Failure to do so will needlessly throw away some marks. It is a good idea to refer to the new information directly, to demonstrate clearly that you are using it.

7.16 These points to some extent overlap and reinforce the slip included with the case study. This shows the serious concern of the examiner's at poor examination technique. You cannot expect to obtain a prestigious examination by three hours of furious copying.

Your preparation including the use of this analysis is vital, but you must also think during the examination and *do what is asked of you*.

8 FOOD FOR THOUGHT

8.1 Have you defined target markets, and appropriate strategies for each one? Do you understand the motivation and composition of each one.

8.2 Have you thoroughly analysed the case. What are the relative strengths of Gravesend as a shopping centre. Are you ready to deal with threats that are posed? To what extent can existing customers be retained, and new ones attracted? What balance will you go for.

8.3 You are likely to be asked to make outline proposals rather than a fully detailed implementation plan, but can you make these as precise and clear as possible, and justified by the material in the examination? Have you considered likely changes in the structure of retailing in Gravesend? To what extent can you offset any decline by growth elsewhere, eg tourism?

8.4 Remember timescale is important in this case. Many of the proposals are long term and will roll out. You must be clear on this. Also what can you be doing in the short term to improve Gravesend's position pending the opening of Bluewater. There is not much financial information in this case, but you must be aware that funding is important. Can you mention potential sources of funds other than Gravesham Borough Council itself? Will tourism provide extra funds or will it initially be another drain on resources?

8.5 Your brief is for Gravesend Town Centre and as such co-ordination with members of the TCI is critical. Have you any proposals to facilitate this? Can your brief be isolated from Gravesham Borough Council? How can co-ordination be achieved with other relevant parties.

8.6 Have you designed suitable promotional strategies? Are your media and creative proposals appropriate for the objectives and target markets in question?

8.7 Is tourism a viable option? At what pace can you implement it? The scale of your promotion will depend on the timing of its development. You should list out the tourism opportunities provided and inferred in the case, and also any reasonable ideas you yourself can generate.

8.8 Is there any further information you would recommend be collected? The existing survey would not necessarily pick up any tourists or visitors from any distance. How might the sampling be modified to achieve this? Are you ready to deal with any further information you are given in the examination?

Chapter 20

MISTRAL: CASE STUDY DOCUMENTATION

> **This chapter includes the case study information sent to candidates.**
> 1   Candidates' brief
> 2   Mistral: text
> 3   Appendices to Mistral: Simon's file contents

INTRODUCTORY NOTE

(a) The second practice case is Mistral a supplier to the European healthcare market.

(b) Remember that the paragraph numbers here have been inserted by BPP for ease of reference. You are unlikely to find such a numbering system in the case itself.

(c) We will remind you of the essentials for each step/stage in panel form. Good luck.

CONSULT THE GUIDANCE NOTES IN CHAPTER 8 PARAGRAPHS 2.1 TO 2.19
STEP 1 READ THE CASE STEP 2 AFTER AN INTERVAL, RE-READ THE CASE STEP 3 REFLECT ON THE INSTRUCTIONS AND CANDIDATES' BRIEF STEP 4 THINK YOURSELF INTO THE ROLE AND THE SITUATION STEP 5 RE-READ THE CASE AND WRITE A PRÉCIS - IN NOT MORE THAN TWO A4 SIDES
ALLOW YOURSELF BETWEEN 3 AND 6 HOURS FOR THESE STEPS

1 CANDIDATES' BRIEF

1.1 You are Simon Walker, a consultant with PACE, a well known firm of marketing strategy consultants. Your firm has recently won, in stiff competition with other similar firms, a prestigious assignment to critically review the marketing strategy of a part of *Mistral UK Limited*, focusing on one of the company's old established product areas.

1.2 Mistral UK Limited is the UK operating division of Mistral Inc, a multinational healthcare company with head offices in Milwaukee, Wisconsin, USA. Your client at Mistral is John Norland who has recently been appointed as Marketing Manager. He is based in Manchester, in the North of England, a reports directly to May Alexander, Director of Marketing.

1.3 John has an informal ('dotted line') relationship with the marketing managers in each of the European subsidiaries of Mistral and with the production managers at the Mistral production facilities in Dublin, Athens and Madrid. These relationships are delicate because, while product development and marketing planning are conducted in the UK, implementation relies on the co-operation of the various European subsidiaries. In particular, John is beginning to form the opinion that the European marketing managers are being reactive to market needs, rather than proactive. Moreover, it has been made clear to him that the European subsidiaries find the involvement of head office in this local markets unnecessary and often misguided.

1.4 Your immediate task is to present your ideas about the bandages market to John Norland and May Alexander at the quarterly strategy meeting which is due to take place in December. In order to get started, you have arranged a meeting with John to gather some background information and he has given you a file containing all the papers on the bandages market which were left by his predecessor.

2 MISTRAL: TEXT

Visit to Manchester in November 1996

2.1 Simon looked out of the window gloomily as the train sped north and wondered how he, a man steeped in fast moving consumer goods marketing (FMCG), could have landed up with this industrial marketing assignment - and in such a high-tech industry as well. 'Still,' he muttered to himself in consolation, 'a bandage is a bandage. At least I don't have to pretend to understand about replacement joints or catheters - not yet anyway.' As he flipped through the sales literature which Mistral had sent him, he began to feel queasy, and heartily regretted the British Rail breakfast which lay uncomfortably in his stomach as page after page of burns, wounds, operations and intravenous drips were revealed in glorious technicolour.

2.2 Simon shuffled his papers together and put them back in his briefcase. He slammed the lid shut, hoping for a few minutes of quiet contemplation before reaching Manchester, only to be startled by the loud fake-melodious electronic ring of a mobile phone in the seat behind him and an even louder voice trying to talk to the caller. Simon sat there and fumed for the rest of his journey.

2.3 He cheered up on reaching Mistral's modern offices and was enthusiastically greeted by John Norland. 'Simon, I can't tell you how pleased I am that you are going to help us out on this project. When I took over this position I had no idea how little attention had been paid to the whole area of bandages and support and I just would not be able to get around to any kind of serious strategic plan this year, with all the other marketing initiatives I am involved in. Now, I am aware that you do not have long so let's get started right away. You ask the questions and I will try to answer them as best I can. Please just bear in mind that I have not been in the job long myself.'

2.4 'Well,' Simon began 'first I must thank you for the most helpful information which you sent me. I have been looking at it on the train but I haven't had a chance to become truly

Notes Part E: Learning from experience: ensuring you pass

immersed in the figures yet. May we begin with the basics such as the background to the company and the industry before we get down to details?'

2.5 Some hours later, Simon found a seat in a first class compartment for the return journey. Heartened by his most interesting and successful day, he decided to pay the extra fare in the hope that he would not meet his friend with the mobile phone again. He pulled out his notepad and began to type.

Note to file - visit to Mistral UK Limited on 6 November 1996 (Verbatim report of interview with John Norland from Mistral by Simon Walker)

'Firstly, please tell me about the company background'

2.6 Mistral UK Limited is a wholly owned subsidiary of Mistral Inc based in Milwaukee, Wisconsin. Mistral Inc is a diversified conglomerate with activities spanning the healthcare, chemicals, pharmaceuticals and food manufacturing industries.

2.7 The UK business was formed out of an established British company, Beaufort, which was founded in 1878 and acquired by Mistral in 1982. The company still sells some old Beaufort products dating back to the 1920s. Subsequent acquisitions have been made over the past ten years to fit in with the global strategic plan. Some of these acquisitions were made to provide geographic coverage of local markets in Europe. Others were acquired for their stage of the art technological expertise.

2.8 After some recent rationalisation, Mistral UK Limited and all the continental European subsidiaries of Mistral Inc now operate principally in the area of medical disposables. The product ranges encompass these areas.

(a) Antiseptic wipes   (g) Splints
(b) Bandages   (h) Surgical instruments
(c) Castings   (i) Swabs
(d) Catheters   (k) Syringes
(e) Dressings   (l) Thermometers
(f) Gloves

2.9 Currently, each of the European companies is an independent profit centre, reporting to the managing director of Mistral UK Limited. All strategic matters concerning medical disposables are managed from the UK. Strategic issues at the moment include product development, marketing planning for all European markets and the monitoring of sales and profits.

2.10 The European companies manage what, to now, have been considered tactical marketing issues such as pricing, distribution and promotion.

'And the industry background?'

2.11 The company's European competitors vary by country but are mainly international conglomerates with medical disposable interests. The competitors vary from one market segment to the next. In the bandages market, for example, there are two German competitors, MTM AG and Brunhoff AG, and two American multinationals, Samuel Inc and BDG Inc. Apart from some obvious cultural differences, these four main competitors are global operations like us and tend to manager their businesses accordingly.

'Having the largest market share in the European bandage market, would you agree that your brands are so well established that they are truly cash cows?'

2.12 Some of our brands are certainly well established - we have been selling them for more than sixty years! What we need to focus on now is the strategies we should employ to maintain the brand and enhance it in the long term but of course we have to take into account short term profit pressures. For example, should the company try to retain market share or profit margins? Some products are becoming commodities, such as surgical instruments and the less sophisticated end of the bandage market. A further question is how can we differentiate sufficiently to justify premium pricing?

2.13 Some of Mistral's bandaging brands have a huge market share, even as high as 60% in some countries, and are years old, having been sold since the 1920s. Others are much more technical and are considered to be an important part of the treatment, rather than merely support.

2.14 Continental Europe tends to have more old products than the UK. These are perfectly good but they are not moving us forward. There is some friction between Europe and UK on this because the Europeans are happy to tender on the basis of the existing product range, while the marketing department in the UK is agitating for progress.

2.15 One thing that we don't appear to be able to grasp though is the difference between developing new products and developing new brands. I am hoping that we can use your experience in consumer markets to help us with this.

'What are the main external factors affecting the business at the moment?'

2.16 Well, hospitals buy established products by tender and there is very little effort required to sell the products. However in recent years credible competitors have been moving in on many product lines and this poses a threat. We tend to rely on our market share and reputation in the bandages market. Although I have only recently arrived I detect that there is a serious lack of product innovation in old-established lines to the extent that I wonder whether the sales force could even cope with innovation if and when it happens.

2.17 In other product areas we have introduced plenty of new products, particularly in the areas of dressings; we are very close to the customers in that area and are improving our product offer all the time. Clearly we need to do the same with bandages and with our channels of distribution, it should be possible. It will require a change in attitude though.

2.18 Superficially, we appear to be doing better in the bandages market than we are in dressings, where we are joint number three in the market. Incidentally, our definition of dressings includes, as well as traditional non-adhesive surface dressings, the much more sophisticated moist wound dressings, deep wound dressings, post-operative dressings and 'incise drapes' which are very clever polyurethane films used throughout long surgical operations to prevent migration of bacteria into the incision. To return to the point, in the dressings market, product development is very important and we are gaining ground. The market leaders are two huge brands which haven't innovated for years - BDG and Samuel - and they are in danger of losing their positions. In bandaging, the situation is reversed and we are in danger of becoming the dinosaur.

2.19 BDG and Samuel have a huge advantage with their great expertise in manufacturing and are able to drive the price down by standardising products to achieve economies of scale in production. However as I have indicated already, they tend to be weak on innovation and clinical expertise, which I believe are the important strategic drivers now and will be in the future.

'Please tell me about the decision making process which your salesmen face in trying to close a sale.'

2.20 The salesmen may have had it easy in the past but the process is becoming much more sophisticated. Products are evaluated by buyers on the basis of cost effectiveness as opposed to just price and the factors taken into account are many and varied. They include the following.

    (a) The type of materials used in the product

(b) The type of waste generated
(c) The impact on nursing time
(d) Time in theatre
(e) Durability
(f) reliability

... and so on, as well as clinical effectiveness.

2.21 The order in which these variables are placed depends, of course, on the particular circumstances of the buyer.

2.22 Added to this, the user group which has a say in the choice of product is vast compared with other marketing situations. It includes the following.

(a) The patient and his/her visitors
(b) The patient's peer group (other patients)
(c) Nurses
(d) Doctors
(e) Clinical directors (who identify treatment regime)
(f) Hospital manager
(g) Purchasing manager
(h) Government (who approve the prescription list)

'And in the future, what will the purchasing trends be?'

2.23 The overriding factor affecting decision making units will be the containment of cost. There are two major issues which will cause the cost of healthcare to escalate in the future. The first is demographics. Currently, approximately 40% - 50% of the population are earning and pay for a little over 30% of the population who are over 65. In only a few years, this situation will reverse. In fact, it will be even worse in Japan, where 20% will pay for 60% - 70%. So the pressures on the workforce to provide care for the elderly will multiply. The second issue is technology. There is an obvious direct effect of technology in medicine, whereby more treatments are being found which keep people alive longer. Then there is the indirect effect whereby technology may save lives, for example in major accidents, but the victims of such accidents are permanently maimed. An example of this would be the driver's air bag. A driver involved in a head-on collision, who would previously have died, may now, with the advent of the air bag, survive but his legs are likely to be crushed and he will require major surgery and rehabilitation. In very blunt terms, it costs a lot less to bury people than to rebuild them! I'm sorry ... you'll never think of your airbag in the same way now, will you?

2.24 Getting back to the point, the purchasing manager will call the tune in future, because we expect to live longer and to be rebuilt if anything goes wrong. I don't want to touch on the ethics of all this, but we continually expect, and receive, ever better healthcare, society in the long run will not be able to bear the escalation of cost.

'Are there other trends which will affect your business in the future?'

2.25 *Yes*. Another 'mega-trend' is the shift away from hospitals in favour of care at home. For example, if a patient has a cartilage operation, or gives birth, they will stay in hospital for much less time than they would have done before, even ten years ago. They also have much more say in how they are treated and with which products. The 1990s is certainly the decade of consumer choice.

2.26 The implication here is that many more healthcare supplies will be bought at the pharmacy and this in turn has a serious effect on the activities of our sales force. Instead of selling to a hospital, which is a 'one shot tender', the salesmen must target the wholesalers, the large chains of pharmacies and the supermarkets. There are positive and negative effects of this. The barriers to entry for a competitors with a credible product selling into a hospital are low because they can simply undercut on price in the tendering process. There is more scope for building brand awareness by selling through pharmacies. However this is a much more complex job for the salesmen. The same clinical standards apply in either situation.

'Since my expertise is in FMCG, I can't help thinking that you could apply the same principles of building up a brand in this situation.'

2.27 I'm sure there is some truth in this as the burden of responsibility is moving from the hospital into the community, allowing consumer marketing opportunities in previously closed product areas. However, I fail to see how we can do this on a Europe wide basis as all these initiatives are coming out of the UK. It seems to me that, on the whole, the European sales force is looking for the easy sale - they are content to pump existing product through the traditional channels to meet preconceived clinical indications. How do you suggest we break out of this mould?

'I'll certainly be thinking about this for our next meeting. May I just ask you now about the different product groups within the bandages market?'

2.28 Of course. Broadly speaking there are four types of bandage.

(a) The first category are known as retention and fixation bandages. These are simply what the name implies - the bandage or tape is there to hold something else in place, such as a dressing or a splint. They are supplied in both adhesive and non-adhesive forms. Our brand name for these products is Victrix.

(b) Next we have light support (crepe) bandages. These are used for the treatment of minor injuries such as sprains and strains and minor sports injuries. These are the Felix group of products.

(c) The more robust version of support bandages - the third category - are simply known as strong support bandages. These days, sports clinics and physiotherapists are using strong support bandages as part of their treatment. These are used to prevent sports injuries, players may strap or tape ankles before a game, or support and protect ligaments and tendons following more serious sprains and strains. We group these products under the Venus brand name.

(d) And lastly, we have compression bandages. These are very much part of the clinical treatment of acute and chronic conditions including venous leg ulcers, oedema, varicose veins, varicose ulcers, pre and post vein stripping. These are normally used in wound healing and in conjunction with other Mistral products such as the Alpha wound dressing. You may have guessed that this is of course the Vulcan product range.

2.29 The most important point for you to understand here is that these product categories form, in effect, a spectrum. The Victrix products serve a very low tech market which is becoming increasingly competitive and we are finding it very difficult to add value here. But the converse is true of our Vulcan range. Here we are beginning to try to look at various medical conditions and add value by packaging complete solutions, rather than just selling existing product.

2.30 The Venus range also provides opportunities in many markets such as the UK to add value to the brand as it is an integral part of high profile sports injury treatment and prevention.

Is this product range uniform across Europe?

2.31 A good question. The regional companies use the same generic terms but there is some disparity between the products offered in each country. However, because the regional companies are responsible for their own sales and profits, it is difficult to withdraw a line which head office may believe adds no strategic value to the portfolio, if it is a good earner in a local market.

And what about promotion?

2.32 Again, the regional companies are responsible for this. Their approach varies widely, but they mainly employ all the obvious techniques. Advertisements in the trade press are commonplace and occasionally even television advertising is used.

2.33 The more imaginative regional companies run a series of nurses conventions whereby clinical experts are engaged to give an explanation of the benefits of using Mistral products. Recently sports injury experts and physiotherapists have been employed in this role.

2.34 Occasionally, when a really new product has been launched, the clinicians involved in the trials may be persuaded to go 'on tour'. For example, when our Vulcan HP sustained compression bandage was launched in the UK, an eminent vascular surgeon from one of the London teaching hospitals took place in a symposium to which both nurses and physiotherapists were invited.

2.35 Since promotion is not a Europe-wide function, we are reliant on the line managers in each of the countries to build up the brand values. In some countries, such as the Netherlands, this is working very well whereas in other countries the promotional activities tend to be 'hit and miss'. Packaging is controlled centrally but the sales forces, local promotional activity, pricing and customer service are managed locally.

Why do you not bring all the marketing functions under one roof?

2.36 You may think this is the obvious thing to do but, even having said all this, the last thing we want to do is to implement the marketing plans centrally. We have always believed that we need locals to understand local issues and that, in order to get close to our customers, we must do a lot of marketing at the regional company level.

2.37 For example, healthcare systems are changing quite radically in many countries in Europe at present. But our customers are inclined to be conservative and stick to what they know, particularly if existing techniques work. Why take a risk if you don't have to? It's rather like the old adage that nobody ever got sacked for buying an IBM. Nobody ever got into trouble for buying an established medical product that has a 40% share of its market. But for buying an untried new product - which may be significantly more expensive on the basis of a direct comparison, even though it's much more durable and reliable and therefore more cost-effective in the long run - well, that's a real risk.

2.38 Pricing has also been a local issue although we have centrally controlled cost of product from the manufacturing facilities to each local company. We have always believed that by measuring the European companies on both sales and profits would avoid any major problems of price differences between countries but I suspect that there may be trouble brewing soon. Also, the role of pricing in customer perception of quality and building brand value in industrial markets such as ours is not well researched or understood. I am starting to wonder whether pricing is really a strategic issue. But to take away any of the local company control over their pricing activities would likely provoke open revolt among European company managing directors.

2.39 New ideas take time and effort and we need to nurture our customers in each country. This is of paramount importance within each country but the situation is very different from one country to the next. However, there is some sign of gradual change here and we are beginning to see possibilities for more international conferences. In time, I think we will begin to fund tat a good idea will travel, and we can encourage this by sponsoring delegates to attend conferences in neighbouring European countries. We are going to have to work hard to overcome parochialism though.

Later on the journey

2.40 Simon looked up at the drab suburban landscape as the train slowed to a crawl. A customer announcement informed passengers that the train was going to be delayed due to a line failure and that British Rail regretted any inconvenience caused. The voice added 'if you were wanting to get to London by 7.30 it wouldn't be this train that you would be wanting to travel on' which was greeted by wry smiles all round the first class compartment in which Simon was seated.

2.41 'Oh well,' he thought to himself 'at least I can get on with looking at the contents of this file which John has given me'. As he flicked through the pages of data he was dismayed to see that it was neither complete nor particularly up to date. It was not the quality of information he was used to dealing with in consumer marketing. 'This assignment is certainly going to be a challenge.'

3 APPENDICES TO MISTRAL: SIMON'S FILE CONTENTS

Ref	Subject matter	Paragraphs
1	Organisation chart	3.1
2	'The world's most intractable problem' - article on demographics	3.2
3	Product portfolio	3.3
4	Mistral sales of bandages by country	3.4
5	Market estimates, total sales by country	3.5
6	Competitor sales by product sector	3.6
7	Average selling prices by selected product and country (£)	3.7
8	Market shares	3.8
9	Memo to Dirk Bradley	3.9
10	Mistral European sales and profits by country 1992 - 1996	3.10
11	Product life cycle	3.11
12	Support bandaging report	3.12

Notes   Part E: Learning from experience: ensuring you pass

Appendix 1: Organisation chart

3.1

ORGANISATION CHART OF RELATIONSHIPS BETWEEN MARKETING, MANUFACTURING AND EUROPEAN SUBSIDIARIES

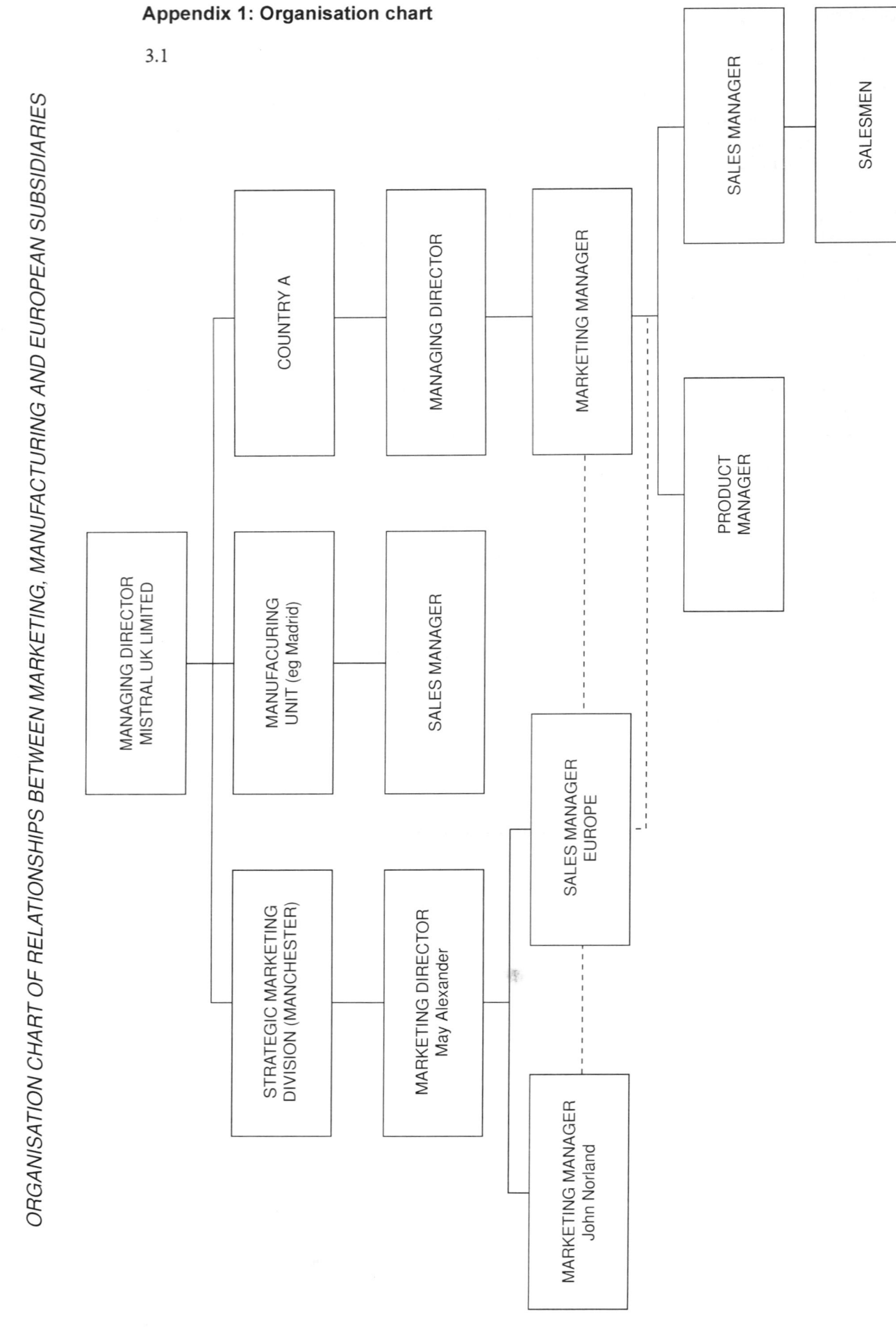

```
                                    ┌─────────────────┐
                                    │   COUNTRY A     │───┬──┌──────────────────┐──┌──────────────────┐──┬──┌───────────────┐──┌──────────┐
                                    └─────────────────┘   │  │ MANAGING DIRECTOR│  │ MARKETING MANAGER│  │  │ SALES MANAGER │  │ SALESMEN │
                                            │             │  └──────────────────┘  └──────────────────┘  │  └───────────────┘  └──────────┘
┌────────────────────┐                      │                                                            │
│ MANAGING DIRECTOR  │──────┬───────────────┤                                                            │  ┌───────────────┐
│ MISTRAL UK LIMITED │      │      ┌─────────────────┐      ┌────────────────┐                           └──│   PRODUCT     │
└────────────────────┘      │      │ MANUFACURING    │──────│ SALES MANAGER  │                              │   MANAGER     │
                            │      │ UNIT (eg Madrid)│      └────────────────┘                              └───────────────┘
                            │      └─────────────────┘
                            │                                                         ┌──────────────────┐
                            │                                                         │ SALES MANAGER    │- - - - - - - - -
                            │                                                         │ EUROPE           │
                            │                                                         └──────────────────┘
                            │      ┌─────────────────────┐   ┌────────────────┐              │
                            │      │ STRATEGIC MARKETING │   │ MARKETING      │              │
                            └──────│ DIVISION (MANCHESTER)│──│ DIRECTOR       │──────────────┤
                                   └─────────────────────┘   │ May Alexander  │              │
                                                             └────────────────┘              │
                                                                                    ┌──────────────────┐
                                                                                    │ MARKETING MANAGER│- - - - - - - -
                                                                                    │ John Norland     │
                                                                                    └──────────────────┘
```

BPP Publishing   **404**

Appendix 2: The world's most intractable problem - article on demographics

3.2 From '*The World in 1996*' (Economist Publications): an article by Barbara Beck

(a) Here is a prediction with a good a chance of coming true. A year from now, if spared by the grim reaper, you will be one year older. And by adding that extra year to your *anno domini*, you will have made your own tiny contribution to making the world grow older. People are living longer, and the number of births is increasing more slowly.

(b) In 1990 some 18% of the OECD countries' population were over 60 years old. By 2030, say experts at the World Bank, that figure will have risen to over 30%. But it is not just the developed countries that are ageing: in most other parts of the world, too, numbers of over-60s are set roughly to double over the next 30 - 40 years. Only Africa, on current form, looks likely to remain a young continent for some decades yet.

(c) Why worry if the world is greying? After all, this is happening for reasons that most people would welcome. Families even in many of the poorer countries are getting smaller because parents no longer have to allow for high infant mortality: and also because better educated parents find it easier to see that more might mean worse. Enthusiasm for babies in the former Soviet Union and in Eastern Europe has waned markedly with the advent of a market economy. And most rich countries have long since adjusted their production of new citizens to what they think they can comfortably afford.

(d) Birth rates in Japan and the European Union are well below replacement level. At the other end of life, improved medical care and healthier lifestyles have seen to it that many more people survive beyond the biblical 'three score years and ten', and that most of them are a great deal fitter than the Methuselahs of old.

(e) The trouble is that most countries have not been very good at adjusting to this rapid change. The prolonged 'baby boom' after the second world war made them think about overpopulation and paying for education rather than provision for old age. Now the debate has changed, but there has been more talk than action.

(f) In most developed countries retirement was originally set at 60 or 65 because people did not live much beyond that age. But life expectancy is rising constantly. In rich countries, a man reaching the official retirement age can now expect to live another 15 years; a woman about 19. In poor countries their post-retirement prospects are even better. And, on present trends, by about 2030 all of them can expect to live ten years longer still. During much of that time they may well be in good shape, spending money on holidays, clothes, housing (perhaps with an alarm bell and a resident warden, just in case things go wrong), entertainments of all kinds, financial products, even going back to school just for fun.

(g) But it also means that in most countries the deal between the generations - pay now, be paid for later - is under severe threat. Most countries' main way of looking after their old folks, the state pension, is becoming too expensive. Already in the OECD countries a quarter of all government spending goes on public-sector pensions. These usually operate on a pay-as-you-go basis, which means that current pensions are paid for by current contributions. In the European Union, for example, at present every five people of working age (not all of whom, remember, will be working) support one pensioner. On present trends, in 30 or 40 years' time they will have to support two. The changes are that this will prove politically impossible.

(h) Already some governments are beginning to wriggle out of earlier promises of ever-bigger pensions, and many have started encouraging their citizens to supplement their state pensions with an occupational or some other kind of private pension.

(i) But the argument between the generations is not just about pensions. Medical expenses too will burgeon as people get older. Already the very old consume a disproportionately large share of the total health-care budget. By one calculation, if people survive into old age, 90% of the cost of medical care they consume over their lifetime is incurred in the six months before their death. New medical techniques and technologies - such as spare-part surgery - seem capable of prolonging life further at ever-greater expense.

(j) Nor is care for the aged just about medical provision. A more people reach a greater age, some of them will need intensive nursing care towards the end of their lives. In the old days, when people became too frail to look after themselves, the family stepped in. In poorer countries it generally still goes. But in richer countries the family is not what it was, and women, who used to be the main carers, are increasingly going out to work. So someone will have to foot the bill for expensive professional nursing care.

(k) In Germany, payroll taxes have recently been raised to pay for nursing-home care. In Britain a newly market-oriented National Health Service has made it clear that it is no longer in the business of providing terminal nursing care for the old. Some old people are having to sell the houses they hoped to leave to their children to pay their nursing-home bills.

(l) The problems surrounding what some gerontologists call the 'fourth age' - from about 75 onwards - seem intractable. Unless a society is prepared to encourage its old folks to wander off into the snow Eskimo-style (or some modern equivalent), it will just have to pay up. Clearly, though, there is likely to be some rationing of benefits. Not many public-health services, for example, will pay for a hearth transplant for an 80-year old.

(m) But the main expense for most countries will be in providing for the huge numbers who in the next few decades will reach the 'third age' - between retirement and infirmity. What can be done to keep that in check?

   (i) Demographers advocate higher birth rates to swell the numbers contributing to the upkeep of pensioners. But before they made a contribution, those extra children would cost money to bring up, putting extra strain on the generation in the middle. Besides, people are not easily persuaded to have more children for the greater good if fewer would be better for them personally.

   (ii) A flow of immigrants of working age helps to lower the age profile in the host country. But absorbing such a flow creates its own problems, and eventually the immigrant population gets older like everybody else.

   (iii) Reduced pensions would bring down costs. But people can vote until they drop dead, and may voice their disapproval at the polling booth. In countries such as the United States older voters ('Grey Panthers') are already flexing their political muscles.

   (iv) Contributions may have to be raised. But the working generation has a vote too, and may demur. Experience in several Latin American countries has shown that if workers get squeezed too hard, they tend to wander off into the black economy.

   (v) Expansion of private provision will have to be encouraged. A number of countries are already doing this, working through occupational schemes. But coverage is patchy, and usually fails to reach the poorest part of the population in greatest need.

   (vi) A compulsory savings scheme may be needed to make people put something by for their old age. Some experts now argue hat the only way of averting a crisis over provision for old age in the early part of the next century is to spread the loan. Three 'pillars' - a state pension, an occupational one and a personal nest egg - are much better than one, they say. Obligatory savings schemes would also do the capital markets a power of good.

   (vii) Sooner or later, the official retirement age will have to go up everywhere. At 60 or 65, many pensioners are now still in their prime. They themselves do not think of themselves as past it.

(n) All the same, raising the retirement age may not go down well with voters who had looked forward to a long and happy period of leisure after decades of grind. Some countries are running into flak over raising the official retirement age for women, which paradoxically is often lower than that or men even though women on average live longer.

(o) But given appropriate incentives, many senior citizens might well enjoy continuing with some form of work, perhaps in a job that is less demanding or only part-time.

Before that happens, though, a lot of ageist prejudices will have to be shed by the corporate world. Over the past decade or two the age at which people retire in practice - as opposed to the official age - has actually come down with a bump. Early retirement has often been used to sweep unemployment under the carpet. In the EU, only about a third of all men aged 60 - 64, and very few women in that age group, are still at work.

(p) None of the more promising - and rather unpleasant - remedies described above will avert the looming crisis on its own. Only a combination of all of them is likely to work. Sounds grim? Sounds better than ending up, some time in 2030, as a destitute oldie.

Appendix 3: Product portfolio

3.3 (a) *Product portfolio*

  (i) *Retention and fixation: Victrix*

   (1) *Victrix Bandage*. This elastic retention bandage is made of viscose and polyamide. The bandage is soft, lightweight, porous, and very comfortable.

   (2) *Victrix CR bandage*. This retention bandage is made from a latex coated polyester/viscose mixture fabric. The bandage is lightweight and porous, it conforms easily. The cohesive properties of the bandages allow swift application and give economical non-slip dressing retention as only a 30% overlap is required.

   (3) *Victrix ZO tape*. This is a traditional zinc oxide tape for use in dressing retention on patients with normal skin. It is tearable by hand making it practical and easy to use for any kind of dressing. It has excellent immediate and lasting adhesion, ensuring prolonged fixation. It is also water resistant, and will therefore not come unstuck if the dressing gets wet. The larger widths are perforated to avoid skin maceration. The tape can be used for fixation of long term dressings on patients with normal skin, wide post-operative dressings and fixation of catheters, drainage tubes etc.

   (4) *Victrix LA tape*. This is a hypoallergenic tape which adheres firmly to the skin with reduced risk of allergic reaction. It is easy to tear by hand making it ideal for fixing medical equipment and lightweight dressings on patients with fragile skin or who are allergic to traditional tapes. It is permeable to air and water vapour and is easily removable. It can be used for dressing fixation and fixation of needles, probes, catheters and other equipment.

   (5) *Victrix HM tape*. This is a microporous hypoallergenic tape used for dressing fixation. The non-woven microporous substrate allows the skin to breathe prevent maceration in normal conditions. The low allergy acrylic adhesive reduces the risk of allergy and skin irritation on patients with sensitive skin. It is easy to remove and is tearable by hand. It can be used for fixation of long term dressings on patients with sensitive skin.

   (6) *Victrix TMH tape*. This is a transparent surgical tape coated with hypoallergenic adhesive. It has a microperforated backing which allows easy tearing both along its length and across its width.

   (7) *Victrix DR sheet*. This is a self-adhesive, non-woven fabric for dressing retention. Excellent comformability simplifies shaping around joints and awkward body contours and being extensible allows the patient greater freedom of body movement. Complete coverage of the dressing reduces the risks of casual contamination. The broad range of sizes increases convenience and patient comfort.

   (8) *Victrix ST 1*. This is a low allergy adhesive surgical tape which is lightweight, non-woven and porous. It can easily be torn length or width-ways before application, and is effective and comfortable in use.

(9) *Victrix ST 2*. This top quality waterproof strapping has a very secure adhesive based upon zinc oxide. It will maintain adhesion even in very hot climate conditions, and the plastic exterior surface is resistant to oil, water and grease.

(10) *Victrix CB*. This is a mix of cotton and nylon fibres woven to produce a product suitable for light levels of support for minor sprains and strains and for dressing retention/cannulae fixation.

(ii) *Light support: Felix*

(1) *Felix prime 2*. This elasticated tubular support bandage is made from rib weave stockinette and covered latex rubber. It provides general light support and can be washed and re-applied. No slipping occurs as with traditional flat bandages.

(2) *Felix ace strapping*. An extensible fabric strapping where comformability and comfort are high priorities, when providing secure fixation or strapping.

(3) *Felix QUO1*. This is a narrow woven cotton, polyamide and elastane bandage. The bandage is comformable, light, strong, durable and suitable for use as a general purpose light support and compression bandage.

(4) *Felix QU02*. This is a narrow woven cotton and polyamide bandage with tailored edges. The bandage is light, durable, comfortable, washable and re-usable. Light support is provided by the elasticated fibres used in the construction of the bandage.

(5) *Felix JAZ*. This flexible cohesive bandage is a combination of high strength nylon fibres and elastic yarns, coated with a latex compound, making the bandages ideal for light support bandage functions, particularly in difficult areas.

(6) *Felix CARE*. This support bandage is a mix of cotton and high strength nylon fibres woven in a way as to produce superior performance over traditional BP quality crepe bandages and making it suitable where support of mild soft tissue injuries is required.

(iii) *Strong support: Venus*

(1) *Venus Ace EAB*. This is a cotton/rayon bandage with a choice of natural rubber and low allergy adhesives both of which are porous allowing the skin to breathe. Easy application is afforded using the central yellow line as a guide and provides the correct tension for the treatment of sprains and strains, and sports injuries.

(2) *Venus Prime 1*. This shaped tubular bandage promotes venous and lymphatic return due to its anatomical design. It is a combination of rib knitted stockinette and covered latex rubber threads. Both full leg and below the knee bandages are available in a variety of sizes. The correct bandage size is selected by measuring the leg circumference at the calf.

(3) *Venus Maxi*. This is a woven product made from high twist cotton/rayon yarns producing the correct tension for the treatment of varicose veins and venous ulcers under rigid compression therapy.

(4) *Venus LAZO tape*. This is a hypoallergenic tape especially for use in rigid joint support due to its strong adhesion and its capability to stay in position.

(iv) *Compression: Vulcan*

(1) *Vulcan 4 × 4 layered*. This contains a simple wound contact layer dressing and four bandages for application of the four layer bandaging system developed by a team at Charing Cross Hospital, London.

(2) *Vulcan LP sustained compression*. These provide for light compression for the treatment of heavy legs, oedema and varicose veins.

(3) *Vulcan HP sustained compression*. These provide for high compression for the treatment of varicose veins, varicose leg ulcers, pre and post vein stripping.

(4) *VulcanEase*. This is a narrow woven extensible bandage made from a blend of cotton and nylon, which incorporates elastane to provide elasticity and is therefore suitable for all light compression needs.

(5) *VulcanIte*. This is a lightweight bandage made from a blend of cotton and rayon which incorporates elastic yarns covered in nylon for patient comfort. It is indicated for the management of superficial early varices, varicosis formed in pregnancy and above and below-the-knee stump bandaging. It is also for use as layer 3 in the 4 layer bandage technique for treating venous leg ulcers.

(6) *VulcanOp*. These are graduated compression hosiery made of polyamide and elastane. They are lightweight, comfortable, air permeable and washable. Colour coded for easy identification. Used to prevent variscosity, deep vein thrombosis and gravitational oedema.

(b) *Key: brands and sales categories*

Category	Brands
Retention	Victrix (not considered strategic - excluded from analysis)
Traditional adhesive	Venus Ace
Low allergy adhesive	No brands mentioned, minor products only so far
Tapes	Venus LAZO, Felix ACE
Tapes accessories	No brands mentioned, minor products only so far
Non-adhesive support	Felix Prime 2, Venus Maxi, Felix QUO1, Felix QUO2, Felix CARE, Venus Prime 1
Cohesive support	Felix JAZ
Compression	Vulcan range

Part E: Learning from experience: ensuring you pass

Appendix 4: Sales of bandages by country

3.4 *Sales 1996 (£'000)*

	United Kingdom Hosp	United Kingdom Non-hosp	France Hosp	France Non-hosp	Italy Hosp	Italy Non-hosp	Belgium Hosp	Belgium Non-hosp	Holland Hosp	Holland Non-hosp	Denmark Hosp	Denmark Non-hosp
Traditional adhesive	5,734	3,238	1,812	592	2,430	7,008	50	73	77	319	284	208
Low allergy adhesive	96	12	47	3	0	0	0	1	12	2	8	1
Functional bandaging total	5,830	3,250	1,859	595	2,430	7,008	50	74	89	321	292	209
Tapes	572	340	47	166	54	299	17	54	10	70	28	109
Functional tapes accessories	260	300	25	18	141	469	0	3	4	12	14	17
Functional taping total	832	640	72	184	195	768	17	57	14	82	42	126
Non-adhesive support	180	108	136	122	77	59	168	8	100	8	122	24
Cohesive support	40	136	44	9	16	247	8	14	31	2	9	6
Support total	220	244	180	131	93	306	176	22	131	10	131	30
Compression bandages	430	1,505	308	2,256	226	72	28	18	1	31	69	12
Total bandages	7,312	5,639	2,419	3,166	2,944	8,154	271	171	235	444	534	377

Appendix 5: Market estimates: total sales of bandages by country

3.5 *Sales 1996 (£'000)*

	United Kingdom Hosp	United Kingdom Non-hosp	France Hosp	France Non-hosp	Italy Hosp	Italy Non-hosp	Belgium Hosp	Belgium Non-hosp	Holland Hosp	Holland Non-hosp	Denmark Hosp	Denmark Non-hosp
Traditional adhesive	7,660	4,040	2,868	940	3,205	8,782	70	102	628	824	345	389
Low allergy adhesive	590	260	276	24	0	0	9	13	123	73	65	4
Functional bandaging total	8,250	4,300	3,144	964	3,205	8,782	79	115	751	897	410	393
Tapes	690	470	129	682	62	408	38	312	190	689	71	252
Functional tapes accessories	380	525	106	88	152	602	7	53	28	153	39	181
Functional taping total	1,070	995	235	770	214	1,010	45	365	218	842	110	433
Non-adhesive support	965	174	864	863	145	77	346	155	1,424	270	860	128
Cohesive support	845	2,595	360	162	297	5,892	40	72	132	75	45	144
Support total	1,810	2,769	1,224	1,025	442	5,969	386	227	1,556	345	905	272
Compression bandages	3,740	14,311	2,374	23,516	2,357	5,894	223	185	1	276	1,988	340
Total bandages	14,870	22,375	6,977	26,275	6,218	21,655	733	892	2,526	2,360	3,413	1,438

Part E: Learning from experience: ensuring you pass

Appendix 6: Competitor sales by product sector

3.6 (a) *Traditional adhesive: competitor sales 1994 (£'000)*

	United Kingdom Hosp	United Kingdom Non-hosp	France Hosp	France Non-hosp	Italy Hosp	Italy Non-hosp	Belgium Hosp	Belgium Non-hosp	Holland Hosp	Holland Non-hosp	Denmark Hosp	Denmark Non-hosp
Mistral	5,505.60	2,998.75	1,781.87	309.22	2,587.33	7,057.61	52.34	77.55	99.59	226.30	266.02	264.70
Competitor 1	1,006.40	325.60	441.30	189.13	450.35	1,079.02	12.60	16.81	279.93	377.75	73.90	91.57
Competitor 2	521.95	287.30	362.49	157.61	90.07	280.46	4.20	6.30	187.11	147.33	22.49	11.25
Competitor 3	208.85	201.96	0.00	0.00	0.00	245.01	0.00	4.20	0.00	73.66	0.00	0.00
Competitor 4	0.00	99.00	0.00	0.00	0.00	170.37	0.00	0.00	0.00	0.00	0.00	0.00
Others	207.93	93.78	157.61	283.69	30.66	39.00	4.20	0.00	36.83	0.00	4.82	0.00
Total market 1994	7,450.73	4,006.39	2,743.27	939.65	3,158.41	8,871.47	73.34	104.86	603.46	825.04	367.23	367.52
Est market 1995	7,580.31	4,035.60	2,811.84	939.64	3,190.00	8,782.77	71.89	103.82	615.53	825.05	356.22	378.54
Est market 1996	7,658.10	4,042.50	2,868.08	939.64	3,205.95	8,782.77	70.45	102.78	627.84	825.05	345.53	389.90
Est market 1997	7,710.75	4,042.50	2,911.10	958.43	3,221.98	8,782.77	69.74	101.75	646.68	825.05	338.62	397.70
Est market 1998	7,993.20	4,042.50	2,969.33	958.43	3,238.09	8,782.77	68.35	100.73	659.61	825.05	328.46	409.63

Notes

(1) Competitors vary by country so have been listed by size not name (eg Competitor in UK is Samuel Inc, while Competitor 1 in France is Brunholt AG)
(2) 1994 data latest available

(b) *Low allergy adhesive: competitor sales 1994 (£'000)*

	United Kingdom		France		Italy		Belgium		Holland		Denmark	
	Hosp	Non-hosp	Hosp	Non-hosp	Hosp	Non-hosp	Hosp	Non-hosp	Hosp	Non-hosp	Hosp	Non-hosp
Mistral	73.21	6.29	38.46	5.36	0.00	0.00	0.09	0.17	16.79	2.06	4.80	1.43
Competitor 1	326.94	159.75	110.32	7.88	0.00	0.00	5.04	6.30	73.66	36.83	41.77	3.22
Competitor 2	131.92	91.61	69.34	6.30	0.00	0.00	4.20	6.30	20.62	20.62	11.25	0.32
Competitor 3	0.00	0.00	0.00	0.00	0.00	0.00	0.00	0.00	0.00	14.14	0.00	0.00
Competitor 4	0.00	0.00	0.00	0.00	0.00	0.00	0.00	0.00	0.00	0.00	0.00	0.00
Others	0.00	0.00	0.00	3.15	0.00	0.00	0.00	0.00	7.37	0.00	1.61	0.00
Total market 1994	532.07	257.65	218.12	22.69	0.00	0.00	9.33	12.77	118.44	73.65	59.43	4.97
Est market 1995	550.02	260.03	239.94	23.15	0.00	0.00	9.51	13.02	120.82	73.66	62.39	4.96
Est market 1996	587.60	258.94	275.93	23.61	0.00	0.00	9.80	13.29	123.24	73.66	65.51	4.96
Est market 1997	635.92	256.39	317.32	24.09	0.00	0.00	10.10	13.55	126.94	73.66	68.79	4.96
Est market 1998	685.73	255.00	364.91	24.57	0.00	0.00	10.39	13.82	129.47	73.66	72.22	4.96

(c) *Tapes: competitor sales 1994 (£'000)*

	United Kingdom Hosp	United Kingdom Non-hosp	France Hosp	France Non-hosp	Italy Hosp	Italy Non-hosp	Belgium Hosp	Belgium Non-hosp	Holland Hosp	Holland Non-hosp	Denmark Hosp	Denmark Non-hosp
Mistral	496.30	329.73	25.00	114.00	46.00	271.00	13.00	38.00	11.00	60.00	25.00	113.00
Competitor 1	97.86	44.03	22.00	252.00	2.00	45.00	8.00	75.00	95.00	364.00	28.00	72.00
Competitor 2	0.00	0.00	15.00	126.00	1.00	27.00	8.00	33.00	47.00	228.00	22.00	48.00
Competitor 3	0.00	0.00	0.00	0.00	0.00	0.00	0.00	25.00	0.00	0.00	0.00	12.00
Competitor 4	0.00	0.00	0.00	0.00	0.00	0.00	0.00	21.00	0.00	0.00	0.00	6.00
Others	30.84	34.56	15.00	126.00	0.00	0.00	4.00	100.00	29.00	0.00	0.00	0.00
Total market 1994	625.00	408.32	77.00	618.00	49.00	343.00	33.00	292.00	182.00	661.00	75.00	251.00
Est market 1995	658.21	439.70	103.00	650.00	59.00	378.00	36.00	304.00	186.00	676.00	73.00	252.00
Est market 1996	693.75	462.37	129.00	682.00	62.00	409.00	38.00	313.00	190.00	689.00	71.00	252.00
Est market 1997	726.95	497.45	161.00	723.00	65.00	437.00	40.00	322.00	194.00	707.00	69.00	252.00
Est market 1998	832.25	531.29	201.00	759.00	68.00	472.00	42.00	332.00	198.00	721.00	67.00	252.00

(d) *Functional tapes accessories: competitor sales 1994 (£'000)*

	United Kingdom		France		Italy		Belgium		Holland		Denmark	
	Hosp	Non-hosp	Hosp	Non-hosp	Hosp	Non-hosp	Hosp	Non-hosp	Hosp	Non-hosp	Hosp	Non-hosp
Mistral	242.37	263.72	19.86	16.70	133.38	401.58	0.34	1.01	3.83	5.30	12.69	18.70
Competitor 1	99.33	204.39	37.82	28.37	5.27	105.40	2.52	4.20	20.62	105.19	20.88	136.54
Competitor 2	0.00	0.00	18.91	15.76	0.00	0.00	0.00	4.20	0.00	36.83	0.00	0.00
Competitor 3	0.00	0.00	0.00	6.30	0.00	0.00	0.00	0.00	0.00	0.00	0.00	0.00
Competitor 4	0.00	0.00	0.00	0.00	0.00	0.00	0.00	0.00	0.00	0.00	0.00	0.00
Others	28.73	21.79	15.76	12.61	0.00	0.00	4.20	42.02	2.94	0.00	5.62	9.64
Total market 1994	370.43	489.90	92.35	79.74	138.65	506.98	7.06	51.43	27.39	147.32	39.19	164.88
Est market 1995	375.26	501.39	96.98	83.74	145.58	557.68	7.20	52.45	27.82	150.28	39.20	173.13
Est market 1996	380.78	523.78	106.67	87.92	152.86	602.30	7.34	53.50	28.37	153.28	39.20	181.78
Est market 1997	397.32	532.81	117.34	92.32	160.50	644.46	7.49	54.57	28.94	157.11	39.20	190.87
Est market 1998	412.40	545.92	129.07	96.94	168.53	696.02	7.64	55.66	29.52	160.26	39.20	200.42

(e) *Non-adhesive support: competitor sales 1994 (£'000)*

	United Kingdom Hosp	United Kingdom Non-hosp	France Hosp	France Non-hosp	Italy Hosp	Italy Non-hosp	Belgium Hosp	Belgium Non-hosp	Holland Hosp	Holland Non-hosp	Denmark Hosp	Denmark Non-hosp
Mistral	172.97	100.46	106.54	16.70	74.83	73.40	202.33	8.15	88.98	5.60	108.74	19.65
Competitor 1	432.74	62.75	0.00	252.17	42.16	0.00	84.02	25.21	589.32	259.59	220.08	72.29
Competitor 2	0.00	0.00	0.00	145.00	28.74	0.00	33.61	21.01	368.33	0.00	216.86	32.13
Competitor 3	0.00	0.00	0.00	100.86	0.00	0.00	0.00	16.81	235.73	0.00	216.86	4.82
Competitor 4	0.00	0.00	0.00	0.00	0.00	0.00	0.00	0.00	0.00	0.00	0.00	0.00
Others	344.36	0.00	851.06	315.21	0.00	0.00	33.61	84.02	73.66	0.00	72.29	0.00
Total market 1994	950.07	163.21	957.60	829.94	145.73	73.40	353.57	155.20	1,356.02	265.19	834.83	128.89
Est market 1995	959.72	169.94	909.73	846.54	145.74	75.60	350.04	155.19	1,389.92	267.85	851.54	128.88
Est market 1996	966.38	174.00	864.24	863.47	145.74	77.86	346.54	155.19	1,424.67	270.52	860.06	128.88
Est market 1997	968.00	178.32	842.63	880.74	145.74	80.20	343.07	155.19	1,460.29	274.58	860.06	128.88
Est market 1998	968.00	184.21	800.50	898.36	145.74	82.61	339.64	155.19	1,496.79	277.33	868.66	128.88

(f) *Cohesive support: competitor sales 1994 (£'000)*

| | United Kingdom || Italy || France || Belgium || Holland || Denmark ||
	Hosp	Non-hosp	Hosp	Non-hosp	Hosp	Non-hosp	Hosp	Non-hosp	Hosp	Non-hosp	Hosp	Non-hosp
Mistral	32.74	99.82	39.72	11.34	11.11	119.30	3.02	5.30	27.40	3.24	1.38	3.81
Competitor 1	582.74	2,218.36	204.89	94.56	258.71	4,662.69	16.81	25.21	58.93	70.42	30.52	77.11
Competitor 2	209.73	161.12	0.00	0.00	19.16	431.67	8.40	16.81	17.68	0.00	0.00	19.28
Competitor 3	0.00	0.00	0.00	0.00	4.31	314.86	6.30	12.60	0.00	0.00	0.00	0.00
Competitor 4	0.00	0.00	0.00	0.00	0.00	124.09	0.00	0.00	0.00	0.00	0.00	0.00
Others	0.00	0.00	94.56	40.98	0.00	11.02	1.68	8.40	22.10	0.00	0.00	0.00
Total market 1994	825.21	2,479.30	339.17	146.88	293.29	5,663.63	36.21	68.32	126.11	73.66	31.90	100.20
Est market 1995	839.62	252.06	349.34	154.23	296.24	5,776.90	38.02	70.36	129.26	74.40	38.29	120.23
Est market 1996	844.82	2,600.00	359.82	161.94	297.72	5,892.43	39.93	72.47	132.50	75.14	45.94	144.28
Est market 1997	852.73	2,687.50	367.02	170.04	299.21	6,069.21	41.92	74.65	135.81	76.27	55.13	173.14
Est market 1998	887.39	2,790.31	378.02	178.54	300.70	6,190.59	44.02	76.89	139.21	77.03	66.15	207.76

Tutorial note from BPP. The normal positions of France and Italy in this appendix have been swapped in the table above. This is how the data appeared in the published case study.

Part E: Learning from experience: ensuring you pass

(g) *Compression bandages: competitor sales 1994 (£'000)*

	United Kingdom Hosp	United Kingdom Non-hosp	France Hosp	France Non-hosp	Italy Hosp	Italy Non-hosp	Belgium Hosp	Belgium Non-hosp	Holland Hosp	Holland Non-hosp	Denmark Hosp	Denmark Non-hosp
Mistral	269.25	98.64	226.63	118.83	153.60	58.26	21.51	8.82	13.85	4.13	37.22	11.38
Competitor 1	926.40	10,673.20	866.82	6,304.18	1,676.85	4,570.61	84.02	50.42	193.89	147.33	819.28	192.77
Competitor 2	732.50	2,025.75	283.69	4,728.14	527.01	1,121.10	33.61	42.02	101.66	88.40	321.29	40.16
Competitor 3	397.20	1,311.13	204.89	2,521.67	0.00	28.74	16.81	33.61	88.40	10.61	144.58	19.28
Competitor 4	391.20	0.00	173.37	0.00	0.00	0.00	16.81	0.00	0.00	0.00	120.48	0.00
Others	870.59	2,807.65	504.34	6,304.18	0.00	0.00	42.02	42.02	73.66	0.00	449.80	48.19
Total market 1994	3,587.14	16,916.37	2,259.74	19,977.00	2,357.46	5,778.71	214.78	176.89	471.46	250.47	1,892.65	311.78
Est mkt 1995	3,675.23	14,207.93	2,316.22	21,774.92	2,357.46	5,894.28	219.06	180.41	480.88	262.98	1,939.96	327.36
Est mkt 1996	3,741.60	14,309.60	2,374.13	23,516.91	2,357.46	5,894.28	223.44	185.82	490.50	276.14	1,988.46	341.34
Est mkt 1997	3,795.72	14,500.00	2,421.62	25,398.26	2,357.46	5,894.28	227.91	191.40	500.31	289.94	2,028.22	354.08
Est mkt 1998	3,840.13	14,500.00	2,482.08	27,430.13	2,357.46	5,894.28	232.47	197.14	510.32	304.44	2,078.94	368.24

Appendix 7: Average selling prices by selected product and country (£)

3.7   1996 (Spring)

Product	United Kingdom Hosp	United Kingdom Non-hosp	France Hosp	France Non-hosp	Italy Hosp	Italy Non-hosp	Belgium Hosp	Belgium Non-hosp	Holland Hosp	Holland Non-hosp	Denmark Hosp	Denmark Non-hosp
1 Felix Jaz												
10cm × 3cm - 'C'	1.22	2.01	1.30	2.21	1.06	1.05	1.27	2.10	1.29	1.95	1.22	1.30
10cm × 3cm - 'M'	1.40	2.30	1.50	2.44	1.22	2.02	1.55	2.41	1.54	2.49	1.45	2.49
10cm × 3cm - 'S'	1.55	2.25	1.46	2.39	1.20	1.79	1.50	2.50	1.87	2.52	1.93	2.63
2 Victrix CR												
10cm × 20cm - 'P'	2.90	4.50	3.25	4.60	2.53	3.76	3.10	4.10	2.95	4.05	3.30	4.30
10cm × 20cm - 'S'	2.59	4.95	2.49	5.20	3.26	4.64	3.20	5.20	2.97	5.10	3.57	5.51
10cm × 20cm - 'E'	2.05	2.76	2.11	2.89	1.96	2.64	2.05	2.72	2.10	2.69	2.15	2.99
10cm × 4cm - 'E'	0.40	0.00	0.37	0.00	0.00	0.98	0.42	0.00	0.50	0.00	0.78	0.00
10cm × 4cm - 'P'	0.68	0.72	0.70	0.33	0.57	0.95	0.63	0.78	0.64	0.82	0.74	1.02
10cm × 4cm - 'S'	0.48	0.98	0.39	0.49	0.70	0.98	0.70	0.97	0.72	1.00	0.89	0.98
3 Felix ACE EAB												
10cm × 4.5cm - 'E'	1.85	2.04	1.78	1.88	1.82	1.96	2.24	2.42	2.32	2.63	2.71	3.22
10cm × 4.5cm - 'P'	3.12	3.12	3.25	3.25	3.25	3.05	3.06	3.06	2.94	2.94	2.66	2.74
10cm × 4.5cm - 'S'	2.97	3.28	3.06	3.44	2.63	2.90	3.02	3.20	2.85	3.05	2.78	3.26
4 Vulcan HP												
10cm × 7cm - 'S'	3.26	4.05	3.02	0.00	0.00	0.00	3.25	0.00	3.62	3.97	4.14	4.26
10cm × 7cm - 'D'	0.00	0.00	3.25	4.38	3.10	4.32	3.70	4.42	3.58	4.06	4.34	4.17
10cm × 7cm - 'E'	3.07	3.27	2.92	3.42	2.10	2.95	3.10	3.59	2.96	3.51	3.33	4.10
10cm × 7cm - 'R'	2.86	2.98	0.00	0.00	0.00	0.00	0.00	0.00	0.00	0.00	3.40	3.70
10cm × 7cm - 'T'	0.00	0.00	2.67	0.00	2.48	0.00	2.73	0.00	2.74	0.00	2.98	0.00

Notes | *Part E: Learning from experience: ensuring you pass*

Appendix 8: Share of European market by product and competitor (1995)

3.8

	FUNCTIONAL BANDAGES (34%)	FUNCTIONAL TAPING (22%)	SUPPORT (44%)	TOTAL MARKET (100%)
90-100%	OTHERS	OTHERS	OTHERS	OTHERS (21%)
80-90%	MTM / BDG	MTM		
70-80%	BRUNHOFF / SAMUEL 68.9%	BDG	MTM	MTM (16%)
50-70%		BRUNHOFF		BDG (11%)
40-50%		SAMUEL	BDG	BRUNHOFF (11%)
30-40%	MISTRAL	36.7%	BRUNHOFF	SAMUEL (6%) / 35.8%
10-30%		MISTRAL	SAMUEL 9.8%	MISTRAL
0-10%			MISTRAL	

Source: Miles & North; Mistral in-house data

20: Mistral: case study documentation Notes

Appendix 9: Memo to Dirk Bradley

3.9

> To: May Alexander, Director of Marketing
> cc: John Norland, Marketing Manager
> From: Dirk Bradley, Financial Controller
> Date: 20 June 1996
> Re: Bandages - financial results for year ending 31 December 1995
>
> I can't give you the precise figures yet, but early indications show that we have increased our 35% market share in taping, despite increased competition. Cohesive bandage sales appear to have risen approximately 24%.
>
> This year seems to be getting off to a good start and with the new manufacturing line for elasticated adhesive bandage in Madrid it's over to your department now!
>
> All the best
>
> Dirk

Appendix 10: Mistral European sales and profit by country 1992 - 1996

3.10

(a)

UK	1992	1993	1994	1995	1996	*Percentage comparisons*			
Sales		47,730.90	52,451.60	58,279.50	64,755.00	0.91%	0.90%	0.90%	
Gross profit		23,388.10	26,750.30	30,888.10	35,615.30	49.00%	51.00%	53.00%	55.00%
Operating expenses		5,665.70	6,136.80	6,702.10	7,213.10	11.90%	11.70%	11.50%	11.00%
Sales and marketing expenses		9,068.90	11,014.80	13,404.30	16,188.80	19.00%	21.00%	23.00%	25.00%
A & P		1,217.10	1,416.20	1,661.00	1,942.70	2.60%	3.00%	2.90%	3.00%
Net profit		7,436.50	8,182.40	9,120.70	10,360.80	15.58%	15.60%	15.65%	16.00%

(b)

France	1992	1993	1994	1995	1996	*Percentage comparisons*			
Sales		21,411.90	23,529.60	26,144.00	27,520.00	0.91%	0.90%	0.95%	
Gross profit		11,134.20	11,764.80	10,980.50	11,008.00	52.00%	50.00%	42.00%	40.00%
Operating expenses		2,355.30	2,588.30	2,875.80	3,027.20	11.00%	11.00%	11.00%	11.00%
Sales and marketing expenses		4,282.40	4,470.60	4,705.90	4,678.40	20.00%	19.00%	18.00%	17.00%
A & P		599.50	611.80	627.50	605.40	2.80%	2.60%	2.40%	2.20%
Net profit		3,897.00	4,094.20	2,771.30	2,697.00	18.00%	17.00%	11.00%	10.00%

(c)

Italy	1992	1993	1994	1995	1996	*Percentage comparisons*			
Sales		46,549.59	50,597.38	53,827.00	56,660.00	0.92%	0.94%	0.95%	
Gross profit		21,831.80	22,566.40	22,768.80	22,664.00	46.90%	44.60%	42.30%	40.00%
Operating expenses		6,051.40	6,577.70	6,997.50	7,365.80	13.00%	13.00%	13.00%	13.00%
Sales and marketing expenses		10,240.90	10,625.40	11,034.50	11,218.70	22.00%	21.00%	20.50%	19.80%
A & P		698.20	759.00	807.40	849.90	1.50%	1.50%	1.50%	1.50%
Net profit		4,841.20	4,604.40	3,929.40	3,229.60	10.00%	9.00%	7.00%	6.00%

421 BPP Publishing

(d)

Belgium	1992	1993	1994	1995	1996	Percentage comparisons			
Sales		1,550.90	1,704.20	1,893.60	2,104.00	0.91%	0.9%	0.9%	
Gross profit		814.20	852.10	899.50	946.80	53.00%	50.00%	48.00%	45.00%
Operating expenses		170.60	187.50	208.30	210.40	11.00%	11.00%	11.00%	10.00%
Sales and marketing expenses		325.70	340.80	359.80	378.70	21.00%	20.00%	19.00%	18.00%
A & P		31.00	34.10	37.90	42.10	2.00%	2.00%	2.00%	2.00%
Net profit		286.90	289.70	293.50	315.60	19.00%	17.00%	16.00%	15.00%

(e)

Holland	1992	1993	1994	1995	1996	Percentage comparisons			
Sales		1,657.10	2,045.80	2,589.60	3,237.00	0.81%	0.79%	0.80%	
Gross profit		911.40	1,227.50	1,683.20	2,265.90	55.00%	60.00%	65.00%	70.00%
Operating expenses		198.90	245.50	310.80	388.40	12.00%	12.00%	12.00%	12.00%
Sales and marketing expenses		348.00	491.00	699.20	971.10	21.00%	24.00%	27.00%	30.00%
A & P		54.70	71.60	103.60	161.90	3.30%	3.50%	4.00%	5.00%
Net profit		309.90	419.40	569.70	744.50	19.00%	21.00%	22.00%	23.00%

(f)

Denmark	1992	1993	1994	1995	1996	Percentage comparisons			
Sales		3,711.70	4,078.80	4,078.80	4,532.00	0.91%	1.00%	0.90%	
Gross profit		1,670.30	1,835.50	1,835.50	1,903.40	45.00%	45.00%	45.00%	42.00%
Operating expenses		426.80	489.50	448.70	498.50	12.00%	12.00%	11.00%	11.00%
Sales and marketing expenses		816.60	1,305.20	815.80	906.40	22.00%	32.00%	20.00%	20.00%
A & P		81.70	89.70	89.70	99.70	2.00%	2.00%	2.00%	2.00%
Net profit		345.20	– 48.90	481.30	398.80	9.00%	–1.00%	12.00%	9.00%

Appendix 11: Product life cycle

3.11

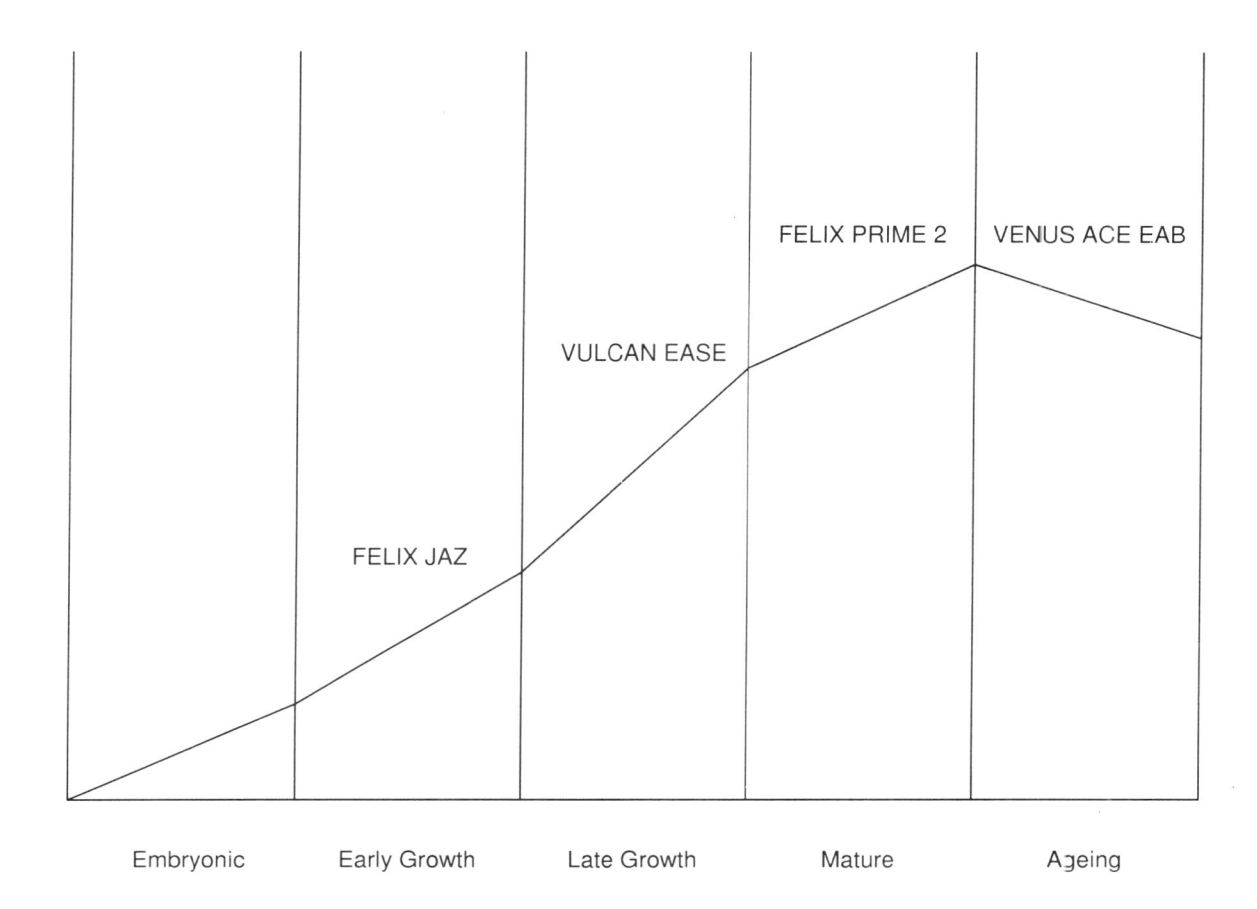

[Product life cycle graph showing products positioned across stages:
- Embryonic: (start of curve)
- Early Growth: FELIX JAZ
- Late Growth: VULCAN EASE
- Mature: FELIX PRIME 2
- Ageing: VENUS ACE EAB]

Appendix 12: Support bandaging report

3.12 (a) *Sales*

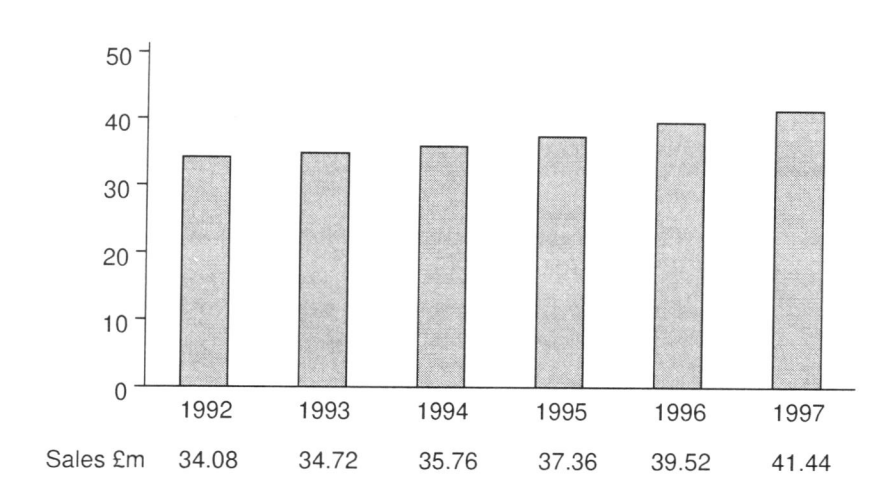

Year	1992	1993	1994	1995	1996	1997
Sales £m	34.08	34.72	35.76	37.36	39.52	41.44

Sales by region

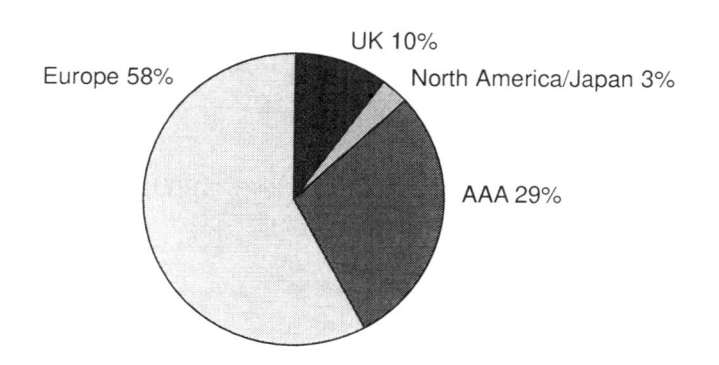

- Europe 58%
- UK 10%
- North America/Japan 3%
- AAA 29%

(b) *Profitability*

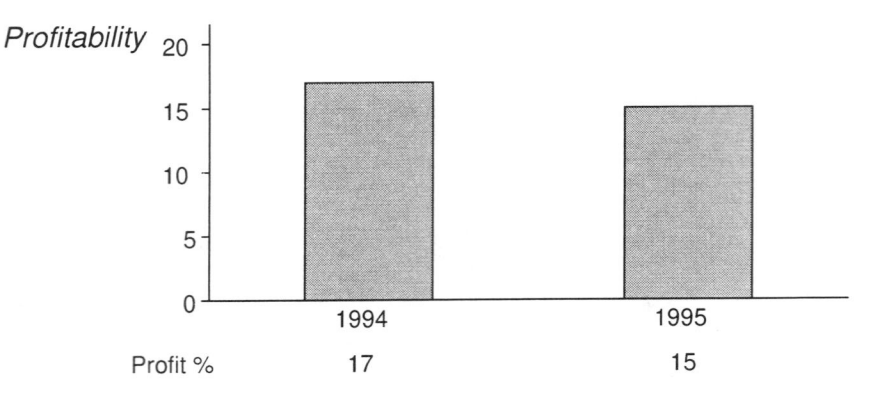

Profitability

	1994	1995
Profit %	17	15

Competitive situation

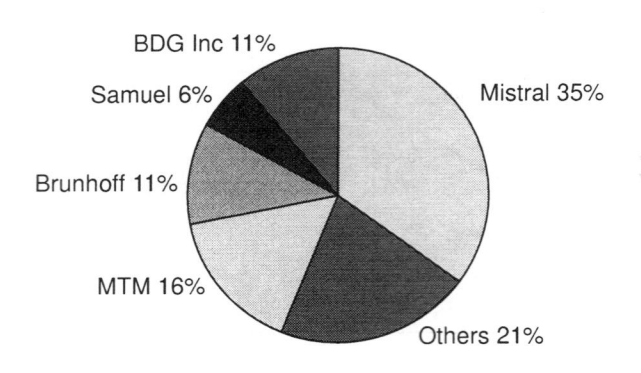

Market shares: Mistral 35%, Others 21%, MTM 16%, Brunhoff 11%, Samuel 6%, BDG Inc 11%

(c) *Environment*

(i) The market for support bandages is currently growing by 2.8% per annum.

(ii) The emergence of low cost/lower quality general support products is starting but has yet to become significant.

(d) *Competitors*

(i) The emergence of credible competitors to our adhesive bandages occurred in 1994, eg Spain and France.

(ii) The growth of off-the-shelf bracing for sports prophylaxis is eroding our potential in functional bandaging.

(e) *Profit*. Net profit has fallen from 17% to 15% in 1995 due to:

(i) the mix change between elasticated adhesive bandages (EABs) and general support, where general support and tape products (which have lower net profit levels) now make a greater proportion of sales;

(ii) the expected lower net profit on EABs, in reflection of the increased competitor activity and defending our business against these competitors.

(f) *Strategies*

(i) Segment the adhesive bandage market through the introduction/ development of product variants.

(ii) Make market supply difficult for our new competitors.

(iii) Segment the traditional EAB (via packaging) to enhance its acceptability in all sectors.

  (1) Vets
  (2) Sports/activity market

(3) Hospital
(4) OTC (over-the-counter)

(iv) Develop a workshop package to support the range in the key areas of use, sports/activity and general physiotherapy.

(v) Aggressively promote a full range of cohesives to strengthen our position in this growing sector.

(vi) Manufacture/source a full range of general support bandages to provide a cost competitive range to be offered on hospital contracts to gain substantial growth with minimal investment.

(vii) Package some key brands to maximise their OTC potential.

Chapter 21

MISTRAL: PRÉCIS, MARKETING AUDIT, SWOT

> **This chapter covers the following topics.**
> 1. Introduction
> 2. Sample précis
> 3. Marketing audit checklist
> 4. Marketing audit 1
> 5. Marketing audit 2
> 6. SWOT analyses

1 INTRODUCTION

1.1 Having now completed your précis you can now compare it with the three specimens which follow. This Tutorial Text tries to help you consider the case from a number of angles, so you will be dealing with material drawn up by a number of syndicates. Key points to watch out for are:

(a) structure;
(b) excessive detail;
(c) value judgements;
(d) jumping the gun - suggesting solutions rather than summarising facts.

1.2 The three specimens are different, reflecting the type of person writing it and his/her background. Sample *précis 1* is rather minimal. The person concerned appears to have gone through the case, Candidates' Brief and pages 1 to 11 extracting bits from the case verbatim, without headings, until two pages have been filled. There are no references to the data given in the appendices. However, it is at least factual and there are no value judgements.

1.3 Sample *précis 2* is by contrast highly structured and in report format rather than essay style. It gets more detail in the allowed space than sample *précis* 1 and has the advantage that some important data from the appendices are included.

1.4 Sample *précis 3* is short. The student concerned is very opinionated and decisive. There are quite a lot of value judgements, although some of the statements ring true. This précis is useful only as a contrast and possibly as a 'devil's advocate'. In doing this exercise you really need to remain objective and deal only in the *facts*.

1.5 Hopefully your own précis will be closer to sample 2. Is it?

21: Mistral: précis, marketing audit, SWOT

2 SAMPLE PRÉCIS

2.1 *Sample précis 1*

I am Simon Walker, a marketing consultant charged with the task of critically reviewing the marketing strategy of part of Mistral UK Ltd, focussing on one of the company's old established product areas - the bandages market.

Mistral UK Ltd is a subsidiary of Mistral Inc and along with other European subsidiaries operates principally in medical disposables. Each European company is an independent profit centre but reports to the Managing Director of Mistral UK which manage all strategic matters concerning medical disposables including product development, marketing planning for all European markets and the monitoring of sales and profits. The European companies manage the tactical marketing issues such as pricing, distribution and promotion.

Mistral's competitors vary by country but are mainly international conglomerates with medical disposable interests. In the bandages market, for example, are two German competitors and two American multinationals.

Some of Mistral's bandaging brands have a huge market share - as high as 60% in some countries, and have been sold for more than 60 years.

Hospitals buy established products by tender and there is very little effort required to sell these. Mistral tend to rely on market share and reputation in the bandages market. Very little innovation has taken place in the bandages market with regard to products and distribution. However, product development is very important in the dressings market which is dominated by the two American multinationals, BDG and Samuel.

Whilst salespeople have had it easy in the past, the buying process is becoming more sophisticated and buyers are evaluating products in terms of cost effectiveness as opposed to just price. Also the user group has a say in the choice of products and comprises a vast array of people such as patients, doctors, nurses, hospital managers, and the Government (who approve the prescription list).

With shorter stays in hospitals and increased care at home there is likely to be a greater need to target the wholesalers, the large chains of pharmacies and the supermarkets.

There are mainly four types of bandages.

1. Those to *hold something else in place* such as a dressing or a splint and known as retention and fixation bandages. They come in adhesive and non-adhesive forms under the brand name VICTRIX.

2. Light support (crepe) bandages used for minor injuries, for which the brand name is FELIX.

3. Strong support bandages used for more serious injuries such as sprains, also to strap or tape ankles etc to prevent sports injuries.

4. Compression bandages used for chronic conditions such as ulcers and wound healing marketing under the brand name VULCAN.

Companies commonly advertise in the trade press and occasionally on TV. The more innovative companies in the Group run a series of nurses' conventions where clinical experts are engaged to explain the benefits of Mistral products. Since promotion is not controlled centrally Mistral rely on companies' line mangers to build up the brand values. Packaging is controlled centrally, but the sales forces, local promotional activity, pricing and customer service are managed locally.

2.2 *Sample précis 2*

1. *Candidates' brief*
    (a) I am Simon Walker, consultant with PACE.
    (b) Client: John Norland, Marketing Manager Mistral UK Ltd.
    (c) John Norland reports to May Alexander, Director of Marketing.
    (d) Task: critical review of marketing strategy for bandages.

Notes *Part E: Learning from experience: ensuring you pass*

2 *Organisation*

   (a) Client company: Mistral UK Ltd (MUK) a subsidiary of Mistral Inc (MINK).

   (b) Other subsidiaries of MINK in European bandages market operate in France, Italy, Belgium, Holland, Denmark - called *regional companies* (RECOS).

   (c) RECOS are independent profit centres but report to the Managing director of MINK.

   (d) European strategies for product development and marketing planning are controlled by MINK who monitor sales and profits.

   (e) RECOS manage tactics such as pricing/distribution/promotion and their salesforces although there is a 'Sales Manager Europe'.

   (f) Client has an informal relationship with the marketing managers of RECOS and with MINK's production managers at the factories in Dublin, Athens and Madrid.

3 *Markets*

Appendices indicate that the markets in which MUK/RECOS mainly operate, segment into:

	Market size 1996 £m	Total %	Market growth 1988/1994 index
Functional bandaging	31.3	28.5	104
Functional taping	6.3	5.7	123
Support	16.9	15.5	108
Compression	55.2	50.3	111
Total	109.7	100.0	-

4 *Competitors*

   (a) Mainly international conglomerates with medical disposable interests.

   (b) Specifically, four main global players in the bandages market - two German (MTM, Brunhoff) and two American multinationals (Samuel, BDG).

   (c) The Samuel and BDG brands dominate the dressings market (but not the bandages market).

5 *Products/brands*

   (a) There are four basic types of bandages.

      1 To hold a dressing or splint in place: VICTRIX (plus adhesive tapes (VICTRIX ZO))

      2 For light support (crepe) - sprains, strains, minor sport injuries: FELIX (plus tapes FELIX ACE)

      3 For strong support and/or to protect against sports injuries: VENUS (plus tapes VENUS LAZO)

      4 Compression bandages for acute conditions like ulcers and serious wounds: VULCAN

   (b) Mistral supply other medial 'disposable' products such as dressings and surgical instruments/accessories which are assumed to be not *directly* part of my brief.

   (c) Some of Mistral's bandaging brands have market shares of up to 50% in some countries which have been selling for over 60 years.

   (d) Very little NPD in bandages in comparison to dressings

6 *Pricing*

Pricing is regarded as a tactical issue to be decided by individual countries and consequently varies widely from country to country (as do profits). John has, however, wondered whether pricing is really a strategic issue.

7 *Sales/distribution*

It is not clear whether individual company salesforces are specialised by type of product or customer. However, there are indications of changes in the DMU and buying motives also in the distribution channels which suggest that the salesforces will require considerable retraining/reorganisation in the future.

8   *Promotion*

   (a) *Advertising.* Advertisements in the trade press are commonly used. Occasionally Mistral advertises on TV. Brand building is sporadic since promotion is locally managed.

   (b) *Sales promotion.* Symposia, nurses' conventions and clinicians' tours occur but only at the instigation of the more imaginative RECOS. Packaging is however controlled centrally.

   (c) *Personal selling* (see 7 above) appears to be locally administered although there is a Sales Manager Europe. Currently selling seems to be somewhat laid back and reactive.

   (d) *Public relations.* No specific activities are stated.

9   *Appendices of major importance*

   Appendix 2 emphasises the social trend of ageing populations and the impossibilities of maintaining the various costs of current healthcare provisions.

   Appendix 4 gives 1996 sales by product by country split into hospital and non-hospital outlets.

   Appendix 5 gives the total market sizes 1996 for bandages by type by country split into hospital/non-hospital outlets.

   Appendix 6 gives Mistral and competitors' 1994 sales by product by country split into hospital/non-hospital.

   Appendix 7 gives average selling prices by country for Spring 1996 for select Mistral products (one for each of the four brands).

   Appendix 10 shows sales and profits by country for 1992 to 1996.

2.3   *Sample précis 3*

As Simon Walker, I have an almost impossible task to perform in light of the time and information constraints.

It would appear that Mistral has been very loosely if not poorly managed as far as marketing is concerned, with the various countries going their own way. This will have to change if Mistral are to succeed in the future.

Marketing will have to centralised and firm discipline applied throughout Europe.

The product range is complicated and old and in need of rationalisation.

Unprofitable products should be removed whilst a programme of new product development based *on customer research* should be instigated.

A pricing review is also urgently required since there are wide discrepancies between profits produced by the different European countries under the present pricing arrangements.

As less and less time is being spent in hospital and more treatment is conducted in the home, the proportions of sales achieved through the various distribution channels will change. Mistral will need to do more direct marketing and retail marketing in future and this will mean an overhaul/retraining of the European salesforce to be drawn up by the Sales Manager, Europe

Changes in the DMU and in the buying motives will call for a re-orientation of the promotional mix and the copy platform.

2.4   So how did your précis shape up? Remember you are not taking any decisions yet. You still need to keep an open mind for further analysis.

3   MARKETING AUDIT CHECKLIST

3.1   *Checklists*

   (a) Before doing the audit proper you might like to try the information checklist mentioned in Chapter 8 Paragraph 3.7 and the checklist format in Chapter 1, Paragraphs 2.8 and 2.9. You should use this checklist to determine the information we have on *Mistral* and the information we do not have. You could use a tick to

Notes   Part E: Learning from experience: ensuring you pass

show the information we have and a *cross* (X) to show the information we do not have (and which might then form the basis of your MkIS/MR recommendations later on in your plan). Further refinements might be to use *P* for information we have in part only and *NA* for *not applicable*. Really organised students might like to note the page numbers on which items ticked or marked P occur. It is easy for people to panic when they realise how little information the case study gives them. However, in real life we often take decisions based on inadequate information: the important thing is to recognise this and make reasonable assumptions.

(b) Having done this operation you might like to compare your results with those of the syndicate which follows, noting that there are likely to be some discrepancies, since this exercise is partly judgmental.

Internal

3.2 (a) *Current position*

(i) *Performance*

- P Total sales in value and in units
- ✓ Total gross profit, expenses and net profit
- P Percentage of sales for sales expenses, advertising etc
- ✓ Percentage of sales in each segment
- P Value and volume sales by year, month, model size etc
- X Sales per thousand consumers, per factory, in segments
- ✓ Market share in total market and in segments

(ii) *Buyers/customers*

- X Number of actual and potential buyers by area
- P Characteristics of consumer buyers, eg income, occupation, education, sex, size of family etc
- P Characteristics of industrial buyers, eg primary, secondary, tertiary, manufacturing; type of industry; size etc
- P Characteristics of users, if different from buyers
- P Location of buyers, users
- X When purchases made: time of day, week, month, year; frequency of purchase; size of average purchase or typical purchase
- ✓ How purchases are made: specification or competition; by sample, inspection, impulse, rotation, system; cash or credit
- ✓ Attitudes, motivation to purchase; influences on buying decision; decision making unit in organisation
- ✓ Product uses - primary and secondary

(b) *Products*

(i) *Mistral*

- P Quality: materials, workmanship, design, method of manufacture, manufacturing cycle, inputs-outputs
- P Technical characteristics, attributes that may be considered as selling points, buying points
- ✓ Models, sizes, styles, ranges, colours etc
- P Essential or non-essential, convenience or speciality
- P Similarities with other company products
- P Relation of product features to user's needs, wants, desires
- P Development of branding and brand image
- P Degree of product differentiation, actual and possible
- X Packaging used, function, promotional
- P Materials, sizes, shapes, construction, closure

21: Mistral: précis, marketing audit, SWOT

- (ii) *Competitors*
  - ✓ Competitive and competing products
  - ✓ Main competitors and leading brands
  - X Comparison of design and performance differences with leading competitors
  - P Comparison of offerings of competitors, images, value etc
- (iii) *Future product development*
  - P Likely future product developments in company
  - P Likely future, or possible future, developments in industry
  - P Future product line or mix contraction, modification or expansion

(c) *Distribution*

- (i) *Mistral*
  - P Current company distribution structure
  - P Channels and methods used in channels
  - X Total number of outlets (consumer or industrial) by type
  - X Total number of wholesalers or industrial middlemen, analysed by area and type
  - P Percentage of outlets of each type handling product broken down into areas
  - P Attitudes of outlets by area, type, size
  - X Degree of co-operation, current and possible
  - P Multi-brand policy, possible or current
  - P Strengths and weaknesses in distribution system, functionally and geographically
  - X Number and type of warehouses; location
  - X Transportation and communications
  - X Stock control; delivery periods; control of information
- (ii) *Competitors*
  - X Competitive distribution structure; strengths and weaknesses
  - P Market coverage and penetration
  - X Transportation methods used by competitors
  - X Delivery of competitors
  - X Specific competitive selling conditions
- (iii) *Future developments*
  - P Future likely and possible developments in industry as a whole or from one or more competitors
  - P Probable changes in distribution system of company
  - P Possibilities of any future fundamental changes in outlets

(d) *Promotional and personal selling*

- (i) *Mistral*
  - X Size and composition of sales force
  - X Calls per day, week, month, year by salespeople
  - X Conversion rate of orders to calls
  - P Selling cost per value and volume of sales achieved
  - X Selling cost per customer
  - P Internal and external sales promotion
  - X Recruiting, selection, training, control procedures

- P Methods of motivation of salespeople
- X Remuneration schemes
- P Advertising appropriation and media schedule, copy theme
- X Cost of trade, technical, professional, consumer media
- X Cost of advertising per unit, per value of unit, per customer
- X Advertising expenditure per thousand readers, viewers of main and all media used
- X Methods and costs of merchandising
- P Public and press relation; exhibitions

(ii) *Competitors*

- X Competitive selling activities and methods of selling and advertising; strengths and weaknesses
- X Review of competitors' promotion, sales contests etc
- X Competitors' advertising themes, media used

(iii) X *Future developments* likely in selling, promotional and advertising activities

(e) *Pricing*

(i) *Mistral*

- P Pricing strategy and general methods of price structuring in company
- X High or low policies; reasons why
- P Prevailing pricing policies in industry
- X Current wholesaler, retailer margins in consumer markets or middlemen margins in industrial markets
- X Discounts, functional, quantity, cash, reward, incentive
- X Pricing objectives, profit objectives financial implications such as breakeven figures, cash budgeting

(ii) *Competitors*

- P Prices and price structures of competitors
- X Value analysis of own and competitors' products
- X Discounts, credit offered by competitors

(iii) *Future developments*

- P Future developments in costs likely to affect price structures
- X Possibilities of more/less costly raw materials or labour affecting prices
- P Possible price attacks by competitors

(f) *Service*

(i) *Mistral*

- X Extent of pre-sales or customer service and after-sales or product service required (by products)
- X Survey of customer needs
- NA Installation, deduction in use, inspection, maintenance, repair, accessories provision
- X Guarantees, warranty period
- X Methods, procedures for carrying out service
- X Returned goods, complaints

(ii) *Competitors*

- X Services supplied by competing manufacturers and service organisations
- X Types of guarantee, warranty, credit provided

(iii) P *Future possible developments* that might require revised service policy

External

3.3 (a) *Environmental audit - national and international*

    P   Social and cultural factors likely to affect the market, in the short and long term

    X   Legal factors and codes of practice likely to affect the market in the short and long term

    P   Economic factors likely to affect market demand in the short and long term

    X   Political changes and military action likely to impact upon national and international markets

    P   Technological changes anticipated and likely to create new opportunities and threats

(b) *Marketing objectives and strategies*

    P   Short-term plans and objectives for current year, in light of current political and economic situation

    X   Construction of standards for measurement of progress towards achieving of objectives; management ratios that can be translated into control procedures

    X   Breakdown of turnover into periods, areas, segments, outlets, salesmen etc

    X   Which personnel required to undertake what responsibilities, actions etc when

    X   Review of competitors strengths and weaknesses likely competitive reactions and possible company responses that could be made

    P   Long-term plans, objectives and strategies related to products, price, places of distribution, promotion, personnel selling and service.

3.4 You are now ready to conduct the marketing audit proper, systematically working your way through the environmental audit, to the marketing functions audit and the other functional audits (financial, production and personnel).

CONSULT THE GUIDANCE NOTES IN CHAPTER 8 PARAGRAPHS 3.1 TO 3.8
STEP 6 CONDUCT A MARKETING AUDIT
ALLOW YOURSELF ABOUT 3 HOURS FOR THIS STEP

Have a thoughtful and *critical* look now at the marketing audits submitted below.

Part E: Learning from experience: ensuring you pass

4 MARKETING AUDIT 1

External audit

Opportunities

4.1 *Opportunities*

(a)	Product life cycle in Europe lags behind UK	(Product)
(b)	Redefine markets in customer terms	(Position)
(c)	Development of brands	(Product)
(d)	Differentiate product offering	(Product)
(e)	Take advantage of market growth and distribution channels	(Position)
(f)	Recognise change in DMU towards customer needs	(Position)
(g)	Develop new organisational and measurement structure	(Organisation)
(h)	Exploit competitor weaknesses in clinical expertise	(Product)
(i)	Rational product range	(Product)
(j)	Key: Organisation = Marketing-orientated structure and culture	
	Product = Consolidate and improve the offering to customer	
	Position = Move ahead of customer	

4.2 *Prioritising opportunities*

Probability of success

	High	Low
High (Attractiveness of opportunity)	Moving ahead of the customer Consolidate and improve offering	Market orientation structure and culture
Low		

Threats

4.3 *Threats*

(a)	Overdependence on hospital channel	(Distribution)
(b)	Competitive cost advantages	(Competition 1)
(c)	Squeeze on state funding of healthcare	(Environment)
(d)	Shift in distribution towards end customer	(Distribution)
(e)	Increased intensity and sophistication of competition	(Competition 2)
(f)	Mistral lose competitive advantage though old brands	(Competition 2)
(g)	Shift in markets, not capturing and analysing	(Distribution)
(h)	Shift toward FMCG	(Distribution)
(i)	Competition gain ground through technology development	(Competition 2)

(j) Key: Competition 1 = Price war
         Competition 2 = Competitors building competitive advantage
         Distribution   = Market moving away from us
         Environment   = Reduced government spending

4.4 *Prioritising threats*

Likelihood of occurrence

	High	Low
Seriousness of threat High	Market moving away from us Reduced government spending Competitors building advantage	
Seriousness of threat Low		Price war

MISTRAL: COMPETITIVE ENVIRONMENT

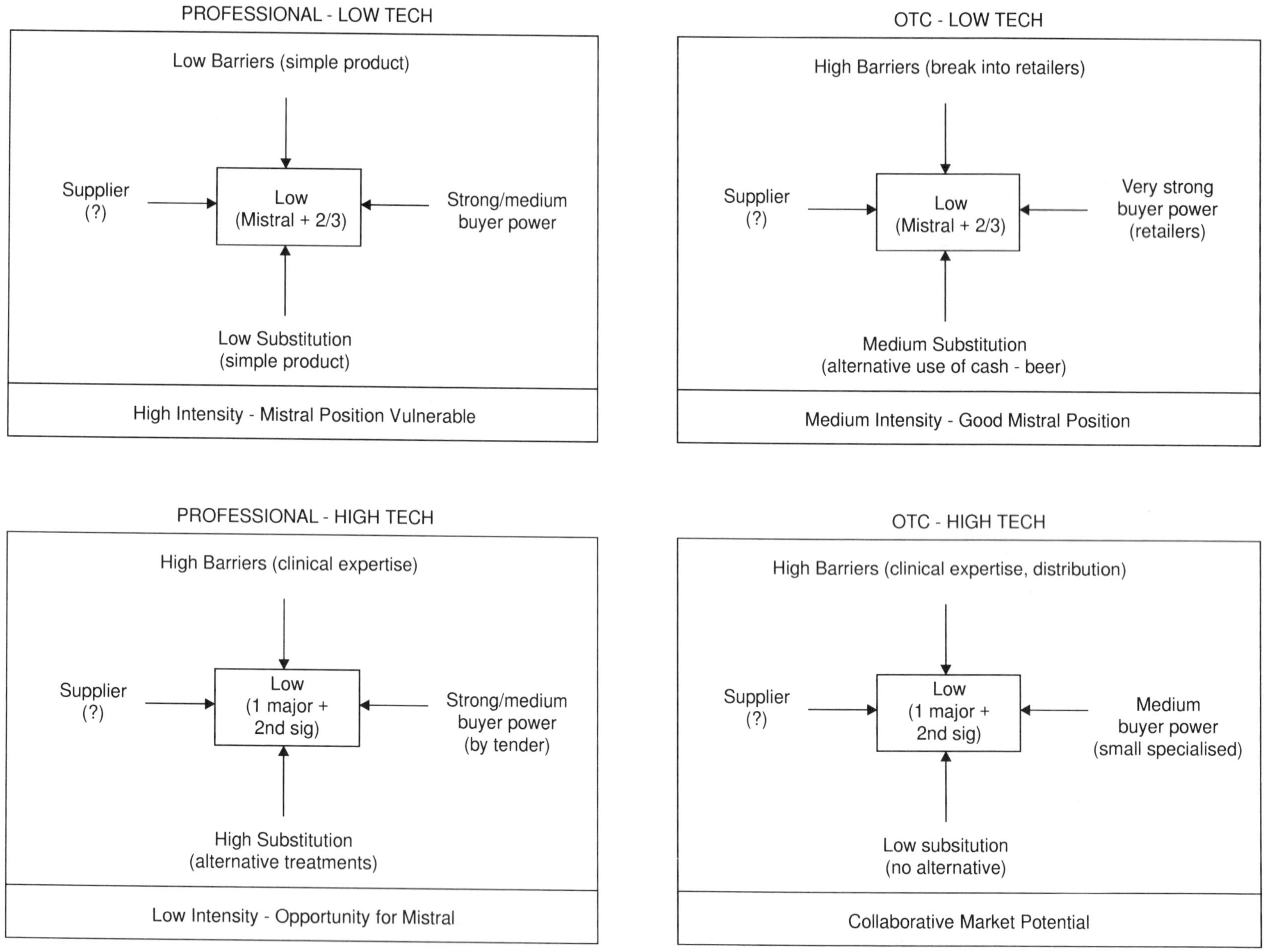

PROFESSIONAL - LOW TECH

Low Barriers (simple product) →
Supplier (?) ↑
Strong/medium buyer power ↓
Low Substitution (simple product) ←

Centre: Low (Mistral + 2/3)

High Intensity - Mistral Position Vulnerable

OTC - LOW TECH

High Barriers (break into retailers) →
Supplier (?) ↑
Very strong buyer power (retailers) ↓
Medium Substitution (alternative use of cash - beer) ←

Centre: Low (Mistral + 2/3)

Medium Intensity - Good Mistral Position

PROFESSIONAL - HIGH TECH

High Barriers (clinical expertise) →
Supplier (?) ↑
Strong/medium buyer power (by tender) ↓
High Substitution (alternative treatments) ←

Centre: Low (1 major + 2nd sig)

Low Intensity - Opportunity for Mistral

OTC - HIGH TECH

High Barriers (clinical expertise, distribution) →
Supplier (?) ↑
Medium buyer power (small specialised) ↓
Low substitution (no alternative) ←

Centre: Low (1 major + 2nd sig)

Collaborative Market Potential

OTC = Over the counter

Competitive stance

4.5 *Competitive strategies*

Strategic position

	Cost leader	Differentiate
Narrow	BDG	Brunhoff
Broad	MTM Samuel	Mistral

Competitiveness

4.6 *Competitive positioning*

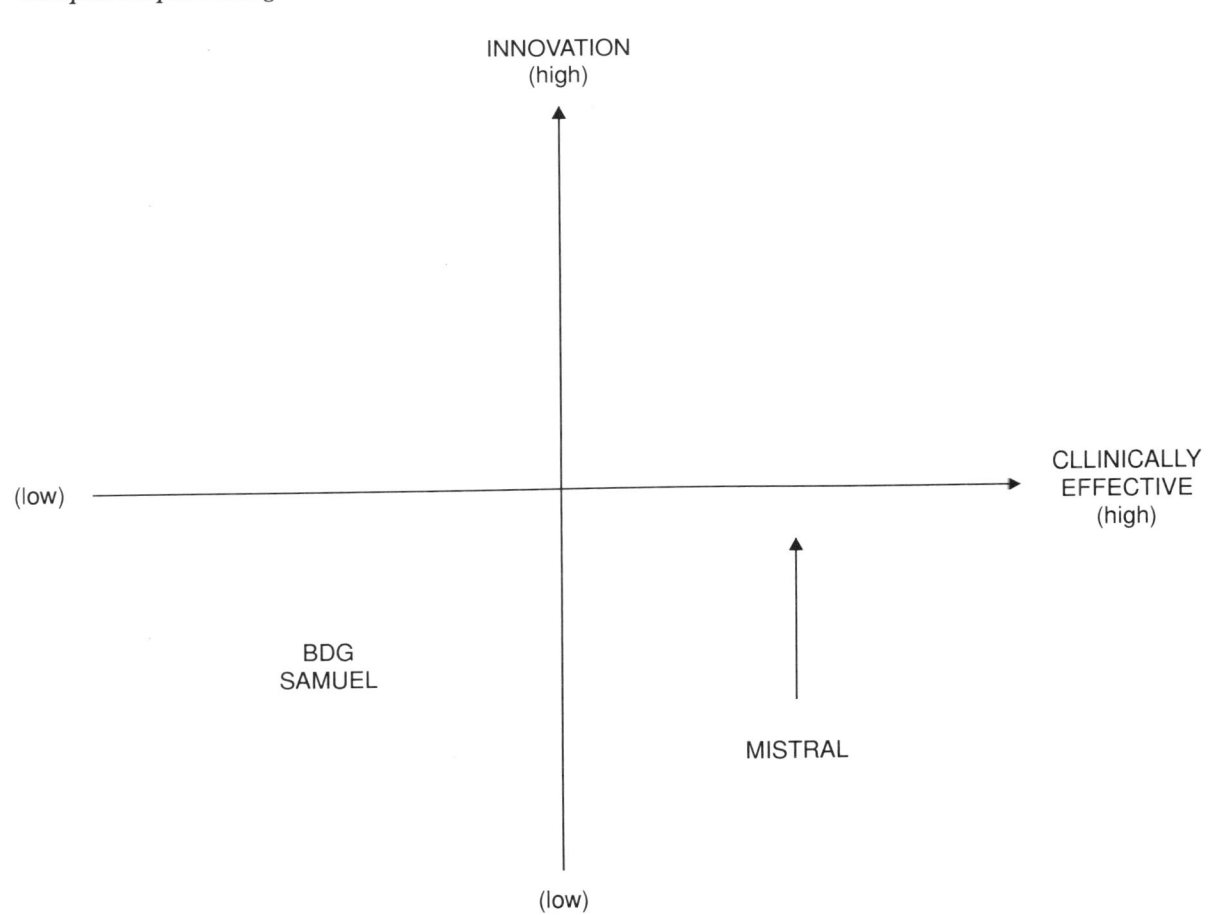

```
                    INNOVATION
                      (high)
                        |
                        |
(low) ------------------+------------------> CLINICALLY
                        |                    EFFECTIVE
                        |                     (high)
                        |
      BDG               |
      SAMUEL            |        ↑
                        |      MISTRAL
                      (low)
```

Part E: Learning from experience: ensuring you pass

4.7 Customer buying behaviour (continued on next page)

External audit: Customer buying behaviour profile

Factor	Hospital (43% sales by value)	Current Non-hospital (57% sales by value)	Research needs
What is bought	1. Traditional adhesives £10 million in 1996 2. Others: less than £5 million combined	1. Traditional adhesives £11 million 2. Compression bandages £4 million 3. Others: £2 million 4. Low allergy: none	1. Hospitals: Private, Government, location. Broken down by product, size, trend (ie product growth or decline). 2. Sales: private, Government, location. Broken down by product size. 3. Audit of financial figures provided because of discrepancies, including exchange rates used.
When is it bought?	Don't know	Don't know	Quantity, frequency
Where is it bought?	Type of hospital: 1 UK: 50% 2 France 20% 3 Italy: 20% (Holland, Belgium, Denmark: total of 10% for all three of sales advised	Don't know UK 30% France: 20% Italy: 45% Holland Belgium Denmark (Holland, Belgium, Denmark: total of 10%)	1 Purchasing council in each country for hospitals? 2 Who are the wholesalers? 3 Are they the same for Mistral's other products, distribution lines? 4 Need figures for other European sales (ie Spain, Ireland, Greece where we manufacture).
How is it bought?	Established products: by tender Non-established products: don't know	Don't know	• Non-established products: how are the influences from symposiums turned into sales? • Need to confirm DMU for hospitals • Non-hospitals: buying behaviour, where do they buy from, how often, influences, details of DMU • Effect of price on behaviour (price elasticity) • Role of pricing in customer perception of quality and building brand value

External audit: customer buying behaviour profile continued

Factor	Hospital (43% sales by value)	Non-hospital (57% sales by value)	Research needs
Buyers	Purchasing manager(?) DMU: 1 Influencers: patients, visitors, other patients, physiotherapist 2 Users: doctors, nurses, physiotherapist 3 Decider: Clinical Director 4 Approver: Hospital Manager 5 Gatekeeper: Government	Don't know Possibilities: 1 Pharmacies 2 Sports clinics 3 Physiotherapist 4 Nursing homes 5 Vets(?)	Confirmation of hospital DMU Composition of DMU of non-hospital
Why do they buy from us?	Because we meet their purchase criteria: 1 Approved list 2 Clinical effectiveness 3 Good reputation 4 Reliability 5 Durability 6 Impact on nursing time 7 Type of waste generated 8 Cost effectiveness 9 Quality	Assumptions: 1 Reputation 2 Quality 3 Effective distribution channels 4 Price/value relationship 5 Terms of trade	Research into actual buying criteria of non hospitals Rating of factors listed for different hospitals/non-hospital outlets
Intermediaries	Buy direct from Mistral: non intermediaries	Wholesalers Retailers	Non-hospitals: need to confirmation of non-hospital intermediaries and their criteria (value chain analysis)

Part E: Learning from experience: ensuring you pass

4.8 Future customer buying behaviour

Future customer buying behaviour

Factor	Hospital	Non-hospital	Research needs
What is driving change?	1. Political: privatised, non privatised, funding 2. Economic: costs of health care and ability to fund will reflect demographic changes, EC funding to poorer areas of community 3. Social: ageing but fitter population, life expectance increase, changing family structure, consumer choice, home/community care, change is family structure growth in nursing home care increase in leisure time. 4. Technological: change in manufacturing process, accident prevention methods (airbags, changing nature of injuries		1. Need to have analysis on different drivers by country, how they differ by country, region 2. Potential EU legislation 3. Impact of Maastricht requirement to meet monetary union on health care funding. 4. Changing governments
Were is it bought?	Move towards privatisation More price sensitive Ownership of private hospitals	Move towards direct purchase by end consumer: • pharmacies • supermarkets • sports retailers • note: supermarket v pharmacy battle • sports clubs, physiotherapists etc	• Decision making criteria that the end purchaser will use • Does branding make a difference? • Order by brand name • Who are our potential end consumer buyers? • What are their needs? • Buying behaviour
Buyers	Purchasing manager more important Changing DMU - increasing consumer power	As above	Identify new hospital DMU Composition of DMU of non-hospital - as above
Why will they buy from us?	Increasing cost sensitivity. Other criteria still valid • Approved list • Clinical effectiveness • Good reputation • Reliability • Durability • Impact on nursing time • Type of waste generated • Cost effectiveness • Quality	Assumptions: Meets needs Reputation Quality Effective distribution channels Price/value relationship Terms of trade	Research into future buying criteria of non-hospitals Rating of factors listed for different hospitals/non hospital outlets

Marketing mix

4.9 Product

Importance to customers	Strengths	Weaknesses
High	• Clinical expertise • Wide range • Established products plus established brands • Market leader • Quality products	• Confusing? • Brands not known by consumers (MR) • Production cost lower (competitors)
Medium	• Packaging centralised? • High technology manufacturing	• Lack of innovation • Ageing product line • Lack of differentiation in market • Lack of 'complete solutions'
Low	• NPD operation is centralised	• Inconsistency of portfolio by country

4.10 Place

Importance to customers	Strengths	Weaknesses
High	Managed locally (in tune with culture)	
Medium	Supermarket opportunities - strength as market leader	Overdependence on hospital Complexity with wholesaler/retailer, salesforce.
Low	*Channels:* Hospital	*Non-hospital* Nursing homes Pharmacies Supermarkets Sports clinics Wholesalers Sports centres/health centres

Notes   **Part E: Learning from experience: ensuring you pass**

4.11 *Price*

Importance to customers

	Strengths	Weaknesses
High		• Competitors have potential to undercut on price
Medium	• Have price differential • (Holland's positive experience suggests...)	• Local pricing (inconsistent) • Parallel imports • ...Not exploiting market position
Low	• Different levels of profitability by product	• No research on price elasticity

4.12 *Promotion*

Importance to customers

	Strengths	Weaknesses
High	• Local - so understands cultural needs	• Ad hoc • No strategic framework • Uncoordinated

Medium	• Pockets of creativity
	   - Nurses conventions
	   - Experts
	• Growth of international conferences
		• Reliant on country managers (varied)
		• No cohesive investment by country
		• Lack of targeting

Low	• Brochures feature bandages alongside other products (cross-sell)	• Lack of communication between country managers

5 MARKETING AUDIT 2

5.1 A vital component of the marketing plan is to first establish the situation which Mistral UK Ltd currently faces. In order to accomplish this, a macro and micro environmental analysis has been conducted, complemented with an internal audit of Mistral UK's strengths and weaknesses, and an external outlook of potential opportunities and threats which may emanate within the five year period (a full 'SWOT' analysis offers a detailed examination and should be referred to in Appendix A). The section concludes by identifying the attributes of the present marketing mix to determine the company's strategic position.

The marketing environment

5.2 To determine the nature of the environment in which Mistral UK Ltd compete, both an external and internal analysis have been completed. In summary, according to P Kotler (1988, p135):

> 'The company's marketing environment is made up of the sectors and forces outside the firm's marketing function which infringe upon the ability of marketing management to develop and maintain a successful relationship with the firm's target group.'

Therefore, a full examination has been made in order to determine how best Mistral can move forward in the forthcoming years.

Macro-environment

5.3 The macro-environment investigation in this section considers the *uncontrollable* elements of the market which ultimately impinge on any strategic marketing planning provided for Mistral UK Ltd. The company recognises that many of its European subsidiaries are reactive in their approach, and therefore the conducting of a SLEPT (Social, Legal, Economic, Political and Legal) analysis will enable a more proactive approach to be taken by the organisation in the future.

Social factors

5.4 (a) The population is ageing, placing increased pressure on healthcare provision and its costs.

(b) Birth rates are continuing to fall, and families are getting smaller as there is lower infant mortality. Parents are increasingly better educated and recognise the economic burden of large families.

(c) Generally, the vast majority of the population are leading healthier lifestyles, and life expectancy is continually rising.

Economic factors

5.5 (a) There are increased financial pressures on NHS and state pension provisions due to the ageing population.

(b) The cost of health care has been predicted to escalate in the future, due to two main causes: *shifting demographics* and *advancing technology*. Technological developments in medicine have a direct effect on the cost of health care. new and improved treatments have been discovered which keep people alive longer. There are also indirect effects of technology which cause the cost of health care to rise whereby technology may save lives.

(c) Currently, approximately 40% - 50% of the UK population are supporting the 30% of the population who are over the age of 65. However, this situation will be reversed within the next few years creating greater pressure on the work-force to provide care for the elderly. In Japan, the pressures on the economically active are even worse: 20% of the population will support 60% - 70%. Ultimately, healthcare is rapidly becoming market-orientated.

Political

5.6 (a) Euromonitor (1996) indicates that many governments throughout the developed world are cutting healthcare budgets by enforcing higher priced prescription charges.

(b) The government is encouraging private and occupational pensions due to increasing pressures on state pensions, created by an ageing population in the UK and throughout of much of Europe.

(c) The NHS has become more market orientated, and patients in the UK, and in many European markets, now have to pay for some treatments. In Germany, an increase in the payroll tax has been enforced to pay for nursing-home care.

(d) In Greece, Spain and Portugal access to OTC (over the counter) products has been restricted by law until the mid 1990s according to Euromonitor (1996), and is thus predicted to increase throughout the latter part of the decade.

Technical

5.7 (a) Technological developments in medicine and lifesaving equipment/machines are escalating costs in health care products.

(b) Competitive advantage may be obtained via innovation, and leverage of clinical expertise across product ranges: many items in the bandages segment are well established, but outdated.

Micro-environment

5.8 Unlike the macro-environment analysis provided above, the micro-environmental examination undertaken below identifies the elements of the market which Mistral UK Ltd have greater control over. This analysis has been accomplished through the application of Porter's (1985) Five Forces Model.

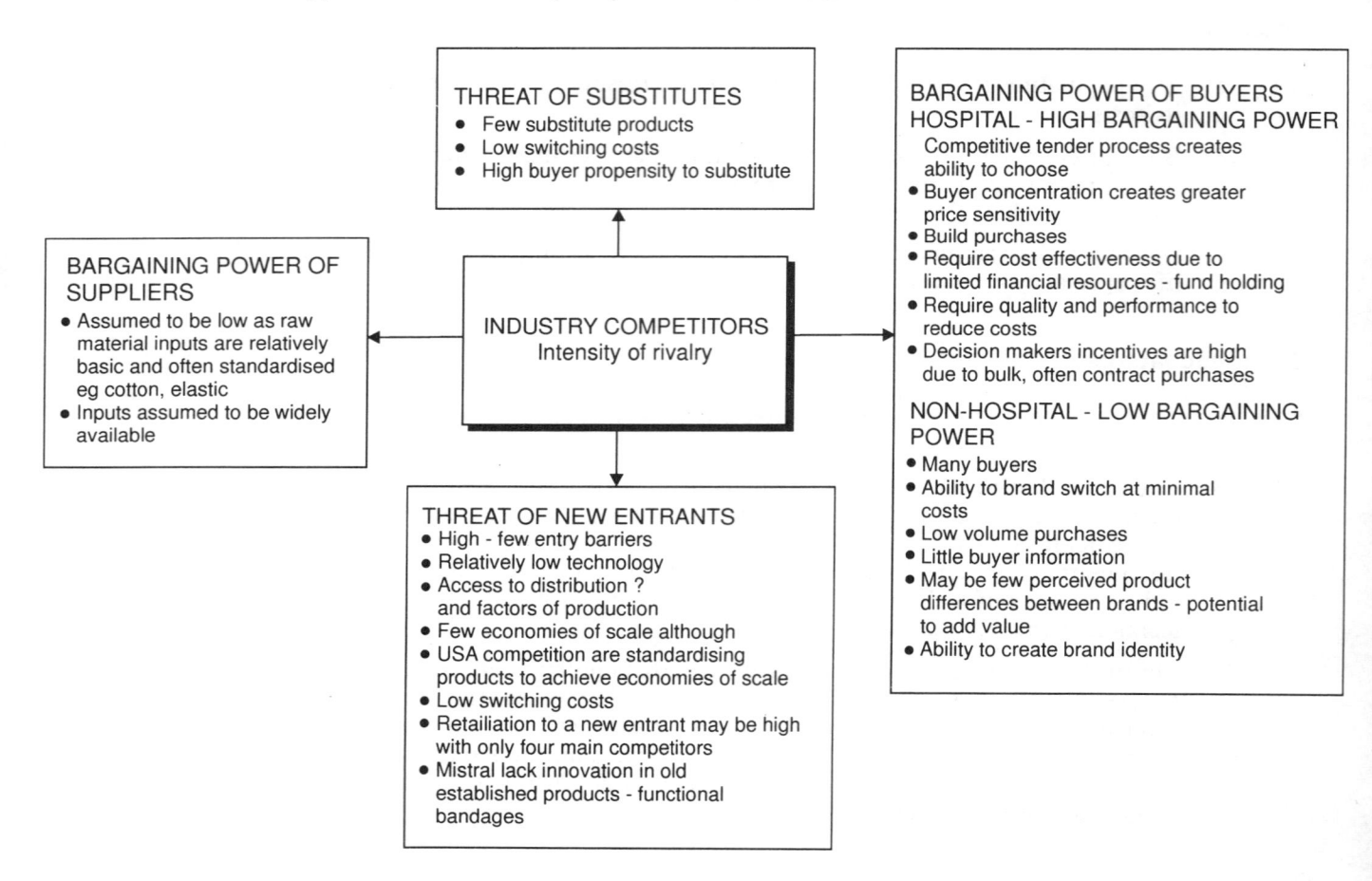

THREAT OF SUBSTITUTES
- Few substitute products
- Low switching costs
- High buyer propensity to substitute

BARGAINING POWER OF BUYERS
HOSPITAL - HIGH BARGAINING POWER
- Competitive tender process creates ability to choose
- Buyer concentration creates greater price sensitivity
- Build purchases
- Require cost effectiveness due to limited financial resources - fund holding
- Require quality and performance to reduce costs
- Decision makers incentives are high due to bulk, often contract purchases

NON-HOSPITAL - LOW BARGAINING POWER
- Many buyers
- Ability to brand switch at minimal costs
- Low volume purchases
- Little buyer information
- May be few perceived product differences between brands - potential to add value
- Ability to create brand identity

BARGAINING POWER OF SUPPLIERS
- Assumed to be low as raw material inputs are relatively basic and often standardised eg cotton, elastic
- Inputs assumed to be widely available

INDUSTRY COMPETITORS
Intensity of rivalry

THREAT OF NEW ENTRANTS
- High - few entry barriers
- Relatively low technology
- Access to distribution ? and factors of production
- Few economies of scale although
- USA competition are standardising products to achieve economies of scale
- Low switching costs
- Retailiation to a new entrant may be high with only four main competitors
- Mistral lack innovation in old established products - functional bandages

The marketplace

5.9 (a) The total market value for the bandages market was valued at £109,732,000 in 1996.

(b) Euromonitor (1996, p 171) suggests that in the non-hospital sector:

'The over-the counter healthcare market in Europe has proved to be one of the strongest growing areas in the consumer economy during recent years, and it is still for further expansion in the later 1990's - the result not just of rising consumer spending power, but also of growing pressure on governments to limit the amount of drugs spending on the part of the state.'

(c) Euromonitor (1996) also reveals that competitive pressures are forcing down prices, whilst there appears to be a problem of '*imminent expiration of many patents on keynote products*' as new entrants begin to offer alternative brands.

(d) In many European countries, old-style pharmacists' shops are protected as OTC products cannot be sold in supermarkets. (Euromonitor (1996)).

(e) German, Swiss and Benelux consumers are deemed to offer the highest expenditure per capita on healthcare products purchased in the non-hospital sector, with strong growth occurring in each of these markets as indicated by Euromonitor (1996).

(f) Euromonitor (1996 p 171) predicts that in the medium term:

'the fastest value growth in the late 1990s will be in Italy and in the Netherlands, which already has the heaviest per capita spending on healthcare in Europe. It will also be strong in Sweden, where economic necessity is forcing the government to point customers toward OTC products instead of prescription goods.'

Customers

5.10 (a) There is increased demand for an improved quality of health care, and so manufacturers such as Mistral are attempting to get closer to the customer by offering total package solutions.

(b) Growing market segment: health care products for the *elderly*.

(c) There has been a shift away from hospitals to care at home which creates greater bargaining power for the consumer who is able to switch brands relatively easily. The 1990s has become the decade of 'consumer choice' as patients have more say in how they are treated and what products are used. Thus, more healthcare supplies will be purchased at pharmacies and during supermarket visits, which will have a direct effect on the activities of the sales force.

(d) Products are now evaluated by buyers on the basis of cost effectiveness as opposed just to price, and include variants such as material used, wastage generated, durability etc. In Europe, however, there is a tendency for consumers to 'stick to what they know' and this may offer a source of loyalty in the future.

Competition

5.11 (a) The competition consists of mainly international conglomerates with interests in disposable medical items.

(b) Competition varies between different countries and markets, as Table 1.5 in Appendix C illustrates.

(c) There are four major players in the bandages market. The two German competitors are *MTM AG* and *Brunhoff AG*. The two American competitors are *Samuel Inc* and *BDG*.

(d) Increased competition is moving into the hospital sector across many product lines as the tendering process diminishes entry barriers.

(e) There has also been an emergence of credible competitors to the adhesive bandages sector which occurred in 1994.

Part E: Learning from experience: ensuring you pass

Suppliers

5.12 (a) Information is not available regarding the suppliers of inputs to the production process. It is assumed that there are many suppliers of the basic raw materials which may include for example, cotton, elastic and plastic wrapping supplied for hygiene.

(b) It is assumed all suppliers must offer high levels of quality in the material they supply if Mistral are to utilise them in their product offering to command premium prices. Similarly, many customers are known to assess quality standards during the selection process.

External environment summary

5.13 The environment analyses identify the uncontrollable, wider market forces impinging on current company activity. Therefore it is important to remember that these factors are subject to change, radical or otherwise, at any time. Subsequently throughout the implementation process of the marketing plan, it is advised that marketing management should seek continually to monitor, anticipate, and evaluate the impact of these forces impinging upon the business. This may ultimately affect the nature of the plan if the company is to be successful in accomplishing its objectives, whilst becoming proactive rather than reactive to market changes. As Wilson et al (1992, p 188) suggest:

> ' Marketing strategy is concerned with matching the capabilities of the organisation with the demands of the environment. There is therefore a need for the strategist to monitor the environment on an ongoing basis so that opportunities and threats facing the organisation are identified and subsequently reflected in the strategy.'

(a) *Opportunities*

Key opportunities for Mistral UK to exploit in the bandages market are these.

(i) Product innovation and clinical expertise combined with leveraging resources available in the dressing segment to outpace the competitors.

(ii) Expansion into the non-hospital market through new market development eg vets, sports clinics, Red Cross.

(iii) Add value to the Venus and Vulcan ranges by offering complete solutions.

(iv) Build a brand identity with which both hospital and non-hospital customers can associate.

(v) New product/packaging developments (functionality). Hospitals demand waste-limitation, quality and durability, whilst non-hospital customers demand products which offer quality, value for money and can be displayed easily. Incidentally, the end-user may require more detailed information regarding product usage, and this may be incorporated at the point of sale (POS) or distributed at the point of treatment within the hospital to initiate a relationship with the end-user.

(vi) The shift away from hospital to care at home provides increased opportunities for advertising and promotion techniques which target the end-user. Product/patient information may be a means of developing a relationship with the brand.

(vii) Expand into new geographic areas such as Greece and Spain where production facilities exist and there continues to be relaxation in legislation which is creating growth in the non-hospital OTC sector.

(b) *Threats*

Potential threats to Mistral presently include the following.

(i) Credible, potentially powerful competitors in an oligopolistic market situation who may create price wars through product standardisation.

(ii) The emergence of low cost/low quality products which may hinder the premium price positioning Mistral UK Ltd wish to establish, particularly if innovation is insufficient to command the price differential.

(iii) Escalating health costs with an ageing population, declining birth rate, and fewer working citizens. Cost effectiveness is vital, predominantly in the hospital sector, whilst end-users in the non-hospital sector are becoming increasingly price sensitive.

(iv) Fewer barriers to entry into the hospital sector as price becomes increasingly important.

(v) European customers who are reluctant to purchase new products.

Internal environment

5.14 The internal environment is composed of many constituents. Those which have been considered here include organisational operations, the internal strengths and weaknesses, and marketing activities which have been identified through each of the four elements of the marketing mix.

Organisational operations

5.15 [The present organisational chart is illustrated in Figure 1.0 of Appendix E.] Operational issues to be aware of currently include the following.

(a) Each European company is an independent profit centre, reporting to the managing director of Mistral UK Ltd.

(b) All strategic matters concerning medical disposables are managed from the UK.

(c) Each European company manages their own tactical marketing issues such as pricing, distribution and promotion on a local level, whereas packaging is controlled centrally.

(d) Duplication of effort exists in the structure of the organisation with managing Directors and Marketing Managers existing in each country. Internal conflict exists between the European subsidiaries and the UK headquarters as managers in Europe tend to be reactive rather than proactive.

(e) There has been an absence of strategic planning for the bandages segment both in the UK and throughout Europe. Incidentally, there is a lack of local market information as well as marketing management experience.

(f) Relationships are sensitive between marketing managers based in the UK and production facilities based outside, creating tensions when proposing new product developments.

(g) Mistral UK Ltd are situated in modern offices suggesting adequate resources and a pleasant working environment as well as projecting a professional image.

(h) Technically, there is a lack of innovation in the old established lines (bandages market), although new product development is extensive in the dressings segment.

(i) Continental Europe are currently satisfied to tender on the basis of the existing product range (which tends to have more old products than the UK) whereas the UK are keen to progress. This has caused tensions.

(j) The current strategic issues for Mistral as these.
   (i) Product development.
   (ii) Marketing planning for the European markets.
   (iii) Monitoring of sales and profits.

Strengths

5.16 Internally Mistral possess the following strengths.

(a) Mistral UK have the largest market share in the bandages market.

(b) In the dressings market, Mistral have developed plenty of new products through innovation and have successfully become close to the customer.

(c) Mistral are a well-established company with a strong reputation and brand name.

(d) Centralised guidelines for promotional activity have enabled an international brand to be established.

(e) Value has been successfully added in some markets through providing complementary products which ultimately give a complete solution.

Weaknesses

5.17 (a) Friction exists between the UK and the European subsidiaries.

(b) Mistral rely on market share and reputation in the bandages market. The company still sell the old Beaufort products, indicating that they may have encountered difficulties in establishing their own brand.

(c) European subsidiaries are reactive rather than proactive to market conditions.

(d) Lack of product innovation in the old established lines.

(e) Little customer research has been conducted in both the hospital and non-hospital sector. Subsequently, the company are unable to clearly define, and subsequently fulfil, customer requirements optimally.

(f) Net profit has fallen in the support bandages market from 17% to 15% during 1995 in the support bandages market.

(g) Victrix retention and fixation bandages are difficult to add value to due to increasing competition.

Market activities

5.18 Mistral UK Ltd and all the continental subsidiaries of Mistral Inc, operating in the principal area of medical disposables. The product ranges include the following.

(a) Antiseptic wipes
(b) Bandages
(c) Castings
(d) Catheters
(e) Dressings
(f) Gloves
(g) Splints
(h) Surgical instruments
(i) Swabs
(j) Syringes
(k) Thermometers

Product ranges

5.19 There are basically four product categories in which Mistral UK Ltd compete.

(a) Retention and fixation
(b) Support - cohesive and non-adhesive support bandages
(c) Compression
(d) Tapes - tapes, functional tape accessories

Brand portfolio

5.20 There are four main brands of bandage.

(a) *Victrix* — *Retention and fixation*. Range comprises two main retention bandage types, four varieties of tape ranging from traditional zinc oxide to hypoallergenic, and a further four bandage/dressing retention types.

(b) *Felix* — *Light support (crepe) bandages*. Consists of seven varieties of product ranging from tubular bandages to support bandages which offer superior performance over traditional crepe products.

(c) *Venus* — *Strong support*. Three different bandage types available ranging from tubular to cotton/rayon bandages, complemented by the availability of a hypoallergenic tape to maintain strong support.

(d) *Vulcan* *Compression bandages.* The range provides six bandage types offering light through to high compression, as well as graduated compression for post-operative application.

Price

5.21 (a) From the information given it appears that Mistral bandages are subject to regional disparities in prices due to local pricing.

(b) Italy displays relatively low average selling prices in all product categories, and in both the hospital and non-hospital sectors with little price variation between the two.

(c) In all other countries stated, the cost of private, non-hospital care appears to be relatively higher.

(d) The average selling prices provided by Mistral UK would suggest that products in the non-hospital market are more likely to obtain a premium price as consumers appear to be spending more. However, USA-based competitors, Samuel Inc and BDG Inc have gained competitive advantage by following a generic low-cost strategy.

(e) Therefore, Mistral should seek to add value through differentiation in comparison to competitors' product offerings, if they are to command premium prices and a quality image.

(f) Due to the lack of local market knowledge and competitor intelligence, more information is required.

Place

5.22 (a) Little information is given as to how Mistral UK distributes products. It is assumed that bandages are distributed directly to both hospital and non-hospital clientele. However, it may be possible that wholesalers are channel members of the non-hospital distribution chain in supplying smaller supermarket and pharmacy retail chains with bandages.

(b) Production facilities exist in Dublin, Athens and Madrid and would appear from the organisation's structure to be distributed via the sales manager.

(c) Distribution of products to the hospital sector adopts a 'push' strategy through personal selling, whilst distribution to the non-hospital sector is via a 'pull' strategy with customers required to purchase the product over the counter (OTC).

Promotion

5.23 (a) Local marketing management and line managers are responsible for implementing marketing communications and building brand values.

(b) Advertising and trade press advertisements are commonly used with occasional television advertising. Local nurses conventions using clinical experts to promote Mistral products have proved successful and should be incorporated throughout Europe where appropriate.

(c) Variations exist between European countries.

(d) Local responsiveness has been successful in understanding local issues, however, the disparities in the level of communication between nations needs to be resolved.

(e) There is a lack of competitor knowledge or evaluation of existing promotional methods.

Part E: Learning from experience: ensuring you pass

Comments on marketing audits 1 and 2

5.24 In appraising the above two marketing audits we need to bear in mind that whilst an audit should deal in *fact* it should also be judgmental. For example: marketing research conducted? Is it adequate? It is also reasonable and legitimate to use general knowledge, particularly in macroenvironmental analysis (PEST).

5.25 *Marketing Audit 1* is somewhat incomplete but contains some good work, particularly in its use of models. Note the use of Porter in analysing the competitive environment and the use of SWOT in auditing the marketing mix. Also innovative is the combining of research needs with the customer buying behaviour audit.

5.26 *Marketing Audit 2* is in the form of a situational analysis by a syndicate comprising Angela Beeston, Michael Bignell, Jon French, Martyn Hilton, Claire Newton and Kelly Rodgers. It is very thorough and comprehensive would you not agree?

6 SWOT ANALYSES

6.1

CONSULT THE GUIDANCE NOTES IN CHAPTER 8 PARAGRAPHS 3.9 TO 3.13
STEP 7 DO A SWOT ANALYSIS
ALLOW BETWEEN 2 AND 3 HOURS FOR THIS STEP

6.2 Look now at the three SWOT analyses conducted by students/syndicates which follow and see how these compare with yours. All three SWOT analyses have their good and not so good points.

(a) *SWOT analysis 1* is a straightforward listing, without any categorisation, purportedly limited to the key items but without any scores and degrees of importance to facilitate prioritisation.

(b) *SWOT analysis 2* by a Singaporean syndicate again contains a limited number of uncategorised items in no priority order. This SWOT attempts to match SWs against OTs to develop extra categories (SO, OW, ST, WT) but such elaboration can result in confusion rather than increased clarity, don't you think?

(c) *SWOT analysis 3* by Angela Beeston, Michael Bignell, Jon French, Martyn Hilton, Claire Newton and Kelly Rodgers - is extremely detailed and comprises six separate SWOTS under the categorisations of the company, sales organisation, product range, geographical sales areas, market segments and competition. You may, however, ask yourself, why *these* six in particular and whether it isn't better to identify strengths and weaknesses first and *then* categorise them - see Guidance Notes.

SWOT analysis 1

6.3

Strengths	Weaknesses
• High market share in bandage industry • Good reputation • Well established company • Profitable organisation • Wide range of bandages brands • Quality products	• Lack of coordination and integrated strategic marketing effort across Europe • Reactive approach by marketing managers • Organisation structure is not aligned to implement strategic marketing • Friction exists between HQ(UK) and European subsidiaries • Lack of product innovation • Poor distribution to non-hospital outlets
Opportunities	**Threats**
• Ageing population trend in the UK and Europe gives us an opportunity to sell more bandages products • The shift from hospital to home care provides an opportunity to build the non hospital market segment • The direct effect of technology on medicine to prolong life provides an opportunity for Mistral to sell more bandages • The growing popularity of sports provides Mistral with additional opportunities to tap this market segment • More sports clinics and physiotherapists using strong support bandages as part of their treatment provide Mistral an opportunity to sell strong support bandages to this market segment	• Competitors moving into our product lines pose a threat to Mistral • Major competitors like BDG and Samuel are exerts in manufacturing and are able to drive the price low through standardising products to achieve economies of scale in production • The emergence of low cost/low quality bandage competitors • The emergence of parallel importing due to low entry barriers in this industry • The technology is changing the bandages market rapidly and if Mistral cannot cope with this change it will lose out

Part E: Learning from experience: ensuring you pass

SWOT analysis 2

6.4

	Strengths	Weaknesses
	S1 High market share in bandages S2 Technology expertise S3 Offer competitively priced bandages S4 Quality products S5 Strong distribution coverage in hospitals market	W1 Lack of product innovation W2 Lack of co-ordination and integrated strategic marketing effort across Europe W3 Fragmented branding approach W4 Weak in distribution to non-hospitals such as pharmacies, super-markets etc
Opportunities	**SO**	**OW**
O1 BDG and Samuel are in danger of losing market leadership positions due to lack of product innovation O2 Shift from hospital from home care provides an opportunity for Mistral to build non-hospital segment O3 Growing popularity of sports - Mistral may tap this segment O4 More sports clinics and physiotherapists using strong support bandages	S2,O1 Enter support bandage market with product innovation S2, S4, O2, O3,O4 To establish our reputation in non-hospital market	W4, O2, O4 To place more emphasis on the non-hospital market
Threats	**ST**	**WT**
T1 Rising cost of healthcare in Europe T2 Emergence of low cost/low quality bandage competitors	S1, S4, T2 To differentiate our products S3, T1 Charge a competitive price to maintain market share	W2, T2 Develop integrated marketing effort between UK and Europe to provide consistency in image among competitors

SWOT analysis 3

6.5 (a) Mistral UK Ltd: the company

Strengths	Weaknesses
• Mistral UK Ltd is a wholly owned subsidiary and operating division of Mistral Inc - a multinational healthcare company with headquarters in Milwaukee, Wisconsin, USA • Established reputable company formed out of an acquisition in 1982 of the British based Beaufort, founded in 1878. • Further acquisitions throughout the globe during the past decade have provided market entry and geographic coverage of local markets in Europe. • Acquisitions have subsequently enabled 'state of the art' technological expertise to be acquired • Modern offices at headquarters • Recent rationalisation has enabled Mistral UK Ltd and the European subsidiaries of Mistral Inc to focus activity in eleven medical disposable ranges from antiseptic wipes to thermometers • Central control of all strategic matters concerning medical disposable including marketing, product development, and monitoring of sales and profits in the UK	• Delicate relationships with marketing and managers in each of European subsidiaries production managers in Dublin, Athens and Madrid because product development, and marketing planning are conducted in the UK and thus requires the cooperation and implementation by the subsidiaries. • European marketing managers are reactive rather than proactive, implying that subsidiaries are followers of the competition rather than market leaders • European subsidiaries find head office involvement in their local market invasive, unnecessary and often misguided • Marketing management currently appear to have no formal strategic planning procedures which would suggest minimal direction In the bandages market, combined with new management of the division becoming acquainted with the markets and product offerings • Duplication of top management and Mistral marketing management in each country UK operates in • European companies manage tactical marketing issues, but are deemed to be reactive as opposed to proactive, thus making the company slow to respond to sector demands in European markets. • Lack of up-to-date and accurate market data
Opportunities	**Threats**
• Opportunity for European subsidiaries to have more local autonomy, and therefore aim to become more locally responsive to consumer demands • Mistral UK Ltd want to get close to their customers, and therefore wish to undertake marketing activities at the regional company level • Introduce a marketing information system to encourage accurate data records	• American companies BDG Inc and Samuel Inc offer low-cost alternative bandages • Italy has low average selling prices, which may pose a threat to Mistral's premium product image

(b) SWOT analysis: sales organisation

Strengths	Weaknesses
• Hospital sales are made by tender - currently little effort to sell the products. Same clinical expertise and knowledge is required to sell to both the hospital sector, and pharmacies in the non hospital sector, enabling Mistral to leverage existing practices • The Vulcan compression bandage was developed by customers at Charing Cross Hospital - this shows ability of company to share knowledge with customers and work as a team	• Conflict between European subsidiaries who are content to sell the existing product ranges whilst the UK marketing staff are keen to innovate and update in order to achieve progress • European salesforce are looking for an easy sale - content with established, existing products to be sold through traditional distribution channels • Salesforce are reluctant to become involved with new innovative products, as they rely on established lines which tend to sell themselves
Opportunities	**Threats**
• Establish a relationship with customers in the hospital sector • Form close relationships with customers through distribution channels to work together with buyers in developing products, and addressing customer requirements • Strength of DMU (decision making unit) in both market sectors - '1990s decade of consumer choice' • 'Mega-trend' is the shift away from hospitals in favour of care at home. Consequently, patients have much greater decision making power in how they are treated and with which products, therefore brand image and positioning will be critical • Potential to target channels of distribution as more healthcare supplies are purchased OTC (over the counter) • Retain salesforce, or recruit a separate division to serve the non-hospital sector • New recruits may be more amenable to product development and innovation • Sales force need to target multiple distributors such as wholesalers, pharmacy chains and supermarkets which require different sales techniques than the 'one-off' hospital tenders	• Pressure to increase the effectiveness of salesforce as the buying process becomes more sophisticated in 'pushing' bandages into stock, 'pulling' through sales at the end-user level • Products are evaluated by buyers on basis of cost effectiveness as opposed to just price • Barriers to entry in the hospital sector are low as competitors with a credible product offering can often undercut on price in the tendering process - eg oligopolistic competition by four major players may create price wars, discouraging innovation at Mistral UK Ltd • Availability of low cost alternative which incur very few switching costs in both hospital and non-hospital sectors

(c) SWOT analysis: product range

Strengths	Weaknesses
• Established brands - some more than sixty years old and are renowned in the market • Some of Mistral's bandaging brands have as high a market share as 60% in some countries and date back to 1920s • Some bandages such as Vulcan compression bandages are considered more technical and considered to be an important part of treatment • In the 'dressings' product segment new products are plentiful, and the company are very close to the customers in new product development and enhancement. These skills could be transferred to the bandages market	• Short term profit pressures delimit new product development, or progression of existing product lines • Continental Europe have more old products than the UK, creating stagnation and inertia in certain markets • Rely on market share and reputation in bandages market • Lack of product innovation, particularly in old-established, traditional product lines.
Opportunities	**Threats**

• To maintain the brand positioning and enhance it in the long-term
• Differentiate to achieve premium pricing
• Leverage expertise in dressings market, to introduce and develop bandages
• Factors which may provide opportunities for products according to some of the buyers' evaluation of bandages include:
  - material type
  - wastage generated
  - impact on nursing time
  - durability
  - reliability
• Communicate features and benefits of alternative products to encourage brand switching and establish a relationship through the brand with customers and end users
• Standardise low-tech bandages to reduce cost
	• Credible competitors are moving in on many product lines and have the ability to be more innovative and to offer updated products
	• Varying exchange rates in European markets
	• Overriding factor affecting DMUs is the containment of costs which will escalate in the future due to demographic trends eg ageing population with a lower proportion of population earning to pay for healthcare and technological advances to prolong lifespans
	• High customer loyalty, a purchaser are inclined to be conservative, especially if they find the product effective and satisfactory - consumers are reluctant to change
	• Competitive pressures continue to force down prices, whilst imminent expiration of many patents on key note products adds to the intensity

(d) SWOT analysis - geographical sales area

Strengths	Weaknesses
• Regional subsidiaries are responsible for promotion enabling Mistral to utilise the appropriate tools for a particular market eg television advertising may be utilised in Italy where the non-hospital sector is greater than the hospital sector and consumers may have greater choice in the products they purchase • Locally responsive as individual sales forces have autonomy for local promotional activity, pricing and customer service	• Difficult to withdraw product lines which headquarters deem to add no strategic value to the product portfolio, if it competes successfully, and earns moderate profits in the local market • Reliant on line manages in each of countries to build brand values - this has been 'hit or miss' in many European countries
Opportunities	**Threats**
• Involve sports injury experts and physiotherapists to become involved with the products, and their promotion by holding conventions which provide information, features and benefits of the products of the products supported by clinical experts • Hold 'tours' similar to those held in other countries to target geographic areas and particular market segments • Possibilities for international conferences in neighbouring European countries • In developing nations birth rates continue to rise to swell the population • Increasing elderly population in developed countries may increase the market size as the old tend to be more accident prone or require nursing care • Future OTC healthcare market in Europe proved to be one of the strongest growing areas in the consumer economy. Euromonitor (1996) indicates huge expansion in the later 1990s due to increased consumer spending power and the reluctance of governments to offer financial assistance in many countries • In the past many European countries according to Euromonitor (1996) have protected old style pharmacists' shops by barring the sale of OTC products in food retail outlets - this is currently diminishing, as larger retail groups consolidate their hold on consumers, and provides the opportunity to penetrate new channels of distribution • German, Swiss and Benelux employers are indicated to be the greatest spenders on healthcare with each offering strong growth markets (Euromonitor 1996). • Greece, Spain and Portugal are currently having non-hospital restrictions lifted and subsequently may offer potential new geographic markets • Euromonitor (1996) predicts Italy and the Netherlands to offer the heaviest per capita spending on healthcare in Europe in the latter part of the decade. Similarly, in Sweden economic necessity is forcing consumers into the non-hospital sector.	• The role of pricing in customer perception of quality and building brand value is not well understood • Parochialism amongst European countries may hinder the promotion of products • Local economic disparities • Declining birth rates, increasing elderly population fewer employed to pay for hospital treatment. Resulting escalating costs across many developed European markets.

21: Mistral: précis, marketing audit, SWOT

(e) SWOT analysis - market segments

Strengths	Weaknesses

• Mistral operate in two customer market segments
  - hospital
  - non-hospital
• Serve four broad product categories:
  - Retention and fixation bandages
  - Light support (crepe) bandages
  - Strong support bandages
  - Compression bandages
• Products range from relatively low-tech Victrix brand (retention and fixation) to high-tech Vulcan (compression) bandage range
• Vulcan range adds value by packaging complete solutions for medical conditions
	• Difficult to add value to Victrix bandages which are relatively low-tech, standardised products

Opportunities	**Threats**
• Venus (strong support) bandages have the ability to add value to the brand as they form an integral part of high profile sports injury treatment and prevention and again the opportunity to increase brand identity and image is available • As institutions like the NHS decline, people are becoming more amenable to paying for their treatment	• Increasing competition in retention and fixation bandages threatens Victrix range • Healthcare systems are undergoing radical change in many European countries

(f) SWOT analysis - competitors

Strengths	Weaknesses
• International conglomerates with medical disposal interests • Intense competition, four main competitors - two German competitors MTM AG and Brunhoff AG, and two American multinationals, Samuel Inc and BDG Inc • Competitors are global operations • BDG and Samuel have gained competitive advantage through great expertise in manufacturing enabling them to lower costs and reduce prices through standardisation of products to achieve economies of scale in production	• BDG and Samuel offer standardised products which may not address special application requirements because they are too basic • BDG and Samuel tend to be weak on innovation and clinical expertise
Opportunities	**Threats**
• Differentiate, and add value by offering products which are innovative and offer more than their basic purpose eg waterproofing self-cleaning, ventilation, flexibility, colour for the image conscious eg Felix and Venus support bandage ranges may be available in colours to match sports strips ie football, rugby, hockey, basketball, tennis, boxing. • Buyers evaluate products on cost effectiveness as opposed to just price • Low-cost alternatives tend to be basic in nature with few added features and benefits other than the main purpose they serve	• Competitors vary country by country • BDG Inc and Samuel Inc provide low-cost bandage alternatives

Part E: Learning from experience: ensuring you pass

6.6 So then, how did your SWOT compare? Ideally it should have been even better by containing indications of the relative importance of each item using the three point scale *high, medium, low,* as well as references and subcategorisation.

Chapter 22

MISTRAL: ANALYSES OF APPENDICES

> **This chapter covers the following topics.**
> 1 Your own analysis
> 2 Appendix analysis 1
> 3 Appendix analysis 2

1 YOUR OWN ANALYSIS

CONSULT THE GUIDANCE NOTES IN CHAPTER 8 PARAGRAPHS 3.14 TO 3.17
STEP 8 CONDUCT ANALYSES/CROSS ANALYSES OF APPENDICES
ALLOW ABOUT 2 TO 3 HOURS FOR THIS STEP

1.1 The next step is to analyse and cross analyse the appendices. Not all the data will be equally meaningful. Before conducting you analysis be sure to read Chapter 8 Paragraphs 3.14 to 3.17 and use the format provided. You will need a clear head and two or three hours to do a reasonable job.

1.2 Remember that the format suggested on Chapter 8 Paragraph 3.17 is a summary document. You will want to underpin this with working papers, perhaps containing graphs, pie-charts and financial analysis.

1.3 Now compare your summary sheets with those on the following pages. To what extent do they broadly agree? If they differ, you are as likely to be right as the syndicate that produced them. The point is to give the difference proper consideration before rejecting or accepting it.

(a) *Appendix analysis 1*, done by a syndicate, is not at all good in many respects. It is minimal and largely negative. There are very few cross references and it is mainly descriptive rather than analytical.

(b) *Appendix analysis 2* is more thorough and organised, would you not agree? It also tries much harder to relate each appendix to others and to the data in the text so as to develop potentially valuable extra insights. The syndicate members doing this analysis were likely to have a better understanding of the case than those doing Analysis 1 and thus be better equipped to handle the examination questions.

1.4 To help you refer back to the relevant appendix, the table below gives the paragraph number of each appendix in Chapter 20.

APPENDICES TO MISTRAL UK LTD: SIMON'S FILE CONTENTS

Ref	Subject matter	Chapter 20 Paragraphs
1	Organisation chart	3.1
2	'The world's most intractable problem' - article on demographics	3.2
3	Product portfolio	3.3
4	Mistral sales of bandages by country	3.4
5	Market estimates, total sales by country	3.5
6	Competitor sales by product sector	3.6
7	Average selling prices by selected product and country (£)	3.7
8	Market shares	3.8
9	Memo to Dirk Bradley	3.9
10	Mistral European sales and profits by country 1992 - 1996	3.10
11	Product life cycle	3.11
12	Support bandaging report	3.12

2 APPENDIX ANALYSIS 1

Appendix 1

2.1 'Form should follow strategy'. There are anomalies. In the text (page 4, Chapter 20, para 2.9) we are told that Mistral UK only monitors sales and on page 10 (Chapter 20, paras 2.35-2.37) that sales forces are managed locally but Appendix 1 shows a Sales Manager Europe reporting to the UK Marketing Director. also the manufacturing units (in Spain, Greece and Ireland) have their own sales managers. the UK Marketing Manager has only a functional relationship with country marketing managers.

Appendix 2

2.2 Assumed to be an article from World in 1996 copyright held by the Economist Publications. We are not told the background of its author, Barbara Beck. The message is that the very old people consume a disproportionately large share of the total healthcare market and that populations are ageing. Current healthcare systems provided by countries will be less and less able to cope with escalating costs.

Appendix 3

2.3 It adds greater detail of the product range (bandages and tapes). Each product carries one of the four brand names (Victrix, Felix, Venus, Vulcan) followed by a product classification. The detail is fairly technical and not greatly beneficial from a strategic point of view.

Appendix 3B

2.4 Tends to add confusion rather than to clarify. Tells us which brands come under which sales categories.

Appendix 4

2.5 This is more helpful. Gives sales of bandages/tapes for seven out of the eight sales categories listing in 3B for each of the six countries, split into hospital and non-hospital categories. Needs further refinement to indicate percentages.

Appendix 5

2.6 Gives market estimated total sales for 1996 in the same format at Appendix 4 enabling market shares to be assessed by further refinement.

Appendices 6.1, 6.2, 6.3, 6.4, 6.5, 6.6, 6.7.

Appendix 6

2.7 Again helpful, in that each of seven sales categories are shown for sales 1994 (by country and by hospital/non-hospital) for Mistral and each of four major competitors plus the group of others. It also shows estimated sales in total for 1994 through to 1998, enabling trends to be assessed.

Appendix 7

2.8 Tells us the average selling prices for Spring 1996 for selected products in a range of sizes by country and hospital/non-hospital sectors. Although very limited, it indicates wide variations between countries.

Appendix 8

2.9 Indicates Mistral's share of the 1995 European market against its four major competitors for three groups of products - 'functional bandages, functional taping and support 'adds more confusion to product groups. Needs to be reconciled with Appendix 6.

Appendix 9

2.10 This is a memo from the UK Financial Controller to the Director of Marketing re the marketing Manager giving some figures for year ended 31 December 1995 for bandages. Despite it being 20 June 1996, precise figures as requested are not available. However, indications are good in that 'cohesive' bandage sales are up 24% whilst taping has increased its market share.

Also 1996 appears to have got off to a good start. Madrid have developed a new line for elasticated adhesive bandage.

Appendix 10

2.11 Shows sales, expenses, gross/net profits by country for 1993 to 1996 enabling trends to be established. Indicates wide variations in net profits between countries.

Appendix 11

2.12 Positions four products on the product life cycle. Importance of these four products in terms of total sales needs to be established.

Appendix 12

2.13 Is a poorly presented report on bandaging which adds little to previous data on sales, profits and competitors. it does, however, indicate some strategies regarding segmentation, new product development, competitors and promotion.

3 APPENDIX ANALYSIS 2

3.1 Consult the table in Section 1 of this chapter for where to find the location of Appendix in the case study documentation. The paragraph references refer to the main text of the case in Chapter 20.

22: Mistral: analyses of appendices

Appendix number	What is it saying?	How does it help us?	Which other appendices or text can it be related to (Chapter 20)	If so, what extra information insights does this reveal?
1	• Organisational relationships between UK and European subsidiaries for marketing and manufacturing show that there is a European Sales Manager and manufacturing unit sales managers as well as country sales managers. Also John Norland the UK Marketing Manager has no formal or line authority over country marketing managers	• In understanding the reporting relationships and the limits of authority of our client John Norland	Text pp Candidates Brief (1.1-1.4), 4, 10 (2.34-2.37) Appendix 9 and others	That tensions between the UK and European subsidiaries as regards marketing decisions are likely to be exacerbated by these organisational relationships. Also that whilst subsidiary marketing managers operate through product managers and sales managers, the UK Marketing Manager does not. Some of the marketing information available to my client John Norland is incomplete, dated and anomalous
2	• In a recent article published in 'World in 1996', (copyright the Economist Publications) concerning the 'intractable' problem of the ageing of the world's population, ranging over birth rates, retirement ages, pensions, healthcare and finance	• Highlights forthcoming changes in Mistral's marketing environment	Text pp 6, 7, 8 (2.20-2.27) Appendix 12	Confirms that European buying behaviour for medical disposables is likely to become more cost-driven in the public sector. Also that the private sector is likely to expand greatly to cater for the needs of an increasingly elderly population. This will affect future strategy and the marketing mix required
3	• Describes the product portfolio in some detail. Shows us that the four major brands are allied to primary purpose ie - retention and fixation: Victrix (10 lines) - Light support: Felix (6 lines) - Strong support: Venus (4 lines) - Compression: Vulcan (6 lines) • Tells us that each product carries a brand name and a line identification also that products tend to bisect into bandages and tapes. • Gives a short technical description of each line and its major benefits from a usage viewpoint	• To understand better the product range and to improve our interpretation of other related data in the case eg the average selling prices and the product life cycle	Text pp 3, 4, 5, 6, 8 (2.6-2.30) Appendices 1, 3B, 4, 5, 6, 7, 8, 9, 11, 12	• Shows that product terminology/use can differ between countries and cause confusion as well as inaccuracies in the marketing data. No clear brand images/ attributes. • Problems in controlling existing product/ brand portfolio and in new product/brand development but also opportunities. Some products becoming commodities

Part E: Learning from experience: ensuring you pass

Appendix number	What is it saying?	How does it help us?	Which other appendices or text can it be related to (Chapter 20)	If so, what extra information insights does this reveal?
3B	Indicates the distribution of brands by eight product categories. Tells us that Victrix is not considered strategic and is excluded from the analysis. Taking away Victrix (10 lines) and Vulcan's six compression lines we cab see how the remaining six Felix lines and the four Venus lines fall into the remanding six product groupings	Not a lot really in itself, but is key to assimilating subsequent sales breakdowns	Text pp8, 9 (2.28-2.31) Appendices 3, 4, 5, 6, 9, 12	Gives us the proportions of total sales for each of the seven product groupings and their market shares. Helps us to access Brand/product line strengths within these groupings or market segments against our competitors
4	Gives us 1996 sales for the seven product groupings or segments referred to in 3B split by country and into hospital/non-hospital outlets. Also indicates four super-segments for bandages market, namely: - adhesive - functional bandaging - functional taping - compression bandages	Tells us the relative importance of sales in each of these segments and in each country bisected into hospital and non-hospital sectors	Text pp 5, 7, 8, 9, 10 (2.16-2.18, 2.23-235) Appendices 3, 5, 6, 8, 9, 12	Some inconsistencies in terminology for market segments/product groupings by cross analysis gives us a better idea of brand strengths By subtracting sales excluding Victrix given in Appendices 4 and 6 from total sales given in Appendix 12 we can establish that Victrix sales for 1994 were £9.35m and for 1996 £7.85m
5	Tells us the estimated 1996 market sizes for the seven segments referred to above by country and by hospital/non-hospital sectors	Enables us to work out market segment sizes by value and % and to assess the relative importance of each segment to the total market	Text pp 4, 5 (2.12-2.18) Appendices 2, 3, 6, 8, 9, 11, 12	By cross references, this gives us our market shares and those of our leading competitors for each segment and the total market. Reinforces statements made in the text
6	Gives us 1994 sales for each of the seven segments for Mistral plus the four leading competitors plus others, by country and for hospital/non-hospital sectors. also estimated total market size for the four years 1995/1998 by country and hospital/non-hospital sectors	Gives us our market shares versus competitors in each market segment by product group, by country and by hospital/non-hospital sectors. Enables us to develop a more effective competitive marketing strategy. Also gives us market segment size trends for the last two and next two years, useful for sales forecasting and objective setting purposes	Text pp 4, 5, 8 (2.12-2.15, 2.27) Appendices 3, 4, 5, 8, 9, 11 12	When cross-referenced with other data eg Appendices 3 and 12 also gives us an idea of our product/brand segment and in each market segment and in the total market
7	Tells us average selling prices for Spring 1996 for four selected products in a number of sizes, by country and by hospital/non-hospital sectors	Gives us an idea of how prices for the same products vary by country and by hospital/non-hospital sector	Text pp 3, 4, 7 (2.8-2.13, 2.23-2.24) Appendices 10,11,12	Gives us an insight into the pricing variability for Felix Jaz which is in the early stage of its plc. Also into the reasons for variations in profitability by country
8	Gives us a bar-chart visual of comparative market shares of Mistral plus the individual leading competitors for 1995 by three product groupings (five market segments)	Gives a good visual indication of our recent competitive positioning in terms of market shares and a means of correlation with other data in the case. Shows us that Mistral commission some market research and have some in-house data	Text pp 4, 5, 8 (2.12-2.15, 2.28) Appendices 3, 4, 5, 6, 9, 11, 12	Adds to the detail of competitor market shares by using different product groupings and a different year. Also names individual competitors

22: Mistral: analyses of appendices Notes

Appendix number	What is it saying?	How does it help us?	Which other appendices or text can it be related to Chapter 20	If so what extra information insights does this reveal?
9	• In an answer by the Financial Controller to the Marketing Director cc John Norland in response to a request for 1995 financial results. Tells us of good results for taping and cohesive bandage sales and indicates that 1996 has got off to a good start	• Indicates poor management accounting in that the memo is dated 20 June 1996, so that even after six months the financial results for the previous year cannot be released internally. Also gives only partial, potentially misleading information, plus information not requested	Text pp 5, 8 (2.4-2.15, 2.28) Appendices 4, 6, 12	• Adds to our organisational knowledge. Indicates that internal data provision to marketing can be unreliable and badly in retrospect
10	• Shows sales, expenses, gross and net profits for each country for the four years 1993 to 1996 in value and percentage terms	• Tells us which countries are doing relatively well/poorly and downward/upward trends. Points towards those countries with the most potential for improvement • Sales and marketing expenses as a proportion of sales can be compared by country. Net profits are shown to vary from 6% in Italy to 23% in Holland in 1996	Text pp 3, 4, 7 (2.6-2.11, 2.23-2.27) Appendices 10, 11, 12	• When cross referenced with average selling price, indicates wide variations in net profit at least partly attributable to price variances. Also a possible reason for low gross margins is a failure to sell stocks
11	• Is a PLC chart showing the growth stage of four products. It tells us that Felix Jaz is in its early growth stage whilst Venus Ace EAB is ageing. However, the date is not yet given	• Reminds us of the need to review sales of all products against the plc test. Also to take appropriate action as suggested in Kotler to maximise sales and profits during each stage	Text pp 4, 5, 6, 7, 8, 9, 10 (2.12-2.35) Appendices 3, 4, 5, 10,12	• Appendix 3 tells us that Felix Jaz is a flexible cohesive bandage whilst Appendix 9 says that cohesive bandage sales appear to have risen by 24% in 1995. • Appendix 3B shows that Felix Jaz is the only cohesive support bandage so that sales and market shares/sizes under this heading in Appendices 4 and 5 can be attributed to Felix Jaz. • Appendix 6.6 indicates considerable growth potential

12	• A somewhat poorly presented Bandaging Report of no stated date giving incomplete information under headings of sales, profitability, competitive situation, environment, competitor, profit and strategies	• Only part of the information adds to our knowledge. However, the other part does at least serve to confirm previous data. We learn that the market for support bandages is growing by 2.8 per cent per annum and that low cost/lower quality general support products are emerging. There are signs that various strategic decisions have been made but not fully integrated	Text 5, 7, 8, 9, 10,11 (2.14-2.18, 2.5-2.39) Appendices 2, 3, 4, 5, 6, 7, 8, 9, 10,11 Candidates Brief	• When cross referenced with appendices 4 and 6, enables us to calculate Victrix sales for 1994 and 1996.
				• Allied to the Candidates' Brief suggests particular strategies
				• Expands on Appendix 10 to tell us the reasons for the net profit falling from 17% to 15% in 1995 were:
				  1 a greater proportion of sales on low profit products
				  2 Increased competition on elasticated adhesive bandages

465 BPP Publishing

Chapter 23

MISTRAL: SITUATIONAL ANALYSIS, KEY ISSUES, MISSION STATEMENT, BROAD AIMS, MAJOR PROBLEMS

> **This chapter covers the following topics.**
> 1 The steps you should take
> 2 Situation analyses
> 3 Decide key issues
> 4 Mission statement and broad aims
> 5 Major problems

1 THE STEPS YOU SHOULD TAKE

1.1 So much for contemplating your appendices. It is now time to move on to the next two steps.

> CONSULT THE GUIDANCE NOTES IN
> CHAPTER 8 PARAGRAPHS 3.18 TO 3.28
>
> **STEP 9 RECONSIDER YOUR PRÉCIS, MARKETING AUDIT AND SWOT ANALYSIS**
> **STEP 10 CONDUCT A SITUATIONAL ANALYSIS**
>
> ALLOW BETWEEN 2 AND 3 HOURS FOR COMPLETING THESE STEPS

1.2 You should reconsider/review your SWOT analysis, précis and marketing audit in the light of new insights gained from your appendix analysis and adjust them accordingly.

1.3 When you have completed your situational analysis please compare it with the specimens which follow, all from syndicates on the CIM ID courses.

1.4 The situation analysis, although wide-ranging, should usually culminate in a statement of not more than half a page summarising the detail. All four situational analyses conform to the brevity requirement.

(a) *Example 1* is about the right length and tries to focus on the key issues as the writer sees them. It is in essay style and does the job reasonably well although you may think it omits too much.

(b) *Example 2* is structured and uses bullet points to cover more ground in the available space. Some of the figures stated need qualifying. Perhaps it leans rather too heavily on weaknesses identified in a SWOT.

23: Mistral: situational analysis, key issues, mission statement, broad aims, major problems

(c) *Example 3* is again structured although somewhat haphazardly. Some of the points made are questionable.

(d) *Example 4* is quite intensive but overlong and more like a minimarketing audit than the situation summary statement required.

Which example in your opinion demonstrates the best overall grasp of Mistral's situation in a clear and succinct manner. Is your own statement better?

2 SITUATION ANALYSES

Situation analysis 1

2.1 *Example 1*

> Mistral (M) is currently faced with declining profits and increased competition from low cost, lower quality products in its traditional markets and is critically reviewing its marketing strategy for the bandages market using a well-known firm of consultants.
>
> M's overall market share has grown from 25% in 1994 to 29% in 1996 in an expanding market but the growth in sales has mainly come from the lower profit products.
>
> European countries' populations are ageing, causing escalated healthcare costs which cannot be borne by state welfare systems indefinitely, hence the increased emphasis on price albeit at the expense of quality which is inconsistent with M's current positioning.
>
> Healthcare is increasingly becoming privatised and conducted in the home so that the market naturally segments into hospital and non-hospital sectors as well as public and private. This leads to changes in the DMU with the patient and private doctor/consultant/nurse having a greater say in the types of bandages used. In future more bandages will be sold through wholesalers and/or direct to pharmacy chains and grocery multiples.
>
> M's European subsidiaries are at present autonomous with regard to pricing, salesforce, distribution and promotion. The extent to which this arrangement will continue to be effective in the changing market is open to debate.

Situation analysis 2

2.2 *Example 2*

> **Current situation and areas of weakness**
>
> (a) *Strategic direction*
>
>   (i) Key strategic issues considered tactical (eg pricing, promotion)
>   (ii) No strategy for bandages market
>
> (b) *Culture*
>
>   (i) No coherent European corporate culture
>   (ii) Not learning from other countries best practice
>
> (c) *Marketing focus*
>
>   (i)   Product rather than customer orientated
>   (ii) Focus on hospital market although non-hospital is larger and growing
>   (iii) Heavy reliance on mature products (eg Venus Ace - 56% of sales)
>
> (d) *Coverage*
>
>   (i) European coverage fragmented
>
> (e) *Profitability*
>
>   (i) Reducing in real terms
>   (ii) 1996 ÷ 1994 = 18% increase in sales but 10% decrease in profit margin

Part E: Learning from experience: ensuring you pass

(f) *Control*

    (i) No marketing information system
    (ii) Financial reporting insufficient/not timely

Situation analysis 3

2.3 Example 3

(a) *What business are we in?* Medical disposables with a diverse product range. Bandages are the part of this market we are concerned with.

(b) *Marketing.* Despite marketing managers in every company, there appears to be a lack of understanding of the difference between products and brands and no strategy for these apart from keeping adding to the product portfolio. Whist an MkIS is apparent, information arrives incomplete and late. Mistral appear to be product/sales led.

(c) *Salesforce.* Somewhat laissez-faire. Needs retraining in order to cope with changing market needs.

(d) *Current plans.* There is a lack of clear objectives and strategies despite an emphasis on profits.

(e) *Organisation.* Informal reporting relationships and unclear demarcation between roles.

(f) *External environment.* People are living longer, birthrates are slowing down, and there is more care at home. Government controls are combining to split the market into cash-strapped state schemes and an increasing private sector for people who can afford it. Porter's 5 Forces Analysis indicates increased threats of new entrants and substitute products. In the public sector, increased bargaining power of hospitals and in the private sector, increased bargaining power of patients, advisers and retailers.

(g) *Marketing mix.* This mirrors strategy in not being clearly thought out and integrated. There are obvious weaknesses in every element.

Situation analysis 4

2.4 Example 4

External

(a) *Market conditions*

    (i) Increased number of older and dependent people
    (ii) Shift towards self-therapy and less time in hospital

(b) *Political*

    (i) Government subsidies to private hospitals
    (ii) Government directives on purchasing of medical disposables
    (iii) Method of procurement for state hospitals is open/selective tender

(c) *Social*

    (i) Greying population is increasing and changing demand
    (ii) Changing lifestyles affect bandage usage

(d) *Economic*

    (i) Single European market facilitates greater standardisation
    (ii) Increased consumer mobility leads to greater awareness/discrimination

(e) *Technological*

    (i) Medical products becoming more sophisticated
    (ii) Research and technology breakthroughs lead to shorter PLCs

23: Mistral: situational analysis, key issues, mission statement, broad aims, major problems

Internal

(a) *Organisation*
- (i) Lack of integration between Mistral UK and its European subsidiaries
- (ii) Existing structure/culture not conducive to good two-way communications
- (iii) A more polycentric outlook

(b) *Product*
- (i) Lack of initiative on new product development
- (ii) Overdependence on traditional adhesive (risky)
- (iii) Threat of cheaper competitive products

(c) *Price*
- (i) Pricing approach is cost-based
- (ii) No linking between price and positioning
- (iii) Widely varying prices between countries (? justified)

(d) *Promotion*
- (i) Salesforce focus on transaction selling and demand stimulation
- (ii) Promotion is ad-hoc
- (iii) Lack of integrated marketing communications

(e) *Distribution*
- (i) No strong network. Over-emphasis on hospital segment
- (ii) Changes in external environment will create the need for new channels.

Implications

(a) Need to change from polycentric to a more geocentric outlook
(b) To stay competitive, must innovate through product developments
(c) Need to reposition and build brand
(d) Could compete on differentiation, particularly in non-hospital segment
(e) Over-emphasis on traditional adhesive at the expense of compression
(f) Distribution strategy in need of radical overhaul
(g) Sales strategy should move towards relationship marketing
(h) More integration required between Mistral UK and European subsidiaries

Part E: Learning from experience: ensuring you pass

2.5 Supporting models and analysis

(a)

Boston Matrix Italy - Italy Hospital

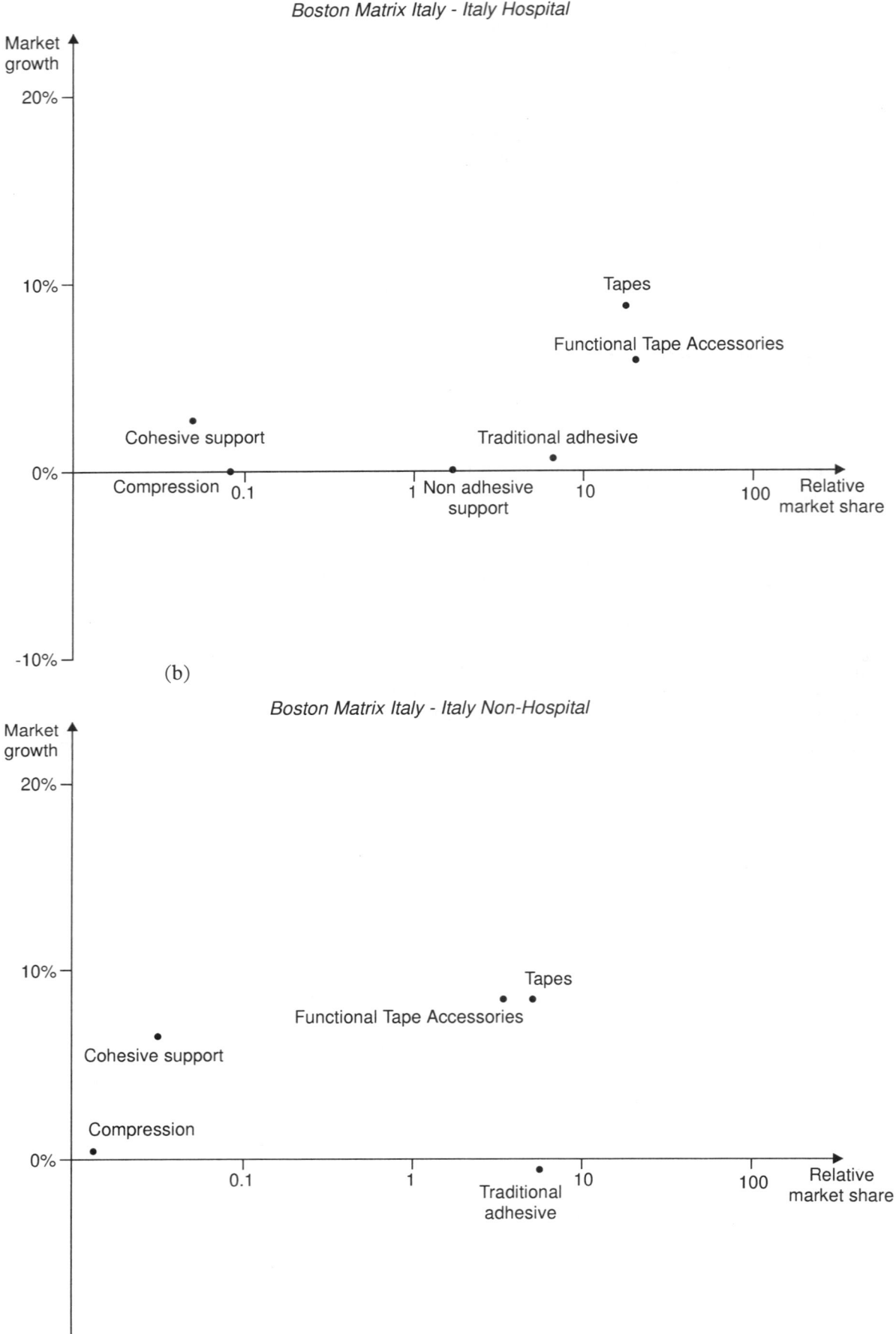

(b)

Boston Matrix Italy - Italy Non-Hospital

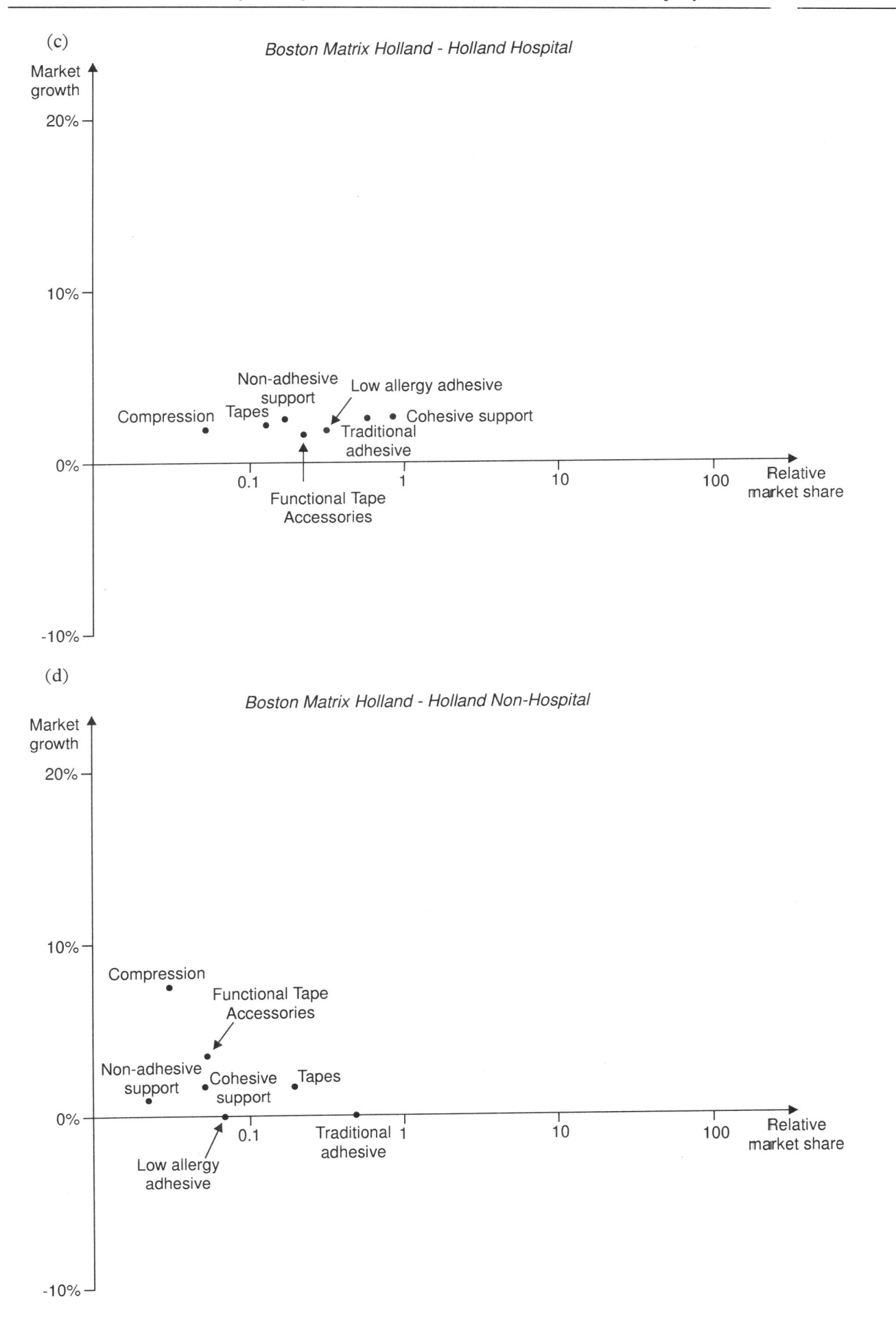

23: Mistral: situational analysis, key issues, mission statement, broad aims, major problems

(c) *Boston Matrix Holland - Holland Hospital*

Points plotted on Market growth (y-axis, 0% to 20%) vs Relative market share (x-axis, logarithmic: 0.1, 1, 10, 100):
- Compression (~0.05, ~2%)
- Tapes (~0.15, ~3%)
- Non-adhesive support (~0.2, ~3%)
- Functional Tape Accessories (~0.2, ~2%)
- Low allergy adhesive (~0.3, ~3%)
- Traditional adhesive (~0.3, ~2%)
- Cohesive support (~0.8, ~3%)

(d) *Boston Matrix Holland - Holland Non-Hospital*

Points plotted on Market growth (y-axis, 0% to 20%) vs Relative market share (x-axis, logarithmic: 0.1, 1, 10, 100):
- Compression (~0.04, ~7%)
- Functional Tape Accessories (~0.06, ~3%)
- Non-adhesive support (~0.03, ~1%)
- Cohesive support (~0.07, ~2%)
- Tapes (~0.25, ~2%)
- Low allergy adhesive (~0.07, 0%)
- Traditional adhesive (~0.4, 0%)

(e)

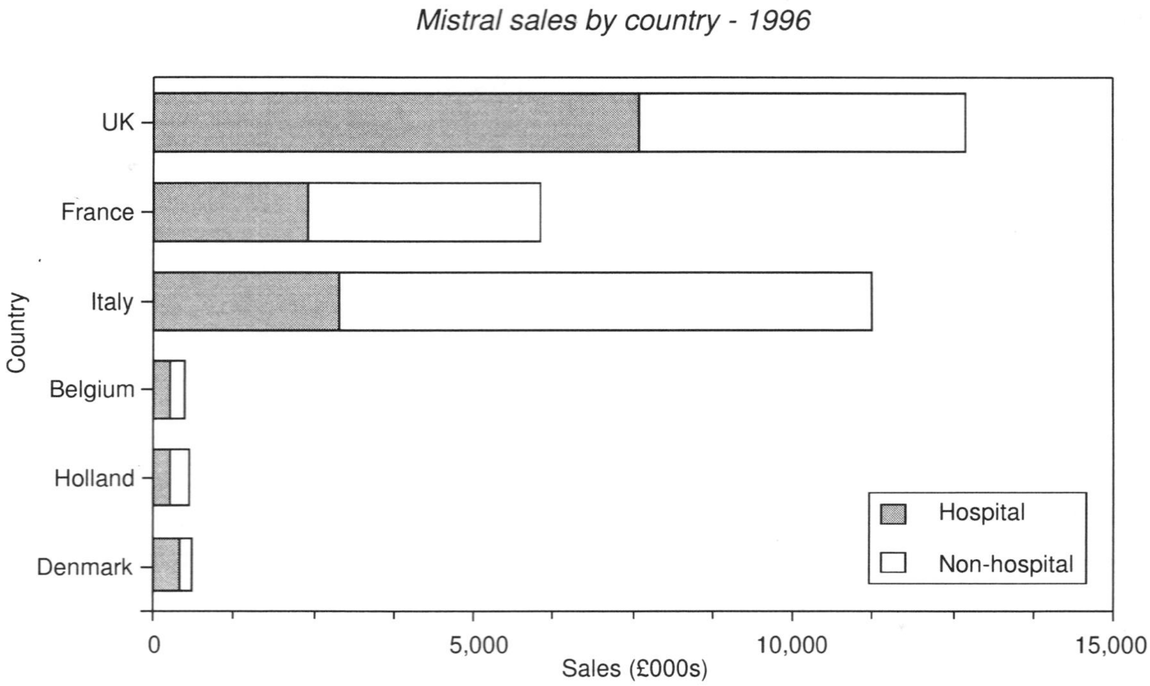
Mistral sales by country - 1996
UK
France
Italy
Belgium
Holland
Denmark
Country
Hospital
Non-hospital
0
5,000
10,000
15,000
Sales (£000s)

(f)

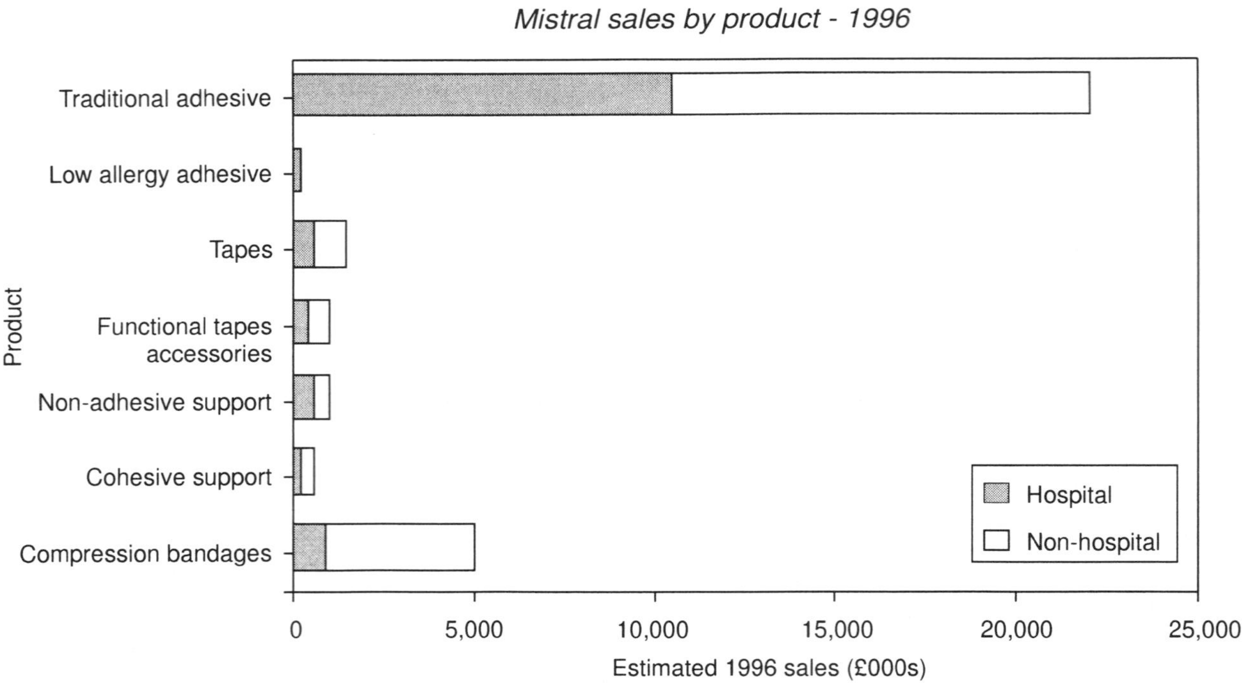
Mistral sales by product - 1996
Traditional adhesive
Low allergy adhesive
Tapes
Functional tapes accessories
Non-adhesive support
Cohesive support
Compression bandages
Product
Hospital
Non-hospital
0
5,000
10,000
15,000
20,000
25,000
Estimated 1996 sales (£000s)

(g)

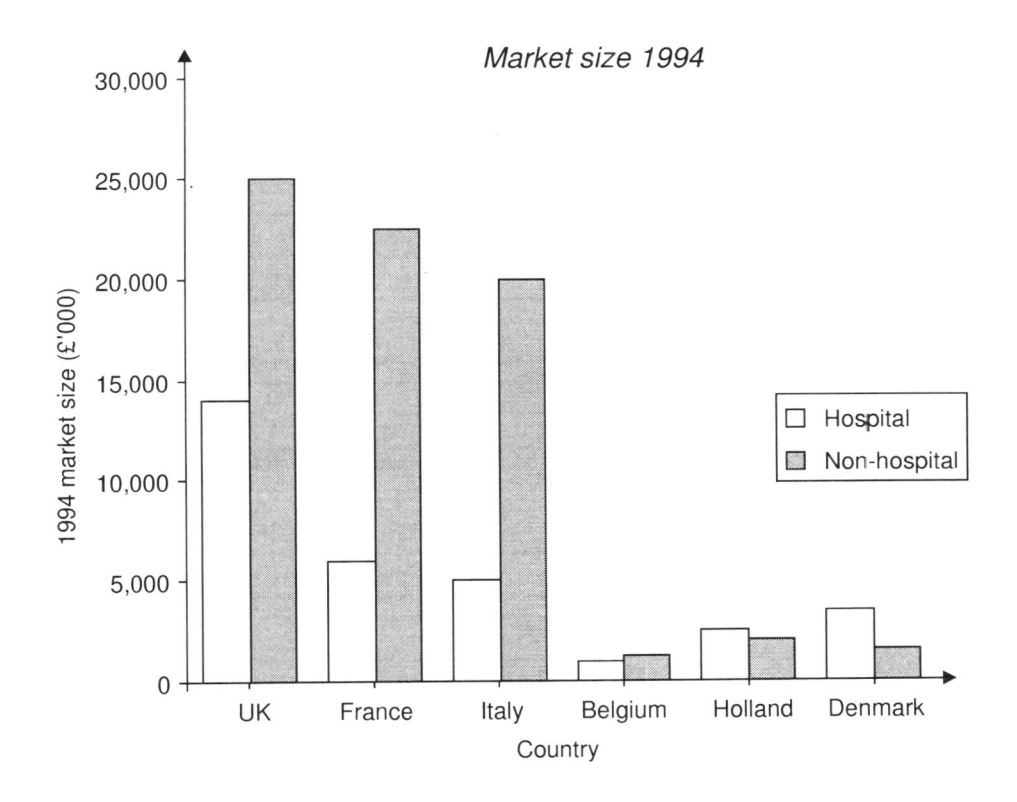

Market size 1994

(h)

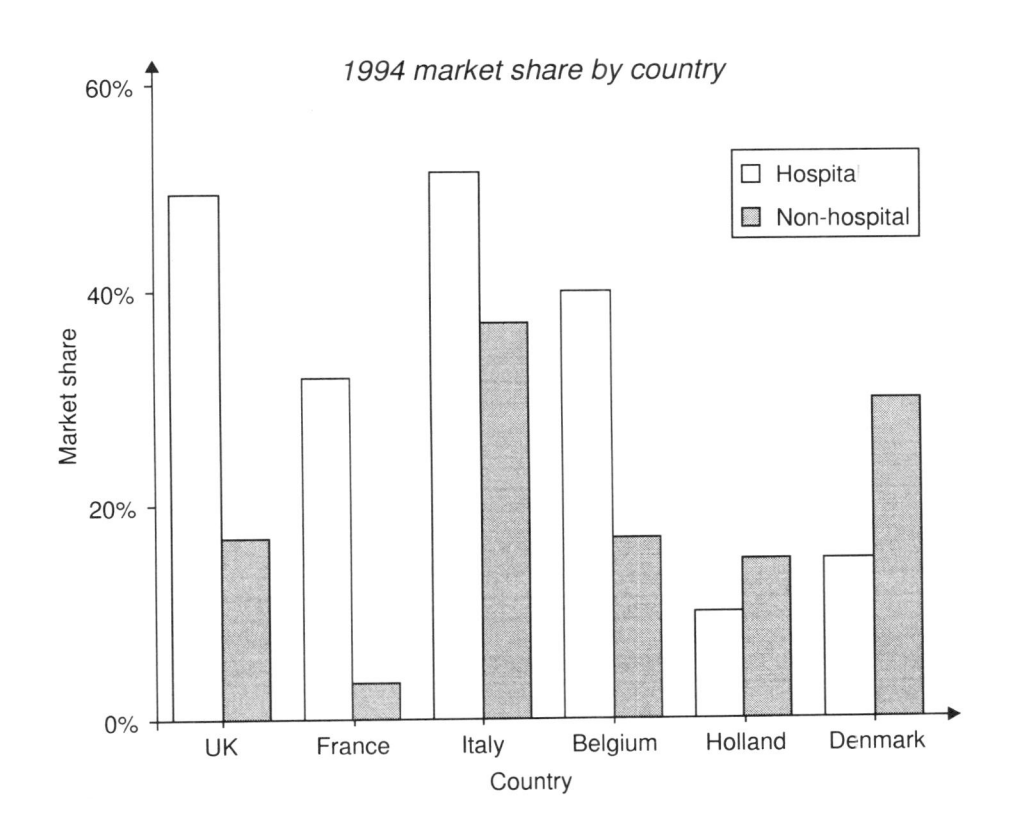

1994 market share by country

Notes   **Part E: Learning from experience: ensuring you pass**

(i)

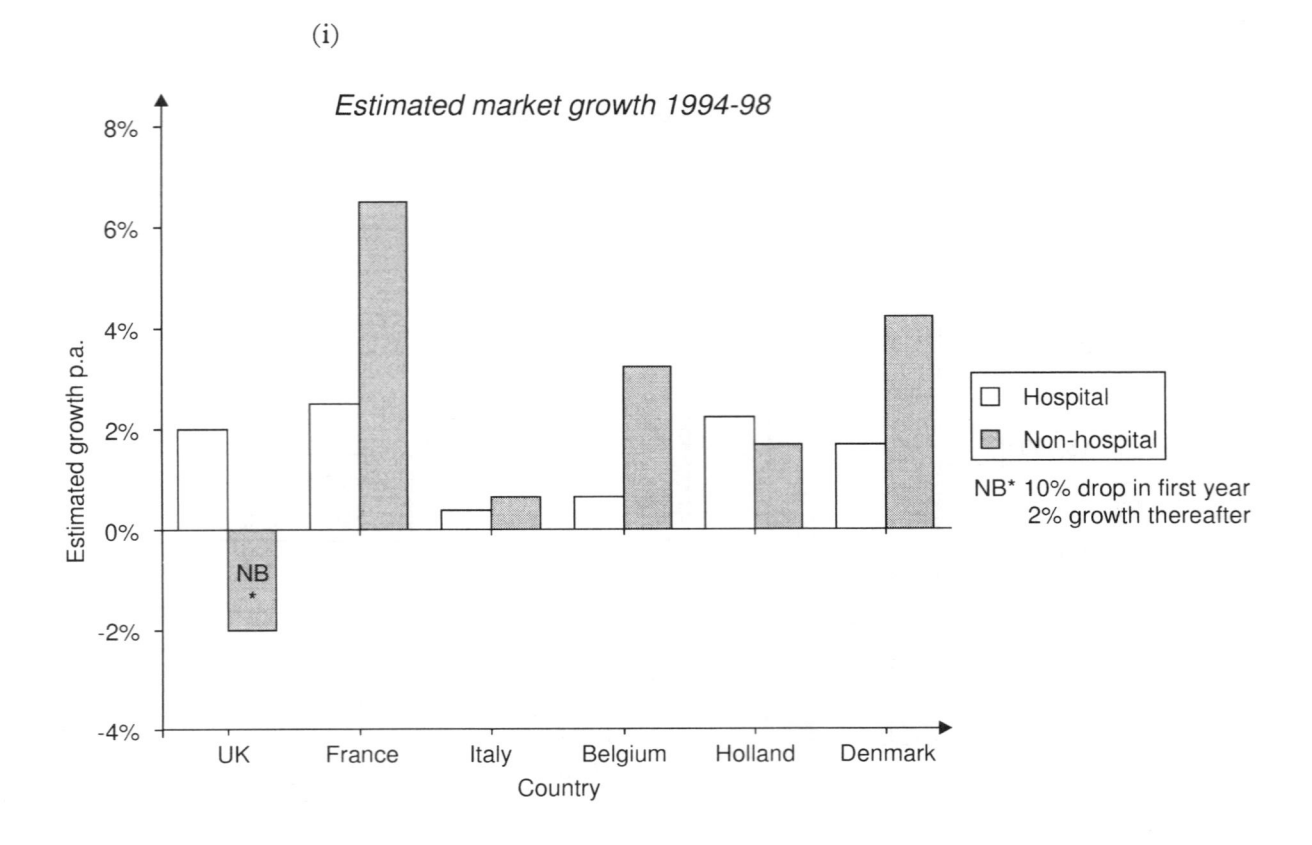

Estimated market growth 1994-98

[Bar chart showing Estimated growth p.a. by Country (UK, France, Italy, Belgium, Holland, Denmark), with Hospital and Non-hospital bars. UK Hospital ~2%, UK Non-hospital ~-2% (NB*); France ~2.5% and ~6.5%; Italy ~0.5% and ~0.7%; Belgium ~0.7% and ~3.3%; Holland ~2.3% and ~1.8%; Denmark ~1.8% and ~4.3%.]

NB* 10% drop in first year
2% growth thereafter

(j)

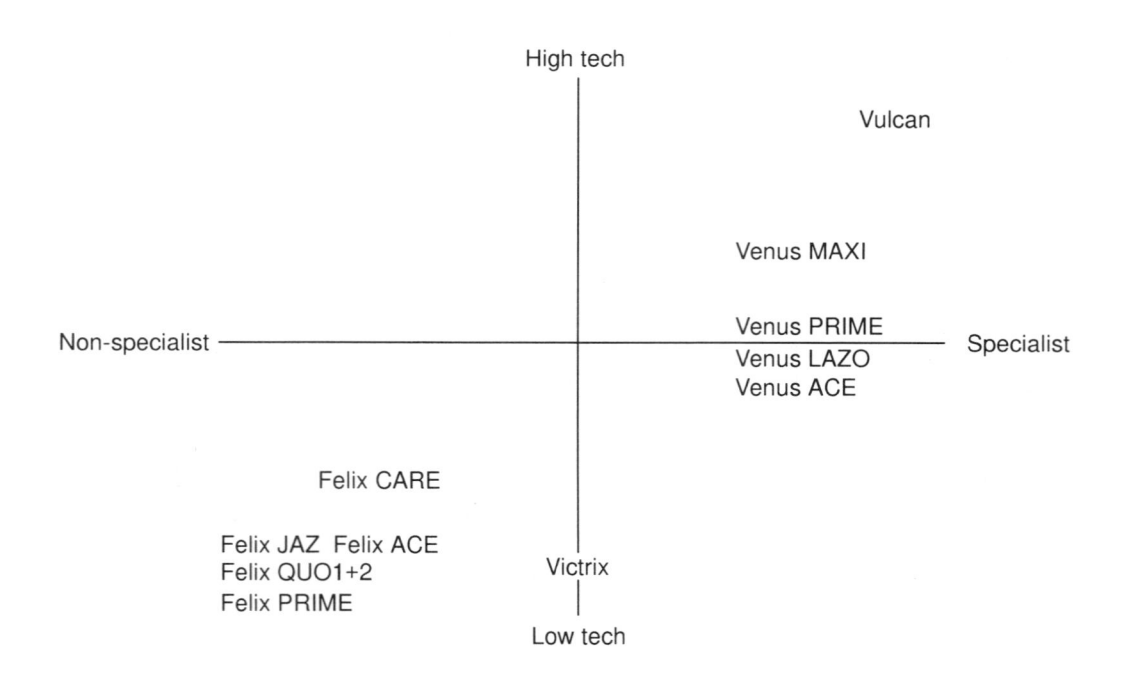

```
                        High tech
                           |
                           |              Vulcan
                           |
                           |           Venus MAXI
                           |
                           |           Venus PRIME
Non-specialist ────────────┼──────────  Venus LAZO    ──── Specialist
                           |           Venus ACE
                           |
                           |
              Felix CARE   |
                           |
     Felix JAZ  Felix ACE  |
     Felix QUO1+2       Victrix
     Felix PRIME          |
                       Low tech
```

23: Mistral: situational analysis, key issues, mission statement, broad aims, major problems

Brands and products

Category	Brands	Materials	Use	Benefits
Traditional adhesive	Venus Ace EAB	Cotton/rayon. Natural rubber adhesive	Sprains and strains. Sports injuries	Porous (allows skin to breathe). Easy application yellow guide line. Correct tension
Low allergy adhesive	Venus Ace EAB	Cotton/rayon. Low allergy adhesive	Sprains and strains. Sports injuries	Porous (allows skin to breathe). Easy application yellow guide line. Correct tension
Tapes	Venus LAZO		Rigid joint support	Hypoallergenic. Strong adhesion stays in position.
	Felix Ace		Secure fixation or strapping.	Extensible, conformable and comfortable
Functional tape accessories				
Non-adhesive support	Felix Prime 2	Rib weave stockinette, covered latex rubber	Elasticated, tubular for general light support	Can be re-used. No slipping.
	Felix QU01	Narrow woven cotton, polyamide and elastane	General purpose light support and compression	Conformable, light, strong and durable
	Felix QU02	Narrow woven cotton, polyamide, elasticated fibres and tailored edges	Light support	Conformable, light durable, washable and re-usable
	Felix CARE	Cotton and high strength nylon fibres	Support of mild soft tissue injuries	Superior performance over BP quality crepe bandages
	Venus Maxi	High twist cotton/rayon yarns	Varicose vein and venous ulcer treatment. Rigid compression therapy	Correct tension
	Venus Prime 1	Rib knitted stockinette and covered latex rubber threads	To promote venous and lymphatic return	Anatomical design, shaped tubular bandage Full leg and below the knee sizes available
Cohesive support	Felix JAZ	High strength nylon fibres and elastic yarns, coated with a latex compound	Light support particularly in difficult areas	Flexible, cohesive

Part E: Learning from experience: ensuring you pass

Category	Brands	Materials	Use	Benefits
Compression bandages	Vulcan 4X4	Four layers of bandages plus wound contact layer dressing	Four layer bandaging system for treating venous leg ulcers	
	Vulcan LP		Light compression for the treatment of heavy legs, oedema and varicose veins	Sustained compression
	Vulcan HP		High compression for the treatment of varicose veins, varicose leg ulcers, pre and post vein stripping	Sustained compression
	VulcanEase	Narrow woven blend of cotton and nylon, includes elastane	All light compression needs	Extensible, elasticity
	Vulcanite	Blend of cotton and rayon with nylon covered elastic yarns	Management of superficial early varices, varicosis formed in pregnancy and below the knee stump bandaging. also layer 3 in Vulcan 4×4	Lightweight
	VulcanOp	Polyamide and elastane	Graduated compression hosiery used to prevent varicosity, deep vein thrombosis and gravitational oedema	Lightweight, comfortable, air permeable and washable. Colour coded for easy identification.
Glossary of terms	Extensible	Will extend (elastic)		
	Conformable	Conforms to irregular shapes		
	BP	British Pharmacoepia (quality standard)		
	Cohesive	Sticks to itself		
	Venous	Veins, blood flow system		
	Lymphatic	Anything to do with the lymphatic system		
	Heavy legs/Oedema	Water retention		
	Varices, varicosis and varicose	Problems caused by poor circulation of blood, ulcers, sores, varicose veins		

2.6 Brand analysis

(a) *What values does it represent?*
- Innovation
- Long established
- Reliable
- Traditional

(b) *What does it say now?*
- Professional - not necessarily to OTC customers
- Will do what it is supposed to do
- No consistent brand value across Europe
- Value for money
- Low risk
- No consistent brand value across Europe

(c) *Now does it say it?*
- Bland packaging
- Inferred through company reputation
- By using professional language - feature driven

(d) *To whom does it say it?*
- The professional or specialist

(e) *What is the competitive advantage?*
- Clinical expertise
- Established relationships with DMU
- Distribution channels

(f) *What scope does it have?*
- New markets, possibly
- Offer greater service (training packages?)
- Bundling product packages
- Credibility in new markets etc

(g) *Rational and emotional mix*

Rational
- Does the job
- Available
- Ease of use
- Cost savings

Emotional
- Security - low risk
- My patients benefit
- Patient compliance
- Professionals feel valued
- Cosmetic appearance

(h) *Reflection of self image*
- Caring
- Accessible
- Professional
- Friendly
- Easy to do business with

(i) *Style language and tone*
- Multi language
- Informative
- Lively

(j) *Research*

Test the brand values through qualitative and quantitative customer research.

(k) *Developing the Mistral brand*

Agree its role

Consolidate--------Stress added value--------→ Transfer established 'profession' values to all market segments

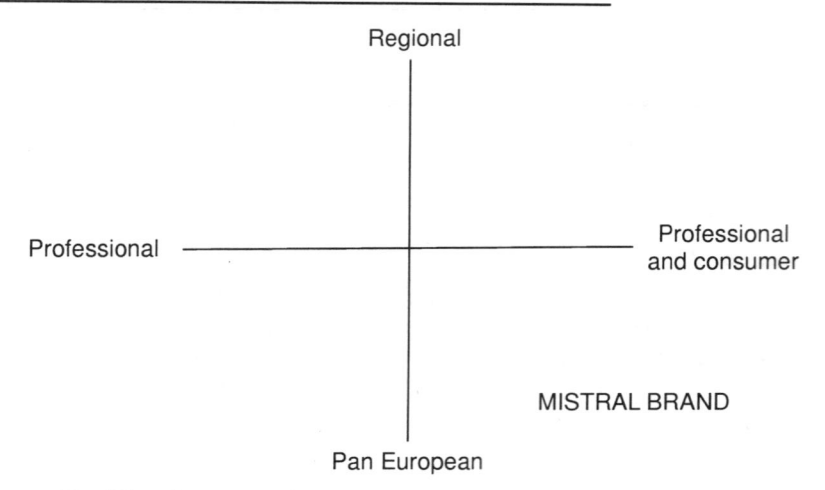

Notes   *Part E: Learning from experience: ensuring you pass*

```
                        Regional
                           |
                           |
                           |
Professional ──────────────┼────────────── Professional
                           |                and consumer
                           |
                           |
                           |         MISTRAL BRAND
                           |
                      Pan European
```

The Mistral name should be an umbrella brand for the entire range.

(l) *Value systems*

- Heritage
- Innovation
- Long established
- Reliable

(m) *What is the rational and emotional mix?*

Rational

- Does the job
- Available
- Ease of use
- Cost savings

Emotional

- Security - low risk
- Patients will benefit
- Patient compliance
- Professionals feel valued

(n) *Does it have a tactical or strategic role?*

At present it has a tactical role as the brand values have been developed.

(o) *Value positioning*

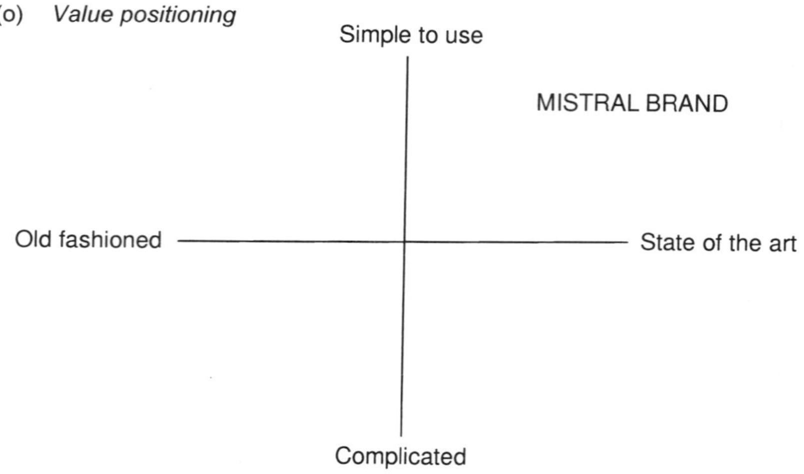

```
                      Simple to use
                           |
                           |        MISTRAL BRAND
                           |
                           |
Old fashioned ─────────────┼───────────── State of the art
                           |
                           |
                           |
                           |
                       Complicated
```

(p) *Relationship with targets*

We will review the marketing mix to ensure that the core brand value reflects the *caring, personnel and professional* elements.

23: Mistral: situational analysis, key issues, mission statement, broad aims, major problems   Notes

3   DECIDE KEY ISSUES

> READ THE GUIDANCE NOTES IN
> CHAPTER 8 PARAGRAPHS 4.1 TO 4.3
>
> **STEP 11 DECIDE THE KEY ISSUES**
>
> ALLOW 1 HOUR TO 1½ HOURS TO DO THIS STEP

3.1   Your next step takes you into decision mode. This step is the most important one, since it has the most bearing on the likely examination areas.

3.2   Bearing in mind that the exam question will normally contain only three questions you are also reminded to limit your key issues to a *maximum of six*. You might like to construct a list of candidate key issues which could then be ranked, as a way of doing this exercise. When deciding key issues, look for clues not only in the case study itself but also in the *Candidates' Brief*.

3.3   Remember also the technique of parcelling up several minor issues into one major issue as described in Chapter 8 Paragraph 4.1.

3.4   Now that you have completed this crucial exercise, please compare your conclusions with those produced by six separate syndicates as given on the next page.

3.5   *Mistral - key issues in rank order (6 Syndicates)*

	A		B
1	Marketing research	1	Brand building
2	Branding	2	Pricing policy
3	Reorganisation	3	Distribution strategy
4	New product development	4	NPD/Rationalisation
5	Distribution	5	Reorganisation
6	Pricing	6	Lack of marketing planning and control

	C		D
1	Lack of integrated marketing	1	External environmental changes
2	Internal frictions	2	Brand building/competitive positioning
3	Competitive strategy	3	Pricing
4	Marketing organisation	4	MR/MkIS
5	Brand building	5	Distribution strategy
6	Price rationalisation	6	Marketing organisation

	E		F
1	Marketing strategy, P&C	1	Marketing segmentation
2	Marketing mix integration	2	Positioning/brand attributes
3	Marketing research	3	Pricing strategy
4	Organisational issues	4	Distribution strategy
5	Environmental issues	5	Marketing management
6	The Mistral brand	6	Marketing research

3.6   Although there is quite a high degree of unanimity, opinion on rank order varies, perhaps reflecting different tutor inputs. Is there a logical rank order? What do you think this should be?

4 MISSION STATEMENT AND BROAD AIMS

> PLEASE CONSULT THE GUIDANCE NOTES IN
> CHAPTER 8 PARAGRAPHS 4.4 TO 4.14
>
> **STEP 12 DEVELOP A MISSION STATEMENT**
> **STEP 13 DECIDE BROAD AIMS**
>
> ALLOW ABOUT AN HOUR FOR EACH OF THESE STEPS

4.1 Let us now move forward to the next decision step, namely that of *creating a suitable mission statement*. Although you will not normally be asked for a mission statement per se in the exam paper, it does of course provide a necessary setting and guide for our marketing plan.

4.2 When you have completed your mission statement go on to your *broad aims*. Remember there should be consistency between your mission statement and your broad aims, also that you should try to limit the latter to *four* bearing in mind the need to convert these into quantified and time-scaled objectives at a later stage.

4.3 In this particular case, no mission statement or corporate aims are provided.

4.4 Having completed these two steps you should now compare your results with those of four separate syndicates which follow.

4.5 *Syndicate B1*

> *Mission statement*
>
> Mistral offers customers 'value for money' medical disposables without compromising our environmental responsibilities. We will continue to be a pro-active market leader through innovation and through providing staff with all necessary skills and information.
>
> *Broad aims*
>
> 1 To become closer to customers so as to achieve an even fuller understanding of their needs
>
> 2 To maintain and improve our position in key markets by the exploitation of new product opportunities
>
> 3 To reduce dependence on one product group
>
> 4 To nurture a marketing orientated structure

23: Mistral: situational analysis, key issues, mission statement, broad aims, major problems

4.6 *Syndicate E1*

Mission statement

Mistral is in the business of medical disposables. We strive to be the market leader by creating total solutions for our customer-partners. We aim to provide customers with the quality of product that they want, at a reasonable price, with the highest level of service in the market.

Broad aims

1   To keep fully informed on customer needs and environmental changes
2   To move away from a product orientation to a customer problem solution concept
3   As a result of 1 and 2 above, to command a higher than market average price and achieve satisfactory profits
4   To back to provision of total solutions with a 'second to none' level of service

4.7 *Syndicate B*

Mission statement

Mistral supplies medical disposables that alleviate pain and suffering and help to save lives on a global basis. It aims to be the most immediately recalled brand in both the public and private sectors of the market

Broad aims

1   To reposition favourably our brand image so as to build up our brand equity
2   To centralise marketing communications strategy
3   To research the private sector
4   To modify our sales approach and distribution channels to suit the changing market.

4.8 *Syndicate D*

Mission statement

Mistral's mission is to be the first-choice supplier of innovative and affordable solutions that meet the needs of existing and new customers within the health Service and consumer markets

Broad aims

1   To be recognised as the market leader throughout Europe in the supply of bandaging solutions
2   To promote and sustain long-term profit growth by investing in people, technology and products
3   To expand and develop the bandages market by opening up new market segments
4   To differentiate Mistral from competitors by positioning the brand as the most cost-effective, high clinical quality solution

4.9 You will note a great deal of conformity between the broad aims stated and the key issues given earlier. This is both usual and healthy. *Key issues* are often better raised in the form of questions eg should the Mistral brand be re-positioned? The implication is that there are criteria and alternatives to consider. A *broad aim* by contrast is a statement of intent in other words a *decision* rather than a *query*. Broad aims should, of course, be capable of conversion into quantified and timescaled objectives in your finalised marketing plan

Notes **Part E: Learning from experience: ensuring you pass**

4.10 How did you mission statement compare? Did you decide on similar broad aims? Were you able to keep your broad aims down to four, consistent with your mission statement?

5 MAJOR PROBLEMS

> CONSULT THE GUIDANCE NOTES GIVEN IN
> CHAPTER 8 PARAGRAPHS 4.15 TO 4.18
>
> **STEP 14 IDENTIFY AND ANALYSE MAJOR PROBLEMS**
>
> ALLOW BETWEEN TWO AND THREE HOURS TO DO THIS TASK

5.1 We are now returning for the last time to analysis or at least some analysis mixed with decision. Your task is:

(a) to decide the six *major problems;*
(b) to identify alternative solutions;
(c) to evaluate those solutions;
(d) to select the best solutions.

5.2 One more necessary discipline is to rank these six major problems in order. The reason this step has been left until now is that experience shows that if people get involved in specific and often minor problems too early on, they lose sight of the broader issues. Problem solution is also related to tactical as well as strategic planning. You will need to decide which are long-term and which need immediate action.

5.3 Students often get confused between *problems* and *key issues* which is quite natural because quite often they can be the same. However, a key issue is not necessarily a problem. To be silly about it, what sort of toilet paper to have in the new office block may be a problem but it is hardly a key issue. Equally, marketing research may be a key issue, but might not be seen as a major problem.

5.4 You will need quite some time for this exercise, probably two to three hours. When you have finished you might like to compare your six major problems with those submitted by the syndicates as in the following table. Note how some of these are sub-elements of a larger problem.

23: Mistral: situational analysis, key issues, mission statement, broad aims, major problems Notes

5.5 *Mistral: major problems*

Item		A1	B1	C1	D1	A2	B2	C2	D2
A	Lack of a clearly thought out marketing strategy and plan	1	2	2	5	1	1	1	1
B	Achieving the correct balance between centralised marketing and regional initiatives (organisation)	5	6	5	1				3
C	How best to re-position the Mistral brand and build up the brand equity	2	4	1	2	6	2	2	
D	Pricing policy: the determination of best prices for maximum profitability			6		2	6		
E	Marketing research and the marketing information system inadequacies	3		3	6 3	4	3 4	6 3	4
F	Lack of consistency and integration in marketing communications				6		3	6	
G	Changing buying behaviour and its effect on distribution channels in non-hospital sector		3						5
H	Ageing populations, escalating healthcare demand/costs and their effect upon buying behaviour in the hospital sector	6							
I	Inadequately trained and motivated sales force		1			3			
J	New product development and the management of the product portfolio	4	5	4	4	5	5	4	2
K	Increasing competition							5	6

5.6 A list of only eleven problems generated by a mix of eight syndicates asked to give six in rank order indicates a high level of certainty. It can be seen that the five major concerns are marketing strategy and planning, brand building, marketing information, product planning, and organisation.

5.7 Once you have decided what the major problems are, you have completed your analysis and are ready to move forward to the decision stage of your plan.

Chapter 24

MISTRAL: OUTLINE MARKETING PLANNING

This chapter contains the following guidance and plans.

1 Introduction: approaching the marketing plan
2 The steps you should follow
3 Outline marketing plan: example 1
4 Outline marketing plan: example 2

1 INTRODUCTION: APPROACHING A MARKETING PLAN

1.1 You will remember the advice we gave you on your first practice run, to produce an outline plan first and then to flesh it out into the required detail. Well we strongly suggest you do this again. Before you do please re-read the rationale for writing an outline plan first, contained in the notes at the beginning of Chapter 16 for the *Gravesend Town Centre* case.

1.2 As before we give below the steps you should follow to produce any marketing plan for your convenience. When you have reminded yourself of the procedure and framework, please take only about an hour to produce an outline plan and then compare yours with the two examples which follow before proceeding to the next chapter.

2 THE STEPS YOU SHOULD FOLLOW

2.1 These are of course the same as for the detailed marketing plan and are given below for your convenience.

> CONSULT THE GUIDANCE NOTES GIVEN IN
> CHAPTER 8 PARAGRAPHS 4.19 TO 6.8
>
> *In outline only*
>
> **STEP 15 DEVELOP QUANTIFIED, TIMESCALED OBJECTIVES**
> **STEP 16 CONSIDER ALTERNATIVE STRATEGIES. SELECT THOSE MOST APPROPRIATE**
> **STEP 17 DRAW UP [DETAILED TACTICAL] PLANS COVERING THE MARKETING MIX**
> **STEP 18 DRAW UP A MARKETING RESEARCH PLAN AND MKIS**
> **STEP 19 CONSIDER ORGANISATIONAL ISSUES, CHANGES AND MARKETING ORIENTATION**
> **STEP 20 CONSIDER ORGANISATIONAL CULTURE AND NEED FOR INTERNAL MARKETING**
> **STEP 21 DETERMINE THE FINANCIAL/HR RESOURCE IMPLICATIONS OF YOUR PLANS**
> **STEP 22 ASSESS COSTS AND DRAW UP INDICATIVE BUDGETS**
> **STEP 23 DRAW UP SCHEDULES GIVING TIMINGS/SEQUENCE OF ACTIONS**
> **STEP 24 SPECIFY REVIEW PROCEDURES AND CONTROL MECHANISMS**
> **STEP 25 DRAW UP OUTLINE CONTINGENCY PLANS**
> **STEP 26 REVIEW YOUR COMPLETE MARKETING PLAN**
>
> YOU SHOULD TAKE ABOUT AN HOUR TO DO THIS OUTLINE

3 OUTLINE MARKETING PLAN: EXAMPLE 1

Marketing objectives, strategies and justification

3.1 *Objectives*

1. Establish the Mistral brand name as a credible and competitive player by the year 1997.
2. Achieve a 40% share of the European bandages market in terms of turnover by the year 2001.
3. Achieve 20% of total sales revenue from new products by the year 2000.
4. Achieve a 60%-40% split of sales revenue in favour of the non-hospital/retail/OTC markets by the year 2001.
5. To achieve 10% of total sales revenue from new European counties by the year 2001.

3.2 *Marketing strategies*

1. *Develop and launch new products*, as well as rejuvenate existing products, under a 'Mistral' umbrella brand name.
2. *Differentiate the Mistral brand* from the competition and seek to *position* Mistral as a high quality clinical brand.
3. *Develop additional market segments* in terms of geography (new European countries) and end user (retail/OTC).
4. *Implement an integrated marketing communications plan* to promote 'Mistral' pro-actively.

3.3 *Justifications*

Three Ansoff strategies are recommended to fill the planning gap over the next five years as shown below.

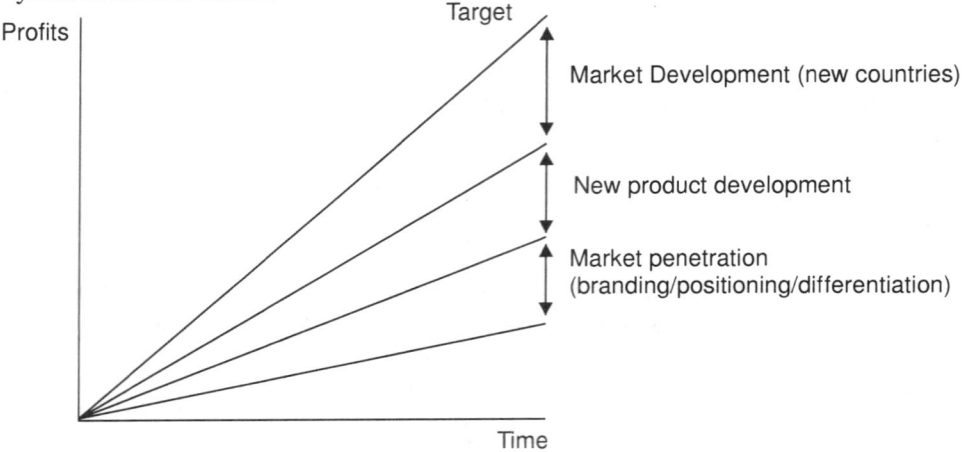

[Graph showing Profits vs Time with Target line, depicting three gaps: Market Development (new countries), New product development, and Market penetration (branding/positioning/differentiation)]

(a) *Justification for branding and positioning (market penetration)*

   (i) Provides differentiation
   (ii) Facilitates automatic rebuy
   (iii) Promotes loyalty

(b) *Justification for NPD (product development)*

   (i) Replace mature products
   (ii) Ensure long term profits/sales income
   (iii) Shows innovation

(c) *Justification for market development*

   (i) Expand overall bandage market
   (ii) Recapture market share
   (iii) Enter retail/OTC market in a more committed way

Segmentation, targeting, positioning

3.4 *Segmentation*

Segments include:

(a) Geography - European countries
(b) End user - hospitals/non-hospitals
(c) Benefits sought - economy/prestige
(d) Psychographics - culture/life style

3.5 *Targeting*

From the highlighted segments the following should be targeted.

(a) *Hospitals*

   European countries such as:

   (i) Germany
   (ii) Scandinavia
   (iii) Spain/Ireland/Greece (current Mistral manufacturing sites)

(b) *Non-hospitals/retail/over the counter*

   I recommend a focus on *young athletic men and women* who will need support bandages to enhance their sporting activities. The following target criteria should be examined.

   (i) Age range 16-45
   (ii) Any class classification - A, B, C, D, E
   (iii) Any ACORN category
   (iv) Active in sports/outdoor activities

(v) Interested in fashion accessories for sport
(vi) Perceive that paying a premium price as obtains quality
(vii) Shop at Olympus other high street sports outlets

3.6 *Positioning*

(a) I recommend that a set of *core values* are assigned to the Mistral brand name. Building upon established reputation and new innovation, suggested brand values are:

(i) Reputation
(ii) Innovation/style
(iii) Quality, clinical expertise

(b) In respect to the current main competition the following *positioning maps* are suggested

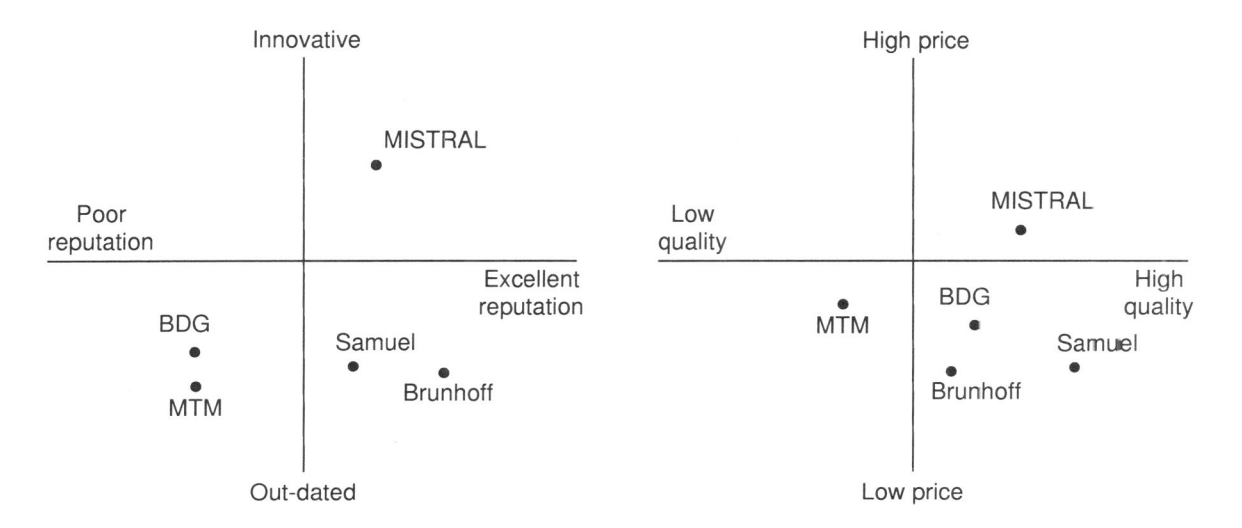

[Positioning map 1: Innovative/Out-dated vs Poor reputation/Excellent reputation — MISTRAL positioned upper right (Innovative, towards Excellent reputation); BDG and MTM lower left (Poor reputation, Out-dated); Samuel and Brunhoff lower right (Excellent reputation, Out-dated)]

[Positioning map 2: High price/Low price vs Low quality/High quality — MISTRAL positioned upper right (High price, High quality); MTM on low quality side; BDG, Brunhoff, Samuel positioned towards high quality at lower price]

(c) *Justification:* this positioning will aid differentiation and awareness of brand values.

Marketing mix

3.7 *Product*

(a) *Objectives*

(i) Increase sales
(ii) Increase profit margins
(iii) Support brand image/positioning
(iv) Support Mistral brand values

(b) *Strategies*

(i) Position as innovative/high quality
(ii) Differentiate
(iii) Capture OTC market share

(c) *Tactics*

(i) Immediate new product development
(ii) NPD in Felix and Venus product ranges for OTC sports market
(iii) Package to reflect style image
(iv) Review product portfolio (BCG analysis)
(v) Rationalise portfolio
(vi) Crate fashionable/stylish products that appear to young sports people ie colour/logo/styling

(d) *Justification:* NPD of innovative/stylish products is required to support branding and change attitudes.

3.8 *Pricing*

    (a) *Objectives*

        (i) Maximise profit margins
        (ii) Support quality positioning
        (iii) Reflect differentiation

    (b) *Strategies*

        (i) Maintain premium pricing
        (ii) Reflect added value
        (iii) Price skimming for new products

    (c) *Tactics*

        (i) Skimming prices
        (ii) Retain regional input on pricing
        (iii) Prevent cross border selling

    (d) *Justification*

        (i) Keep profit margins up
        (ii) Support brand values

3.9 *Promotion*

    (a) *Objectives*

        (i) Achieve 90% awareness of Mistral brand in all markets by year 2001

        (ii) Position Mistral brand as high quality, based on reputation and innovation

        (iii) Position Felix and Venus products as 'must have sports/fashion accessories for athletes ie Mistral support to go with Reebok trainers

    (b) *Strategies*

        (i) 'Pull' in consumers

            (1) Create awareness
            (2) Utilise above the line methods
            (3) Adopt pan-European promotion of brand values

        (ii) 'Push' to lower distribution channels

    (c) *Tactics: Non-hospital/OTC*

        (i) Advertising

            1 Consumer magazines
            2 GQ/Marie Claire/sports
            3 National Press
            4 Posters (sports events)

        (ii) Public relations

            1 Advertising in sporting magazines
            2 Endorsement from celebrity athletes

        (iii) Sales promotion

            1 Exhibitions
            2 Direct mail catalogues (Innovations)
            3 Point of sale material

        (iv) Personal selling

            1 Relationship marketing with major retailers

    (d) *Tactics: hospital*

        (i) Advertising: medical journals

        (ii) Public relations

            1 Trade journal editorials
            2 Reputed physiotherapist endorsement

(iii) Sales promotion
1 Conventions
2 Road shows
3 Exhibitions
4 Direct mail shots

(e) *Justifications*

(i) 'Pull': better for consumer marketing (awareness creation)
(ii) 'Push': better for direct contact with clinical buyers/retail distributor chains

3.10 *Place*

(a) *Objectives*

(i) Increase sales
(ii) Increase outlets

(b) *Strategies*

(i) Build relations with retail trade
(ii) Encourage stocking
(iii) Seek outlets via mail order

(c) *Tactics*

(i) Incentivise the sales force
(ii) Push products down the retail chain
(iii) Retrain sales force to cope with selling to retail trade

(d) *Justification*

(i) Better targeting of sales force resources
(ii) Better communication of brand values

Notes **Part E: Learning from experience: ensuring you pass**

3.11 *Timetables*

Promotion	1997		1998		1999		2000		2001	
	1	2	1	2	1	2	1	2	1	2
Advertising										
Specialist magazines	←――――――――→									
Press		←――→								
Posters					←――――――――→					
PR			←―――→							
Sales promotions					←―――→					
• Exhibitions					←―――――――――――――→					
• Point of sale					←――→					
• Direct mail					←―――――――――――――→					
Personal selling					←―――――――――――――→					

NB Assume new product launches in early 1998

Marketing information system (MkIS)

3.12 From the data provided to me it appears obvious that Mistral does not have an adequate MkIS in place.

3.13 I recommend that resources are put in place to help set one up as this is vital for decision making support. Specific data required includes:

  (a) internal records (sales margins, etc);
  (b) marketing intelligence (competitor sales, response profits etc);
  (c) marketing research (new country/segment data).

  I recommend work on this starts immediately within the Mistral UK marketing offices.

Organisation

3.14 Currently, the company is focused on products not customers. I recommend the following steps are examined to change the culture round.

  (a) Each European country should report on sales and marketing to the UK.
  (b) Appoint separate sales director and marketing director.
  (c) Introduce a matrix management structure for sales and marketing.
  (d) Encourage a greater marketing orientation.
  (e) Secure top level support for marketing.
  (f) Are individual managing directors necessary in each European country?

Budgets - advertising and promotion

3.15 No exact figures have been provided for future sales, marketing, advertising and promotional budgets.

3.16 Assumption: approximately 20% of sales revenue is to be allocated and I recommend the following breakdown for advertising and promotion.

(a) *Next five years*

1997	30%
1998	30%
1999	20%
2000	10%
2001	10%

(b) *Further broken down each year*

Advertising	50%
Public relations	5%
Sales promotion	10%
Personal selling	20%
Direct mail	10%
Contingency	5%
Total	100%

Contingencies

3.17 It is important to consider 'what if' scenarios.

(a) Plans should be drawn up for:
  (i) re-evaluating marketing mix
  (ii) competitor response profiling
  (iii) benchmarking against competition

(b) Lists of possible events should be produced ie:
  (i) EU law changes on healthcare
  (ii) Environmental issues for medical disposables
  (iii) competitor launching new products

Always be prepared for the unexpected.

Control

3.18 Control can be described as follows.
  (a) Setting standards
  (b) Measuring actual performance
  (c) Comparing actual performance
  (d) Evaluating reasons for variances
  (e) Taking corrective action

3.19 In this case, control needs to be effected upon the following.
  (a) Budgets (sales/advertising spend)
  (b) Forecasts (sales, number of new outlets)
  (c) Positioning)perception of quality, price, value for money of brands)
  (d) Awareness levels from advertising

4 OUTLINE MARKETING PLAN: EXAMPLE 2

Objectives

4.1 *Mission statement*

Mistral is dedicated to providing stakeholder value through the profitable provision of ancillary healthcare products

Mistral works closely with healthcare experts to develop leading edge accessories which aid injury prevention, assist surgical procedures, improve quality of life and aid healing.

4.2 *Marketing objectives*

(a) Increase total European market share from 29% to 40% over the next five years.
(b) Increase non-hospital market penetration from 24% to 35% over the planning period.
(c) Widen product mix so that no one product has more than 30% of total sales volume
(d) Enter new European markets by 1999
(e) Harmonise European pricing by 1999

Marketing strategy

4.3 A clear strategy will enable Mistral companies to work towards a common aim.

4.4 *Competitive forces*

An awareness of emerging trends is essential to select the correct strategy

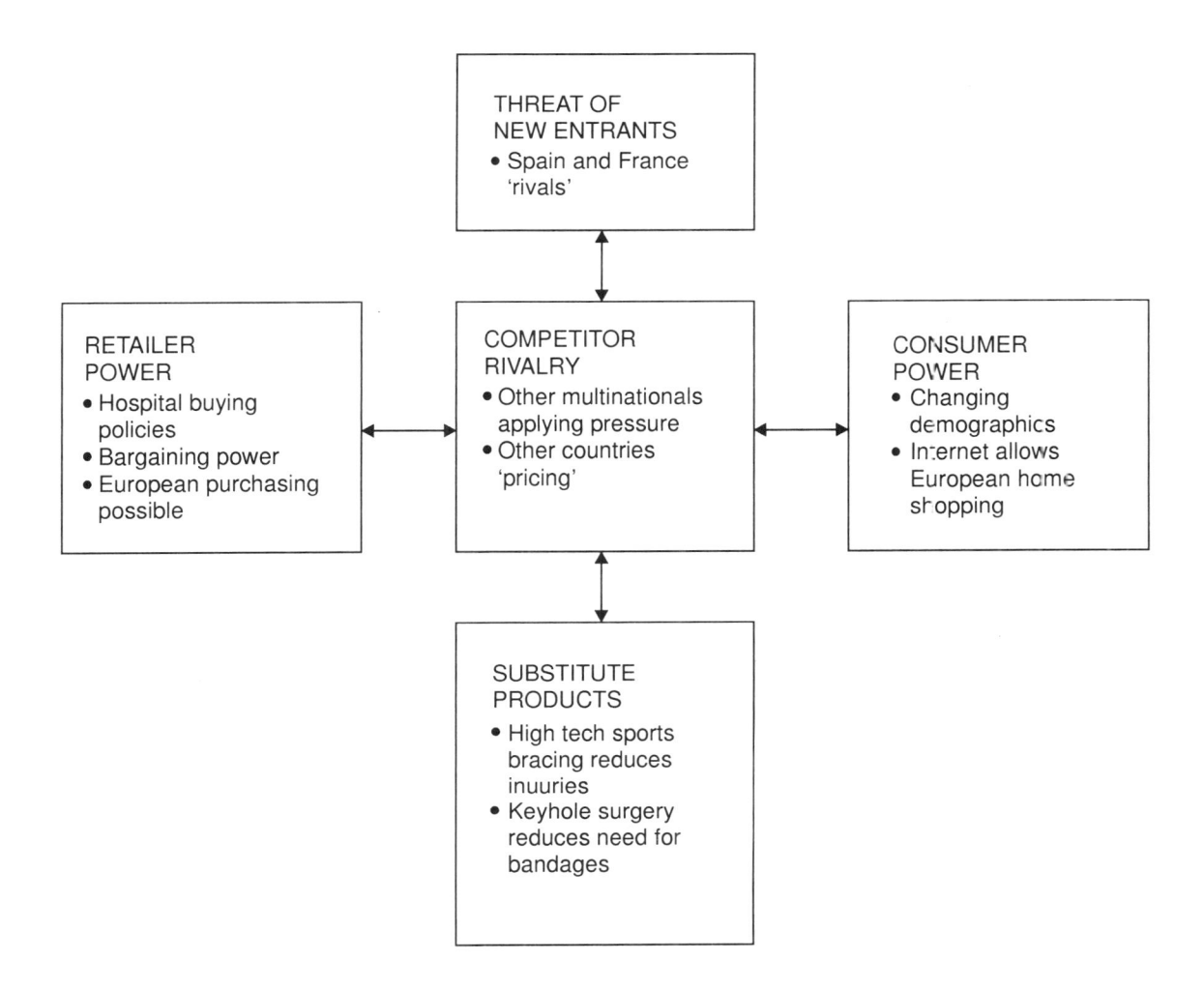

```
                    THREAT OF
                    NEW ENTRANTS
                    • Spain and France
                      'rivals'
                          ↕
RETAILER          COMPETITOR              CONSUMER
POWER             RIVALRY                 POWER
• Hospital buying • Other multinationals  • Changing
  policies          applying pressure       demographics
• Bargaining power ↔ • Other countries   ↔ • Internet allows
• European purchasing  'pricing'             European home
  possible                                   shopping
                          ↕
                    SUBSTITUTE
                    PRODUCTS
                    • High tech sports
                      bracing reduces
                      injuries
                    • Keyhole surgery
                      reduces need for
                      bandages
```

4.5 Strategic options

To respond to these forces, three strategies are possible.

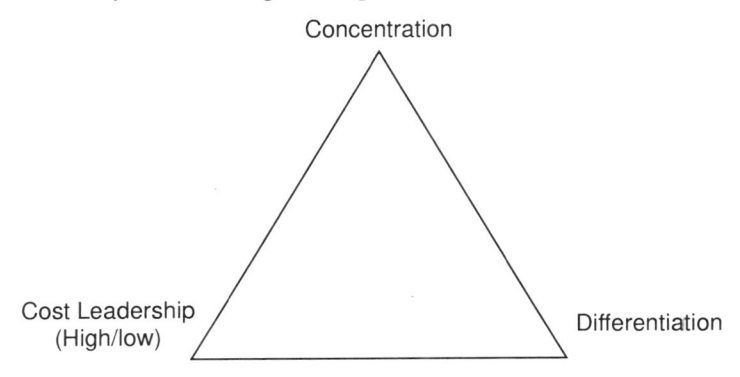

```
                    Concentration
                         /\
                        /  \
                       /    \
                      /      \
                     /        \
                    /          \
     Cost Leadership ---------- Differentiation
     (High/low)
```

(a) *Concentration (focus):* the wide range of markets and Mistral's wide product range make this option unfeasible.

(b) *Cost leadership:* Mistral's commitment to leading edge products and established 'traditional' products require a polarisation policy, which would be confusing to the customer.

(c) *Differentiation:* achieved through the provision of value added products, product innovation and strong branding. This strategy is recommended to achieve sustained competitive advantage.

4.6 *Market attack strategies*

The generic strategy identified in 4.5 identities the type of products and markets aimed at by Mistral. Competitive marketing approaches are considered below.

(a) *Frontal attack*

 (i) Takes on competitors across the marketing mix.

 (ii) Could lead to promotional wars, and requires consistent and aggressive marketing approach.

(b) *Flank attack*

 (i) Attack where opponents are weakest.

 (ii) As Mistral's main competitors are also multi-national companies this is unlikely to lead to sustained advantage.

(c) *Guerrilla attack*

 (i) Unpredictable and regional approach
 (ii) Not suitable in a 'homogenised Europe'

(d) *Bypass: recommended for Mistral*

 (i) Avoids direct competition by differentiating products and attacking new markets.

 (ii) Value added brand creation will complement this approach.

4.7 *Product portfolio/life cycle*

The reliance on ageing products demonstrates the urgent need for product relaunch, brand building and increased sales penetration

(a) *Product portfolio (from BCG)*

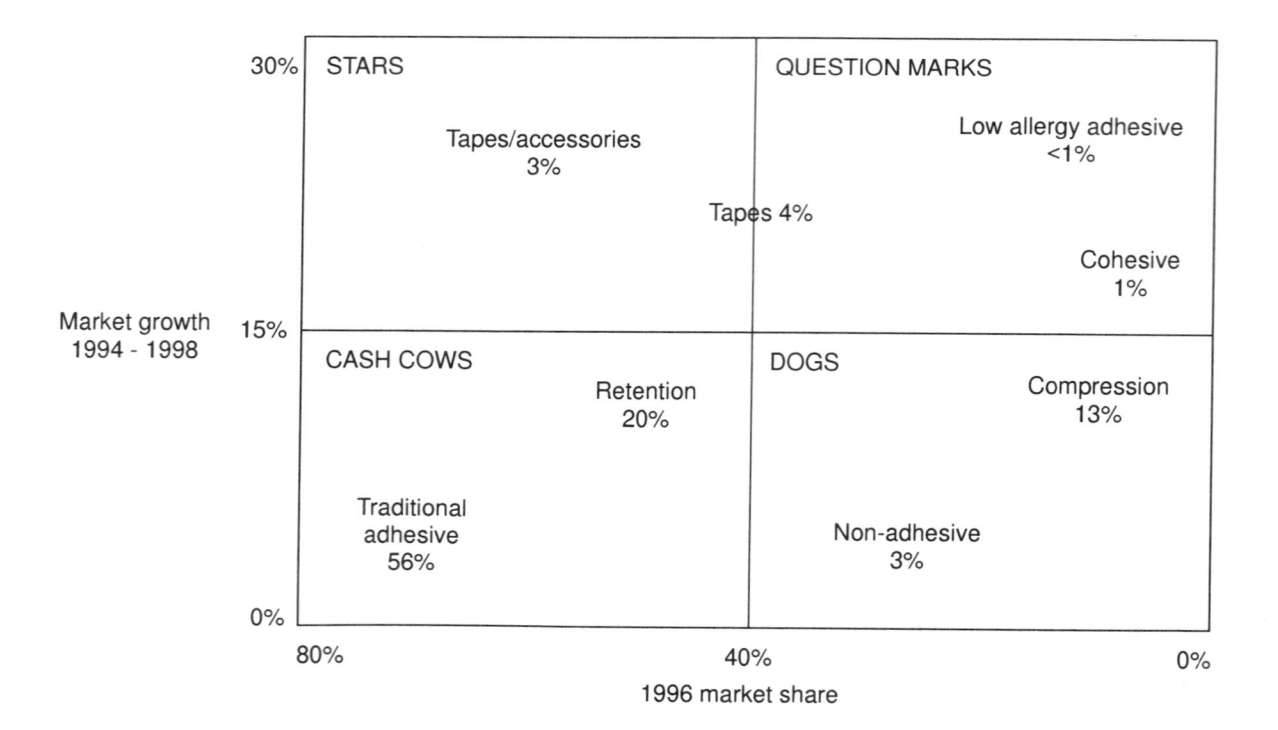

	80% – 40% market share	40% – 0% market share
15%–30% growth	STARS Tapes/accessories 3%	QUESTION MARKS Low allergy adhesive <1% Tapes 4% Cohesive 1%
0%–15% growth	CASH COWS Retention 20% Traditional adhesive 56%	DOGS Compression 13% Non-adhesive 3%

Market growth 1994 - 1998 (vertical axis); 1996 market share (horizontal axis)

(b) *Product life cycle (PLC*

INTRODUCTION	GROWTH	MATURITY	DECLINE
Push for awareness	Create pull	Relaunch	Redesign and relaunch

Curve points:
- Tapes/accessories (Introduction)
- Cohesive (Growth)
- Compression (Growth)
- Non-adhesive (Growth/Maturity)
- Retention (Maturity)
- Traditional adhesive (Decline)

4.8 *Strategic recommendations*

Presented in an *Ansoff Matrix*, also categorising risk.

	Existing Products	New Products
Existing Markets	MARKET PENETRATION • Compression market • Penetration strategy in Holland, France and Denmark • Cohesive support	PRODUCT DEVELOPMENT • Victrix and dressings as packages • High tech products developed with leading surgeons
New Markets	MARKET DEVELOPMENT • Products for older people • Eu and production markets	DIVERSIFICATION • Sports braces, developed with sportswear company

Justification

(a) *Low risk:* market penetration
  (i) Reduces reliance on mature products
  (ii) Increases control in individual markets
  (iii) compression market - growing due to demographic change

(b) *Medium risk.* Product and market development
  (i) Bypass competitors, value added solutions

(ii) Capitalises on demographic changes
(iii) Prestige as product innovator
(iv) Expand EU coverage, increasing turnover

(c) *High risk - diversification*

(i) Expand product base in competitive sports bracing market, reduce risk with joint venture.

Target markets for bandages

4.9 Mistral has an increasingly diverse range of user groups and customers.

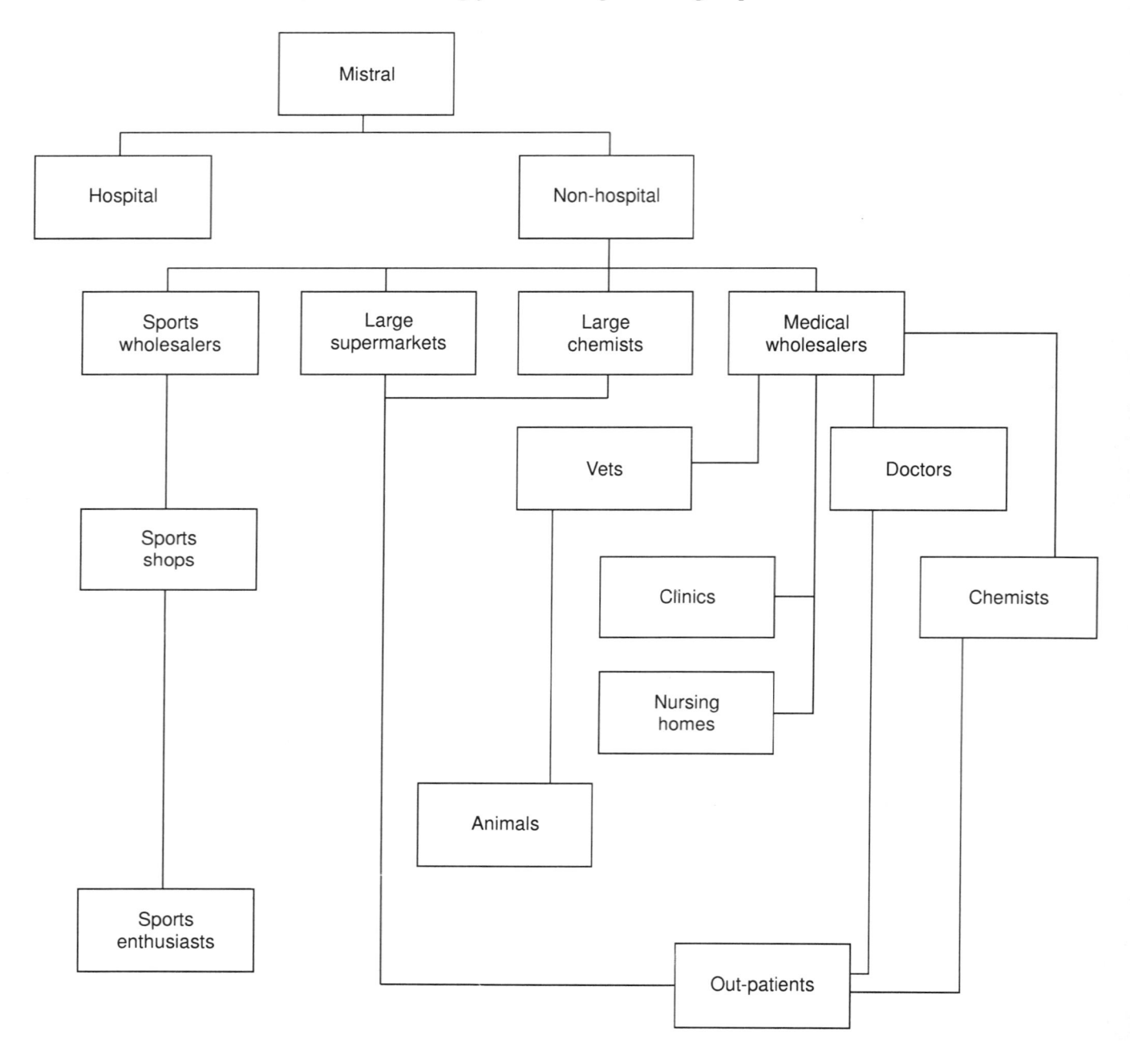

```
                          ┌─────────┐
                          │ Mistral │
                          └────┬────┘
                    ┌──────────┴──────────┐
              ┌─────────┐           ┌──────────────┐
              │Hospital │           │ Non-hospital │
              └─────────┘           └──────┬───────┘
                    ┌──────────┬──────────┬──────────┐
              ┌──────────┐┌──────────┐┌──────────┐┌──────────┐
              │  Sports  ││  Large   ││  Large   ││ Medical  │
              │wholesalers││supermarkets││ chemists ││wholesalers│
              └──────────┘└──────────┘└──────────┘└──────────┘
                   │                ┌────────┐   ┌─────────┐
                   │                │  Vets  │   │ Doctors │
                   │                └────────┘   └─────────┘
              ┌──────────┐          ┌────────┐   ┌──────────┐
              │  Sports  │          │ Clinics│   │ Chemists │
              │  shops   │          └────────┘   └──────────┘
              └──────────┘          ┌────────┐
                   │                │Nursing │
                   │                │ homes  │
                   │                └────────┘
                   │                ┌────────┐
                   │                │Animals │
                   │                └────────┘
              ┌──────────┐          ┌──────────────┐
              │  Sports  │          │ Out-patients │
              │enthusiasts│         └──────────────┘
              └──────────┘
```

Note. Non-hospital markets are becoming more important to Mistral due to the change in healthcare practices across Europe.

Targeting and positioning

4.10 An increased amount of consumer promotion and targeting will be required to take into account the trend towards homecare, private nursing homes, decreased prescription lists and an 'older' population.

4.11 Therefore, four clearly defined brands should be established to aid consumer understanding.

(*Note*. Brands can contain similar products but with clearly different uses.)

Brand	Product uses	User groups
Victrix	Dressing fixation, packaged most with dressings	In - and out-patients Animals
Felix	Injury support	In- and out-patients Animals
Venus	Sports injury prevention	Amateur/professional sports-people - all sports
Vulcan	Medical treatment	Older people

4.12 *Unique positioning*

   (a) Price/innovation

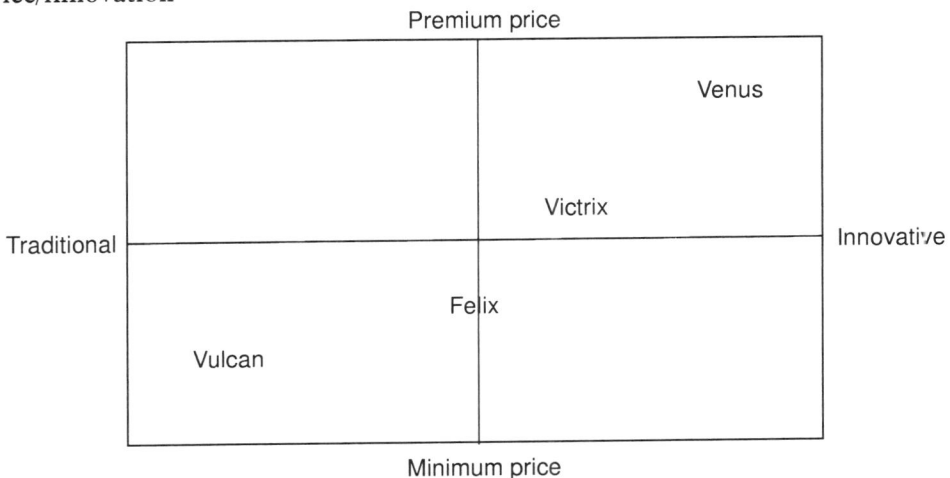

```
                    Premium price
         |                    |
         |                    |      Venus
         |                    |
         |                    |   Victrix
Traditional|--------------------|-----------Innovative
         |                    | Felix
         |                    |
         |   Vulcan           |
         |                    |
                    Minimum price
```

   (b) Durability/innovation

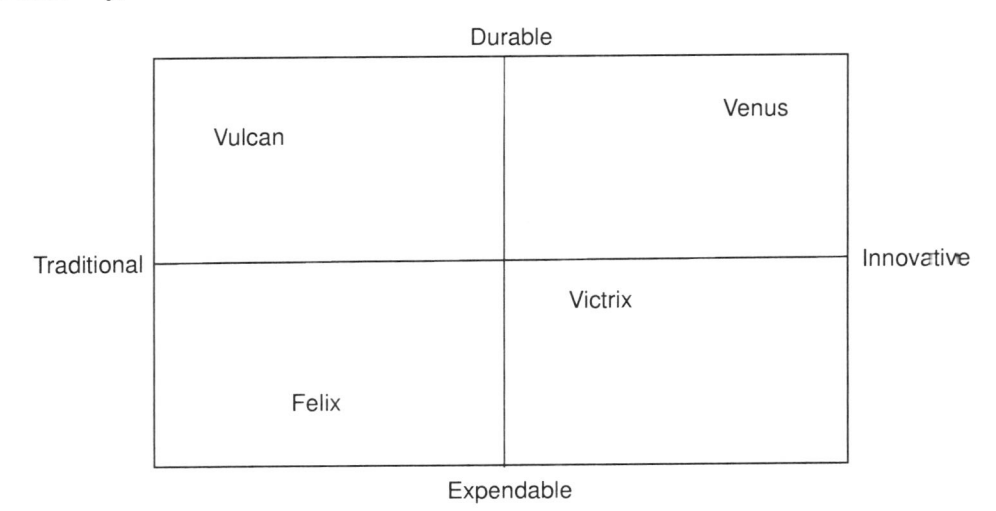

```
                      Durable
         |                    |
         |                    |      Venus
         |   Vulcan           |
         |                    |
Traditional|--------------------|-----------Innovative
         |                    |
         |                    |   Victrix
         |                    |
         |   Felix            |
                     Expendable
```

(c) Durability/attractiveness

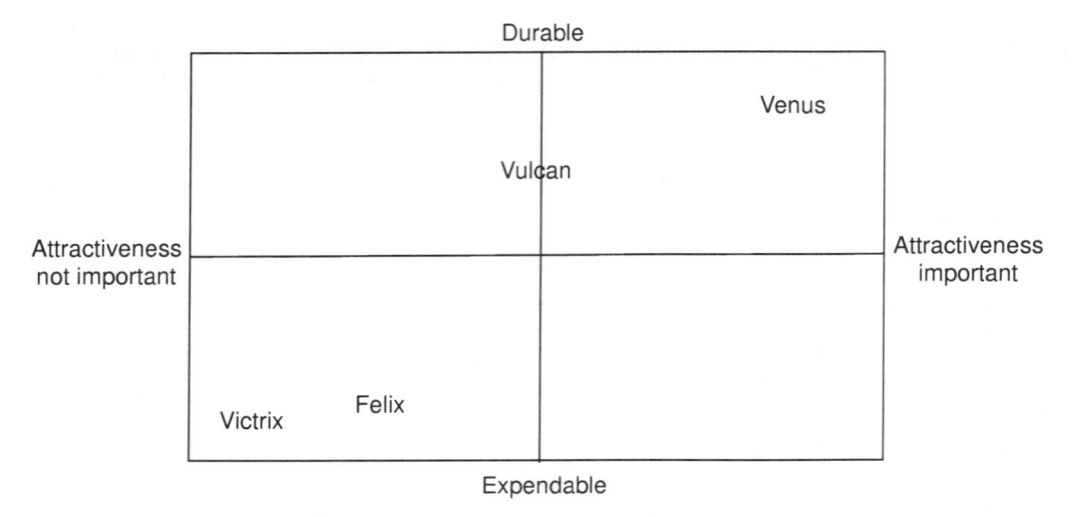

```
                        Durable
         ┌───────────────┬───────────────┐
         │               │               │
         │               │         Venus │
         │          Vulcan              │
Attractiveness         │           Attractiveness
not important          │               important
         │               │               │
         │               │               │
         │     Felix    │               │
         │ Victrix       │               │
         └───────────────┴───────────────┘
                      Expendable
```

Note. If competitor information were available this would also be shown above, to establish the degree of differentiation.

Marketing programmes

4.13

		From
1	*People (internal marketing)*	
	• Formal reporting structure, subsidiaries: head offices	6/97
	• Marketing forums for international know-how exchange	6/97
	• International assignments, develop future leaders	12/97
2	*Processes*	
	• International marketing information system (MkIS), database generation, information dissemination through Intranet, including research to identify major trends	12/97
3	*Product*	
	• Recategorise products into brands	12/97
	• Fixation packaged with dressings	12/97
	• Joint venture, sports bracing product	12/99
4	*Price*	
	• Geocentric pricing strategy, with local adaptation to market needs	6/98
5	*Distribution*	
	• To countries with manufacturing plants	12/99
	• Conquer other EU markets	1/2001
6	*Promotion*	
	• Industrial markets - push strategy	6/97
	• Consumer markets - pull strategy	6/97
	• Brand: local research	6/97
	• Advertising - central strategy, central and local production	1/98
	• Personal selling: international trade fairs	1/99
	• Public relations: central responsibility, local coordination	1/98
	• Sales promotion: local responsibility	3/97
	• Marketing mix: differentiated for industrial and consumer markets	1/98
7	*Research*	
	Market/marketing research	
	• Identify information gaps	6/97
	• Select agencies	6/97
	• Process data for input to MkIS (demographic changes and trends in healthcare particularly important)	12/97

Budgets

4.14 *Budget*

(a) Approved centrally, controlled locally

(b) Between 3-5% of sales turnover. 1996 spend on bandages *should* be:

Bandage turnover: £39,520,000. Therefore a 4% marketing budget = £1,580,800.

(c) Total European budget split

	Consumer £'000	Industrial £'000	Total £'000
Advertising - brand	100	200	300
- tactics	200	150	350
Merchandising POS	150	-	150
Trade fairs	-	200	200
Public relations	50	700	200
Sales provision	200	-	200
Research	75	25	100
Contingency	35	40	75
Marketing information system	35	40	75
Total	845	755	1,600

Comments

4.15 Both example marketing plans are very good don't you think? Example 2 makes more use of strategic modelling although it could have benefited from some notes on control. If yours is as good then you should be well satisfied.

Chapter 25

MISTRAL: DETAILED MARKETING PLANNING

> **This chapter contains the following information and plans.**
> 1 Introduction to detailed plans and the steps you should follow
> 2 Detailed marketing plan example
> 3 The examination

1 INTRODUCTION TO DETAILED PLANS AND THE STEPS YOU SHOULD FOLLOW

1.1 What you need to do now is to expand your outline plan into as much detail as possible an critically examine the completed final plan to ensure it covers everything, I well integrated and convincing.

1.2 At this point we need to advise that whereas a complete marketing plan is intended to cover you for all eventualities, it *cannot provide all the detail that might be needed for a specific examination question.* You will therefore have to add detail as required in the examination itself. Moreover, the CIM reserves the right to introduce additional material to you in the examination hall.

1.3 However, in anticipation of examination questions signalled in the case study some syndicates will prepare extra materials on, say, organisation or financial implications or marketing research.

1.4 With the above in mind we are reminding you of the steps you need to take in creating your detailed marketing plan having conducted the necessary prior analysis.

> CONSULT THE GUIDANCE NOTES GIVEN IN
> CHAPTER 8 PARAGRAPHS 4.19 TO 6.8
>
> **STEP 15 DEVELOP QUANTIFIED, TIMESCALED OBJECTIVES**
>
> **STEP 16 CONSIDER ALTERNATIVE STRATEGIES. SELECT THOSE MOST APPROPRIATE**
>
> **STEP 17 DRAW UP DETAILED TACTICAL PLANS COVERING THE MARKETING MIX**
>
> **STEP 18 DRAW UP A MARKETING RESEARCH PLAN AND MKIS**
>
> **STEP 19 CONSIDER ORGANISATIONAL ISSUES, CHANGES AND MARKETING ORIENTATION**
>
> **STEP 20 CONSIDER ORGANISATIONAL CULTURE AND NEED FOR INTERNAL MARKETING**
>
> **STEP 21 DETERMINE THE FINANCIAL/HR RESOURCE IMPLICATONS OF YOUR PLANS**
>
> **STEP 22 ASSESS COSTS AND DRAW UP INDICATIVE BUDGETS**
>
> **STEP 23 DRAW UP SCHEDULES GIVING TIMINGS/SEQUENCE OF ACTIONS**
>
> **STEP 24 SPECIFY REVIEW PROCEDURES AND CONTROL MECHANISMS**
>
> **STEP 25 DRAW UP OUTLINE CONTINGENCY PLANS**
>
> **STEP 26 REVIEW YOUR COMPLETE MARKETING PLAN**
>
> YOU WILL NEED BETWEEN 15 AND 18 HOURS TO DO THIS MAJOR TASK

1.5 Having completed your own detailed marketing plan you might like to compare your efforts with that of the syndicate which follows.

1.6 The detailed marketing plan example has been chosen largely on account of its coverage within the time available It suffers a *lack of strategic models* (compared with the example outline plans). Also, strictly speaking, segmentation/target markets and positioning should come under the general heading of Marketing Strategy. A major omission is that of marketing research. However, overall this plan serves as a good example of what could constitute a comfortable pass in the examination, given a section on marketing research.

How does your detailed plan compare?

2 DETAILED MARKETING PLAN EXAMPLE

Marketing objectives

2.1

1. To increase total bandage sales by 25% from £40 million (1996) to £54 million by 2001
2. To achieve a gross profit level of not less than 50% and a net profit margin of about 20%
3. To achieve a 2:1 (67%:33%) ratio for the community market to the hospital market by 2001
4. To increase market shares in the compression bandages and adhesive support lines from 15.6% to 50% and from 5.3% to 15%, respectively (rationale provided later in this report).
5. To increase proportion of sales from Belgium Denmark and Holland to at least 30% of total Mistral sales.

Target markets and segmentation

2.2 *Current situation*

(a) Our current stance is not strategic, since it is based on product types, institutions (hospital and non-hospital) and countries.

(b) It does not take into account similar characteristics of *strategically equivalent segments* across Europe's Single Market, mobility of people, and common lifestyles.

(c) The growing importance of the community sector requires more relevant classification of customers.

2.3 *Segmentation approach*

(a) Consider customers' needs and expected perceived benefits, since *solutions* are bought, not commodities as such.

    (i) *Hospital sector*

        (1) Private vs public
- Price sensitivity
- Buying policies
- Cost consciousness

        (2) Size (big vs small)
- Volume of purchases
- Complexity of decision-making unit (DMU)
- Key account management

        (3) Location
- Distribution logistics
- National vs regional
- Servicing attention required

        (4) Sophistication
- Product specifications to match treatment for bandaging needs
- High tech range of products
- Affordability to the affluent

    (ii) Trade sector (wholesalers, distributors, pharmacies, clinics, vets)

        (1) Size and number of outlets or branches
- Purchasing policies
- Buying power
- Bulk discounts expected
- Margins
- Availability of shelf space
- Competitors represented, including exclusivity arrangements
- House brands, labels

    (iii) End-user sector (individuals)

        (1) Based on psychographics/life style

(b) Recognise that markets are interlinked regionally and vertically

    (i) *Regional*

        (1) Hospitals may operate in groups or chains through affiliation, joint ventures, management agreements.

        (2) Trade customers may be part of common wholesale or retail pharmacy chain.

        (3) End users may move or travel from one place to another in Europe.

    (ii) *Vertical*

    Hospitals may be linked by referral to specialists, general practitioners, physiotherapists, pharmacies and patients in a vertical chain.

(c) Consider similarities in bandage markets which might exist in other areas.
   (i)   End-user applications
   (ii) Purchase criteria
   (iii) benefits sought

Positioning

2.4 Mistral previously positioned itself as a leading low-cost supplier of traditional adhesives. However, competition is intense here and its product, Venus Ace, is at the ageing stage of product life cycle.

2.5 Mistral should re-position itself as a brand leader at the high end of the bandages industry, in the compression (Vulcan) and cohesives (Felix Jaz) ranges, where growth potential is greatest.

2.6 Mistral should adopt a differentiation-focus strategy instead of the cost-leadership strategies of its major competitors, to avoid head-on confrontation with them.

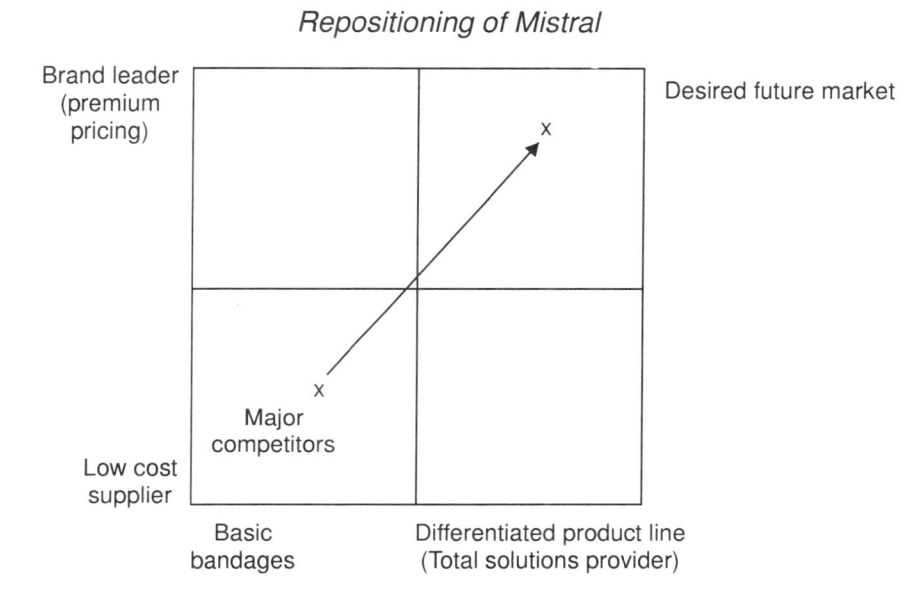

Repositioning of Mistral

```
Brand leader
(premium                                    Desired future market
pricing)                              x

                              
                        x
                    Major
                    competitors
Low cost
supplier
            Basic           Differentiated product line
            bandages        (Total solutions provider)
```

Marketing strategy

2.7 In the short-term to 2001 (the next five years), a *market penetration* strategy is advocated.

Rationale: supposedly the easiest method which produces results soonest.

(a) Gain new customers
   (i) Target customers not currently using Mistral bandages.
   (ii) Target private institutional customers whose end-users could afford high-end lines like Felix Jaz and Vulcan.

(b) Obtain more value from existing customers.
   (i)   Focus on customer retention (relationship marketing).
   (ii) Preserve the key accounts (eg the 15 product-market sectors whose 1996 sales exceeded £1 million).
   (iii) Cross-sell the full range, especially the compression and cohesive lines.
   (iv) Emphasise benefits to differentiate from the competition.

(c) Improve profitability of the current business

    (i) Examine current supplier relationship with factories in Dublin and Athens to negotiate more equitable transfer pricing.

    (ii) Alter sales mix by increasing the proportion of high margin lines.

    (iii) Review level of marketing and sales expenditure (average of 21% is too high!)

Product strategy

2.8 *Tapes and accessories* (where Mistral is leader in a small market)

Defend/increase market share by seeking to become customers' first choice, especially the *Venus Lazo* and *Felix Ace* lines

2.9 *Compression and cohesive* support (where Mistral is a small player in a big market).

    (a) Increase turnover as well as margins from premium pricing by differentiation.

    (b) Differentiate the high-tech range (Vulcan) from the competition to prevent customers from treating all bandages alike.

    (c) Emphasise reliability and hence value for money to justify premium pricing in general.

2.10 *Traditional adhesives* (where Mistral is leader in a mature market)

    (a) Strive to achieve greater cost efficiency through economies of scale by negotiating lower transfer price from factories or consider outsourcing (subject to Mistral Inc approval).

    (b) Stress cost-effectiveness since prices have been driven low, and the ageing stage of the PLC is reached.

    (c) Saturate the trade customers sector which provides wide distribution networks.

    (d) Rejuvenate product to extend its life or repackage to renew its appeal especially toward OTC end-user customers.

2.11 *Non-adhesive support and low allergy adhesives* (which are of low profit importance and low existing and future sales importance).

    (a) Limit sales and marketing costs to commensurate level, since Felix Prime 2 has reached maturity stage in PLC.

    (b) Review significance of these products in relation to Mistral's other products to consider a possible phased withdrawal from the market.

Pricing strategy

2.12 *The current situation*

    (a) The absence of standard pan-European pricing policy (not the same as absolute prices) has these implications.

        (i) Inconsistent pricing to customers (who may be mobile, knowledgeable of our prices and operating regionally).

        (ii) Over-pricing is uncompetitive or under-pricing sacrifices potential profits.

        (iii) Unethical practices such as parallel importing could happen.

        Note. Major lines (Felix Jaz, Venus Ace, Vulcan) are priced at 4p to 8p per cm^2, other than Victrix which is priced at 1p to 2p per cm^2 - Spring 1996 prices).

    (b) Pricing has not been based on *value* or *perceived benefits* to customers but on outcome of competitive bidding or price-discounting.

(c) *Premium pricing* cannot be *commanded* on high-end products because customers may not understand the 'economic value' concept ie *hidden costs* on top of purchase price are not considered, such as:

    (i)   the adverse effect of poor quality bandages;

    (ii)   the extended healing time due to ineffective bandages;

    (iii)   the costs of disposal;

    (iv)   the staff (nurses and hospital assistants) cost of training to use high-tech, special bandages).

Premium pricing must be justified.

2.13 *Suggested pricing strategies*

(a) Develop consistent policy on pricing across the entire UK and European companies. There is a need for consensus of pricing to prevent:

    (i)   parallel importing, hence prices being pressed down in France by Italy;
    (ii)   confusion among Mistral's regional customers (especially institutional);

(b) Pursue a policy of non-price competition and use product and service differentiation to justify our price premium, especially when targeting the more quality-conscious and affluent customers (private hospitals and individuals).

(c) Train the marketing staff and also educate customers (by seminars and conventions) on our philosophy of 'higher price but better quality' for high-tech ranges like Vulcan.

(d) Promote and ensure *quality assurance* in our products so that if we can sustain a quality differential, customers will pay our price.

(e) Set up joint working committees to determine common pricing basis for negotiating with clients that operate across Europe.

2.14 *Segmentation approach*

Using the *price segmentation model*, four price categories of customers could be envisaged.

(a) *'Price' segment* most likely applies to customers of Victrix range who are indifferent to quality. This could be used by small clinics treating outpatient end-users for minor injuries.

(b) *'Convenience' segment* represents those who are indifferent to differentiation but who are prepared to pay for easy availability. could apply to consumers who buy OTC for common self-manageable injuries. Packaging may be the basis of choice. Products: Felix Prime 2 and Venus Ace.

(c) *Value segment* could be found in the institutional private sector hospitals which are both brand conscious and cost-conscious, eg Venus and Vulcan lines where quality justifies price.

(d) The *loyal segment* are those straight rebuy customers who make Mistral the market leader. Prices will have to be kept competitive to maintain volume.

Sales and distribution strategy

2.15 Increase the *'life-time value'* of each existing customer. Selling activities will entail both *account penetration* and *order filling*.

2.16 *Prioritise new account* penetration as a counter-defensive measure to the big four competitors by penetrating *their* customer base by promoting our value-added solutions.

2.17 Develop *distribution channels* in the community (trade) sector to ensure a wide coverage.

Part E: Learning from experience: ensuring you pass

2.18 Stress the 'economic-value to the customer' concept by emphasising the real benefits of our bandaging solutions compared to the low prices of our competitors, which may not reveal hidden usage costs.

2.19 *Relationship marketing* is an effective counter strategy to the threat of customer loss.

Promotions strategy

2.20 Develop an awareness of the Mistral family brand name throughout UK and European markets.

2.21 Devise pan-European promotion initiatives to project a common approach to the homogeneous, interlinked European markets.

2.22 Increase advertising and promotions budget (above and below the line) to fund the brand building activity over the next five years.

Brand development in Europe

2.23 *Current situation*

(a) Mistral's current brands are 'fragmented' and not associated with its corporate name and identity.

(b) To command a regional market, a pan-European approach to the development of new brands, currently non-existent, will be essential.

2.24 *Proposed process*

(a) Commission a *pan-European market research* project on branding.

Purpose: to determine which of Mistral's brands are preferred and what they mean to customers.

(b) *Investigate the customer's possible reactions* if certain existing brands are deleted only to be re-named.

Purpose: to assess strength of brand names in differentiation against the competition, as well as perception of quality by customers.

(c) *Develop and consider possible individual brand names*, and consult with UK and European subsidiaries on acceptability based on cultural language, religious and other relevant points of view.

(d) *Obtain consensus* from May Alexander and, if necessary, Mistral Inc's approval on the proposed new branding exercise.

(e) Current individual brands have already been prefixed in name by the four major product lines.

(i) The next logical step is, preferably to link the names to the corporate identity of Mistral.

(ii) However, to do so may make the brand names too cumbersome and lose their effectiveness.

(f) Mistral will have to determine which branding approach to use.

(i) Use new names as discussed.
(ii) Use existing names together with the Mistral name.

We recommend that the combination branding method be used so that the Mistral label is used but without cluttering the individual brand names.

(g) Once the new brand identities have been decided on, work on an internal communication exercise to inform all levels of staff of the intended changes.

(h) *Appoint an agency* to assume the responsibility of communicating the new brands across the region, after due deliberation over the budgeted advertising and promotion expenditures allocated to this brand development exercise.

(i) Ensure that all corporate livery and communications, whether internal or external, convey the intended message of the new brands eg 'preferred medical products supplier'.

(j) As future sales endeavours are made, train the sales force to remind Mistral customers of the new brands which are aimed to differentiate from others and which convey the Mistral pledge of quality and cost-effectiveness.

(k) Annually, continue to invest appropriate sums of expenditure to promote the new brands.

Quantitative projections

2.25 *Sales (in £ million)*

1977	1998	1999	2000	2001
42	44	47	50	54

Justifications

(a) Market penetration
(b) Brand development

2.26 *Sales mix*

(a) *By sector (%)*

	1997	1998	1999	2000	2001
Hospital	41	39	37	35	33
Non-hospital	59	61	63	65	67

Justifications

(i) To re-align with overall market mix
(ii) To develop the non-hospital market to take advantage of 'megatrend shift'
(iii) To reap benefits of market-orientation strategy instead of product-push strategy

(b) *By product line*

1996 to 2001

	%		%
Functional bandaging	69.5	→	25
Functional taping	9.6	→	10
Support	5.3	→	15
Compression	15.6	→	50
	100.0		100

(c) *By country*

1996 to 2001

	%		%
UK	41	→	25
Italy	35	→	25
France	18	→	20
Belgium		→	10
Denmark	6	→	10
Holland		→	10
	100		100

(d) Financial budget (£ million)

	1997	1998	1999	2000	2001
Sales	42.0	44.0	47.0	50.0	54.0
Gross profit	21.0	22.0	23.5	25.0	27.0
Marketing expenses	6.3	6.6	7.1	7.6	8.1
General expenses	4.2	4.4	4.7	5.0	5.4
Advertising and promotions	2.1	2.2	2.3	2.4	2.7
Net profit	8.4	8.8	9.4	10.0	10.8

3 THE EXAMINATION

3.1 You must now get your preparations finalised for the second mock exam before turning to the exam paper which follows in the next chapter.

3.2 Just in case you have forgotten, you need to conduct two final steps in the recommended methodology.

3.3

CONSULT CHAPTERS 8 AND 10 FOR GUIDANCE NOTES.
STEP 27 DRAW UP YOUR EXAMINATION PLAN **STEP 28 PRACTICE WRITING IN TRUE REPORT STYLE (CHAPTER 10)**
ALLOW AS LONG AS NECESSARY FOR THESE LAST TWO STEPS

3.4 Good luck in your second practice run exam!

Chapter 26

MISTRAL: THE EXAMINATION PAPER, EXAMINER'S REPORT AND INDICATIVE MARKING GUIDES

This chapter contains the following.

1 The examination paper
2 Examiner's report
3 Indicative marking guides
4 A final word

MISTRAL

THE EXAM QUESTIONS ARE ON THE NEXT PAGE

DO NOT LOOK UNTIL YOU ARE READY TO SPEND
THREE HOURS ON DOING THESE AS A MOCK EXAM

Notes **Part E: Learning from experience: ensuring you pass**

1 THE EXAMINATION PAPER

Additional information - to be taken into account when answering the questions set.

MEMORANDUM

To: John Norland
From: May Alexander
Subject: Parallel importing
Date: 1 December 1996

I thought you should be aware of a very heated discussion I have just had with Jean-Michel le Mesurier in Paris. If I have understood him correctly, there seems to be a problem with the autonomous pricing strategies in the various European countries because, without trade barriers, wholesalers are able to nip across the border and buy the same Mistral product in a neighbouring country, sometimes for a fraction of the Price. Such parallel importing activities appear to be driving prices down to the lowest common denominator and causing great embarrassment. Jean-Michel was furious because, having endeavoured to keep his prices up to retain the position of price leader in his market he now finds he is being undercut, indirectly, by our Italian colleagues. This needs further investigation but I just thought that you should be aware of the problem and include some consideration of this matter in the presentation to the quarterly strategy meeting later this month.

I am looking forward to hearing your presentation and also Simon Walker's on the bandages market.

With best wishes

May Alexander

You have had a month to analyse the information which John Norland has given you and to prepare your presentation in discussion with your colleagues at PACE Marketing Consultants. Your presentation, *in report format,* will cover the following.

Question 1 - (50 marks)

Present a strategic marketing plan for the European bandages business of Mistral, looking ahead five years. Your plan should take into account the major trends affecting the business, including demographics, technology and the switch in influence away from hospitals in favour of the community.

Question 2 - (25 marks)

Based on your strategic marketing plan, make recommendations to Mistral for a European pricing policy that will support the company's marketing objectives and overcome problems of parallel importing.

Question 3 - (25 marks)

Propose a process by which Mistral can begin to develop new brands in Europe.

26: Mistral: the examination paper, examiner's report and indicative marking guides

2 EXAMINER'S REPORT

General comments

2.1 Unfortunately, results in this paper are still generally disappointing. Too many candidates are still failing to deal with the constraints of a three-hour examination and so failing to demonstrate their ability to apply marketing principles.

2.2 The Mistral case found far too many candidates unable to address the question posed on examination day. Work prepared before the examination was too often regurgitated without thinking or taking account of the additional information or the marks allocated on the paper.

2.3 The list of reasons for failure in the case were (yet again):
   (a) failure to answer the questions posed on the day;
   (b) regurgitation of case material;
   (c) presentation of pre-prepared answers regardless of questions set;
   (d) lack of knowledge on strategic marketing issues;
   (e) inclusion of irrelevant data, numbers and SWOT analysis;
   (f) ignoring the additional information provided;
   (g) poor time management;

2.4 The last again requires special mention. In this case the questions carried marks of 50:25:25. Question 1 was rightly anticipated by most candidates but was often answered as if it carried 80% of the marks. Questions 2 and 3 were often answered quite superficially and covered in two or three pages each - or even ignored completely!

2.5 Examiners try hard to award marks but to do so we need something to mark! Time management is a critical skill for the practising marketer - not just useful to pass exams.

Question 1 (50 marks)

> *'Present a strategic marketing plan for the European bandages business of Mistral, looking ahead five years. Your plan should take into account the major trends affecting the business, including demographics, technology and the switch in influence away from hospitals in favour of the community'.*

2.6 Most candidates had properly forecast this question. Having been asked so many times in the past, this question is beginning to focus attention on the contents of a strategic marketing plan and generally the structures (if not the contents) of plans are improving. Unfortunately, for some candidates it is obviously the only thing that they prepare. In this case the strategic marketing plan attracted only 50% of the marks and too few candidates modified their approach accordingly.

2.7 One by-product of an easily predictable question is the reliance on group preparation or even completely pre-prepared answers simply copied out on the day of the examination. Such collusion is easily spotted by examiners and always rewarded with a fail grade. Remember, you can prepare with others but the examination is a test of individual, not group, ability. The questions and the additional information are constructed in such a way to make pre-prepared answer difficult to use so candidates should read the question *very* carefully on the day.

2.8 SWOT and PEST analyses continue to take up pages of examination scripts but still attract relatively few marks because they are not applied to strategic action and recommendations.

2.9 The major problems in answer to this question on the Mistral case centred around the following.

(a) Concentration on tactics rather than longer term strategy.

(b) A tendency to give top-level views on what should be done without any indication of *how* this might be achieved.

(c) Inadequate understanding of targeting and positioning although Porter and BCG models were used extensively.

(d) Failure to identify target markets thereby producing a wide range of conflicting objectives and actions and a tendency to produce 'product-led' strategies.

(e) Not all candidates submitted budgets and the control aspects were generally weak.

(f) General confusion about the difference between strategy and tactics.

(g) Too many candidates, working to a predictable question, are contenting themselves with a 'tick-box' answer that concentrates on getting the headings to a strategic plan right and not worrying too much about the content.

2.10 The major comment from examiners is that while many candidates can identify strategic alternatives by using Ansoff/Porter, far too few seem capable of making an informed choice and proposing action. The majority of the marks available to candidates are awarded for *decisions* not analysis. Once again we found too few opportunities to award marks for this aspect.

Question 2 (25 marks)

'Based on your strategic marketing plan, make recommendations to Mistral for a European pricing policy that will support the company's marketing objectives and overcome the problems of parallel importing'.

2.11 This question proved difficult for candidates who had only prepared a strategic plan before the examination. Those who had succeeded in understanding the Mistral situation in a wider, more strategic, context managed better. Those candidates unable to think on the day fared badly.

2.12 This question was looking for two things, in recommendations for a European pricing policy:

(a) to support Mistral's marketing objectives (from Question 1);
(b) to overcome problems of parallel importing (from additional information).

2.13 Candidates who thought this simply meant writing out the pricing section they had prepared for the strategic plan tended to fail this question.

2.14 The main problems encountered on this question were these.

(a) Offering simplistic solutions like 'standardised pricing' for all countries without regard to local conditions or implementation.

(b) Not understanding or trying to find out what 'parallel importing' means (this is an open book examination so the reference material is available!).

(c) Certificate level explanations of 'penetration' or 'skimming' without any attempt to relate to the case.

(d) Answers that directly contradicted proposals made in Question 1, for example reducing prices while proposing a market-leading position!

Question 3 (25 marks)

> 'Propose a process by which Mistral can begin to develop new brands in Europe'.

2.15 This question proved the downfall of far too many candidates. Even allowing for thinking and planning the answer, 25 marks should justify in excess of 30 minutes writing time. Examiners offered just two or three pages found it difficult to award pass marks.

2.16 A surprising number of candidates appeared to have little understanding of branding, despite its coverage in Marketing Communications Strategy (Diploma) and the attention given to this subject in the recent marketing literature. The Leffe case was the last case to look at branding as a strategic issue; sadly there is little evidence of progress being made.

2.17 The main problems encountered on this question were these.

   (a) Confusing 'brands' with 'products' and offering ideas on new product development processes.

   (b) Not offering a 'process' but a textbook definition of what brands are.

   (c) Little consideration of the special nature of international branding.

   (d) Answers that directly contradicted proposals made in question one.

Conclusions

2.18 Mistral again proved to be a difficult case for too many candidates.

2.19 Questions 2 and 3 have highlighted the dangerously superficial knowledge held by a number of candidates on key strategic issues such as pricing and branding. Previous cases have also shown this problem in areas such as forecasting and strategic alliances (Gravesend), positioning and promotion (Leffe), marketing organisation (FirsrATE) and segmentation (Australian Tourist Commission)

2.20 Future cases will continue to explore these areas.

3 INDICATIVE MARKING GUIDES

3.1 *Overview*

   (a) *The case.* The case study presented for this examination has been disguised. However the data and financial/pricing figures have been produced (after modifications) from the real data drawn from the sponsor organisation. The case represents a real situation and a real problem that the organisation faces today.

   (b) The organisation has a long history and controls many extremely successful brands across Europe. These brands are under competitive pressure mainly from low priced alternatives. There are pressures from the market, and more recently from inside Mistral, to cut prices to compete. So far Mistral management have resisted these pressures but cannot continue to do indefinitely without other affirmative action in the market place to support their position.

   (c) *Key points*

   (i) Mistral is an organisation with a history.

   (ii) Mistral has successfully managed brands in this market for over 60 years!

   (iii) Mistral is a multi-national organisation facing multi-national competition.

   (iv) Mistral is a price leader in most markets.

   (v) Mistral is facing price competition.

Notes   *Part E: Learning from experience: ensuring you pass*

- (vi) Products are driven by technology and softer issues.
- (vii) Mistral must deal with a complicated industrial buying process.
- (viii) The future promises major changes to Mistral's markets.
- (ix) Mistral operates a decentralised planning process.
- (x) Mistral has a history of success but it may have to change to continue that success into the future.

3.2 *The answers.* In awarding marks in this case, the key points are these.

- (a) We are looking for application, not just the statement of theory.
- (b) We are assessing marketing answers, not product-led sales answers.
- (c) We are assessing marketing strategy, not tactics.
- (d) The answer must be practical given the case situation.
- (e) The acid test remains - would you give this person a job as a marketer?

3.3 *The additional information.* The problems (potential and real) associated with pricing policy were clearly signposted in this case. The additional information puts the final touches to that discussion and shows where the problem will lead if not tackled directly.

The pricing issue has a question (Question 2, 25%) dedicated to it. We should expect to pick up reference to the additional information in this question.

For the unwary (and product-led mind) all this data could suggest a purely economic solution to the problem. This will not do at all!

Question 1

3.4 *Question 1 - 50 marks.* (Present a strategic marketing plan for the European bandages business of Mistral, looking ahead five years. Your plan should take into account the major trends affecting the business, including demographics, technology and the switch in influence away from hospitals in favour of the community.)

- (a) *Approach*

    This question is similar to those asked in previous papers so should have been predicted by most candidates - marks should not be awarded too easily. Given that developing a strategic marketing plan is what most candidates will have spent most of the past four weeks doing, we can be demanding. Models will be popular, of course, but should only be used as a guide to strategic recommendations that must be firmly linked to Mistral's particular situation.

    (*Note,* In an open book examination no marks are gained by simply copying models out of books.)

    - (i) The question is asking for:
        - (1) a strategic marketing plan;
        - (2) for bandages;
        - (3) for Europe;
        - (4) for the period 1996-2001.
    - (ii) The question also clearly defines some of the environmental factors that the plan needs to take account of:
        - (1) demographics;
        - (2) technology;
        - (3) shift of influence from hospitals to community.

        There are of course others!

- (b) As with all cases of strategic marketing plans, success is much more likely if driven by customers and their needs rather than by competition or products. Targeting and positioning (of the brands in the minds of Mistral's customers and prospects) must be the key for the future. Some short-sighted people are calling for margin reduction and price cutting to meet short-term competitive pressure but this must be resisted. The company has always been premium priced and has offered 'superior' products to its market. Mistral must look to:

- (i) 'rediscover' the needs of its customers;
- (ii) 'reinvent' the brands to make them relevant to today's needs;
- (iii) compete from a premium price position;
- (iv) continue to add value above that offered by the competition.

3.5 *Good answers to Question 1*

We can expect to see a logical sequence of steps that might look like this.

(a) *Current situation*
- (i) What is going on?
- (ii) What is the problem?
- (iii) PEST/SWOT

(b) *Corporate objectives/mission statement vision*
- (i) What business are we in?
- (ii) What do we want to achieve?

(c) *Target market*
- (i) What are we aiming at?
- (ii) What are key needs/want/motivators?
- (iii) Segmentation
- (iv) Other 'stakeholders' and their interests

(d) *Marketing objectives*
- (i) What should we be trying to do?
- (ii) Quantifications
- (iii) SMART

(e) *Targeting and positioning*
- (i) How do we differentiate Mistral?
- (ii) How do we position Mistral in the customers' minds?
- (iii) Key 'product-market matches'?

(f) *Marketing strategy*
- (i) What are the alternatives?
- (ii) Which route is best?
- (iii) Why?
- (iv) Porter/Ansoff/GEC/ADL models - if relevant

(g) *Marketing programmes*
- (i) Product policy
  - product/packaging/source etc
- (ii) Pricing policy
  - relating to competition and position
  - relate to additional information
- (iii) Distribution policy
  - local environment driven
- (iv) Customer service
  - relate to position
- (v) Process policy
- (vi) People policy
- (vii) Promotional policy
  - related to position and vision

(h) *Ensuring implementation*
- (i) Budgets
- (ii) Timetables
- (iii) Control system

Notes **Part E: Learning from experience: ensuring you pass**

(iv) Contingency planning

3.6 Best answers will:

(a) apply environmental analysis to Mistral;
(b) identify target market(s) and position Mistral to meet them;
(c) set marketing objectives;
(d) propose marketing strategy - alternatives and selection;
(e) propose marketing programmes - to deliver the strategy;
(f) outline budgets and control systems for implementation.

Question 2

3.7 *Question 2 - 25 marks.* (Based on your strategic marketing plan, make recommendations to mistral for a European pricing policy that will support the company's marketing objectives and overcome problems of parallel importing.)

(a) *Approach*

(i) This question can be expected to cause candidates some problems.

(ii) It is the first time that we have asked candidates a specific question on pricing and, although it was clearly signposted in the case, it may catch come candidates unprepared.

(iii) The question is also linked to an international aspect - parallel importing. Again the data was all contained within the case but may not have been considered properly.

Note. It is an open book examination and texts can be consulted on the day to clarify certain terms.

(b) The questions asks for:

(i) an answer to Question 2 based on the strategic marketing plan presented in Question 1;

(ii) recommendations for a European pricing policy to:

(1) support Mistral's marketing objectives (from Question 1);
(2) overcome problems of parallel importing (from Additional information).

3.8 Good answers to Question 2 will build on the answer presented in Question 1. We are looking for a clear continuation of the marketing plans, not a short-term fix that goes against Question 1 proposals. Naturally the answers will be dependent upon answers given to Question 1 and should be marked in this light.

(a) *Part one*

We are looking for evidence that the candidates understands the strategic role and significance of price, the nature of pricing objectives and the factors which need to be taken into account when setting a price. Good answers will probably follow the sequence:

(i) Pricing objectives (what are we trying to do?)

The most common are these.

(1) Survival
(2) Return on investment
(3) Market stabilisation
(4) Maintenance/implementation of market position
(5) Meeting/following competition

Answers will depend on Question 1, but objective (4) is favoured.

(ii) Factors influencing pricing

The most common are theses.

(1) Corporate objectives
(2) Competitive stance
(3) Nature and structure of competition

26: Mistral: the examination paper, examiner's report and indicative marking guides

              (4) Product life cycle
              (5) Legal considerations
              (6) Consumers needs and responses
              (7) Cost structures

       (iii) Pricing methods

           The two most common are:

           (1) cost driven
           (2) market driven

           Option (2) should be adopted.

Purposefully, little information on costs was included in the case so as not to mislead candidates. We are looking for an overall answer which takes a *market-led approach to pricing* and uses price as an integrated element of the marketing mix. Pricing policy should be used to support the proposed marketing objectives over the longer term. Answers which suggest a short-term solution that includes a long-term cost (erodes Mistral's price leading/market leading position) will attract few marks.

An analysis of case data will show that while Italy (the source of the parallel imports) has one of the largest market shares - Appendix 4 divided by Appendix 5, it also has a declining net profit figure - Appendix 10. Holland on the other hand, is maintaining a premium price strategy - Appendix 7 and is showing rising net profit figures - Appendix 10.

(b) *Part two*

Parallel importing, sometimes known as 'grey marketing' tends to occur when there are significant differences in prices for the same product in different countries.

Appendix 7 shows the relative prices charged by Italy and France.

Some measures that could be taken include these.

    (i)   Better price planning on a pan-European basis
    (ii)   Educate/replace managers
    (iii) Confront parallel imports with tactical pricing
    (iv) Build brand loyalties in import market
    (v)   Develop better management information systems
    (vi) Change measurement systems for subsidiaries

3.9 Best answers will:

(a) identify pricing objectives

(b) describe factors affecting price

(c) select pricing method

(d) describe how price policy will control parallel importing

(e) describe non-pricing actions that may be needed to better resolve parallel importing problems

Question 3

3.10 *Question 3 - 25 marks.* (Propose a process by which Mistral can begin to develop new brands in Europe.)

    (a) *Approach*

This question again approaches the question of branding, first raised seriously in the Leffe paper (December 1995). There is a difference between 'brands' and 'products' and candidates taking the opportunity to develop everything they know about new Product Development will be unlikely to gain many marks. Remember this is an open-book examination so candidates can refer to texts on the subject *during the examination.*

'Brands are more than products. Brands are designed to help customers identify products/services which promise specific benefits. As such they create a set of expectation in the minds of customers about performance, quality and price. This in turn allows the strategist to build added-value into products and to differentiate them from competitors.' (Wilson, Gilligan and Pearson)

(c) The answer to this question will vary according to the answers presented for Question 1 and 2. The answer should be compatible given recommendations offered by the candidate in the areas of marketing objectives, marketing strategy and pricing policy. Wilson, Gilligan and Pearson (pp 298-300) describe Davidson's approach to brand development. Davidson suggests five steps to development.

  (i) What is the meaning of the brand today and what do we want it to mean in five years time?

  (ii) What line extensions and new products do we wish to develop under this brand name?

  (iii) What changes in market needs and consumer demographics do we foresee that will require us to modify or change the brand meaning?

  (iv) What are the detailed plans by year for actioning these changes in the next five years? What are the sales, spending and profit implications?

  (v) Bearing in mind the new markets we wish to enter, which ones can be covered with existing brand names and which need new brand names.

3.11 Best answers will describe new brand development process of Mistral which:

  (a) takes into account current role of Mistral's brands
  (b) accounts for major expected changes in customer needs
  (c) matches process to proposed marketing objectives and strategy in (Question 1)
  (d) describes control system for process

4 A FINAL WORD

4.1 So how did it go? Hopefully your performance will have improved. Now, try to hone your skills on the third and final case, *Sentinel Aviation* which, you will find, offers quite a few surprises.

Chapter 27

SENTINEL AVIATION: CASE STUDY DOCUMENTATION

> **This chapter includes the case study information sent to candidates.**
> 1 Candidates' brief
> 2 Sentinel Aviation: text
>
> *Tutorial note.* No appendices accompanied this case study

INTRODUCTORY NOTE

(a) The third practice case is Sentinel Aviation, involved in business-to-business marketing.

(b) Remember that the paragraph numbers here have been inserted by BPP for ease of reference. You are unlikely to find such a numbering system in the case itself.

(c) We will remind you of the essentials for each step/stage in panel form. Good luck.

CONSULT THE GUIDANCE NOTES FOR THESE STEPS IN
CHAPTER 8 PARAGRAPHS 2.1 TO 2.19

STEP 1 READ THE CASE
STEP 2 AFTER AN INTERVAL, RE-READ THE CASE
STEP 3 REFLECT ON THE INSTRUCTIONS AND CANDIDATES' BRIEF
STEP 4 THINK YOURSELF INTO THE ROLE AND THE SITUATION
STEP 5 RE-READ THE CASE AND WRITE A PRÉCIS - IN NOT MORE THAN TWO A4 SIDES

ALLOW YOURSELF BETWEEN 3 AND 6 HOURS FOR THESE STEPS

Part E: Learning from experience: ensuring you pass

1 CANDIDATES' BRIEF

1.1 You are Jim Converre, marketing director of Sentinel Aviation. You report to Mike Flynn, managing director, and have been given responsibility for improving marketing performance worldwide. You were recruited from outside the industry, to your present position, just over a year ago.

1.2 Your background is not in the aircraft industry but in computing where you have a successful track record in marketing both hardware and software. Mike Flynn is also from outside the industry. His previous experience was in the leisure industry. This fact has not gone unnoticed in the ultra-traditional aviation industry.

1.3 Since taking up your position as marketing director you have begun to draw together the strands of the marketing job previously handled by a number of different managers. You have appointed agencies to help in areas such as market research and marketing communications and have started to make sense of the product range. A year into the job it is time to start thinking about more strategic issues.

1.4 The company has never before had a strategic plan or marketing plan and neither OmniCorp nor Sentinel are planning driven cultures. Nevertheless, you know that, with or without formal plans, Sentinel must start to address its markets more strategically - it is the only way that the company can realise its full potential and OmniCorp's return-on-net-asset targets can be met.

2 SENTINEL AVIATION: TEXT

Sentinel Aviation

2.1 Sentinel Aviation is a member of the Aviation Division of *OmniCorp*, an American industrial conglomerate and the company must meet group performance targets, based on *return on assets*.

2.2 Sentinel Aviation has a turnover of £4.25 million (1996) and operates in more than 45 countries. Key export territories include France, Germany, Italy, Spain and USA. The company employs around 60 people and retains a hierarchical management structure (as is shown on the chart on the next page).

2.3 Sentinel Aviation's product portfolio includes the largest range of autopilots and *chartplotters* in the world. It consists of the following.

    (a) Autopilots, including 'Navigaid', considered to be the finest autopilot on the market.

    (b) Chartplotters for the commercial and leisure sectors marketed under the brand name 'Chartwell'.

    (c) The 'Firstaid' instrument range covering most leisure aircraft applications.

    (d) Products from other group companies, including hydraulic systems, control systems, cables and radar equipment.

2.4 Sentinel's turnover by product type is:

    (a) Autopilots   40%
    (b) Instruments   12%
    (c) Chartplotters   31%
    (d) Distributed products   17%

27: Sentinel Aviation: case study documentation

Exhibit 1: organisation structure

OMNICORP ORGANISATION

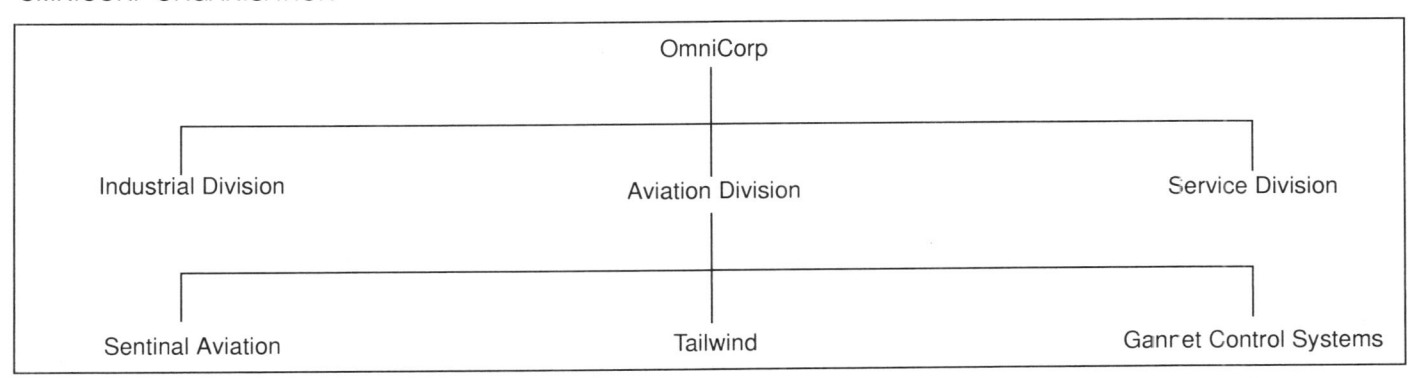

- OmniCorp
  - Industrial Division
  - Aviation Division
    - Sentinal Aviation
    - Tailwind
    - Ganret Control Systems
  - Service Division

SENTINEL AVIATION ORGANISATION

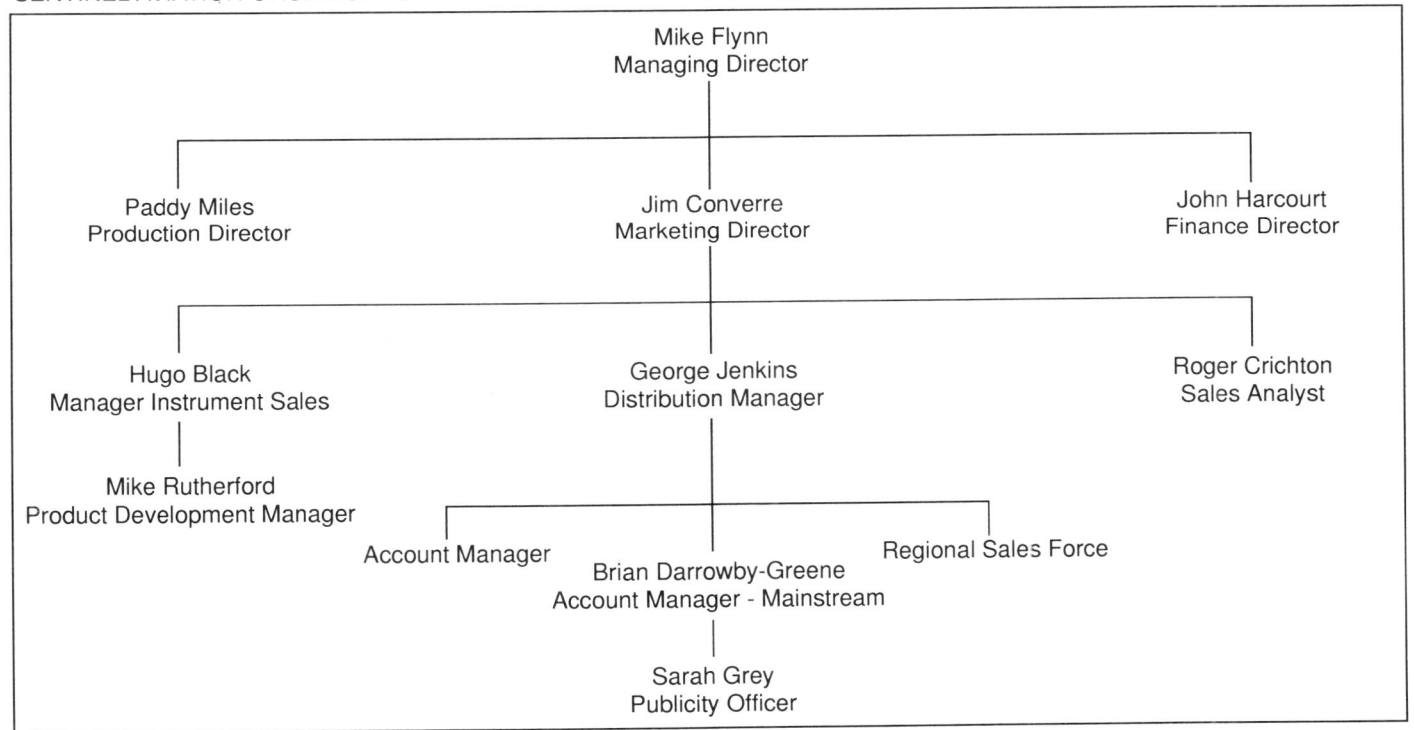

- Mike Flynn — Managing Director
  - Paddy Miles — Production Director
  - Jim Converre — Marketing Director
    - Hugo Black — Manager Instrument Sales
      - Mike Rutherford — Product Development Manager
    - George Jenkins — Distribution Manager
      - Account Manager
      - Brian Darrowby-Greene — Account Manager - Mainstream
        - Sarah Grey — Publicity Officer
      - Regional Sales Force
  - John Harcourt — Finance Director
    - Roger Crichton — Sales Analyst

2.5 Sentinel's turnover by region is:
   (a) UK   23%
   (b) US   20%
   (c) Europe   42%
   (d) Rest of world 15%

2.6 Although Sentinel has a broad product range, it is perceived by most of its customers as a single product company because of the long-term success of *Navigaid*.

Storm clouds

2.7 There was a strong wind blowing as Jim Converre looked out over the airfield. 'Not like that when you were flying round the world,' said Mike Flynn, the managing director. 'You don't always need a strong wind,' said Jim, thinking that a little calm might not be a bad thing now and again. The pace of change had been frantic since the Americans took over and he still wasn't sure whether they had taken the right course.

   (a) 'Have you had a chance to finalise the strategy document we discussed?' asked Mike. 'I know the pressure has been on but the Americans are keen to know how we are going to meet our targets. They like things to be tidy. I'm over there on Thursday so I'll be able to get the latest figures for you.'

   (b) 'To be honest Mike, it's the sheer choice that is holding me back. There are so many opportunities and I'm not sure which is the best.'

   (c) 'That sounds great,' said Mike, 'but we still need a report. Can we say Monday? Don't forget, you've got old Jack's retirement presentation this afternoon. Just remind everyone of the good old days and they'll be happy.'

   (d) 'That's the trouble,' thought Jim, 'everyone else in the company is stuck in the good old days'.

The 'good old days'

2.8 'Ladies and gentlemen, if I could have your attention for a few minutes. I am as you know a comparative newcomer to the company and I've been given the task of paying tribute to a man who has given fifty years of his life to the company in its various forms. I have to say it was fascinating looking back over the history of this great company and it's even more fascinating to see what an important role Jack has played over the years.'

2.9 'Jack confessed that he had always wanted to be a pilot. He didn't do that but he did the next best thing and joined a company that made equipment for pilots. When Jack joined, the company was called Scutts and Neville. I believe the original partners were still working then - if you can call it work. They developed one of the earliest autopilot systems and they guaranteed every piece of equipment personally. They supervised installation themselves and they insisted on joining the air trials with the customer. That's customer service for you.'

2.10 'The original owners moved on and fortunately those extremes of service have changed too. Jack told me the company has changed hands at least five times but he survived all the changes. Most of the owners treated the business as a hobby, they were pilots first and businessmen second. Running out of money was the favourite pastime and the company suffered what seemed like a long steady decline right through to the 1970s.'

2.11 'There must be something about Jack, he just kept rising through the ranks and he reached the position of works manager nearly 25 years ago. The real breakthrough for the company came just after that when Reg Cowley turned up at the factory with his new invention in the back of an estate car. That was the first generation Navigaid. It was a huge clumsy thing but it revolutionised the industry and the company has never looked back. When it was first launched, it represented a genuine state-of-the-art product and it was the first to make full use of electronics in the leisure sector.'

2.12 'The company has refined Navigaid since then and brought it into the digital age. As you all know, the Navigaid has built up a tremendous following over the years and it is still the first product customers associate with the company. Not surprisingly, the success of the Navigaid attracted other companies and there were several unsuccessful takeover bids by competitors. The company finally changed hands three years ago when it joined our parent company OmniCorp. Fortunately, OmniCorp was not a competitor and the company was given a free hand to do what it is best at. Navigaid remains a key product and it has now benefited from some sophisticated input from OmniCorp's central research laboratories.'

2.13 'But what was Jack doing all this time? He confessed to me that he still knows very little about electronics, but that's not his job. Jack says his job is to get the orders out and I think we would all agree that he has done a superb job.'

2.14 Jim could hear the mutterings from the audience, 'Electronics company, what is he on about? We're aircraft navigation specialists. Everyone in the industry knows that'. It was not the first time he had come across the complaint. 'These new managers don't understand the aviation industry. They're trying to turn us into a computer company. All we make now is electronics components. So much for 70 years of heritage.'

2.15 'Forget all that,' thought Jim, 'this is Jack's retirement and he deserves a good time.'

2.16 'So there we are, 50 years of achievement and change. I think that's a proud record Jack and you deserve credit for everything you've done. The rumour is that you are going back to your original boyhood ambition and take flying lessons. It has been a long wait but we hope it has been worth it.'

The press enquiry

2.17 When Jim got back to the office, there was a message on his desk from Jack's daughter, Sarah Grey, the publicity officer.

2.18 'Jim, while you were out, Andy Law from Aviation Times called. He is doing a feature on navigation aids and would like some information on our products. Shall I send him the press pack? He wants to include a list of distributors as well.'

2.19 'Here we go again,' though Jim, 'sending out standard press packs whenever a journalist rings up. If we had a proper public relations strategy, we wouldn't have to respond at the last minute like this.'

2.20 He hesitated, then picked up the telephone. 'Sarah, it's Jim. That Aviation Times feature, yes just send them the usual press pack. Can you tell Andy I'll get back to him about the distributors. I might have some interesting information for him.'

Part E: Learning from experience: ensuring you pass

2.21 *Exhibit 2: press information*

> **Press information**
>
> *The Sentinel product range*
>
> Sentinel make the largest range of autopilots and chartplotters in the world, including the renowned Navigaid, which is generally considered to be the finest autopilot in the market.
>
> Sentinel made its name with the first generation Navigaid which was adopted by virtually every leisure aircraft builder when it was first introduced. It was the first practical, reliable product of its type on the market. The range was completely upgraded in 1994 and now includes eight different systems including variants for specific applications such as twin-engine, executive jets and light aircraft.
>
> Chartplotters are an important part of Sentinel's product range. We make six different products for the commercial and leisure sectors marketed under the brand name Chartwell. We offer different types of LCD* or CRT* screen, a choice of cartridges, different types of cartography and the option of a GPS* antenna.
>
> Sentinel's Firstaid instrument portfolio covers most aircraft applications with a range of well designed, highly-functional products that provide reliable performance in all conditions.
>
> Sentinel is able to offer an increasing range of complementary products from other companies within the OmniCorp Aviation Division. The portfolio includes hydraulic systems, control systems and radar equipment.
>
> *(For further information, please contact Sarah Grey at Sentinel Aviation)*
>
> (*Tutorial note*
> LCD: Liquid Crystal Display
> CRT: Cathode Ray Tube display
> GPS: Global Positioning System used for navigation and establishing location)

Product development

2.22 Jim glanced over a copy of the press pack before it was mailed to Aviation Times. The paragraph about instruments reminded him that he needed to reply to Hugo Black's memo. He picked up the memo.

2.23 *Exhibit 3: Hugo Black's memo*

> **MEMORANDUM**
>
> To: Jim Converre
> From: Hugo Black, Manager Instrument Sales
> Subject: Instrument range rationalisation
>
> The Firstaid range of instruments was first launched in 1991 and currently accounts for around 12% of sales. Unfortunately it has suffered from low funding, poor design input and a consequent lack of interest by the salesforce. This is despite the fact that we offer a much more sophisticated product than our competitors at a similar price.
>
> The Firstaid range is very broad but we are not exploiting the strength of the range. The products don't look as though they come from the same stable and some of our customers believe that a number of our products are manufactured by competitors.
>
> Where we should be differentiating our products - between the commercial/ executive jet and leisure ranges - we are failing to establish a separate identity and customers are confused by the fact that we have several similar products with different names, sold by the same people.
>
> We do need to deal with the issue of range rationalisation as a matter of urgency. Can we arrange a meeting please?

The American briefing

2.24 'Jim,' it's Mike Flynn. 'Before I leave for the States tomorrow, can you do me a short briefing document for Ed Quorn, the new OmniCorp vice-president. He will be visiting us next month but wants a quick run down on the marketplace. Less than a page, he said.' 'If it can't be said in a page, it ain't worth saying' were his exact words.

2.25 *Exhibit 4: briefing document*

> **Briefing document**
>
> Sentinel currently specialises in aviation electronics for the executive jet and leisure sector, and is believed to be one of the world's top five suppliers. Sentinel products are currently sold in 45 countries, either directly to aircraft builders or through a network of specialist dealers. The total worldwide aviation electronics market is believed to be worth around £425 million and our overall share is about 1% of that. In the UK leisure sector, we currently hold around 20% of the market and in the executive jet sector about 8%. Executive jet and leisure sectors are becoming increasingly competitive as supplier rationalisation intensifies and other sectors such as defence suffer a severe downturn. The majority of our competitors are also members of larger industrial groups and only one independent remains.

The problem of research

2.26 'Thank goodness he wanted less than a page,' thought Jim. 'We don't actually have much more information. If he is visiting next month, I'd better finalise the research agency briefing so that we can get some proper research underway.'

2.27 *Exhibit 5: market research brief*

Market research brief

Sentinel Aviation, the international aviation electronics group, seeks to appoint a research consultancy to carry out a variety of market research projects. The successful consultancy will be responsible for obtaining primary and secondary data and managing that data via a database.

Background

Sentinel competes in the global aviation electronics industry believed to be worth around £425 million. There is, at present, no definitive study of the market, and no way in which we can judge the size of the market opportunity available to us.

The market is traditionally split into four main sectors.

- Leisure
- Executive jet (commercial)
- Light aircraft
- Defence

Sentinel competes in the first two sectors and information on our estimated share in each of the sectors is attached. For information, we have also attached a brief customer profile for the leisure sector. We have no comparable information for the executive jet sector.

Requirements

We require a proposal for ongoing research to support our marketing activities.

The research should cover the following broad areas.

- Size of the global leisure and executive jet markets
- Growth of those markets
- Competitor profiles for Europe, USA and UK
- Attitudes to Sentinel and competitors
- Product pricing
- Channel efficiency and effectiveness
- Key purchasing considerations for aviation electronics products
- Competitor advertising and marketing activities by territory
- Other aspects the agency considers important for Sentinel

Appendix: Sentinel's current market share in selected sectors

In the sectors in which Sentinel competes, the breakdown is as follows.

A Leisure sales account for 73% of all sales:

- leisure twin-engine sector accounts for 49%
- leisure single-engine sector accounts for 24%

B Sales to executive jet sector account for 23% of all sales

C Sales to OEM manufacturers account for 4% of all sales

A *The UK leisure market.* This covers all aircraft not build specifically for commerce and includes single and twin engine aircraft. Sentinel's UK market penetration is around 20% of a market worth approximately £3.8 million.

B *The UK executive jet market.* This consists mainly of small 'company' jets or small fleets of planes. Sentinel has a market share of around 8% in a market worth approximately £2.9 million.

C *The UK OEM market.* This market includes all sales to other equipment manufacturers, but not to aircraft builders. Figures on Sentinel's existing penetration are not currently available.

Customer profile: UK leisure sector

- Aircraft owners are lifestyle oriented and are technically knowledgeable.
- Customers are 35 - 64 years old; more than 80% are senior or middle management.
- 85% of owners keep their aircraft on a serviced, operational airfield.
- 26% intend to purchase navigation or communications equipment in the next two years.

The distributor network

2.28 The phone rang, it was Sarah Grey. 'I called Andy Law to confirm that the information was on the way. He wants to know more about the distributor story. We seem to have whetted his appetite. What should I tell him?'

2.29 'Tell him he'll just have to be patient for a few more days. We'll get back to him as soon as some details have been finalised. Let him know it will be an exclusive for Aviation Times. I've got a meeting to discuss the matter with George Jenkins tomorrow. I should know more then.'

2.30 He turned over the memo again.

2.31 *Exhibit 6: Memo from George Jenkins re: distribution*

MEMORANDUM

To: Jim Converre
From: George Jenkins, Distribution Manager
Subject: Swiftair distributerships

We have an opportunity to improve our international presence. Swiftair Instruments is rationalising its distributor network and dropping about 15% of its current distributors. It's not clear why they are dropping so many distributors; the official line is that those distributors are underperforming but that seems a rash solution. Whatever the reason, this has left a lot of distributors feeling very uncertain and it has damaged Swiftair's credibility.

We can capitalise on that and I think we should give serious consideration to talking to those distributors who have been dropped. We shouldn't just take on new distributors indiscriminately, there might be something wrong with their performance, but some of them are located in territories where we don't have an effective presence. Others are located in territories where a little local rivalry might stir things up in our favour. I have attached a profile of our current network. Before I talk to them individually, we should draw up a 'shopping list'.

Sentinel dealer network

In the UK we operate a two-tier distribution system.

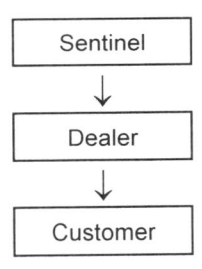

```
Sentinel
   ↓
Dealer
   ↓
Customer
```

In the rest of the world, we operate a three-tier system.

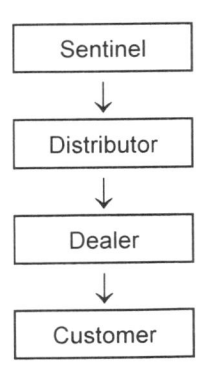

```
Sentinel
   ↓
Distributor
   ↓
Dealer
   ↓
Customer
```

> *UK distribution*
>
> In the UK, we sell to accredited dealers, mail order companies, OEM manufacturers, and aircraft builders. One dealer group, Corby Air, dominates the business with 18% of our total UK dealer sales. If we look at the rest of our UK dealer sales, average order size is low and there is considerable scope for improving business. Taking Corby out, we have more than 50 accounts spending just over £5,000 each annually.
>
> *European distribution*
>
> The four major European markets are France, Italy, Germany and Spain, although the majority of aircraft building takes place in Holland, France and Scandinavia. We have had problems with continuity in Germany and France. With three changes of distributor in the last five years, sustained growth has been difficult in the major markets.
>
> *USA distribution*
>
> The USA is a completely different market. It is the largest single aircraft products market in the world, volumes are much higher and manufacturers take a much more aggressive approach to marketing. We don't have specific figures for aviation electronics, but the USA aircraft accessories market, which includes electronics, was worth more than a billion dollars in 1995. Marketing techniques are different too and mail order is extremely successful. Although that is good for volume, it does tend to make the market price sensitive and it is hard for anyone to sell premium products. Dealers tend to concentrate on more complex products where the customer requires more advice and guidance. Our US distributor (Sentinel US, reporting to OmniCorp) combines a successful retail and mail order business but so far we have not accounted for a major part of their business. Sentinel US sales in 1996 were approximately £840,000 and our main dealer, Aerotec, took about 14% of that.

Lunch with the IT consultant

2.32 Despite the other 'priorities' that were building up all around him, Jim decided to keep a long-standing lunch meeting with a former colleague, Ray Molloy, development manager for European Software Consultants. He wanted to sound out Ray on future developments.

2.33 'So how's the world of flying?' said Ray. 'You must feel at home with all those propellors and rudders. Do your customers still wear flying goggles and steer by the sun and the stars?'

2.34 'That age has gone, Ray, tough there are a few diehards about still. These days we're in the digital age - GPS, Fly-by-wire, VGA, fuzzy logic and Windows.'

Tutorial note	
GPS:	Global Positioning System used for navigation and establishing location
Fly-by-wire:	computer controlled automation
VGA:	a standard for computer graphics
Fuzzy logic:	a computer-based approach to decision making
Windows:	Microsoft's operating system for personal computers

2.35 'I'm impressed,' said Ray. 'So what are you an aircraft equipment company, or an IT company?'

2.36 'Funny you should say that, Ray, we ask the same question ourselves. Some of the older employees say it with a sneer, but these days we are recruiting more and more people with a software background. A love of planes is no longer a prime qualification. As you would imagine, that causes a lot of resentment. Mike Flynn and I get it all the time but at least I fly at the weekends so the staff give me some credibility.'

2.37 'We have to look to the future,' said Jim. 'Our customers are talking about interfaces and systems integration and they are getting very sophisticated. The salesforce is suffering. They used to fill their diaries with the dates of air shows. Now they have to fit in the major electronics exhibitions and they have to learn a new language. We recruit more salespeople via Computer News than Aviation Weekly.'

2.38 'We are also looking at opportunities outside the aviation industry. This is strictly off the record by the way. We have developed some really sophisticated control and monitoring systems. I believe there are some huge application opportunities in industrial control, security and a lot of other industries. The Americans are very keen on crossing boundaries and one of the other aviation companies in the group is already selling hydraulic systems to the construction industry.'

2.39 'We have a lot of experience in GPS technology but only apply it to the air sector - do you know that a few nights ago I saw a television programme about how GPS was being used in a Middle East country to keep tract of a city's taxis and get them to customers faster. I can't help feeling that opportunities are popping up everywhere while we always look up to the skies.'

2.40 'We make most of our own components you know and we've got some very talented software designers and systems engineers. Our traditional aviation markets are growing, but I can't help feeling we could grow even faster if we looked outside the aviation industry. To be blunt, an electronics solution is the same in any industry.'

2.41 'I'm glad I've had the opportunity to tell you about this, Ray. I wanted to sound you out about your own situation. Next month, we've got a meeting with the Americans and we want to float the idea of a "ventures company" that looks for new opportunities. If we get the go ahead, would you be interested?'

Motivating the salesforce

2.42 Later that afternoon, Jim was due to brief the sales team at their monthly meeting. With so many positive developments in the air, Jim felt upbeat. He wanted to enthuse the salesforce. He knew they were encountering problems with competitors; they were struggling with the new technology and they were uncertain where the new management team was taking them. There were rumours about reorganisation. It was time for reassurance.

2.43 He want through his presentation notes in the taxi on the way back from lunch.

2.44 *Exhibit 7: Jim's presentation notes*

> **PRESENTATION**
>
> 1 'We must look on our business as a global business. We have the reputation and an established sales structure and we must build on that. Many of you regard ourselves as regional sales executives responsible for specific territories. We have to change that perspective and think globally.
>
> 2 Over the next six months, we will be making some fundamental changes to the salesforce structure so that we can focus our resources on our customers, wherever they are. For some of you, that will mean changes in territorial responsibility while others will be switching from OEM sales to dealer support. We will be talking to you individually about the changes, but today I want to paint the broad picture.
>
> 3 *Improving understanding of the market.* Let's look at the market. It is a global market and, as we keep on reminding you, we only have about 1% of a market that is worth about £425 million - plenty of opportunity for growth there. We are already present in 45 countries, but the problem is we don't know very much about the market. It came as a real surprise to me that there is no definitive study of the market. We think there should be, so we are talking to a number of market research consultancies and we will be

putting one of them to work within the next few weeks. The aim is to get a much better picture of individual markets. We also want to track our competitors more effectively and to find out what customers think of us and our competitors. The information will be managed on a database and you will all have access to this via the network. You will get a summary of any new data on your sales bulletins and you will be able to extract data that relates to your individual territories and responsibilities.

4   *Refining market support*. The research will give us a clearer indication of where our sales and marketing priorities lie and we will use the information to plan your new responsibilities. We will also use the information to refine our advertising and marketing support strategy. As you know, we advertise in the aviation trade press in the UK and selected European territories. In the past, a lot of our European advertising has been what I call 'blackmail' advertising - a dealer is offered an opportunity to advertise in a special supplement or air show edition and we have to respond very quickly with an advertisement.

5   The research will allow us to assess advertising opportunities in relation to market potential. We are considering a number of options - standard distributor advertisements, corporate advertisements to run across all territories, and the appointment of local advertising specialists to work with territory managers. If we can develop an effective way of measuring the return on our marketing budget, we will increase the proportion of company turnover we spend from its current 5% to the 7 or 8% we used to spend a few years ago.

6   *Improving distribution performance*. We are also looking at ways in which distributor coverage and performance can be improved. You will play a key role in this. At present, coverage is sporadic and is based on a historic network of distributors that does not reflect current market conditions. By a fortunate coincidence, there are a number of distributors who are looking for a new opportunity thanks to Swiftair. We will be talking to a number of them about taking on the Sentinel franchise so that we can increase our coverage.

7   It is important to improve distributor performance. Product knowledge has been a problem in the past and we are currently developing a training programme to improve that. This will have three elements: distributor sales staff will attend a series of workshops on software and systems integration; we will be providing a technical support service using a combination of helpline and field visits; and we will be building a database of software applications which can be used to identify sales opportunities.

8   *Cross-selling within the group*. We aim to build on the strengths of our overall resources by exploiting links with other companies in the OmniCorp group. As you know, there are a number of group companies which operate in markets with characteristics similar to ours. Gannet control systems is a leading player in the helicopter sector where we do not compete and we are working on a joint project to develop a group product portfolio. Tailwind, who make mechanical and hydraulic steering systems are talking to us about developments that incorporate our autopilot products.

9   We keep hearing the term 'synergy' - it will become increasingly important. Our customers don't really care where the products come from. They want an integrated suite of products that work together and they are happy to deal with a single source because it is more convenient. Our customers should see us as a single integrated group able to provide them with complete solutions. If we don't achieve that, we may end up as components suppliers, selling our products to systems integrators. If we lose control and contact with the customer we would be forced into competing on price. Mike Rutherford, our product development manager, is spending time with each of the other companies in the aviation division and we will be running a series of workshops for you in the next quarter.

10 Yes, the business is changing and I think the pace of change will accelerate over the next few years. We shouldn't forget our heritage but we must not let it limit our growth potential. We are a solutions company and we have to expand our horizons. There are some superb opportunities out there if we are flexible enough to adapt.'

Living luxury

2.45 The sales meeting had, Jim felt, gone reasonably well. There was, however, a concern that the sales team was unlikely to change suddenly on the strength of a single presentation. It would take time. But there could be no going back. The memo from Brian Darrowby-Greene, account manager for Mainstream, the executive jet manufacturer, was a classic example of the way things used to be done.

2.46 Mainstream is a long-established customer and provides a significant amount of regular business. Although Mainstream is not one of Sentinel's top six customers, it provides an excellent reference for Sentinel quality. Mainstream is widely regarded as *the* executive jet and the company protects its reputation jealously. The company only endorses products with guaranteed quality and the association has proved valuable for Sentinel. Mainstream want Sentinel to place an advertisement in a glossy, lifestyle magazine which they distribute to their customers. The cost will be £1,200. Brian Darrowby-Greene argues that this is a small investment to protect a valuable customer relationship, but Jim has other priorities for his marketing budget.

2.47 *Exhibit 8: 'Mainstream' advertisement*

MEMORANDUM

To: Brian Darrowby-Greene
From: Jim Converre
Subject: Mainstream advertisement

Thank you for your memo about the advertisement in Mainstream's customer magazine. I appreciate that Mainstream is a long valued customer and we have advertised in this magazine for at least ten years, but I think it may be time to say enough is enough. If we look at Mainstream's purchase record, the year-on-year increase is minimal and, in real terms, the value of the business has declined over the last three years. We need to grow on a wider front and I don't believe that this advertisement will help us to achieve that. It is aimed primarily at existing Mainstream customers. They don't choose the instrumentation. The advertisement is not going to broaden our customer base.

I am sorry if this sounds negative but I am anxious to build business for the company as a whole. We should certainly continue to reinforce our relationship with customers like Mainstream and I would like to discuss some options with you.

Adding value

2.48 While sales team enthusiasm was high, Jim decided to take a further initiative. He was concerned that the distribution chain was not adding real value to the company's products. He dictated a memo.

2.49 *Exhibit 9: Jim's memo on adding value*

MEMORANDUM

To: The sales team
From: Jim Converre
Subject: Adding value

We face increasing competition across our product range and this is likely to intensify as competition increases. We also face a new threat from competitors outside the industry - systems integrators who buy products and components and provide the customer with an integrated solution. We have premium products with strong brand values and we ought to be in a position to dominate the market. However, competitive threats could force a price war and there is a long-term threat that our high value products could become commodities. It is essential that we add value to the products by introducing other services that are relevant to the customer. To help you identify opportunities, here are brief guidelines on the services that we could offer.

Fitting	A rudder adaptor should ideally be built in to our offer for optimum performance. Encourage customers to use our network of service dealers to fit and test our products.
Kits	There is a significant do-it-yourself market, particularly in the small leisure sector. We can provide kits which 'enthusiast' owners can fit themselves. The cost is around £250 and we should not lose sight of this market.
Entry-level service	We should also monitor trends in the small plane leisure market. As customers become more sophisticated, they may switch to more advanced products. We will be offering an entry-level autopilot product, sold together with a cost-effective dealer fit service and we will promote it through the trade press.
Calibration	The growing sophistication of aircraft instruments will increase the demand for calibration services. We have an international dealer network and we should promote the after-sales services available through the network.
Upgrade services	The rapid development of software means that the current installed systems will provide excellent opportunities for regular upgrades. We should also ensure that our customers are aware of the latest versions available, and we should stress the cost-effectiveness of our upgrade services.

Pricing issues

2.50 Added-value services would be vital if the company is to maintain its position as a supplier of premium products. The whole question of pricing was one that had been distorted by recent difficulties in the distribution network. Pricing had to be tackled head on if Sentinel was to maintain share and profitability.

2.51 John Harcourt, the financial director, has provided some background information on current pricing policy.

2.52 *Exhibit 10: Memo from John Harcourt re: pricing*

MEMORANDUM

To: Jim Converre
From: John Harcourt, Financial Director
Subject: Pricing

Although we position ourselves as a supplier of premium products, in reality our prices appear to be driven by our competitors. Sentinel retail prices are calculated on a 'going rate cost plus' basis. The level of margin as calculated is tailored to keep prices at or below those of our major competitors. We also face considerable psychological barriers, pricing some of our executive jet autopilot units at £1,995 or £2,995, below the £2,000 or £3,000 barriers. We are currently carrying out detailed cost calculations so that we can establish the true relationship between retail prices and profit.

Export distributor prices are calculated as a percentage discount from the UK retail price list. The levels are based on the going rate, but in an *ad hoc* way. The UK discount level has now been linked to purchase commitment, but this process cannot be applied so easily to overseas distributors where the sales force seems to negotiate prices to keep the business.

Heavy discounting to end users, mainly through competitors' mail order operations in the UK and USA has made both markets very price sensitive. The customer no longer sees a direct relationship between the value of the product and the price paid. True value-added products are relegated to a niche market where price is not an issue. This situation is not the norm in the rest of Europe, although the Chartplotter market does suffer from cheap, inferior imports.

Because of legislation barring price control by manufacturers, there is little possibility of reclaiming markets blighted by heavy discounting. The cycle starts when retailers operating in an increasingly competitive market cannot resist discounting to increase turnover. Their profits drop, so they ask for more discount, and our profits drop. We have to break the cycle.

The agency pitch

2.53 Summers Associates has recently been appointed as Sentinel's new advertising agency with a wide-ranging brief to review all communications. The appointment surprised the Sentinel sales team, as well as industry observers, because Summers have no aviation industry experience. The agency made its mark by working for many leading IT companies and helping them to communicate the value of new technologies across broad industrial bases.

2.54 The agency is presenting its initial recommendations for short and long-term communications. Jim had thought to use these recommendations as part of his overall marketing strategy.

2.55　*Exhibit 11: Agency presentation*

> ### Agency presentation
>
> When we were appointed, we promised you that we would not make predictable recommendations. We were not looking for a comfortable relationship. We are also ignoring tradition by not showing you creative ideas at this stage. The real challenge goes deeper than that. Our task is to reposition Sentinel for the next decade and we cannot do that with pictures of aeroplanes.
>
> The real questions are:
>
> 1　Who are you?
> 2　Where are you going?
>
> We started with the first question and asked some of your customers what they thought of you. There is good news and bad news.
>
> You have a superb reputation for quality and many customers felt that you made the finest autopilot on the market. The problem is, they could not name any other Sentinel products and they see you as a single product company. The question of where you are going is rather irrelevant in those circumstances.
>
> We also asked a selection of aircraft builders what they were looking for from companies like Sentinel. They see partnership as the key factor in future buying decisions. They will rely on the supplier's expertise to keep them ahead of the marketplace. They don't want to specify their instrumentation requirements in detail. They want an integrated solution that they can just 'plug into'. When we asked them what sort of company they saw as a potential partner, they told us that it didn't really matter. Systems integration skills would be as important as aviation expertise.
>
> The implications are clear - to maintain your current position as an aircraft equipment specialist is going to limit your options in the long term. We have seen the same problem throughout the IT sector. Companies focus on their product range and not their customers' requirements. You have to step back and look at your core competencies.
>
> So what have you got to offer? Software development, data processing, the ability to interpret and present complex data, controlling complex processes, presentation of control information, systems integration developing simple, clear interfaces. When you present that to the marketplace, your opportunities may be much greater.
>
> In developing our advertising campaign, we must reinforce your position in your traditional markets, but we must also change the perceptions and position you as a partner on a global scale. The market is becoming increasingly global and there is rationalisation amongst both suppliers and customers. If the aircraft equipment industry follows the pattern of the automotive sector, companies could reduce the number of suppliers and source on a global scale. The opportunities are greater but so too is the risk of being locked out. We have to emphasise the strengths of the group so that you are seen as a major player capable of handling large-scale projects.
>
> That will form the basis of our long-term communications strategy. We also need to consider how the messages are communicated. Advertising will continue to play a role in raising your profile in key markets, but we also recommend increased use of direct marketing to key prospects. The research you are carrying out will help to identify the most important sectors and provide a platform for planning and monitoring marketing campaigns.

Competitor profile

2.56 Jim was pleased, everything was falling into place. He would be in a good position to work on the marketing strategy. He had constructive feedback from the sales team, the agency had given a useful perspective on the future, and the Swiftair distributor opportunity had come at just the right time. Mike would have the latest figures from America. Sales analyst Roger Crichton's competitor profile was just coming in on the fax.

2.57 *Exhibit 12: Competitor profiles*

FASCIMILE

To: Jim Converre
From: Roger Crichton
Subject: Competitor profiles

Here are the first results from the competitor profiling exercise. Being in such a fragmented marketplace, building a complete picture is going to take some time. I have started with the biggest organisations and I am sending you the initial data that I have been able to uncover. More will come as I receive it. I hope this 'first-cut' is useful for your strategy job.

Sentinel's main competitors

In the global aircraft electronics market, Sentinel does not compete in specialist sectors such as radar, flightdeck systems and radio communications. Competitors in these sectors have not been included.

In the executive jet and leisure sectors, Sentinel has *two main competitors* and *three minor competitors*. The Swiftair Group and Eagle Electronics almost divide the world between them with just under 50% market share across all sectors between them. Eagle dominate the US market while Swiftair has a stronger presence in Europe. The remaining market is divided between Sentinel, Airway and Kestrel in the leisure sector, and Peregrine, Controllair and Wing Electronics in the commercial sector.

In specialist markets like Global Positioning Systems, specialist manufacturers such as Gamma, Starburst, Mapping, and Technair have an increasing presence.

In each of the three main product sectors, there are a large number of competitors, many only operating in their domestic market. Attached is a list of competing products in each sector.

Instruments	Chartplotters	Autopilots
Sentinel (Firstaid)	Sentinel (Chartwell)	Sentinel (Navigation)
Autosteer	Apache	Autosteer
Breen	Autosteer	Braemar
Datastor	Breen	Breen
DINstruments	Codesteer	Commander
Faeroe	Orville	Firstsite
Goldstar	Datastor	Navigator
KPM	Firstsite	Pantheon
Airship	Fortune	Ronaldson
Navigator	Gannet	Flightmate
Northern	Gremlin	Tango
Pantheon	KPM	Tiptop
Flightmate	Lawrence	Victor
Victor	Lodestar	
	Microplot	
	Navigator	
	Navirum	
	Pantheon	
	Robinson	
	Airpilot	
	Wilbur	
	Trueplot	
	Victor	

The Swiftair Group

Swiftair Europe is a division of the US-based Topflight Group, responsible for marketing the company's leisure and executive jet brands in Europe, the Middle East and North Africa. The rest of the world is handled by Swiftair USA.

In 1996, the company had a turnover in excess of £24 million, and claimed market share of around 38% in instruments and 63% in autopilots, 35% in radar and 27% in VHF radio, where we do not compete.

The company markets its products under three different brand names: Autosteer, Pantheon and Apache. The brands address different sectors and there is little product overlap. However, Swiftair is now beginning to impose a secondary corporate branding which may dilute the established brand names.

Autosteer targets the leisure market with three instrument ranges, three types of autopilots, three chartplotters and a branded LCD radar unit. The company came into the Swiftair portfolio in 1990 and turnover has almost doubled since the takeover.

Pantheon focuses on executive jets and has a specialist support group for large aircraft. The range is mainly radar, although they have an autopilot, chartplotter and a new instrument system.

Apache specialise in VHF radios and target the leisure market.

The company appears to be targeting the top end leisure market traditionally held by Breen and is also strengthening its commercial operations through strategic alliances with a Japanese organisation.

Eagle Electronics

Eagle Electronics is a German-owned group which has grown rapidly by acquisition. Strategic takeovers have given the company a strong presence in the leisure sector, adding to its existing portfolio in defence, exploration and offshore electronics.

Although Eagle's largest market is the USA, the company claim a 10% share of the worldwide leisure and light commercial sectors and this accounts for around 28% of group turnover. There is a considerable degree of product overlap in different sectors and there has been considerable customer confusion as a result of frequent name changes amongst recently-acquired companies. Eagle is now trying to group its products under the overall Eagle brand but this is proving to be a difficult process. The change is complicated by the fact that some of the existing names are well known in the marketplace.

Flightmate, for example, has a good reputation in the leisure sector, but this name has been grouped with an earlier company name, Robinson, which was unknown outside the commercial/executive jet sector. We understand that both of these brand names are to be phased out over the next few years.

The group is anxious to improve its performance in the commercial sector, where sales have been static for the last two years. They are also looking at the European region as a key growth sector and are believed to be targeting the executive jet sector with a new product.

Navigator

Navigator is one of the last independents in the aviation electronics sector. Their main product line is VHF radios and autopilots. They have recently launched a range of instruments for the first time.

They concentrate on the leisure sector and position themselves as specialists. The company claims a 1996 turnover of nearly £10 million, almost treble the 1991 figures. They spend a considerable amount of money on promotion and this investment appears to have paid off.

Breen Electronics

Breen was the first manufacturer to incorporate electronics in aircraft equipment in the mid-1950s. Since 1979, the company has had five separate owners and has twice been on the verge of bankruptcy.

Their pioneering work gave them a considerable reputation in the market but they tended to concentrate on luxury aircraft which has turned out to be a declining market.

Recently, the company has tried to overcome this narrow focus by launching a range of autopilots, chartplotters and instruments for a light aircraft. Despite its positioning as a value-for-money range, the products are in fact expensive compared to competitive offerings and they are regarded as unattractive.

They have also tried to adapt jet fighter technology for the executive jet market with a range of head-up displays. This has not been widely accepted and is causing confusion about the company's future direction.

The American visit

2.58 Mike Flynn had just returned from a visit to group headquarters. He walked into Jim's office.

2.59 'Jim, we've agreed the figures with the Americans. I think you should be aware of them before you finalise your plans. They aren't making any demands about our direction or our policies, but they have set out the performance requirements quite clearly.'

2.60 'They are looking for somewhere between 15 and 20% return on net assets. It's tough, but I think we can achieve it if we take the broader view of our business. I don't think we can get that sort of return if we just stick to our traditional markets. The business is too cyclical. We could be in for a mini-boom if that European legislation on air safety goes through, but that only takes us about two years on.'

2.61 'While I was over there, I ran through our figures with Kurt Grain the financial controller. You ought to have an up-to-date set.

2.62 *Exhibit 13: Financial forecasts - Sentinel Aviation*

	1994	1995	1996	1997E	1998E	1999E	2000E
Sales £'000s	2,601	3,230	4,250	5,440	6,800	8,330	10,030
RONA %	(4.1)	3.9	10.4	8.0	-	-	-
Gross profit %	32	26.9	29.4	25.6	31	34	32
Operating profit %	(4.5)	3.3	15.3	5	7	12	14
Inventories £'000s	450	1,100	780	1,200	600	500	650
Inventory days	135	258	124	110	46	27	32
Debtor days	50	78	100	65	-	-	-
Creditor days	48	142	92	85	-	-	-

2.63 'Those figures we discussed for five year growth require something else. We're about £4.25 million now. If we just gain market share, we could grow at around 10% a year, but that is not going to do it. The Americans really want us to be a £25 million a year subsidiary within five years. We are going to have to look seriously at other opportunities.'

Chapter 28

SENTINEL AVIATION: PRÉCIS, MARKETING AUDIT, SWOT

This chapter covers the following topics.

1. Introduction
2. Sample précis
3. Marketing audit: information checklist
4. Sample marketing audit 1
5. Sample marketing audit 2
6. SWOT analyses

1 INTRODUCTION

1.1 Having now completed your précis you can now compare it with the three specimens which follow.

1.2 *Sample précis 1* uses a series of questions and then provides partial answers in a very staccato form. This is quite a useful technique, providing the questions are pertinent (which they are) but this précis omits quite a lot of other data, don't you think?

1.3 *Sample précis 2* is in essay form and perhaps explains the position more clearly than Sample 1 but unfortunately appears to have petered out when the writer got about half way through the case.

1.4 *Sample précis 3* is an interesting approach using marketing plan headings to categories the summary and quoting page references.

Which of the three précis do you prefer.

2 SAMPLE PRÉCIS

2.1 *Sample précis 1*

Who are Sentinel Aviation?

(a) Division of Aviation Division of Omnicorp, USA
(b) Turnover £4.25m over 45 countries
(c) Employees: 60

What markets are Sentinel in?

(a) Global aviation Market - <1%

(b) Leisure and executive jet markets

    (i) Leisure aircraft owners: 73% of sales
    (ii) Executive jet owners: 23% of sales
    (iii) OEM: 41% of sales

What products do they sell?

(a) Autopilots - Navigaid brand (considered the finest on the market)
(b) Chartplotters - Chartwell brand
(c) Instruments - Firstaid brand
(d) Distributed products

How does turnover split geographically?

UK 23%, Europe 42%, US 20%, Rest of world 15%

What is Sentinel's share of the markets in UK?

Leisure: 20%, Executive jet: 8%, OEM: ?%

Who are Sentinel's competitors?

The Swiftair Group (US)
Eagle Electronics (German)
Navigator
Breen Electronics

What are Sentinel's distribution channels?

(a) Dealers, distributors, mail order companies, OEMs
(b) In the UK, through dealers
(c) Rest of the world, through distributors to dealers

What are Sentinel's financial targets?

(a) To increase turnover to £25m in five years
(b) To achieve 15% to 20% return on net assets

2.2 **Sample précis 2**

I am the marketing director working out a marketing strategy for Sentinel Aviation (SA) which is a member of the Aviation Division of Omnicorp, an American conglomerate, and committed to group performance targets based on return on assets.

SA, with 60 staff turned over £4.25m in 1996 and operates in over 45 countries. Its product portfolio includes the largest range of autopilots and chartplotters in the world. Its autopilot 'Navigaid' is considered the finest on the market. Other products include instruments and distributed products. Autopilots and chartplotters account for 71% of turnover, 65% of turnover comes from the UK and Europe.

SA's share of the world's aviation electronics market is only about 1% but it has around 20% of the UK leisure sector and 8% of the executive jet sector. SA is steeped in the tradition of aviation as a hobby and staff are generally reluctant to accept that SA is now in the highly competitive business of electronics rather than aviation navigation equipment *per se*. SA does not currently compete in the light aircraft or defence sectors and 71% of sales are to the owners of leisure aircraft, 23% to executive jet owners with 4% being to OEMS

SA markets through dealers in the UK and through distributors to dealers elsewhere but also supplies mail order companies and OEMs and aircraft builders. One of SA's competitors, Swiftair Instruments, is rationalising its distributors and dropping about 15%, some of which are in territories where SA does not have an effective presence. In the UK one dealer (Corby) accounts for 18% of SA's total UK dealer sales. The USA is a completely different and much larger market but SA's US Distribution (part of Omnicorp) did only £0.84m sales in 1996.

Notes **Part E: Learning from experience: ensuring you pass**

There are many opportunities for SA technology to be applied outside the aviation industry in the form of sophisticated control and monitoring systems for industrial control, security and other industries.

2.3 Sample précis 3

		Page numbers
1	Sentinel Aviation SA and role	1,2
	• Member of Aviation Division Omnicorp USA	(Chapter 27,
	• Turnover of £4.25m, 60 staff, 745 countries	paras 21.-2.3)
	• I am its Marketing Director of one year's standing, ex computing	
	• No previous strategic or marketing plan, now working on this	
2	Markets, market shares, sales	3, 9, 10
	• *Key markets*: France, Germany, Italy, Spain, USA	(Chapter 27
	• *Market shares*: World Aviation Electronics = <1% (total market £425m)	paras 2.4-2.7,
	UK leisure sector = 20% (total market £3.8m)	2.27)
	UK executive jet sector = 8% (total market £2.9m)	
	• *Sales*: UK 23%, Europe 42%, US 20%, Rest of world 15%	
	Autopilots 40%, chartplotters 31%, Instruments 12%	
	Distributed products 15%	
	Leisure sector 73%, executive jet sector 23%, DEMS 4%	
3	Competitors	26
	• Two main competitors in leisure and executive jet sectors = Swiftair and Eagle Electronics with 50% of the world market across all sectors between them. Eagle dominate the US while Swiftair is stronger in Europe	(Chapter 27 para 2.61)
4	Customer profile	10
	• Aircraft owners are lifestyle oriented and technically knowledgeable	(Chapter 27
	• Customers are 35-64 years old, >80% middle/senior managers	para 2.27)
	• 85% of owners keep their aircraft on a serviced, operational airfield.	
	• 26% intend to buy navigation or communications equipment in the next two years.	
5	Marketing research	9
	• SA have drawn up an agency brief requesting information on the global leisure and executive jet markets naming size, growth, competitor profiles, attitudes to SA and competitors, pricing, channel efficiency/effectiveness, buying criteria, competitor marketing/ advertising activities by territory and area.	(Chapter 27 para 2.27)
6	Objectives	
	• Group performance targets based on return on assets	
	• Turnover to increase from £4.25 to £25m in five years	
	• 15% to 20% return on net assets	
7	Strategies	19, 23,5,14,24
	• Internal conflict between being an electronics company and remaining traditional	(Chapter 27 paras 2.12-
	• Omnicorp keen to cross boundaries eg Hydraulic systems sold to construction industry	2.16, 2.45, 2.49-2.50, 2.59
	• Opportunities outside aviation for SA with recently developed sophisticated control and monitoring systems - applications in industrial control, security and other industries. Experience in GPS can be put to new uses eg taxis	
	• Customers want integrated solutions, need to reinforce relations	
	• Agency suggests repositioning	
	• New ventures company being suggested	
8	Products/services	21
	• See 2 above plus NPD as 7 above plus added value services (fitting, kits, entry level services, calibration, upgrades)	(Chapter 27 paras 2.54, 2.55)

			Page numbers
9	Pricing		22
	• Premium. Psychological pricing barriers eg executive jet autopilot units at £1,995 or £2,995		(Chapter 27
	• Heavy discounting to end users mainly through mail order UK/USA		para 2.56)
	• Cost calculations being conducted to determine relationship between retail prices and profit		
10	Promotion		5, 15-18, 25
	• No proper public relations strategy, need to formulate long-term communications strategy		(Chapter 27 paras 2.12-2.16
	• Direct mail to key prospects		2.48-261)
	• Advertising's key role in raising profile, currently 'blackmail' advertising		
	• Salesforce changes - need to remotivate, cross-selling opportunities		
	• Cross-selling		
11	Distribution		8
	• Either direct to aircraft builders (OEMs) or through network of specialist dealers, also to mail order companies. Use dealers UK but distributors to dealers elsewhere. Main European markets = France, Germany, Italy and Spain		(Chapter 27 para 2.27)
	• Major UK dealer (Corby) = 18% of SA's total dealer sales UK		
	• US distributor (Owned by Omnicorp) only did £0.84m in 1996		

3 MARKETING AUDIT: INFORMATION CHECKLIST

Checklist

3.1 (a) Before doing the audit proper you might like to try the information checklist mentioned in Chapter 8 Paragraph 3.7 and the checklist format in Chapter 1, Paragraphs 2.8 and 2.9.

(b) You should use this checklist to determine the information we have on Sentinel Aviation and the information we don't have. You could use a tick to show the information we have and a cross (x) to show the information we don't have (and which might then form the basis of your MkIS/MR recommendations later on in your plan). Further refinements might be to use P for information we have in part only and NA for not applicable. Really organised students might like to note the page numbers on which items ticked or marked P occur.

(c) Having done this operation you might like to compare your results with those of the syndicates which follow noting that there are likely to be some discrepancies, since this exercise is partly judgmental.

Internal

3.2 (a) *Current position*

    (i) *Performance*

        P   Total sales in value and in units
        ✓   Total gross profit, expenses and net profit
        X   Percentage of sales for sales expenses, advertising etc
        ✓   Percentage of sales in each segment
        P   Value and volume sales by year, month, model size etc
        X   Sales per thousand consumers, per factory, in segments
        ✓   Market share in total market and in segments

    (ii) *Buyers/customers*

        X   Number of actual and potential buyers by area
        P   Characteristics of consumer buyers, eg income, occupation, education, sex, size of family etc

Part E: Learning from experience: ensuring you pass

- P Characteristics of industrial buyers, eg primary, secondary, tertiary, manufacturing; type of industry; size etc
- NA Characteristics of users, if different from buyers
- P Location of buyers, users
- X When purchases made: time of day, week, month, year; frequency of purchase; size of average purchase or typical purchase
- P How purchases made: specification or competition; by sample, inspection, impulse, rotation, system; cash or credit
- P Attitudes, motivation to purchase; influences on buying decision; decision-making unit in organisation

(b) *Products*

(i) *Sentinel Aviation*
- X Quality: materials, workmanship, design, method of manufacture, manufacturing cycle, inputs-outputs
- P Technical characteristics, attributes that may be considered as selling points, buying points
- P Models, sizes, styles, ranges, colours etc
- P Essential or non-essential, convenience or speciality
- ✓ Similarities with other company products
- P Relation of product features to user's needs, wants, desires
- P Development of branding and brand image
- P Degree of product differentiation, actual and possible
- X Packaging used, function, promotional
- X Materials, sizes, shapes, construction, closure

(ii) *Competitors*
- ✓ Competitive and competing products
- ✓ Main competitors and leading brands
- X Comparison of design and performance differences with leading competitors
- P Comparison of offerings of competitors, images, value etc

(iii) *Future product development*
- ✓ Likely future product developments in company
- P Likely future, or possible future, developments in industry
- P Future product line or mix contraction, modification or expansion

(c) *Distribution*

(i) *Sentinel Aviation*
- P Current company distribution structure
- ✓ Channels and methods used in channels
- X Total number of outlets (consumer or industrial) by type
- X Total number of wholesalers or industrial middlemen, analysed by area and type
- X Percentage of outlets of each type handling product broken down into areas
- X Attitudes of outlets by area, type, size
- X Degree of co-operation, current and possible
- X Multi-brand policy, possible or current
- X Strengths and weaknesses in distribution system, functionally and geographically
- X Number and type of warehouses; location

- X Transportation and communications
- X Stock control; delivery periods; control of information

(ii) *Competitors*
- P Competitive distribution structure; strengths and weaknesses
- X Market coverage and penetration
- X Transportation methods used by competitors
- X Delivery of competitors
- X Specific competitive selling conditions

(iii) *Future developments*
- P Future likely and possible developments in industry as a whole or from one or more competitors
- P Probable changes in distribution system of company
- P Possibilities of any future fundamental changes in outlets

(d) *Promotional and personal selling*

(i) *Sentinel Aviation*
- X Size and composition of sales force
- X Calls per day, week, month, year by salesmen
- X Conversion rate of orders to calls
- P Selling cost per value and volume of sales achieved
- X Selling cost per customer
- X Internal and external sales promotion
- X Recruiting, selection, training, control procedures
- X Methods of motivation of salesmen
- X Remuneration schemes
- X Advertising appropriation and media schedule, copy theme
- X Cost of trade, technical, professional, consumer media
- X Cost of advertising per unit, per value of unit, per customer
- X Advertising expenditure per thousand readers, viewers of main and all media used
- X Methods and costs of merchandising
- P Public and press relation; exhibitions

(ii) *Competitors*
- X Competitive selling activities and methods of selling and advertising; strengths and weaknesses
- X Review of competitors' promotion, sales contests etc
- X Competitors' advertising themes, media used

(iii) X *Future developments* likely in selling, promotional and advertising activities

(e) *Pricing*

(i) *Sentinel Aviation*
- P Pricing strategy and general methods of price structuring in company
- P High or low policies; reasons why
- P Prevailing pricing policies in industry
- X Current wholesaler, retailer margins in consumer markets or middlemen margins in industrial markets
- X Discounts, functional, quantity, cash, reward, incentive
- X Pricing objectives, profit objectives financial implications such as breakeven figures, cash budgeting

(ii) *Competitors*
- P Prices and price structures of competitors
- X Value analysis of own and competitors' products
- X Discounts, credit offered by competitors

(iii) *Future developments*
- X Future developments in costs likely to affect price structures
- X Possibilities of more/less costly raw materials or labour affecting prices
- X Possible price attacks by competitors

(f) *Service*

(i) *Sentinel Aviation*
- P Extent of pre-sales or customer service and after-sales or product service required (by products)
- X Survey of customer needs
- P Installation, deduction in use, inspection, maintenance, repair, accessories provision
- X Guarantees, warranty period
- X Methods, procedures for carrying out service
- X Returned goods, complaints

(ii) *Competitors*
- X Services supplied by competing manufacturers and service organisations
- X Types of guarantee, warranty, credit provided

(iii) P Future possible developments that might require revised service policy

External

3.3 *Environmental audit - national and international*
- X Social and cultural factors likely to affect the market, in the short and long term
- X Legal factors and codes of practice likely to affect the market in the short and long term
- X Economic factors likely to affect market demand in the short and long term
- X Political changes and military action likely to impact upon national and international markets
- P Technological changes anticipated and likely to create new opportunities and threats

3.4 *Marketing objectives and strategies*
- ✓ Short-term plans and objectives for current year, in light of current political and economic situation
- ✓ Construction of standards for measurement of progress towards achieving of objectives; management ratios that can be translated into control procedures
- P Breakdown of turnover into periods, areas, segments, outlets, salesmen etc
- P Which personnel required to undertake what responsibilities, actions etc when
- P Review of competitors' strengths and weaknesses likely competitive reactions and possible company responses that could be made
- X Long-term plans, objectives and strategies related to products, price, places of distribution, promotion, personnel selling and service.

3.5 You might like to look back at the sample information checklists for the previous cases in this text (*Gravesend Town Centre* and *Mistral*) and compare these with Sentinel Aviation. You should be able to observe differences in the types of information provided and the information gaps. For a non-manufacturing company/organisation, for example, some of the items in the checklist will not apply. You must recognise that every case is different and that standardised lists of marketing information required which are *not specific to the case* will be frowned upon.

3.6 You are now ready to conduct the marketing audit proper, systematically working your way through the environmental audit, to the marketing functions audit and the other functional audits (financial, production and personnel).

> CONSULT THE GUIDANCE NOTES FOR THIS STEP IN
> CHAPTER 8 PARAGRAPHS 3.1 TO 3.8
>
> **STEP 6 CONDUCT A MARKETING AUDIT**
>
> ALLOW YOURSELF ABOUT THREE HOURS FOR THIS STEP

Have a thoughtful and *critical* look now at the marketing audits submitted in Section 4 below. These are both reasonably good efforts. The first syndicate have not only audited generally in accordance with the recommendations but they have also added a column for *issues* so as to derive added value from the process. They could also have added a column for *information needs* to make it even better. The second sample is not so well formatted as the first but contains some useful insights and the competitor analysis is better than average.

4 SAMPLE MARKETING AUDIT 1

External analysis

4.1 *Macro environment*

   (a) *Technology*

Situation	Issues
Increased application of advanced electronics systems in aviation	Product development in electronics-based applications continues to exercise the greatest influence in the industry. Advancements aim at efficiency, enhanced performance, safety and ease of operation of aircraft
The impact of the information technology industry on travel	Teleconferencing facilities, E-mail and the Internet may limit the need for corporate travel.

   (b) *Political*

Situation	Issues
Product standards must confirm with Government civil aviation regulations of each country	Product quality as regards standards, performance, safety must be strictly enforced
Incidences of accidents involving instrument failure	This would cause greater Civil Aviation monitoring of product standards
Defence spending in developed countries is on the decline	This will increase competition in the commercial, executive jet and leisure markets

(c) *Social*

Situation	Issues
'Jet setting' lifestyles among the wealthy and corporate executives	This would promote aircraft sales
Increased international tourism and travel	Promotes aircraft sales
Incidences of aircraft accidents	Raise concern regarding safety of aircraft travel
Increased consumer familiarity with electronic products	Promotes greater appreciation of aviation electronics particularly in the leisure market

(d) *Economic*

Situation	Issues
Corporate spending is tied to economic growth	Economic performance is a prerequisite to corporate and individual purchases of aircraft
Internationalisation of corporate operations	Promotes aircraft sales
Exchange rates on foreign currencies	Gain/losses will impact company profits

4.2 *Market*

(a) *Market*

Item	Company position/issues
(i) Aviation	
World market	Company's achievement to date is 1% of an estimated £425 million market
US market	Largest single market in the world. Company's achievement to date is less than 1% of US 1 billion
Company sales	Company's sales are based (73%) on the leisure sector instilling the image in the market that is Sentinel a low end product company
	Company's sales are confined to UK and Europe (65%). Globalisation of operations is limited
(ii) OEM	Comprises only 4% of sales. The market remains largely uninvestigated though the opportunities may be potentially high

(b) *Customers*

Item	Company position/issues
Product awareness	Buyers are well informed about the technical issues regarding the products
Brand consciousness	Buyers are sensitive to established brands and the reputation of the market
Decision-making	Buyer decision-making is influenced by aircraft builders who may endorse specific brands
Company image	Customers view Sentinel as a 'one product' company, limiting its potential in other product areas

(c) *Competitors*

Item	Company position/issues
Market leaders	The world market for leisure and executive jet sector is dominated by Swiftair and Eagle who have just under 50% market shares between them
	Swiftair has introduced secondary branding that is expected to affect its established brands. In addition they have dropped 15% of their dealers in Europe
	Eagle's current customers are confused by product overlap and frequent name changes of acquired brands
	Both companies have grown by acquiring of existing companies; which have been maintained as distinct and separate operations. Accordingly, the leaders are untested on the issue of *integrating systems* and *joint collaboration* on product development among their companies
Other competitors	*Breen Electronics* is a pioneer in applying electronics to aviation. Their reputation is good but their performance has been dogged by poor strategic planning. The company has good exposure to higher end applications. The company would make a good candidate for acquisition at a fair price
	Navigator concentrates on leisure market with radio, autopilots and instrumentation. Financially sound and independent
Competitive forces	The lower end of the market is facing competition from low quality imports, particularly in chartplotters
	Systems integrators are a new force in the market, offering integrated solutions to customers

(d) *Stakeholder*

Situation	Issues
Omnicorp is the parent company	Introduce prospects for product/corporate development and long-term stability
	Facilitate growth in the US market
	Parent is seeking a new dimension of growth in Sentinel

Internal analysis

4.3 *Company*

Company	Strengths	Weaknesses
(a) Organisation	• Good reputation in leisure sector as autopilot pioneer • Omnicorp involvement provides the company with added strengths and financial backup	• Not planning driven and no strategic direction • Research and development is narrow and limited • Structure is vague with no customer orientation • Information on customers and competitors is lacking
(b) Product	• Purpose added value and expand the product scope • Brand/products of good quality and well known	• Continue product research and innovation • Poor product quality is not well communicated to customer
(c) Price	• Prices at going rate, cost plus • Company competitiveness in sales	• Frequent discounting • Inability to command price based on quality is eroding profits
(d) Promotions		• Campaign promotion practised ad-hoc • Uncreative public relations is providing poor support to company image

5 SAMPLE MARKETING AUDIT 2

5.1 *Sales data*

(a)

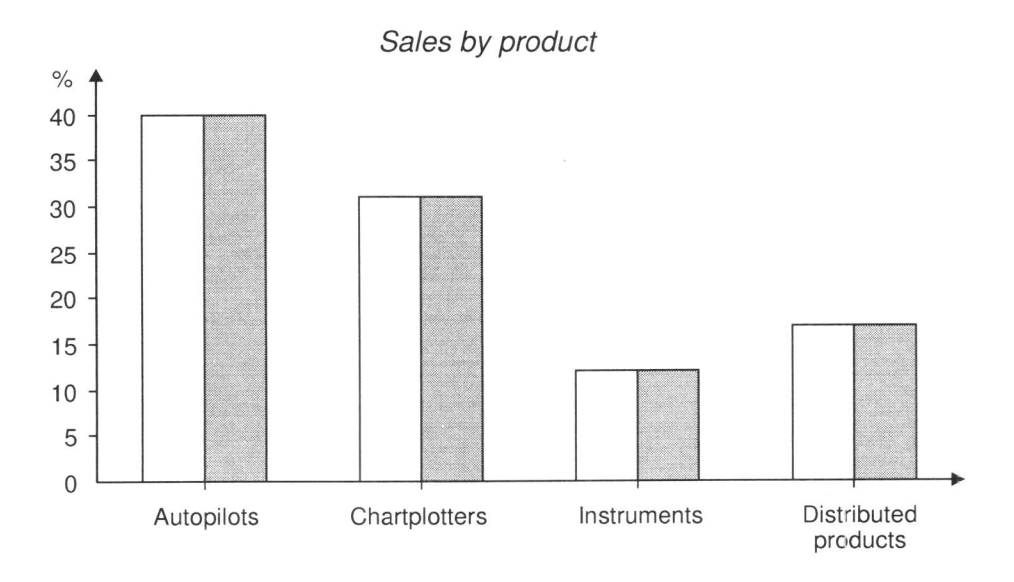

Sales by product

[Bar chart showing percentages: Autopilots 40%, Chartplotters 31%, Instruments 12%, Distributed products 17%]

(b) *Statistics*

(i)	Total sales	£4.5m
(ii)	Gross profit	£1.25m
(iii)	Net profit	£0.65m
(iv)	Expenses	£0.6m

(c)
(i)	Leisure sales	£3.1m
(ii)	Executive jet	£98m
(iii)	OEM	£17m

(d) *Market share*

(i)	Aviation electronics market	£425m
(ii)	Sentinel share	1%

(e) *Sales by region*

(i)	UK	£98m
(ii)	Europe	£178m
(iii)	US	£85m
(iv)	Rest of world	£64m

5.2 *Customer information*

(a) Relatively little information on customers
(b) Split into Leisure and Executive
(c) Leisure - consumer is the pilot
(d) Executive - purchaser unlikely to be the user
(e) Dealers are highly influential in purchase
(f) Customers look for integrated solutions
(g) Customers are happy to deal with a single source because it is more convenient
(h) Purchasing patterns: Leisure, one at a time; Executive, in multiples
(i) Airshows/other events are likely to be influential

5.3 *Competitor analysis: general*

(a) *Further information needs*

(i) Competitive profile for Europe/US
(ii) Pricing
(iii) Distribution channels
(iv) Customer perceptions

(v) Competitors in potential new market areas

(b) *Competitor presence by sector*

Direct competitors	Leisure	Executive jet	Light aircraft	Defence	OEM
Swiftair	yes	yes	yes	yes	(yes)
Eagle	yes	yes	yes	yes	(yes)
Navigator	yes				
Breen Electronics		yes	yes		
Airway	yes				
Kestrel	yes				
Peregrine			yes		
Controllair			yes		
Wing electronics			yes		
Sentinel	yes	yes	no	no	yes

(c) *Indirect competitors and new entrants*

(i) Radar/flight-deck and radio communications
(ii) System solutions providers - aircraft general
(iii) OEMs
(iv) Software houses
(v) GPS manufacturers: Gamma, Starburst, Mapping, Technair
(vi) Sentinel US and other large distributors
(vii) Omnicorp: Tailwind, Gannet control system
(viii) Mail-order companies
(ix) Industrial control and security systems providers
(x) Other leading edge technological companies forming joint ventures

5.4 *Competitor profiles*

(a) *Eagle Electronics*

Strengths	Weaknesses
• Division of large industrial group • Important share of group turnover • Leisure • USA • Aggressive	• Confused branding • Confused product portfolio • Static growth in commercial sector • Two strong brands to be phased out
Strategy	
To grow in commercial sector, especially in Europe, targeting the executive jet sector with a new product	

(b) *Breen Electronics*

Strengths	Weaknesses
• Reputation	• Multiple ownership • Strategic focus on luxury aircraft • Marketing mix
Strategy	
Unclear	

(c) *Navigator*

Strengths	Weaknesses
• Independent • Rapid growth • Investment in promotion • Investing in new products	• Independent - vulnerable to takeover • Limited product range

Strategy
Focus on leisure and position as specialists

(d) *Swiftair*

Strengths	Weaknesses
• High market share • Global distribution • Division of larger industrial group • Established brand • Clear positioning • Strategic alliance • Premium product focus • Growing steadily (financial resources)	• Secondary corporate branding

Strategy
• Focus on top end of market and look for strategic alliances
• Distribution, rationalisation

5.5 *General issues*
(a) Supplier rationalisation
(b) Decline in defence contracts
(c) Mail order is leading to the commoditisation of the market
(d) Sophistication of market: move towards integrated solutions
(e) Competitors offer a broader product range
(f) Distributor power: is there threat of vertical integration?

5.6 *Future trends/developments*
(a) The market is becoming increasingly competitive.
(b) Increasingly sophisticated customers - talking about *interfaces* and *integration*.
(c) Customers do not really care where products come from - they want an integrated suite of products that work together.
(d) Customers are happy to deal with a single source.
(e) Substitute products might come from companies which purchase components and integrate them themselves.
(f) The market is increasingly fragmented.

5.7 *Products*
(a) Sentinel is a product push company with no real market orientation
(b) High potential for sorting out the product range and developing it
(c) High reputation and quality - Navigaid
(d) Questionable - Firstaid
(e) More sophisticated than competitors
(f) Convenience products
(g) Range seen as 'things for planes' - no integration as range
(h) Features are not based on market research
(i) Mixed identity - similar products with different names

5.8 *Place (channels)*

   (a) Sentinel operates in 45 countries with 60 staff.

   (b) Depends on dealer network, most of whom hardly sell enough to cover servicing costs.

   (c) Distribution in France and Germany is weakened by dealer turnover.

   (d) Domination by Corby Aero (18% sales).

   (e) Distribution chain is not seen as adding value to products.

5.9 *Promotion and personal selling*

   (a) No obvious public relations strategy or marketing communications plan.

   (b) Efforts to build awareness have obviously failed. Sentinel is seen as a 'one product company'.

   (c) Other products are either unknown, poorly differentiated, incorrectly positioned in the minds of customers - or a combination of all these.

   (d) Standard promotional pack for any media enquiry.

   (e) Lack of strategy.

   (f) Advertising on a 'blackmail by dealers' basis.

   (g) No measurement of effectiveness.

   (h) Agency appointed.

   (i) Planned improvements.

   (j) Everything above (especially (h) and (i)) happened very recently.

5.10 *Pricing*

   (a) Lack of coherent pricing strategy.

   (b) Pricing bears little relation to product positioning.

   (c) Cost-based approach is inadequate.

   (d) Price is set independently of the rest of the mix.

   (e) Pricing is driven by competitors.

   (f) Prices are calculated on cost plus basis.

   (g) Overseas distributors renegotiate prices to keep business.

   (h) UK and US markets are highly price sensitive (mail order).

   (i) Detailed calculations are only now underway to establish links between retail prices and profit.

5.11 *Physical evidence*

   (a) Elements outside the core product - packaging and support services.
   (b) Lost opportunity for differentiation in the mind of the customer.
   (c) Sentinel's product range is not perceived as coming from one company.
   (d) Dealers' lack of product knowledge does not help.
   (e) Reference from Mainstream (the executive jet company) seems the only good news.

5.12 *Positioning grid*

Positioning grid

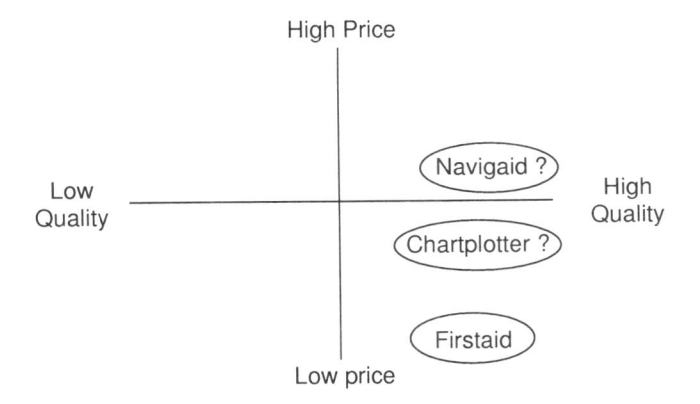

```
                    High Price
                        |
                        |
                        |
              ┌─────────┐
              │Navigaid ?│
  Low         └─────────┘       High
  Quality ────────────────────  Quality
                    ┌──────────┐
                    │Chartplotter ?│
                    └──────────┘
                        |
                    ┌────────┐
                    │Firstaid│
                    └────────┘
                        |
                    Low price
```

5.13 *Strengths and weaknesses analysis summary*

(a) *Organisational factors.* No strengths: it will be impossible to deliver significant changes in strategic direction without cultural change.

(b) *Manufacturing factors.* This is an areas of significant strength although workforce is seen as a marginal strength because of its resistance to change. UK supplier sourcing flexibility is a strength.

(c) *Financial factors.* This is a weak area and highly important. Availability of development capital is likely to depend on parent company - without significant investment, Sentinel is unlikely to achieve Omnicorp's RONA targets.

(d) *Marketing factors*

   (i)   Strengths relate to Navigaid and its reputation.

   (ii) Significant weaknesses relate to market share, competitive stance, distribution channels, pricing and advertising.

   (iii) Other serious weaknesses include salesforce motivation and the distribution network.

6 SWOT ANALYSES

6.1

CONSULT THE GUIDANCE NOTES FOR THIS STEP IN CHAPTER 8 PARAGRAPHS 3.9 TO 3.13
STEP 7 DO A SWOT ANALYSIS
ALLOW BETWEEN 2 AND 3 HOURS FOR THIS STEP

6.2 (a) *Sample 1* is quite nicely formatted and succinct but somewhat minimal.

(b) *Sample 2* is a little more extensive.

(c) *Sample 3* is the most extensive and makes its points well.

However, none of these three examples makes any attempt to *score* and/or *allocate degrees of importance* to the items so as to facilitate prioritisation for decision making purposes, as recommended. Does yours?

Part E: Learning from experience: ensuring you pass

6.3 *SWOT analysis: Sample 1*

Strengths	Weaknesses
1 Excellent software designers and systems engineers 2 Reputation for quality - heritage 3 Premium products 4 Makes own components 5 Management/engineering change 6 Omnicorp backing 7 Established distribution network 8 'Navigaid' brand	1 Product led 2 Myopic culture 3 No MkIS 4 Sentinel is regarded as a single product company 5 Product portfolio - not managed/brand marketing 6 Poor salesforce 7 Strategy and planning 8 Does not exploit synergy 9 Poor communications
Opportunities	Threats
1 Light aircraft 2 Expanding distribution network eg Swiftair (new customers) 3 Expected Euro-legislation → mini-boom (new customers) 4 Opportunities for diversification, branching further into electronics sector (market development etc) 5 Opportunities for joint venture with aircraft manufacturers 6 US market 7 Intergroup sales	1 Rationalisation of suppliers by aircraft manufacturers 2 Competition outside the industry buying components and supplying integrated solutions 3 Threat of price war 4 Swiftair - alliance with Japan 5 Eagle is targeting Europe with a new product

6.4 *SWOT analysis: Sample 2*

(a) *Strengths*

(i) Wide range of products offered
(ii) Wide markets - 45 countries indicates good global presence
(iii) A free hand, but with financial support from Omnicorp
(iv) Growth in sales averages 28% from 1994 to 1996
(v) Good reputation for quality as an autopilot pioneer
(vi) 70 years of heritage
(vii) Synergistic advantage - cross selling with Omnicorp US

(b) *Weaknesses*

(i) Only have 60 employees. A confused management structure
(ii) Not planning driven and no strategic direction
(iii) Conflict among the employees; inconsistent goals; a reluctance to accept change
(iv) Lack of proper identity or branding of products; can confuse
(v) Salesforce's lack of product and IT knowledge
(vi) The inability to command price based on quality is eroding profits
(vii) Promotions are not campaign-based but practised *ad-hoc*
(viii) Standard press pack and no proper public relations strategy

(ix) Dealer performance and dealer support

(x) Inventory levels are high and debtor days have been increasing since 1994

(xi) Customers perceive our products to be manufactured by *competitors;* wrong perception by our customers.

(xii) Lack of MkIS, no database system

(xiii) Salesforce think regionally and not globally

(c) *Opportunities*

(i) 99% of total market share is still available.

(ii) Synergy is available between the combination of products from Sentinel and Omnicorp's aviation division to produce integrated systems to serve the target market with our total solution products.

(iii) Lapse in competitor operation (Swiftair) creates an opportunity to increase our market penetration.

(iv) New product development in OEM market such as shipping and leisure crafts, automative, production machinery, measuring and control instruments.

(v) Aircraft builder looking for venture company and partnership

(vi) Significant DIY, increasing demand for calibration in sophisticated aircraft instruments and upgrading of systems markets.

(vii) US is the single largest market worth more than US £1 billion. It offers the chance of developing volume sales through successful use of mail order.

(viii) Take on new distributors dropped by Swiftair, whose credibility has been damaged. Introduce Sentinel franchise to improve weak market areas.

(ix) Globalisation and rationalisation amongst suppliers; customers sourcing on a global scale.

(x) Asia has a very high market potential for the aviation industry.

(d) *Threats*

(i) Price war between competitors, heavy discounting.

(ii) Cheap inferior quality imports in leisure market may drain revenue from low end applications.

(iii) New entrance outside the aviation industry may find application for their products in aviation.

(iv) UK leisure and executive jet sectors are facing increasing competition which could force a price war and long term threat to high value products to become commodities.

(v) Declining markets for different aircraft due to absence of 'cold war' situation.

(vi) Perceived by customers as a single product company in the cyclical and fragmented market place.

6.5 *SWOT analysis: Sample 3*

(a) *Strengths*

(i) Largest range of autopilots (finest in the world) and chartplotters (71% of total sales) in the world - but only a 1% share of worldwide sales.

(ii) Sentinel is given a free hand by Omnicorp to plan directions and policies.

(iii) Technology is input from Omnicorp's central research and development.

(iv) Omnicorp's aviation division includes Tailwind (hydraulic system, control system, etc) and Gannet (control systems for helicopters), where cross selling within group and packaging the product (integrated products to add value) are planned - a potential growth opportunity. Also, the aviation division can be presented to the customers as a group to market complete package.

(v) Several after-sales and supplementary services can add value to Sentinel's products - installation services, calibration and upgrading services will be introduced.

(vi) The newly appointed advertising agency, Summer Associates, is experienced in IT industries and will help Sentinel communicate the value of new technologies across different industries.

(b) *Weaknesses*

(i) Sentinel never before had a strategic marketing plan.

(ii) Based on the organisation chart, Sentinel lacks an international marketing division. Separate manager for instruments sales (Hugo Black). Separate account manager for one customer (Mainstream aircraft manufacturer) which is not a top-six customer. Why is product development under instruments sales? Why is the publicity officer under account manager - Mainstream?

(iii) Despite a broad product range, most customers still perceive Sentinel as a single product (Navigaid) company.

(iv) Conservative selling practice and culture; narrow focus - 'aircraft navigation business'.

(v) Firstaid's relatively poor performance (12% of total sales) is due to low funding (resources) and poor design input, resulting in lack of interest from the salesforce. Failure to differentiate the products within the range causes customer confusion.

(vi) Sentinel is territory-oriented, as opposed to pursuing global marketing opportunities.

(vii) Sentinel's premium quality products are in danger of losing that position because of price discounting and lack of marketing support from dealers and distributors.

(c) *Opportunities*

(i) 26% of aircraft owners in UK intend to purchase navigation or communications equipment in the next two years - aftersales market.

(ii) The major competitor, Swiftair, has dropped 15% of its distributors - some could be experienced, with existing distribution network knowledge of the market place, and can provide information about Swiftair (a competitor).

(iii) Opportunities exist to apply existing technology (especially GPs) to industries outside the aviation industry.

(iv) Aircraft builders value the expertise from suppliers who are able to provide them with complete, integrated packages using IT.

(v) A mini-boom in the market is expected when European (EU) legislation on air safety is passed - increasing the demand for Sentinels' products.

(d) *Threats*

(i) Traditional markets (leisure and executive) are becoming increasingly competitive with fewer but larger competitors, shifting focus on those markets as the defence (airforce) market declines. The global market is dominated by two main players (Swiftair and Eagle) holding a 50% market share.

(ii) Customers are getting more sophisticated in their application of computerisation and IT.

(iii) Threats from a new type of competitor, 'system integrators', who package products and components from various sources and market complete packages (added-value) to the customers. Customers have expressed a strong desire for such integrated products.

Chapter 29

SENTINEL AVIATION: SITUATIONAL ANALYSIS, KEY ISSUES, MISSION STATEMENT, BROAD AIMS, MAJOR PROBLEMS

> **This chapter covers the following topics.**
> 1 Appendix analysis
> 2 The steps you should take
> 3 Situation analysis
> 4 Decide key issues
> 5 Mission statement and broad aims
> 6 Major problems

1 APPENDIX ANALYSIS

1.1 For the first time in at least the last eight years and 15 cases, this case contains no appendices and therefore no Appendix analysis is required. However, there is instead a number of exhibits in the text itself which have had to be taken into account in prior analysis.

2 THE STEPS YOU SHOULD TAKE

2.1 In this chapter you will complete your analysis, make judgements and move to decision making mode.

2.2 Firstly you are asked to re-visit your précis, marking audit, SWOT etc and to add further analysis so as to be able to draw up a situation analysis statement summarising all the information, not just the marketing bits.

CONSULT THE GUIDANCE NOTES IN CHAPTER 8 PARAGRAPHS 3.18 TO 3.28
STEP 9 RECONSIDER YOUR PRÉCIS, MARKETING AUDIT AND SWOT ANALYSIS STEP 10 CONDUCT A SITUATION ANALYSIS
ALLOW BETWEEN 2 AND 3 HOURS FOR COMPLETING THESE STEPS

2.3 When you have completed your situational analysis statement please compare it with the specimens which follow.

Notes   **Part E: Learning from experience: ensuring you pass**

2.4 (a) *Specimen 1* is really an expansion on the key issues (which come later). This format works only to a limited extent.

(b) *Specimen 2* starts with our role and finishes with the implications of the new targets. This is good but perhaps what comes in between could be improved.

(c) *Specimen 3* is formatted under headings of External and Internal. It contains more detail than Specimen 2 and is probably the best of the three for our purposes

3 SITUATION ANALYSES

3.1 *Specimen situation analysis 1*

Situation analysis

Given Sentinel's current situation and the new targets agreed with Omnicorp a number of key issues need to be addressed.

(a) *What business are we in?*

We need to decide whether to stay in the aviation business or whether our technological expertise can provide solutions for other industries. From my Managing Director's recent comments we have no other option but to look outside aviation in the medium term.

(b) *What are the critical success factors?*

We need to know these for the navigational aids segments within the aviation market and for selected new markets outside aviation.

(c) *For what new markets are Sentinel the best 'fit'?*

This would entail comparing Sentinel's strengths against the critical success factors identified for new attractive markets in order to make the best selection(s).

(d) *To what extent can targets be met from existing markets?*

There are numerous initiatives such as new products/services, re-organisation/ motivation of the salesforce, new distribution outlets, pricing, communications and market research which if embodies n a short-term marketing plan would contribute to growth. These, plus exploiting synergistic opportunities within the Group and the potential mini-boom in Europe arising from increased safety legislation, should close some of the gap and we can then establish how much needs to come from new market opportunities.

3.2 *Specimen situation analysis 2*

The situation is that I am the marketing director of Sentinel Aviation (SA) part of the Aviation Division of Omnicorp (and American conglomerate) with a brief to develop a long-term strategic plan which will meet Omnicorp's expansion and return on assets expectations.

My major problems are that SA is steeped in tradition and is still mainly a product orientated company, that there are almost too many product/market opportunities to choose from, and that SA is unsure as to what business it is in or should be in.

I am currently consulting market research and advertising agencies for specialist assistance whilst endeavouring to handle new product/service, pricing and distribution issues personally.

Competition is increasing and market segmentation/positioning strategies relevant to competitors are in need of urgent review. My managing director has recently agreed figures with Omnicorp which amount to increasing turnover almost six times by the end of the next five days, consistent with a return on net assets of between 15% and 20%. Only part of this expansion can come from gains in market share, so that opportunities outside current product-markets will have to be considered.

3.3 Specimen situational analysis 3

External

Competition is increasing and there is a danger we will be reduced to being a components supplier competing on price unless we react positively to the opportunity to move to new markets, offering integrated solutions based on our distinctive competences. Moves to exploit synergies within the Group include working with Gannet to develop a group product portfolio and with Tailwind on developments that incorporate our Autopilot products.

Our experience in GPS could be applied outside the aviation industry eg GPS is already being used to track a city's taxis in the Middle East.

New targets agreed with Omnicorp call for a six-fold increase in turnover over the next five years.

The indications are that aircraft builders will look increasingly for integrated solutions. The market is becoming more global and supplier rationalisation could follow.

Internal

We have quite a number of marketing weaknesses, not the least of which is lack of a long-term strategic marketing plan based on a clear understanding of what business we want to be in and of our distinctive competences. More information is being sought to facilitate the making of the correct strategic decisions.

However, a number of improvements are being made to our marketing mix, including the provision of added-value services and the reorganisation and remotivation of our salesforce. Marketing communications should become much more effective following the recent appointment of a new advertising agency.

We are also adding new distribution outlets as a result of Swiftair's rationalisation and we are reviewing our price setting procedures.

Depending upon being able to *measure* the return on our marketing budget, it will be increased form the current 5% of turnover to the 7% or 8% that applied a few years ago.

It is now incumbent on me to develop an effective marketing strategy to meet Group targets over the next five years which includes new product concepts and new markets outside aviation.

4 DECIDE KEY ISSUES

CONSULT THE GUIDANCE NOTES FOR THIS STEP IN CHAPTER 8 PARAGRAPHS 4.1 TO 4.4
STEP 11 DECIDE THE KEY ISSUES
ALLOW 1 HOUR TO 1½ HOURS FOR THIS STEP

4.1 You are reminded that the next step is the most important one, since it has the most bearing on the likely examination areas.

4.2 You are also reminded to limit these to a *maximum of six* and that you might like to construct a list of candidate key issues which could then be ranked, as a way of doing this exercise.

4.3 Remember also the technique of parcelling up several minor issues into one major issue as described in Chapter 8 paragraph 4.1.

4.4 Now that you have completed this crucial exercise, please compare your conclusions with those produced by six separate syndicates as given on the next page.

4.5 Sentinel Aviation - Key issues

Syndicate A2	*Syndicate B2*
1 Are objectives achievable with current markets? 2 New product development 3 Organisation culture 4 Image perceptions 5 Distribution 6 Pricing	1 What business should we be in? 2 What are our distinctive competences? 3 How to develop new products for new markets 4 How to change our image 5 Distribution channel effectiveness 6 Internal marketing
Syndicate C2	*Syndicate D2*
1 Achievement of new targets 2 Developing an effective strategy 3 Creating a five year plan 4 Changing the company culture 5 Motivating the salesforce 6 Direct marketing	1 Lack of information - new markets, customers, competitors 2 No marketing plan 3 Distribution 4 Current product-markets are insufficient 5 Confusing product lines 6 Low market awareness
Syndicate A1	*Syndicate B1*
1 Development of new products/markets 2 Achieving greater synergy 3 Internal marketing 4 Relationship marketing 5 Segmentation and positioning 6 Marketing research	1 Marketing planning and control 2 New market evaluation and entry 3 NPD 4 Lack of full marketing orientation 5 Salesforce efficiency 6 Distribution

4.6 As in previous cases, the results of syndicate work in Key Issues indicate quite a strong consensus. Do you agree with the consensus? What are your best bets with regard to potential exam question areas?

4.7 You are now about to enter the stage when you need to make the big decisions. Hopefully, the standard of your previous analysis will help you to make the right decisions.

5 MISSION STATEMENT AND BROAD AIMS

CONSULT THE GUIDANCE NOTES IN CHAPTER 8 PARAGRAPHS 4.4 TO 4.14
STEP 12 DEVELOP A MISSION STATEMENT STEP 13 DECIDE BROAD AIMS
ALLOW ABOUT AN HOUR FOR EACH OF THESE STEPS

5.1 Remember there should be consistency between your mission statement and your broad aims, also that you should try to limit the latter to four bearing in mind the need to convert these into quantified and time-scaled objectives at a later stage.

5.2 Having completed these two steps you should now compare your results with those of four separate syndicates which follow. Please be critical when looking at these syndicates' work.

5.3 *Syndicate C*

Mission statement

Sentinel's aim is to provide leading edge electronic positioning solutions through investments in staff and new technology, meeting the changing needs of our customers.

Broad aims

1. To increase market share in existing markets
2. To develop new market/new product opportunities
3. To establish a marketing philosophy throughout the company
4. To adopt relationship marketing

5.4 *Syndicate D*

Mission statement

To open up the world by improving communications in the field of navigation through offering sate of the art integrated solutions. This will be achieved through partnerships with customers, suppliers and employees.

Broad aims

1. To engender a customer focused reactive culture
2. To seek out new product-market opportunities
3. To be the most responsive supplier to customers
4. To bring new opportunities to our customers

5.5 *Syndicate E*

Mission statement

To be the first choice supplier of integrated electronics solutions to customers with navigation needs by providing the highest standards of service using technical expertise to ensure complete customer satisfaction.

Broad aims

1. To establish strategic planning and direction processes within a marketing culture
2. To develop a fully customer-focused organisation
3. To establish a comprehensive MkIS
4. To achieve superior growth and profitability
5. To maximise appropriate market opportunities
6. To improve distribution coverage and performance
7. To establish a core product portfolio

Notes *Part E: Learning from experience: ensuring you pass*

5.6 Syndicate F

> *Mission statement*
>
> Sentinel will be the preferred provider of integrated Navigational solutions in key global markets. The company will be at the leading edge of technological innovations and of quality and service excellence.
>
> *Broad aims*
>
> 1. To develop a more market orientated culture
> 2. To develop closer relationships with our customers
> 3. To achieve and if possible exceed our financial targets
> 4. To supply innovative products to new and existing customers
> 5. To develop a clear brand strategy, and to communicate this to customers
> 6. To develop synergistic sales within the Omnicorp Group
> 7. To develop a more cost-effective distribution network

5.7 You were asked to be critical when assessing the work of the above four syndicates. Let us compare notes. If there is woolly thinking at this stage (the initial broad decisions) it is likely to permeate right down through the detail of the ensuing plan. You must ask yourself 'can I convert these broad aims into quantified and time-scaled objectives which will be acceptable to the Board?'

(a) More often than not syndicates *confuse strategies with objectives* in their minds when drawing up their broad aims. All four syndicates have fallen into this trap to some extent. This leads to the writing of objectives in the examination paper which are really strategies and signals to the examiner that you have not really got your thinking straight at the start.

(b) Too many broad aims = too many objectives and supporting plans. Syndicates E and F have gone beyond the four required and perhaps simply repeated their Key Issues. Also, when looking critically at the Mission Statements we should remember that these are intended to be short corporate positioning statements of what business the company is in and its aims for the benefit of target audiences including staff, investors and customers.

It is the word 'Navigation' too constraining? What about potential customers? Should something be included about service and value?

5.8 Let us now move on to the next step, that of identifying problems which will get in the way of achieving our mission and broad aims.

6 MAJOR PROBLEMS

CONSULT THE GUIDANCE NOTES GIVEN IN CHAPTER 8 PARAGRAPHS 4.15 TO 4.18
STEP 14 IDENTIFY AND ANALYSE MAJOR PROBLEMS
ALLOW BETWEEN TWO AND THREE HOURS FOR THIS STEP

6.1 Remember to restrict yourself to six major problems in rank order.

6.2 Do not worry if your major problems relate closely with the key issues. This is quite usual.

6.3 Having done this, you can now compare your ranking with those of six syndicates provided below.

6.4 *Sentinel Aviation: six major problems ranked by syndicates*

Problem		B1	A2	B2	C1	D2	A1
1	No clear marketing strategy or history of marketing strategy	1	2	2	1	2	2
2	Unsure of what business they are in	6		3	5		3
3	How to achieve a six-fold increase in sales over five years	2	1	1	2	1	1
4	Too many opportunities versus no strategic selection criteria				5	4	
5	Predominantly a product rather than a marketing orientated company	3		6		3	
6	No real understanding of customer needs/markets		3				5
7	Inaccurate perception of company by customers		4			4	
8	Have not clearly differentiated its products and established competitive advantage			6		5	
9	Salesforce disoriented and demotivated	4		4			6
10	Wide distribution base in need of rationalisation and integration				6		4
11	Insufficient MR and a lack of MkIS		5		3		
12	No apparent integrated MARCOMS	5				6	

6.5 It is to be expected that some correlation should emerge between key issues and major problems. There is also quite a strong consensus between the syndicates (only 12 items) and it seems clear that if Sentinel could overcome these major problems, there would be little left in the way of achieving broad aims of increasing sales market share, and achieving its return on net assets targets.

6.6 You should now be ready to move forward to your outline plan

Chapter 30

SENTINEL AVIATION: OUTLINE MARKETING PLANNING

> **This chapter contains the following guidance and plans.**
> 1   The steps you should follow
> 2   Examples of outline marketing plans
> 3   Brand building and communications
> 4   Distribution
> 5   Pricing
> 6   Marketing information system

1   THE STEPS YOU SHOULD FOLLOW

1.1   We strongly recommend you now re-read the notes provided for the Gravesend Town Centre practice run in Chapter 16, and that you opt to produce an outline plan for Sentinel Aviation before developing this into the complete detailed marketing plan required. You are reminded of the steps for the marketing plan proper as follows.

CONSULT THE GUIDANCE NOTES GIVEN IN CHAPTER 8 PARAGRAPHS 4.19 TO 6.8
In outline only
STEP 15 DEVELOP QUANTIFIED, TIMESCALED OBJECTIVES
STEP 16 CONSIDER ALTERNATIVE STRATEGIES. SELECT THOSE MOST APPROPRIATE
STEP 17 DRAW UP DETAILED TACTICAL PLANS COVERING THE MARKETING ORIENTATION
STEP 18 DRAW UP A MARKETING RESEARCH PLAN
STEP 19 CONSIDER ORGANISATIONAL ISSUES, CHANGES AND MARKETING ORIENTATION
STEP 20 CONSIDER ORGANISATIONAL CULTURE AND NEED FOR INTERNAL MARKETING
STEP 21 DETERMINE THE FINANCIAL/HR RESOURCE IMPLICATIONS OF YOUR PLANS
STEP 22 ASSESS COSTS AND DRAW UP INDICATIVE BUDGETS
STEP 23 DRAW UP SCHEDULES GIVING TIMINGS/SEQUENCE OF ACTIONS
STEP 24 SPECIFY REVIEW PROCEDURES AND CONTROL MECHANISMS
STEP 25 DRAW UP OUTLINE CONTINGENCY PLANS
STEP 26 REVIEW YOUR COMPLETE MARKETING PLAN
YOU WILL NEED ABOUT ONE HOUR TO DO YOUR OUTLINE

30: Sentinel Aviation: outline marketing planning

2 EXAMPLES OF OUTLINE MARKETING PLANS (based upon previous analysis, mission and broad aims)

2.1 This being a somewhat unusual case with clear signals that diversification into new markets with new systems would be required in order to meet new targets agreed with Omnicorp, most Groups opted to draw up the outline plans for particular aspects rather than to attempt an overall outline plan. What follows therefore are examples of these mini plans done by individual syndicates. Whilst as you can see, such an approach can produce some good results, there is a danger of generating too much output for outline planning purposes and difficulties in putting the various aspects together into a coherent whole.

Example plan: B1

2.2 Example of overall objectives and strategies by Nottingham Trent University syndicate B1.

(a) *Objectives*

    (i) To reach a sales turnover of £25m by the year 2002
    (ii) To achieve a return on net assets of 15% by the year 2002
    (iii) To increase aviation electronics market share to 2% by 2002

(b) *Strategies*

Products

	Existing	New
	Market penetration	**Product development**
1	*Increase purchases* — Increase end user sales using upgrades via direct mail; Increase distributor sales via trade push eg loyalty scheme promotions, PO, training	*New features* — Add-on value - fitting, kits, entry-level service, calibration, upgrades; Product technology innovation
2	*Gain customers from competitors* — Buy competitors	*Quality levels* — Range from premium price to lower quality, lower priced goods
3	*Convert non-users* — Increased awareness via introductory promotions	*New products* — Via strategic alliance/partnerships/joint ventures
	Market development	**Diversification**
1	*New markets:* eg ships, yachts, helicopters, light aircraft and cars	Personal security - guidance for the blind, orienteering/rambling, car tracking/security, tagging criminals
2	*New distribution channels* — Take up redundant Swiftair distributors; Intergroup (Omnicorp) sales; Mail order in UK/Europe, rest of world	Via: acquisition, take-over or joint ventures with: 1 *Horizontal integration* — Other aviation equipment manufacturers 2 *Vertical integration* — Suppliers/customers
3	*New geographic areas* eg Middle East/South East Asia OR, rationalisation	

Part E: Learning from experience: ensuring you pass

Outline marketing plan Group A (overall strategy evaluation and choice)

2.3   *Ansoff matrix*

Market penetration	*Product development*
1 Relationship marketing management 2 USA - Eagle customers 3 Acquire small manufacturing companies 4 Mail order - USA, Europe 5 More manufacturers to be targeted	1 Integrated systems 2 'Cheap' range 3 Rationalisation of product range 4 DIY kits 5 Customised range
Market development	*Diversification*
1 Non aviation 2 Internet 3 New countries 4 Travel - taxis etc 5 Defence 6 Light aircraft 7 Retail	1 Research and development only 2 Entertainments industry 3 Tagging ie wildlife, prisons 4 Training centre 5 Planes - building

30: Sentinel Aviation: outline marketing planning

(b) Evaluating the role of each option

	Feasible? 1 2 3	Acceptable? 1 2 3	Achievable? 1 2 3	Suitable? 1 2 3	Exploit core competences 1 2 3	Valued by customer 1 2 3	Level of risk 1 2 3	Score
Market penetration								
Relationship management (business-to-business)	X	X	X	X	X	X	X	7
USA market	X	X	X	X	X	X	X	9
Acquisition of manufacturers	X	X	X	X	X	X	X	17
Product development								
Aviation systems integration	X	X	X	X	X	X	X	8
Introduction of cheap range	X	X	X	X	X	X	X	16
Rationalise the range	X	X	X	X	X	X	X	11
Market development								
Non aviation navigation	X	X	X	X	X	X	X	11
Use of the Internet	X	X	X	X	X	X	X	7
Enter into new countries	X	X	X	X	X	X	X	17
Diversification								
Concentrate on research and development	X	X	X	X	X	X	X	18
Entertainment (flight simulators)	X	X	X	X	X	X	X	19
Control/tagging systems	X	X	X	X	X	X	X	13

Key

1 = Low risk or *yes* to taking on an idea
2 = Medium risk or *unsure* as to potential
3 = High risk or *no* to taking the idea further

Part E: Learning from experience: ensuring you pass

    (c) *Strategic choice*

        (i) *Market penetration:* relationship management (RM) (business-to-business) USA

        (ii) *Product development:* systems integration

        (iii) *Market development:* Internet
                              Non aviation navigation

        (iv) *Year 1 focus:* RM plus Internet
                             Research USA
                             Research and development systems

        (v) *Year 2-3 focus:* Action USA plus systems integration
                                   Research non aviation navigation

    (d) *Justification*

        (i) *Strategies chosen:* Lowest scores
                                   Exploiting core competence
                                   A good balance

        (ii) *Strategies rejected:* Highest scores
                                       Not as good exploiting core competences
                                       Tended to be higher risk

Outline market development plan (Group B Nottingham Trent University)

2.4   *Market choice: the police force*

    (a) We are a small company.

    (b) Initially we need to *target* precisely. We thus believe that the whole of the emergency services sector would be too large.

    (c) The police force appeared to exploit core competences of navigation and technology.

2.5   *Situation analysis*

    (a) *Internal*

        (i) We offer suitable products which can be modified to suit needs.
        (ii) Technological expertise to do any adaptation.
        (iii) Research centre at Omnicorp can be used for backup.
        (iv) Core knowledge of countries and their culture (as this market could be worldwide).

    (b) *External*

        (i) Police in every country.
        (ii) UK and Europe are regionalised (so we need to research key areas).

2.6   *Target market*

    (a) *Who?* Police forces in the markets in which we currently operate.

    (b) *Needs?*

        (i) Cost effectiveness   (v) Tracking
        (ii) Speed of reaction   (vi) Use 'people' resource more effectively
        (iii) Low maintenance/reliability   (vii) Integrated systems eg traffic
        (iv) Support services   (viii) Regional force interaction

2.7   *Objectives*

    (a) Achieve 50% penetration of UK regional police forces within three years.
    (b) Achieve 50% penetration in another market outside the UK within four to five years.
    (c) To break even by the end of year 2 leading to profit in year 3.

2.8 *Marketing strategy*

(a) Research the market, identify competitors.

(b) Research product modification in partnership with reputable regional forces eg Metropolitan and West Midlands.

(c) Position as high quality, cost effective, reputable company.

(d) Period of trial/market testing with chosen forces.

(e) Presentation to all forces through personal selling.

(f) Launch in UK during the year.

2.9 *Tactics*

(a) *Product*
   (i) Core package of navigation and tracking system specifically for cars.
   (ii) Extras for other police vehicles: boats, bikes, helicopters.
   (iii) Software updates.
   (iv) Service deal to install, train and maintain.
   (v) Branding: one *umbrella brand* for Police products '*Crimeroute*', with subrands: '*Navigate*'; '*Tracker*'; '*Rider*'; '*Pilot*'.

(b) *Price*
   (i) Consider elasticity of demand
   (ii) Adopt market orientated pricing
   (iii) Perceived value should decide price

(c) *Promotion*
   (i) Personal selling: recruit three key staff initially
   (ii) Police conventions
   (iii) Trade magazines/editorials
   (iv) Public relations: editorials in local newspapers, videos, literature
   (v) TV (eg Tomorrow's World)
   (vi) Combination of push and pull strategy
   (vii) Endorsement from heads of trial areas

(d) *Place:* Sell direct to forces

2.10 *Implementation*

(a) *Allocating*

Budget 7% of Sentinel's total turnover = £297,500
         Allocate 30% of that for the first year = £89,250

Year 1 budget

	J	F	M	A	M	J	J	A	S	O	N	D	£
Recruit													1,000
Train													2,000
Research and trial													76,250
Video and literature													5,000
Initial PR													5,000

Year 2

	J	F	M	A	M	J	J	A	S	O	N	D
Conventions	As they occur											
Personal selling												
PR												
Advertising												

Part E: Learning from experience: ensuring you pass

- (b) *Organising*
    - (i) Jim has ultimate responsibility
    - (ii) Appoint *police sector product manager:* possibly an internal recruit
    - (iii) Two account managers should liaise with trial areas
    - (iv) Dealt with as a separate entity
- (c) *Control/monitoring*
    - (i) Monthly meeting with the four main people involved
    - (ii) Jim to report formally to MD quarterly
    - (iii) Set targets quarterly, to enable review
    - (iv) Review budget quarterly
- (d) *Internal marketing*
    - (i) Jim to be 'champion'
    - (ii) Task force of four people
    - (iii) Meet with directors, to get their commitment
    - (iv) Distribute details of revised structure
    - (v) Presentation by Jim to all staff (informal)
    - (vi) Liaise closely with R & D

Market development plan - Marine navigation (Group C Nottingham Trent University)

2.11 *Situation analysis*

- (a) *Market*
    - (i) Ocean going marine boats
    - (ii) Assumption: this is almost a *mirror* market to executive and leisure jets which Sentinel currently supplies, and includes large commercial ships, speedboats, sailboats, yachts.
- (b) *Customers*
    - (i) Distributors
    - (ii) Boat manufacturers
    - (iii) Fleet rental operators
    - (iv) Private boat owners
- (c) *Competitors*
    - (i) Established marine electronic companies
    - (ii) Need market research to find out competitive forces at work

2.12 *Macro*

- (a) *Aim:* to establish a presence in the market by 2002.
- (b) *Objectives*
    - (i) To achieve £5m turnover by 2002
    - (ii) To conduct market research within three months, so that more objectives can be set.

2.13 *Strategy*

- (a) *Segment:* Ocean going leisure and pleasure market
- (b) *Target*
    - (i) Distributors
    - (ii) Ship builders
    - (iii) Private owners
    - (iv) Fleet rental market
- (c) *Positioning.* Product approach: quality, reliability, ease of use, easy to install, sturdy, rugged.

(d) *Product.* Chartplotters and Navigaid.

(e) *Differentiation.* Quality premium product must be consistent with Sentinel aircraft.

(f) *Method of market entry.* Need research but will enter major markets where we already have strong presence (UK, USA, Europe eg France).

2.14 *Tactics*

(a) *Product*
   (i) Chartwell and Navigaid
   (ii) Most easily adopted, already have customers in that market

(b) *Place/distribution*
   (i) Distributors
   (ii) Mail order
   (iii) Internet to end user

(c) *AIDCA*
   (i) *Awareness.* Advertising, advertorial in trade press
   (ii) *Interest*
      (1) Glossy brochures
      (2) Exhibit at key events eg Earls Court, the Boat Show
      (3) Point of sale materials
   (iii) *Desire.* Personal selling, direct mail
   (iv) *Conviction.* Testimonials from key people, friends etc via publicity
   (v) *Action*
      (1) Sales promotion to make the product easy to buy (eg 'push' down distribution chains via *trial use* of Navigaid).
      (2) Aid to distributors, ship builders etc.
      (3) Relationship marketing.
      (4) Ease of repeat orders.
      (5) Good customer service.
      (6) Training and help lines.

(d) *Price*
   (i) Research existing competitors' prices.
   (ii) Set prices to reflect premium product positioning.
   (iii) Must be consistent with prices of aircraft navigation aids.
   (iv) Be price competitive: try to reduce costs that do not add value.

2.15 *Implementation*

(a) *People*
   (i) Skills audit
   (ii) Targets and recruitment plans
   (iii) Training plan
   (iv) Specialised knowledge
   (v) Become more customer-oriented
   (vi) Train distributors

(b) *Financial*

This programme will start 18 months from now. It proceeds from market penetration, so the budget will have to increase to £408,000 for advertising costs.

1998 < 1 year of marketing development plan.

Other costs are:

	£,000
Research - year prior	10
Promotion adverts	50
Exhibition	30
POS	20
PR attendance	40
Direct mail	15
Sales literature	20

Justification: we are new to the market so we need to establish ourselves.

(c) *Control/measures*

(i) Awareness studies/tracking, recall tests
(ii) Feedback from salesforce
(iii) RONA
(iv) Market share obtained
(v) Profitability
(vi) Sales turnover
(vii) Customer surveys/phone polls

Market development plan - Automotive market (Group D Nottingham Trent University)

2.16 *Justification*

(a) Increase in profits and turnover set down by Omnicorp cannot be achieved by *market penetration* alone.

(b) *Product development* is too time consuming and takes up significant resources.

(c) *Market development* is in line with company core competences.

(d) Strong strategic fit, compared with other alternatives.

2.17 *Identify market*

(a) Automotive market - supplying a product which satisfied navigational needs within the automotive market.

(b) Additional market - net market.

(c) This market can be segmented further into sub-segments.

2.18 *Key customers and needs*

(a) Original equipment manufacturers (OEM). (Private and commercial vehicle manufacturers: cars, buses, motorbikes, taxis, HGVs etc).

OEM need a product which enhances their own *product* through efficiency, safety, user cost savings and navigational capabilities, therefore adding value to their product.

(b) Subcontractors.

(c) Dealers.

(d) DIY (retail outlets).

(e) End users - need a product which allows them to reach their destination effectively and satisfies aspirational requirements because of the perceived prestige of the product arising from its positioning and branding.

2.19 *Objectives*

(a) To achieve £5 million turnover by 2001.
(b) To achieve 30% gross profit.
(c) To achieve 15% RONA.

2.20 *Strategies*

(a) Segmentation: geographically, commercially, private vehicles.

    (i) USA – an established and large market; the product is at growth stage in its product life cycle in USA, therefore the opportunity exists to exploit market opportunity through positioning.

    (ii) UK and Europe - relatively new markets with significant market share/market leader, innovator opportunities. The product is still at launch/introduction stage of its product life cycle.

(b) Targeting:

    (i) UK/Europe - commercial and private vehicles.
    (ii) USA - commercial and private vehicles.

Target markets represent high potential with medium risk.

(c) Positioning: *differentiation* through innovative products, technical expertise and enhanced customer service, allowing premium pricing, moving away from the price discounting trends, and therefore achieving Omnicorp's gross profit and growth objectives.

2.21 *Tactics:* adapted to each market segment.

(a) *Price:* premium; skim in UK and Europe and USA in both private and commercial vehicles sectors

(b) *Product:* premium, modifications to suit automotive needs, stronger service levels, branding, technical advances of products

(c) *Promotion*

    (i) Personal selling - training, review of structure of salesforce, motivation/ remuneration/ performance evaluation.

    (ii) Public relations - develop corporate and product portfolio identity through international public relations strategy; seek publicity with launch into new markets.

    (iii) Sales promotion - develop company literature specific to the needs of each market, dealer incentives, exhibitions, direct mail, trade presentations.

    (iv) Advertising will be a small part of promotional mix, concentrating on trade journals.

(d) *Distribution:* channel negotiations with potential customers through dealers, direct supply of actual product.

2.22 *Control*

(a) Implementation: see Gantt chart
(b) Organisations: see organigram (not supplied)
(c) Internal marketing: workforce training, managing a change of culture and objectives
(d) Control: against turnover, profitability and corporate objectives

Notes   *Part E: Learning from experience: ensuring you pass*

IMPLEMENTATION CHART - GANTT CHART
AUTOMOTIVE MARKET

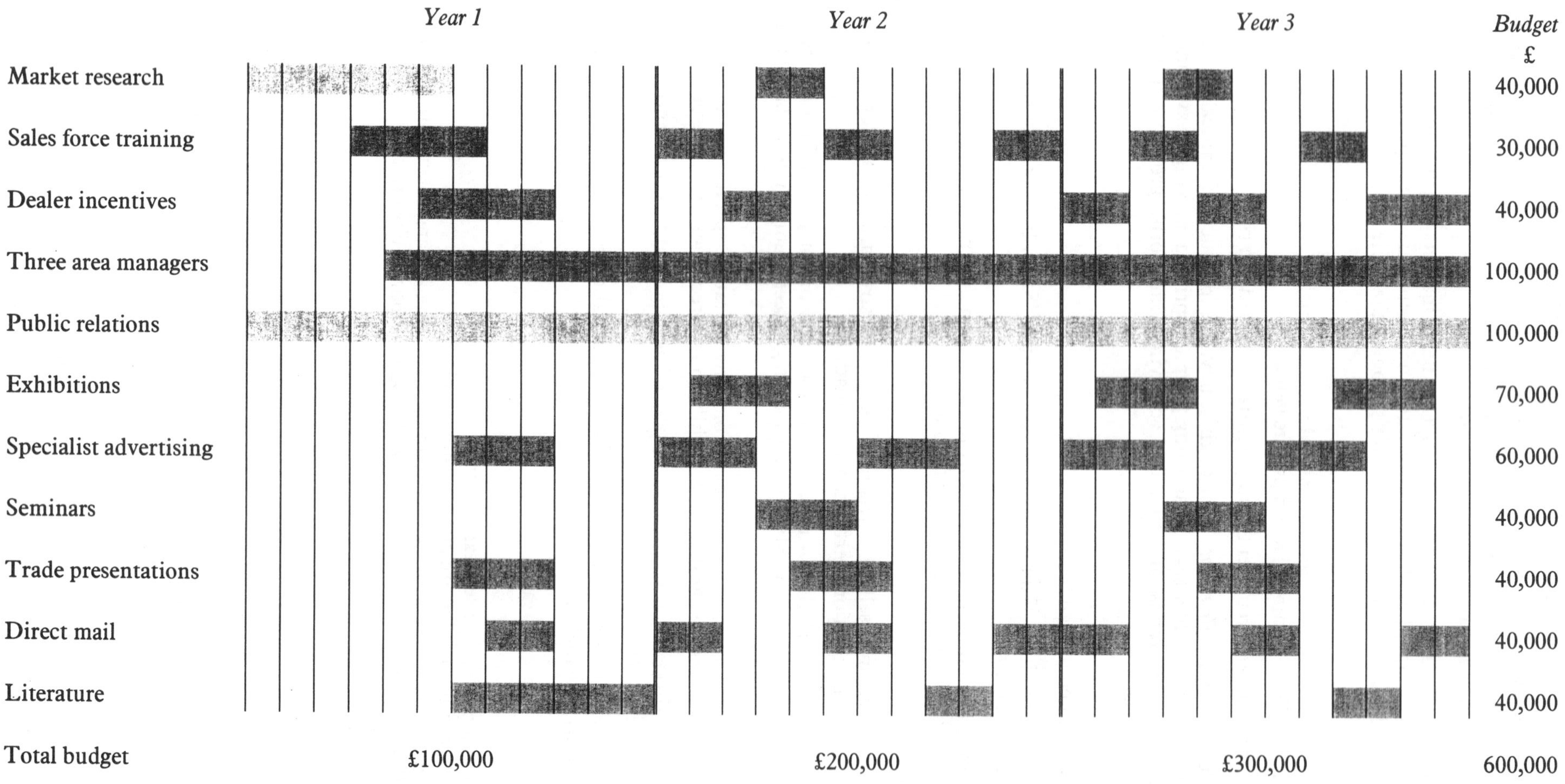

	Year 1	Year 2	Year 3	Budget £
Market research				40,000
Sales force training				30,000
Dealer incentives				40,000
Three area managers				100,000
Public relations				100,000
Exhibitions				70,000
Specialist advertising				60,000
Seminars				40,000
Trade presentations				40,000
Direct mail				40,000
Literature				40,000
Total budget	£100,000	£200,000	£300,000	600,000

Operational marketing plan for related diversification (CIM Intensive Diploma Syndicate)

2.23 *Background*

(a) Experts in navigation equipment

(b) Current focus is on the aviation industry

(c) The parent company has set a sales target of £25m within five years

(d) Several strategies are needed to address the planning gap

(e) Related diversification - navigational equipment in boats?

    (i) Little knowledge of nautical market
    (ii) Synergy with navigation expertise

2.24 *Objective*

(a) *Business strategy*

To achieve £3m revenue within the market of navigational equipment for boats over a period of five years.

(b) *Marketing objective*

To gain 5,000 customers of the nautical navigation product within five years.

2.25 *Marketing strategy*

(a) *Segments* of the boat market are:

- Shipping
- Leisure
- Sport
- Commercial

(b) *Criteria* for segmentation

    (i) Comparative technology
    (ii) Existing customers
    (iii) Disposable income
    (iv) Life style
    (v) Potential market profitability
    (vi) Access/distribution network
    (vii) Competition
    (viii) East of market entry - tariffs/controls

(c) *Target: leisure*

    (i) 35-36 year olds
    (ii) Synergy with aviation market
    (iii) CEO/senior managers
    (iv) Boat owners
    (v) France, Spain, UK

(d) *Positioning*

Values

    (i) High quality
    (ii) Innovative
    (iii) High level of support
    (iv) Nautical expertise

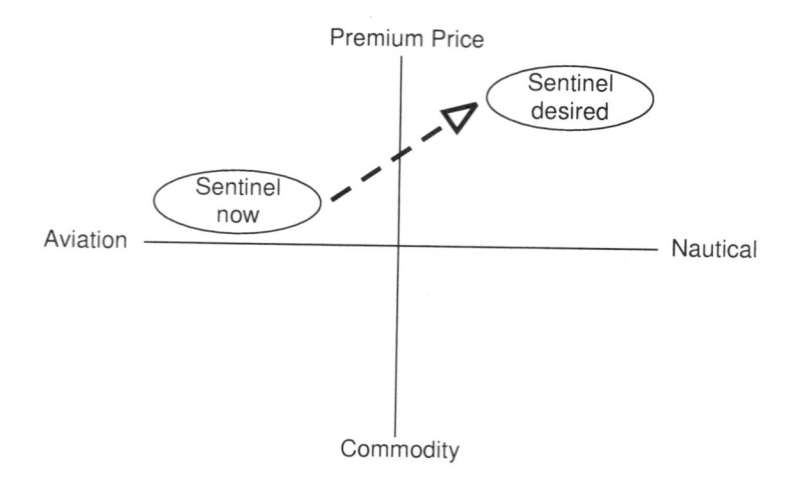

Part E: Learning from experience: ensuring you pass

Positioning

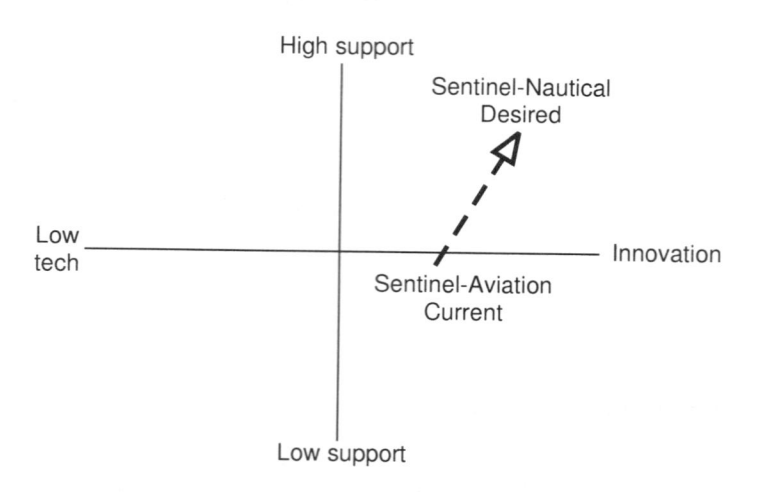

2.26 Tactics

	Objective	Budget	Time	Controls
Product	Develop product for leisure boat market	£100,000	First product six months ongoing R&D	MkIS
Price	£1,000	-	Immediate, plus ongoing	Sales statistics
People	Highly trained staff at all levels	£200,000	Six months ongoing	Customer satisfaction survey
Place	New/existing distribution, France, Spain, UK	£50,000	Immediate start Six months in place	Sales returns Customer satisfaction
Physical evidence	Warranty/guarantees develop materials	£10,000	Start immediately	Customer feedback
Promotion	Launch event Above/below line marcomms	£80,000	Six months	Awareness survey
Process	To engender customer care culture	£30,000	Immediate	Cost satisfaction survey

30: Sentinel Aviation: outline marketing planning Notes

3 BRAND BUILDING AND COMMUNICATIONS

Brand strategy for Sentinel - Nottingham Trent University syndicate

3.1 *Situation analysis*

   (a) *Weaknesses*

      (i) Wide range of products with similar names - confuses the customer
      (ii) Names are not representative of product (*First aid* = instruments?!)
      (iii) No strategic approach to branding
      (iv) Promotions/branding are currently unfocused
      (v) Low awareness - people think they are made by competitors

   (b) *Strengths:* the one well known brand is 'Navigaid' - autopilot

   (c) *Competitors*

      (i) Brand identities should be directed towards the market sector rather than the product type
      (ii) Have a smaller product range than Sentinel
      (iii) Main competitors having branding problems - therefore opportunities for Sentinel
      (iv) *Navigator:* heavy focused promotion has earned considerable growth.

3.2 *Brand strategy: as identified in Ansoff matrix*

   (a) *Improve segmentation and targeting:*

      Focus on leisure and commercial sectors
      Develop a product range branding for each sector

   (b) *Develop stronger branding.*

      (i) *Brand fit:* develop relationships between brand names

          (1) Sentinel is associated with aviation - but is not well known
          (2) 'Navigaid' - global recognition of product and quality - already the *preferred choice*.

      For a family umbrella brand name use '*Navigaid*' for both sectors with a sub-brand name for product identification. This offers scope for brand extensions.

      (ii) *Brand names* should suggest benefits and qualities, be easy to pronounce and remember, and be distinctive and meaningful.

	(Leisure sector) NAVIGAID *Adventure range*	(Commercial sector) NAVIGAID *Star Master range*
Autopilot	'Adventure Pilot'	'Master Pilot'
Chartplotter	'Adventure Planner'	'Master Planner'
Instruments	'Adventure Instruments'	'Master Instruments'

      (iii) *Positioning:* needs to be clear, consistent, competitive and consistent (offering functional and symbolic benefits)

'The ultimate choice in complete navigation systems.
Leading the way though quality, innovation and attention to customer needs.'

Positioning maps

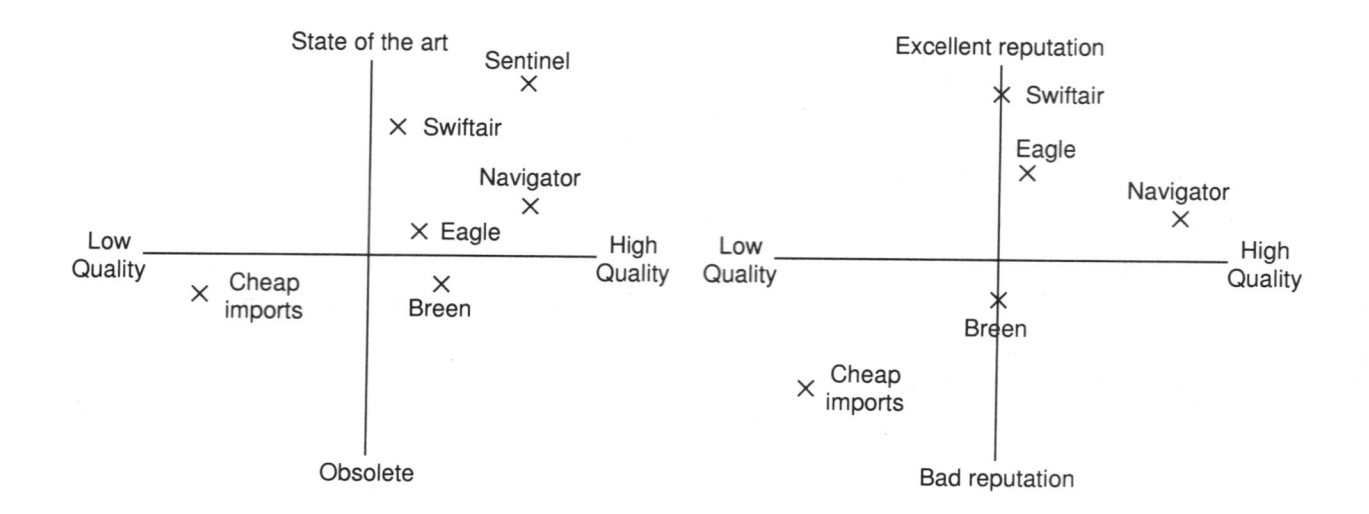

```
        State of the art                          Excellent reputation
              |     Sentinel                             |  × Swiftair
              |        ×                                 |
              |  × Swiftair                              |     Eagle
              |      Navigator                           |      ×           Navigator
              |         ×                                |                     ×
Low           |  × Eagle         High      Low           |                  High
Quality _____|_____ Quality  Quality _____|_____ Quality
       × Cheap |   ×                                     | ×
        imports|  Breen                                  | Breen
              |                                × Cheap   |
              |                                  imports |
              |                                          |
           Obsolete                               Bad reputation
```

    3.3   *Outline*

        (a) *Objectives*

           (i)   To change the *perception* of Sentinel from being a single product company to a *complete solutions* company within all target markets within two years.

           (ii)   To increase target customer awareness of all products by 50% in two years, increasing to 90% in five years.

           (iii) To increase the number of enquiries by 30% by year 2.

           (iv) To increase conversion levels by 30% by year 2 increasing to 60% by year 5.

           (v)   To position *Navigaid brand products* as the preferred choice amongst the leisure and commercial sector by year 3.

           (vi) To increase customer loyalty amongst current customers by 30% in year 2.

        (b) *Target audience*

           (i)   End user = ABC1 affluent, lifestyle oriented, innovators and succeeders.

           (ii)   Manufacturers - such as Mainstream - want complete solutions and partnerships.

           (iii) Dealers/distributors - want added value, support, high turnover.

        (c) *Positioning statement (as before):* differentiate Sentinel from competitors on quality and service.

        (d) *Message:* 'Navigaid - the ultimate navigation system'. It should have a rational content allowing people to draw their own conclusions.

        (e) *Media*

           (i)   Print - high impact, colour use, space for technical/explanatory copy.
           (ii)   Quality, prestigious specialist publications. Space purchased by agency.

(f) *Pre-testing*
- (i) Attitudinal tests - current perceptions (omnibus survey/focus groups).
- (ii) Focus groups/hall tests with target group - test effectiveness of number of advertisements.
- (iii) Aided or unaided recall.

3.4 *Campaign implementation ('Push and pull' strategy)*

(a) *Personal selling*
- (i) 'Push' to dealers/distributors or direct to manufacturers and OEMs.
- (ii) Structure selling effort by customer/sector, as their needs will differ.
- (iii) Prioritise customers by turnover and determine the number of calls required per customer.
- (iv) Use relationship marketing - regular contact, two way communications - to build loyalty.
- (v) Remuneration: by salary and commission.

(b) *Advertising*

'Push' to trade, 'pull' for consumers.
- (i) *Trade:* manufacturer/dealer support advertisements in specialist trade aviation magazines.
- (ii) *Consumer:* professional, aviation magazines, high circulation, colour, prestigious magazines.

We need a high impact, high reach, high frequency schedule for 'burst' launch, then 'drip' campaign for constant reminders and quality assurance.

(c) *Public relations*
- (i) Editorial in quality press.
  - (1) Consumer: Times, Telegraph, Guardian
  - (2) Trade: top aviation magazines - high circulation, high profile
- (ii) Encourage journalists by offering fight simulator trials
- (iii) Endorsements by celebrities - Red Arrows
- (iv) Raise awareness - offering competition winners flight on Concorde; 'Top Gun' training schools to see new 'brands' in action.

(d) *Direct mail*
- (i) *To end users:* generate requests for further information/special offers from selected dealers (links in to dealer support).
- (ii) *To manufacturers,* offering partnership development - encourage responses for sales people to visit, and can be used to build a data base. Costs suggest one mail shot per year.

(e) *Exhibitions:* use to build brand name and generate awareness/sales leads. Attend prestigious consumer/trade air shows and technology shows (be selective).

(f) *Sales promotions*
- (i) Trade: sales literature and display material; dealer incentives; contests for dealer's sales staff; special quantity trade terms.
- (ii) Consumer: cross selling promotions, competitions, free trials.

(g) *Packaging:* should enhance quality image and premium pricing. Logos need to be clearly identifiable and should be integrated with all other promotional tools.

(h) *Internal communications*

Staff to be made aware of new campaigns, and kept up to date with all changes. Regular communications through company newsletter videos and conferences/meetings.

3.5 *Budget*

(a) This will be based on 5% of year 1 turnover = £212,000
(b) This should rise to 7% of projected turnover by year 5 = £750,000

3.6 *Campaign evaluation*

(a) *Selling:* increases in sales, retention of customers, repeat orders (data files and sales records)

(b) *Post-testing of advertisements*
   (i) Attitude and perception changes
   (ii) Increase in awareness
   (iii) Number of responses

(c) *Public relations:* number of column inches, number of photos

(d) *Direct mail:* coupon responses and requests for information

(e) *Exhibitions:* number of new leads, number of customers met

(f) *Sales promotions:* increases in stock held and stock turnover, new customers/distributors

(g) *Internal staff*
   (i) Staff meetings and communications team meetings (monthly)
   (ii) Monthly meetings with agencies
   (iii) De-brief of communications project group

Communication strategy for Sentinel (CIM Intensive Diploma Course syndicate)

3.7 *Background*

(a) Single product company
(b) Low market share (1%)
(c) Focused on aviation market
(d) Not providing integrated solutions
(e) Confused distribution channels

3.8 *Brand audit*

Undertake quantitative and qualitative research to establish the following about the brand.

(a) The values it represents.
(b) What the brand says now.
(c) How does it say it?
(d) To whom does it say it?
(e) What is its competitive advantage?
(f) What scope does it have?
(g) What is the rational and emotional mix?
(h) Does the current brand have a tactical or strategic role?

3.9 *Communications objectives*

(a) To communicate the fact that Sentinel is an integrated solutions provider.

(b) To achieve 25% awareness in target global markets over five years.

(c) Communicate the brand values of:
   (i) quality
   (ii) innovation, and
   (iii) integrated solutions

3.10 *Tactics.* The next stage will be to look at:
   (a) timetable;
   (b) budgets;
   (c) targets (specific);
   (d) monitoring;
   (e) contingency planning.

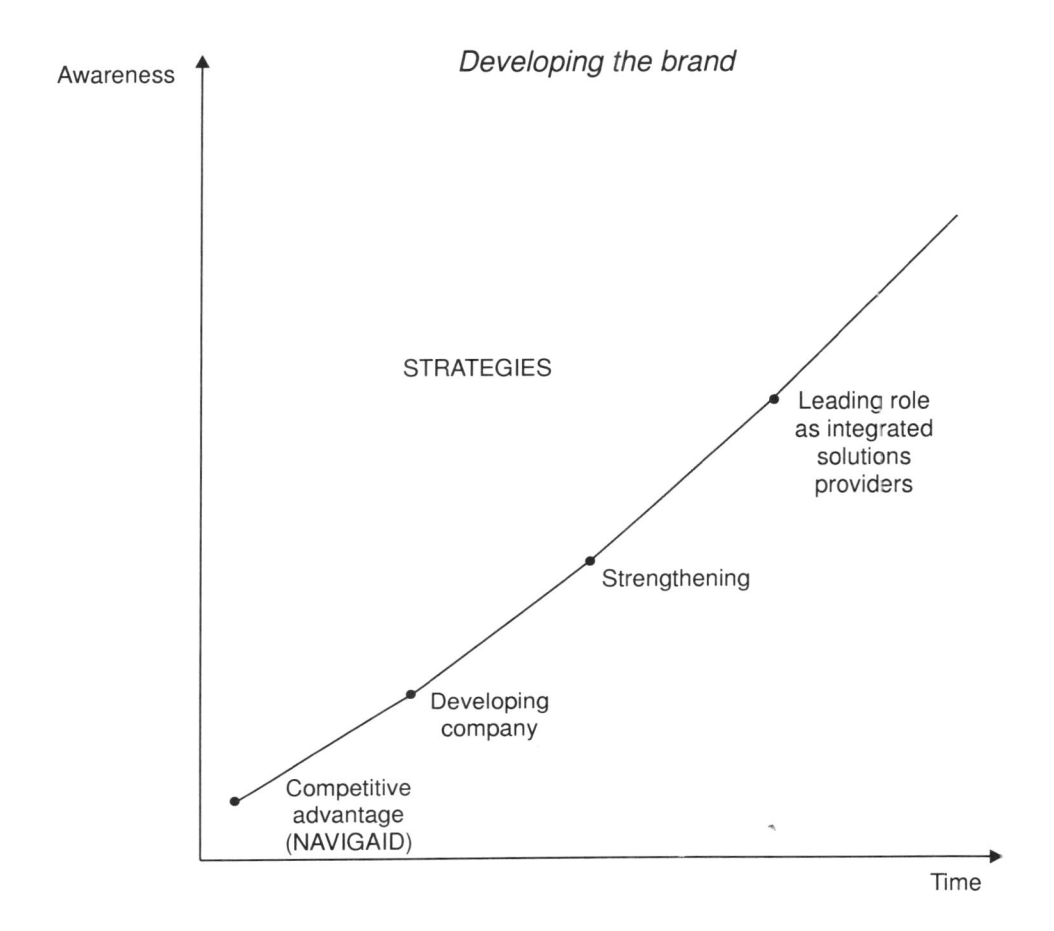

Developing the brand

Awareness ↑

STRATEGIES

- Leading role as integrated solutions providers
- Strengthening
- Developing company
- Competitive advantage (NAVIGAID)

→ Time

4 DISTRIBUTION

Strategic distribution plan - aviation and automotive market (Nottingham Trent University syndicate)

4.1 *Introduction*

In order to position the Sentinel corporate brand within the mind of the customer, Sentinel Aviation should change its name to Sentinel Navigation Systems and have (for now) two main divisions - *Aviation* and *Automotive*. Careful thought needs to be given to the establishment of *distribution* channels to reach customers and end users. This is a strategic distribution plan outlining Sentinel's intended routes to its customers.

Part E: Learning from experience: ensuring you pass

4.2 *Current position*

(a) *Aviation*

(i) *UK (excluding rest of Europe).* Sentinel has a two tier system - direct to customers or dealers.

Breakdown of dealer sales	*Customer sales*
1 Corby = 18% of sales = 54,878	Total UK turnover = 23% of £4.25m = £977,500. Removing dealers sales of £304,878 gives £672,621: ie in UK, over *two thirds sales are direct to customers*, with a plethora of small dealers. Costs serving these dealers must be relatively high for the turnover.
2 50 dealers × 5,000 – £250	
Total = £304,878	

(ii) *Europe* is a three tier system.

Sentinel→Distributor→Dealer

(1) The four main markets are France, Italy, Germany and Spain. There is a problem with continuity in France and Germany.

(2) Aircraft manufacture occurs in Holland (although if this if Fokker, it is no longer a manufacturer since Daimler Benz withdrew financial support), Scandinavia and France. Therefore the aircraft industries in Scandinavia and perhaps Holland are not closely serviced by Sentinel.

(3) *Swiftair* is poised to lose 13% of dealerships, a possible opportunity for Sentinel to fill gaps in Europe. Must be strategically acceptable, and necessary if selected, to maintain quality of service.

(iii) *USA* is the biggest market. Sales through Sentinel US are disappointing - reasons are unknown, and therefore need to be found out. The main dealer (Areotec) accounts for 14% of US turnover, ie £117,600.

(b) *Automotive*

(i) The automotive sector is growing and purchasers are requiring increasing levels of technological sophistication. In addition, manufacturers are always looking for new features and the competitive advantage.

(ii) Sentinel's range of *Chartplotters* could be easily adapted for vehicle use and provide an invaluable navigation aid for drivers.

4.3 *Trends*

(a) A possibility is that distribution of aviation products via the Internet will grow, although like catalogue sales this will eventually flatten out. This channel has been rejected to avoid a price war.

(b) The final design specifications of modern cars and vans are becoming more complex. The end user demands reliability, simplicity of use and innovation. In order for these criteria to be satisfied, the automotive sector needs to incorporate more and more design sophistication and more technology. Sentinel's 'Navcar' is a first product offering to satisfy a growing market of 'in-car navigation systems'.

Distribution aims and objectives

4.4 *Aviation*

(a) *Aim:* To establish profitable and efficient distribution channels to enable our channel members to deliver products to our customers quickly and efficiently.

(b) *Objectives*

(i) To increase net profit through channel members by 10% in the first year, increasing to 15% in year 5.

(ii) To rationalise geographically the distributor/dealer network within the first quarter.

(c) To implement and complete initial dealer/distributor training plans within first year, and to establish a regular programme of maintenance training each year.

(d) To create and implement training programmes for key account managers within six months of year one.

4.5 *Automotive*

(a) *Aims.* To create close supply links with our customers - the automobile manufacturers.

(b) *Objectives*

(i) To develop profitable channel businesses as in other words to establish net profits of 15% in Year 1 rising to 25% in Year 5.

(ii) To create training programmes for client service team and KAMs within first quarter of year 1.

(iii) To have trained 90% of the selected customer engineers in Sentinel's products by the end of year 1.

4.6 *Factors in developing the distribution strategy*

(a) *Geography.* Sentinel's UK base and a transnational marketing policy would lead to the continued use of intermediates in all aviation markets except the UK. Customers are widely dispersed, and Sentinel does not have the resources to approach them all directly.

(b) *Channel length.* Longer channels mean more intermediaries but lower costs for Sentinel. Loss of control is the price Sentinel has to pay. However, control is a central issue in relation to the automotive and aircraft manufacturer strategies. Sentinel *must* be close to these people.

(c) *Buyer behaviour.* Sentinel must be able to match their intermediaries with customers and therefore must have accurate information on buyer behaviour: in aviation this means the end users; in the automotive sector, the customer is the manufacturer, the end user the driver.

(d) *Product support.* Intermediaries must be able to offer technical support to customers. Sentinel must ensure regular dealer/distributor product training if they are to serve their aviation customers satisfactorily.

(e) *Channel co-operation.* Dealers and distributors of Sentinel's various products should work together and work towards common goals.

(f) *Channel leadership (aviation).* Sentinel should lead the channel and be quite clear as to its expectations of channel member performance and standards. Channel members who do not fulfil Sentinel's criteria (which will relate to profitability, stock levels, promotional activities, delivery dates etc) will not be included.

Distribution strategies

4.7 *Options for Sentinel*

Initially, these will be quite simple: do Sentinel deal *directly* with their customers or use intermediaries? In terms of geographical dispersion, the major motor manufacturers are spread around the world. Dealing directly with them would reduce channel length and give greater control. Channel co-operation may be difficult between distributors and dealers as automotive manufacturers would require clear, specific advice - particularly on design.

(a) *Direct (to customers)*

Sentinel will deal directly with:

(i) aviation OEMS in the UK;

(ii) aircraft manufacturers world-wide (this is due to the limited number of 'customers' and will negate the necessity of Sentinel approaching a distributor in Holland/Scandinavia);

(iii) automobile manufacturers in Europe and USA.

Notes Part E: Learning from experience: ensuring you pass

4.8 Distribution

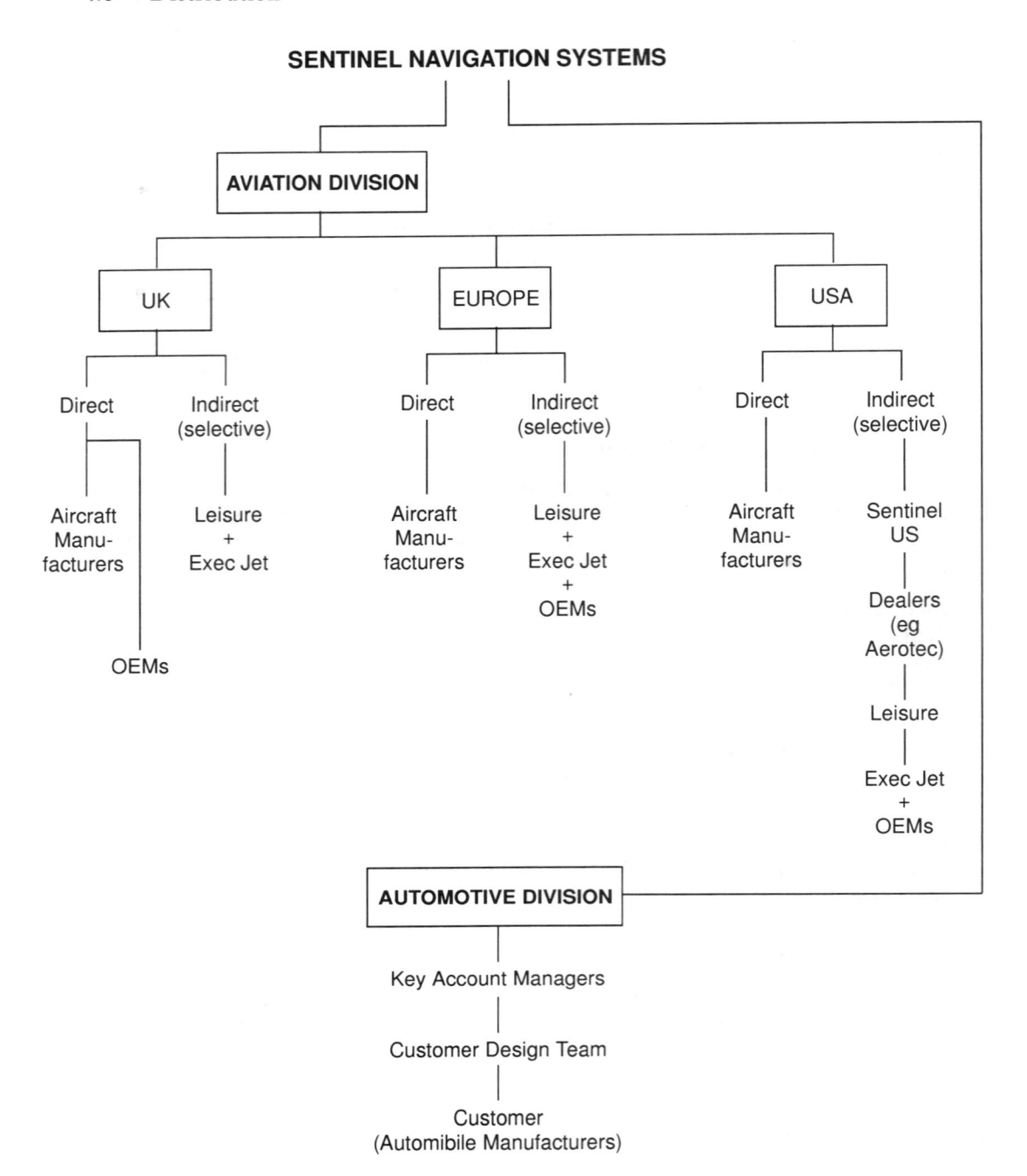

SENTINEL NAVIGATION SYSTEMS

- **AVIATION DIVISION**
  - **UK**
    - Direct
      - Aircraft Manufacturers
      - OEMs
    - Indirect (selective)
      - Leisure + Exec Jet
  - **EUROPE**
    - Direct
      - Aircraft Manufacturers
    - Indirect (selective)
      - Leisure + Exec Jet + OEMs
  - **USA**
    - Direct
      - Aircraft Manufacturers
    - Indirect (selective)
      - Sentinel US
      - Dealers (eg Aerotec)
      - Leisure
      - Exec Jet + OEMs

- **AUTOMOTIVE DIVISION**
  - Key Account Managers
  - Customer Design Team
  - Customer (Automibile Manufacturers)

4.9 Geographic structure and support

GEOGRAPHICAL STRUCTURE & SUPPORT

AUTOMOTIVE DIVISION

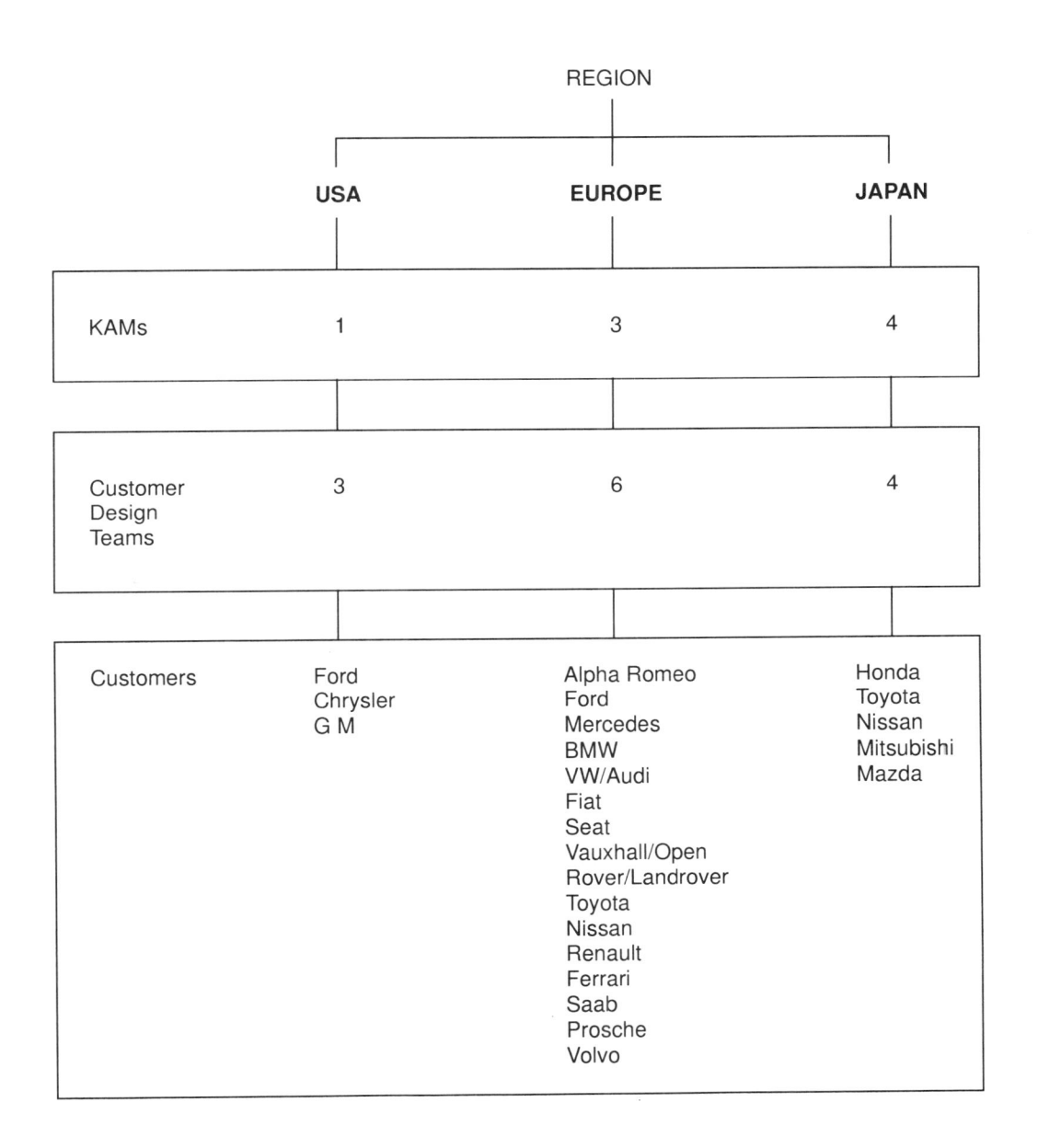

```
                    REGION
         ┌────────────┼────────────┐
        USA        EUROPE         JAPAN
```

	USA	EUROPE	JAPAN
KAMs	1	3	4
Customer Design Teams	3	6	4
Customers	Ford Chrysler GM	Alpha Romeo Ford Mercedes BMW VW/Audi Fiat Seat Vauxhall/Open Rover/Landrover Toyota Nissan Renault Ferrari Saab Prosche Volvo	Honda Toyota Nissan Mitsubishi Mazda

All KAMs and CDTs would be regionally based (Polycentric)

(b) *Indirectly (via dealers and distributors - aviation market only)*

   (i) Leisure buyers - worldwide (ie UK, Europe and USA)
   (ii) OEMs - Europe and USA
   (iii) Executive jet - Europe, USA and UK.

4.10 *Distribution channel penetration*

The options are *intensive*, *selective* and *exclusive*.

(a) *Intense* distribution normally applies to manufacturers of high volume, low-value products in mass demand - products typically purchased of habit an convenience eg cigarettes, food and other consumer packaged items.

(b) *Selective* distribution is for buyers who invest time in 'shopping around'. This type is used when the manufacturer requires a degree of control and after sales service is important.

(c) In *exclusive* distribution, only one outlet is used in a relatively large geographical area and the product sold require service or information to fit them to bigger needs.

4.11 *Selection for Sentinel*

The strategic choice for Sentinel is as follows.

(a) *Aviation*

   (i) Sentinel will offer *selective distribution rights* to its distributors and dealers in all markets *except the US*, where Sentinel US will be made an 'exclusive' dealer and Aerotec will be relegated to a prescribed dealer under contract to Sentinel US.

   (ii) The *justification* is that Sentinel will need the specialist services of dealers and distributors in UK and Europe. This will given them a high degree of control and ensure that customers will receive the necessary levels of service choice, availability and price they demand. However, in the USA, Sentinel US holds massive potential in terms of knowing the market well. They have an established mail order and retail network. As they are already part of Omnicorp, possibilities for synergy exist (also cross-selling of products), the channel length is short, thus giving greater control.

(b) *Automobile*

   (i) Sentinel would establish direct links with the automotive manufacturers, via a team of *key account managers* (KAMs) who will guide and support a new team of customer design engineers. Sentinel's design engineers will be allocated a client or clients and will work very closely with the customer's in-house design teams on the design and application of Sentinel's products during the manufacture and assembly processes. With larger customers, Sentinel would establish a Sentinel office on the customer's site, close to the design facility so that Sentinel becomes seen as almost part of the in-house team.

   (ii) In addition, Sentinel would take two design engineers from each customer on secondment for a two week training programme on Sentinel's products. These engineers would then return to the manufacturer and be the key contact points for the Sentinel customer design team, thus aiding the design process.

4.12 *Channel management tactics*

(a) *Key issues (aviation)*

   (i) Rationalisation of existing network of dealer distributors
   (ii) Investigation of problems in France and Germany
   (iii) Investigation of current relationships with Sentinel US
   (iv) Determine sales force status, including key account management
   (v) Dealer/distributor support/incentivisation/contracts
   (vi) Examine status of MkIS to facilitate 'direct' distribution to customers

(b) *Key issues (automotive)*

    (i) The key issue for Sentinel will be to build long-lasting *relationships* with *each customer* and integrate its support and products as closely as possible with those of the customer. The customer must perceive Sentinel's design team as an invaluable help in designing bespoke systems and be a cost-effective resource.

    (ii) For luxury models, Sentinel must be able to incorporate customers' needs with a view to satisfying the end user. Sentinel must also maximise its sales and revenue through this direct channel approach and must therefore review carefully the profitability of this strategy.

4.13 *Tactics*

(a) *Aviation*

    (i) Conduct MR on existing dealerships/distributors and sort criteria for inclusion/exclusion. Criteria should include turnover, facilities, loyalty, efficiency etc. Establish final number of dealer/distributor networks. This should include specialist investigations in France and Germany.

    (ii) I should visit the US to meet with Sentinel US to define reasons for relatively low sales in the past. Establish action plan to rectify situations, draft exclusivity agreement and decide on the principal customer-focused strategies and objectives.

    (iii) Recruit and train KAMs for all direct sales and dealer operations. Train existing sales force to support dealers. Develop incentives for KAMs and sales support team.

    (iv) Organise dealer/distributor conferences in UK and Europe (1 UK, 2 Europe) to explain new structure, objective, strategies, incentive and training programmes and contracts.

    (v) Devise dealer/distributor training ad incentive programmes.

    (vi) Draft standards of performance and related contracts. Offer trade support to dealers/distributors with POS materials, demonstration equipment and guidance on bulk purchasing. Run incentive schemes for top three dealer distributors to pay for private pilot training to top performing sales personnel.

    (vii) Evaluate coverage by existing MkIS of UK OEMs and world-wide aircraft manufacturers. Incorporate improvements where necessary.

    (viii) (1) Create customer design teams who will be responsible for specific customer(s). The role of these teams will be to work closely with customers (all aircraft manufacturers, UK, Europe and US and OEMs in the UK) preferably on the customer's manufacturing site - developing and applying new technologies to designs. The target would be to establish a Sentinel 'cell' with each customer, who would then be a key point of focus for development ideas and thus bring customers and Sentinel closer together.

    (2) In addition, create an induction programme for up to two flight engineers from each customer to be trained by Sentinel's aviation division, in Sentinel's premises in autopilot and chartplotter design and applications. These two engineers will then be key contacts to work with Sentinel on home development projects.

(b) *Automotive*

    (i) Recruit and train KAMs. Establish sales objectives, plans and incentives, such as a racing experience at Brands Hatch Formula 3 cars or a trip to the Monaco Grand Prix.

    (ii) Recruit and train customer design teams. Establish objectives and introduce to KAM. The team supporting the successful KAM will also win similar prizes.

(iii) Take two engineers from each customer and train them for two weeks on Sentinel's products. Establish a rapport between these engineers and Sentinel's KAM and customer design team.

4.14 *Implementation timetable*

	Year 1 Q1 Q2 Q3 Q4	Year 2 Q1 Q2 Q3 Q4	Year 3 Q1 Q2 Q3 Q4
Aviation			
1 MR on dealerships/distributors	←→		
2 Sentinel US investigation and plan	←→		
3 Recruit KAMs and incentivise	↔ ↔	↔	↔
4 Dealer distributor training and incentive schemes	←——————————————————————→		
5 Dealer/distribution conference	↔		
6 Update MkIS	←——————————————————————→		
7 Control			
- APC	x x x x	x x x x	x x x x
- SC	• •	• •	• •
Automotive			
1 Recruit and train KAMS	—		
2 Recruit and train customer design teams	—		
3 Train customer's engineers	———— ————	————	
4 Evaluation and control meetings	x x	x x x x	x x x x

4.15 *Budget/annum - combined aviation and automotive*

Staff	No.	Average cost (salary plus)	S/T	Equipment	T&S	Total £
KAMs	12	70,000	348,000	18,000	36,000	472,000
CDTs	40	38,500	1,000,000	60,000	120,000	1,218,500
Customer training (Customers' engineers)	70				140,000	140,000
Market research						20,000
Sentinel US investigation						3,000
Dealer/distributor training						100,000
Dealer/distributor conference *3						50,000
Update MkIS						10,000
Total						£2,013,500

Notes *1 - one off cost
       *2 - one off cost
       *3 - alternate years

NB. The majority of the salary costs are already being incurred by Sentinel - ie they are *not* taken out of the marketing budget.

Evaluation and control

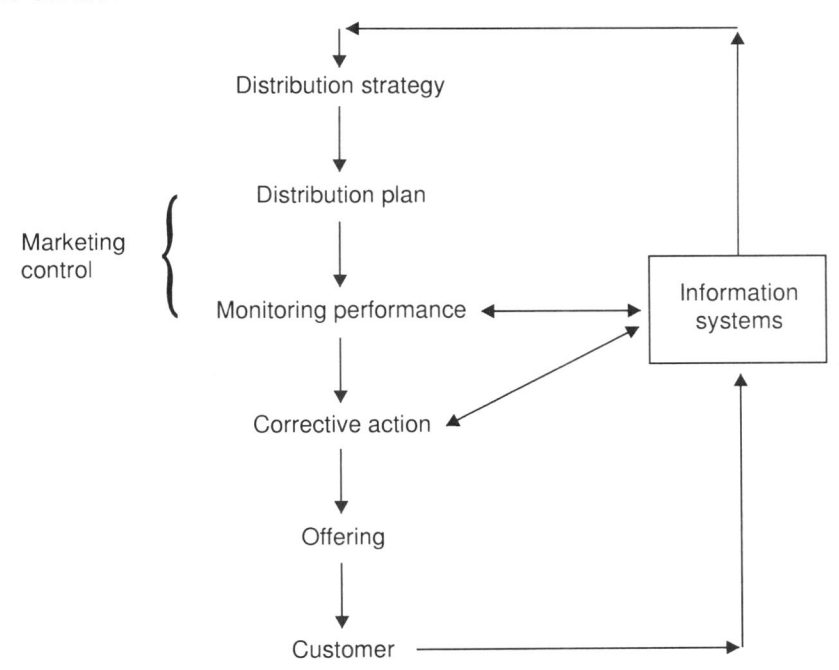

```
                    ┌──────────────────────────────┐
                    ↓                              │
            Distribution strategy                  │
                    │                              │
                    ↓                              │
            Distribution plan                      │
   Marketing  {     │                    ┌──────────────┐
   control          ↓                    │ Information  │
            Monitoring performance ←────→│   systems    │
                    │                    └──────────────┘
                    ↓                         ↑   ↑
            Corrective action ────────────────┘   │
                    │                              │
                    ↓                              │
                Offering                           │
                    │                              │
                    ↓                              │
               Customer ───────────────────────────┘
```

4.16 *Evaluation criteria*. Different criteria are to be applied to each channel, but they should basically incorporate the following.

(a) *Financial*

  (i) Cost of the channel
  (ii) Profitability of the channel (compared to overall gross profit targets)
  (iii) Turnover of Navigaid, NavPlot and NavCar

(b) *Non-financial*

  (i) Market share achieved.
  (ii) Growth (or decline) in channel.
  (iii) Opportunities exploited by dealerships dealers and KAMs.
  (iv) Speed and reliability of delivery of aviation equipment to end users.
  (v) Channel willingness to support marketing activity, ie point of sales, trade literature etc.
  (vi) Number of engineers trained.
  (vii) Strength of relationship with manufacturers.

4.17 *Control*

(a) *Annual planning control*

Steps taken throughout the year: Jim Converre and Mike Flynn should meet once every three months to check ongoing performance against the plan.

(b) *Profitability control*

Efforts to check channel profitability against targets.

(c) *Strategic control*

Biannual meeting of Sentinel Board should approve Mistral's fit with the opportunities and threats of general environment. After year 3, a full evaluation meeting will take place to define action and implementation plants for years 4 and 5.

Notes | *Part E: Learning from experience: ensuring you pass*

Conclusion

4.18 *Aviation*

(a) If Sentinel is to deliver technologically advanced, premium priced navigation equipment and solutions to its aviation clients, it must have distribution channels which are effective, profitable, provide a high level of advice and backup service to its customers and serve the customers' needs well.

(b) By applying different criteria and different channel solutions, Sentinel should be able to deliver on its customer promises and reinforce its position as a reliable provider of high quality navigation equipment.

4.19 *Automotive*

(a) The automobile sector represents a vast market for Sentinel.

(b) Sentinel's track record with reliable technology will stand them in good stead when developing relationships with the automobile manufacturers.

(c) Although the budgeted costs are high, the potential unit sales are astronomical. If Sentinel can provide the close design support and key account management skills that are needed, it can expect to enjoy high turnover and profitability.

5 PRICING (Nottingham Trent University Syndicate)

5.1 *Introduction*

Price is the only element of the marketing mix which generates income. It does not add value but it is seen as a value indicator.

Pricing considerations

5.2 *Corporate objectives (SMART)*

(a) To achieve £25 million turnover by 2001.

(b) To achieve RONA between 15% and 20%.

(c) To increase market share to 3% in UK, Europe and the USA.

(d) To generate £5 million turnover in the chosen market development area (ie automotive).

(e) To achieve £5 million turnover from new product development.

(f) Establish Sentinel as a high quality manufacturer and supplier.

5.3 *Demand*

(a) The aviation market worldwide is worth £425m - we assume it will grow to £500m by 2001.

(b) Automotive market: USA is a growth market; however, UK and Europe are still in the introduction stage for navigation equipment.

(c) Demand can become less elastic for products with added value and high quality.

5.4 *Demand effects*

(a) *Uniqueness*. Differentiation might increase demand for Sentinel products.

(b) *Substitutes*. Swiftair and Eagle products.

(c) *Availability*. Supply is meeting demand in the aviation market at present.

(d) *Who's buying*. The end user is not price sensitive, and has high disposable income.

(e) *Our customers*. Dealers and distributors are price sensitive as they have margins to support and are presently driving prices down.

5.5 *Costs.* Ensure total awareness of fixed and variable costs. Costs will increase in absolute terms due to increased turnover and implementation of the marketing plan. However, percentage costs will be reduced due to economies of scale.

5.6 *RONA.* This is a major factor affecting cost/price relationship. We will not be able to go below a certain price.

The product

5.7 *Position*

(a) Sentinel is currently viewed as a one product company (ie Navigaid, high quality product), but there is lack of brand recognition across the range. Desired position will carry Navigaid brand across the range to justify premium pricing of all products.

(b) *PLC.* Currently at the mature stage. Integrated systems will extend the life cycle. (In the diagram below, Year 0 is 1996.)

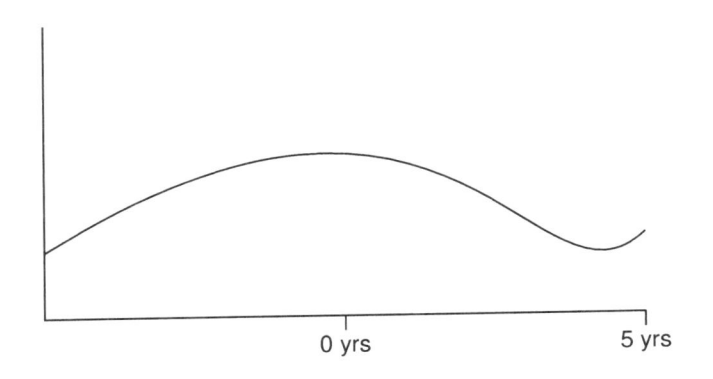

5.8 *Competition*

(a) Swiftair/Eagle/Breen appear to be following the market trend by *discounting*. All are part of large companies, therefore with a low cost basis due to economies of scale.

(b) Breen are expensive in relation to their perceived position.

5.9 *Pricing objectives* will be linked to the corporate and marketing objectives. The overall objective is to achieve the £25 million turnover by year 5, 2001.

5.10 *Pricing strategies*

(a) *Standardised.* Country to country variations are caused only by costs of transit. This prevents grey and parallel markets. This related to ethnocentric orientation. The weakness is that it does not take into account the influences of each individual market.

(b) *Geocentric.* Prices are adapted but subsidiaries do not have complete control. Coherent with all country markets, this offers a broad and consistent strategy within which final price may be adjusted. The weakness is that it may encourage grey markets. Its strength is that it does take account of market influences.

(c) *Adaptation* relates to MNE's with *polycentric orientation:* each local subsidiary calculates its own price. This is *not relevant* to Sentinel.

(d) *Market skimming.* High price, niche market. The product has to be proportionately beneficial. Fast cash recovery but encourages competitors to enter the market.

(e) *Market penetration.* A low price is charged speedily to gain market share. It requires high sales volumes and economies of scale. Discourages competition.

5.11 Sentinel's strategy should be *geocentric*, due to different stages of the product life cycle, the amount of competition and the fact that the USA is more price sensitive than UK and Europe.

The pricing strategy adopted needs to be flexible to take account of the characteristics of each market.

5.12 *Tactics*

(a) *Price*

   (i) To achieve 30% gross profit and 15% RONA.
   (ii) Cost plus 45% will be the minimum price to sell to distribution channels.
   (iii) Sentinel's cost = 45% = net ex work price minimum.

(b) *Place.* Relationship marketing with chosen distributors. Distributors will be able to choose the final price within the parameters set by Sentinel.

(c) *Promotion*

   (i) Brand values and product benefits will be communicated to justify premium pricing.
   (ii) Cost of promotion strategy is justified in relation to turnover and objectives.

(d) *Product.* Premium high quality product with added value?

5.13 *Implementation/control*

(a) A pricing policy document should be produced as a guideline to distributors and regional managers (KAM).

   (i) This will detail minimum selling prices and set pricing/cost thresholds.
   (ii) This could also act as a mechanism for coping with fluctuating revenues.

(b) There should be regular meetings between RM's and KAM's to discuss performance and changes in demand in the market or additional competition that might affect pricing.

(c) Revenue targets should be set for distributors to ensure pricing structure will contribute to corporate objectives.

(d) Does pricing reflect Sentinel's high quality products?

(e) Is the pricing effective in meeting revenue objectives?

(f) *Ratio analysis.* This could be assessed historically to act as a control mechanism to highlight any negative or positive trends.

5.14 *Summary*

(a) *Current situation*

   (i) No pricing policy at present
   (ii) Price sensitivity
   (iii) Poor control
   (iv) Price wars
   (v) Going rate: cost plus
   (vi) Cannot afford to compete on price

(b) *Factors that influence pricing decisions*

   (i) Corporate objectives
   (ii) Stage in PLC: growth
   (iii) Legal constraints
   (iv) Competition: need to assess the strength
   (v) Customer: level of demand
   (vi) Costs: fixed and variable

(c) *International considerations*

   (i) Standardisation or adaption
   (ii) Exchange rate

(iii) What currency to price in
(iv) When to quote price - ex factory, FOB, CIF, DDP
(v) Transfer pricing
(vi) Distribution costs
(vii) Documentation
(viii) Tariffs

(d) *Pricing policy decisions for Sentinel*

(i) Must be integrated with the rest of the marketing mix
(ii) Pricing objective - price to differentiate
(iii) Pricing method - market orientated - perceived value
(iv) Consider discount for early payment

6 MARKETING INFORMATION SYSTEM (Nottingham Trent University syndicate)

6.1 A *marketing information system* (MkIS) consists of people, equipment and procedures to gather, sort, analyse, evaluate and distribute needed, timely and accurate information to marketing decision makers. In seeking data for decision making purposes a marketing manager should follow a logical series of steps starting with internal sources and ending with the conducting of ad-hoc surveys.

6.2 A well structured MkIS is vital to successful implementation and development of plans, and will contribute to control and monitoring. How can a customer's needs be satisfied if we do not know what they are?

(a) *Contributions to planning*

(i) A better understanding of the market (general and specific trends as well as customer and competitor information).
(ii) A more precise evaluation of the nature and causes of market changes.
(iii) A reduction in the likelihood of being taken by surprise.
(iv) Improved sharing of information.
(v) More informed decision making.
(vi) Higher levels of performance.
(vii) Better feedback and control of the plan.

(b) The MkIS will provide quantitative and qualitative data on:

(i) *customers* who they are, buyer behaviour, expenditure, tastes
(ii) *trade:* attitudes, trends, positions, motivation
(iii) *sales:* volume, price, areas, stocks seasonality
(iv) *environment:* PEST factors

The principal contribution needs to be seen in terms of improvements to the *implementation* process by virtue of better analysis and improvements to the formulation of strategy and tactics.

6.3 *Establishing an MkIS*

McDonald suggests four stages.

(a) Identify all the data and information currently produced;

(b) Get managers to list the decision they have to make, together with the information essential to making these decisions. Think about true information needs and develop the system around these.

(c) Combine the two in the most logical manner to identify gaps, duplication of information and occasions where redundant information is produced.

(d) Organise a focused and cost effective system.

6.4 *Structure*

The MkIS should contain the following interactive subsystems.

(a) *Internal records* - eg orders, invoices, customer details, sales patterns, prices, inventory levels.

(b) *Marketing intelligence system* - for market and competitor activity (eg trade journals, professional bodies, government statistics, AGB, Mintel. Sales force can be used).

(c) *Marketing research* systematic collection and analysis of information relevant to specific marketing situations faced by the organisation.

(d) *Analytical decision making:* models and PC programmes to explain, predict and improve processes.

Marketing research and the marketing information system will provide essential underpinning to the planning and control of marketing strategies.

6.5 *Design*

(a) Data collected needs to be processed to produce coherent information. Therefore storage and retrieval considerations should include these.

    (i) Manual or computerised?
    (ii) Hard copy back up
    (iii) Cross referencing of data
    (iv) Data protection legislation consideration

(b) Irrelevant data should be eliminated

(c) Information must be:

    (i) concise
    (ii) relevant
    (iii) accurate
    (iv) as detailed as required
    (v) cost effective
    (vi) directed to the right person
    (vii) timely

(d) The designers of any MkIS should also:

    (i) recognise user limitations in defining and using information
    (ii) ensure users understand the system and can evaluate and control it
    (iii) improve feedback
    (iv) clarify meaning of data and highlight limitations of information
    (v) ensure the system is flexible
    (vi) recognise that it is only as effective as its designers and users make it.

(e) *Remember*

    (i) Managers may not know what they need and want
    (ii) Managers may not make good use of the information
    (iii) Better communication means better performance

(f) *Cost and organisation implications*

    (i) Training
    (ii) Recruitment of specialist skills
    (iii) Reallocation of duties
    (iv) Centralisation of information-gathering function
    (v) Equipment
    (vi) Running costs
    (vii) Time taken to realise the benefits

(g) *Benefits*

    (i) Control of costs
    (ii) Diagnosis of poor sales performance
    (iii) Flexible promotion strategy
    (iv) Forecasting
    (v) Better planning
    (vi) Credit management
    (vii) Purchasing automation
    (viii) Advertising strategy

(ix) Pricing strategy
(x) Evaluation of advertising expenditure
(xi) NPD direction
(xii) Buyer behaviour

6.6 *Methods for collecting information specified in Sentinel's research brief.*

(a) *Size of markets.* Try sources such as Nielsen or AGB. Sentinel may need to commission a special project. Exploit contacts at Omnicorp who may have more comprehensive information.

(b) *Growth of markets* - as (a) above.

(c) *Competitor profiles.* Internal sources include salesforce questionnaires. Use the salesforce as intelligence agents to obtain company brochures and financial reports. Use desk research with World Bank, DTI etc.

(d) *Customer attitudes.* Primary research should take the form of telephone questionnaires or focus groups with dealers, distributors and end users.

(e) *Product pricing.* This could be incorporated into the above research to establish the pricing perceptions, and be supported by a 'comp shop' carried out by salesforce to establish the pricing reality. This would then be disseminated and analysed internally.

(f) *Channel efficiency and effectiveness.* Internal sales records and invoices will provide a picture of effort versus achievement by each distribution channel. Some dealer and distributor questionnaires would provide explanations and potential solutions. The Centre for Interfirm Comparison in the UK can give indications of percentage of distribution costs to total sales for similar companies.

(g) *Purchasing considerations.* Customer and dealer incentive schemes will assess post purchase satisfaction or dissonance and reasons for choice. A freephone number or returnable form on packaging offering money off next purchase, free gift, free holiday flight etc.

(h) *Competitor advertising and activity.* The salesforce should include this information in their monthly reports. Mintel produce a brand expenditure document by four week period to monitor this.

(i) Other information required should include the following.

(i) Sales reporting
(ii) Reasons for lack of distribution in Holland and Scandinavia
(iii) Sentinel US relationship
(iv) Mail order opportunities
(v) Distribution issues in Germany and France
(vi) Swiftair distribution network
(vii) Potential areas for market development

Part E: Learning from experience: ensuring you pass

Types of marketing research

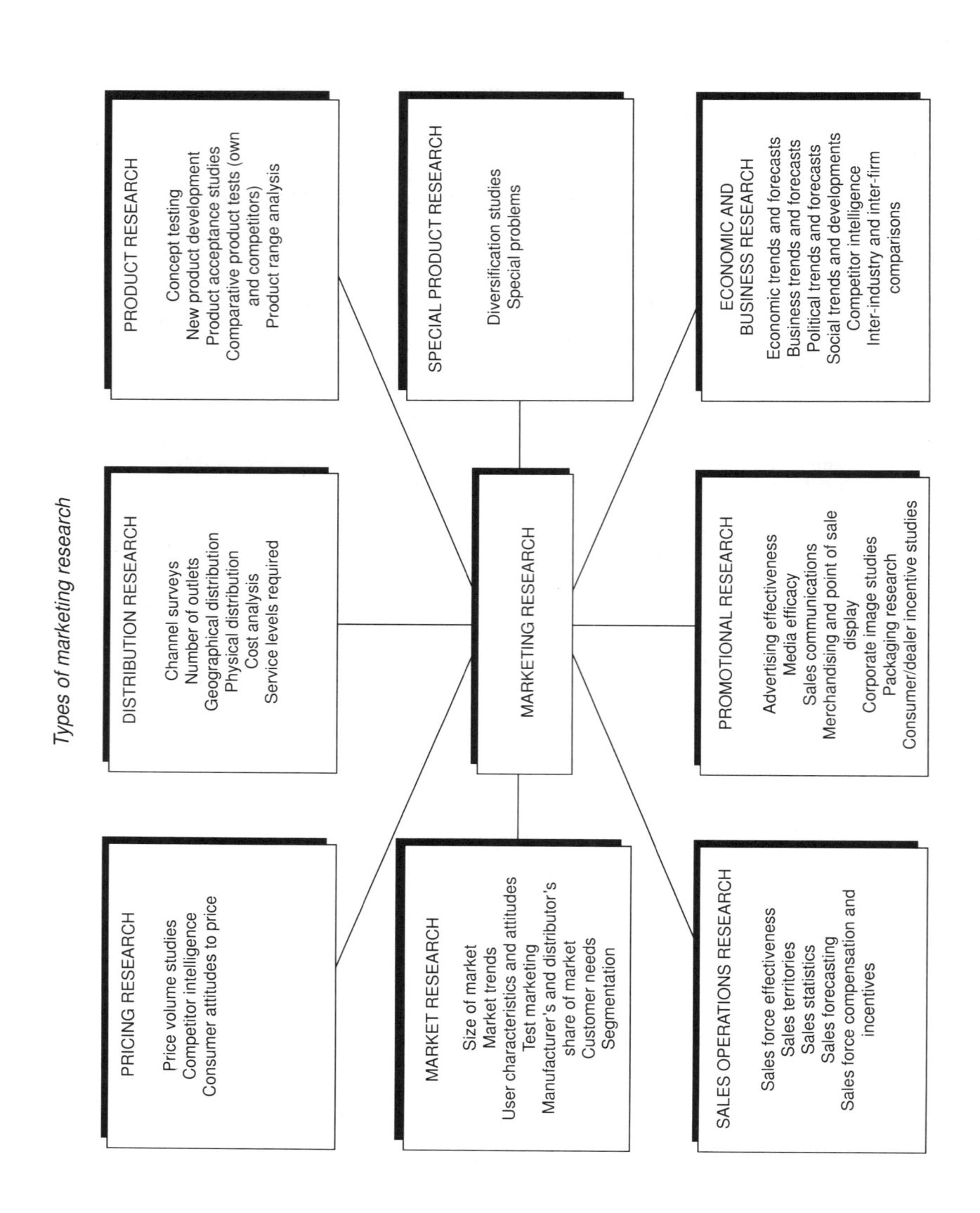

PRODUCT RESEARCH
- Concept testing
- New product development
- Product acceptance studies
- Comparative product tests (own and competitors)
- Product range analysis

SPECIAL PRODUCT RESEARCH
- Diversification studies
- Special problems

ECONOMIC AND BUSINESS RESEARCH
- Economic trends and forecasts
- Business trends and forecasts
- Political trends and forecasts
- Social trends and developments
- Competitor intelligence
- Inter-industry and inter-firm comparisons

DISTRIBUTION RESEARCH
- Channel surveys
- Number of outlets
- Geographical distribution
- Physical distribution
- Cost analysis
- Service levels required

MARKETING RESEARCH

PROMOTIONAL RESEARCH
- Advertising effectiveness
- Media efficacy
- Sales communications
- Merchandising and point of sale display
- Corporate image studies
- Packaging research
- Consumer/dealer incentive studies

PRICING RESEARCH
- Price volume studies
- Competitor intelligence
- Consumer attitudes to price

MARKET RESEARCH
- Size of market
- Market trends
- User characteristics and attitudes
- Test marketing
- Manufacturer's and distributor's share of market
- Customer needs
- Segmentation

SALES OPERATIONS RESEARCH
- Sales force effectiveness
- Sales territories
- Sales statistics
- Sales forecasting
- Sales force compensation and incentives

Chapter 31

SENTINEL AVIATION: DETAILED MARKETING PLANNING

> **This chapter contains the following information and plans.**
> Introductory note: the steps you should follow
> 1-8 Detailed marketing plan
> 9   The examination

INTRODUCTORY NOTE: THE STEPS YOU SHOULD FOLLOW

Well now, you are almost there save for the finishing touches. Just how much work you need to do depends upon the amount of detail in your outline plan but we suggest you make one last big effort to ensure your plan makes the grade for this important examination.

At this point we need to advise that whereas a complete marketing plan is intended to cover you for all eventualities, it cannot of course provide all the detail that might be needed for a specific examination question. You will therefore have to *add detail as required in the examination itself*. Moreover, the CIM reserves the right to introduce additional material to you in the examination hall.

However, in anticipation of examination questions signalled in the case study some syndicates will prepare extra materials on, say, organisation or market segmentation or marketing research.

CONSULT THE GUIDANCE NOTES GIVEN IN CHAPTER 8 PARAGRAPHS 4.19 TO 6.8
STEP 15 DEVELOP QUANTIFIED, TIMESCALED OBJECTIVES **STEP 16 CONSIDER ALTERNATIVE STRATEGIES. SELECT THOSE MOST APPROPRIATE** **STEP 17 DRAW UP DETAILED TACTICAL PLANS COVERING THE MARKETING MIX** **STEP 18 DRAW UP A MARKETING RESEARCH PLAN AND MKIS** **STEP 19 CONSIDER ORGANISATIONAL ISSUES, CHANGES AND MARKETING ORIENTATION** **STEP 20 CONSIDER ORGANISATIONAL CULTURE AND NEED FOR INTERNAL MARKETING** **STEP 21 DETERMINE THE FINANCIAL/HR RESOURCE IMPLICATIONS OF YOUR PLANS** **STEP 22 ASSESS COSTS AND DRAW UP INDICATIVE BUDGETS** **STEP 23 DRAW UP SCHEDULES GIVING TIMINGS/SEQUENCE OF ACTIONS** **STEP 24 SPECIFY REVIEW PROCEDURES AND CONTROL MECHANISMS** **STEP 25 DRAW UP OUTLINE CONTINGENCY PLANS** **STEP 26 REVIEW YOUR COMPLETE MARKETING PLAN**
YOU WILL NEED BETWEEN 15 AND 18 HOURS TO DO THIS MAJOR TASK

Having made your last one big effort how does your plan compare with the specimen which follows prepared by a Nottingham Trent University syndicate comprising Siobhan Dean, Ian Ewers, Sue Hart, Aidan Nicholson, Hayden Rees and Scott Snell. This plan may not be totally perfect but it is a very fine effort indeed and it is extremely well presented.

DETAILED MARKETING PLAN

CONTENTS

1 **Executive summary**

2 **Company background**

3 **Strategic business objectives**
Corporate objectives
Mission statement

4 **Situational analysis**
The aviation market
The competition
The customer
The products
Key points from marketing audit
Key considerations

5 **Marketing objectives**

6 **Strategic direction**
Porter's generic strategies
Ansoff matrix
Strategies for Europe
Strategies for USA

7 **Action plan**
Product
Pricing
Relationship marketing and distribution
Promotion and communication
People
Process
Physical evidence

8 **Implementation and control**
Creating a marketing orientation
Control
Contingencies

9 **Timescales and budgets**

Appendix A: Financial analysis

Appendix B: Competitor analysis

Appendix C: Customer analysis

Appendix D: Product analysis

Part E: Learning from experience: ensuring you pass

1 EXECUTIVE SUMMARY

1.1 *The market*

(a) The aviation electronics market is split into four key sectors - leisure, executive, light aircraft and defence.

(b) Sentinel's key business areas are *leisure* and *executive*.

(c) Main competitors are the Swiftair Group and Eagle.

(d) The market is valued at an estimated £425m of which Sentinel has a 1% market share.

(e) Opportunities for organic growth are limited, and to achieve the corporate objectives Sentinel need to target new markets.

1.2 *Marketing objectives*

To have a 3% market share in aviation electronics by 2002.

1.3 *Strategic direction*

(a) *Short term*

(i) Market penetration: improve distribution channel management.
(ii) Differentiation: added value service.
(iii) Geographical focus on Europe.

(b) *Medium-term*

(i) Product development: integrated solutions.
(ii) Market development: move to a related market (eg maritime).

(c) *Long-term:* market and product development, with NPD for automotive and security markets.

1.4 *Action plan*

(a) To ensure transformation from being a product-led company to being customer-led.

(b) Rationalisation of the present product ranges.

(c) Emphasis on relationship marketing.

(d) Formulation of effective communications plan to establish brand entities.

(e) Create partnerships and close links with dealers and distributors to encourage better performance.

2 COMPANY BACKGROUND

2.1 Sentinel Aviation is a traditional, well established English company steeped in the aviation industry. It was a pioneer of aviation instrumentation in the 1970s with the introduction of the Navigaid autopilot, which revolutionised the avionics industry and has since been their leading product. Their key markets are currently the UK, France, Italy, Germany, Spain and the US with a presence in 40 other countries.

2.2 The company was acquired by Omnicorp, a large American industrial conglomerate, three years ago. In 1996, Sentinel Aviation's turnover was £4.25 million, resulting in an operating profit of £650,000. The total worldwide aviation electronics market is believed to be worth around £425 million of which the company as a 1% share. Currently, 60 staff are employed with a hierarchical management structure; the Managing Director, Mike Flynn, has fairly recently joined the company after having spent many years working in the leisure industry.

2.3 With an increasing number of staff being recruited from outside the aviation industry, as well as intensive competition, it has been realised that organic growth will not provide the return on assets and turnover required to fulfil the expectations of the parent company.

3 STRATEGIC BUSINESS OBJECTIVES

3.1 *Mission statement*

Sentinel is committed towards providing the highest quality transport guidance and control solutions, while continuously focusing and building on our partnerships with customers and personnel.

3.2 *Corporate objectives*

(a) To be a £25m subsidiary by 2002.

(b) To achieve a RONA of between 15-20% in present and future businesses.

(c) To create a customer-orientated company by Quarter 4, 1998.

(d) To reduce inventory days from 124 to 32

In order to establish Sentinel's financial situation, an analysis of how effectively the company has used its assets and assessment of its liquidity position. This is enclosed as Appendix 1.

4 SITUATIONAL ANALYSIS

4.1 *The aviation market*

The worldwide aviation electronics market is worth £425 million and is split into four market sectors:

(a) leisure;
(b) executive jet (commercial);
(c) light aircraft;
(d) defence.

4.2 The leisure market covers all aircraft not specifically intended for commerce. They need not be jet aircraft. The executive jet/commerce market includes planes for individual companies and also small fleets of planes. The third and fourth sectors are light aircraft and defence.

4.3 Since there has been no previous definitive study on the aviation electronics industry, it is difficult for Sentinel to have a clear understanding of their market. However, the chart below outlines Sentinel's key areas of business.

Sentinel's key areas of business

Market	Value £m	Share %	Sales £'000
UK Leisure	3.8	20	760
Executive jet	2.9	8	230
Total			990

4.4 The OEM market includes all sales to other equipment manufacturers, but not to aircraft builders. However, figures on Sentinel's existing penetration are not currently available.

4.5 Another way to break down the market would be by geography, and Sentinel currently operates in over 45 countries. Their two major country markets, the UK and the US, account for 43% of sales (£1.83m). Therefore the remaining £2.43m is spread across 43 counties, which means average sales of £56,500 each. Regional sales are as follows.

Sales by region (1996)

Region	Share of sales %	Sales £'000
UK	23	980
Europe	42	1,790
US	20	850
The rest	15	640

4.6 *The competition*

Sentinel has two main competitors and three minor competitors in the executive jet and leisure sectors. The Swiftair Group and Eagle Electronics almost divide the world between them with just under 50% market share across all sectors between them. (Please refer to appendix 2 for a detailed competitor analysis.)

Customers

4.7 *The customer*

As the pie chart below suggests, Sentinel's most important customers are within the leisure segment of the market, dominated by sales for twin-engine aeroplanes. This is probably due to the fact that twin-engine aeroplanes will fly longer distances and, therefore, more sophisticated equipment is required.

Total sales by market 1996 (£m)

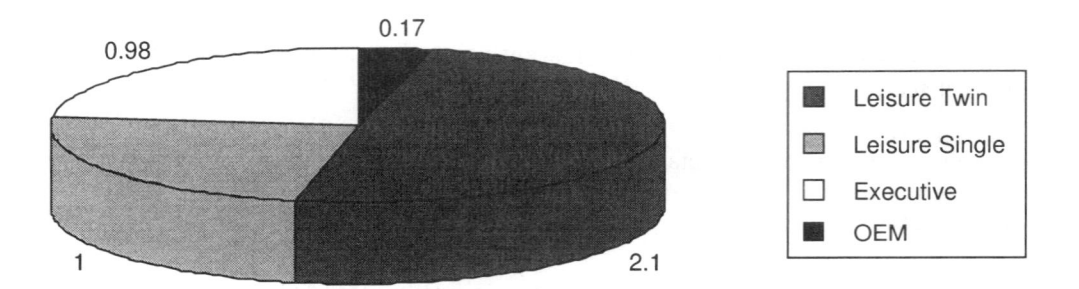

- Leisure Twin: 2.1
- Leisure Single: 1
- Executive: 0.98
- OEM: 0.17

The buyers within each market sector and the extent to which Sentinel deals with them at present are unclear due to lack of market information. However, the customer base is split into three main buyer categories; leisure, executive and aircraft manufacturers/OEM. These are described below.

4.8 *Leisure*

(a) Personal or syndicate purchase of an aircraft - single-twin aeroplane, helicopter, glider etc.

(b) Leasing from an airfield is also an option.

(c) Likely to be wealthy individuals:
   (i) 34-64 years old
   (ii) middle/senior managers, or company owners
   (iii) innovators
   (iv) early adopters.

(d) Influences on purchase decision:
   (i) family status
   (ii) financial status and credit rating
   (iii) advice of dealer/airfield staff
   (iv) advice of fellow air club members
   (v) trade and specialist press.

31: Sentinel Aviation: detailed marketing planning

(e) Customer profile - Appendix 3

4.9 *Executive*

(a) Such planes are used for business travel.

(b) Firms might have contracts with lease companies.

(c) Maintenance services will be sought, including fitting.

(d) Similar socio-economic group as the leisure market.

(e) Influences on purchase decision.
   (i) Financial director
   (ii) Managing director
   (iii) Transport department
   (iv) Maintenance costs and value added services eg service support

(f) Customer profile - Appendix 3.

4.10 *Aircraft manufacturers/OEM*

(a) Business-to-business relationship (exclusive contracts).

Likely to be smaller aircraft manufacturers supplying to leisure, executive and light aircraft markets.

(b) People influencing the purchasing decision:
   (i) Production director
   (ii) Purchasing director

(c) Look to develop partnerships to exploit market opportunities.

(d) Key product attributes sought:
   (i) 100% efficiency and reliability
   (ii) Quality
   (iii) Features (aesthetics)

4.11 Due to the nature of the distribution channels, it is important for Sentinel to bear in mind their relationship with their dealers and distributors, as they are the 'middle men' between the company and the end users described above. Therefore, relationship marketing will play an important part.

Products

4.12 *The products*

Sentinel Aviation's product portfolio includes the largest range of autopilots and chartplotters in the world.

(a) Autopilots, including Navigaid, which is considered to be the finest autopilot on the market.

(b) Chartplotters for the commercial and leisure sectors marketed under the brand name 'Chartwell'.

(c) The 'Firstaid' instrument range covers most leisure aircraft applications.

(d) Products from other group companies, include hydraulic systems, control systems, cables and radar equipment.

Although Sentinel has a broad product range in its industry, it is perceived by most of its customers as a single product company due to the long-term success of the Navigaid brand. The figure below shows the sales performance of products and the potential for these figures to be improved upon through an effective communications strategy.

Total sales by product 1996 (£m)

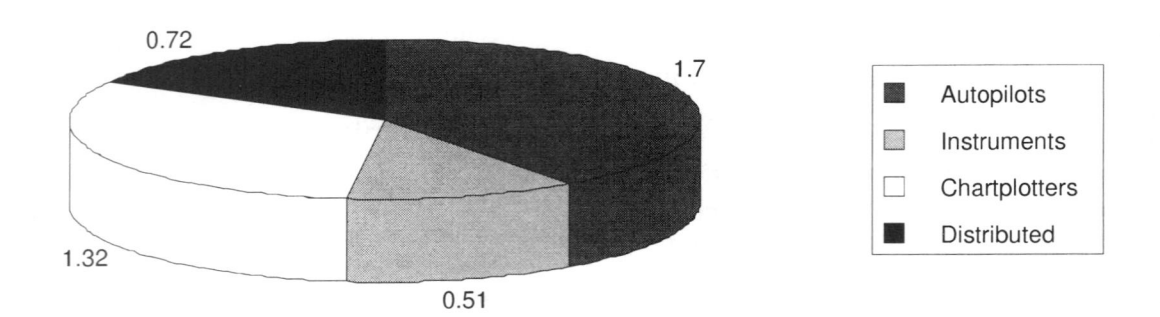

[Pie chart showing: Autopilots 1.7, Instruments 0.51, Chartplotters 1.32, Distributed 0.72]

4.13 *Key points from marketing audit*

After conducting a full marketing environmental audit on Sentinel to establish where the company is now, the key points were extracted and summarised as follows.

4.14 *Internal strengths*

(a) A well established tradition of quality which has existed for over 70 years.

(b) Strong brand reputation, for Navigaid.

  (i) A dedicated work force, strong in-house capabilities and management experience from a range of different backgrounds.

  (ii) Strong parental support from Omnicorp which boasts three other aircraft divisions and other expertise.

  (iii) Sentinel understand their technical capabilities but realise that they need to be developed and geared towards customer needs.

(c) Recognition of current problems.

4.15 *Internal weaknesses*

(a) No corporate or marketing planning or strategy formulating unit.

  (i) Utilisation of marketing techniques is weak through lack of marketing knowledge - no MkIS.

(b) The current distribution network is haphazard and reactive.

  (i) Confused corporate image and lack of brand consistency - perceived as a one-brand company.

  (ii) The cost-plus pricing policy is ineffective and therefore the targets set by Omnicorp will be difficult to achieve.

  (iii) Sentinel is a product-orientated company, as is emphasised by the current organisational structure.

(c) No integrated system is yet available - customers do not realise such an offering is possible.

(d) Cultural issues: internal conflict and resistance to change.

  (i) The background of the sales force and distributors is in the traditional aviation industry.

(e) Pareto Rule - 80% of business comes from 20% of customers.

4.16 *External opportunities*

(a) *Aviation market*

    (i) Growth in the leisure, executive markets and light aircraft.

    (ii) Product extension and modification for further market segments (light market) particularly GPS systems.

        (1) Hang glider   (3) Glider
        (2) Balloons   (4) Helicopter

(b) *Technology options*

    (i) Guidance systems
    (ii) Positioning
    (iii) Security
    (iv) Industrial control data processing
    (v) Tracking

(c) *Market options*

    (i) Maritime market - similarities in product application and customer profile - 'plug and play'.

    (ii) Land-based market - automotive, parcels.

    (iii) Integrated solutions - 'one stop' shop.

    (iv) Geographical markets - Scandinavia, Holland, Far East, 'old empire'.

4.17 *External threats*

(a) Increased competition due to the slack in the industry and the reduction in military aircraft contracts.

(b) The fast pace of technology demands continuous product improvement and development.

(c) Exchange rate fluctuations could harm export sales.

(d) Trading partnerships could increase competitors' strengths and market share.

(e) Price war (discounting): Sentinel is not in a position to follow suit and this could affect their quality image.

(f) Lockout, from customers rationalising their suppliers

Key considerations

4.18 *Company-wide considerations*

(a) *What businesses are Sentinel in?* Sentinel has been traditionally perceived as an aviation company but must now assess what they actually offer their customers and why customers buy Sentinel's products. The conclusions led us to redefining your business as providing guidance and control solutions which could be applied to various sectors of the transport industry.

(b) *What are Sentinel's core competencies?* Quality production and reputation, expertise in R&D, technology and design with great potential for customer service and support.

4.19 *Key factors for success*

(a) Customer focus.

(b) An effective brand strategy.

(c) A marketing orientated culture to facilitate the implementation of marketing plans.

(d) Market understanding and proactive PR/promotional policies.

(e) Product rationalisation and changes to the marketing mix.

(f) Capability for NPD through synergy and involving partners and employees.

(g) A well-established distribution network with mutual understanding and direction between Sentinel and the dealer/distributor.

5 MARKETING OBJECTIVES

5.1 *Objectives*

(a) To have a 3% market share in the aviation market by 2002.

(b) To gain £5m yearly sales in the maritime market by 2002.

(c) To increase corporate awareness by 40% by 2000.

(d) To have an in-depth understanding of the aviation and maritime markets.

(e) To achieve a marketing orientated culture with quality standard recognition.

(f) To create an information system to improve NPD and operational efficiency by spending 10% on R&D.

(g) To increase dealers' turnover from 2 to 8-10 units pa on average by 2000.

6 STRATEGIC DIRECTION

6.1 After analysing Sentinel's current situation, it became apparent that *organic growth is not sufficient* to satisfy the corporate and financial objectives. Therefore further strategies must be considered to achieve the target revenues, as the gap analysis below depicts.

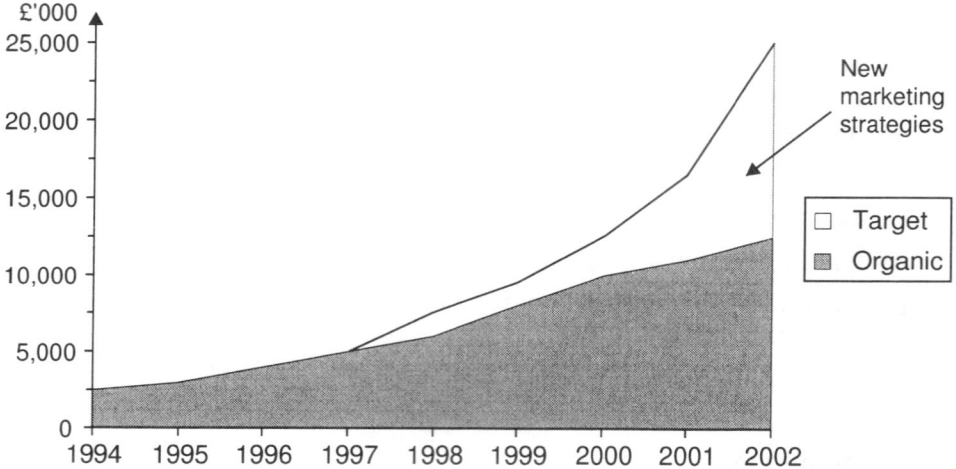

6.2 By applying various strategic models realistically, Sentinel can assess and adopt an appropriate strategy that will help to achieve the marketing and appropriate objectives.

6.3 *Porter's generic strategies*

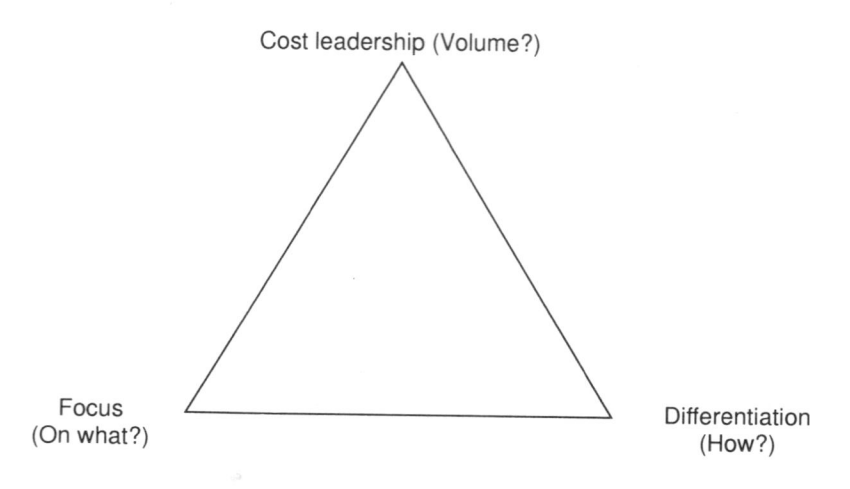

In order to meet the 15-20% RONA target set by Omnicorp, Sentinel needs to achieve above-average performance in the medium to long term, which can only be achieved through exploiting a *sustainable competitive advantage*.

6.4 *Cost leadership*

The *cost leadership* method of achieving sustainable competitive advantage is not a realistic option for Sentinel to pursue for two main reasons.

(a) The company is a market follower and too small to achieve significant economies of scale.

(b) A low price policy would not portray the premium image sought by Sentinel for its product offerings.

6.5 *Focus*

A *focus strategy was also rejected* due to Sentinel's lack of market knowledge and poor market orientation within the company. To become expert at market segmentation, Sentinel would have to understand their customers and be able to *implement* the focus concept effectively. However, in its present situation the company is unable to do this.

6.6 *Differentiation*

(a) The most appropriate strategy to adopt would be *differentiation*, which can be used as a basis from which Sentinel can expand rapidly. The key aspect on which Sentinel will base differentiation should be added value, in particular, customer focus, service and support.

(b) In light of the current geographical sales characteristics and performance, Sentinel should be focusing on two specific *areas* where potential growth is the highest: Europe and the USA.

(c) Europe, (including the UK), is a highly developed economic community and has high potential for development due to several factors.

   (i) Sentinel is already established.
   (ii) There is a high number of aircraft manufacturers in all market segments, particularly, Airbus the world's second largest commercial aircraft manufacturer.
   (iii) Many aircraft builders are located in Holland, France and Scandinavia.
   (iv) We assume there are many consumers who match the consumer profile within the leisure segment (ie lifestyle orientated).
   (v) It has strong maritime links, particularly UK, France and Italy.

(d) The USA has a high development potential as it is the largest single aircraft market in the world, but has intensive competitive markets than Europe. The reasons for high potential are similar to Europe but the reasons for not entering the market alone are as follows.

   (i) Sentinel is not big enough currently to penetrate the market.
   (ii) Lack of expertise in the American market.
   (iii) High concentration of competition.
   (iv) Highly price sensitive market which is volume led.
   (v) Use of much more aggressive marketing tactics.

6.7 *Ansoff matrix*

	Current products	New products	Risk level
Current markets	MARKET PENETRATION STRATEGY 1 More purchase and usage by existing customers 2 Gain customers from competitors 3 Convert non-users into users (where both are in the same market) **1**	PRODUCT DEVELOPMENT STRATEGY 1 Product modification with new features 2 Different quality levels 3 New product **2**	Low = 1 High = 4
New markets	MARKET DEVELOPMENT STRATEGY 1 New markets 2 New distribution channels 3 New geographical areas - exports **3**	DIVERSIFICATION STRATEGY 1 Vertical integration 2 Horizontal integration 3 Concentric integration 4 Conglomerate integration **4**	

To meet medium term corporate objectives, the following tactics need to be implemented in this logical format.

Strategies for Europe

6.8 *Product development strategy*

(a) Sentinel needs to work in conjunction with other members of the Omnicorp group aviation divisions, to be able to offer complete solutions. Central research and development will allow costs of the project to be both shared and minimised, whilst 'pooling' knowledge. These solutions will provide 'one stop shopping' both for the commercial and industrial customers.

(b) In terms of the entry into markets with similar characteristics (eg maritime) Sentinel's existing products will have to be adopted and 'hardened' to meet the less-favourable operating conditions (movement, weather conditions etc). This process will require testing and trial periods; but with the technology remaining the same, the lead time should be minimal compared to completely new product development.

6.9 *Market penetration strategy*

(a) With the majority of European aircraft being manufactured in Holland, and Scandinavia, it is proposed that Sentinel should aim to make these their target markets.

(b) The development of complete solutions will allow the company, or the distributor*, to open new industrial sales channels. This will mean that by offering a complete solution Sentinel can begin to target the major players within the world aviation market such as Boeing, McDonnell Douglas, Airbus, Jet Stream, Saab, Shorts, Fokker etc.

* It is not known which member of the Omnicorp group will distribute the complete solutions or whether a separate company will be created.

6.10 *Market development strategy*

(a) With the aviation supplies market predicted to intensify and combined with the company's predicted sales increasing to only £10 million (refer to gap analysis), new markets with similar attributes need to be entered to meet Omnicorp's financial objectives.

(b) The closest related market, which requires the least product adaptation, providing the lowest lead times, is the maritime market. This market will utilise the same technology used in the aviation market, but will require basic adaptations (see product development).

(c) Entering into this market without any knowledge or expertise will require the formation of a strategic alliance with a boat builder or distributor, with whom the products can be developed and promoted. This will involve research of the various players within this market prior to deciding on a suitable partner that best compliments Sentinel's corporate image.

(d) Transferring the aviation technology into the maritime industry is a short to medium term expansion strategy, due to the short lead times involved, which will have little impact on Sentinel's net assets. The long-term aim would be to transfer the aviation technology into other similar markets which have suitable applications, but longer lead times, such as these.

 (i) Car security
 (ii) Emergency services
 (iii) Parcel tracking
 (iv) Taxis
 (v) Defence (vehicle tracking and recognition to combat 'friendly fire' scenarios)
 (vi) Ecological studies (tracking dolphins etc)
 (vii) People (prison, hospital, school security, children)
 (viii) Containers
 (ix) Road recovery companies (AA, RAC, Green Flag etc)

Strategies for USA

6.11 *Market penetration strategy*

Using the Sentinel US division of Omnicorp, Sentinel Aviation should continue to use mail order as a distribution method and should remain controlled by the US company. Sentinel Aviation will then simply supply each product to the US counterpart, to be distributed centrally. This is for the following reasons.

(a) Sentinel Aviation's limited understanding of the US market.

(b) Sentinel US is established.

 (i) Sentinel US understands the market at an operational level and the appropriate tools required.

 (ii) Mail ordering is not a core competence of Sentinel Aviation and can therefore be outsourced.

6.12 *Strategic summary*

As a summary to Porter's generic strategies and Ansoff's matrix, the model featured below clarifies, in a visual format, the short, medium and long-term strategies that are recommended to Sentinel.

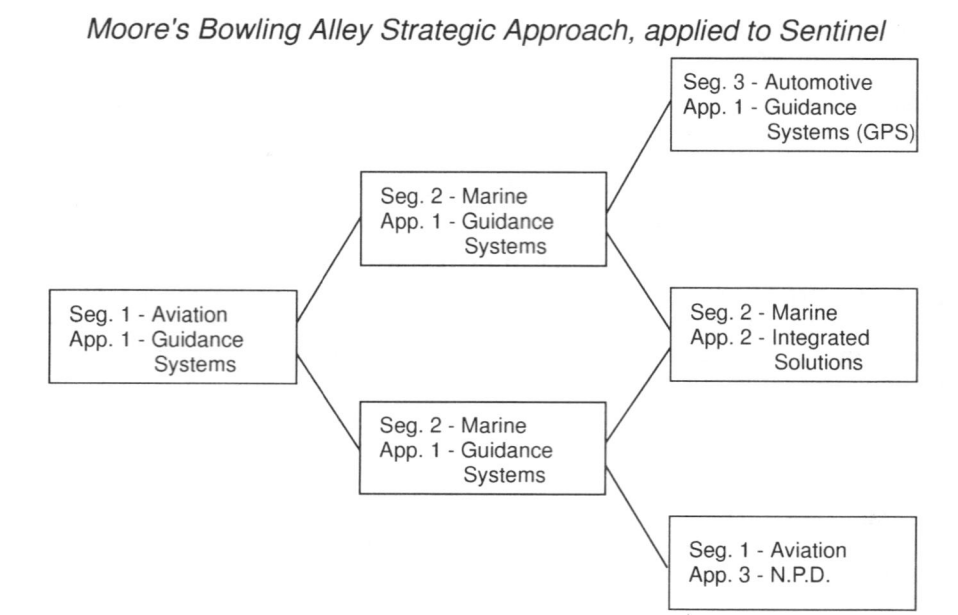

Notes   Part E: Learning from experience: ensuring you pass

Moore's Bowling Alley Strategic Approach, applied to Sentinel

```
                                              Seg. 3 - Automotive
                                              App. 1 - Guidance
                                                       Systems (GPS)

                       Seg. 2 - Marine
                       App. 1 - Guidance
                                Systems

Seg. 1 - Aviation                             Seg. 2 - Marine
App. 1 - Guidance                             App. 2 - Integrated
         Systems                                       Solutions

                       Seg. 2 - Marine
                       App. 1 - Guidance
                                Systems

                                              Seg. 1 - Aviation
                                              App. 3 - N.P.D.
```

Time ⟶

7 ACTION PLAN

7.1 *Product*

Sentinel need to rationalise their product range in order to concentrate on their key qualities and competencies. With the current market segments identified, it is suggested that only three product options per range to suit the three markets.

(a) Deluxe - dealers, distributors and manufacturers
(b) Premium - dealers, distributors and manufacturers
(c) High quality (for direct mail sales)

This will create a more responsive product portfolio addressing the needs of each customer group.

7.2 *Brand positioning*

The company needs to highlight its strengths to create a brand image.

(a) History/prestige   (d) Reliability
(b) Quality   (e) Technical expertise
(c) Efficiency

7.3 We suggest that Sentinel focuses on using only two brand names, which are *Sentinel* as corporate umbrella branding and *Navigaid* for the leisure and executive markets. A recommended corporate logo is enclosed as Appendix 6, which will be featured on the instrumentation itself and the packaging. A communications package will be implemented to promote awareness of the new umbrella branding and the range of products offered.

7.4 In order to differentiate Sentinel's products and keep their position in the high value market, the company should also offer after-sales services such as these.

(a) Fitting   (c) Support help-line
(b) Training   (d) Upgrades

7.5 *Product development*

Sentinel should create two types of product offering.

(a) 'Plug and play', a simple plug in and use product range which can be easily replaced, an 'out of box experience' for the leisure market.

(b) *Complete solutions* - sourcing radar and radio communications from Omnicorp for leisure, commercial and light aircraft sectors.

Sentinel need to adapt and create new products for the aviation, maritime and other new markets through product development, creating a venture company or forming strategic alliances. This is with particular reference to the GPS system.

7.6 *Pricing*

(a) Adopt a premium pricing policy to enhance the brand image.

(b) Differentiation to be seen through the quality of the products and added value elements - training, support, upgrading etc, justifying the premium pricing policy.

(c) Offer incentives/discounts only on the integrated systems range.

(d) Work alongside dealers/distributors to agree a maximum/minimum pricing - price fixing is illegal in the EU but we need to discourage parallel imports.

(e) Review new methods of formulating price - the present strategy of cost-plus is completely inappropriate.

7.7 *Relationship marketing and distribution*

(a) The key aspect of the distribution strategy, which the company has not actively been pursuing, is *relationship marketing*. Sentinel need to build relationships with dealers, distributors and aircraft manufacturers to increase sales and distribution channels.

(b) The objective is to create long term relationships where both parties learn over time how best to interact with each other, which leads to decreasing relationship costs for both customer and supplier.

(c) Sentinel should look at achieving results by understanding their customers and developing relationships rather than concentrating on achieving scale economies (lower costs). The idea of the 'promise concept' also needs to be adopted by Sentinel Aviation. This concept suggests that as new business develops, the supplier or service provider will make promises to the new customers. These promises have to be kept in order to maintain and enhance the two way relationship. In terms of Sentinel, this will mean not expanding faster than production can deal with, which will mean good communication between both the distribution manager and the production manager to meet pre-set sales targets (reduction in inventory days).

(d) In order for the company to add value to both the product and the individual relationships that are to be developed they need to look at key elements of customer service. Outlined below are eight aspects of *customer service* which will meet the added value requirements.

 (i) Key account managers.
 (ii) On-site engineers for key accounts.
 (iii) Call-out engineers.
 (iv) Customer inquiry and support lines.
 (v) Internet page for inquiries and to act as a point of reference.
 (vi) Annual equipment checks/services.
 (vii) Customer and distributor training courses.
 (viii) Customer friendly manuals.

7.8 *Possible and existing distribution channels*

```
SENTINEL → MANUFACTURER → CUSTOMER
SENTINEL → MANUFACTURER → DEALER → CUSTOMER
SENTINEL → DISTRIBUTOR → DEALER → CUSTOMER
SENTINEL → DEALER → CUSTOMER
SENTINEL → DISTRIBUTOR → CUSTOMER
SENTINEL ----> OMNICORP ----> CUSTOMER
SENTINEL → CUSTOMER
```

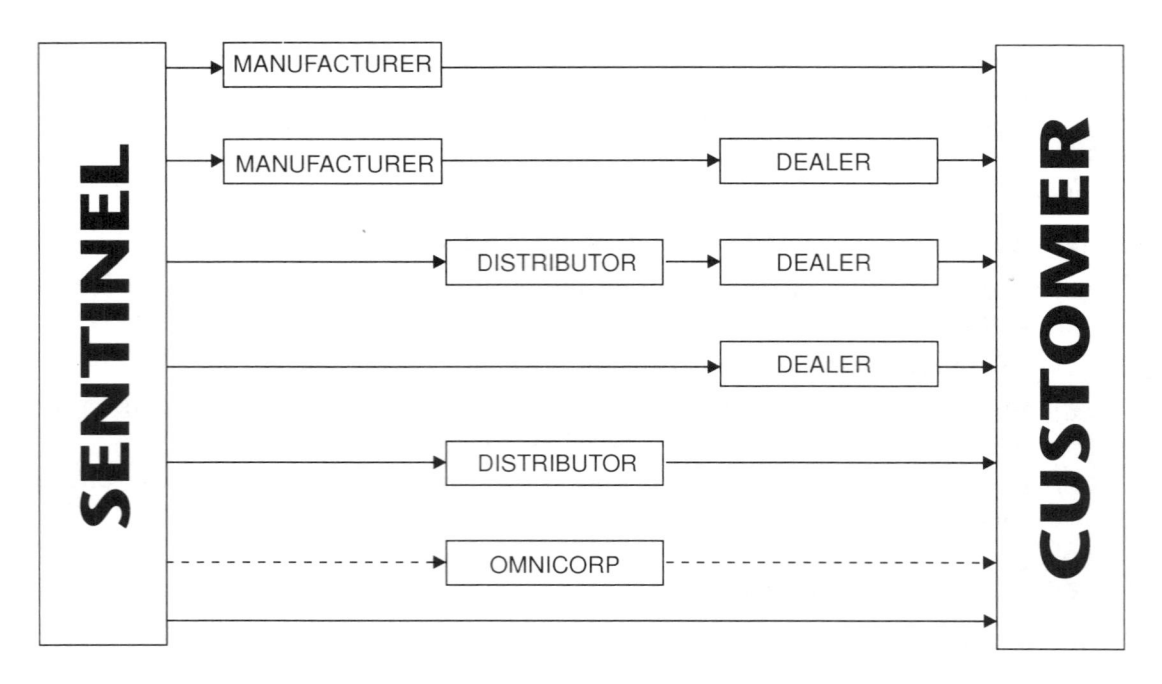

7.9 The above diagram illustrates the distribution options available to Sentinel.

(a) Review and rationalise current dealer/distributor networks.

(b) Source and evaluates appropriateness of potential new dealerships (ie from Swiftair).

(c) Develop a system for assessing and monitoring channel performance and efficiency.

(d) Set performance objectives and targets for dealers and distributors in line with the corporate objectives.

(e) Establish distribution channels in Holland and Scandinavia.

(f) Supply to the US though Omnicorp using 'box and ship' policy for direct mail sales.

(g) Assess the viability of contract discounting and volume discounting with distributors and manufacturers. (*NB.* Emphasis on long-term relationships.)

7.10 *Promotion and communication*

Promotion and communication are key factors that Sentinel should consider in order to meet their marketing objectives and improve customer awareness. The following recommendations outline the kind of activities that should be undertaken.

(a) Use direct marketing to build the customer base and help develop the MkIS.

(b) Focus on personal selling technical support, channel sales, end-user support.

(c) Public relations

    (i) Internal: Train and inform (the group motivation exercises) to move to a marketing orientation

    (ii) External: Establish and shape relationships with trade press
Nurture partnership with clients

(d) Exhibitions, trade fairs, corporate events etc in aviation and maritime.

(e) *Advertising*. Assess and select several agencies to pitch for the business (including Summers) in order to obtain a variety of ideas to promote brand strengths and target the correct people/channels.

(f) Introduce promotional goods (eg pens, badges and wind socks, with Sentinel's name) strategically placed in airfields.

(g) Use the Internet to service and inform the dealers/distributors.

(g) Use the Internet to service and inform the dealers/distributors.

7.10 *People*

(a) Train people to become customer-orientated.

(b) Encourage all staff to contribute their knowledge and learn further about the market through the creation of an MkIS system.

(c) Promote the values of customer service to employees.

(d) Obtain feedback through employee focus groups and regular team meetings.

(e) Encourage empowerment through offering incentives and reward systems.

(f) Implement further training for the salesforce in technology, competitive and customer relation developments.

7.11 *Process*

(a) Establish a greater degree of customer contact through the process of building relationships, focusing on the service side of the business.

(b) Quality systems such as ISO 9000 should be introduced to maintain quality levels and enhance the reputation of the company with dealers, distributors and customers.

(c) Any further production could be outsourced in order to keep the core skills within the business and keep asset liability to a minimum.

7.12 *Physical evidence*

(a) Point of sale information such as stands, signs etc should be considered to increase awareness of Sentinel's corporate identity.

(b) Create a good, aesthetic environment that motivates and facilitates work, eg open plan offices, plants, air conditioning etc.

8 IMPLEMENTATION AND CONTROL

8.1 *Creating a marketing orientation*

(a) In pursuing a marketing orientated strategy, Sentinel Aviation needs to adapt its structure to accommodate the new strategy. At present the company is very product-led, and the structure reflects this. There is no marketing plan and more importantly no 'planning-driven' culture.

(b) The culture of the organisation needs to be re-directed in order to address the idea of providing 'the highest quality transport guidance and solutions, while continuously focusing and building on our partnerships with customers and personnel'. Currently many of the existing staff are resisting any move away from the traditional aviation industry and this is a key problem which could affect future company development. This problem will be addressed through the appointment of both a process director and a human resources manager.

(c) New positions have been created and can be slotted into a revised organisation structure.

Job title	Key responsibilities
1 Process director	To oversee 'cultural' transformation, implementation of stronger recruitment policies (investors in people), and ensuring quality standards (IS 9002) reporting directly to Mike Flynn
2 Commercial director	Total responsibility for sales and marketing functions, reporting directly to Mike Flynn
3 Marketing manager	Establishing venture company, implementing marketing strategy, managing PR, the market research agency and the advertising agency, reporting to the commercial director
4 Sales manager	Managing, retraining (towards a customer focused attitude),and motivating the sales force, as well as overseeing relationship marketing, reporting to the commercial director
5 Client planner	Implementing and management of information systems (eg MkIS), and analysing sales and client performance, reporting to the commercial director
6 Human resource manager	Defining job descriptions, recruitment and selection, and personnel management, reporting to the process director
7 Production manager	Ensuring product volumes and quality, and advising on production processes, reporting to the production director.

8.2 *Control*

(a) Measure against set corporate and marketing objectives.
(b) Use market data to assess competitors and find strategic opportunities.
(c) Assess plans, compare with budgets and variances on a monthly basis.
(d) Feedback from the sales force.
(e) Use MkIS to assess strategic direction.

8.3 *Contingencies*

(a) Discuss exit strategy for the maritime market and the venture company.

(b) Look for individual product solutions, not *just* integration of products.

(c) Research alternatives now for future market penetration - ie GPS in cars, trucks containers, parcels etc.

(d) Consider further corporate strategic moves - alliances, acquisitions (Breen?).

9 TIMESCALES AND BUDGETS

9.1 The Gantt chart below illustrates the proposed timescales and budgets for the recommended strategies.

31: Sentinel Aviation: detailed marketing planning

Time scale

Product Development
- R + D
- H R M
- Market Research

Market Penetration
- Communications
- Distribution

Market Development
- Market research
- Distribution
- Communication

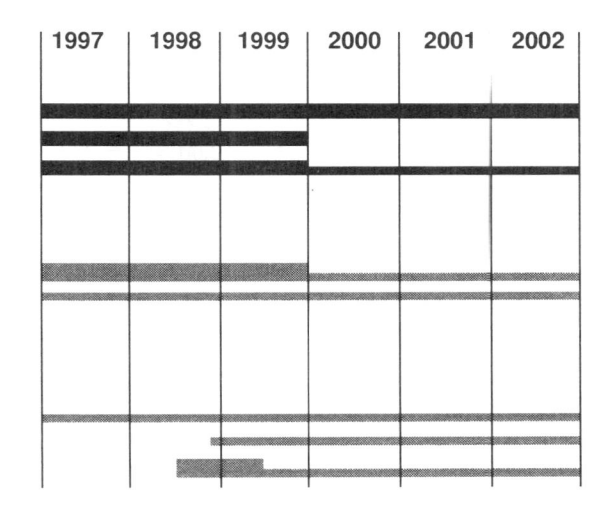

Budgets	1997 £m	1998 £m	1999 £m	2000 £m	2001 £m	2002 £m
Organic growth	5.44	6.80	8.33	10.03	11.84	13.61
Market penetration	0.8	2.50	2.75	3.17	5.7	6.58
Market development (Maritime)	-	-	1.00	2.75	3.75	5.00
Projected turnover	6.24	9.30	12.08	15.95	21.29	25.19

Budget marketing expenditure	1997 %	1998 %	1999 %	2000 %	2001 %	2002 %
(% of turnover)	Q3 & Q4					
Research and development	5	10	10	10	10	10
Human resource management	12	20	20	15	15	12
Marketing	5	10	10	8	7	7

Notes Part E: Learning from experience: ensuring you pass

APPENDIX A - FINANCIAL ANALYSIS

Outline profit and loss account for Sentinel 1994 to 2000 in £,000

E = Estimated figures

The advertising budget shown here relates to the overall marketing/administration budget.

	1994	1995	1996	1997E	1998E	1999E	2000E
Sales	2,601	3,230	4,250	5,440	6,800	8,330	10,030
Cost of goods sold (COGS)	1,769	2,381	3,000	4,047	4,692	5,498	6,820
Gross profit	832	849	1,250	1,393	2,108	2,832	3,210
Marketing/admin costs	715	742	600	1,121	1,632	1,832	1,806
Operating profit	117	107	650	272	476	100	1,404
Advertising cost			213 (5%)	408 (7.5%)	510	625	752
Return on net Assets (RONA)	(4.1)	3.9	10.4	8.0	-	-	-

Predicted company sales against predicted operating profit

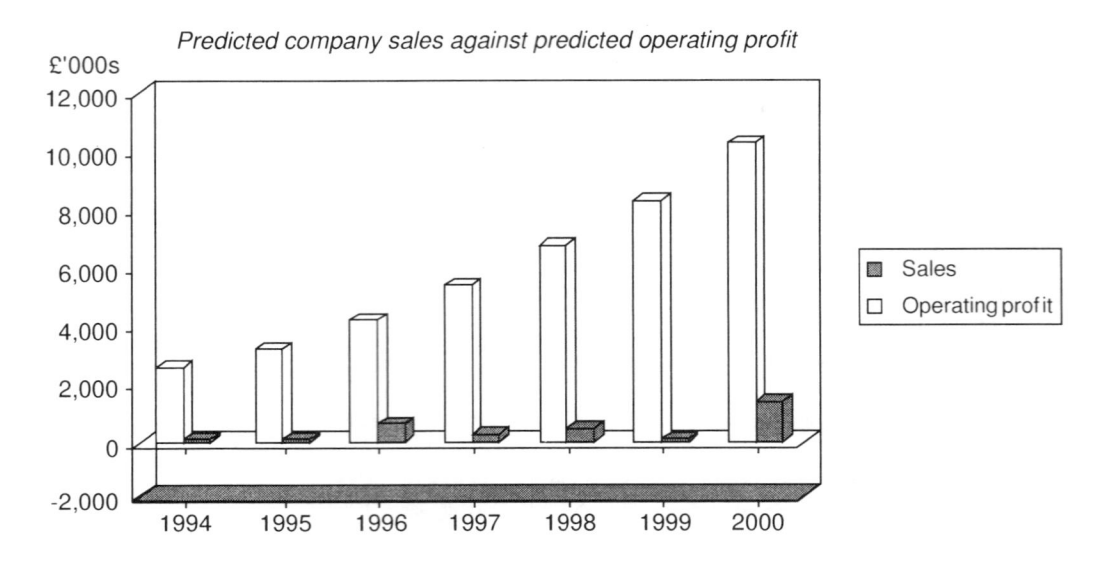

Ratio analysis

The main target set for Sentinel by Omnicorp is a return of net assets (RONA) of between 15% and 20%.

RONA is calculated as follows.

$$\frac{\text{Operating profit}}{\text{Net assets}} \times 100$$

As the operating profit and the % RONA are known can be calculated for each year, indicating funding needs.

$$\text{Operating profit} \times \frac{100}{\text{RONA}} = \text{net assets} \qquad 1995: \frac{3,230}{2,743} = 1.18$$

	Net assets £,000	Asset utilisation ratio
1994	2,854	0.91
1995	2,473	1.18
1996	6,250	0.68
1997E	3,400	1.60
1998E	-	-
1999E	-	-
2000E	9,360 (15% RONA)	1.07
	7,020 (20% RONA)	1.43

The net assets ratio has also been calculated:

Utilisation ratio $= \dfrac{\text{Turnover}}{\text{Net assets}}$ 1995: $\dfrac{3,230}{2,743} = 1.18$

For the asset utilisation ratio, control of assets including stock, debtors and creditors is vital. Therefore control of all costs not just marketing costs are important and all departments have a key role to play in hitting sales and RONA targets.

1996 was a year with good profitability on high turnover, but a poor use of assets, ie 0.68 asset utilisation ratio: the increase in turnover required a large increase in assets. This has implications for the year 2000 where the achievement of the higher RONA will only result from better asset utilisation: this means lower net assets and funding are required.

The next ratio that can be considered is the current ratio: $\dfrac{\text{Current assets}}{\text{Current liabilities}}$

The change is due to the proposed rapid fall in inventory levels, which in the past these have been excessive. Are dealers going to be asked to carry stock or is Sentinel going to have to manufacture to order?

Figures for debtors and creditors are needed.

Debtor days is $\dfrac{\text{Debtors}}{\text{Sales}} \times 365 =$ debtor days

This can be adapted to:

Sales $\times \dfrac{\text{Debtor days}}{365} =$ debtors   1995: £3,230,000 $\times \dfrac{78}{365} =$ £690,000

Creditors are calculated in a similar way except that as the involved purchase price cost of goods sold (COGS) is more appropriate than sales.

COGS $\times \dfrac{\text{Creditor days}}{365} =$ creditors   1995: 2,381 $\times \dfrac{142}{365} =$ £926,000

The following guide to liquidity can be produced, assuming the level of days is at 1997 levels for the three future years.

	1994	1995	1996	1997E	1998E	1999E	2000E
Current assets							
Stock	450	110	780	1,200	600	500	650
Debtors	356	690	1,164	968	1,210	1,483	1,786
	806	800	1,944	2,168	1,810	1,983	2,436
Current liabilities							
Creditors	232	926	756	643	1,092	1,280	1,588
Current ratio	3.5	1.9	2.6	3.4	1.7	1.5	1.5

It is accepted that the desired current ratio is 2:1 and in the past it can be seen that there has been a liquidity problem due to poor credit and inventory control. In the next three years, a ratio of 1.5 is not a major problem: the analysis does not take cash balances into account.

Summary

Many aspects of the company performance affect the return on net asset and asset utilisation ratios, not just marketing performance.

The required level performance and higher levels or operating profit will require a higher level of funding. The availability of such funds from Omnicorp or other sources will influence the objectives proposed.

The threat of liquidity problems is not too serious and should be controllable. The asset information available is not complete as no figures on Sentinel's cash position are available and, assuming cash surpluses, it should be possible to reduce the number of creditor days if so desired.

APPENDIX B - COMPETITOR ANALYSIS

Sentinel has two main competitors and three minor competitors in the executive jet and leisure sectors. The Swiftair Group and Eagle Electronics almost divide the world between them with just under 50% market share across all sectors between them.

The Swiftair Group

Swiftair Europe is a division of the US-based Topflight Group, responsible for marketing the company's leisure and executive jet brands in Europe, the Middle East and North Africa. The rest of world is handled by Swiftair USA.

Swiftair claimed 63% share of the autopilot markets, which makes it market leader in that field and its share of 38% on instruments probably makes it the market leader there.

The company markets its products under three different brand names, AutoSteer, Pantheon and Apache. The brand address different sectors and there is little product overlap. However Swiftair is now beginning to impose a secondary corporate branding, which may dilute the established brand names.

Swiftair's AutoSteer range has three autopilot systems compared with Sentinel's eight and three different chartplotters against Sentinel's six.

Pantheon focuses on executive jets and has a specialist support group for large aircraft. The range is mainly radar, although they have an autopilot, chartplotter and a new instrument system. Apache specialise in VHF radios and target the leisure market.

The company appears to be targeting the top end leisure market traditionally held by Breen and is also strengthening its commercial operations through strategic alliances with a Japanese organisation.

Eagle electronics

Eagle is a German owned group, which has grown rapidly through acquisitions and strategic takeovers.

However, this acquisition policy has caused confusion due to many brand names and product overlaps in different sectors. Its present policy of trying to regroup everything under the Eagle name, means the loss of some existing well respected names, and therefore an opportunity for Sentinel.

Although Eagle's largest market is the USA, the company claim a 10% share of the worldwide leisure and light commercial sectors, and this accounts for around 28% of group turnover. They are currently targeting the executive jet sector with a new product and are also looking at the European region as a key growth sector.

Navigator

Navigator has succeeded with a strategy of focusing on a particular market, ie leisure, with autopilots and VHF radios, and promoting them heavily. This is different from the broad approach of Swiftair and Eagle.

The company is one of the last independents within the aviation electronics sector and the turnover in 1996 was nearly £10 million.

Breen

Breen has suffered by concentrating on the declining luxury aircraft market. They are now trying to reposition themselves as a value for money provider which is, however, expensive. They have also tried to make sales for light aircraft, and sell adapted jet fighter technology with little success. Given this company's past history of being on the verge of bankruptcy, it now appears to be extremely vulnerable.

It is important to note that the rest of the industry appears to be extremely fragmented, and there is also another source of competition. These are the system integrators, who put together a range of products and software to offer complete solutions.

However, they do not necessarily manufacture any of the individual elements of the system themselves. Therefore if they go on to achieve greater success, companies like Sentinel will have opportunities to supply them, but with little power so their products will have to sell on price, since the final buyer will not be interested in the source of the component parts themselves.

APPENDIX C - CUSTOMER ANALYSIS

Some profiles

Ed Entrepreneur

Ed is 39, he is married to Sarah. They have two children Robert, who is 8 and Elizabeth, who is 5. Ed set up his own IT consultancy firm when he left Hewlett Packard three years ago. He lives in Horsham, West Sussex, in a house set in two acres of land and commutes to work in the city. He drives a BMW 3 Series for work and has a classic Triumph Spitfire, which he drives during the summer.

Ed spends his weekends with his family or at the airfield where he has been taking flying lessons for 18 months and has recently received his flying licence. He has recently become part owner of a twin engine plane with three other members of his flying club, Peter, Melissa and Michael. Sarah is excited at the prospect of him flying her to Paris for shopping and cultural activities.

Tom Techno

Tom is single, and has worked at Jet Stream Aircraft Manufacturers since he left the Royal Air force, after completing his three years service. Prior to joining the Air Force he graduated from Bristol University with a degree in economics, where he actively participated in the University Air Corps. His role at the company involves purchasing the technical equipment for the aircraft that Jet Stream produce, including navigation autopilots and GPS.

APPENDIX D - PRODUCT ANALYSIS

The complete product

Core

1. Customers who buy these products need to be able to navigate safely in all conditions. Therefore Sentinel products must provide reliable guidance solutions and information.

2. Pilots may be under a legal obligation to fit and use navigation equipment, if the 'European Legislation on air safety goes through', (Mike Flynn). Standards may be raised or tightened, meaning a mini-boom in the market and an additional need for system upgrades.

3. Pilots need to be able to *depend* upon such products to function at all times when flying, without the fear of the equipment breaking down or not functioning correctly. Sentinel products are sought for their reputation for reliability, quality and functionality, attributes that have been built up over the firm's seventy year history. The need for functionality is met well in Sentinel's current instruments range 'Firstaid'.

4. Sentinel's reputation for high quality products could be utilised to make them a symbol of status.

Physical

1. Sentinel is known by its customer as a single product company, due to the long term success and good reputation of 'Navigaid'. This is evidence that the design and branding of Sentinel products does not give a 'family' identity and image.

2. Instruments consist of a glass fronted dial, normally with a black background overlaid with white digits. Behind the dial is a black box containing the workings of the instruments, with wires connecting it to the various sensors or part of the plane.

3. Chartplotters consist of either a liquid crystal display (LCD) or cathode ray tube display (CRT), a choice of cartridges (PCB/processor) and the option of a global positioning system (GPS) antenna. These components are connected together by wires with only the display being visible to the pilot whilst inside the cockpit. The software for the chartplotters consist of different types of cartography which can be loaded onto the processor to specifically meet the needs of the customer.

4. Autopilots are devices, which enable the pilot to watch the control of navigating the plan to and from an automatic mode.

Augmented

The augmented product includes things which add value to the product or aid in its use. Examples are service and delivery of the products, training in how to fit, use of sell the products and solutions, which could be carried out on site or at Sentinel's offices. Provision of a help facility such as manuals, telephone customer service line or via the internet, safety features add-ons and up-grades also add value to the products.

Range considerations

Sentinel's two main product ranges are autopilots under the 'Navigaid' name and chartplotters under the name 'Chartwell'. These two groups of products account for 71% of the company's sales and are stated in the case study to represent the widest range of their kind in the world.

The range is certainly not matched by equivalent success on a world wide scale, therefore we must consider is this range *too wide* and so some rationalisation is necessary.

The *candidate's brief* states that Sentinel has never before had a strategic plan or strategic marketing plan, and this fact gives weight to the argument that product development has not been matched by attention to the development of segments of the market.

The instrument portfolio under the name 'Firstaid' accounts for 12% of sales. However this group of products does not seem to be performing to potential. Hugo Black's memo says its strengths are sophistication above its price, therefore it is presumably good value for money. This range is confused by customers with competing products with different names and suffers from a lack of design input from the sales force, so it is no surprise that its performance is disappointing.

Distributed products, we assume, are products from other companies in the group, including hydraulic equipment, control systems, cables and radar equipment. It is likely that this group has good potential since it accounts for 17% of Sentinel's sales, and these would have developed since the takeover by Omnicorp three years ago. The future for cross selling looks good, therefore other subsidiaries of Omnicorp would perhaps do the same for Sentinel in the US.

Total sales by product (£m)

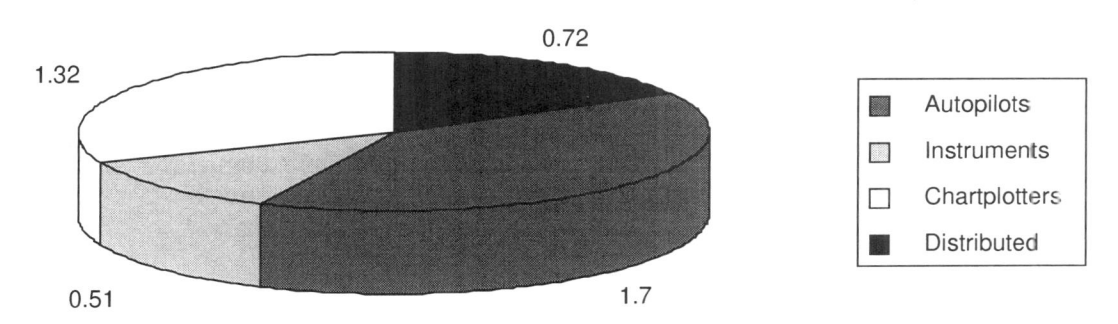

- Autopilots: 1.7
- Instruments: 0.51
- Chartplotters: 1.32
- Distributed: 0.72

Autopilots

Sentinel made its name with the first generation Navigaid, which was adopted by virtually ever leisure aircraft builder when it was first introduced. It was the first practical and reliable product of its type on the market.

The range was completely upgraded in 1994 and now includes eight different systems, including variants for specific applications such as twin engine, executive jets and light aircraft.

Chartplotters

Chartplotters are an important part of Sentinel's product range, with six different products for the commercial and leisure sectors, which are sold under the band name 'Chartwell'.

They offer different types of liquid crystal display (LCD), cathode ray tube (CRT) display screens, a choice of cartridge, different types of cartography and the option of a global positioning system (GPS) antenna. However, the chartplotter market does suffer from cheap, inferior imports within Europe.

Instruments

Sentinel's 'Firstaid' instrument portfolio covers most aircraft applications with a range of well designed, highly functional products, that provide reliable performance in all conditions.

The 'Firstaid' range was launched in 1991 and currently accounts for around 12% of sales turnover. However, it has suffered from low funding, poor design input and consequent lack of interest from the salesforce. This is despite the fact that Sentinel offer a much more sophisticated product than their competitors at a similar price.

Sentinel needs to establish a brand identity and to differentiate products between the leisure and executive jet sectors.

Part E: Learning from experience: ensuring you pass

APPENDIX E - MARKETING ENVIRONMENT AUDIT

E1 *Macro analysis*

Political

- Foreign and home market government stability
- EU legislation on air safety.
- Manufacturer price control legislation.
- Reduced government spending in the aviation defence market, leading to increased competition in commercial and leisure markets.

Economic

- Exchange rates (USA) transfer pricing to Omnicorp.
- European recession compared to the UK.
- Level of disposable income.

Social

- Increased sophistication of customers (partnership and solutions).
- Demographics, ageing population.
- General decline in leisure time due to trend toward longer working hours.
- Increased end-user familiarity with graphical user interfaces (Windows).

Technological

- Demand for total integrated solutions.
- Transfer of technology from information technology sector.

E2 *Micro analysis*

Customers

- Rationalisation of suppliers. Customers are able to source from suppliers on a global scale.
- New markets, Scandinavia, Holland and the Far East 'old Empire'.
- Change of attitude in the UK and US market as regards the direct relationship between quality and price, due to the increase in sales through mail order selling.

Competitors

- Fragmented market place.
- Market size = £425m.
- Major competitors include Swiftair, and Eagle who together hold 49% global market share. Navigator are the only independent company and operate in the radio and leisure markets. The majority of competitors are owned by large industrial groups and therefore share resources such as R&D.
- Future competitors include systems integrators.
- In the European market the competitive position of chartplotters suffers from cheap inferior imports.

Distribution

- New channels as Swiftair are restructuring their dealer network.
- Different distribution structure in US market, eg three tier network.

E3 *Internal*

Strategy and objectives

- Poor corporate strategic planning, eg no clear objectives and no mission statement.
- Confused corporate image.
- No public relations strategy.

Structure

- Well established company

31: Sentinel Aviation: detailed marketing planning

- Organisational structure: product orientated rather than customer focused.
- No clear lines of communication, eg salesforce report to distribution manager.
- Not fully utilising Omnicorp's resources such as research and development.
- Cultural problems, eg two distinct groups of employees with conflicting views on the company's activities within the market place. Some employees are traditionalists who view that the company is primarily in aviation whereas others see Sentinel as a software company.

Systems

- No feedback system from dealers and customers via the sales force.
- No market information system.
- No control system on company's activities.

People

- Dedicated workforce and top management from different industries including leisure and computing.
- Good technical expertise.

Salesforce

- Lack of market and competitor awareness this could be addressed through training.
- No involvement in new product development process.

E4 **4 Ps**

Product/service

- Well established tradition of service.
- Broad range of products, eg manufacture the largest range of autopilots in the industry.
- Poor brand identity, eg Sentinel are renowned for only one product (Navigaid).
- Strong brand reputation for Navigaid.
- Lack of market-focused product development.

Price

- A price war must be avoided at all costs, as to meet Omnicorp's targets for profitability would only be achievable through standardisation and high volume, not attributes associated with Sentinel.
- Goals can be achieved through customers' perception of quality and performance. This recognition can be achieved through strong branding.
- In general, prices are based on a *cost plus system*, which is a weak pricing strategy and it does not relate to customer perception.
- A perception of quality (perhaps reinforced by strong branding).

Place

- Distribute to 45 countries.
- UK distribution: operate a two tier distribution system, Sentinel > dealer > customer.
- Europe (four major markets; France, Italy, Germany and Spain): three tier distribution system, Sentinel > distributor > dealer > customer.
- USA: Sentinel should supply through US distributor (Sentinel US reporting to Omnicorp) combines a successful retail and mail order business.

Promotion

- Advertise in Aviation Times and attend trade exhibitions.
- Mail advertising for dealers.

Notes   *Part E: Learning from experience: ensuring you pass*

APPENDIX F - BRAND LOGO IDEAS

Proposed corporate logo

Sentinel

Guiding You Into The Future

Proposed product branding

Corporate Umbrella Brand

Sentinel Navigaid

Product Brand

APPENDIX G - BUDGETS AND TIMESCALES EXPLAINED

Product development

Action	Explanation
R&D (Research and development)	• To adapt products to the maritime market • Then adapt to other future markets • To provide an integrated product solutions to existing markets via Omnicorp).
HRM (Human resource management)	• Implementation of new structure and culture. • staff recruitment, selection, and re-training of sales force.
Market research	• to establish what potential customers want within the maritime market • to test the product launch within particular market segments

Market penetration

Action	Explanation
Communication	• To communicate the new corporate image and brand strategy via a variety of communication mediums, eg advertising, PR promotional goods etc.
Distribution	• To evaluate and rationalise the distribution network • To introduce checking/reward systems to improve dealer/distributor performance. • To improve relationships with distributors/dealers via social events, training seminars etc

Market development

Action	Explanation
Market research	• To research new markets such as security and automotive to measure the potential of entering these sectors
Distribution	• To Whom It May Concern: source and establish new channels of distribution, manufacturers and the interest.

9 THE EXAMINATION

9.1 You must now get your preparations finalised for your first mock exam before turning to the exam paper which follows in the next chapter.

9.2 Just in case you have forgotten, you need to conduct two final steps in the recommended methodology.

9.3
> CONSULT CHAPTERS 8 AND 10 FOR GUIDANCE NOTES.
>
> **STEP 27 DRAW UP YOUR EXAMINATION PLAN**
> **STEP 28 PRACTISE WRITING IN TRUE REPORT STYLE**
>
> ALLOW AS LONG AS NECESSARY FOR THESE LAST TWO STEPS

9.4 Good luck in your final practice exam!

Chapter 32

SENTINEL AVIATION: THE EXAMINATION PAPER, EXAMINER'S REPORT AND INDICATIVE MARKING GUIDES

This chapter contains the following.

1　The examination paper
2　Examiner's report
3　Indicative marking guides

SENTINEL AVIATION

THE EXAM QUESTIONS ARE ON THE NEXT PAGE

DO NOT LOOK UNTIL YOU ARE READY TO SPEND
THREE HOURS ON DOING THESE AS A MOCK EXAM

Notes   **Part E: Learning from experience: ensuring you pass**

1 THE EXAMINATION PAPER

Additional information - to be taken into account when answering the questions set.

> *The news from Gannet*
>
> Mike Flynn was on his way out to a meeting with Sentinel's bankers and met Jim on the stairs.
>
> 'Jim, I've been talking with my opposite number in Gannet Control Systems, I wanted to know whether they undertake any strategic planning in their operations.
>
> 'Although they are not much advanced on us, he did mentioned one thing - market segmentation. They seem to have abandoned the traditional classifications used by the industry and developed a new approach based on customer needs rather than product specification.
>
> 'He is sending across their methodology but it won't necessarily work for us since our businesses are different. Still, I wondered whether you could build something into your research plans. You never know, we might be able to jump ahead of the competition with a new approach. Gannet are obviously enthusiastic but it started to get too technical for a non-marketer like me.
>
> 'I'll be interested to see what you come up with.'

It has become clear from discussions with Mike Flynn that there is little point in presenting a full strategic marketing plan to Omnicorp at this stage, their only real concern is that Sentinel reaches its financial targets. Nevertheless you have agreed with Mike that, by this time next year, a detailed strategic marketing plan must in be in place if the company is to grow in a planned and profitable manner.

You have agreed, also, that there are three clear questions that must be addressed before any detailed planning can take place. You are therefore required to prepare a report for Mike Flynn which will cover the following.

Question 1 - (30 marks)

It is clear that Sentinel will not reach the financial targets set by Omnicorp if it remains a supplier only to the Aviation sector. What 'business' do you think Sentinel is or should be in and, therefore, in which additional sectors would you suggest Sentinel should be seeking business?

Question 2 - (30 marks)

Which single strategic model can best be used to describe Sentinel's situation and should be used as the basis of the strategic plan? Show how this model might be used to guide Sentinel's move into new sectors.

Question 3 - (40 marks)

What are the critical strategic information gaps and how might they be filled? How might the information collected be used to develop the segmentation, targeting and positioning policy?

2 EXAMINER'S REPORT

General comments

2.1 The Sentinel case saw pass rates falling yet again in the Analysis and Decision paper. Too many candidates are still failing to deal with the constraints of a three-hour examination set at post-graduate level. For a professional qualification rated at 70 'M' level CATS points it is appropriate that candidates be given the opportunity to apply their knowledge. There are still too many candidates who either do not have sufficient knowledge to pass this examination or who are unable to apply it in a business situation.

2.2 This paper is set as an *'open book' examination* which means that candidates do not have to memorise anything but are free to refer to texts, models, frameworks and key criteria as they would in a business situation. Free from the burden of testing knowledge, the case study can concentrate on testing the candidates' ability to apply their knowledge in relation to the questions posed on examination day. Unfortunately, the Sentinel case found far too many candidates unable to address the question posed and work prepared before the examination was too often regurgitated without thinking or taking account of the *additional information* or the marks allocated in the paper.

2.3 Many of the past cases included a 'predictable' question on preparing and producing a strategic marketing plan as a major part of the paper. Many candidates may have expected its practice to continue - bad mistake. There is no doubt that the development of a strategic marketing plan should play a central role in the candidate's preparation for the examination, but this time it was not requested as a specific question. Future candidates are urged not to rely on the ability to guess examination questions and expect to pass by simply copying out pre-prepared answers on the examination day.

2.4 We expected a number of weaker candidates to offer their full marketing plans regardless of the actual question asked but we were surprised by the relatively small numbers of candidates who succumbed to this temptation. Still, the absence of a specific question on a strategic plan identified candidates who are still unready to pass the paper and enter the profession. Marks, as always, were only awarded for answers which tackled the specifics of the questions posed. Additional data offered, no matter how good, did not attract marks if it did not relate to the questions.

2.5 The list of reasons for failure in the case were (yet again):
 (a) failure to answer the questions posed on the day
 (b) regurgitation of case material
 (c) presentation of pre-prepared answers regardless of questions et
 (d) lack of knowledge on strategic marketing issues.
 (e) inclusion of irrelevant data, numbers and SWOT analyses
 (f) ignoring the additional information
 (g) poor time management

*Candidates and tutors should note that the above list seems to remain unchanged from one examiners report to the next. Regardless of the type and approach of the case study set, the reasons for failure are **always** the same.*

2.6 The issue of time management again requires special mention. In this case the questions carried marks of 30:30:40. The absence of a question on the strategic plan confused a number of candidates but many still answered question two (it mentioned 'models') as though it were worth half the marks on the paper. Question three was often answered quite superficially and covered in three or four pages only - or even ignored completely! Examiners try hard to award marks but to do so we need something to mark! Time management is a critical skill for the practising marketer - not jut useful to pass exams.

Part E: Learning from experience: ensuring you pass

The questions

2.7 In order to ensure that candidates were aware that the previously 'standard question' on the strategic marketing plan was not to appear in this paper, an introduction to the question was added.

> 'It has become clear from discussions with Mike Flynn that there is little point in presenting a full strategic marketing plan to Omnicorp at this stage, their only real concern is that Sentinel reaches its financial targets. Nevertheless you have agreed with Mike that, by this time next year, a detailed strategic marketing plan must be in place if the company is to grow in a planned and profitable manner.
>
> You have agreed, also, that there are three clear questions that must be addressed before any detailed planning can take place. You are therefore required to prepare a report for Mike Flynn which will cover the following.'

The likelihood that a full strategic plan would not be required was clearly flagged in the case study text.

Question 1

2.8 This is a fundamental question for marketing and marketing strategy. The question 'What Business' was originally raised in Levitt's famous article 'Marketing Myopia' (HBR) in 1960. it remains a topic for discussion even today with too few organisations dealing with the problem effectively.

2.9 This question was answered by most candidates with a reasonable if not thorough approach. The 'PESTs' and 'SWOTs' were again in evidence as most candidates had considered 'where are we now' as part of their preparation. In the instances where Ansoff was used in this question answers started to achieve the depth of thinking required. Unfortunately, some weaker candidates were determined to turn this question into an opportunity to 'unload' all their previously prepared work on situational analysis and hope that some marks would be gained.

2.10 Given the fundamental nature of this question in developing marketing strategy, it is an aspect which we can justifiably expect candidates to address in an effective and reasoned manner. It was therefore rather worrying that too many candidates appear to be very product oriented in their views of what constituted Sentinel's existing and future business. This, unfortunately, demonstrates an almost complete lack of knowledge of the basics of marketing and marketing planning and a complete lack of a strategic grasp of the situation.

2.11 Happily, a number of candidates did show that they were aware of the need for a more customer based definition of the business and that defining Sentinel's business as being primarily 'the aviation business' was a dangerously myopic view. Some better candidates came up with some pleasingly creative and very marketing oriented approaches to defining Sentinel's business based on much wider conceptions of what Sentinel's core competencies might be used for in seeking new business opportunities.

Question 2

2.12 This question gave candidates a real opportunity to integrate theory with practice - unfortunately, few candidates rose to this challenge.

2.13 The weakest candidates failed completely to answer this question as it was set: they had placed their SWOT etc into Question 1 and now tried to put the next part of their pre-prepared strategic plan into Question 2. The question exposed some candidates' inadequate knowledge of the models themselves as well as their strengths and

32: Sentinel Aviation: the examination paper, examiner's report and indicative marking guides

weaknesses relative to the case situation. Some candidates were simply unable to come to a decision!

2.14 In too many cases answers were presented which were simple text book explanations of a marketing model (often Ansoff) with little or no application to the Sentinel case.

2.15 Over half the candidates used Ansoff as the preferred model and then 50% of these immediately demonstrated they had no understanding of the model and how it could be used as the basis of a strategic plan A smaller number of candidates used more useful portfolio models such as BCG, GE or ADL. A basic (not extended) Ansoff made it hard to draw out the situation and once the chosen model has been reproduced too few candidates showed any signs of using it to drive and direct the business. Very few answers clearly demonstrated how the models could be used to guide Sentinel's expansion to new sectors.

2.16 Regrettably, extremely few candidates considered the softer issues of Sentinel's and Omnicorp's culture and the need to select a model which would be acceptable to this non-planning mentality.

2.17 Through the entire series of papers the examiners saw all models known to marketing and some which were completely new! The answers to this question clearly demonstrated the gulf which still exists between knowing a marketing model and knowing how to apply the model in practice. There is obviously no point in releasing more people into the marketing profession who know all the theory but can do nothing with it - future cases will continue to test this crucial ability to apply knowledge.

Question 3

2.18 This question carried 40 marks so, allowing for planning time on examination day, the prepared candidates should have been writing for approximately 60 minutes on the answer. This is especially important when we note that this is question three, it carried the highest marks of all three questions, bad time management typically causes many examination failures.

2.19 This question as the most troublesome for candidates. Many acquitted themselves adequately on the information requirements since the lack of good marketing data was clearly flagged in the case text. Unfortunately, marks were not collected in quantity since too many candidates failed to relate the information to their answers to question one (new sectors) and two (strategic models and expansion routes) or to the case in general. Too many answers were offered in 'splendid isolation' from Sentinel's situation and in a simple list format.

2.20 The real problem with this question came in part two, where candidates were asked to show how the information might be used in developing segmentation, targeting and position policy. Too many candidates gave simple definitions of segmentation and positioning, or bland unrelated statements as to why these were important but failed to answer the question set. The weakest candidates used this section to ignore the parameters of the question set and instead used it as a dumping ground for their pre-prepared material on the 4Ps or 7Ps. Where segmentation was mentioned, the additional information was too often ignored and there was a return to demographics and geographics when relating information to segmentation.

2.21 The second part of the question was also hit by lack of time in badly managed papers. For some reason, many candidates still seem to disregard the fact that the question with the most marks (in this case 40%) should have the most time allocated to it.

2.22 In fact the question was straightforward and, for the well prepared candidate, it posed few problems. The better answers linked the additional information in the earlier part of the question to the steps in market segmentation, targeting and positioning and the

Notes   **Part E: Learning from experience: ensuring you pass**

highest marks were awarded to those showing a strong awareness of how this related to the Sentinel case in particular.

Conclusions

2.23 Sentinel again proved a testing case for too many candidates.

2.24 Overall, answers were not well integrated, there were even some papers which attempted the question in an order other than that set - with predictable results. Also, there is still a tendency for some candidates to spend their time 'rearranging' the case material in their answers rather than developing any additional insight.

2.25 Generally, the Sentinel case has followed in the wake of previous cases (Mistral, Gravesend, Leffe and others) and has demonstrated the existence of a core problem in this examination. Candidates have a reasonably good grasp of key concepts and techniques and are able to define and describe these. The Analysis and Decision paper, however, requires that candidates demonstrate their ability to *apply* these concepts and techniques in a business situation. Too many candidates are still unable to do this.

3   INDICATIVE MARKING GUIDES

3.1 *Overview*

    (a) *The case.* The case study presented for this examination has been heavily disguised. However, the data and financial/pricing figures have been produced (after modifications) from real data drawn from the sponsor organisation. The case content describes a real problem that the organisation faces today.

    The organisation has a reasonably long history and has grown into its present situation rather haphazardly from its early flying origins. Like similar businesses in aviation, sailing and other leisure/hobby sectors, there is a historical conflict between the people in it for 'love' and the people in it for profit. Emotions (about history and heritage) tend to run high in the traditional management of these businesses. Since the takeover of Sentinel by Omnicorp, the relative importance of profit and 'love of flying' is no longer in doubt. The senior managers understand this fundamental shift of emphasis, it is less clear that the rest of the organisation has yet appreciated the nature of the change.

    (b) *Key points*

      (i) Sentinel is an organisation with a sense of history and heritage.

      (ii) Sentinel has been managed and staffed by people who feel 'involved' in flying.

      (iii) Sentinel's growth has been good enough in the past to keep it in business but has been patchy and relatively uncontrolled.

      (iv) Sales have been opportunistic rather than planned and co-ordinated.

      (v) Sentinel is product-led rather than customer-led.

      (vi) The company has little knowledge or understanding of its customers or their needs.

      (vii) Omnicorp purchased Sentinel because it saw potential in the organisation.

      (viii) Omnicorp has placed demands on Sentinel for significant additional financial returns, in its view, Sentinel should be capable of achieving these returns.

      (ix) About Omnicorp's financial demands on Sentinel:

        (1) If they are not met, Sentinel's senior managers will probably be replaced - not achieving the financial targets is not an option.

        (2) Can they be met solely by Sentinel being more 'efficient' at what it does now? - unlikely.

32: Sentinel Aviation: the examination paper, examiner's report and indicative marking guides

(3) Can they be met solely by Sentinel being more 'effective' at what it does not? - unlikely

(4) Efficiency and effectiveness are both *necessary* but unlikely to be *sufficient* to achieve the set financial targets. Sentinel will have to find something *different* to add to the equation

3.2 The answers

In awarding marks, the key points are these.

(a) We are looking for application, not just the statement of theory.

(b) We are assessing marketing answers, not product-led sales answers.

(c) We are assessing marketing strategy, not tactics.

(d) The answer must be practical given the case situation.

(e) The 'acid test' remains - would you give this person a job as a marketer?

(f) And...

(i) Many of the past cases included a 'predictable' question on preparing and producing a strategic marketing plan as a major part of the paper. Many candidates may have expected this practice to continue - bad mistake. There is no doubt that the development of a strategic marketing plan should play a central role in the candidate's preparation for the examination, but this time it has not been requested as a specific question.

(ii) A number of weaker candidates can be expected to offer their full marketing plans regardless of the actual questions asked - this will identify candidates who are still unready to pass the paper. *Marks will only be awarded for answers which tackle the specifics of the questions posed.* Additional data offered, no matter how good, will not attract marks if it does not relate to the questions.

3.3 The additional information

(a) The additional information raised a number of points, none of which should have surprised the well-prepared candidate.

(b) The *lack of planning* in the organisation (Omnicorp and Sentinel) is a function of the corporate culture as well of the industry. This was flagged clearly in the case so that absence of a specific question on a strategic marketing plan should be no surprise.

(c) The question about segmentation is important and should be tackled specifically in question three.

3.4 The questions

(a) In order to ensure that candidates were aware that the 'standard question' on the strategic marketing plan was not to appear in this paper, an introduction to the question paper was added:

> 'It has become clear from discussions with Mike Flynn that there is little point in presenting a full strategic marketing plan to Omnicorp at this stage, their only real concern is that Sentinel reaches its financial targets. Nevertheless you have agreed with Mike that, by this time next year, a detailed strategic marketing plan must be in place if the company is to grow in a planned and profitable manner. You have agreed, also, that there are three clear questions that must be addressed before any detailed planning can take place. You are therefore required to prepare a report for Mike Flynn which will cover the following.'

(b) The likelihood that a full strategic plan would not be required was clearly flagged in the study too.

Notes **Part E: Learning from experience: ensuring you pass**

Question 1

3.5 *Question 1 - 30 marks* (It is clear that Sentinel will not reach the financial targets set by Omnicorp if it remains a supplier only to the Aviation sector. What 'business' do you think Sentinel is or should be in and, therefore, in which additional sectors would you suggest Sentinel should be seeking business?)

(a) *Note*. This question carries 30 marks so, allowing for planning time on examination day, the prepared candidate should be writing for approximately 45 minutes on the answer.

(a) *Approach*

(i) This is a fundamental question for marketing and marketing strategy. The question 'What Business' was originally raised in Levitt's famous article 'Marketing Myopia' (HBR) in 1960. It remains a topic for discussion even today with too few organisations dealing with the problem effectively.

(ii) Clearly, Sentinel will have to do a number of things if it is to achieve the financial targets set upon it. It will have:

(1) to be more efficient at servings its Aviation customers - control costs, enhance profitability per customer etc;

(2) to be more effective at serving its Aviation customers - serve customers better, improve retention, sell more products per customer etc;

(3) to gain more Aviation customers - compete better, improve market share, grow international business etc.

(iii) But all this is unlikely, on its own, to meet the target. Sentinel is going to have to expand its business outside 'Aviation'. To do this in a manner which is anything other than a sales-led approach will require some analysis and understanding of what business Sentinel is in so that the organisation can expand into areas which the marketplace considers 'logical' and in which Sentinel can be considered to have some degree of competitive advantage.

(iv) The question is in *two* parts and is asking for:

(1) what business is, or should Sentinel be in?
(2) *therefore*, what other sectors should it be looking at?

3.6 *Good answers*

We can expect to see a logical sequence of steps that might look like this.

(a) *Part one* (What business is, or should Sentinel be in?)

(i) Analysis of the current situation at Sentinel

(1) SWOT
(2) PEST

(ii) What business in Sentinel in at the moment?

(1) This question is concerned with identifying the nature of the business which will allow Sentinel to expand in a logical manner. The candidate may consider the nature of the business that Sentinel thinks it is in but we are concerned more with a marketing definition of the business.

(2) There are three traditional ways of determining the nature of the business than an organisation is in:

- The *customer groups* that are approached and/or served.
- The *customer needs* which the organisation will satisfy.
- The *technology* which the organisation uses to satisfy those needs.

(3) In the case of Sentinel, the examples might be:

- We are in the *Aviation* business. This definition might be extended to cover ideas such as the *leisure* business, *hobby* business, *commercial transport* business etc.
- We are in the *location/movement* business.
- We are in the *automatic pilot/radar/gps* business.

32: Sentinel Aviation: the examination paper, examiner's report and indicative marking guides

(4) Any of these definitions may be acceptable if the case is argued properly and from sound marketing principles. Suggestions such as 'we sell autopilots' are clearly unacceptable.

(b) Part two (*Therefore, what other sectors should it be looking at?*)

What sectors should Sentinel be considering for expansion?

(i) Clearly, this part of the question (and indeed the rest of the candidate's paper) needs to follow on logically from the answer offered in part one above. We are looking for clear evidence that the candidate has investigated the situation properly and has considered expansion of the Sentinel operation from a longer term marketing perspective and not just from a short term sales perspective.

(ii) Ansoff should be used at this point to explain what penetration, product development, market development and diversification means from the definition of Sentinel's business as proposed. We should also expect a clear statement of the prioritisation of the various activities according to the *relative risk* involved in each.

3.7 Best answers will:

(a) analyse Sentinel's current position
(b) identify what business Sentinel is/should be in
(c) identify areas for future expansion of Sentinel

Question 2

3.8 *Question 2 - 30 marks* (Which *single strategic model* can best be used to describe Sentinel's situation and should be used as the basis of the strategic plan? Show how this model might be used to guide Sentinel's move into new sectors.)

(a) *Note.* This question carries 30 marks so, allowing for planning time on examination day, the prepared candidates should be writing for approximately 45 minutes on the answer.

(b) *Approach*

This question is likely to attract a wide range or responses from candidates. It has been purposefully phrased to ask for just *one* model from the whole range at the disposal of the candidate, that should be used to 'best describe' Sentinel's situation and eventually 'be used as the basis of the strategic plan'.

Therefore, it can be seen that the question is asking for:

(i) the choice of a single model...
(ii) to explain Sentinel's situation...
(iii) to be used as the basis of the strategic plan; and
(iv) a demonstration how this model can be used to guide Sentinel's expansion into new sectors.

Note. This is an open book examination and texts are available to the candidates to be consulted on the day to identify all strategic models and their characteristics.

3.9 *Good answers* can then be expected to follow a sequence of thinking such as this.

(a) Choosing a single model.

(i) There is a raft of models that can be chosen, some obviously offer more potential for doing what Sentinel wants than others. The models we can expect to see might include:

(1) Porter (generic strategies)
(2) Ansoff (and Ansoff 'expanded')
(3) BCG
(4) GEC/McKinsey
(5) Shell (directional policy)

Part E: Learning from experience: ensuring you pass

(6) ADL

(ii) Of these, I would expect GEC/Shell/ADL to offer the most mileage in the context of the case.

(iii) Ansoff would *not* be my first choice (especially as it should be included in question one) but I expect it to be a popular choice. If the candidate can make it work then marks should be awarded accordingly.

(iv) In any event, *only one* model is requested by the question and, where a candidate offers more than one, only the principal model should be considered.

(b) *To explain Sentinel's situation*

(i) This examination (as all Diploma examinations) is designed to be a test of the candidate's ability to apply strategic marketing knowledge, not just be a test of what they know. Therefore we are concerned with the candidate's ability to apply models within the context of the question posed and the case in general.

(ii) Question 1 will have proposed a 'business' for Sentinel and the candidate is now to show how the model they have selected describes the current situation faced by the company as well as its options for expansion in the future.

(iii) There is a hidden dimension to this question which should be worth bonus points: describes the situation to whom? If the situation (on the proposed expansion plans) has to be described to Omnicorp and the Sentinel workforce, then a model which is easily understood by these two groups should be selected.

(c) *To be used as the basis of the strategic plan*

The candidates should show how the model selected will form the basis of the strategic plan which will be developed over the coming year. The model should be capable of being used to do the following.

(i) Set corporate objectives
(ii) Identify target markets
(iii) Set marketing objectives
(iv) Design marketing strategy and tactics
(v) Design control systems

(d) Demonstrate how this model can be used to guide Sentinel's expansion to new sectors.

(i) This section of the question asks the candidate to link questions one and two and to use the selected model to show how, *in the case of Sentinel as described in the case study*, the model can be used to identify areas of potential growth for the company.

(ii) The methods of analysis and potential growth areas (if identified) will, of course, vary with the model selected. Marks should be awarded according to the relevance and use of the selected model.

3.10 Best answers will do the following.

(a) Select a single strategic model
(b) Show how it explains Sentinel's situation
(c) Show how it can be used as the basis of the strategic plan
(d) Demonstrate how this model can be used to guide expansion

Question 3

3.11 *Question 3 - 40 marks* (What are the critical strategic information gaps and how might they be filled? How might the information collected be used to develop the segmentation, targeting and positioning policy?)

(a) *Note.* This question carries 40 marks so, allowing for planning time on examination day, the prepared candidate should be writing for approximately 60 minutes on the

32: Sentinel Aviation: the examination paper, examiner's report and indicative marking guides

answer. This is especially important when we note that this is Question 3, it carries the highest marks of all three questions and bad time management typically causes many examination failures.

(b) *Approach*

This question is straightforward and comes in two parts. The question is asking for:

(i) Gathering the information

(1) What are the critical gaps?
(2) How might these gaps be filled?

(ii) Using the information, for:

(1) segmentation policy
(2) targeting policy
(3) positioning policy

(iii) Again, the prepared candidate will probably have covered these points in their four week analysis period although they may have expected a planning questions to have appeared on the day. Beware answers which present the data in pre-prepared formats not related to the question posed.

Finally, question 3 has been placed in its position because it follows on naturally from the answers given in the previous two questions. It is important that question 3 answers build on question 1 and 2.

3.12 *Good answers* will follow the question and answer in two parts.

(a) *Part one - gathering the information*

(i) The question asks the candidate to identify the *critical strategic information gaps* and how the *might be filled*. The answer can be presented in a tabular form although simple lists (without explanation) are not acceptable.

(ii) Critical strategic information gaps will be:

(1) a function of the model selected and the expansion routes identified;
(2) focused on customer, competitor and market information - in the markets identified previously;
(3) possibly influenced by Hamel's model (spoken/unspoken needs and served/unserved customers);
(4) driven by the strategic decisions that have to be made, not driven by curiosity;
(5) driven by the additional information, the importance of customer needs as a potential segmentation base;
(6) about the longer rather than the short term;
(7) what Sentinel needs to know before it can progress, not a list of 'nice to know' items.

(iii) Filling the gaps will be dependent upon the nature of the gaps identified and should take into account the normal sources of data (internal, government and private) and should be relevant given:

(1) the resources of Sentinel;
(2) the timescales involved;
(3) the marketing and planning knowledge of Sentinel.

(iv) Simply 'briefing an agency' will not be sufficient.

(b) *Part two - using the information*

(i) This part of the question is inextricably linked to part one and cannot be answered in a vacuum.

(ii) This part is also strongly linked to the additional information and should build in the idea of market segments based on customer needs rather than product variations. Other customer-related bases of segmentation may be acceptable as long as the candidate fully justifies the choice and makes the connection to the additional information and explains why their approach is more appropriate.

  (iii) Candidates should show that they understand the role of segmentation, targeting and positioning for Sentinel and how the information collected in part one of the question will be used to develop these policies. From the candidate's previously argued case for Sentinel's expansion into identified target markets:

    (1) Who are we aiming at?
    (2) What are the key wants/need/motivators?
    (3) What bases for segmentation?
    (4) Tests of segmentation
    (5) Prioritisation of segments (targeting)
    (6) How do we differentiate Sentinel in the segments?
    (7) Ho do we position Sentinel in the target customers' mind?

3.13 Best answers will:

  (a) identify critical information gaps;

  (b) suggest how these gaps might be filled;

  (c) show how to use the information to develop segmentation, targeting and positioning policy.

4 A FINAL WORD

4.1 Well, how did you get on with your final mock exam? If you are still dissatisfied with your performance please do not despair. Further help is available at a price.

  (a) A consultants' analysis is provided in the next chapter.

  (b) You can obtain individual past cases, analysed in a similar way to the cases in this Tutorial Text, for further practice. See the back of this text for details.

Chapter 33

CONSULTANTS' ANALYSIS OF SENTINEL AVIATION

> This chapter contains an analysis of Sentinel Aviation by Northern Consultancy Associates.
>
> 1   How to use this analysis
> 2   Strategic considerations
> 3   The market
> 4   The marketing mix
> 5   Organisation
> 6   Financial analysis
> 7   Planning considerations
> 8   Food for thought
>
> *Note.* The address of Northern Consultancy Associates is 8, Church Chare, Ponteland, Newcastle on Tyne NE20 9XT, Phone 01661 820633 (administrative queries only).

1   HOW TO USE THIS ANALYSIS

1.1   It is intended that this analysis be used in conjunction with a copy of the Sentinel Aviation case study obtained from the Chartered Institute of Marketing. It is designed for students preparing for the Institute's Analysis and Decision examination, but may be of value to other users. The following comments are intended for those taking the CIM examination.

1.2   This document was designed to help you think through the problem areas confronting you as Jim Converre, marketing director. Its purpose is to save you valuable study time. However, we do not point to a particular solution, and this analysis is *not* an examination answer.

1.3   You are likely to have to make firm recommendations at the time of the examination. Make these, with appropriate justification, without regurgitating tracts of the case study itself, or this analysis.

1.4   You must answer the questions that are set for you. Do not allow preconceived notions to deflect you from this task. You must adopt a *report style* in the examination. Not only will this be required by instructions given, it will aid clarity of thought and save you time. Please read carefully out comments in this document on examination technique.

1.5   You have been in the post for a year, and are now ready to think about strategic issues. You need to think very clearly about broad strategy and any detailed issues must be considered in relation to strategy. You will be aware of the shortcomings of implementation of existing strategy, and need to make up your mind whether the targets for profitability and growth can be met by improvements to what is being done now, or whether new ventures are necessary.

1.6 You must use the information given in the case study. You will, however, be given additional information during the examination itself, and it is important that you incorporate it in your answer.

1.7 This document will be lodged with the Chartered Institute of Marketing's examiners. You will not gain marks by simply copying sections of it. Use it instead to arrive at and justify recommendations.

1.8 This publication is of necessity produced at great speed, but with every possible care. However, all material should be carefully scrutinised before basing recommendations on it as errors are not impossible.

2 STRATEGIC CONSIDERATIONS

The process

2.1 Whenever one approaches a case study it is necessary, after analysing it, to decide on the basic strategy that the organisation should follow. A strategy is a long term/important decision which will determine that the organisation is moving in the right direction. Then the tactics or operating plans can be determined coherently following the overall direction which is laid down for the organisation. It is often said that strategic decisions ensure that the organisation does the right thing, whilst operating plans concentrate on 'doing things right'.

2.2 It must also be understood that strategies exist at different levels in the organisation and are hierarchical. Thus there will be a corporate strategy which will help determine the marketing strategy, which itself will constrain/direct the advertising strategy. Similarly, the strategy of the corporate headquarters will to an extent determine that of its subsidiaries.

2.3 Since case studies are complex it is considered desirable to adopt a specific process to assist in drawing up a strategy. You may have met this before, but it is important enough to outline here before considering the specific case.

(a) *Mission.* Here one decides the basic business the organisation is in. It is expressed fairly broadly so as not to constrain subsequent thinking. It takes into account customer need, the organisation's distinctive competences and any basic history/philosophy that may have become integral to the organisation.

(b) *Objectives.* If asked to prepare a plan at any level you should specify objectives, and at least some of these should be quantified (eg sales, market share, percentage profit).

(c) *Analysis or audit.* This is the basis of any proposals and much of this analysis is to assist you in making such an audit (ie the selection of strategies and plans is left to you). Basically *internal factors* are considered (strengths and weaknesses) and *external factors* (opportunities and threats). Such an exercise is known as a SWOT analysis.

(d) *Strategy selection.* Your analysis has outlined your current position and prospects; your objectives have stated where you wish to be in the future. Your strategies will reflect the amount of change required if the organisation is to meet its objectives. If the current situation is very inadequate then a dramatic change is required; if it is slightly inadequate then slight changes may be required. Usually the greater change in direction the greater the risk

2.4 Ansoff specified some broad alternative strategies, most appropriate in growth situations, on the basis of a combination of existing or new products, or existing or new markets.

(a) *Existing product/existing market.* Market penetration
(b) *Existing product/new market.* Market development strategy
(c) *New product/existing market.* Product development strategy
(d) *New product/new market.* Diversification strategy

2.5 Porter proposed three alternative generic strategies.

(a) *Overall cost leadership.* A large market share tends to follow from this strategy.

(b) *Differentiation.* Differentiate the offering to offer some customer benefit eg style, quality, technology.

(c) *Focus* is really about market segments. Clearly identify those customers whom you can satisfy most effectively.

2.6 Critically Porter argues that an organisation must determine its generic strategy, its strengths within that strategy and outpoint its competitors in that area if it is to succeed.

Strategic considerations in this case

2.7 As Jim Converre, marketing director of Sentinel Aviation, reporting directly to the managing director you are in an influential position within that company. However, Sentinel is a small company with only 60 employees and is part of the much larger US conglomerate Omnicorp. Whilst the parent company sets ambitious objectives for you, it is not at all prescriptive about means of achieving these. Thus, creative thinking is left to you.

2.8 First of all there is much debate on *the business Sentinel is in.* You must consider this most carefully and whilst you may not be required to produce a mission statement as such you must have a very clear and justifiable recommendation in this area. At present in the very clearly defined executive jet and leisure aircraft market and with your limited portfolio you are one of the top five companies in the world; yet yours is a small company and there is a justifiable view that it is defining its role too narrowly. Questions are asked whether Sentinel is in the aircraft or IT business. Is it a Solutions company? One US aircraft company is selling systems to the construction industry.

2.9 There is clearly a view from the board to take a broad view of the business, but how broad? Texts remind us that firms must be aware of their core business. In section 2(a) of this analysis, Porter states that the generic strategy must identify the company's strengths and outpoint competition in that direction if it is to succeed. The mission will be broader than the strategy, but it must not be so broad as to be meaningless. This is a consideration which will inform your overall thinking and the strategies that you propose.

2.10 Whilst Omnicorp may not be prescriptive about business definitions and strategies it is very clear about objectives (this is not an unusual approach by parent companies). They seek a return on net assets of about 15-20%. You will be expected to achieve this and will have to produce very strong arguments if you wish to demonstrate that they are unrealistic. Whether objectives are unreasonable will be determined by your analysis. The analysis will also provide justification for many of your strategies and thus it is a very important exercise. Indeed it is possible that a specific question may ask for an analysis. If so, and indeed to help your general thinking, it is useful to use a framework for this, and a SWOT has already been mentioned. An alternative is a PEST analysis whereby one considers the political, economic, social and technological factors affecting the organisation. These are external issues and basically an expansion of the external/uncontrollable variables (opportunities/threats) within the SWOT.

2.11 Note that we do not provide a comprehensive SWOT or PEST within this analysis. Remember the examiner sees this document, and such a listing would not be in your best interest, but you must prepare a SWOT fully.

2.12 As a guide, however, strengths for Sentinel would be their quality product range and the existence of three aircraft divisions within Omnicorp; a weakness is the attitude/background of the sales force and distributors, rooted in the aircraft industry. A threat would be increasing competition due to the slack in the industry due to the reduced need for military aircraft, whilst many opportunities are mentioned providing you with opportunities for action.

2.13 The general tone of the case and the objectives set suggest that growth will be necessary, and therefore the Ansoff model may be most appropriate. Sentinel could consider greater penetration, with, for example, the Firstaid product, currently underperforming, or use the synergistic opportunities within existing markets; alternatively new markets may be sought. This may mean much greater effort within existing markets in the US and Europe. It may mean looking to the main commercial sector of the aircraft industry or to new industrial sectors altogether. The further the company moves from its existing markets, the more will this need to be matched with new products ie the diversification strategy with its attendant risks. Systems for control and monitoring would be examples here. Strategic issues are important in this case. You will certainly need to propose strategies within the framework of the mission selected. Only then can research and marketing mix elements be in any focused. Whilst we have outlined the issues in this section, decisions cannot be made until you have considered the various elements in the case more thoroughly in the following sections.

3 THE MARKET

General

3.1 Knowledge of the market is clearly important in any marketing plan. Only then can one determine the size of the market and the growth and share within that market that the Boston Consulting Group insists are vital for profitability. Yet, in practical terms to establish any of the above quantitatively it is essential that the market be clearly defined. This has not yet been done. We are told that in aviation electronics for the executive jet and leisure aircraft markets, Sentinel is one of the top five suppliers in the world, yet sales are only £4.25 million. On the other hand it is also stated that the world wide aviation electronics market is worth £425 million. Moreover Sentinel is considering venturing into industrial sectors other than aviation.

3.2 Decisions on the direction of Sentinel's business are clearly essential before attempting to quantify the market in any practical meaningful way. Also the traditional split in the market provided in the market research brief does not help clarify the situation. The four main sectors are said to be leisure, executive jet (commercial), light aircraft and defence. The leisure market covers all aircraft not *specifically* for commerce. They need not be jet aircraft. The executive jet/commerce market includes planes for individual companies and also small fleets of planes. The third grouping is light aircraft, and it is not clear how these differ from the two previous sectors, nor is it clear where the major commercial airlines and large jets fit into this scenario; why are they not specifically included here? To what extent do they use autopilots and chartplotters?

3.3 Apart from the world-wide aviation electronics market figure (£425 million) mentioned earlier, the only market data is for the UK, from the market research brief.

Market	*Size*	*Share*	*Sales*
		%	£'000
UK Leisure	£3.8m	20	760
Executive jet	£2.9m	8	230
			990

3.4 The OEM (original equipment manufacturers) market is also mentioned but neither the market nor Sentinel's penetration of the UK market seem to be known. We are told that OEMs account for 4% of all (world-wide) Sentinel's sales. Moreover within this case this term appears to incorporate component manufacturers but not the aircraft manufacturers themselves. The extent to which Sentinel sell direct to aircraft manufacturers is not at all clear, but we know they do and Mainstream is an example.

3.5 Another way to break down the market would be geographically. Again we have no market information but Sentinel's use of geographic segmentation indicates their approach.

Region	Share of sales	Sales £'000
UK	23	980
Europe	42	1,790
US	20	850
Rest	15	640

3.6 We are told that Sentinel operates in over 45 countries. Two of them (UK and US) account for 43% of sales (ie £1.830 million). Therefore the remaining £2.43 million is spread across 43 countries, averaging about £56,500 each. Given that we know four countries dominate Europe the average figure for the remaining 39 will be considerably lower.

3.7 Thus we have a very confused picture from the case of Sentinel's market, and this is probably intentional. The sectors of the aircraft industry provided are blurred and incomplete. Who the buyers are within each sector and the extent to which Sentinel deals with them at present is unclear. What is clear is that Sentinel's efforts are fragmented world-wide.

3.8 Thus it would appear that Sentinel's efforts are currently unfocused; in other words they are giving no attention to segmenting their markets. This will be something you must attend to if research and mix efforts are not to be squandered. The fact that Sentinel is considering moving to new markets makes this even more imperative. You may be given more information on the market in the examination. Regardless, some decision on market targets will need to be made and assumptions, based perhaps on inferences within the case, may be necessary.

Buyer behaviour

3.9 Within the market it is also important to understand the behaviour of individual buyers. Very generally, this will depend on the risk perceived by the buyer in the purchase, which will determine the amount of search/investigation to be undertaken. Thus a normal individual consumer for an important purchase will expect informative advertising, some testing/trial opportunity and reassurance from experts. Companies may not need much research for routine purchases, but when buying a new product or from a new source they rely heavily on relevant expertise within the firm and on committee decisions if the purchase is sufficiently important.

3.10 Sentinel appears to have some information on its most important leisure sector. Whilst lifestyle oriented and technologically knowledgeable we would expect buyers to be cautious in purchasing aircraft equipment, for example seeking advice from dealers. However increasingly price (rather than quality) is becoming a factor and purchase is through mail order. Possibly this reflects the confidence of the established buyer; will newcomers be as knowledgeable? The greater importance of mail order in the US is perhaps a reflection of the maturity of that market, and future if not present orientation of others.

3.11 Apart from customers of this type, Sentinel must clearly understand its *corporate buyers*. This will range from dealers and distributors to the manufacturers of aircraft. They are aiming to sell not just products but integrated systems which will be more complex and costly. The buying decision will be much more involved and the advertising agency suggests a close relationship with specific customers so that needs can be anticipated. This suggests *relationship marketing* of which you should have heard and careful selection of potential partners, given the time and investment necessary.

Part E: Learning from experience: ensuring you pass

Additional information

3.12 All the above points to the need for additional information. Sentinel is aware of this need and within the market research brief, various areas are listed for attention. These are a reliable guide but tend to consider *current* problems. Note that key additional information could be provided internally. Rapid analysis of sales data by product, market, and outlet type would give a much clearer overall picture and assist in the analysis of the mix elements mentioned in the brief.

3.13 It is clear, however, that Sentinel intends to expand by product and market. The market research agency appointed has a right to expert guidance in such investigations. From the information available you should be able to select options on which you seek further information before reaching a decision. Only then can the agency make progress and enable you to refine your thinking. The size, growth and competition within markets will be obtained largely from secondary data. Information on attitudes and buying decisions will require personal questioning. End users are relatively few, and therefore telephone surveys could be used. Alternatively researchers could go where customers are clustered (eg airfields), and conduct interviews or organise focus groups and the like. Interviews with companies could also be carried out by phone, but for some potentially critical customers open interviews with senior executives would seem advisable.

3.14 As Jim Converre is aware, there is a real lack of information within the firm. It seems important that you are aware of these gaps at least so that you can make sensible assumptions when proposing strategies. It could be, however, that a question on this appears in the examination and you should be able to detail the information you require (and why you require it) and in broad terms the way in which you expect it might be collected.

4 MARKETING MIX

Product

4.1 There are many issues associated with existing products in the range and potential new products. For convenience we shall treat these under a number of headings, but they are strongly interlinked.

Range

4.2 The company has its own backbone *autopilots*, which account for 40% of its sales. It is for these that it is well known, especially the 'Navigaid' autopilot which enjoys a very good reputation. Chartplotters account for 31% of the company's sales, under the name 'Chartwell'. These two groups of products are said in the case study to represent the widest *range* of their kind in the world. This leads us to consider is this range too wide? Is some rationalisation necessary? The range is certainly not matched by an equivalent success on a world wide scale, and it may be that product development has not been matched by attention to the development of segments of the markets. We do not have sufficient information in the case study to know if this is true, although we may strongly suspect it, especially as we are told on page one of the case study that the company has never before had a strategic or marketing plan.

4.3 The instrument portfolio under the name '*Firstaid*' accounts for 12% of sales, and covers most aircraft applications according to the press release on page six of the case study (Chapter 29, para 2.21), or most leisure applications according to page three of the case study (Chapter 29, para 2.3). Whichever it is, this group of products does not appear to be performing to potential. Its strengths, according to the memo of Hugo Black, manager of instrument sales are sophistication above its price, and therefore presumably good value for money, and that the range is broad. However, its weaknesses are that the design does not give a 'family' identity and image. The range of instruments seems to be confused with some very similar products with different names. Hugo Black blames design input and lack of investment for neglect by the sales force. If we combine lack of customer awareness with a confused product range and a lack of attention from the sales force, it is not surprising that this group of products disappoints in its performance. This does not mean that it does not have potential.

4.4 The picture of the three product groups so far is that it is one of a company struggling to break out of the success and good reputation for autopilots that has been established.

4.5 Given less space in the case study, but already accounting for 17% of turnover is the group of 'distributed' products. This, we assume, is made up mainly from products from other companies in the group, and includes hydraulic equipment, control systems, cables and radar equipment. This seems to be a group with a good potential, since these sales are likely to have developed only since the take-over by Omnicorp three years ago. Presumably this success is without realignment of sales, promotion or distribution arrangements to suit it, or the integration of the products of the two companies to produce complete systems. Future potential therefore looks good for this cross selling. Could the US parent do the same for the existing Sentinel products?

New product development

4.6 As Jim Converre said to Mike Flynn in the case study, there is a huge range of opportunities, and many of these might involve issues related to product development. However, the company cannot do everything, and great dangers could lie in trying, but the company must relate its specific product development to its product strategy, which in turn must be related to its overall strategy. The growth and profit targets mean that the company cannot be conservative, but the product strategy must be thought out. Thus, the memo from Jim Converre to the sales team about added value has within it evidence of both encouragement and dangers. It may encourage people to think about added value, it may help the sales force to feed back ideas for products that are market-led, but it is essentially ad hoc, whatever the merits or demerits of the ideas themselves, which do not appear to have gone through any rational system of appraisal.

4.7 Decisions on whether to develop particular products should be taken in the light of their role in the company's strategy and the other products in the range. The apparent need for rationalisation seems to indicate that this has not happened in the past. With the present emphasis on expansion, there is a danger that uncontrolled development will lead to a waste or resources and both overlap and gaps in the product range. The company has to manage to innovate and to screen out unsuitable ideas at the same time. You might consider an organisational new product development model that is some variant of the following

Product strategy
↓
Idea generation
↓
Assessment
↓
Business plans
↓
Development
↓
Testing
↓
Launch

4.8 The current lack of market information makes the formulation of product strategy difficult and the assessment of potential very difficult, but the implementation of the market research brief will help greatly.

4.9 The advertising agency presentation makes clear that their research indicates that aircraft manufacturers require integrated solutions and less and less a focus on individual components. This is a threat if the company continues only to develop individual products but it is an opportunity, in the sense that synergy is available between the combination of products from Sentinel and the parent to produce integrated systems, and these can be sold to the same end user using the same channels of distribution. Thus Omnicorp and Sentinel together can sell not just autopilots and steering systems, but a total solution that controls where the plane will fly. The opportunities here have to be balanced against using Sentinel's expertise and technology wherever it may be applied. Thus Sentinel *could* develop and sell GPS systems for automotive and marine applications, but it has no branding or distribution systems in place. This does not mean that these factors are insurmountable obstacles but they must be very seriously considered.

4.10 Many companies are so involved in day to day activities that they find it difficult to progress new ideas. This may be especially so in large companies, where politics and bureaucracy may block innovation. Many solutions have been proposed. One is *intrapreneurship* where a small sub group is formed within the company that will act like a small company and develop and launch products, which if successful then enter the normal portfolio. Another is the creation of *venture teams* which are typically interdisciplinary teams that work together on particular new ventures until they become established. In this case study, what is being advocated is a venture company, that would presumably be charged with creating innovation. Its advantage would be that it would be free from the constraints that would hamper innovation. Its disadvantage might be that it would not be likely to capitalise on the synergy possible (bringing together strengths within the group), and might be difficult to control.

Branding strategy and competition

4.11 The company at the moment has one well known brand, 'Navigaid', its best known autopilot. The company name is known for autopilots. Promotional efforts may be required to establish others, but before resources are allocated to this it is necessary to establish:

(a) is a group of products substantial enough to merit a separate brand?

(b) so particular market segments need to be sold brands with a separate image from others? If so what should it be?

(c) How far do the good associations of a strong brand travel to different products or different market segments?

4.12 Questions like these need to be answered before decisions are made, for example to try to differentiate instruments for the commercial/executive jet and leisure ranges as proposed in Hugo Black's memo.

4.13 The case study gives a profile of the most direct competitors. If we take the potential opportunities at their widest, then this misses out many and possibly powerful competitors, because these would be different outside the aviation business, and there is the potential for the company's technology to take in to land, sea or air. We shall consider the most direct competition first, and then consider the less direct aspects.

4.14 Roger Crichton's fax tells us that Swiftair and Eagle Electronics have 50% of the world market between them. This makes Sentinel's 1% look very insignificant, but these companies operate in segments in which Sentinel do not compete, so that the market share difference in the segments where they do compete is not likely to be as large as the difference between 1% and 50% would appear to show.

4.15 Swiftair operates in Europe, the Middle East and Africa. Its claimed share of 63% of the autopilot market makes it a market leader in that field, and its share of 38% in instruments probably makes it market leader there. It is instructive therefore to compare its product range and branding policy with that of Sentinel. Sentinel makes eight different systems of autopilot, but Swiftair's Autosteer has only three. Autosteer has three different chartplotters against Sentinel's six. Swiftair's Pantheon brand name has one autopilot, one chartplotter and one instrument system. Swiftair's Autosteer is targeted towards the leisure market, whilst Pantheon is directed at the executive jet market. Pantheon targets executive jets, but also large aircraft. There seems to be a clear lesson here - branding directed towards market sector rather than product type seems to be effective, and coverage of a large part of the market seems to be possible with a smaller range of products than that of Sentinel. Hugo Black's memo to Jim Converre about instruments seems to back this up.

4.16 Given the substantial market share held by Sentinel in the UK, and the overall high share of Swiftair, it is likely that Swiftair has a very strong position in Europe. Some potential chinks in Swiftair's armour are that its proposed distributor rationalisation may cause some disquiet amongst its customers, and trying to impose a secondary overall corporate branding may dilute the brand strengths it already has.

4.17 Whereas Swiftair is strong in Europe, Eagle is strong in the USA. Its acquisition policy, with many brand names, has caused confusion, but its present policy of trying to regroup everything under the Eagle name means the loss of some existing well respected names, and therefore an opportunity for Sentinel.

4.18 Navigator has succeeded on a strategy of focusing on a particular market (leisure) with autopilots and VHF ratios, and promoting them heavily. This is different from the broad based approach of Swiftair and Eagle. Its new foray into instruments may reduce its narrow focus somewhat, but it still seems to be concentrating on the leisure sector.

4.19 Breen has suffered by concentrating on a declining market, the luxury market. They are now trying to position themselves as a value for money provider (who is, however, expensive) and have tried to make sales for light aircraft, and sell jet fighter technology with little success. Given this company's past history of being on the verge of bankruptcy, it now appears to be extremely vulnerable.

4.20 Given the large numbers of competitors listed in the fax, the rest of the industry appears to be extremely fragmented. There is one source of competition not mentioned in that fax. These are the systems integrators, who put together a range of products and software to offer complete solutions. They do not necessarily manufacture any of the individual elements of the system themselves. If they go on to achieve greater success, companies like Sentinel will have opportunities to supply them, but with little power, and therefore their products will have to sell on price, since the final buyer will not be interested in the source of the component parts themselves. If Sentinel counter this threat by producing integrated systems, as they are capable of doing, especially with the synergy achievable through Omnicorp, then they will have to be good systems integrators themselves, providing a good service to their customers by understanding their needs.

Price

4.21 Not only has Omnicorp given ambitious targets for the growth in turnover, there are also ambitious targets for profitability at 15% to 20% return on net assets, a level that Sentinel has not managed to achieve to date. This means that market share cannot be 'bought' by low prices, and price wars have to be avoided at all costs. A low price strategy is usually only feasible through low costs, which typically means high volumes and standardisation, neither of which reflects the current situation of the company.

4.22 High market share can be achieved with higher than average prices - the market leader in most markets is not the lowest priced provider. How can low prices be avoided? One route is quality and performance. Here Sentinel have an advantage in 'Navigaid', considered to be the finest autopilot in the market, and where customers appear often to regard it as such. Quality on its own is not enough - the market has to recognise it as such, and the mechanism of this identity is normally through powerful brands. Here Sentinel seem to have a problem for its products other than autopilots since the agency research provided in its presentation indicates very a low awareness of these products in the Sentinel range.

4.23 In John Harcourt's (financial director) memo to Jim Converre on pricing, he says that the level of prices is tailored to keep prices at or below competitors, and below psychological price barriers. This seems to be a mistake, since for the 'Navigaid' range at least, its quality and reputation ought to allow the charging of a premium price. Depending on the brand policy chosen, this might eventually feed through to help the other products in the range. It is likely, however, that price competition is likely to continue to be strong in the American market due to competition, but to offset that, higher volumes are possible, and if the company can manage to differentiate its products enough, it might still be possible to charge a premium over some competitors.

4.24 If Hugo Black is correct in his memo about instruments, then this is a much more sophisticated product than competitors' at a similar price. This ought to allow for a very strong competitive position, or for the company to charge higher prices for these products than it does. What appears to prevent this is lack of identity - some customers think the products are not made by Sentinel, and the lack of standard appearance and good design. If these things can be put right, the problems involved in pricing will ease.

4.25 If a client can be provided with a complete answer to a problem, through the combination of several products and appropriate software, then the price of the individual components will not be important. Here the increasing availability of complementary products from the Omnicorp range can be utilised, if the company can organise to combine them in integrated solutions for clients, well promoted and branded with adequate distribution, sales input and after sales service.

4.26 The globalisation of the market, and the opportunity to provide system made up from various parts of the Omnicorp group raises the issue of transfer pricing (prices for goods transferred from one company to another within the group). Often companies will try to make charges in such a way as to lower the overall tax liability, but care then has to be taken in interpreting data on profitability of parts of the group.

Distribution

General

4.27 A company uses intermediaries to distribute its products who typically carry out a number of functions. Typically distributors and retailers will hold stock, break large bulk orders down, will sell, promote, provide information and perhaps after sales service. They therefore are effectively carrying out some marketing activities on a subcontracting basis, in return for the percentage mark-up they make on the products sold. Despite this mark-up, it may be more economic to distribute this way rather than direct to the customer, as the facilities and the costs of the dealer can be shared by the sales of a number of suppliers. Thus a manufacturer might sell direct to the largest customers, but indirect to others.

4.28 An intensive distributions system represents a situation where the manufacturer obtains as many outlets as possible, on the basis that the final customer is not willing to travel to gain the product they want and maximum convenience is the goal. On the other hand, a selective distribution policy is one where the manufacturer limits the outlets to those that have the right image or competence, or to those who will buy in big enough quantities in relation to the cost of supplying with them and dealing with them. In either case, there needs to be dealers available where customers want to buy, providing a good quality of service.

UK distribution

4.29 In the UK, Sentinel sell either direct to the customer, or to dealers. One group of dealers, Corby, accounts for 18% of UK business, the rest going through over 50 dealers with an average turnover for Sentinel of £5,000. Order size is also said to be low. This could mean that there are too many small dealers, costing too much to service, and creating difficulties in supporting them so that they can provide the right kind of service. The presentation of Jim Converre to the sales force recognises that there has been in the past problems of dealers having inadequate product knowledge, and a programme of training and technical support is being arranged to overcome this. A question is whether all dealers provide enough business to justify this investment in them.

4.30 We have enough information in the case study to calculate an approximation of how much of the UK turnover goes direct to customers and how much goes through dealers. Corby account for 18% of UK dealer sales. The rest, therefore, account for 82% of dealer sales. There are over 50 dealers, each with an average turnover of £5,000 per annum. If we assume just 50 dealers, this total comes to 50 × 5,000 ie £250,000. Total UK dealer sales are therefore 100/82 × £250,000 ie £304,878. We know that the whole UK sales for Sentinel are 23% of their world sales of £4.25 million, ie £977,500. Thus, in the UK more than two thirds of sales are direct to the customers. Is the company geared up to this sector, or is it more dealer oriented?

Europe

4.31 Outside the UK, the company has a three tier system, reaching dealers through distributors. Of the four main European markets of France, Italy, Germany and Spain, we are told that in two of them, France and Germany, there have been problems with continuity, presumably retaining particular dealers or distributors. An anomaly is that the majority of aircraft building takes place in Holland, Scandinavia and France. The first two of these are not major markets. Does this mean that there are distribution problems in Holland and Scandinavia that prevent adequate coverage for Sentinel?

4.32 Jim Converre's memo to George Jenkins, the distribution manager, points out that Swiftair are poised to jettison 15% of their dealerships. Since Swiftair are particularly strong in Europe, this represents and opportunity to fill gaps in the European distribution system. Great care is required however. If any of these dealers are taken on, it will be important to avoid those who are unsatisfactory. It would also be wise to avoid those who would simply duplicate existing provision, possibly making it difficult for existing and new distributors to provide a good service.

Distribution in the USA

4.33 Sentinel appears to be underperforming in the US market, which is possibly the most important in the world. A slight change in market share here could have major effects. The US distributor, Sentinel US is owned by the group, reporting to Omnicorp, and is a successful business. Despite this, Sentinel does not account for a major part of Sentinel US' business. The reason is unknown, but priority should be given to finding out. It could be that Sentinel are not providing some aspect of product or service for the very competitive US market, or not providing sufficient promotional support. On the other hand, for some reason Sentinel US may be neglecting Sentinel's product range. The main dealer, Aerotec is taking 14% of the US turnover, ie £117,600. If more dealers like that could be provided by Sentinel US, a major improvement would result.

Promotion

4.34 It is necessary for us here to deal with separate elements of the promotional mix - advertising, personal selling, public relations etc. It is important, however, to keep in mind that they are all part of an effort in marketing communications, and that they must blend together in achieving strategic objectives. This means that communications objectives must be defined for clearly established target markets.

Advertising and public relations

4.35 Advertising expenditure in the company appears to be about to increase substantially. Present expenditure is 5% of sales, and in Jim Converre's presentation to the sales force, we are told that this will rise to between seven and eight per cent of turnover. If sales projections are correct, this will lead to a very big increase in expenditure, since the increased percentage will be of a greater amount. Thus, at the present time, the advertising budget will be 5% of 1996 turnover of £4.25 million, which is £212,500. At (say) 7.5% of the 1997 turnover of £5.44 million the budget will be £408,000. In the same way, by the year 2000 it will be £752,250. We see in the case study that the Navigator company has spent heavily on promotion, and this seems to have paid off. On this basis prospects look good.

4.36 There is, however, strong evidence in the case study that both the advertising and the public relations efforts are reactive rather than fitting in with any strategy. Brian Darrowby-Greene's memo requesting authorisation of an advertisement to support Mainstream may be justifiable as supporting an important customer, but it is an examples of the lack of a planned approach to the use of advertising resources. Similarly reacting to a press enquiry with an information pack will achieve something, but there is no evidence of planned PR activities to support the marketing strategy of the company.

4.37 The presentation by the advertising agency, Summers Associates does not recommend a media strategy or present any creative ideas, but it is to be commended for fundamental questions about the business that need to e answered before a logical campaign can be planned.

4.38 Once main strategic issues such as branding policy have been established, and the nature of the distribution network established, communications tasks can be defined, and market targets identified. After that, the media and the message can be clearly and logically worked out. We know that there is a very good reputation for 'Navigaid' autopilots, but the image of the instruments range is confused, and the agency research shows that customers could not name any Sentinel product other than autopilots.

4.39 Jim Converre's statement to the sales force about advertising expenditure is conditional, in that it is subject to an effective means being developed to assess advertising effectiveness. This is always difficult, but methods could include awareness measures, measures of response - eg coupon return for more information or for a salesman to call. Similar measures could be used for the direct marketing advocated by the advertising agency, especially for measures dealing with response. What would be hardest of all would be to attribute specific amounts of sales to the advertising.

Personal selling

4.40 In industrial markets such as those in which Sentinel operate, personal selling typically takes up a very important role in the promotional mix. There are many reasons for this, such as the variety and complexity of organisational buying behaviour, the need to convey information both to and from customers, and the size of individual orders justifying selling cost.

4.41 Although the case study tells us (page 15 of the case Chapter 29 para 2.46) that substantial change is anticipated in responsibility eg territory change and some people moving from OEM to dealer support, we know very little of the sales force deployment. We are told that it regionally based, although we cannot be sure whether this means simply within the UK, or on an international basis.

4.42 The organisation chart on page two (Chapter 29, para 2.2) of the case study gives us something of a clue. There are two account managers, one dedicated to the Mainstream company, an aircraft manufacturer. These two account managers may be the sum total of aircraft manufacturer support. If this is the case is it wise? We have already seen that it looks as though aircraft manufacturers represent the biggest sector for Sentinel, at least in the UK. There is an impression that the main thrust of the sales force is in contact with dealers, but we cannot be absolutely sure of this. If this is the case, it would explain why aircraft manufacturing centres in Scandinavia and Holland are not major markets. If this is so major potential is being missed. The possibility is that buyers buy globally, but Sentinel only sell locally.

4.43 We are aware from Jim Converre's presentation to the sales force that he is aware of the importance of keeping it well motivated, and indeed we can see that the sales force's lack of enthusiasm for the instrument range has helped to deny it success. It is easy to assume that simply creating payment schemes with a high proportion of commission will solve the problem. This is rarely the case, and where business takes some time to be established, and where teamwork is required, high commission can create more problems through fostering a short term mentality than are solved. Some financial incentives such as bonuses or modest commission are possible, but they should be used with care.

4.44 It is clear that education and training will be required. We know from the reaction to the 'Good Old Days' presentation that some of the most experienced personnel do not have a concept of the business in tune with current and future conditions, and retain a company culture from a bygone age. It is also clear that if the sales force is going to be reorganised and duties changed there will be a need for training. This need will be even greater, if products are sold that come from a combination of hardware and software from a range of sources in the group, sold as a system solution.

Exhibitions

4.45 Little mention is made of exhibitions, and presumably the company is represented at the most important of these. If the company spreads its effort outside the aviation industry, then it policy concerning which exhibitions to use will have to be reviewed.

5 ORGANISATION

5.1 Sentinel's organisation structure is shown on page 2 of the case (Chapter 29 para 2.2, chart ref). It looks hierarchical, and there seem to be clear reporting relationships. The established dictum that 'structure follows strategy' however, suggests that even if the organisation is logical at present, it may not be so when rapid expansion has taken place through implementation of the new strategies that you propose. Is the structure logical at present? Certainly there are questions you may ask.

5.2 Typically a marketing department might be organised on product or brand lines where every product has a champion to look after its interest; this structure lends itself to the criticism that it appears to lack market orientation. An alternative is a market structure where managers are organised by some customer base (eg industry or country). Neither system is perfect, but at least there is clarity. Sentinel appears to be falling between these two models.

5.3 Reporting to Jim Converre is Hugo Black, the manager for instrument sales; where are the managers for the other three groups within the portfolio? Why should the product development manager report to Hugo Black? What exactly is the role of the distribution manager? Does he really organise promotion/sales? The two account managers presumably sell to major accounts (eg Mainstream) and in that sense are market based; have they any interest in the strategic development of products? Why does the publicity officer report to one of them? What does the *regional* sales team mean - UK only? There appears to be no one with a specific overseas interest at present.

5.4 You will need to think through a more appropriate structure for Sentinel. It would appear that there should be managers for product groupings. Possibly sales/distribution could look after broad groupings of customers. Sales persons in technical companies such as this should naturally take an interest in customer needs and product features and feed back valuable information to the firm. Distributors of course will continue to work with the sales force and training of both will be necessary.

5.5 What of the service activities such as research and promotion? Should they be incorporated into a marketing support limb? What of product development and the ventures company if floated? If there is to be a stronger link with Omnicorp this may need to be acknowledged.

5.6 Whatever structure you propose you must be aware of the rapid change which will overtake the company. Conferences and training will be necessary and the structure must be flexible to take on new tasks and problems. This in turn leads to its own management problems however. The difficulties of the rapid growth and change of culture being proposed must not be underestimated.

6 FINANCIAL ANALYSIS

6.1 Students are constantly reminded by examiners that they must show an awareness of the financial implications of their proposals, even when little information is given. In this case a fair amount of financial data is given and more can be inferred. This will be considered here. Students should try to understand this and it will add confidence to planning proposals. Certainly they must note the conclusion drawn. The main source of data is the financial forecast on page 29 (Chapter 29, para 2.66) and by inference this can be considerably expanded. For example, sales figures are given and therefore from the percentage profit figures actual figures for gross profit and operating profit (ie net profit excluding interest and tax, and extraordinary items) can be calculated. This allows us to distinguish between the cost of preparing the goods for sale and the costs of marketing/administration.

OUTLINE PROFIT AND LOSS ACCOUNT

	1994	1995	1996	1997E	1998E	1999E	2000E
Sales	2,601	3,230	4,250	5,440	6,800	8,330	10,030
Cost of goods sold (COGS)	1,769	2,381	3,000	4,047	4,692	5,498	6,820
Gross profit	832	849	1,250	1,393	2,108	2,832	3,210
Marketing/admin costs	715	742	600	1,121	1,732	1,832	1,806
Operating profit	117	107	650	272	476	1,000	1,404
Advertising cost			213	408	510	625	752
Advertising % sales			(5%)	(7.5%)			

6.2 The advertising budget shown earlier is shown here to relate it to the overall marketing/administration budget. Assuming the sales force falls within the marketing/administration cost, is the balance reasonable?

6.3 When considering financial accounts, ratios are often used for comparison purposes (eg overtime). These are used in the financial forecasts provided (eg percentage profit, debtors/creditors days). The main objective set for Sentinel is also a ratio, return on net assets (RONA) which is calculated as follows.

$$\frac{\text{Operating profit}}{\text{Net assets, ie Total assets - current liabilities}} \times 100$$

6.4 One benefit of considering RONA is that it indicates the return on the long term funding committed to the firm. Consider that if in a balance sheet total assets = total liabilities (shareholder equity + long term loan + current liabilities), the deduction of current liabilities from each side will leave equivalent amounts: therefore net assets as defined will equate to equity + long term loan - or long term funding. Now since we have the percentage RONA and the operating profit, the net assets can be calculated for each year indicating funding needs.

$$\frac{\text{Operating profit}}{\text{Net assets}} \times 100 = \text{RONA}$$

Therefore operating profit $\times \dfrac{100}{\text{RONA}}$ = net assets

Thus consider 1995: $107 \times \dfrac{100}{3.9} = £2,743\text{m}$

The net assets for 1995 = £2.743m

The net assets for each year can be similarly calculated giving:

	Net assets	Asset utilisation ratio
	(£'000)	
1994	2,854	0.91
1995	2,743	1.18
1996	6,250	0.63
1997E	3,400	1.60
1998E	-	-
1999E	-	-
2000E	9,360 (15% RONA assumed)	1.07
	7,020 (20% RONA assumed)	1.43

Having calculated the net assets another major ratio can now be established, the asset utilisation ratio = $\dfrac{\text{Turnover}}{\text{Net assets}}$

This demonstrates the efficiency of asset use and for 1995 is $\dfrac{3{,}230}{2{,}743} = 1.18$

6.5 Other years are shown in the table above. What does it tell us? Firstly that the chosen ratio for objectives (RONA) is a function of two other ratios, return on sales, and the asset utilisation ratio. This can be demonstrated if we show the ratios as follows.

$$\dfrac{\text{Profit}}{\text{Sales}} \times \dfrac{\text{Sales}}{\text{Assets}} = \dfrac{\text{Profit}}{\text{Assets}}$$

Thus for return on sales the control of all costs, not just marketing costs, are important. For the asset utilisation ratio control of assets (including stock, debtors and creditors) is vital. Whilst marketing has a key role in hitting sales targets, managers in other functional areas also have responsibility for hitting RONA targets. Also higher profits frequently need more assets, and therefore funding from somewhere. The year 1996 is a year with good profitability on high turnover, but poor use of the additional assets (asset utilisation ratio). Therefore a large increase in assets was required to achieve that increased turnover. The relationship is clearer for 2000, when two possible figures for RONA have been used. The higher RONA (20%) results from better asset utilisation and therefore requires lower net assets and funding. Of course if Sentinel failed to achieve even the 15% RONA (and this could be because it misses turnover or targets for percentage operating profit) then an even higher level of net assets will be required and there will be more concern on long term funding.

6.6 Another issue that students must consider is *liquidity*. The relevant ratio here is the current ratio, ie

$$\dfrac{\text{Current assets}}{\text{Current liabilities}}$$

The information we have is not complete but we have the information on the most important items (Current assets: stock and debtors, Current liabilities: creditors). What alerts us to a potential problem is the proposed very rapid fall in inventory levels in the future. (To date these levels have been excessive, but to achieve the new figures will be a major challenge to Sentinel, both in the production and sales process. Are distributors being asked to carry larger stocks?) If inventory levels fall, the current ratios must fall. Perhaps this needs further investigation.

6.7 What is required is a figure for debtors and for creditors. Now the ratio to calculate debtors days is:

$$\dfrac{\text{Debtors}}{\text{Sales}} \times 365 = \text{debtors days}$$

This can be adapted to:

$$\text{Sales} \times \dfrac{\text{Debtors days}}{365} = \text{debtors}$$

eg 1995: $3{,}230 \times \dfrac{78}{365} = £690{,}000$

6.8 Creditors are calculated similarly except that as they are involved in purchases (cost price) cost of goods sold (COGS) is more appropriate.

$$\dfrac{\text{Creditors}}{\text{COGS}} \times 365 \text{ days} = \text{creditor days}$$

$$\text{COGS} \times \dfrac{\text{Creditor days}}{365} = \text{creditors}$$

Again take 1995:

$$2{,}381 \times \dfrac{142}{365} = £926{,}000$$

We can thus provide a guide to liquidity.

	1994	1995	1996	1997	1998	1999	2000
Current assets							
Stock	450	1,100	780	1,200	600	500	650
Debtors	356	690	1,164	968	1,210	1,483	1,786
Current liabilities							
Creditors	232	926	756	643	1,092	1,280	1,588
Current ratio	3.5	1.9	2.6	3.4	1.7	1.5	1.5

Note. Level of days is assumed at 1997 level for three future years.

6.9 In the past, liquidity has probably been too high due to poor credit and inventory control. If one accepts a desirable current ratio of 2:1 and that inventory target will be met then there is some cause for concern. However for the three future years a ratio of 1.5 is not disastrous, (remember we have no cash figures) and if necessary reducing the number of creditor days from 85 to 65 will resolve the position and restore the ratio to 2:1.

6.10 In summary, the main conclusions from the above are as follows.

(a) Whilst the normal measure of marketing efficiency is a variant of profit/sales, to translate this to return on net assets, the asset utilisation ratio is also a crucial consideration. Many elements impact on these ratios, not just marketing performance.

(b) Other things being equal a higher level of operating profit will require a higher level of funding. The availability of such funds from Omnicorp or elsewhere might influence the objectives proposed.

(c) Whilst there is a threat of liquidity problems, this does not seem too serious, and should be controllable.

(d) Advertising expenditure has traditionally been a high proportion of the marketing budget.

7 PLANNING CONSIDERATIONS

7.1 It seems likely that you will have to make a variety of recommendations within the examination on elements such as the Marketing Mix, but the key planning issue is undoubtedly proposing a strategic marketing plan. There is much information missing and how formal these plans can be in a relatively short time (eg for Ed Quorn's visit next month) is debatable. However you must carefully have considered your SWOT and more market information may be available in the examination. You certainly should have selected options and listed pros and cons of each and then would be wise to devise more detailed plans for the most promising.

33: Consultants' analysis of Sentinel Aviation

7.2 Mike Flynn has just returned with the latest detailed figures from America. These are agreed but surprisingly the RONA objective seems vague at 15 - 20%. The forecast is until 2000, with a turnover of £10,030m in that year. Yet he adds that the Americans 'really want' Sentinel to be a £25m pa subsidiary within five years. As four years are estimated in the forecast plan, is he talking of the year 2001, or does he mean within five years from the end of that plan (ie 2005)? There seems to be a need for a clear assumption from you or some scope for your own proposals.

7.3 Certainly the growth within the plan does not seem excessive merely reflecting the growth since Omnicorp took over the company three years ago.

	1994	1995	1996	1997E	1998E	1999E	2000E
	£'000	£'000	£'000	£'000	£'000	£'000	£'000
Turnover	2,601	3,230	4,250	5,440	6,800	8,330	10,030
Growth %		24	32	28	25	32	20

7.4 Mike Flynn seems to envisage a 10% growth if Sentinel stays within current markets. This indicates how much he believes might come from new business.

	1996	1997	1998	1999	2000
	£'000	£'000	£'000	£'000	£'000
Turnover	4,250	5,440	6,800	8,330	10,030
Current markets + 10%		4,675	5,143	5,656	6,222
New ventures		765	1,657	2,674	3,808

7.5 Of course this is merely his opinion and you may believe that correct strategic management may allow you to grow faster than this in your current markets. There are products within the portfolio which are underperforming and regions exploited. Strategic thinking allied to reorganisation of mix elements could meet forecast requirements. Then you could please the Americans by moving towards the £25 million target with new developments.

7.6 You will probably wish to break down sales within your plan in more detail to reflect your proposed developments. Do not become involved in *too* much detail, however. Remember the *funding* developments of your plans, but again over involvement in figures should not be necessary.

7.7 Another important factor to remember when devising plans is timescale. The financial forecasts remind you of this but remember you are about to propose plans to achieve targets. This may mean that you have to adjust the rate of development initially, possibly exceeding the targets set eventually to satisfy the Americans.

7.8 For example, initially you have little information. How long will it take to appoint an agency and obtain information? It would be foolish to progress too far without this. You must revise your product portfolio. Then you need to reorganise and match strategies, retrain and recruit to the sales force. The advertising agency needs to start establishing brands. You will not stagnate initially, but all forecasts seem to envisage a steady rate of growth at present. You may expect greater acceleration from a more stable base.

7.9 Generally in this section you are being reminded that after all the analysis from this document you will need to be considering proposals and putting some figures to them. Here we have been discussing mainly the strategic plan but this can be expanded to other areas. What is your promotion budget? How will it be split by media? What balance of business is to go through distributors? How many people do you need in the sales force and of what type?

7.10 You may not be able to use all the quantitative data you have considered from the last two sections in a formal plan, but instead incorporate them into alternative answers, and the degree of precision you have incorporated should increase your confidence considerably. However, remember that it is the quality of your thought and the justification of your proposals which will determine your success or otherwise in the examination.

8 FOOD FOR THOUGHT

8.1 Are you prepared to make an analysis of Sentinel Aviation's position making sensible assumptions or incorporating additional information provided in the examination?

8.2 Have you prepared a list of options and are you able to argue for and against each? You should develop strategic plans for the most promising to give yourself some flexibility. The examiner does not always give you an open ended choice on which to develop/launch. You should be able to argue a broad case for penetration versus diversification.

8.3 Have you decided on market targets? Where will your emphasis be by country, by industry, via middlemen or direct?

8.4 Have you listed all the gaps in information which Sentinel needs to fill? Are you clear how this information assists proposed strategies? How would you collect it?

8.5 Using the quantitative data in the case can you draw up a time phased and quantitative strategic plan? Can you provide quantitative support for your mix plans?

8.6 What reorganisation is necessary for company personnel to implement your proposed strategy? How would you change the culture of the company?

8.7 It appears that an increased advertising budget is to be available. Can you create advertising objectives? How would you evaluate the effectiveness of the advertising expenditure? Who would be your principal targets?

8.8 How would your product range fit into your strategic plan? What should the main direction of new product development be? What would your branding policy be?

8.9 Can you avoid competing mainly on price, and if so, how?

8.10 Given your objectives and target markets, will your distribution arrangements be appropriate? If not, how will you change them?

8.11 Have you decided how to allocate the efforts of the sales force, for example across the product range and between distributors and dealers and direct to large customers such as plane manufacturers? Have you made arrangements for recruitment, training and motivation? Do you need any special arrangements for overseas sales?

GOOD LUCK!

Index

Index

This index covers Chapters 1 to 11 only

7 S framework, 176

ABC circulation, 113
Absorption costing, 161
Accounts or billing department, 104
Acid test ratio, 153
Acruals, 145
Additional information, 189
Advertiser, 103
Advertising, 82
   agency, 103
   budget, 31, 85
   content, 94
   decisions, 85
   objectives, 85, 100
   Standards Authority (ASA), 95
   strategy, 99
Ansoff matrix, 41, 44
Assets, 143
Audit Bureau of Circulations (ABC), 113
Avoidable costs, 164

Balance of Payments, 121
Balance sheet, 143
Banded offers, 88
BARB, 113
Basic approach to a case study, 202
Behaviour observation, 63
Benefits, 50
Boston Matrix, 42
BRAD, 113
Brainstorming, 53
Brand, 114, 143
   management, 177
   mark, 114
   name, 114
British Code of Advertising Practice (BCAP), 95
British Code of Sales Promotion Practice (BCSPP, 1982), 96
British Rate and Data (BRAD), 113
Broad aims, 213
Broadcasters' Audience Research Board (BARB), 113
Broadcasting Acts, 94, 95
Budgets, 30
Budget period, 26
Budget process, 26
Business schools, 60
Buyers, 35
   intentions, 21
Buying behaviour analysis, 34

Campaign planning, 97
Candidates' brief, 190, 204
Candidates' notes, 190
Case study examination role, 185
Case study method of learning, 185
Case study rationale, 192
Cash flow forecasting, 167
Cash flow statement, 147
Cinema, 94
Clearing banks, 136
Commission rebating, 107
Communications research, 116
Comparative advantage, 121
Comparative advertising, 96
Competitions (sales promotion), 89
Competitive strategies, 46
Competitor audit, 8
Competitor response, 47
Complaints files, 52
Conflicting accounts, 105
Consistency, 213
Consumer panels, 59, 68
Contract manufacturing, 132
Contribution, 160
   analysis, 25
Control, 55
Controllable costs, 162
Copyright, 114
Corporate identity, 75
Corporate management, 6
Corporate objectives, 5, 6
Corporate plan, 22
Corporate public relations, 75
Cost, 24
   centre, 155
   leadership, 46
   plus pricing, 158
   ratios, 26
Cravens and Lamb, 199
Creative team, 104
Creditor turnover, 153
Critical success factors, 43
Culture, 177
   differences affecting marketing, 125
Current ratio, 153
Customer audit, 8

Debtor turnover, 153
Deciders, 35
Decision making, 158, 162
   unit (DMU), 35
Decisions, 193
Decline, 40
Depreciation, 145
Derived demand, 179
Diagrams, 234
Differential cost, 164

Index

Differentiation, 46
Diffusion of innovation, 36
Direct mail, 90
Directional policy matrix, 44
Discounted cash flow, 164
Distribution, 24, 49, 131
   budget, 31
   strategies, 129
DTI, 60
Dumping policies, 30
Dupont, 78

Easton, 200
Economic factors, 16, 127, 128
Edge and Coleman, 200
Environmental audit, 8
Europa Yearbook, 136
Expense budgets related to marketing, 30
Experimentation, 47
Export facilitating agencies, 135
External variables, 11

Fair Trading Act 1973, 93
False trade description, 93
Feasibility studies, 170
Field surveys, 60
Financial implications checklist, 169
Financial ratios, 154
Fixed costs, 25
Fixed element, 159
Focus, 46
Follow the leader strategy, 46
Forecast, 167
Forecasting, 19
   techniques, 20
Franchising, 132
Functional budget, 27
Further research, 194

Gap Analysis, 42
Gate keepers, 36
Gearing, 152, 154
Generic competitive strategies, 46
Gross profit, 146
   percentage, 151
Group interview, 62
Guidance Notes, 191

Historical cost, 143
Hoover, 93

Ideas for new products, 52
Implementation and control, 54
Important notes, 204
Incremental costs, 164

Industrial (business to business) marketing, 178
Inflation, 156
Influencers, 35
Information specification, 56
Integration of marketing communications, 76
Internal communication, 117
Internal marketing, 174, 176
International division, 139
International market entry, 129
International marketing, 120
   mix, 128
   planning and control, 137
   research, 134
International pricing, 128
Investment centre, 155
ITC (Independent Television Commission), 95

JICNARS, 113
JICPAR, 114
Joint Industry Committees or JIC's, 113
Joint venture, 132

Key issues, 212
Knocking-copy, 96

Legal factors, 15
   and promotion, 93
Legal requirements, 128
Liabilities, 143
Licensing, 131
Liquidity ratios, 153
Long-term decision making, 164

Manager's role, 4
Marginal cost, 160, 162
Market follower strategy, 46
Market leader, 46
Market research, 53, 56
   agency, 63
   report, 65
Market structure analysis, 34
Marketing, 4
   and TQM, 175
   audit, 9
   budgets, 23
   communications strategy, 74
   costs, 31
   information system (MkIS), 8, 68, 56
   mix, 47
   myopia, 172
   objectives, 5
   orientation, 175
   plan, 4, 9

Marketing research, 8, 56
   agencies and consultants, 60
   data, 58
   programme, 65
Master budget, 28
Matching principle, 145
'Me too' strategy is, 46
Media
   buying, 102
   decisions, 85
   independent, 110
   independents, 110
   owner, 108
   planner, 104
   research, 112
   scheduling, 86
   selection, 99
Message, 97
   decisions, 85
Midgeley and Wills, 40
Mini cases, 197
Mission statement, 33, 212
Mode of entry, 129, 133

Net profit percentage, 151
New product development (NPD), 39, 52
Newspapers, 32
Non-legal constraints on promotion, 92
Non-tariff barriers, 123

Objectives of the case study, 201
Observational methods, 63
Off-price labels, 88
Omnibus surveys, 59
Opportunity costs, 164
OSCAR (Outdoor Site Classification and Audience Research), 114
Overseas production, 131
Overseas sales office, 131

Panel, 62
Participant observation, 63
Passenger counts, 63
People, 51
Periodicals, 59
Personal interview, 60
Personal selling, 82
Personality promotions, 89
PEST, 15
Physical evidence, 52
Piercy, 8
PIMS Data Base, 43
Planning and Control exam, 3
Political factors, 16, 126, 129
Porter, 46
Postal or mail survey, 61

Posters, 94
Précis, 205
Premium offers, 88
Prepayment, 145
Press, 94
Pre-testing, 100
Price earnings ratio, 154
Pricing, 48
Principal budget factor, 27
Process, 51
Product, 48
   life cycle (PLC), 37
   portfolio analysis, 8
Productivity analysis, 18
Profit, 146
   loss account, 145
   centre, 155
Progress or traffic department, 104
Promotion, 48, 54
   mix, 78, 81
   strategies, 129
Psychographic segmentation, 36
Public relations, 91
Publicity, 82, 91
Pull and push promotional strategies, 82, 91

Quality circles, 52
Question design, 192
Quick ratio, 153

Radio, 32, 94
RAJAR (Radio Joint Audience Research), 114
Ratio analysis, 18, 150
Rationale of case study, 201
Relationship marketing, 172
Report style, 234
Research and development budget, 31
Respondent, 60
Response rates, 62
Responsibility centre, 155
Retail audits, 59, 66
Retained profit, 146
Return on capital employed, 151
Risk, 170
Role of case study, 205
Rolling budget, 27

Sales budget, 28
Sales decisions, 84
Sales force, 53, 84
   opinion, 20
Sales forecast, 8
Sales promotion, 82, 86
   budget, 31

Index

tasks, 88
   in current use, 88
Sales quantity budget, 28
Sales revenue budget, 28
Scaling techniques, 53
Schedule improvement, 102
Screening, 53
Segmental productivity analysis, 155
Segmental reporting, 146
Segmentation, 173
   analysis, 36
   variables, 36
Selecting an agency, 104
Selling decisions, 84
Selling expenses budget, 30
Services, 49, 177
Shared cost/syndicated research, 59
Short term such decisions, 158
Situational analysis, 210
SLEPT, 15
Socio-cultural trends, 15, 128
Sources of finance, 169
Stakeholders, 6, 33, 212
   roles, 187
Stepped fixed costs, 159
Stock, 145
   audits, 63
   turnover, 152
Strategic evaluation, 43
Strategy, 7
Sunk costs, 164
Supply of Goods (Implied Terms) Act 1973, 93
SWOT analysis, 17, 207
Syndicate groups, 187

Tactics, 7
Tariff barriers, 123
Technological factors, 16, 127, 129
Technological forecasting, 22, 53
Telephone interview, 60
Television, 94
Test marketing, 47
Time series analysis, 21
Time value of money, 165
Total marketing, 173
Total quality management (TQM)., 173
Trade Descriptions Acts, 93
Trademark, 114
Transfer pricing, 139
Trends in the examination paper, 189

Uncontrollable variables, 11
Universities, 60
Users, 35

Value added statement, 156
Value analysis, 52

Working capital, 1527 S framework, 176

CIM - Diploma: Strategic Marketing Management: Analysis and Decision (9/97)

ORDER FORM

For further practice, or for experience of different industry contexts, you might like to try one or more of the *Solo Cases* below. These are past CIM case studies, analysed in a similar way to the case studies in this Tutorial Text. Each is printed separately and costs £6.95.

To order your Solo Cases, telephone 0181-740 2211. Alternatively, send this page to our Freepost address or fax it to us on 0181-740 1184.

To: BPP Publishing Ltd, FREEPOST, London W12 8BR   **Tel: 0181-740 2211**
                                                         Fax: 0181-740 1184

Forenames (Mr / Ms): _____

Surname: _____

Address: _____

_____

Post code: _____   Date of exam (month/year): _____

Please send me the following Solo Cases	Date	Quantity	Price	Total
Leffe	12/95	....	£6.95	....
FirstATE	6/95	....	£6.95	....
Australian Tourist Commission	12/94	....	£6.95	....
Purbeck Financial Services	6/94	....	£6.95	....
GT Student Aids Ltd	12/93	....	£6.95	....
Royal Mail	6/93	....	£6.95	....
Regional Railways	12/92	....	£6.95	....
Euro Airport	6/92	....	£6.95	....

Please include postage:

UK: Solo Case £2.00 for first plus £1.00 for each extra.   ....

Europe (inc ROI): Solo Case £2.50 for first plus £1.00 for each extra.   ....

Rest of the World: Solo Case £5.00 for first plus £3.00 for each extra.   ....

I enclose a cheque for £ _____ or charge to Access/Visa/Switch

Card number ☐☐☐☐ ☐☐☐☐ ☐☐☐☐ ☐☐☐☐

Start date (Switch only) _____ Expiry date _____ Issue no. (Switch only) _____

Signature _____

To order any further titles in the CIM range, please use the form overleaf.

CIM - Diploma: Strategic Marketing Management: Analysis and Decision (9/97)

ORDER FORM

Any books from our CIM range can be ordered by telephoning 0181-740 2211. Alternatively, send this page to our Freepost address or fax it to us on 0181-740 1184.

To: BPP Publishing Ltd, FREEPOST, London W12 8BR   **Tel: 0181-740 2211**
                                                          Fax: 0181-740 1184

Forenames (Mr / Ms): _____

Surname: _____

Address: _____

_____

Post code: _____   Date of exam (month/year): _____

Please send me the following books:

	Price* Text (5/97)	Price* Kit (2/97)	Quantity Text	Quantity Kit	Total £
Certificate					
Marketing Environment	16.95	7.95	....	....	....
Understanding Customers	16.95	7.95	....	....	....
Business Communications	16.95	7.95	....	....	....
Marketing Fundamentals	16.95	7.95	....	....	....
Advanced Certificate					
Promotional Practice	16.95	7.95	....	....	....
Management Information for Marketing and Sales	16.95	7.95	....	....	....
Effective Management for Marketing	16.95	7.95	....	....	....
Marketing Operations	16.95	7.95	....	....	....
Diploma					
Marketing Communications Strategy	17.95	8.95	....	....	....
International Marketing Strategy	17.95	8.95	....	....	....
Strategic Marketing Management: Planning and Control	17.95	8.95	....	....	....
Strategic Marketing Management: Analysis and Decision	24.95	-	....	....	....
Solo cases (each)	-	6.95	....	....	....

* Please state whether you want the current edition of the Kit or the new edition to be published in February 1998. New editions of the Study Text will be published in May 1998. Prices above are for 1997 editions.

Please include postage:

UK: Texts £3.00 for first plus £2.00 for each extra   ....

   Kits and solo cases £2.00 for first plus £1.00 for each extra   ....

Europe (inc ROI): Texts £5.00 for first plus £4.00 for each extra   ....

   Kits and solo cases £2.50 for first plus £1.00 for each extra   ....

Rest of the World: Texts £8.00 for first plus £6.00 for each extra   ....

   Kits and solo cases £5.00 for first plus £3.00 for each extra   ....

                                                                 Total _____

I enclose a cheque for £ _____ **or charge to Access/Visa/Switch**

Card number [ ][ ][ ][ ][ ][ ][ ][ ][ ][ ][ ][ ][ ][ ][ ][ ]

Start date (Switch only) _____ **Expiry date** _____ **Issue no. (Switch only)** _____

Signature _____

CIM - Diploma: Strategic Marketing Management: Analysis and Decision (9/97)

REVIEW FORM & FREE PRIZE DRAW

All original review forms from the entire BPP range, completed with genuine comments, will be entered into one of two draws on 31 January 1998 and 31 July 1998. The names on the first four forms picked out on each occasion will be sent a cheque for £50.

Name: _____   Address: _____

How have you used this Text?
(Tick one box only)
- [ ] Home study (book only)
- [ ] On a course: college _____
- [ ] With 'correspondence' package
- [ ] Other _____

Why did you decide to purchase this Text?
(Tick one box only)
- [ ] Have used BPP Texts in the past
- [ ] Recommendation by friend/colleague
- [ ] Recommendation by a lecturer at college
- [ ] Saw advertising
- [ ] Other _____

During the past six months do you recall seeing/receiving any of the following?
(Tick as many boxes as are relevant)
- [ ] Our advertisement in the *Marketing Success*
- [ ] Our advertisement in *Marketing Business*
- [ ] Our brochure with a letter through the post
- [ ] Our brochure with *Marketing Business*
- [ ] The BPP Publishing Web-site

Which (if any) aspects of our advertising do you find useful?
(Tick as many boxes as are relevant)
- [ ] Prices and publication dates of new editions
- [ ] Information on Text content
- [ ] Facility to order books off-the-page
- [ ] None of the above

Your ratings, comments and suggestions would be appreciated on the following areas

	Very useful	Useful	Not useful
Introductory section (How to use this text etc)	[ ]	[ ]	[ ]
Background knowledge in Parts A and D	[ ]	[ ]	[ ]
Practical advice in Part C and D	[ ]	[ ]	[ ]
Overall treatment of cases	[ ]	[ ]	[ ]
Précis, marketing audit, SWOT	[ ]	[ ]	[ ]
Appendix analysis	[ ]	[ ]	[ ]
Situational analysis etc	[ ]	[ ]	[ ]
Outline marketing planning	[ ]	[ ]	[ ]
Detailed marketing planning	[ ]	[ ]	[ ]
Consultants' analysis	[ ]	[ ]	[ ]

	Excellent	Good	Adequate	Poor
Overall opinion of this Text	[ ]	[ ]	[ ]	[ ]

Do you intend to continue using BPP Study Texts/Kits   [ ] Yes   [ ] No

Please note any further comments and suggestions/errors on the reverse of this page

Please return to: Neil Biddlecombe, BPP Publishing Ltd, FREEPOST, London, W12 8BR

REVIEW FORM & FREE PRIZE DRAW (continued)

Please note any further comments and suggestions/errors below

FREE PRIZE DRAW RULES

1 Closing date for 31 January 1998 draw is 31 December 1997. Closing date for 31 July 1998 draw is 30 June 1998.

2 Restricted to entries with UK and Eire addresses only. BPP employees, their families and business associates are excluded.

3 No purchase necessary. Entry forms are available upon request from BPP Publishing. No more than one entry per title, per person. Draw restricted to persons aged 16 and over.

4 Winners will be notified by post and receive their cheques not later than 6 weeks after the relevant draw date. Lists of winners will be published in BPP's *focus* newsletter following the relevant draw.

5 The decision of the promoter in all matters is final and binding. No correspondence will be entered into.